FEUDAL SOCIETY

FEUDAL SOCIETY

by

MARC BLOCH

Translated from the French by
L. A. MANYON

Foreword by
M. M. POSTAN

THE UNIVERSITY OF CHICAGO PRESS

THE UNIVERSITY OF CHICAGO PRESS, CHICAGO 37
UNITED STATES OF AMERICA
Routledge & Kegan Paul Ltd, London E.C.4, England
The University of Toronto Press, Toronto 5, Canada

Translated from the French LA SOCIÉTÉ FÉODALE. *English
translation* © *Routledge & Kegan Paul Ltd 1961. Printed
in Great Britain. Published 1961. Second Impression 1962
All rights reserved*

CONTENTS

v

CONTENTS

CONTENTS

CONTENTS

PLATES

PLATES

FOREWORD

By M. M. POSTAN

I

MARC BLOCH'S book, now the standard international treatise on feudalism, is the last product of his scholarly activities. Yet it must not be read as an epitome of his life's work. The second volume appeared in 1940 and was circulated to his friends in this country as from the 'author on active service': *de la part de l'auteur aux armées*. But although his wartime readers could have had no premonition of his tragic end three years later, and had every reason for expecting him to go back to the study of the Middle Ages, the book must have struck them then, as it must strike the informed reader now, as part of a serial, *un traité fleuve*, on the Middle Ages of which the other instalments had appeared a few years earlier. The best known and the most important of these earlier instalments, *Les Caractères originaux de l'histoire rurale française*, like the several studies which preceded and accompanied it,[1] presented an image of the medieval world, which from Bloch's own point of view was incomplete. In spite of the generous sweep of their ideas, those earlier books did not illuminate the entire range of medieval culture and society. Their interest was sharply (in writing about Bloch we cannot use the word narrowly) focused on the material basis of medieval existence: soil, topography, technique of cultivation, forms of settlement; or else on those social relations through which the material basis plainly showed.

That this was not Bloch's full view of the middle ages must be obvious not only from his writings, but also from innumerable hints and references all over his *Caractères originaux* itself. True enough, his predilections and his preoccupations as a historian were with 'rational' aspects of history, with tangible facts capable of being understood, i.e. ordered and analysed in the way in which most modern scientists order and analyse their data. Students of ideas who happen to have preserved a vocabulary uncorrupted by recent usage will therefore recognise Bloch's approach as 'positivist' in the proper sense of the word. Bloch himself might have fought shy of this appellation. In his posthumously published

---

[1] More especially *Rois et Serfs*, Paris, 1920; 'Liberté et servitude personelles au moyen âge', Madrid, 1933; and 'The Rise of Dependent Cultivation', in *Cambridge Economic History*, I.

notes on the historian's craft he dissents from positivists of the wrong kind, the *positivistes de stricte observance* or the *positivisme un peu rudimentaire* or *positivisme mal compris*.[1] But this very anxiety to dissociate himself from the misconceptions of positivism displays an affinity with positivism properly conceived. To him history is a science in the true epistemological sense of the term: a *connaissance* which offers us *un classement rationel et une progressive intelligibilité*. And he accordingly defends history's claim to the name of science (*au nom scientifique*) even though it be incapable of Euclidean demonstration of immutable laws.[2]

Yet this attitude, even though positivist and rational in the proper sense of the terms, did not restrict him to economic phenomena, to the mere business of earning and spending, or to those social problems which Marxists would classify as 'social relations of production'. Everything in historical inquiry capable of being tested by verifiable proof and of yielding useful sense was grist to his mills. And those powerful millstones of his ground fine sense out of the greatest possible variety of historical facts—men's ideas, beliefs, fears and political incentives as well as their material needs and economic devices.

Hence his plan to pass from the *Caractères originaux* and similar studies to a treatise on feudalism considered as a system of human relations. In so far as the earlier studies dealt almost entirely with agriculture and village society, they bypassed many other topics of medieval history and gave no more than part of Bloch's full design. In order to complete his picture and to do so in a manner appropriate to his outlook he had to follow his earlier studies with a further treatise analysing the medieval world from the point of view of its social order, or rather of those elements in the social order which were not involved in productive processes or directly determined by them. And that meant writing the story of the social ties embodied in vassalage, fealty, personal dependence, private authority over men, as well as of the older ties of family and tribal system which the feudal system absorbed or replaced.

II

It is on these relations that the present volume concentrates and thereby complements Bloch's other studies. Yet even taken by itself it opens up a view of the Middle Ages much wider and perhaps truer than most other studies dealing ostensibly with the same subject. A hasty reader, trained in the British or German tradition of medieval studies, may consider the book as yet another recapitulation of the ideas which form the main corpus of academic thought about the Middle Ages. In this corpus 'feudalism' is merely a name for the legal or customary principles embodied in the

---

[1] *Le métier d'historien*, Paris, 1948 (English translation under the title of *The Historian's Craft*), pp. xii, 4.   [2] *Ibid.*, pp. xvi, xii–xiii, 72.

feudum as the universal principle of military organization. Thus told the history of feudalism is mainly the story of baronial and knightly contracts of service. In tracing their origin constitutional historians are often content to demonstrate how military necessities of the earlier centuries of the Middle Ages called into existence the knights' fees with their baronial and honorial superstructures. In tracing the subsequent mutations of English or German feudalism, they try to show how the military system of fees broke up, was replaced, revived or bastardised, and how new contractual principles—indenture or plain hire—replaced the older contract of military fief.

This identification of feudalism with military service is bound to narrow the history of feudalism down to a single issue and to remove out of its history a vast range of subjects which other historians habitually weave into it and to which the word and concept of feudalism owes its prominent place in historiography. How far this difference of approach can some-times go has recently been demonstrated at an Anglo-Soviet occasion, when the two principal speakers, the Russian and the English, gave carefully composed disquisitions on feudalism which hardly touched at a single point. The English speaker dwelt learnedly and gracefully on military fiefs, while the Russian speaker discoursed on class domination and exploitation of peasants by landlords. Needless to say the Russian dis-quisition was packed tight with familiar Marxist furniture: the state as a vehicle of class rule, 'commodity exchange' as a solvent of feudalism, feudal economy as an antecedent of early capitalism. Yet for all its dogmaticism and ancient verbiage, the Russian use of the term appeared to bear more directly on the intellectual enterprise of history than the conventional connotation adopted by the English speaker.

Needless to say, the concept of feudalism as it figures in English and perhaps German historiography has its uses. The English and German lawyers who gave it birth and the constitutional historians who developed it have brought to its study a great deal of juristic and scholastic rigour. This rigorous tradition has now deposited a body of ideas which university teachers can usefully employ for pedagogical purposes, mainly as a vehicle of intellectual discipline and an antidote to the journalistic levities of modern historiography. But regarded as an intellectual tool, to be used in the study of society, the conventional Anglo-German approach has been, to say the least, unhelpful. In so far as it concentrates on military service it cannot provide a key to the fundamentals of medieval society or indeed any society; in so far as it concerns itself with contractual principles it conceals from the view the underlying social realities. And even within the narrow range of legal and contractual problems it cannot allow for the time lag between the evolution of legal forms and the changing needs of society.

Of course, from some points of view the legalistic formulation of feudal-ism is no worse than its other generalized formulations. It is indeed possible

(and some writers have also found it convenient) to argue that no port-
manteau formula and certainly no single term can do what we expect the
term feudalism to do, i.e. to sum up the essentials of a social system or of
a historical situation. Such comprehensive words, be they mercantilism,
capitalism, or socialism, must over-simplify the reality they purport to
epitomize. In some contexts the practice of giving general names to whole
epochs can even be dangerous. It may lure its practitioners into the worst
pitfalls of the nominalist fallacy, and may encourage them to endow
their terms with real existence, to derive features of an epoch from the
etymology of the word used to describe it or to construct edifices of historical argument out of mere semantic conceits.

These are all very real dangers. But the same dangers are inherent in
all general terms. If pressed consistently this objection to general terms
will hold good against such humdrum concepts as war, peace, state, estate,
class, industry, agriculture. Indeed, without generalized terms representing
entire groups of phenomena not only history but all intelligent discourse
would be impossible.

Of this Bloch was well aware. Why he asks 'be afraid of general words?
No science can do without abstractions . . . and is the chlorophylic function
more "real" than the economic function?'[1] But if generalized concepts are
to be used, there is much to be said for employing only the useful ones,
i.e. those which help us to distinguish one historical situation from another,
and to align similar situations in different countries and even in different
periods.[2] And in order that the concept of feudalism could be thus useful
it must invoke the really essential features of an historical situation or an
epoch and show them in their interdependence.

This the constitutional and legal concepts of feudalism cannot do, but
this is what Bloch obviously had in mind. True enough, his definition of
feudalism, where he attempts it (e.g. in Part VIII), might at first sight bear
strong resemblance to conventional definitions of text books. But looked
at more closely it will be found to embrace most of the significant features
of medieval society. 'A subject peasantry; widespread use of the service
tenement (i.e. the fief) instead of salary; supremacy of a class of specialized warriors; ties of obedience and protection which bind man to man;
fragmentation of authority; and, in the midst of all of this, survival of
other forms of association, family and State.'[3] This is certainly an approach much wider than the one which equates feudalism with *feudum*
and begins and ends its history with that of the knight service. In Bloch's
definition the fief is only an element, albeit a very important one, of the
whole situation. But to him a society might still be feudal even if the fief
occupied a more subordinate position. This latitude might strike the

[1] *The Historian's Craft*, p. 74.
[2] '*un lexique* . . . . *dont la généralité se veut supérieure aux résonances d'aucune
époque particulière*', *ibid.*, pp. 87–8; also p. 72.   [3] Below, p. 446.

orthodox as incompatible with the etymology of the term. But, he argues, etymological rectitude is not the final test of an historical concept. 'What', he asks in his *Métier d'historien,* 'if the term is currently used to characterize societies in which the fief is not the most significant trait. There is nothing in this contrary to the practice of all the sciences. Are we shocked by the physicists persisting to apply the term atom, i.e. indivisible, to an object they subject to the most audacious division?' [1]

III

A connotation of feudalism in which fief is merely a part clearly derives from the assumption 'that the framework of institutions which govern a society can in the last resort be understood only through the knowledge of the whole human environment', and is equally clearly implied in his insistent references to the *ambiance sociale totale.*[2] It is therefore not surprising to find him introducing his story of feudalism by a stimulating and perceptive discussion of medieval mentality. For not only are men's ideas embedded in the *ambiance sociale,* but they are of the very essence of social structure. To quote him again, 'social classification exists in the last analysis only by virtue of the ideas which men form of it.' [3]

However, what makes this epigram significant is not only its emphasis on ideas but its underlying assumption that the true universe of discourse of an historian of feudalism is social classification. And once social classification becomes the main theme in the history of feudalism, that history must inevitably concern itself with the masses of people below and outside the system of military fiefs.

Bloch may insist that the manor had a history separate from that of the feudal system, but he repeatedly emphasizes that it was 'an essential element in feudal society'. He in fact begins his final definition of feudalism with 'a subject peasantry'. If he does not deal with a subject peasantry in greater detail in the main body of this book, this is merely because he has already done so in the *Caractères originaux.* From this point of view the two studies are complementary and cannot display Bloch's view of feudal society except in combination. And even then the view might be capable of yet another enlargement. For all we know, had Bloch survived the war he might have rounded off his account of the Middle Ages by a major work on the history of medieval ideas: *les caractères orginaux d'histoire morale et intellectuelle européenne.*

M. M. POSTAN

[1] P. 86.   [2] *Métier d'historien,* p. 8 and *passim.*
[3] Below, p. 268, also p. 59.

INTRODUCTION

GENERAL SCOPE OF THE INQUIRY

ONLY within the last two centuries or so could the words 'Feudal Society', as the title of a book, have conveyed an idea of what the book was about. Yet the adjective itself is a very old one. In its Latin form, *feodalis*, it dates from the Middle Ages. The French noun *féodalité*, feudalism, though of more recent origin, goes back at least to the seventeenth century. But for a long time both these words were used only in a narrowly legal sense. The fief (*feodum*) was, as we shall see, a form of real property, and *féodal* was therefore understood as meaning 'that which concerns the fief' (this was how the French Academy defined it); and *féodalité* might mean either 'the quality peculiar to a fief' or the obligations incident to such tenure. The French lexicographer, Richelet, in 1630, described these terms as 'lawyers' jargon'—not, be it noted, historians' jargon. When did it first occur to anyone to enlarge their meaning so as to designate a state of society? *Gouvernement féodal* and *féodalité* are used in this sense in the *Lettres Historiques sur les Parlemens*, published in 1727, five years after the death of their author, the Comte de Boulainvilliers.[1] This is the earliest example that I could find, after fairly extensive research. Perhaps one day another inquirer will be more fortunate. Until this happens, however, this strange man Boulainvilliers, at once the friend of Fénelon and the translator of Spinoza, above all an impassioned apologist of the nobility whom he believed to be descended from Germanic chieftains—a sort of prototype Gobineau with less enthusiasm and more learning—may be regarded as having a presumptive claim to be the inventor of a new historical classification. For that is what it really amounts to, and in the study of history there have been few stages so decisive as the moment when 'Empires', dynasties, famous periods identified with some great name—in a word, all the old arbitrary divisions born of a monarchical and oratorical tradition—began to give place to another system of classification, based on the observation of social phenomena.

It was however a more celebrated writer who first gave wide currency to this conception and to the terminology that expressed it. Montesquieu

---

[1] *Histoire de l'ancien gouvernement de la France avec XIV Lettres Historiques sur les Parlemens ou Etats-Généraux*. The Hague, 1727. The fourth letter is entitled *Détail du gouvernement féodal et de l'établissement des Fiefs* (1, p. 286) and contains (p. 300) this sentence: 'Je me suis étendu dans l'extrait de cette ordonnance, la croyant propre à donner une idée exacte de l'ancienne féodalité'.

had read Boulainvilliers. The vocabulary of the lawyers, moreover, held no terrors for him: was not the literary language of France to emerge from his hands greatly enriched with the gleanings of the Bar? If he seems to have avoided the term *féodalité*, which was doubtless too abstract for his taste, it was unquestionably he who convinced the educated public of his time that the *lois féodales* were the distinguishing marks of a particular period of history. From the French the words, along with the idea, spread to the other languages of Europe, being in some cases merely transcribed, and in others translated, as with the German word for feudalism, *Lehnwesen*. At length the French Revolution, in its revolt against what remained of the institutions but lately christened by Boulainvilliers, completed the popular diffusion of the name which he, with entirely opposite sentiments, had conferred upon them. 'The National Assembly', declares the famous decree of the 11th August 1789, 'totally abolishes the feudal régime'. How could one thenceforth deny the reality of a system which it had cost so much to destroy?[1]

Nevertheless, it must be admitted that the word feudalism, which was to have so great a future, was very ill-chosen, even though at the time the reasons for adopting it appeared sound enough. To Boulainvilliers and Montesquieu, living in an age of absolute monarchy, the most striking characteristic of the Middle Ages was the parcelling out of sovereignty among a host of petty princes, or even lords of villages. It was this characteristic that they meant to denote by the term feudalism, and when they spoke of fiefs they were referring sometimes to territorial principalities, sometimes to manors. But not all the manors were in fact fiefs, nor were all the fiefs principalities or manors. Above all, it may be doubted whether a highly complex type of social organization can be properly designated either by concentrating on its political aspect only, or—if 'fief' be understood in its narrowest legal sense—by stressing one particular form of real property right among many others. But words, like well-worn coins, in the course of constant circulation lose their clear outline. In the usage of the present day, 'feudalism' and 'feudal society' cover a whole complex of ideas in which the fief properly so called no longer occupies the foreground. Provided that he treats these expressions merely as labels sanctioned by modern usage for something which he has still to define, the historian may use them without compunction. In this he is like the physicist who, in disregard of Greek, persists in calling an 'atom' something which he spends his time in dividing.

It is a question of the deepest interest whether there have been other societies, in other times and in other parts of the world, whose social

---

[1] Among the French people whose buttonholes are today adorned with a red ribbon or rosette, how many know that one of the duties imposed on their order by its first constitution of the 19th May 1802 was 'to combat . . . any enterprise tending to re-establish the feudal régime?'

structures in their fundamental characteristics have sufficiently resembled that of our Western feudalism to justify us in applying the term 'feudal' to them as well. This question will turn up again at the end of this book, but it is not the subject of our present study. The feudalism which we shall attempt to analyse here is that to which the name was first applied. Apart from some problems of origin or of later developments, the inquiry will be confined to that period of our history which extends roughly from the middle of the ninth century to the first decades of the thirteenth; and it will be restricted to western and central Europe. The reasons for the choice of dates will become clear in the course of the work itself, but the geographical limits seem to call for a brief explanation.

Ancient civilization was centred about the Mediterranean. 'I believe that the earth,' wrote Plato, 'is very large and that we who dwell between the pillars of Hercules and the river Phasis live in a small part of it about the sea, like ants or frogs about a pond.'[1] These same waters remained through many centuries the axis of the Roman world, even after conquest extended that world. A senator from Aquitania could make his career on the shores of the Bosporus; he could own vast estates in Macedonia. The great fluctuations of prices that shook the Roman economy were felt from the Euphrates to Gaul. Without the grain of Africa, the existence of Imperial Rome is as little conceivable as Catholic theology without the African Augustine. On the other hand, anyone crossing the Rhine found himself at once in a strange and hostile land, the vast territory of the Barbarians.

Now, on the threshold of the period that we call the Middle Ages, two far-ranging movements of peoples had destroyed this equilibrium—there is no need at present to inquire how far it had already been shaken from within—and replaced it by a very different pattern of peoples. The first of these was the Germanic invasions; the second, the Moslem conquests. The Germans penetrated the greater part of the countries formerly included in the western section of the Roman Empire, and the territories occupied by them became united, sometimes through subjection to the same political régime, but always and in any case by the common mental habits and social customs of the invaders. Little by little, the small Celtic groups in the British Isles were linked up with this Romano-Germanic society and more or less assimilated to it. North Africa, on the other hand, was to follow an entirely different course. The counter-offensive of the Berber tribes had prepared the breach with Rome: Islam completed it. Elsewhere, on the shores of the Levant, the victories of the Arabs had isolated the former East Roman Empire in the Balkans and Anatolia and transformed it into the Greek Empire. Difficulties of communication, a distinctive type of social and political structure, and a religious mentality and

[1] *Phaedo*, 109b.

ecclesiastical organization very different from those of Latin Christianity combined to cut off this Empire more and more from the Christian communities of the West. The West, it is true, exercised a wide influence among the Slav peoples in the eastern parts of Europe, among some of whom it introduced not only the Catholic form of Christianity, but also Western modes of thought and even certain Western institutions; but, none the less, the societies which were linguistically Slavonic evolved, for the most part, on quite independent lines.

Hemmed in by these three blocs, Mohammedan, Byzantine, and Slav, and ceaselessly engaged in pushing forward its ever-changing frontiers, the Romano-Germanic world was itself by no means homogeneous. Differences arising from their different backgrounds had deeply marked the various societies of which it was composed, and had lasting effects. Even where the points of departure were almost identical, the lines of development might subsequently diverge. Yet, however pronounced these differences may have been, how can we fail to recognize, over and above them, the predominant quality of a common civilization—that of the West? If in the following pages where the phrase 'Western and Central Europe' might have been expected, we say simply 'Europe', this is not merely to avoid the repetition of cumbersome adjectives. What does it matter, after all, how the name and its limits were defined in the old artificial geography, with its 'five parts of the world'? All that counts is its human significance. European civilization arose and flowered, until in the end it covered the face of the earth, among those who dwelt between the Tyrrhenian, the Adriatic, the Elbe, and the Atlantic Ocean. It had no other homeland. The eighth-century Spanish chronicler who, after their victory over Islam, styled 'Europeans' the Franks of Charles Martel, had already dimly perceived this. So, some two hundred years later, had the Saxon monk, Widukind, who, when Otto the Great had driven back the Hungarians, enthusiastically hailed him as the liberator of 'Europe'.[1] In this sense of the word— and it is the richest in historical content—Europe was a creation of the early Middle Ages. It was already in being at the beginning of the feudal age proper.

The term 'feudalism', applied to a phase of European history within the limits thus determined, has sometimes been interpreted in ways so different as to be almost contradictory, yet the mere existence of the word attests the special quality which men have instinctively recognized in the period which it denotes. Hence a book about feudal society can be looked on as an attempt to answer a question posed by its very title: what are the distinctive features of this portion of the past which have given it a claim to be treated in isolation? In other words, what we are attempting here is to analyse and explain a social structure and its unifying principles. A

[1] *M.G.H., Auctores Antiquissimi*, XI, p. 362; Widukind, I, 19.

similar method—if in the light of experience it should prove fruitful—might be employed in other fields of study, under a different set of limiting conditions. I hope that what is undeniably new in the present enterprise will make amends for the defects of execution.

The very magnitude of the inquiry, so conceived, has made it necessary to divide the material. The first book will describe the social background generally and the growth of those bonds of interdependence between men which, more than anything else, gave the feudal structure its special character. The second book will be concerned with the development of social classes and the organization of governments. It is always difficult to divide up a living organism. Yet the final differentiation of the old social classes, the emergence of a new class, the *bourgeoisie*, and the resuscitation of the authority of the State after long eclipse, coincided with the time when the most specifically feudal characteristics of Western civilization began to disappear; and this explains why, though no strictly chronological division has seemed possible, the first book is concerned above all with the birth of feudal society, the second with the way it developed, extended and declined.

But the historian is in no sense a free man. Of the past he knows only so much as the past is willing to yield up to him. What is more, when the subject he is attempting to cover is too vast to allow him to examine personally all the sources, he is conscious of being constantly frustrated in his inquiry by the limitations of research. No survey will be made here of those paper wars in which scholars have sometimes engaged. History, not historians, is my concern. But whatever may be the reasons for them I resolved never to conceal the gaps or uncertainties in our knowledge. In this I felt I should run no risk of discouraging the reader. On the contrary, to impose an artificial rigidity on a branch of knowledge which is essentially one of movement—that would be the way to engender boredom and indifference. One of the men who have gone furthest in the understanding of medieval societies, the great English jurist Maitland, said that a historical work should make its readers hungry—hungry to learn, that is, and above all to inquire. If this book does that, I shall be well content.[1]

---

[1] Every historical work, if it happens to be addressed to a relatively large public, confronts its author with a practical problem of the most difficult kind—the problem of references. Justice perhaps required that the names of all the learned works but for which this book would not exist be set out in full array at the foot of each page. At the risk of being thought ungrateful, I decided to leave such references, for the most part, to the bibliography at the end of the book. I have, however, made it a rule never to cite an original source without affording every student with a little experience the means of finding the passage referred to and verifying my interpretation of it. If the reference is not given, the reason is that the information given in my text, supplemented by well-arranged tables in the publication in which the document appears, makes it easy to find. Where these are lacking, a note serves as a pointer. In a court of justice, after all, the status of the witnesses is much more important than that of counsel.

BOOK ONE: THE GROWTH OF TIES OF DEPENDENCE

PART I

The Environment: The Last Invasions

I

MOSLEMS AND HUNGARIANS

1 EUROPE INVADED AND BESIEGED

'YOU see before you the wrath of the Lord breaking forth. . . . There is naught but towns emptied of their folk, monasteries razed to the ground or given to the flames, fields desolated. . . . Everywhere the strong oppresseth the weak and men are like fish of the sea that blindly devour each other.' Thus, in 909, the bishops of the province of Rheims assembled at Trosly. The literature of the ninth and tenth centuries, the charters, and the deliberations of councils are full of such lamentations. When all allowance has been made both for exaggeration and for the pessimism natural to religious orators, we are forced to see in this incessantly recurring theme, supported as it is by so much contemporary evidence, the proof of a state of affairs regarded as intolerable even in those days. Certainly it was a period when those who were capable of observing and making comparisons, the clergy in particular, felt themselves to be living in a hateful atmosphere of disorder and violence. Feudalism was born in the midst of an infinitely troubled epoch, and in some measure it was the child of those troubles themselves. But some of the causes which helped to create or maintain this disorderly environment were altogether foreign to the internal evolution of European societies. Forged several centuries earlier in the fiery crucible of the Germanic invasions, the new civilization of the West, in its turn, seemed like a citadel besieged—indeed more than half overrun. It was attacked from three sides at once: in the south by the devotees of Islam, Arabs or their Arabized subjects; in the east by the Hungarians; and in the north by the Scandinavians.

2 THE MOSLEMS

Of the enemies just enumerated, Islam was certainly the least dangerous, although one would hesitate to speak of its decline. For a long period neither Gaul nor Italy, among their poor cities, had anything to offer which approached the splendour of Baghdad or Cordova. Until the twelfth century the Moslem world, along with the Byzantine world, exercised a true economic hegemony over the West: the only gold coinage still circulating in our part of Europe came from Greek or Arab mints, or at least

3

—like more than one of the silver coinages too—were copies of their productions. And if the eighth and ninth centuries witnessed the final breakdown of the unity of the Caliphate, the various states which at that time arose from the wreckage remained formidable powers. But thereafter it was much less a question of invasions properly so-called than of frontier wars. Let us leave aside the East, where the emperors of the Amorian and Macedonian dynasties (828–1056) painfully and valiantly set themselves to reconquer Asia Minor. Western societies came into collision with the Islamic states on two fronts only.

First, southern Italy. This region was, as it were, the hunting-ground of the sovereigns who ruled over the ancient Roman province of Africa—the Aghlabite emirs of Kairouan, succeeded, at the beginning of the tenth century, by the Fatimite caliphs. The Aghlabites had wrested Sicily little by little from the Greeks who had held it since Justinian's time and whose last stronghold, Taormina, fell in 902. Meanwhile the Arabs had gained a footing in the peninsula. Across the Byzantine provinces of the south they threatened the semi-independent cities of the Tyrrhenian coast and the little Lombard principalities of Campania and of the Beneventino, which were more or less dependencies of Constantinople. At the beginning of the eleventh century they could still carry their raids as far as the Sabine mountains. One band, which had made its stronghold in the wooded heights of Monte Argento, very close to Gaeta, could only be destroyed, in 915, after twenty years of marauding. In 982, the young 'emperor of the Romans', Otto II, set out to conquer southern Italy. Though Saxon by origin, he considered himself nevertheless to be the heir of the Caesars, in Italy as elsewhere. He committed the surprising folly, so often repeated in the Middle Ages, of choosing the summer season as the time for taking to these scorching regions an army accustomed to entirely different climates, and on the 25th July he encountered the Moslem bands on the east coast of Calabria and suffered a most humiliating defeat.

The Moslem peril continued to press heavily on these regions till, in the eleventh century, a handful of adventurers from Normandy routed both Byzantines and Arabs. Uniting Sicily with the southern part of the peninsula, the vigorous state which they eventually created was destined both to bar for ever the path of the invaders and to act as an inspired intermediary between the Latin and Islamic civilizations. On Italian soil the struggle against the Saracens, which had begun in the ninth century, continued for a long time—with small and fluctuating territorial gains on either side. But in relation to Christendom as a whole, it was only a remote territory that was at issue.

The other field of conflict was in Spain. There, it was for Islam no longer a question of raids for plunder or temporary annexations; populations of Mohammedans lived there in great numbers and the states founded by the Arabs had their centres in the country itself. At the beginning of the tenth century the Saracen bands had not yet completely forgotten the way over the Pyrenees. But these long-distance raids were becoming more and more infrequent. Starting from the extreme north, the Christian reconquest, in spite of many reverses and humiliations, slowly progressed. In Galicia and on those plateaux of the north-west which the emirs and caliphs of Cordova, established too far to the south, had never held with a very firm hand, the little Christian kingdoms, sometimes divided, sometimes united under a single ruler, moved forward to the region of the Douro from the middle of the eleventh century; the Tagus was reached in 1085. At the foot of the Pyrenees, on the other hand, the course of the Ebro, although so near, remained for a long time Moslem; Saragossa fell only in 1118. These struggles, though they did not by any means preclude more peaceful relations, were as a rule interrupted only by brief truces, and they stamped the Spanish societies with a character of their own. With the Europe 'beyond the passes' they had scarcely any dealings, save in so far as they furnished its nobility—especially from the second half of the eleventh century—with the opportunity for brilliant, profitable and pious adventures, while at the same time providing its peasants with the opportunity of sett-ling on the unoccupied lands at the pressing invitation of Spanish kings and nobles. But along with the wars properly so-called went piracy and brigandage, and it was chiefly through these that the Saracens contributed to the general disorder of the West.

From an early date the Arabs had been sailors. From their lairs in Africa, Spain, and especially the Balearics, their corsairs attacked the western Mediterranean. Nevertheless, in these waters, traversed by only a very few ships, the trade of pirate in the true sense of the word had not been very profitable. In the mastery of the sea, the Saracens—like the Scandi-navians in the same period—saw above all the means of reaching coasts whence they could carry out profitable raids. From 842 they went up the Rhône as far as the approaches of Arles, plundering both banks on their way. The Camargue at that time was their normal base. But soon an accident was to procure them not only safer headquarters, but also the possibility of extending their ravages very considerably.

At a date not precisely ascertained, probably somewhere about 890, a small Saracen vessel coming from Spain was driven by the winds on to the coast of Provence, on the outskirts of the present town of Saint-Tropez. Its crew hid themselves during the day, then at nightfall emerged and massacred the inhabitants of a neighbouring village. Mountainous and wooded—it was called at that time the land of ash-trees (*frênes*), or 'Freinet' [1]—this secluded place was easy to defend. Like their compatriots of Monte Argento in Campania, at the same period, this band of Arabs

---

[1] The memory of this name is preserved in the name of the existing village of La Garde-Freinet. But the citadel of the Saracens was situated on the sea-coast and was not, therefore, at La Garde, which is inland.

fortified themselves on a height, in the midst of thickets of thorns, and summoned their comrades to join them. Thus was created a most dangerous nest of robbers. With the exception of Fréjus, which was pillaged, it does not seem that the towns, protected as they were by their walls, were direct victims. But in the neighbourhood of the coast the country districts were appallingly devastated. The brigands of Le Freinet also took numerous prisoners whom they sold in the Spanish markets.

Moreover, they were not slow to carry their incursions well inland. Very few in number, they seem to have been reluctant to face the risks of the Rhône valley, relatively populous and protected by fortified cities or castles. But the Alpine massif made it possible for small bands of practised mountaineers to steal far forward, from one range of mountains to another, from thicket to thicket, and coming as they did from the Sierras of Spain or the mountainous Maghreb, these Saracens were, in the words of a monk of Saint-Gall, 'real goats'. Moreover, the Alps, in spite of appearances, were not to be despised as a field for raids. Nestling in their midst were fertile valleys, on which it was easy to descend without warning from the surrounding mountains. Such a valley was Graisivaudan. Here and there, abbeys stood forth, ideal objectives for the raider. (Above Susa, the monastery of Novalesa, whence most of the monks had fled, was sacked and burned as early as 906.) Best of all, there journeyed through the passes small parties of travellers, merchants, or even pilgrims on their way to Rome to pray at the tombs of the Apostles. What could be more tempting than to ambush them on the road? As early as 920 or 921, some Anglo-Saxon pilgrims were battered with stones in a defile, and from then on such crimes were of frequent occurrence. The Arab *djichs* or armed bands were not afraid to venture astonishingly far north. In 940, we find them in the neighbourhood of the upper Rhine valley and in the Valais, where they burned the famous monastery of Saint-Maurice d'Agaune. About the same time, one of their detachments riddled with arrows the monks of Saint-Gall as they walked peacefully in procession round their church. This band, at any rate, was dispersed by the little group of defenders whom the abbot hurriedly gathered together; a number of prisoners, brought into the monastery, heroically allowed themselves to die of starvation.

To police the Alps or the Provençal countryside was beyond the power of contemporary states. There was no other remedy than to destroy the lair at Le Freinet. But here a new obstacle arose. It was practically impossible to lay siege to this citadel without cutting it off from the sea, whence it received its reinforcements. Now, neither the kings of this region—in the west, the kings of Provence and Burgundy, in the east, the king of Italy—nor their counts had fleets at their disposal. The only skilled sailors among the Christians were the Greeks who, however, occasionally turned their skill to account, just as the Saracens did, by taking to piracy. (It was Greek pirates who plundered Marseilles in 848.) On two occasions, in 931 and

942, the Byzantine fleet appeared off the coast of Le Freinet; on the second at least, and probably on the previous occasion also, they had been summoned by the king of Italy, Hugh of Arles, who had important interests in Provence. Nothing was achieved on either occasion. What is more, in 942, Hugh changed sides, even while the struggle was in progress, planning to make the Saracens his allies and with their aid to close the Alpine routes against the reinforcements which one of his rivals for the Lombard crown was awaiting. Then in 951 Otto the Great, king of East Francia—Germany of today—made himself king of the Lombards. His purpose was to build up in central Europe and even as far as Italy a power like that of the Carolingians, a Christian power and a promoter of peace. Regarding himself as the heir of Charlemagne whose imperial crown he was to assume in 962, he believed it to be his mission to put an end to the depredations of the Saracens. First trying the diplomatic approach, he sought to persuade the caliph of Cordova to order his people to evacuate Le Freinet. Then he formed the project of leading an expedition himself, but never carried it out.

Meanwhile, in 972, the marauders made the mistake of capturing too illustrious a prize. On the route of the Great Saint Bernard, in the valley of the Dranse, the abbot of Cluny, Maïeul, while returning from Italy, was ambushed and taken to one of those mountain refuges which the Saracens frequently used when they were not able to get back to their base. He was only released in return for a heavy ransom paid by his monks. Now Maïeul, who had reformed so many monasteries, was the revered friend, the director of conscience and, if one may venture to say it, the *saint familier* of many kings and barons; notably of William, count of Provence. The latter overtook on their way back the band who had committed the sacrilegious outrage and inflicted on them a severe defeat; then, gathering together under his command a number of nobles from the Rhône valley, to whom were to be distributed subsequently the lands brought back into cultivation, he launched an attack against the fortress of Le Freinet. This time, the citadel fell.

This for the Saracens was the end of large-scale brigandage on land, though naturally the coastline of Provence, like that of Italy, remained exposed to their outrages. Even in the eleventh century we find the monks of Lérins actively engaged in buying back Christians whom Arab pirates had captured and taken to Spain; in 1178 a raid near Marseilles yielded many prisoners. But the cultivation of the fields could be resumed in the coastal and sub-alpine regions of Provence, and the Alpine routes became again neither more nor less safe than any others traversing the mountains of Europe. Moreover, on the Mediterranean itself, the merchant cities of Italy, Pisa, Genoa and Amalfi, had since the beginning of the eleventh century passed over to the offensive. They chased the Moslems from Sardinia, and even hunted them down in the ports of the Maghreb (from 1015) and of Spain (in 1092). Thus they began to clean up those seas on the security of which their trade was so largely dependent. It was only a relative security, but until the nineteenth century the Mediterranean was not to know anything better.

3 THE HUNGARIAN ASSAULT

Like the Huns before them, the Hungarians or Magyars had appeared in Europe almost without warning, and at an early date the writers of the Middle Ages, who had learned to know them only too well, showed a naive astonishment that the Roman writers should not have mentioned them. Their early history is in any case much more obscure than that of the Huns, for the Chinese sources which, well before the Western records begin, enable us to follow the trail of the 'Hiung-Nu', are silent on the subject of Magyars. It is certain that the new invaders also belonged to the peculiar and highly characteristic world of the nomads of the Asiatic steppes: peoples often of very diverse languages, but astonishingly alike in their manner of life, because of the similarity of their surroundings; horse-breeders and warriors, living on the milk of their mares or the fruits of their hunting and fishing; natural enemies especially of the agriculturalists on the fringes of their territory. In its basic structure, the Magyar speech belongs to the linguistic type called Finno-Ugrian; the idioms to which it is closest today are those of certain aboriginal peoples of Siberia. But in the course of its wanderings the original ethnic stock had been mixed with numerous Turkish-speaking elements and had received a strong imprint from the civilizations of that group.[1]

As early as 833 we find the Hungarians, whose name appeared then for the first time, disturbing the settled populations—the Khanate of the Khazars and the Byzantine colonies—in the neighbourhood of the sea of Azov. Soon, they are threatening at any moment to cut the Dnieper route, at this time an extremely active commercial highway by which, from portage to portage and from market to market, the furs of the North, the honey and wax of the Russian forests, and the slaves bought on all sides went to be exchanged against the merchandise or gold of Constantinople or Asia. But new hordes—the Petchenegs—starting out after them from beyond the Urals, harassed them unceasingly. The road to the south was successfully barred to them by the Bulgarian empire. Thus driven back, one of their groups preferred to bury itself in the steppe further to the east, but the greater number crossed the Carpathians in about 896, to spread over the plains of the Tisza and the middle Danube.

These vast areas, so often ravaged by invasion since the fourth century, formed at that time on the map of Europe a sort of enormous blank patch.

[1] The very name Hungarian is probably Turkish. The same perhaps is true, at least in one of its elements, of the name Magyar, which seems moreover to have been applied originally to only one tribe.

'Solitudes' is the word used to describe them by the chronicler Regino of
Prüm, though it is not necessary to take the expression too literally. The
varied populations which had formerly had important settlements in these
regions, or had merely passed through them, had in all probability left
behind small groups of stragglers. Above all, a great many Slav tribes had
by degrees infiltrated there. But settlement unquestionably remained very
sparse: witness the almost complete recasting of the geographical nomenclature, including that of the rivers, after the arrival of the Magyars.
Furthermore, after Charlemagne had crushed the Avar power, there was
no longer any solidly organized state capable of offering serious resistance
to the invaders. Their only opponents were some chiefs of the Moravian
people who a short time before had succeeded in establishing in the north-
west corner a tolerably strong principality, already officially Christian—
the first attempt, in fact, to form a genuine, purely Slav state. The attacks
of the Hungarians destroyed it once and for all in 906.

From this moment, the history of the Hungarians took a new turn. It is
scarcely possible any longer to speak of them as nomads in the strict sense
of the word, since they now had a permanent settlement in the plains
which today bear their name. But from there they sallied forth in bands
over the surrounding countries: not, however, to conquer territories. Their
sole purpose was to plunder and return loaded with booty to their permanent location. The decline of the Bulgarian empire after the death of the
tsar Simeon (927) opened the way to Byzantine Thrace, which they
plundered on several occasions. The West, much less well defended, had a
special attraction for them, and they came into contact with it at an early
date.

As long ago as 862, before they had even crossed the Carpathians, a
Hungarian expedition had penetrated as far as the borders of Germany.
Later on, some of these men had been engaged as auxiliaries by the king of
that country, Arnulf, in one of his wars against the Moravians. In 899,
their hordes swooped down on the plain of the Po; the following year, on
Bavaria. From this time onward, scarcely a year passed in which the annals
of monasteries in Italy and Germany, and soon afterwards Gaul, did not
record, sometimes of one province, sometimes of another: 'ravages by the
Hungarians'. Northern Italy, Bavaria and Swabia were especially afflicted;
all the region on the right bank of the Enns, where the Carolingians had
established frontier commands and distributed lands to their abbeys, had
to be abandoned. But the raids extended well beyond these limits. The
radius covered would confound one's imagination, if one did not take into
account the fact that the long pastoral journeys to which the Hungarians
were formerly accustomed in the open steppe and which they continued
to practise in the more restricted circle of the Danubian *puszta* had been a
wonderful apprenticeship. The nomadism of the herdsman of the steppes
—who was already a robber as well—was a preparation for the nomadism

9

of the bandit. Towards the north-west, Saxony—that is to say the vast territory which extended from the Elbe to the middle Rhine—was attacked as early as 906, and from then on was repeatedly ravaged. In Italy, the Hungarian hordes drove on as far as Otranto. In 917, they penetrated, by way of the Vosges forest and the Saales pass, to the rich abbeys grouped about the Meurthe. From that time onwards, Lorraine and northern Gaul became one of their familiar hunting-grounds. Thence they ventured into Burgundy and even south of the Loire. Men of the plains, they were nevertheless not afraid to cross the Alps if the need arose. It was 'by the devious ways of these mountains' that, coming from Italy, they descended in 924 upon the district of Nîmes.

They did not always avoid battles against organized forces, and in these engagements they met with varying success. Nevertheless they preferred as a rule to glide rapidly across country: true savages, whom their chiefs drove to battle with blows of the whip, but redoubtable soldiers, skilful in flank attacks, relentless in pursuit and resourceful in extricating themselves from the most difficult situations. Perhaps they needed to cross a river, or the Venetian lagoon. They hurriedly made boats of skins or of wood. At their halting places they set up their tents—the kind used by the people of the steppes; or they entrenched themselves in an abbey abandoned by its monks and from that point assailed the surrounding country. Artful as savages, provided when necessary with intelligence by the ambassadors whom they sent on ahead, less to parley than to spy, they had very quickly penetrated the rather clumsy artifices of Western policy. They kept themselves informed about interregna, which were particularly favourable to their incursions, and they were able to profit by the dissensions among the Christian princes to place themselves at the service of one or other of the rivals.

Sometimes, following the normal practice of bandits in every age, they demanded sums of money from the conquered populations in return for sparing their lives; from some they even exacted a regular tribute: Bavaria and Saxony were obliged for several years to submit to this humiliation. But these methods were scarcely practicable save in the territories bordering on Hungary itself, and elsewhere they simply killed and robbed outrageously. Like the Saracens, they seldom attacked fortified towns; where they ventured to do so, they usually failed, as they had done under the walls of Kiev in the early days of their expeditions in the region of the Dnieper. The only important city they captured was Pavia. They were especially dreaded by the villages and the monasteries, frequently isolated in the country districts or situated in the suburbs of towns, outside the walls. Above all, they seem to have been bent on taking prisoners, carefully choosing the best, and sometimes, among a whole population put to the sword, sparing only the young women and the very young boys—to serve their needs and their pleasures, no doubt, but mostly to be sold. On occasion, they had no compunction about selling this human cattle even in the markets of the West, where not all the customers were of a mind to be fastidious over the nature of their purchases; in 954 a girl of noble family, captured in the outskirts of Worms, was put up for sale in the city.[1] More often these unfortunates were dragged as far as the Danubian regions, to be offered to Greek traders.

4 END OF THE HUNGARIAN INVASIONS

Meanwhile, on the 10th of August 955, the king of East Francia, Otto the Great, who had received intelligence of a raid on southern Germany, attacked the returning Hungarian band on the banks of the Lech. After a bloody battle he was victorious, and was able to press home his advantage. The marauding expedition thus dealt with was destined to be the last. On the confines of Bavaria hostilities were henceforth limited to border warfare. Soon, in accordance with the Carolingian tradition, Otto reorganized the frontier commands. Two marches were created: one in the Alps, on the Mur; the other, further north, on the Enns. The latter, soon to acquire the name of the eastern command—*Ostarrichi*, from which Austria is derived—reached the forest of Vienna as early as the end of the tenth century, and the Leitha and Morava towards the middle of the eleventh.

Brilliant though it was and despite its resounding moral effect, an isolated feat of arms like the battle of the Lechfeld would clearly not have sufficed to put an end to the raids. The Hungarians, whose own territory had not been touched, were far from having undergone such a crushing defeat as the Avars had earlier at the hands of Charlemagne. The defeat of one of their bands, of which several had already been likewise vanquished, would have been powerless to change their mode of life. The truth is that, from about 926, their long-distance raids, though furious as ever, were none the less becoming more infrequent. In Italy, without battle, they also ceased after 954. In the south-east, from 960 on, the incursions into Thrace dwindled to modest little freebooting ventures. There is no doubt at all that this was the result of a number of deep-seated causes which had by degrees become effective.

The long forays across western Europe, carrying on an ancient traditional behaviour, had not always been ultimately profitable. The hordes created frightful havoc as they passed, but it was hardly possible for them to load themselves with enormous quantities of booty. The slaves, who must have followed on foot, always tended to slow down their movements, and moreover could not easily be prevented from escaping. The sources often speak of fugitives: an instance was that parish priest from the neighbourhood of Rheims who, forced to accompany his captors as far as Berry, gave them the slip one night, remained hidden in a swamp for several days

[1] Lantbertus, *Vita Heriberti*, c. I in *M.G.H., SS.*, IV, p. 741.

and finally succeeded in getting back to his village, bursting with the tale of his adventures.[1] For the removal of treasure, the wagons, moving along the wretched tracks of the time and traversing hostile territories, provided a means of transport much more cumbersome and much less reliable than the ships of the Northmen did on the fine rivers of Europe. The devastated fields often gave insufficient fodder for the horses: the Byzantine generals well knew that 'the great obstacle encountered by the Hungarians in their wars resulted from lack of pasturage'.[2] On their journeys the bands were obliged to fight many a battle; and even if victorious, they returned decimated by this guerilla warfare. Disease also fought against them. Bringing to a close in his annals (which he compiled from day to day) his account of the year 924, the cleric Flodoard of Rheims joyfully records the news, just received, that the majority of the pillagers of the Nîmes region had succumbed to a 'plague' of dysentery. As time went on, moreover, the fortified towns and castles increased in number, breaking up the open spaces which alone were really favourable to raiders. Finally, from about the year 930, the continent had become practically free from the nightmare menace of the Northmen, so that thenceforth kings and nobles had their hands free to turn against the Hungarians and to organize a more methodical resistance. Looking at the situation from this aspect one sees that the decisive importance of Otto's work lay much less in his splendid victory of the Lechfeld than in his creation of the marches.

Many motives therefore came into play to turn the Magyar people away from a type of enterprise which was undoubtedly yielding less and less in profit and costing more and more in lives. But the influence of these motives could not have been so effective had not Magyar society itself been undergoing important changes.

On this point, unfortunately, the sources fail us almost completely. Like so many other nations, the Hungarians began to keep annals only after their conversion to Christianity and Latin culture. We gain the impression nevertheless that agriculture little by little took its place by the side of stock-raising: a slow metamorphosis, in any case, and one which involved for a long time modes of life intermediate between the true nomadism of the pastoral peoples and the absolute stability of the communities of agriculturalists pure and simple. In 1147, the Bavarian bishop, Otto of Freising, when on crusade, descended the Danube and was able to observe the Hungarians of his own day. Their huts of reeds (more rarely of wood) were used as shelter only during the cold season: 'in the summer and autumn, they lived in tents.' This is the same alternation which a little earlier an Arab geographer noted among the Bulgars of the Lower Volga. The villages—very small affairs—were movable. Some time after the introduction of Christianity, between 1012 and 1015, a synod decreed that

[1] Flodoard, *Annales*, 937.
[2] Leo, *Tactica*, XVIII, 62.

villages must not move too far away from their churches. If they did so, they were obliged to pay a fine and 'return'.[1]

So, in spite of everything, the practice of extended raids disappeared. Above all, there is no doubt that solicitude for the harvests ran counter to the great summer migrations that brigandage involved. Favoured perhaps by the absorption of foreign elements—Slav tribes that had long all but ceased to be nomadic, and captives coming from the old rural civilizations of the West—these modifications in the Magyar mode of life were in harmony with profound political changes.

We perceive dimly, among the early Hungarians, above the little societies united by blood-relationship actual or reputed, the existence of larger but not very stable groupings: 'the battle once ended,' wrote the Emperor Leo the Wise, 'they disperse to their clans ($\gamma \varepsilon \nu \acute{\eta}$) and tribes ($\phi \upsilon \lambda \acute{\alpha} \iota$)'. It was a type of organization rather similar, on the whole, to that still to be found at the present day in Mongolia. As far back as the sojourn of the Magyar people in the region to the north of the Black Sea, an attempt had been made, in imitation of the Khazar state, to set above all the chiefs of the hordes a 'Great Lord' (such is the name employed by both the Greek and Latin sources). The leader elected was a certain Arpad. From then on, although it would be quite inaccurate to speak of a unified state, the Arpad dynasty clearly regarded itself as destined for leadership. In the second half of the tenth century it succeeded, not without a struggle, in establishing its power over the entire nation. Populations which were settled, or which moved about only in the interior of a restricted territory, were easier to subdue than nomads devoted to a life of constant roving. The work of stabilization seems to have been complete when in 1001, Vaik, a prince descended from Arpad, took the title of king.[2]

A rather loose association of plundering and roving hordes had been transformed into a state firmly rooted in its own soil, after the fashion of the kingdoms or principalities of the West—indeed to a large extent in imitation of them. As so often the fiercest conflicts had not prevented contact between civilizations, and the more advanced had influenced the more primitive.

The influence of Western political institutions had, moreover, been accompanied by a deeper penetration involving the whole outlook of the people; when Vaik proclaimed himself king, he had already received baptism under the name of Stephen, which the Church has preserved for him by ranking him among its saints. Like all the vast religious 'no man's land' of eastern Europe, from Moravia to Bulgaria and Russia, pagan Hungary had from the first been disputed by two teams of evangelists, each

---

[1] K. Schünemann, *Die Entstehung des Städtewesens in Südosteuropa*, Breslau, n.d., pp. 18–19.
[2] On the somewhat obscure circumstances of the establishment of the Hungarian kingdom, cf. P. E. Schramm, *Kaiser, Rom und Renovatio*, I, 1929, p. 153 *et seq.*

of which represented one of the two great systems, from that time quite clearly distinguishable, into which Christianity was divided: that of Byzantium and that of Rome. Hungarian chiefs got themselves baptized at Constantinople, and monasteries observing the Greek rite subsisted in Hungary till well on into the eleventh century. But the Byzantine missions, which came from too great a distance, were destined finally to be eclipsed by their rivals.

Initiated in the royal houses by marriages in which the desire for *rapprochement* was manifest, the work of conversion was actively carried on by the Bavarian clergy. Bishop Pilgrim in particular, who from 971 to 999 occupied the see of Passau, made this his concern. He conceived of Passau as playing for the Hungarians the same rôle of missionary metropolis as Magdeburg was to play for the Slavs beyond the Elbe, and Bremen for the Scandinavian peoples. Unfortunately, unlike Magdeburg and Bremen, Passau was only a simple bishopric, a suffragan diocese of Salzburg. Did that make any difference? The bishops of Passau, whose diocese had really been founded in the eighth century, regarded themselves as the successors of those who, from the time of the Romans, had had their see in the fortified burg of Lorch, on the Danube. Yielding to the temptation to which so many of his cloth on every hand were succumbing, Pilgrim caused a series of false bulls to be fabricated, by which Lorch was recognized as the metropolitan see of 'Pannonia'. All that remained was to reconstitute this ancient province. Around Passau, which would break all ties with Salzburg, and resume its pretended ancient rank, would be grouped, as satellites, the new bishoprics of a Hungarian 'Pannonia'. However, neither the popes nor the emperors could be persuaded to give their consent.

As for the Magyar princes, even if they felt ready for baptism they were yet firmly resolved not to be dependent on German prelates. As missionaries and later as bishops, they preferred to appoint Czech priests or even Venetians; and when about the year 1000 Stephen organized the ecclesiastical hierarchy of his state, it was placed, by papal consent, under the authority of its own metropolitan. After his death, the struggles for the succession, though they temporarily restored some prestige to certain chiefs who had remained pagan, did not in the end seriously affect his achievements. Ever more deeply penetrated by Christianity, provided with a crowned king and an archbishop, the latest arrival among the peoples of 'Scythia' had—in the words of Otto of Freising—finally renounced the tremendous raids of former days to shut itself up within the henceforth unchanging horizon of its fields and pastures. Wars with the sovereigns of neighbouring Germany remained frequent. But it was the kings of two settled nations who thenceforward confronted each other.[1]

[1] The history of the ethnological map of 'extra-feudal' Europe does not here concern us directly. It may be noted nevertheless that the settlement of the Hungarians in the Danubian plain ended by cutting the Slav bloc in two.

II

THE NORTHMEN

1 GENERAL CHARACTER OF THE SCANDINAVIAN INVASIONS

FROM the time of Charlemagne, all the populations of Germanic speech living to the south of Jutland, being thenceforward Christians and incorporated in the Frankish kingdoms, came under the influence of Western civilization. But farther to the north lived other Germans who had preserved their independence and their own traditions. Their speech, differing among themselves, but differing much more from the idioms of Germany properly so-called, belonged to another of the branches that sprang originally from the common linguistic stock; we call this today the Scandinavian branch. The contrast between their culture and that of their more southerly neighbours had been clearly marked after the great migrations which, in the second and third centuries of our era, had almost depopulated the German lands along the Baltic and about the mouth of the Elbe and thus removed many intermediate and transitional elements.

These natives of the far north formed neither a mere sprinkling of tribes nor yet a single nation. The following groups were distinguishable: the Danes, in Scania, on the islands, and, a little later, on the peninsula of Jutland; the *Götar* whose memory is preserved today in the names of the Swedish provinces of Oester- and Vestergötland;[1] the Swedes, round the shores of lake Mälar; finally, the various peoples who, separated by vast stretches of forest, by partly snowbound wastes and icy tracts, but united by a common sea, occupied the valleys and coasts of the country which was soon to be called Norway. Nevertheless there was a sufficiently pronounced family likeness among these groups, doubtless the result of much intermingling, for their neighbours to attach a common label to them. Since nothing seems more characteristic of the foreigner—a being by nature mysterious—than the direction from which he appears to spring forth, the Germans on the hither side of the Elbe formed the habit of saying simply: 'men of the North', *Nordman*. It is a curious thing that this word, despite its outlandish form, was adopted unaltered by the Roman populations of Gaul; either because, before they came into direct contact with 'the savage

---

[1] The relationship of these Scandinavian Götar to the Goths, whose rôle was so considerable in the history of the Germanic invasions, poses a difficult problem on which the specialists are far from agreement.

nation of the Northmen', its existence had been revealed to them by reports emanating from the border provinces; or, more probably, because the common people had first heard the name used by their leaders—royal officials most of whom, at the beginning of the ninth century, were descended from Austrasian families and normally spoke the Frankish tongue. Moreover, the use of the term was strictly confined to the continent. The English either tried to the best of their ability to distinguish among the different peoples, or simply designated them collectively by the name of one of them, the Danes, with whom they had most to do.[1]

Such were the 'pagans of the North' whose incursions, suddenly launched about the year 800, were destined for nearly a century and a half to afflict the West. We today are naturally better able to place the raids of the 'Northmen' in their historical setting than were the look-out men, searching the seas with their eyes and trembling when they descried the prows of the enemy ships, or the monks busy in their *scriptoria* recording the acts of pillage. Seen in their true perspective, the raids seem to us but an episode— a particularly blood-stained one, it is true—of a great human adventure: those far-ranging Scandinavian migrations which at about the same time, from the Ukraine to Greenland, were creating so many new commercial and cultural ties. But the task of showing how, by those epic achievements of peasants and merchants as well as of warriors, the horizon of European civilization was enlarged is not within the scope of the present work; we are here concerned with the ravages and conquests of the Northmen in the West only in so far as they constituted a leavening element in feudal society.

Thanks to the burial customs of the Northmen, we can form an exact idea of their fleets, for a ship concealed under a mound of earth was the chosen tomb of a chief. Modern excavations, mainly in Norway, have brought to light several of these ship-burials: ceremonial boats, it is true, intended for peaceful movement from fiord to fiord rather than for voyages to distant lands, yet capable at need of very long journeys; a vessel copied exactly from one of them—the Gokstad boat—was able in the twentieth century to cross the Atlantic from shore to shore. The 'long ships', which spread terror in the West, were of an appreciably different type—not so different, however, but that the evidence of the burials, supplemented by documentary evidence, enables us to reconstruct their appearance without much difficulty. They were deckless boats, masterpieces of joinery by a race of craftsmen in wood, and in their skilfully proportioned lines worthy of a great seafaring people. A little more than 65 feet long as a rule, they could either be propelled by oars or sailed, and each carried an average of forty to sixty men, no doubt closely packed. The

[1] The 'Northmen' to whom records of Anglo-Saxon origin sometimes give prominence are—according to the usage even of the Scandinavian texts—Norwegians, as distinct from Danes *stricto sensu*.

speed of these vessels, judging by the model constructed from the Gokstad find, was easily as much as ten knots. They were of shallow draught—not much more than three feet; a great advantage when they left the high seas and ventured into the estuaries or even up the rivers.[1]

For, to the Northmen, as to the Saracens, the waters were only a pathway to the plunder of the land. Although they did not disdain at times to learn from Christian renegades, they possessed a sort of intuitive river lore of their own, becoming so quickly familiar with the complexities of this means of travel that, as early as 830, a contingent had escorted the archbishop Ebbo from Rheims on his flight from his emperor. The prows of their ships moved forward among intricate networks of tributaries with innumerable windings, favourable to surprise attack. Navigating the Scheldt, they got as far as Cambrai; on the Yonne, as far as Sens; on the Eure, as far as Chartres; on the Loire, they reached Fleury, well upstream from Orleans. Even in Britain, where the waterways beyond the tidal reaches are much less favourable to navigation, the Ouse was nevertheless able to convey Northmen as far as York, and the Thames and one of its tributaries as far as Reading. If sails or oars could not be used, they resorted to towing. Often, in order not to overload the ships, a detachment would follow by land. Sometimes the water might be too shallow for the ship to approach the banks, or perhaps in order to carry out a raid it might be necessary to follow a shallow river, and in such cases small boats were launched from the ships. To turn the fortifications barring the river route, a portage would be improvised; this was done in 888 and 890, in order to by-pass Paris. Over towards the east, in the Russian plains, the Scandinavian merchants had had long experience in these alternations between the navigation and the portaging of ships from one river to another or alongside rapids.

Moreover, these marvellous sailors had no fear of the land—of land routes or land battles. When necessary they did not hesitate to leave the river to set out in pursuit of plunder; like those who in 870 followed through the forest of Orleans, along the tracks left by the vehicles, the trail of the monks of Fleury as they fled from their abbey on the banks of the Loire. Increasingly they learnt to use horses (this for their journeys rather than for fighting) which they usually obtained from the very district they were plundering. Thus, in 866, they rounded up a great number of horses in East Anglia. Sometimes they transported them from one field of plunder to another; in 885, for example, from France to England.[2] In this way, they became more and more independent of the waterways: in 864, for instance, they abandoned their ships on the Charente, and ventured as far as Clermont d'Auvergne, which they captured. Capable now of moving swiftly overland, they were better able to take their enemies by surprise; they were also very skilful at constructing earthworks and defending themselves.

[1] See Plate I.   [2] Asser, *Life of King Alfred*, ed. W. H. Stevenson, 1904, c. 66.

17

What is more—and they were superior in this respect to the Hungarian horsemen—they knew well how to attack fortified places. By 888 the list of the towns which in spite of their ramparts had succumbed to the assault of the Northmen was already long: among them were Cologne, Rouen, Nantes, Orleans, Bordeaux, London and York, to mention only the most famous. The truth is that, leaving aside the part sometimes played by the element of surprise, as at Nantes, captured on a feast-day, the old Roman walls were by no means always well maintained, still less were they always resolutely defended. When at Paris, in 888, a handful of energetic men put the fortifications of the *Cité* in order and found the heart to fight, this town, which in 845 had been sacked after being almost abandoned by its inhabitants, and which on two subsequent occasions appears to have suffered the same fate, for once put up a successful resistance.

The raids were profitable. The terror which they inspired in advance was not less so. Some communities (for instance, as early as 810, certain Frisian groups), recognizing that the government was incapable of defending them, and some isolated monasteries, had from the first begun to buy immunity. Later the sovereigns themselves grew accustomed to this practice: for a sum of money they would obtain from the marauders the promise to discontinue their ravages, at least for the time being, or to turn towards other prey. In West Francia, Charles the Bald had set the example in 845; in 864 it was followed by Lothar II, king of Lorraine; and in East Francia, in 882, it was the turn of Charles the Fat. Among the Anglo-Saxons, the king of Mercia paid for immunity, perhaps as early as 862; as did the king of Wessex, certainly, in 872. It was in the nature of such ransoms to act as a perpetual lure and in consequence to be repeated almost indefinitely. Since the princes were obliged to collect the necessary sums from their subjects and, above all, from their churches there finally developed a regular drain of Western wealth in the direction of Scandinavia. Today, among so many reminders of those heroic ages, the museums of the North preserve in their glass cases surprising quantities of gold and silver: largely the proceeds of commerce, no doubt; but much of it also, as the German priest Adam of Bremen remarked, 'fruits of brigandage'. It is a striking fact that these precious metals stolen or received as tribute sometimes in the form of coins, sometimes as jewellery of the Western type, should usually have been refashioned into trinkets conforming to the taste of their new owners—evidence of a civilization singularly sure of itself.

Prisoners were also carried off, and unless they were afterwards bought back, transported overseas. Thus, a little after 860, black prisoners rounded up in Morocco were sold in Ireland.[1] Finally, these warriors of the North were men of strong and brutal sensual appetites, with a taste for bloodshed

[1] H. Shetelig, *Les origines des invasions des Normands* (*Bergens Museums Årbog, Historisk—antiqkvarisk rekke*, nr. 1), p. 10.

and destruction, which manifested itself at times in great outbreaks partaking of madness, when violence no longer knew any restraint: one such occasion was the famous orgy in 1012, during which the Archbishop of Canterbury, whom till then his captors had carefully guarded with an eye to ransom, was pelted to death with the bones of the animals eaten at the banquet. Of an Icelander who had campaigned in the West the saga tells us that he was surnamed 'the children's man', because he refused to impale children on the point of his lance, 'as was the custom among his companions'.[1] All this sufficiently explains the terror spread by the invaders wherever they went.

2 FROM RAID TO SETTLEMENT

Nevertheless, since the time when the Northmen had pillaged their first monastery on the Northumbrian coast (793), and had compelled Charlemagne hurriedly to organize the defence of the Frankish littoral on the Channel (800), the nature and scope of their enterprises had gradually undergone a considerable change. The earliest raids, limited to northern shores—the British Isles, the low-lying country bordering the great northern plain, the cliffs of Neustria—had been seasonal affairs carried out in fine weather by small bands of 'Vikings'. The etymology of this word is disputed.[2] But that it stood for a pursuer of profitable and warlike ventures is not in doubt, and no more is the fact that the Viking bands were generally constituted, in disregard of family or national ties, expressly for the enterprise itself. Only the kings of Denmark, heads of a state with at least a rudimentary organization, were already, on their southern frontiers, attempting genuine conquests—though indeed without much success.

Then, very rapidly, the radius of Viking activity expanded. The ships fared as far as the Atlantic and farther still towards the south. As early as 844, certain ports of western Spain had been visited by the pirates. In 859 and 860, it was the turn of the Mediterranean. The Balearics, Pisa, the Lower Rhône were reached, and the valley of the Arno was penetrated as far up as Fiesole. This Mediterranean inroad was, however, to be the only one of its kind. Not that distances frightened the discoverers of Iceland and Greenland. Did not the Barbary corsairs in the seventeenth century venture in the opposite direction to within sight of Saintonge, nay, even as

---

[1] *Landnámabók*, cc. 303, 334, 344, 379.

[2] Two principal interpretations have been advanced. Some scholars derive the word from the Scandinavian *vik*, bay; others see in it a derivative of the common Germanic *wik*, meaning a town or market. (Cf. the Low-German *Weichbild*, urban law, and a great number of place-names, such as Norwich in England, or Brunswick—*Braunschweig*—in Germany.) In the former case, the Viking would have taken his name from the bays where he lurked waiting to attack; in the latter, from the towns which he sometimes frequented as a peaceful merchant and sometimes pillaged. No one so far has been able to furnish a decisive argument for one theory or the other.

far as the banks of Newfoundland? But the truth is that the seas of southern Europe were too well guarded by the Arab fleets.

On the other hand, the raids ate farther and farther into the body of the continent and into Great Britain. No diagram is more eloquent than the wanderings of the monks of Saint-Philibert, with their relics. The abbey had been founded in the seventh century on the island of Noirmoutier—an abode well suited to monks, so long as the sea remained more or less free from marauders, but one which became extremely dangerous when the first Scandinavian ships appeared in the Bay. A little before 819, the monks had a refuge built on the mainland, at Dées, on the shore of the Lac de Grandlieu. Soon they formed the habit of going there every year from the beginning of spring and remaining there until the bad weather towards the end of autumn seemed to afford a safe barrier against their seafaring enemies, so that the church on the island could once more be opened for the divine offices. Nevertheless, in 836, Noirmoutier, continually devastated and experiencing growing difficulties in supplying itself with food, was judged to be no longer tenable, and Dées, formerly only a temporary refuge, was raised to the status of a permanent establishment, while farther to the rear a little monastery recently acquired at Cunauld, upstream from Saumur, served thenceforward as a position on which to fall back. In 858 a further retreat was necessary, and Dées, still too near the coast, had in its turn to be permanently abandoned in favour of Cunauld. Unfortunately this site on the easily navigable Loire had not been judiciously chosen. By 862 the monks had judged it necessary to move away from the river to Messay in Poitou—only to realize, after about ten years, that they were still perilously close to the sea. This time the entire extent of the Central Massif did not seem too great a protective barrier, and in 872 or 873 the monks fled to Saint-Pourçain-sur-Sioule. Even there, however, they could not remain for long, and eventually the fortified town of Tournus, on the Saône, still farther to the east, was the asylum where, from 875, the saintly community, after so many weary journeys, finally found the 'place of tranquillity' of which a royal charter speaks.[1]

These long-distance expeditions of the Northmen naturally required an organization very different from that which had served for the lightning raids of earlier days. In the first place, they called for much larger forces. The small bands, each grouped about a 'sea king', united by degrees until true armies came into being; an example is the 'Great Host' (*magnus exercitus*) which, having been formed on the Thames, and then—after plundering the Flemish coast—reinforced by the adhesion of several isolated bands, ravaged Gaul atrociously from 879 to 892, to return at last and disband on the coast of Kent. Above all it became impossible to return every year to the North, and accordingly the Vikings took to the

[1] R. Poupardin, *Monuments de l'histoire des abbayes de Saint-Philibert*, 1905, with the *Introduction*, and G. Tessier, *Bibliothèque de l'École des Chartes*, 1932, p. 203.

practice of wintering between two campaigns in the country which they had chosen as a hunting-ground. This they did in Ireland from about 835; in Gaul for the first time at Noirmoutier in 843; and in the Isle of Thanet, at the mouth of the Thames, in 851. They had first established themselves on the coasts, but soon they were not afraid to penetrate far into the interior. Often they entrenched themselves on a river island, or they settled down somewhere within easy reach of a stream. For these protracted visits some of them brought over their wives and children. In 888, the Parisians could hear from their ramparts female voices in the enemy camp, chanting the dirge of the dead warriors. Despite the terror inspired by these nests of brigands, from which fresh raids were constantly launched, some natives would venture into the winter quarters to sell their produce, so that the robbers' den for the moment became a market. Buccaneers still, but by now half-sedentary buccaneers, the Northmen were getting ready to become conquerors of the soil.

Everything indeed disposed the simple bandits of former days to such an evolution. These Vikings, who were attracted by the opportunities for plunder that the West afforded, belonged to a race of peasants, black-smiths, wood-carvers and merchants, as well as warriors. Drawn from their homes by the love of gain or adventure, sometimes forced into this exile by family feuds or rivalries between chieftains, they none the less felt behind them the traditions of a society with a fixed framework. It had been after all as colonists that the Scandinavians had settled in the islands, from the Faroes to the Hebrides, and as colonists again, true reclaimers of virgin territory, that from 870 onwards they carried out the great 'taking up of the land', the *Landnáma* of Iceland. Accustomed to mixing commerce with piracy, they had created round the Baltic a whole ring of fortified markets, and the common characteristic of the early principalities founded by various chieftains during the ninth century at either end of Europe—in Ireland round Dublin, Cork and Limerick; in Kievian Russian along the stages of the great river-route—was that they were essentially urban, dominating the surrounding territory from a town selected as centre.

It is necessary at this point to pass over the history, interesting though it is, of the colonies established in the western isles: the Shetlands and Ork-neys, which were annexed from the tenth century to the kingdom of Norway and were only to pass to Scotland at the very end of the Middle Ages (1468); the Hebrides and Man, which till the middle of the thirteenth century con-stituted an autonomous Scandinavian principality; and the coastal king-doms of Ireland, which after their expansion had been checked at the beginning of the eleventh century did not finally disappear till about a century later, under the impact of the English conquest. In these lands situated at the extreme edge of Europe, it was with the Celtic societies that Scandinavian civilization clashed. Here the account of the settlement of the Northmen will be confined to the two great 'feudal' countries: the old

21

Frankish state and Anglo-Saxon Britain. Although between these two territories—as among the neighbouring isles—human intercourse continued, and the war-bands always crossed the Channel or the Irish Sea with ease, while the leaders, if disappointed by a reverse on one shore, habitually turned to seek better fortune on the opposite coast, it will none the less be necessary, for the sake of greater clarity, to examine the two fields of conquest separately.

3 THE SCANDINAVIAN SETTLEMENTS: ENGLAND

Their first wintering on British soil in 851 initiated the Scandinavians' new policy of settling there permanently. From that time on, their bands, working more or less in relays, never let go their prey. Of the Anglo-Saxon states some, whose kings had been killed, disappeared: such were Deira, on the east coast, between the Humber and the Tees; and East Anglia, between the Thames and the Wash. Others, like Bernicia in the extreme north and Mercia in the centre, survived for some time, although much reduced in size and placed under a sort of protectorate. Only Wessex, which extended at that time over the whole of southern England, succeeded in preserving its independence, though not without bitter fighting in campaigns made illustrious from 871 by the clear-sighted and patient heroism of King Alfred.

A finished product of that Anglo-Saxon civilization which, more successfully than any other in the barbarian kingdoms, had managed to weld together in an original synthesis the contributions of contrasted cultural traditions, Alfred, the scholar-king, was also a soldier-king. He succeeded (c. 880) in conquering what still remained of Mercia, which was thus withdrawn from Danish influence, although in the same period it became necessary to abandon to the invader by regular treaty the whole of the eastern part of the island. Yet it should not be supposed that this immense territory, roughly bounded on the west by the old Roman road from London to Chester, formed at that time a single state in the hands of the conquerors. Scandinavian kings or 'jarls', with here and there, no doubt, a petty Anglo-Saxon chieftain, like the successors of the princes of Bernicia, divided up the country, being sometimes united among themselves by various bonds of alliance or subordination, and sometimes at odds with each other. Elsewhere small aristocratic republics were set up, similar to those of Iceland. Fortified boroughs had been constructed which served as strong-points as well as markets for the various 'armies', now become sedentary; and since it was necessary to provide sustenance for the troops arrived from overseas, land had been distributed among the warriors. Meanwhile, on the coasts, other bands of Vikings continued their pillaging. Is it surprising that, towards the end of his reign, his memory still burdened with so many scenes of horror, Alfred, translating the picture of

22

the Golden Age in the *Consolation* of Boethius, could not refrain from adding this touch to the original: 'in those days one never heard tell of ships armed for war'?[1]

The state of anarchy prevailing in the Danish part of the island explains the fact that from 899 the kings of Wessex, who alone in the whole of Britain disposed of extensive territorial power and relatively large resources, were able to undertake the reconquest of the country. Their campaigns were based on a network of fortifications they had gradually constructed. From 954, after an extremely bitter struggle, they succeeded in getting their authority recognized as supreme over all the territory previously occupied by the enemy. This certainly did not mean, however, that the traces of Scandinavian settlement were effaced. It is true that a few jarls, with their followers, had more or less voluntarily taken to the sea again. But most of the former invaders stayed where they were: the leaders retained their authority under the royal hegemony, and the rank and file kept their lands.

Meanwhile, profound political changes were at work in Scandinavia itself. Above the chaos of small tribal groups, real states were being consolidated or established: states as yet very unstable, torn by innumerable dynastic conflicts and ceaselessly engaged in war with each other, yet capable, at least spasmodically, of formidable concentrations of their forces. Alongside Denmark, where the royal power had grown considerably by the end of the tenth century; alongside the kingdom of the Swedes, which had absorbed that of the Götar, there now stretched the latest-born of the northern monarchies, created initially in the relatively open and fertile lands about Oslo fjord and Lake Mjösen. This was the kingdom of the 'north way' or, as the English say, Norway: the very name, a simple matter of location and without any ethnic implications, signifying the unified authority which had been imposed by degrees on the particularism of peoples once quite distinct. The rulers of these more powerful political unities were still familiar with the Viking's way of life. As young men, before their accession, they had roamed the sea; later, if some reverse compelled them to flee for the time being before a more fortunate rival, they set off again on the great adventure. Is it not understandable that, once having been in the position to order substantial levies of men and ships over an extensive territory, they should again have cast their eyes towards the sea to seek, beyond the horizon, the opportunity for new conquests?

When from 980 on the incursions into Britain were once more intensified, it is characteristic that we should soon find at the head of the principal bands two pretenders to Scandinavian thrones: one to that of Norway, the other to that of Denmark. Both subsequently became kings. The Norwegian, Olaf Tryggvason, never returned to the island. The Dane, on the other hand, Sweyn Fork-Beard, did not forget the way back. He seems to

[1] *King Alfred's Old English Version of Boethius*, ed. W. J. Sedgefield, § XV.

have been recalled in the first instance by one of those feuds which a Scandinavian hero could not renounce without dishonour. In his absence, the pillaging expeditions had continued under other leaders, and Ethelred, king of England, decided that there was no better way to defend himself against the marauders than by taking some of them into his service. To oppose Vikings to Vikings in this way was an old game that had been practised on several occasions by the princes of the continent, but in most cases with very limited success.

Experiencing in his turn the faithlessness of his 'Danish' mercenaries, Ethelred, on the 13th November 1002 (St. Brice's Day), revenged himself on them by ordering the massacre of all those within reach. According to a later tradition, which it is impossible to verify, the victims included Sweyn's own sister. From 1003 onwards the king of Denmark was burning English towns, and thenceforward war almost incessantly ravaged the country, continuing till after the death of both Sweyn and Ethelred. In the early days of the year 1017, the last representatives of the house of Wessex having taken refuge in Gaul or having been sent by the Danish conquerors into the distant country of the Slavs, the 'wise' of the land—that is to say, the assembly of the great nobles and bishops—acknowledged Sweyn's son, Cnut, king of all the English.

This was not a simple matter of a change of dynasty. At the time of his accession to the English throne, Cnut was not yet king of Denmark, where one of his brothers reigned; but he became so two years later. Subsequently he conquered Norway, and at least attempted to establish his power over the Slavs and Finns beyond the Baltic, as far as Esthonia. It was natural that the freebooting expeditions by sea should be succeeded by attempts to found a maritime empire. England figured in this enterprise as the most westerly province. It was on English soil that Cnut chose to pass the whole of the last period of his life, and it was to the English clergy that he readily appealed to organize the missionary churches of his Scandinavian dominions. The son of a heathen king, perhaps converted late in life, Cnut himself was devoted to the Roman Church; he was a founder of monasteries, a religious-minded and moralizing legislator in the manner of Charlemagne.

Thus he was in full accord with his subjects in Britain when, faithful to the example of several of his Anglo-Saxon predecessors, he made his pilgrimage to Rome in 1027, 'for the redemption of his soul and the salvation of his peoples'. He was present at the coronation of the greatest sovereign of the West, the Emperor Conrad II, king of Germany and Italy; he also met the king of Burgundy, and as a good son of a people who had always been merchants as well as warriors, he contrived to obtain from these gate-keepers of the Alps profitable exemptions from tolls for the merchants of England. But it was from the Scandinavian countries that he derived the major part of the forces with which he held the great island. 'Aale caused this stone to be erected. He levied taxes for King Cnut in England. God rest his soul.' Such is the inscription in runic characters which today can still be read on a funeral stele, near a village in the Swedish province of Upland.[1] This state, centred about the North Sea, was a cross-roads where many different currents of civilization met. Officially it was Christian, despite the presence in its various territories of numerous elements still pagan or very superficially Christianized; and through the channel of Christianity it was accessible to the influence of the ancient literatures. Finally, it was a blend of the native traditions of the Scandinavian peoples with the heritage of Anglo-Saxon civilization, itself at once Germanic and Latin.

Perhaps it was about this time, but more probably a little earlier, that in Northumbria, which was peopled with former Vikings, an Anglo-Saxon poet, putting into verse old legends of the country of the Götar and the Danish islands, composed the *Lay of Beowulf*, full of the echoes of an epic vein still completely pagan. As further evidence of the play of opposing influences, this strange and sombre poem with its fabulous monsters is preceded in the manuscript in which it has been transmitted to us by a letter from Alexander to Aristotle, and followed by a fragment translated from the Book of Judith.[2]

But this remarkable state had always been rather loosely knit. Communications over such great distances and by turbulent seas involved many risks. For some it must have been disquieting to hear Cnut declare in the proclamation which in 1027, on his way from Rome to Denmark, he addressed to the English: 'I intend to come to you, once my eastern realm is pacified . . . as early this summer as I am able to procure myself a fleet.' The parts of the empire from which the sovereign was absent had to be entrusted to viceroys, who were not invariably loyal. After the death of Cnut the union which he had created and maintained by force fell to pieces. Norway having finally seceded, England, as a separate kingdom, was first allotted to one of his sons, then for a brief period reunited to Denmark. Finally in 1042, it was once more a prince of the house of Wessex, Edward, later called 'the Confessor', who was acknowledged king.

Meanwhile, the Scandinavian inroads on the coasts had not completely ceased, nor had the ambitions of the northern chiefs been quenched as yet. Bled white by so many wars and pillagings, disorganized in its political and ecclesiastical structure, troubled by the dynastic rivalries of the nobles, the English state was plainly no longer capable of more than a feeble resistance.

[1] Oskar Montelius, *Sverige och Vikingafäderna västernt* (Sweden and the Viking Expeditions in the West) in *Antikvarisk Tidskrift*, XXI, 2, p. 14 (several other examples).

[2] Klaeber's edition, 1928, furnishes a guide to the enormous literature relating to the poem. The date is in dispute, the linguistic evidence proving singularly difficult to interpret. The opinion advanced in the text seems to me to tally with historical probabilities: cf. L. L. Schücking, *Wann entstand der Beowulf?* in *Beiträge zur Gesch. der deutschen Sprache*, XLII, 1917. More recently, Ritchie Girvan (*Beowulf and the Seventh Century*, 1935) has attempted to put back the composition to some time about 700. But he does not explain the Scandinavian influence, so perceptible in the subject itself.

The prey was ready for the kill and it was being watched from two sides: from beyond the Channel by the French dukes of Normandy, whose subjects during the whole of the first half of the reign of Edward (who had himself been brought up at the ducal court) already figured among the king's entourage and in the ranks of the higher clergy; and from beyond the North Sea by the Scandinavian kings. When, after the death of Edward, one of the chief magnates of the realm, Harold (himself Scandinavian by name and half-Scandinavian by birth), had been crowned king, two armies landed on the English coast at intervals of a few weeks. One army, on the Humber, was led by the king of Norway, another Harold or Harald—the Harald Hardrada ('of hard counsel') of the Sagas: a true Viking who had attained the crown only after long adventurous wanderings, a former captain of the Scandinavian guards at the court of Constantinople, commander of the Byzantine armies sent out against the Arabs of Sicily, son-in-law of a prince of Novgorod, and lastly an intrepid explorer of the Arctic seas. The other army, on the coast of Sussex, was commanded by the duke of Normandy, William the Bastard.[1] Harald the Norwegian was defeated and slain at Stamford Bridge. William was victorious at Hastings.

It is true that the successors of Cnut did not immediately renounce their inherited ambitions; on two occasions during William's reign the Danes reappeared in Yorkshire. But these warlike enterprises soon degenerated into simple brigandage. In their final phase the Scandinavian expeditions reverted to their original type. Withdrawn from the Nordic sphere, to which for a brief period it had seemed destined to belong for good, England was for nearly a century and a half incorporated in a state that compassed both sides of the Channel, and was permanently involved in the political interests and the cultural currents of Western Europe.

4 THE SCANDINAVIAN SETTLEMENTS: FRANCE

This same duke of Normandy, the conqueror of England, completely French though he was by speech and manner of life, was also one of the authentic descendants of the Vikings. For, on the continent, as in the island, more than one 'sea-king' had in the end made himself a territorial lord or prince.

The process there had begun very early. From about 850, the Rhine delta had seen the first attempt to establish a Scandinavian principality within the political edifice of the Frankish state. About this date, two members of the royal house of Denmark, exiles from their country, received as a 'benefice' from the emperor Louis the Pious the country round Duurstede, then the

---

[1] C. Petit-Dutaillis (*The Feudal Monarchy in France and England*, p. 63) considers that there was probably an entente between the two invaders, who may have contemplated a treaty of partition. The hypothesis is ingenious, but it is scarcely susceptible of proof.

principal commercial centre of the Empire on the North Sea. Enlarged later by other fragments of Frisia, the territory thus conceded was to remain almost continuously in the hands of representatives of this family till 885, when the last of them was treacherously slain by the orders of Charles the Fat, his lord. The little that we are able to discern of their history suffices to show that, with their eyes turned sometimes towards Denmark and its dynastic quarrels, sometimes towards the Frankish provinces—where, though they had become Christians, they did not hesitate to undertake profitable raids—they proved faithless as vassals and useless as guardians of the land. But this Netherlandish Normandy, which did not survive, possesses for the historian all the value of a premonitory symptom.

A little later a group of Northmen, still pagans, appear to have lived for a considerable time at Nantes or in its neighbourhood on good terms with the Breton count. On several occasions the Frankish kings had taken Viking leaders into their service. If, for example, that Völundr, whose homage Charles the Bald had received in 862, had not been killed shortly afterwards in a judicial duel, there can be no doubt that it would soon have been necessary to provide him with fiefs and that this inevitable consequence was accepted in advance. At the beginning of the tenth century the idea of such settlements was clearly in the air, and at last one of these projects took shape. But exactly how and in what form? We are very ill-informed on these questions. The technical problem here is so serious that the historian cannot in honesty refrain from taking the reader into his confidence. Let us therefore, for a moment, open the door of the laboratory just a little.

There were at this period, in various churches, clerics who made it their business to keep an annual record of events. This was an old custom, connected with methods of chronological reckoning, the practice being to note down at the same time the salient events of the past and the present year. At the beginning of the Middle Ages, when dates were still reckoned by consuls, this was the procedure for the consular *fasti*; and also later for the Easter tables which determined the continually varying dates of this feast, which is what mainly regulates the order of the liturgies. Then, towards the beginning of the Carolingian period, the historical epitome was detached from the calendar, though its strictly annual divisions were preserved. Naturally, the perspective of these chroniclers differed greatly from our own. They were interested in hailstorms, in the scarcity of wine or corn, and in prodigies, almost as much as in wars, the deaths of princes, or the revolutions of State or Church. They were in addition unequal, not only in intelligence, but also in the amount of information they possessed. Curiosity, skill in investigation, and zeal varied from individual to individual. Above all, the quantity and quality of the information collected depended on such factors as the situation of the religious house, its importance, its links—close or otherwise—with the court or the nobility.

At the end of the ninth century and during the tenth, the best annalists of Gaul were, beyond question, an anonymous monk of the great abbey of Saint-Vaast at Arras, and a priest of Rheims, Flodoard, the latter combining the advantage of a particularly subtle mind with residence in a unique centre of information and intrigue. Unfortunately the annals of Saint-Vaast stop short in the middle of the year 900, while those of Flodoard, at least in the form in which they have come down to us—for we have also, of course, to reckon with the ravages of time—do not begin before 919. Now, by the most exasperating mischance, the hiatus in the records happens to coincide exactly with the settlement of the Northmen in the West Frankish kingdom.

It is true that these memorials are not the only historical works left by an epoch much preoccupied with the past. Less than a century after the foundation of the Norman principality on the Lower Seine, Duke Richard I, the grandson of its founder, decided to have a record made of his ancestors' exploits as well as his own. He entrusted this task to a canon of Saint-Quentin named Doon. The work, executed before 1026, is full of information. We catch a glimpse of a writer of the eleventh century at work, occupied in putting together the evidence extracted from earlier annals, which he never cites, and adding to it some oral information, by which he sets great store, together with the embellishments suggested either by recollections of things he had read or purely and simply by his own imagination. Here we find displayed the ornaments which a learned clerk thought worthy to heighten the colour of his narrative, and the devices used by a cunning flatterer out to gratify the pride of his patrons. With the help of some authentic documents which enable us to check the narrative, we are here in a position to measure the depth of forgetfulness and the degree of distortion to which, after the lapse of some generations, the historical memory of the men of those times was prone. In short, as revealing the mentality belonging to a particular environment and age this narrative is an infinitely precious piece of evidence; but for the facts themselves, at least so far as the early history of the duchy of Normandy is concerned, its testimony is almost valueless.

Here then is what we are able to ascertain of these extremely obscure events, with the aid of some indifferent annals and a very small number of records.

Without entirely neglecting the mouths of the Rhine and the Scheldt, the Vikings' activities from about 885 were directed more and more to the valleys of the Loire and the Seine. In the region of the Lower Seine, for instance, one of their bands was permanently installed in 896, and thence sallied forth in all directions in search of booty. But these long-distance raids were not always successful. The marauders were defeated in Burgundy on several occasions, and under the walls of Chartres in 911. In the Roumois and the neighbouring region, on the other hand, they were masters, and there is no doubt that in order to feed themselves during the winter seasons they were already obliged to cultivate the land or have it cultivated for them; the more so since this settlement was a centre of attraction and the first arrivals, few in number, had been joined by other waves of adventurers.

If experience had shown that it was not impossible to curb their ravages, it yet seemed that to dislodge them from their lairs was beyond the powers of the sole authority whose business it was to do so, i.e. the king. For regional government no longer existed: in this horribly devastated area, whose centre was now the mere ruin of a town, the machinery of local command had totally disappeared. Apart from that, the new king of West Francia, Charles the Simple (crowned in 893 and universally acknowledged after the death of Odo, his rival), appears from the time of his accession to have planned to come to an agreement with the invader. This plan he tried to put into effect during the year 897, by summoning to his court the chief who at that time commanded the Northmen of the Lower Seine, and making him his godson, but this first attempt was unsuccessful. But after this it is not surprising that, fourteen years later, he should have taken up the idea again, addressing himself this time to Rollo, who had succeeded Charles' godson in the command of the same 'army'. Rollo, for his part, had just been defeated before Chartres and this reverse had not failed to open his eyes to the difficulties with which the pursuit of plunder was beset. He considered it wise to accept the king's offer. This meant that both sides recognized the *fait accompli*—with the additional advantages, so far as the king and his counsellors were concerned, of reuniting to their dominions, by the ties of vassal homage and the accompanying obligations of military aid, an already full-blown principality which thenceforward would have the best reasons in the world for guarding the coast against any further depredations by pirates. In a charter of the 14th March 918, the king mentions the concessions granted 'to the Northmen of the Seine, that is to say Rollo and his companions . . . for the defence of the realm'.

The reconciliation took place at a date which we have no means of determining precisely: certainly after the battle of Chartres (20th July 911), and probably soon after it. Rollo and many of his followers received baptism. He was thenceforward to exercise powers broadly equivalent to those of a count, the highest local official of the Frankish government. These powers, which were virtually hereditary, he was to enjoy throughout the area ceded, which is defined by the only trustworthy source—Flodoard's *History of the Church of Rheims*—as 'some counties' round Rouen. These probably comprised that part of the diocese of Rouen lying between the Epte and the sea, together with part of the diocese of Évreux. But the Northmen were not the men to be content for long with so restricted a living-space; moreover new influxes of immigrants drove them irresistibly to extend their territories. The renewal of the dynastic wars in the West Frankish kingdom soon provided them with the opportunity to sell their intervention. In 924, King Raoul handed over the Bessin to Rollo;[1] in 933, he ceded to Rollo's son and successor the dioceses of Avranches and Coutances. Thus, progressively, the Neustrian 'Normandy' had assumed the shape that it was henceforth to retain.

There remained, however, the Lower Loire with its Vikings—the same problem as on the other estuary, and at first the attempt was made to solve it by the same method. In 921, the duke and marquis Robert—brother of the former king Odo—who held a great command in the West where he ruled all but autonomously, ceded the county of Nantes to the pirates of the Loire, of whom only a few had been baptized. The Scandinavian band, however, appears to have been less strong, and the attraction exercised by the settlements of Rollo, regularized about ten years earlier, hindered its growth. What is more, the Nantes region, unlike the counties about Rouen, was no vacant property, nor was it an isolated one. It is true that, in the kingdom or duchy of the Armorican Bretons, in which it had been incorporated soon after 840, the struggles between the pretenders as well as the Scandinavian inroads themselves had led to extreme anarchy. Nevertheless the dukes or the pretenders to the ducal dignity, notably the counts of the adjacent Vannes region, considered themselves the lawful masters of this Romance-speaking march, and for its reconquest they had the help of the forces which they were able to levy among their followers in Brittany proper. Alan Crooked-Beard, who returned in 936 from England where he had taken refuge, expelled the invaders. The Normandy of the Loire, unlike that of the Seine, had only an ephemeral existence.[2]

The settlement of the companions of Rollo on the Channel coast did not at once put an end to the depredations. Here and there isolated chiefs, all the more avid for plunder because they were angered at not having received lands themselves,[3] continued to overrun the countryside. Burgundy was again ravaged in 924. Sometimes the Northmen of Rouen joined these brigands, and even the dukes themselves had not altogether abandoned their old habits. The monk Richer, of Rheims, who wrote in the last years of the tenth century, rarely fails to call them 'dukes of the pirates'. In truth, their warlike expeditions did not differ greatly from the raids of former times, more especially as they frequently employed bands of Vikings newly arrived from the North: such were the adventurers, 'panting with desire for plunder',[4] who in 1013, more than a century after Rollo had done homage, arrived under the leadership of Olaf, a pretender to the crown of Norway.

---

[1] At the same time, apparently, as Maine, the cession of which was later revoked.

[2] Later, several noble families, in various parts of France, claimed to be descended from chiefs of the Northmen: among them were the lords of Vignory and La Ferté-sur-Aube (Chaume, *Les Origines du duché de Bourgogne*, I, p. 400, n. 4). One scholar, Moranvillé, has ascribed the same origin to the house of Roucy (*Bibl. Éc. Chartes*, 1922). But definite proof is lacking.

[3] Flodoard, *Annales*, 924 (concerning Rögnvald).

[4] William of Jumièges, *Gesta*, ed. Marx, V, 12, p. 86.

This chieftain was at that time a pagan, but was destined to become after his baptism the national saint of his country. Other bands operated independently along the coast. One of them (966 to 970) even ventured as far as the coasts of Spain and captured St. James-of-Compostela. In 1018 yet another band appeared on the coast of Poitou.

Little by little, however, the Scandinavian ships abandoned their long-distance expeditions. Beyond the frontiers of France the Rhine delta also became almost free from Northmen, so that in about 930 the bishop of Utrecht could return to his city, where his predecessor had been unable to set up any permanent residence, and have it rebuilt. But the shores of the North Sea remained exposed to many surprise attacks. In 1006, the port of Tiel on the Waal was pillaged and Utrecht was threatened; the inhabitants themselves set fire to the installations of the wharves and the mercantile quarter, which were not protected by any fortifications. A Frisian law of a slightly later date takes account of what was apparently quite normal: the case of a native of those parts being carried off by the Northmen and forcibly enrolled in one of their bands. For many years the Scandinavian seafarers continued in this way to maintain that state of insecurity so characteristic of a certain phase of civilization. But the age of the long-distance expeditions with their winter camps was past and so—after the defeat of Stamford Bridge—was that of conquests overseas.

5 THE CONVERSION OF THE NORTH

Meanwhile, the North itself was gradually being converted to Christianity. The case of a civilization passing slowly over to a new faith provides the historian with some of his most exciting material, especially when, as in this case, the sources, despite irremediable *lacunae*, permit its vicissitudes to be followed sufficiently closely for it to throw a light on other movements of the same order. But a detailed study would go beyond the scope of this book. A few salient points must suffice.

It would not be correct to say that Nordic paganism failed to put up a serious resistance, since three centuries were necessary to overcome it. We can discern, however, some of the internal causes which led to eventual defeat. To the strongly organized clergy of the Christian peoples Scandinavia opposed no corresponding body. The chiefs of kinship groups or peoples were the only priests. It is true that the kings, in particular, might be afraid that if they lost their rights of sacrifice an essential element of their power would thereby be destroyed, but as we shall explain later, Christianity did not compel them to renounce altogether their sacred attributes. As to the chiefs of families or tribes, it is probable that profound changes in the social structure, connected with the migrations and with the formation of states, dealt a formidable blow to their sacerdotal prestige. The old religion not only lacked the framework of a Church; it seems at the time of the conversion to have shown many symptoms of spontaneous decomposition. The Scandinavian texts introduce us fairly often to real unbelievers. In the long run, this crude scepticism was to lead, less to the absence of any faith, something which would have been almost inconceivable, than to the adoption of a new faith.

Finally, polytheism itself offered an easy approach to the new religion. Minds that are strangers to any critical examination of evidence are scarcely inclined to deny the supernatural, from whatever quarter it may come. When the Christians refused to pray to the gods of the various pagan cults, it was not as a rule for any want of belief in their existence; on the contrary, they regarded them as evil demons, dangerous indeed, but weaker than the sole Creator. Similarly, as we know from numerous texts, when the Northmen came to know of Christ and his saints, they quickly became accustomed to treat them as alien deities whom, with the aid of one's own gods, one could oppose and mock, but whose obscure power was too much to be feared for the wise man, in other circumstances, not to propitiate them and respect the mysterious magic of their cult. It is on record that, in 860, a sick Viking made a vow to Saint Riquier. On the other hand, a little later an Icelandic chieftain genuinely converted to Christianity continued nevertheless in various predicaments to invoke the aid of Thor.[1] From recognizing the God of the Christians as a formidable force to accepting him as the sole God was an easy transition.

Interrupted by truces and *pourparlers*, the pillaging expeditions themselves played a part in the process. More than one seafarer from the North, on returning from his warlike cruises, brought home the new religion, almost as if it were part of his booty. The two great Christianizing kings of Norway, Olaf son of Tryggvi and Olaf son of Harald, had both received baptism—the first on English soil in 994, the second in France in 1014—at a time when, as yet without kingdoms, they were leaders of Viking bands. These transitions, gradual or otherwise, to the law of Christ increased in number as the adventurers, newly arrived from overseas, encountered along their route more and more of their compatriots permanently settled in lands long Christian, most of whom had been won over to the beliefs of the peoples who were now their subjects or neighbours.

Commercial relations, which had begun earlier than the great warlike enterprises and had never been interrupted by them, were also favourable to the conversions. In Sweden the majority of the first Christians were merchants who had frequented Duurstede, at that time the principal centre of communications between the Frankish empire and the northern seas. An old chronicle of Gotland says of the inhabitants of that island: 'They travelled with their merchandise to every land . . . among the Christians, they changed over to Christian customs; some were baptised and brought back priests with them.' It is a fact that the oldest Christian

[1] Mabillon, *AA. SS. ord. S. Bened.*, saec. II, 1733 ed., II, p. 214; *Landnamabók*, III, 14, 3.

communities of which we find traces were formed in the trading towns: Birka, on Lake Mälar, Ripen and Schleswig at the two extremities of the route which traversed the isthmus of Jutland from sea to sea. In Norway, towards the beginning of the eleventh century, according to the penetrating remark of the Icelandic historian Snorri Sturluson, 'most of the men who lived along the coasts had been baptized, while in the high valleys and on the mountainous expanses the people remained completely pagan'.[1] For a long time these contacts between man and man, incidental to temporary migrations, were much more effective in propagating the alien religion than were the missions sent out by the Church.

The latter had nevertheless begun at an early date. To work for the extinction of paganism seemed to the Carolingians at once a duty inherent in the vocation of Christian princes and the surest way of extending their own hegemony over a world destined to be united in one faith. And the same was true of the great German emperors, the heirs of their traditions: once Germania proper had been converted, their attention naturally turned to the Germans of the North. On the initiative of Louis the Pious missionaries went forth to preach the gospel to the Danes and Swedes. As Gregory the Great had once contemplated doing with English children, young Scandinavians were bought in the slave markets to be prepared for the priesthood and the apostolate. Finally, the work of conversion acquired a permanent base by the establishment of an archbishopric at Hamburg, to which the Picard monk Anskar, on his return from Sweden, was the first to be appointed. It was a metropolitan church, at that time without suffragans, but beyond the frontiers of the Scandinavians and Slavs there was an immense province for it to conquer. Nevertheless, ancestral beliefs were still too firmly rooted, the Frankish priests, regarded as servants of foreign princes, aroused too sharp a suspicion, and the teams of preachers themselves, in spite of some fiery souls like Anskar, were too difficult to recruit for these great dreams to be quickly realized. After Hamburg had been pillaged by the Vikings in 845, the mother-church of missions only survived because of a decision to unite it, while detaching it from the Cologne province, with the older and wealthier see of Bremen.

This at least afforded a position on which to fall back and wait, and in fact from Bremen-Hamburg a new and more successful campaign was launched in the tenth century. At the same time, coming from another sector of the Christian world, English priests disputed with their German brothers the honour of baptizing the pagans of Scandinavia. Long accustomed to the calling of 'fishers of men', helped by the constant communications which linked the ports of their island to the opposite coasts, above all less suspect than the Germans, their harvest seems indeed to have been more abundant. It is significant that in Sweden, for example, the vocabulary of Christianity should be composed of borrowings from the Anglo-Saxon

[1] *Saga of St. Olaf*, c. LX.

33

rather than from the German. Not less so is the fact that numerous parishes in that country should have taken English saints as patrons. Although, according to hierarchical rules, the more or less ephemeral dioceses founded in the Scandinavian countries were supposed to be dependent on the province of Bremen-Hamburg, the Christian kings frequently had their bishops consecrated in Britain. English influence was still more widely disseminated over Denmark, and even over Norway, in the time of Cnut and his immediate heirs.

For the truth is that the attitude of the kings and principal chiefs was the decisive factor. This was fully understood by the Church, which always did its utmost to win them over. Especially as the Christian groups grew in number and, from the very fact of their success, found themselves confronted by pagan groups more conscious of danger and consequently more resolute in the struggle, the two parties increasingly came to rely upon the power of coercion exercised—often with an extreme harshness—by the sovereigns. Moreover, without royal support, how would it have been possible to cast over the country that network of bishoprics and abbeys, in the absence of which Christianity would have been incapable of maintaining its spiritual order and of reaching the lower strata of the population? Conversely, in the wars between rival claimants which unceasingly rent the Scandinavian states, religious conflicts were fully exploited: more than one dynastic revolution temporarily destroyed an ecclesiastical organization in process of being established. Victory could be considered certain from the time when, in each of the three kingdoms in turn, Christian kings succeeded consecutively to the throne. This happened first in Denmark, with the accession of Cnut; then in Norway, with Magnus the Good (1035); and considerably later in Sweden, with King Inge who, towards the end of the eleventh century, destroyed the ancient sanctuary of Upsala, where his predecessors had so often offered in sacrifice the flesh of animals and even of human beings.

As in Hungary, the conversion of these northern lands, so jealous of their independence, was inevitably to lead to the establishment by each of them of a hierarchy of its own, directly subordinate to Rome. In due course the archiepiscopal see of Bremen-Hamburg came to be occupied by a politician sufficiently astute to bow before the inevitable and, cutting his losses, to try to save something of the supremacy traditionally claimed by his church. Archbishop Adalbert—from 1043—conceived the idea of a vast Nordic patriarchate, within which national metropolitan sees should be created under the tutelage of the successors of St. Anskar. But the Roman curia, which had no great love for intermediate authorities, withheld its support from this scheme; in addition the quarrels of the nobility in Germany itself prevented its author from pursuing it with much vigour. In 1103 an archbishopric was founded at Lund, in Danish Scania, with jurisdiction over all the Scandinavian lands. Then in 1152, Norway obtained one of its own, which was set up at Nidaros (Trondhjem) close to the tomb—the true national palladium—where rested the remains of the martyr king Olaf. Sweden finally (1164) established its Christian metropolis hard by the site where had stood in pagan times the royal temple of Upsala. Thus the Scandinavian Church escaped from the control of the German Church. Similarly, in the political field, the sovereigns of East Francia, despite their innumerable interventions in the dynastic wars of Denmark, never succeeded in imposing a permanent tribute (the normal sign of subjection) on the Danish kings, or even in advancing their frontiers to any considerable extent. The separation of the two great branches of the Germanic peoples had become more and more pronounced. Germany was not—was never to be—the whole of Germania.

6 IN SEARCH OF CAUSES

Was it their conversion that persuaded the Scandinavians to renounce their habits of pillage and of distant migrations? To conceive of the Viking expeditions as religious warfare inspired by the ardour of an implacable pagan fanaticism—an explanation that has sometimes been at least suggested —conflicts too much with what we know of minds disposed to respect magic of every kind. On the other hand it is surely possible to believe in a profound change of mentality under the influence of a change of faith. Certainly the history of the voyages and invasions of the Northmen would be unintelligible without the passionate love of war and adventure which, in this society, co-existed with devotion to more peaceful arts. The same men who, as shrewd merchants, frequented the markets of Europe from Constantinople to the ports of the Rhine delta, or who in freezing temperatures reclaimed the wastes of Iceland, knew no greater pleasure nor any higher source of renown than 'the clang of iron' and 'the clash of shields': witness so many poems and narratives, set down in writing only in the twelfth century, but faithfully echoing the age of the Vikings; witness also the *stelae*, grave-stones or simple cenotaphs, which on the burial mounds of Scandinavia, along the roads or near the places of assembly, today still display their runes, engraved in bright red on the grey rock. These do not for the most part commemorate, like so many Greek or Roman tombs, the dead who had passed away peacefully by their native hearth. The memories they recall are almost exclusively of heroes struck down in the course of bloody expeditions. This attitude of mind may seem incompatible with the teaching of Christ. But, as we shall often have occasion to observe in the following pages, among the peoples of the West during the feudal era there was apparently no difficulty in reconciling ardent faith in the Christian mysteries with a taste for violence and plunder, nay even with the most conscious glorification of war.

Thenceforth the Scandinavians joined with other members of the Catholic Church in the same profession of faith, were brought up on the same pious legends, followed the same routes as pilgrims, read or had read to them, if ever they had any desire for instruction, the same books in which —in a more or less distorted shape—the Romano-Hellenic tradition was reflected. Yet has the fundamental unity of Western civilization ever prevented intestine strife? At most it may be granted that the idea of a single and omnipotent God, joined to entirely new conceptions of the other world, dealt in the long run a severe blow to that *mystique* of destiny and glory which characterized the old poetry of the North and in which more than one Viking had no doubt found the justification of his passions. But it is surely not to be supposed that this was sufficient to extinguish in the chiefs all desire to follow in the footsteps of Rollo and Sweyn, or to prevent them from recruiting the warriors necessary to realize their ambitions.

As a matter of fact, the problem as set out above suffers from having been incompletely stated. Before inquiring why a phenomenon came to an end, should we not first ask what produced it? This is perhaps in a sense merely to shelve the difficulty, for the causes which produced the Scandinavian migrations are scarcely less obscure than those that led to their cessation. Not that we should in any case need to spend time examining at length the reasons for the attraction exercised on the northern peoples by the countries—generally more fertile and of older civilization—which spread out to the south of them. Is not the history of the great Germanic invasions and of the movements of peoples that preceded them essentially the account of a long migration towards the sun? The tradition of sea-borne raids was itself an old one. By a remarkable coincidence, Gregory of Tours and the poem of Beowulf have both preserved the memory of the expedition which, about 520, a king of the Götar undertook on the coast of Frisia; other similar enterprises are doubtless unknown to us only because of the dearth of records. It is none the less certain that quite suddenly, towards the end of the eighth century, these long-distance expeditions developed on a scale hitherto unknown.

Are we to believe therefore that the West, ill-defended as it was, was at that time an easier prey than in the past? Apart from the fact that this explanation could not be applied to strictly contemporaneous events, such as the colonization of Iceland and the foundation of the Varangian kingdoms on the rivers of Russia, it would be absurdly paradoxical to maintain that the Merovingian state, during the period of its disintegration, appeared more formidable than the kingdom of Louis the Pious, or even of his sons. Clearly it is by the study of the northern countries themselves that we must seek the key to their destiny.

A comparison of the ships of the ninth century with some other finds of earlier date proves that in the period immediately preceding the age of the Vikings the seafarers of Scandinavia had greatly improved the design of

36

their boats. There is no doubt that without these technical developments the far-ranging expeditions across the oceans would have been impossible. But was it really for the pleasure of utilizing these better ships that so many Northmen decided to go in search of adventure far from their native land? It is more reasonable to suppose that they devoted attention to the improvement of their naval equipment so as to venture farther.

Another explanation was suggested in the eleventh century by the actual historian of the Northmen of France, Doon of Saint-Quentin. He saw the cause of the migrations in the over-population of the Scandinavian countries; and the origin of this he ascribed to the practice of polygamy. We may at least discount this second hypothesis: apart from the fact that the chiefs alone maintained real harems, demographic observations have never proved—far from it—that polygamy is particularly favourable to the growth of population. The explanation of over-population itself might well seem suspect. Peoples who have been subjected to invasions have almost always advanced it, in the somewhat naive hope of excusing their defeats by the supposed influx of a prodigious number of enemies. It was thus that the Mediterranean peoples used to explain their defeats by the Celts, the Romans their defeats by the Germans. In the present case, however, the theory deserves more consideration: partly for the reason that Doon probably took it, not from the tradition of the conquered, but from that of the conquerors; and, especially, because it has a certain inherent probability. From the second to the fourth century, the movements of peoples which were finally to bring about the destruction of the Roman Empire had certainly had the effect of leaving in the Scandinavian peninsula, in the islands of the Baltic and in Jutland, extensive territories empty of people. The groups that remained could for several centuries freely multiply. Then a time must have come round about the eighth century, when they began to lack living-space, particularly in view of the state of their agriculture.

It is true that the object of the first Viking expeditions in the West was much less to acquire permanent settlements than to capture booty and take it home. But this was itself a means of making up for the scarcity of land. Thanks to the spoils of southern civilizations, the chieftain who was worried by the constriction of his fields and pastures could keep up his way of life and continue to bestow on his companions the gifts necessary to his prestige. Among people of humbler status, emigration provided the young with a means of escape from the indifferent prospects of an over-crowded home. Lastly, suppose that by one of those quarrels or vendettas which the structure and manners of Scandinavian society made all too frequent a man was forced to abandon the ancestral *gaard*. The diminishing areas of unoccupied land would make it more difficult than in the past for him to find a new home in his own country; and if he were a hunted man he would seldom find any refuge but the sea or the far-off countries to which it opened the door. This was especially the case if the enemy from whom he fled was one of those kings who, owing to increased density of settlement, were able to extend a more effective control over wide areas. Fostered by custom and encouraged by success, inclination very soon reinforced necessity, and to adventure abroad (which generally proved profitable) became at once a profession and a sport.

If the onset of the Scandinavian invasions cannot be explained by the state of government in the countries invaded neither can their termination. Doubtless the Ottonian monarchy was better able than that of the last Carolingians to defend its seaboard; whilst in England William the Bastard and his successors could have proved redoubtable adversaries. But it so happened that neither the German nor the Anglo-Norman rulers were ever seriously put to the test. And it is hard to believe that France from the middle of the tenth century and England under Edward the Confessor seemed prizes too difficult to win. In all likelihood the very strengthening of the Scandinavian kingships, after having at the outset momentarily stimulated the migrations by throwing on to the ocean routes many exiles and disappointed pretenders, had ultimately the effect of drying up the source of them. Henceforward, the levies of men and ships were monopolized by the governments, which organized the requisitioning of shipping with particular care. Moreover the kings were not very favourable to the isolated expeditions which kept alive a turbulent spirit and furnished outlaws with too easy a refuge, just as they provided conspirators—as the saga of St. Olaf shows—with the means of accumulating the riches necessary to their dark designs. It was said that Sweyn, once he had made himself master of Norway, prohibited overseas raids.

The chiefs gradually accustomed themselves to the limitations of a more regular life, in which ambition sought its gratification in the mother-country itself, in the service of the sovereign or his rivals. In order to acquire new lands, men pursued more actively the work of internal colonization. Conquests by kings, like those that Cnut accomplished and Harald Hardrada attempted, continued; but the royal armies were cumbersome machines difficult to set in motion in states whose political organization was so unstable, and the last assault upon England planned by a king of Denmark, in the time of William the Bastard, failed even before the fleet had weighed anchor, owing to a palace revolution. Soon the kings of Norway limited their designs to reinforcing or establishing their dominion over the Western Isles, from Iceland to the Hebrides. The kings of Denmark and Sweden became occupied with long campaigns against their Slav, Lettish and Finnish neighbours; campaigns which were at once punitive expeditions—for, by a fitting retribution, the piracies of these peoples constantly troubled the Baltic—wars of conquest and crusades, but which also at times closely resembled the raids from which the Scheldt, the Thames, and the Loire had so long suffered.

III

SOME CONSEQUENCES AND
SOME LESSONS OF THE INVASIONS

1 DISORDER

FROM the turmoil of the last invasions, the West emerged covered with countless scars. The towns themselves had not been spared—at least not by the Scandinavians—and if many of them, after pillage or evacuation, rose again from their ruins, this break in the regular course of their life left them for long years enfeebled. Others were even less fortunate: the two principal ports of the Carolingian empire on the northern seas, Duurstede on the Rhine delta, Quentovic at the mouth of the Canche, sank once and for all to the status, respectively, of a modest hamlet and a fishing village. Along the river routes the trading centres had lost all security: in 861, the merchants of Paris, escaping in their boats, were overtaken by the ships of the Northmen and carried off into captivity.

Above all, the cultivated land suffered disastrously, often being reduced to desert. In the Toulon region, after the expulsion of the bandits of Le Freinet, the land had to be cleared anew, because the former boundaries of the properties had ceased to be recognizable, so that each man—in the words of one charter—'took possession of the land according to his power'.[1] In Touraine, so often overrun by the Vikings, a document of 14th September 900 throws a spotlight on a little manor at Vontes, in the valley of the Indre, and on an entire village at Martigny, on the Loire. At Vontes, five men of servile status 'could have holdings if we were at peace'. At Martigny the dues are carefully enumerated; but this is a thing of the past; for, though seventeen units of tenure, or *mansi*, are still listed, they no longer have any meaning. Only sixteen heads of families live on this impoverished soil; one less than the number of *mansi*, in fact, whereas normally some of the latter would each have been occupied by two or three households. Several of the men 'have neither wives nor children'. And the same tragic refrain is heard: 'these people could have holdings if we were at peace'.[2] Not all the devastation, however, was the work of the invaders. For, in order to reduce the enemy to submission, it was often necessary to starve him out. In 894, a band of Vikings having been compelled

[1] *Cartulaire de l'abbaye de Saint-Victor-de-Marseille*, ed. Guérard, no. LXXVII.
[2] Bibl. Nat. Baluze 76, fol. 99 (900, 14th September).

to take refuge within the old Roman walls of Chester, the English host, says the chronicle, 'carried off all the cattle round about, and burned the harvests and caused the whole of the surrounding countryside to be eaten up by their horses'.

Naturally the peasants, more than any other class, were driven to despair by these conditions—to such a degree that, on several occasions in the country between the Seine and the Loire and in the region of the Moselle, they united under oath and hurled themselves frenziedly upon the marauders. Their ill-organized forces, however, were invariably massacred.[1] But peasants were not the only ones to suffer severely from the devastation of the fields, and the towns, even when their defences held firm, risked starvation. The lords, who derived their revenues from the land, were impoverished. In particular, the ecclesiastical manors survived now only with difficulty; the result was—as also later, after the Hundred Years' War—a profound decay of monasticism and, in consequence, of intellectual life. England was particularly severely affected. In the preface to the *Pastoral Rule* of Gregory the Great, translated under the auspices of King Alfred, the latter sadly recalls 'the time, before everything was ravaged and burned, when the churches of England overflowed with treasures and with books'.[2] This was in fact the knell of that ecclesiastical culture of the Anglo-Saxons whose radiance had till lately spread over Europe. But undoubtedly the most widespread and enduring effects resulted from the tremendous waste of resources won by human effort. When a condition of relative security had been re-established, a diminished population was confronted with vast stretches of land, formerly cultivated, but now once more reduced to scrub. The conquest of the virgin soil, still so abundant, was retarded by more than a century.

But the material damage was not all. The mental damage must also be reckoned. This was the more profound because the storm, especially in the Frankish empire, followed what had been at least a relative calm. It is true that the Carolingian peace was not of long standing and had never been really complete. But the memory of men is short and their capacity for illusion unbounded. Consider, for example, the history of the fortifications of Rheims, which was repeated, with some variations, in more than one other city.[3] Under Louis the Pious, the archbishop had begged the emperor's permission to remove the stones of the ancient Roman wall and use them in the rebuilding of his cathedral. The king who, in the words of Flodoard, 'enjoyed at that moment a profound peace and, proud of the illustrious might of his empire, feared not any invasion of barbarians',

[1] *Ann. Bertiniani* 859 (with the correction proposed by F. Lot, *Bibl. Éc. Chartes*, 1908, p. 32, n. 2); Regino of Prüm, 882; Dudo of Saint-Quentin, II, 22.

[2] *King Alfred's West Saxon Version of Gregory's Pastoral Care*, ed. Sweet (E.E.T.S., 45), p. 4.

[3] Cf. Vercauteren, *Étude sur les cités de la Belgique seconde*, Brussels 1934, p. 371, n. 1; cf. for Tournai, *V. S. Amandi*, III, 2, *M.G.H., Poetae aevi carol.*, III, p. 589.

gave his consent. Scarcely fifty years had passed before the 'barbarians' returned and it became necessary to build new ramparts with all possible speed. The walls and palisades with which Europe then began to bristle were the visible symbol of a great anguish. Pillage henceforth became a familiar event of which prudent people took account in their legal agreements. For example, there was the rural lease from the neighbourhood of Lucca, drawn up in 876, which provided for the payment of rent to be suspended 'if the heathen nation should burn or lay waste the houses and their contents or the mill';[1] or again, ten years earlier, the will of a king of Wessex, wherein he declares that the benefactions which he makes a charge on his property 'will be paid only if on each estate so burdened there remain men and cattle, and it is not changed into desert'.[2]

Different in purpose but similar in sentiment were the tremulous prayers —preserved for us in a number of liturgical books—which echoed throughout the West. In Provence they cried 'Eternal Trinity . . . deliver thy Christian people from the oppression of the pagans' (in this case certainly the Saracens); in northern Gaul: 'from the savage nation of the Northmen, which lays waste our realms, deliver us, O God'; at Modena, where prayers were addressed to S. Gimignano: 'against the arrows of the Hungarians, be thou our protector'.[3] Let us try for a moment to imagine the state of mind of the devout souls who daily uttered these supplications. A society cannot with impunity exist in a state of perpetual terror. The incursions, whether of Arabs, Hungarians, or Scandinavians, were certainly not wholly responsible for the shadow that lay so heavy on men's minds, but they were without doubt largely responsible.

The havoc had nevertheless not been merely destructive. The very disorder gave rise to certain modifications—some of them far-reaching—in the internal organization of Western Europe.

Movements of population occurred in Gaul which, if we could discover more about them instead of merely guessing, would no doubt be revealed as highly important. From the time of Charles the Bald the government undertook, without much success, the task of sending back to their homes the peasants who had fled before the invader. The texts show us the people of the Bas-Limousin seeking refuge in the mountains on several occasions and it is hardly to be supposed that they all reached their homes again. The plains, particularly in Burgundy, seem to have been more affected by depopulation than the highlands.[4] Of the old villages which disappeared on

---

[1] *Memorie e documenti per servir all'istoria del ducato di Lucca*, V, 2, no. 855.

[2] Will of King Aethelwulf, in Asser's *Life of King Alfred*, ed. W. H. Stevenson, c. 16.

[3] R. Poupardin, *Le Royaume de Provence sous les Carolingiens*, 1901 (*Bibl. Éc. Hautes Études, Sc. histor.* 131), p. 408; L. Delisle, *Instructions adressées par le Comité des travaux historiques . . . Littérature latine*, 1890, p. 17; Muratori, *Antiquitates*, 1738, I, col. 22.

[4] *Capitularia*, II, no. 273, c. 31; F. Lot, in *Bibl. Éc. Chartes*, 1915, p. 486; Chaume *Les origines du duché de Bourgogne*, II, 2, pp. 468–9.

every hand, not all had been destroyed by fire and sword. Many were simply abandoned in favour of safer refuges: as usual the general danger encouraged a concentration of population. We know most about the wanderings of the monks. As they carried along the roads of exile their reliquaries and their pious traditions, a great mass of legend sprang up along their paths—a potent reinforcement of Catholic unity and the cult of the saints. In particular, the great exodus of the Breton relics spread far and wide the knowledge of a new hagiography, readily accepted by minds impressed by the very fabulousness of its miracles.

But it was in England, where the foreign occupation was particularly widespread and prolonged, that the political and cultural map underwent the most noticeable changes. The collapse of two kingdoms till recently powerful—Northumbria in the north-east, and Mercia in the centre—favoured the rise of Wessex, which had already begun during the preceding period; it was this, indeed, that made the kings from that southern land, in the words of one of their charters, 'emperors of all Britain'[1]—a heritage which Cnut, and after him William the Conqueror, would merely gather in. The towns of the south, Winchester, and later London, could thenceforth add to the contents of the treasuries in their castles the yield from the taxes levied on the country as a whole.

The abbeys of Northumbria had been famous homes of learning. There Bede had lived; thence Alcuin had set out for the continent of Europe. The ravages of the Danes, followed by the systematic devastation wrought by William the Conqueror in his determination to punish and prevent revolt, put an end to this intellectual hegemony. What is more, a part of the northern zone was detached for ever from England proper. Cut off from other populations of Anglo-Saxon speech by the settlement of the Vikings in Yorkshire, the lowlands round about the Northumbrian citadel of Edinburgh fell under the domination of the Celtic chiefs of the hills. Thus the bilingual kingdom of Scotland was by a sort of backhand stroke a creation of the Scandinavian invasions.

2 THE HUMAN CONTRIBUTION: THE EVIDENCE OF LANGUAGE AND NAMES

Neither the Saracen marauders, nor—outside the Danubian plain—the Hungarian raiders, mixed their blood in any significant proportion with that of the older Europe. The Scandinavians, on the other hand, did not confine themselves to pillage: in their settlements in England and Normandy they unquestionably introduced a new human element. How is this contribution to be measured? In the present state of knowledge, anthropological data afford no certain indications. While taking such data into account we are obliged to appeal to various scraps of indirect evidence.

[1] J. E. A. Jolliffe, *The Constitutional History of Medieval England*, 1937, p. 102.

Among the Northmen of the Seine, the Nordic language was from about 940 no longer in general use in the region of Rouen. On the other hand, it was still being spoken during that period in the Bessin, which may have been occupied at a later date by a new batch of immigrants; and it remained sufficiently important in the principality for the reigning duke to find it necessary for his heir to learn it. By a striking coincidence we find for the last time, at about the same date, considerable groups of heathens in the area; groups sufficiently strong to play a part in the troubles which followed the death of Duke William Longsword, who was assassinated in 942. Till the first years of the eleventh century, in the entourage of these 'jarls of Rouen', long faithful—as one of the sagas tells us—'to the memory of their cousinship' with the northern chieftains, there must still have been men, doubtless bilingual, who were capable of expressing themselves in the Scandinavian dialects. How otherwise explain the fact that, about the year 1000, the kinsmen of the viscountess of Limoges, who had been kidnapped on the coast of Poitou by a band of Vikings and carried off by her ravishers 'beyond the seas', had recourse, in order to obtain her freedom, to the good offices of Duke Richard II? Or the fact that this same prince, in 1013, should have been able to take into his service the hordes of Olaf, and that the following year some of his subjects appear to have fought in the army of the Danish king of Dublin?[1]

The process of linguistic assimilation must by this period have been almost complete. It was favoured both by the growth of religious unity and by the dwindling flow of Scandinavian colonists, who had arrived at frequent intervals in the period immediately following the first settlement. Adhemar of Chabannes, who wrote in 1028 or shortly after, was of the opinion that assimilation was total.[2] Neither the Romance dialect of Normandy nor, through its agency, ordinary French borrowed anything from the speech of the companions of Rollo, save a few technical terms, almost all of them—if for the moment we disregard the terminology of agrarian life—relating either to navigation or to coastal topography: 'havre' and 'crique' for example. If words of this type remained in current use despite the ascendancy of Romance speech, it was because it had been impossible to find equivalents for them in the language of a nation of landlubbers, as incapable of building ships as they were of describing the physical features of a coastline.

In England the evolution of language was along altogether different lines. Here, as on the continent, the Scandinavians did not continue in their linguistic isolation. They learnt Anglo-Saxon—but only to handle it in a very extraordinary way. While adapting themselves as best they could

---

[1] Adhemar of Chabannes, *Chronique*, ed. Chavanon, III, c. 44 (for the adventure of the viscountess); H. Shetelig, *Vikingeminner i Vest Europa* (Archaeological Relics of the Vikings in Western Europe), Oslo, 1933 (*Institutet for sammenlignende Kulturforksning*, A. XVI), p. 242 (for the presence of the Norman contingents at the battle of Clontarf).

[2] *Chronique*, III, c. 27.

to its grammar and adopting a large part of its vocabulary, they none the less persisted in mixing with it a great number of words from their original tongue. The natives, in their turn, being in close contact with the new-comers, became accustomed to using this foreign vocabulary extensively. Nationalism in language and style was at that time an unknown sentiment even among those writers most attached to the traditions of their people. One of the most ancient examples of borrowings from the language of the Vikings is provided by the song of the battle of Maldon, which celebrates the glorious deeds of the warriors of Essex, fallen in 991 in a battle against a band of these 'murderous wolves'. There is no need here to thumb the technical dictionaries. The evidence lies in perfectly familiar nouns like 'sky' or 'fellow'; in adjectives as frequently employed as 'low' or 'ill'; in verbs which everyone is constantly using, such as 'to call' or 'to take'; in certain pronouns, even (those of the third person plural)—so many terms which seem to us English of the English, but which, together with many others, were in fact born in the North. So much is this the case that the millions of people who in the twentieth century, somewhere in the world, speak the most widely diffused of the European languages, would express themselves quite differently in their everyday speech if the shores of Northumbria had never seen the ships of the 'men of the sea'.

That historian would be very imprudent, however, who, comparing those linguistic riches with the small contribution made to French by the Scandinavian tongues, inferred that the difference between the numbers of the immigrant populations was in exact ratio to the extent of these linguistic borrowings. The influence of a dying language on a rival which survives does not necessarily correspond to the number of individuals originally using the former one; the nature of the languages themselves is a no less important factor. The Danish and Norse dialects of the Viking period were utterly different from the Romance dialects of Gaul, but approximated closely to old English, which like them was descended from a common Germanic source. Certain words in both tongues were identical alike in meaning and in form; others with the same meaning presented similar forms which might easily be used alternatively. Even where the Scandinavian term supplanted an English one seemingly very different, its introduction was often facilitated by the presence in the native language of other words which were from the same root and belonged to an analogous order of ideas. It is none the less true that the formation of this sort of mixed speech would remain inexplicable if numerous Scandinavians had not lived on the soil of England and there maintained close contact with the old inhabitants.

Moreover, if many of these borrowings ended by infiltrating into the common language it was almost always through the medium of the speech peculiar to northern and north-eastern England. Other borrowings appeared only in the dialects of these regions. There indeed—particularly in Yorkshire, Cumberland, Westmorland, north Lancashire and the district of the 'Five Boroughs' (Lincoln, Stamford, Leicester, Nottingham and Derby)—the *jarls* from beyond the seas had carved out their most important and most enduring lordships. This was also the main area in which the invaders had taken possession of the soil. The Anglo-Saxon Chronicle records that in 876 the Viking leader dwelling at York handed over the district of Deira to his companions 'who thenceforward went on ploughing and tilling it'. And farther on, under the year 877 it is stated that: 'after the harvest, the Danish army went into Mercia and some of it they shared out'. The important linguistic evidence concerning this peasant occupation fully confirms the evidence of the chroniclers. For the majority of the words borrowed described humble objects or familiar actions, and only peasants rubbing shoulders with peasants would have been able to teach their neighbours new names for 'bread', 'egg' or 'root'.

The importance on English soil of this contribution at the deeper levels emerges no less clearly from the study of personal names. The most significant are not those used by the upper classes, among whom the choice of names was mainly dictated by a hierarchical tradition followed the more readily because no other principle in the tenth and eleventh centuries had developed to replace it. The practice of naming children after their parents had fallen into desuetude; godfathers had not yet formed the habit of conferring their own names on their godsons nor had fathers and mothers—even among the more pious folk—learnt to name their children only after saints. Before 1066 names of Scandinavian origin had been much in vogue among the English aristocracy, but little more than a century after the Conquest they were abandoned by everyone with any pretensions to social distinction. On the other hand they remained in use much longer among the peasant, and even the urban, populations, who were not inspired by the unrealizable aim of assimilating themselves to a victorious caste; and at these lower levels they persisted in East Anglia till the thirteenth century, in Lincolnshire and Yorkshire till the fourteenth, and in Lancashire till the very end of the Middle Ages. There is certainly no ground for thinking that these names were then borne exclusively by the descendants of the Vikings. For it is evident that in the country districts, within one and the same class, imitation and inter-marriage had exerted their wonted influence, though this influence could not have operated unless numerous immigrants had settled in the midst of the old inhabitants, sharing the same humble life.

So far as Normandy is concerned, the little that we can glimpse—in the present unsatisfactory state of scholarly investigation—leads us to imagine an evolution closely parallel to that of the English counties where the Scandinavian influence was strongest. Although the use of some names of Nordic origin, such as Osbern, persisted among the nobility till the eleventh century at least, it seems that the upper classes as a whole decided at an early date to adhere to French naming. Did not Rollo himself set the example by having his son, born at Rouen, baptized under the name of William? From that time on no Norman duke reverted in this matter to the traditions of his ancestors; clearly the dukes had no desire to set themselves apart in this way from the other great nobles of the realm. On the other hand, the lower strata of the population, as in Britain, showed themselves much more faithful to tradition—as is seen in the survival in the Norman districts even today of a certain number of patronymics derived from old Scandinavian names. All that we know of family name systems in general forbids us to suppose that these names could have assumed a hereditary character before the thirteenth century at the earliest. As in England, these facts reflect a certain amount of peasant settlement; since the examples are less numerous than in England, these suggest that the settlement was less dense.

The study of place-names moreover affords ample evidence that in the countries where they had themselves created so many empty spaces the Vikings had founded more than one new settlement. In Normandy, admittedly, it is not always easy to draw a distinction between the Scandinavian place-names and an older Germanic set derived from a Saxon colonization about the time of the barbarian invasions, of which there is clear evidence in the Bessin at least. It seems however that in most cases the dispute must be settled in favour of the more recent immigration. If, for example, we draw up a list—as it is possible to do with some precision—of those lands in the Lower Seine region which were owned towards the end of the Merovingian period by the monks of Saint-Wandrille, two characteristic facts emerge. First, the names are all Gallo-Roman or of the Frankish period, with no possibility of being confused with the later Nordic contribution; secondly, a very large number are today quite impossible to identify, for the reason, unquestionably, that at the time of the invasion of the Northmen most of the places themselves were destroyed or renamed. In any case it is the general phenomena which are important here and these are the ones least in doubt. The villages whose names show Scandinavian influence are crowded together very closely in the Roumois and the Caux district. Beyond, they are farther apart, though in places there are still little groups relatively compact, such as the one between the Seine and the Risle, on the edge of the forest of Londe (whose name is itself Scandinavian), which recalls the pioneer labours of colonists whose homeland had made them familiar with the life of trappers. To all appearance the conquerors avoided both dispersing themselves excessively and straying too far from the sea. No trace of their occupation appears to exist in the Vexin, the region of Alençon or the district of Avranches.

On the other side of the Channel we find the same contrasts, but spread

[1] Cf. F. Lot, *Études critiques sur l'abbaye de Saint-Wandrille*, 1913 (*Bibl. Écoles Hautes Études, Sc. histor.*, fasc. 204), p. xiii *et seq.*, and p. l, n. 2.

over much greater areas. Extremely dense in Yorkshire and in the regions bordering the Irish Sea to the south of the Solway Firth, the characteristic names—wholly Scandinavian or sometimes only Scandinavian in form —tend to become more scarce as one moves down towards the south or the centre, till they are reduced to a mere sprinkling when, with Buckinghamshire and Bedfordshire, one approaches the hills which form the north-eastern boundary of the Thames valley.

To be sure, not all the places with these Viking names were necessarily new settlements or places which had been entirely repopulated. By way of exception we can point to a few indisputable facts. The settlers who established themselves on the banks of the Seine at the entrance to a little dell and had the idea of calling this settlement, in their language, 'the cold brook' (it is today Caudebec) must have been all, or nearly all, of Nordic speech. Several places in the north of Yorkshire are called 'village of the English', *Ingleby* (the word *by*, moreover, being incontestably Scandinavian)—a name which obviously would have had no meaning if in this region at some particular period it had not been a most unusual thing for a place to have an English population. Sometimes not only the centre itself but also the various divisions of its farmlands acquired imported names, and clearly only peasants would have troubled to alter the humble toponomy of the fields. Cases of this kind are common in north-eastern England, but in Normandy, once again, it is necessary to admit the inadequacy of research.

Other pieces of evidence unfortunately offer less certainty. Many villages, in Britain as in the area about the Seine, are known by a composite name, the first part of which is a man's name of Scandinavian origin. The fact that this eponymous personage (who can hardly have been anything but a chieftain) was a foreign settler does not necessarily imply that his subjects were also of foreign birth. Of the poor devils who laboured to feed the lord Hastein of Hattentot in Caux, or the lord Tofi of Towthorpe in Yorkshire, who can say how many had already, before the arrival of these masters, lived from father to son on the land which they enriched with their toil? All the more must these reservations be taken into account when, in the double name, the second part, which in the preceding examples was, like the first, of foreign derivation, belongs on the contrary to the native language. The men who, in speaking of the lord Hakon's land, called it Hacquenville had assuredly forgotten the tongue of the invaders or, more probably, had never used it at all.

3 THE HUMAN CONTRIBUTION: THE EVIDENCE OF LAW AND SOCIAL STRUCTURE

In the field of law, likewise, not all the evidence is of equal significance, and the influence of a handful of foreign rulers suffices to explain certain borrowings. Since the *jarls* administered justice in conquered England, their subjects—even the English ones—were accustomed to invoke the law under the name (*lagu*) familiar to the men from beyond the seas. The occupied zone was divided into districts on the Scandinavian pattern as *wapentakes* or *ridings*. Under the influence of the leaders of the colonists an entire new legal system was introduced. About 962, after the victories of the kings of Wessex, one of them, Edgar, declared: 'I desire that among the Danes the secular law continue to be regulated according to their good customs.'[1]

In fact, the shires which Alfred not so long before had been obliged to surrender to the Vikings remained for the most part united till the twelfth century under the common designation of 'Danelaw'. But the region so named extended well beyond the limits within which the study of place-names reveals intensive Scandinavian settlement. The fact is that in each territory the prevailing usages were fixed by the big local judicial assemblies where the magnates, even if their origin was different from that of the majority, had a preponderant voice. In Normandy, though the *féal*, or vavasour, continued for some time to be known by the imported name *dreng*, and the peace legislation preserved to the end a Scandinavian imprint, these survivals are not such as to afford any certainty about the extent of the colonization: for the *drengs* were only a restricted group and public order was, by its very nature, the concern of the prince.[2] Generally speaking, Norman law very quickly lost all ethnic colouring (apart from certain characteristics relating to the hierarchical organization of the military classes, which we shall notice later). Doubtless the very concentration of authority in the hands of the dukes, who at an early date gladly adopted the customs of the greater French baronage, was more favourable to juridical assimilation than was the subdivision of powers in the Danelaw.

On both sides of the Channel, in order to measure the profounder effects of the Scandinavian occupation, one should look to the structure of groups smaller in size than the province or county: to the English boroughs of which several, like Leicester and Stamford, long remained faithful to the judicial traditions of the warriors and merchants who had settled there at the time of the invasion; above all, in Normandy as well as in England, to the small rural communities.

In medieval Denmark, the aggregate of the lands appertaining to the

---

[1] Laws of Edgar, IV, 2, 1.

[2] For the word *dreng*, J. Steenstrup, 'Normandiets Historie under de syv förste Hertuger 911–1066' (with a summary in French) in *Mémoires de l'Académie royale des sciences et des lettres de Danemark*, 7e Série, Sections des Lettres, V, no. I, 1925, p. 268. For the peace legislation, J. Yver, *L'Interdiction de la guerre privée dans le très ancien droit normand* (*Extrait des travaux de la semaine d'histoire du droit normand*), Caen, 1928. The article of K. Amira (in reference to Steenstr, up*Normannerne*, I) is still worth reading: *Die Anfänge des normannischen Rechts* in *Hist. Zeitschrift*, XXXIX, 1878.

peasant household was called *bol*. The word passed to Normandy, where it later became a component of certain place-names or was simply used in the more restricted sense of an enclosure, including the farm buildings as well as the garden or orchard. In both the plain of Caen and a large part of the Danelaw, an identical term was used to describe the groups of elongated lots running parallel to each other and side by side, in the heart of the agricultural lands: the word was *delle* in Normandy, 'dale' in England. So striking a similarity of terms used in two zones having no direct relations with each other can be explained only by a common ethnic influence. The Caux district is marked off from the neighbouring French regions by the peculiar shape of its fields, which are roughly square and divided in an apparently haphazard manner; this peculiarity seems to indicate a rural reorganization subsequent to the settlement of the surrounding territories. In 'Danish' England, the upheaval was sufficiently serious to lead to the disappearance of the primitive agrarian unit, the 'hide', and its replacement by another of smaller size, the 'ploughland'.[1] Is it conceivable that a few chieftains, content to take the place of the former lords—over peasants born on that very soil—would have had the desire or the power thus to transform even the names of the fields and meddle with the pattern of agrarian boundaries?

The argument can be carried farther. Between the social structure of the Danelaw and that of Normandy we find a common feature which reveals a profound interrelationship of institutions. The servile bond which in the rest of northern France created such a strong hereditary link between the lord and his 'man' was quite unknown to the rural districts of Normandy; if conceivably it had begun to take shape before Rollo's time, its development then stopped short. Similarly, the north and north-east of England was long characterized by the degree of freedom enjoyed by its peasantry. Among the small cultivators many, while in general subject to the jurisdiction of the lords' courts, had the status of full free men; they could change their masters as they wished; they were accustomed in any case to alienate their lands at will, and altogether their burdens were lighter and more precisely fixed than those which weighed so heavily on some of their less favoured neighbours and indeed, outside the 'Danish' region, on the majority of peasants.

Now it is certain that in the age of the Vikings the manorial system was absolutely unknown to the Scandinavian peoples. Is it conceivable that a small body of conquerors who, because so few in number, would have had to live by the labour of the vanquished populations, should have had any scruples about keeping them in their former state of subjection? That the

---

[1] I believe that Mr. Jolliffe is in error in refusing—against the general opinion of English scholars—to recognize in the 'ploughland' of north-eastern England a result of the upheaval caused by the Scandinavian invasion. See especially 'The Era of the Folk' in *Oxford Essays in Medieval History presented to H. E. Salter*, 1934.

invaders should have taken with them into their new settlements their traditional habits of peasant independence obviously implies a much more massive colonization, and evidently the ordinary warriors, who after the distribution of the soil exchanged the lance for the plough or the hoe, had not come so far merely to find a servitude unknown in their mother-country. It is true that quite soon the descendants of the first arrivals had to accept in part the framework of authority imposed by the conditions of their environment. The leaders of the settlers strove to imitate the profitable example of their counterparts among the other race; and once reinstated, the Church, which derived the best part of its subsistence from manorial revenues, behaved in like manner. The manor existed both in Normandy and in the Danelaw; but for many centuries, the subordina-tion in those regions was less stringent and less general than it was elsewhere.

Thus everything leads to the same conclusion. Nothing could be more untrue than to conceive of the Scandinavian settlers as being—after the manner of the 'French' companions of William the Conqueror—solely a class of chieftains. It is beyond dispute that in Normandy, as in the north and north-east of England, many peasant warriors like those depicted in the Swedish stele landed from the ships of the North. Established sometimes on territory wrested from its previous occupants or abandoned by those who fled, sometimes in the gaps that had remained in the primitive settle-ments, these colonists were sufficiently numerous to found or rename whole villages, to spread about them their vocabulary and their place-names, and to modify in vital respects the agrarian machinery and even the very structure of the rural societies, already in any case thrown into chaos by the invasion.

In France, however, the Scandinavian influence was on the whole less strong and except in rural life, which is by nature conservative, it proved less lasting than on English soil. There the testimony of archaeology con-firms the other types of evidence invoked above. Despite the sad in-completeness of our inventories, it cannot be doubted that the remains of Nordic art are much more rare in Normandy than in England. Several reasons explain these contrasts. In France, the smaller size of the area of Scandinavian settlement rendered it more accessible to external influences. The much more pronounced contrast between the indigenous civilization and the imported one, by the very fact that it did not favour reciprocal exchanges, led to the assimilation pure and simple of the less resistant of the two. The region appears to have been always more populous than the corresponding area of England; consequently, except in the Roumois and the Caux district, which had been terribly ravaged, the native groups that stayed where they were after the invasion preserved a greater density. Finally, whereas in England the influx had continued in successive waves for more than two centuries, in Normandy the invaders had arrived in several batches over a fairly short period and were beyond question—even in proportion to the area occupied—appreciably fewer.

4 THE HUMAN CONTRIBUTION: PROBLEMS OF ORIGIN

Settlement, more or less intensive, by the people of the North may be accepted as a fact. But from what regions of the North did they come? Even contemporaries did not always find it easy to discriminate. It was still possible for those who spoke one Scandinavian dialect to understand another without too much difficulty, and the early bands especially, composed of adventurers assembled for the purpose of pillage, were probably very mixed. Yet the different peoples each had their own traditions, and their consciousness of individual nationality, always lively, seems indeed to have sharpened with the progressive establishment of large kingdoms in the mother-country. In the fields of foreign conquest fierce wars were waged between Danes and Norwegians. These enemy brothers contended with each other for the Hebrides, for the little coastal kingdoms of Ireland and for the kingdom of York; in the Five Boroughs the Danish garrisons called in the English king of Wessex against the opposing army.[1] These rivalries, which rested on differences in ethnic customs that were sometimes profound, only make it the more desirable to determine, settlement by settlement, the precise origin of the invaders.

Some Swedes figured, as we have seen, among the conquerors of England under Cnut. Others took part in the pillage of the Frankish states: such a one was that Gudmar whose cenotaph in the province of Södermanland records his death 'yonder, towards the west, in Gaul'.[2] Most of their compatriots, however, preferred other paths: the eastern and southern shores of the Baltic were so near, the loot offered by the trading-stations on the Russian rivers so tempting, that these were the primary attraction. The Norwegians, familiar with the northern sea-route round the British Isles, formed the largest contingent to colonize the archipelagos scattered all along this periphery, as also in the region of Ireland: it was from there, even more than from the Scandinavian peninsula, that they set forth to conquer England. This explains the fact that they were almost the only invaders to people the counties of the western coast, from the Solway Firth to the Dee. Farther inland, traces of them are still to be found, relatively numerous in the west of Yorkshire, much more scarce in the remainder of the country and round about the Five Boroughs—but in this case everywhere mixed with those of the Danish settlements. The latter, throughout the mixed zone, were on the whole far more densely

---

[1] Cf. Allen Mawer, 'The Redemption of the Five Boroughs', in *Eng. Hist. Rev.*, XXXVIII, 1923.

[2] O. Montelius, 'Sverige och Vikingäfaderna västernt', in *Antikvarisk Tidskrift*, XXI, 2, p. 20.

concentrated. Clearly most of the immigrants permanently established on English soil belonged to the southernmost of the Scandinavian peoples.

The narrative sources for Normandy are of disheartening poverty. What is worse, they contradict each other: while the dukes seem to have made themselves out to be of Danish stock, a Norse saga makes Rollo a Norwegian. There remains the evidence of place-names and of agrarian customs: both these sources have until now been insufficiently investigated. The presence of Danish elements appears certain; likewise that of men from southern Norway. In what proportions? And according to what geographical distribution? At present it is impossible to say: and here I will venture to point out that the clearly marked contrasts between the agricultural lands of the Caux district on the one hand and those of the Caen plain on the other, might well be attributed in the last analysis to differences of settlement—the irregular fields of the Caux recalling those of Norway, the elongated fields of the Bessin those of Denmark. I risk putting forward this very tentative hypothesis only through fidelity to a cherished principle of mine—never to allow the reader to forget that history has still all the excitement of an unfinished excavation.

5 LESSONS

That a handful of robbers perched on a hill in Provence should have been able for nearly a century to spread insecurity all along an immense mountain chain and partially close some of the vital routes of Christendom; that for even longer little detachments of horsemen from the steppes should have been left free to ravage the West in all directions; that year after year, from Louis the Pious to the first Capetians, nay, in England till William the Conqueror, the ships of the North should with impunity have hurled against the shores of Germany, Gaul and Britain pirate bands eager for pillage; that, in order to appease these brigands, it should have been necessary to pay heavy ransoms and ultimately yield extensive territories to the most redoubtable of them—all these are surprising facts. Just as the progress of a disease shows a doctor the secret life of a body, so to the historian the progress of a great calamity yields valuable information about the nature of the society so stricken.

It was by sea that the Saracens of Le Freinet received their reinforcements; and it was the sea that carried the ships of the Vikings to their familiar hunting-grounds. To close it to the invaders would undoubtedly have been the surest way of preventing their ravages: witness the Arabs of Spain denying the southern waters to the Scandinavian pirates, the victories of the fleet eventually created by King Alfred, and the cleaning up of the Mediterranean by the Italian cities in the eleventh century. Now, at the outset at least, the Christian authorities almost all displayed the utmost incompetence in this respect. Were not the masters of the Provençal coast, where so many fishing villages nestle today, to be found imploring the aid of the distant Greek navy? It is no use saying that the rulers had no warships. At that stage in the development of the art of maritime warfare it would certainly have been enough to commandeer fishing or trading vessels, if necessary enlisting the services of a few caulkers to make some of them more seaworthy; and any seafaring population could have provided the crews. But the West seems to have become by that time almost completely unaccustomed to seafaring, and this strange deficiency is not the least curious of the revelations afforded by the history of the invasions. On the coast of Provence the towns, which in Roman times were situated right on the edge of the creeks, were now set back in the hinterland.[1] Alcuin, in the letter which he wrote to the king and the magnates of Northumbria, after the first raid by the Northmen—that on Lindisfarne —makes a comment that sets one thinking: 'Never', he says 'would one have believed in the possibility of such a voyage.'[2] Yet it had only been a matter of crossing the North Sea! When, after an interval of nearly a century, Alfred decided to fight his enemies in their own element, he had to recruit some of his sailors in Frisia, whose inhabitants from an early date had specialized in the business, almost abandoned by their neighbours, of coastal trading along the northern shores. It was left to his great-grandson, Edgar (959–75),[3] to organize a proper native fleet. Gaul showed herself even slower to learn to look beyond her cliffs and dunes. It is significant that the largest portion of the French maritime vocabulary, at least in the western sector, should be of late formation and made up of borrowings, some from the Scandinavian, others even from the English.

Once they had gained a foothold, the bands of Saracens or Northmen, like the Hungarian hordes, were difficult to check. It is not easy to maintain order save where men live close together. Now, at this time even the most favoured regions were by our present standards only sparsely populated. Everywhere empty spaces, dunes, forests offered terrain suitable for the purposes of surprise attack. The marshy thickets which screened the flight of King Alfred could also easily conceal the advance of the invaders. The problem, in short, was the very same one which French officers encounter today when they try to maintain security on the Moroccan borders or in Mauretania—made ten times worse, needless to say, by the absence of any higher authority capable of exercising effective control over vast areas.

[1] E. H. Duprat,' A propos de l'itinéraire maritime: I Citharista, La Ciotat' in *Mém. de l'Institut Historique de Provence*, IX, 1932.

[2] *Ep.* 16, *M.G.H., Epistolae*, IV, p. 42.

[3] On the slowness of English maritime development, cf. F. Liebermann, 'Matrosenstellung aus Landgütern der Kirche London um 1000' in *Archiv für das Studium der neueren Sprachen*, CIV, 1900. The naval battle fought in 851 by the men of Kent is an isolated event; moreover, on this sector of the coast, relations with the nearby ports of Gaul had doubtless maintained maritime life in a less sluggish condition than elsewhere.

Neither the Saracens nor the Northmen were better armed than their adversaries. In the tombs of the Vikings the finest swords bear the marks of Frankish manufacture. They are the 'blades of Flanders', of which the Scandinavian legends so often speak. The same texts frequently speak of the 'Welsh (= foreign) helms' worn by their heroes. Riders and hunters of the steppes, the Hungarians were probably better horsemen, better archers especially than the men of the West; but they were none the less on several occasions defeated by them in pitched battle. If the invaders possessed a military superiority, it was much less technical than social in its origin. Like the Mongols later, the Hungarians were fitted for warfare by their way of life itself. 'When the two sides are equal in numbers and in strength, the one more accustomed to the nomadic life gains the victory.' This observation is from the Arab historian Ibn-Khaldun.[1] In the ancient world it had an almost universal validity—at least till such time as the sedentary peoples could call to their aid the resources of an improved political organization and of a really scientific military machine.

The nomad, in fact, is a 'soldier born', always ready to take the field with his ordinary resources, his horse, his equipment and his victuals; and he is also served by a strategic sense of direction, as a rule quite absent in settled peoples. As to the Saracens and above all the Vikings, their detachments were from the outset designed expressly for combat. Of what use against these highly aggressive troops were improvised levies, brought together in haste from the four corners of a country already invaded? Compare, in the narratives of the English chronicles, the spirited tactics of the *here*—the Danish army—with the clumsiness of the Anglo-Saxon fyrd, the heavy militia which could not be employed in even the shortest operation save by permitting each man, under a system of reliefs, to return periodically to his farm. These contrasts, it is true, were especially pronounced at the beginning. As the Vikings were transformed into settlers, and the Hungarians round about the Danube into peasants, new preoccupations came to interfere with their movements. The West, by means of the system of vassalage or of the fief, provided itself at an early date with a class of professional fighting men. The comparative failure of this military machine, at any time, to provide the means of a really effective resistance speaks volumes as to the internal weaknesses of the system. Were these professional soldiers really willing to fight? 'Everyone runs away,' wrote the monk Ermentarius,[2] about 862 or a little later. Even among those who were apparently the best trained, the first invaders seem to have produced a panic terror whose paralysing effects remind one irresistibly of the accounts given by ethnographers of the headlong flight

---

[1] *Prolégomènes*, trans. Slane, I, p. 291. On the Mongols, see the shrewd observations of Grenard, in *Annales d'hist. économ.*, 1931, p. 564; I have borrowed some expressions from him.

[2] *Monuments de l'histoire des abbayes de Saint-Philibert*, ed. Poupardin, p. 62.

before any stranger of certain warlike but primitive tribes.[1] Brave in the face of familiar dangers, untutored minds are as a rule unable to endure surprise and mystery. The monk of Saint-Germain-des-Prés, writing very soon after the event, related how the ships of the Northmen sailed up the Seine in 854. Notice the agitated tone in which he observes that 'one had never heard speak of such a thing or read anything like it in the books'.[2] This emotionalism was sustained by the atmosphere of legend and apocalypse in which men's minds were steeped. Rémi of Auxerre states that 'innumerable persons' believed that in the Hungarians they recognized the peoples of Gog and Magog, forerunners of Antichrist.[3] The universal belief that all these calamities were a divine chastisement produced a mood of resignation. The letters which Alcuin sent to England after the disaster of Lindisfarne are merely exhortations to virtue and repentance; of the organization of resistance there is not a word. However, the well-authenticated examples of such cowardice belong for the most part to the earliest periods. Later on people gained a little more courage.

The truth is that the leaders were far more capable of fighting (if their own lives or property were in jeopardy) than of methodically organizing a defence. Moreover with very few exceptions they were unable to understand the connection between their particular interests and the general interest. Ermentarius was right in attributing the Scandinavian victories, not only to the cowardice and 'torpor' of the Christians, but also to their 'dissensions'. That a king of Italy, Hugh of Provence, should have come to terms with the terrible bandits of Le Freinet, that another king of Italy, Berengar I, should have taken Hungarians into his service, and a king of Aquitaine, Pepin II, Northmen; that the Parisians, in 885, should have let loose the Vikings on Burgundy; that the town of Gaeta, long allied with the Saracens of Monte Argento, should have agreed only in return for land and gold to lend its support to a league formed to expel these brigands — these episodes, among many others, throw a very harsh light on the common mentality of the age. But suppose the sovereigns, in spite of everything, did attempt to fight. Too often the enterprise ended like that of Louis III, who in 881, having built a castle on the Scheldt in order to bar the way to the Vikings, 'could find no one to defend it'. There were not many royal armies of which one could not have repeated what a Parisian monk said (probably not without a touch of optimism) of the levy of 845; among the warriors summoned many came—not all.[4] But undoubtedly the most revealing case is that of Otto the Great, who, though the most powerful monarch of his time, never succeeded in assembling the small force which was all that was needed to put an end to the scandal of Le Freinet. If in England the kings of Wessex, until the final collapse, valiantly

---

[1] Cf., for example. L. Lévy-Bruhl, *La Mentalité primitive*, p. 377.
[2] *Analecta Bollandiana*, 1883, p. 71.   [3] Migne, *P.L.*, CXXXI, col. 966.
[4] *Analecta Bollandiana*, 1883, p. 78.

and effectively conducted the struggle against the Danes, if in Germany Otto did as much against the Hungarians, in the West as a whole the most successful resistance came rather from the regional powers which, stronger than the kingdoms because they were nearer to the human material and less preoccupied with inordinate ambitions, slowly emerged from among the clutter of petty lordships.

However much may be learnt from the study of the last invasions, we should nevertheless not allow their lessons to overshadow the still more important fact of their cessation. Till then these ravages by hordes from without and these great movements of peoples had in truth formed the main fabric of history in the West as in the rest of the world. Thenceforward the West would almost alone be free from them. Neither the Mongols nor the Turks would later do more than brush its frontiers. Western society would certainly have its clashes; but they would take place within a closed arena. This meant the possibility of a much more regular cultural and social evolution, uninterrupted by any attack from without or any influx of foreign settlers. Consider by contrast the destiny of Indo-China where, in the fourteenth century, the splendour of the Chams and Khmers collapsed under the blows of Annamite or Siamese invaders. Consider above all, nearer home, eastern Europe, trampled underfoot until modern times by the peoples of the steppes and by the Turks. Let us ask ourselves for one moment what Russia's destiny might have been without the Polovtsi and the Mongols. It is surely not unreasonable to think that this extraordinary immunity, of which we have shared the privilege with scarcely any people but the Japanese, was one of the fundamental factors of European civilization, in the deepest sense, in the exact sense of the word.

PART II

The Environment: Conditions of Life and Mental Climate

IV

MATERIAL CONDITIONS
AND ECONOMIC CHARACTERISTICS

1 THE TWO AGES OF FEUDALISM

THE framework of institutions which governs a society can in the last
resort be understood only through a knowledge of the whole human environment. For though the artificial conception of man's activities which
prompts us to carve up the creature of flesh and blood into the phantoms
homo oeconomicus, philosophicus, juridicus is doubtless necessary, it is
tolerable only if we refuse to be deceived by it. That is why, despite the
existence of other works on the various aspects of medieval civilization,
the descriptions thus attempted from points of view different from ours
did not seem to us to obviate the necessity of recalling at this stage the
fundamental characteristics of the historical climate in which European
feudalism flourished. Need I add that in placing this account near the
beginning of the book there was no thought of claiming any sort of illusory
primacy for facts of this kind? When it is a question of comparing two
particular phenomena belonging to separate series—a certain distribution
of population, for example, with certain forms of legal groups—the delicate
problem of cause and effect undoubtedly arises. On the other hand, to
contrast two sets of dissimilar phenomena over a period of several centuries,
and then say: 'Here on this side are all the causes; there on that are all
the effects', would be to construct the most pointless of dichotomies. A
society, like a mind, is woven of perpetual interaction. For other researches,
differently oriented, the analysis of the economy or the mental climate are
culminating points; for the historian of the social structure they are a
starting-point.

In this preliminary picture, designedly limited in scope, it will be necessary to retain only what is essential and least open to doubt. One deliberate
omission, in particular, deserves a word of explanation. The wonderful
flowering of art in the feudal era, at least from the eleventh century on, is
not merely the most lasting glory of that epoch in the eyes of posterity. It
served in those times as a vehicle for the most exalted forms of religious
sensibility as well as for that interpenetration of the sacred and profane
so characteristic of the age, which has left no more spontaneous witness

59

than the friezes and capitals of certain churches. It was also very often the refuge, as it were, of certain values which could not find expression elsewhere. The restraint of which the medieval epic was incapable must be sought in Romanesque architecture. The precision of mind which the notaries were unable to attain in their charters presided over the works of the builders of vaults. But the links that unite plastic expression to the other features of a civilization are still insufficiently understood; from the little that we know of them they appear so complex, so subject to delays and divergences that it has been necessary in this work to leave aside the problems posed by connections so delicate and contradictions that to us seem so astonishing.

It would, moreover, be a grave mistake to treat 'feudal civilization' as being all of one piece chronologically. Engendered no doubt or made possible by the cessation of the last invasions, but first manifesting themselves some generations later, a series of very profound and very widespread changes occurred towards the middle of the eleventh century. No definite break with the past occurred, but the change of direction which, despite inevitable variations in time according to the countries or the phenomena considered, affected in turn all the graphs of social activity. There were, in a word, two successive 'feudal' ages, very different from one another in their essential character. We shall endeavour in the following pages to do justice as much to the contrasts between these two phases as to the characteristics they shared.

2 THE FIRST FEUDAL AGE: DENSITY OF POPULATION

It is and always will be impossible for us to calculate, even approximately, the population of Western countries during the first feudal age. Moreover, there undoubtedly existed marked regional variations, constantly intensified by the spasms of social disorder. Compared with the veritable desert of the Iberian plateaux, which gave the frontier regions of Christendom and Islam the desolate appearance of a vast 'no man's land'—desolate even in comparison with early Germany, where the destruction wrought by the migrations of the previous age was being slowly made good—the country districts of Flanders and Lombardy seemed relatively favoured regions. But whatever the importance of these contrasts and whatever their effect on all the aspects of civilization, the fundamental characteristic remains the great and universal decline in population. Over the whole of Europe, the population was immeasurably smaller than it has been since the eighteenth century or even since the twelfth. Even in the provinces formerly under Roman rule, human beings were much scarcer than they had been in the heyday of the Empire. The most important towns had no more than a few thousand inhabitants, and waste land, gardens, even fields and pastures encroached on all sides amongst the houses.

This lack of density was further aggravated by very unequal distribution. Doubtless physical conditions, as well as social habits, conspired to maintain in the country districts profound differences between systems of settlement. In some districts the families, or at least some of them, took up their residence a considerable distance apart, each in the middle of its own farmland, as was the case, for example, in Limousin. In others on the contrary, like the Île-de-France, they mostly crowded together in villages. On the whole, however, both the pressure of the chiefs and, above all, the concern for security militated against too wide dispersal. The disorders of the early Middle Ages had in many cases induced men to draw nearer to each other, but these aggregations in which people lived cheek by jowl were separated by empty spaces. The arable land from which the village derived its sustenance was necessarily much larger in proportion to the number of inhabitants than it is today. For agriculture was a great devourer of space. In the tilled fields, incompletely ploughed and almost always inadequately manured, the ears of corn grew neither very heavy nor very dense. Above all, the harvests never covered the whole area of cultivation at once. The most advanced systems of crop-rotation known to the age required that every year half or a third of the cultivated soil should lie fallow. Often indeed, fallow and crops followed each other in irregular alternation, which always allowed more time for the growth of weeds than for that of the cultivated produce; the fields, in such cases, represented hardly more than a provisional and short-lived conquest of the waste land, and even in the heart of the agricultural regions nature tended constantly to regain the upper hand. Beyond them, enveloping them, thrusting into them, spread forests, scrub and dunes—immense wildernesses, seldom entirely uninhabited by man, though whoever dwelt there as charcoal-burner, shepherd, hermit or outlaw did so only at the cost of a long separation from his fellow men.

3 THE FIRST FEUDAL AGE: INTERCOMMUNICATION

Among these sparsely scattered human groups the obstacles to communication were many. The collapse of the Carolingian empire had destroyed the last power sufficiently intelligent to concern itself with public works, sufficiently strong to get some of them carried out. Even the old Roman roads, less solidly constructed than has sometimes been imagined, went to rack and ruin for want of maintenance. Worse still, bridges were no longer kept in repair and were lacking at a great number of river-crossings. Added to this was the general state of insecurity, increased by the depopulation to which it had itself in part contributed. Great was the surprise and relief at the court of Charles the Bald, when in the year 841 that prince witnessed the arrival at Troyes of the messengers bringing him the crown jewels from Aquitaine: how wonderful that such a small number of men, entrusted with such precious baggage, should traverse without accident those vast areas infested on all sides by robbers![1] The Anglo-Saxon Chronicle shows much less surprise when relating how, in 1061, one of the greatest nobles of England, Earl Tostig, was captured and held to ransom by a handful of bandits at the gates of Rome.

Compared with what the world offers us today, the speed of travel in that age seems extremely slow. It was not, however, appreciably slower than it was at the end of the Middle Ages, or even the beginning of the eighteenth century. By contrast with today, travel was much faster by sea than by land. From 60 to 90 miles a day was not an exceptional record for a ship: provided (it goes without saying) that the winds were not too unfavourable. On land, the normal distance covered in one day amounted, it seems, to between nineteen and twenty-five miles—for travellers who were in no hurry, that is: say a caravan of merchants, a great nobleman moving round from castle to castle or from abbey to abbey, or an army with its baggage. A courier or a handful of resolute men could by making a special effort travel at least twice as fast. A letter written by Gregory VII at Rome on the 8th December 1075 arrived at Goslar, at the foot of the Harz, on the 1st of January following; its bearer had covered about 29 miles a day as the crow flies—in reality, of course, much more. To travel without too much fatigue and not too slowly it was necessary to be mounted or in a carriage. Horses and mules not only go faster than men; they adapt themselves better to boggy ground. This explains the seasonal interruption of many communications; it was due less to bad weather than to lack of forage. The Carolingian *missi* had earlier made a point of not beginning their tours till the grass had grown.[2] However, as at present in Africa, an experienced foot-traveller could cover astoundingly long distances in a few days and he could doubtless overcome certain obstacles more quickly than a horseman. When Charles the Bald organized his second Italian expedition he arranged to keep in touch with Gaul across the Alps partly by means of runners.[3]

Though poor and unsafe, the roads or tracks were in constant use. Where transport is difficult, man goes to something he wants more easily than he makes it come to him. In particular, no institution or method could take the place of personal contact between human beings. It would have been impossible to govern the state from inside a palace: to control a country, there was no other means than to ride through it incessantly in all directions. The kings of the first feudal age positively killed themselves by travel. For example, in the course of a year which was in no way exceptional, the emperor Conrad II in 1033 is known to have journeyed in turn from Burgundy to the Polish frontier and thence to Champagne, to return

[1] Nithard, *Histoire des fils de Louis le Pieux*, ed. Lauer, II, c. 8.
[2] Loup de Ferrières, *Corréspondance*, ed. Levillain, I, no. 41.
[3] *Capitularia*, II, no. 281, c. 25.

eventually to Lusatia. The nobleman with his entourage moved round constantly from one of his estates to another; and not only in order to supervise them more effectively. It was necessary for him to consume the produce on the spot, for to transport it to a common centre would have been both inconvenient and expensive. Similarly with the merchant. Without representatives to whom he could delegate the task of buying and selling, fairly certain in any case of never finding enough customers assembled in one place to assure him a profit, every merchant was a pedlar, a 'dusty foot' (*pied poudreux*), plying his trade up hill and down dale. The cleric, eager for learning or the ascetic life, was obliged to wander over Europe in search of the master of his choice: Gerbert of Aurillac studied mathematics in Spain and philosophy at Rheims; the Englishman Stephen Harding, the ideal monachism in the Burgundian abbey of Molesmes. Before him, St. Odo, the future abbot of Cluny, had travelled through France in the hope of finding a monastery whose members lived strictly according to the rule.

Moreover, in spite of the old hostility of the Benedictine rule to the *gyrovagi*, the bad monks who ceaselessly 'vagabonded about', everything in contemporary clerical life favoured this nomadism: the international character of the Church; the use of Latin as a common language among educated priests and monks; the affiliations between monasteries; the wide dispersal of their territorial patrimonies; and finally the 'reforms' which periodically convulsed this great ecclesiastical body and made the places first affected by the new spirit at once courts of appeal (to which people came from all parts to seek the good rule) and mission centres whence the zealots were despatched for the conquest of the Catholic world. How many foreign visitors came to Cluny in this way! How many Cluniacs journeyed forth to foreign lands! Under William the Conqueror almost all the dioceses and great abbeys of Normandy, which the first waves of the 'Gregorian' revival were beginning to reach, had at their head Italians or Lorrainers; the archbishop of Rouen, Maurille, was a man from Rheims who, before occupying his Neustrian see, had studied at Liège, taught in Saxony and lived as a hermit in Tuscany.

Humble folk, too, passed along the highways of the West: refugees, driven by war or famine; adventurers, half-soldiers, half-bandits; peasants seeking a more prosperous life and hoping to find, far from their native land, a few fields to cultivate. Finally, there were pilgrims. For religious devotion itself fostered travel and more than one good Christian, rich or poor, cleric or layman, believed that he could purchase salvation of body and soul only at the price of a long journey.

As has often been remarked, it is in the nature of good roads to create a vacuum around them—to their own profit. In the feudal age, when all roads were bad, scarcely any of them was capable of monopolizing the traffic in this way. Undoubtedly such factors as the restrictions of the terrain, tradition, the presence of a market here or a sanctuary there, worked to the advantage of certain routes, although far less decisively than the historians of literary or artistic influences have sometimes believed. A fortuitous event—a physical accident, the exactions of a lord in need of money—sufficed to divert the flow, sometimes permanently. The building of a castle on the old Roman road, occupied by a race of robber knights— the lords of Méréville—and the establishment some distance away of the St. Denis priory of Toury, where merchants and pilgrims found by contrast a pleasant reception, were sufficient to divert the traffic from the Beauce section of the road from Paris to Orleans permanently westward, so that the ancient roadway was abandoned from that time on. Moreover from the beginning of his journey to the end, the traveller had almost always the choice of several itineraries, of which none was absolutely obligatory. Traffic, in short, was not canalized in a few great arteries; it spread capriciously through a multitude of little blood-vessels. There was no castle, burg, or monastery, however far from the beaten track, that could not expect to be visited occasionally by wanderers, living links with the outer world, although the places where such visits were of regular occurrence were few.

Thus the obstacles and dangers of the road in no way prevented travel. But they made each journey an expedition, almost an adventure. If men, under pressure of need, did not fear to undertake fairly long journeys (they feared it less, perhaps, than in centuries nearer to our own) they shrank from those repeated comings and goings within a narrow radius which in other civilizations form the texture of daily life; and this was especially so in the case of humble folk of settled occupations. The result was an ordering of the scheme of human relations quite different from anything we know today. There was scarcely any remote little place which had not some contacts intermittently through that sort of continuous yet irregular 'Brownian movement' which affected the whole of society. On the other hand, between two inhabited centres quite close to each other the connections were much rarer, the isolation of their inhabitants in-finitely greater than would be the case in our own day. If, according to the angle from which it is viewed, the civilization of feudal Europe appears sometimes remarkably universalist, sometimes particularist in the extreme, the principal source of this contradiction lay in the conditions of communi-cation: conditions which favoured the distant propagation of very general currents of influence as much as they discouraged, in any particular place, the standardizing effects of neighbourly intercourse.

The only more or less regular letter-mail service which functioned during the whole of the feudal era was that which linked Venice to Constantinople. Such a thing was practically unknown in the West. The last attempts to maintain a royal posting-service, on the model left by the Roman govern-ment, had disappeared with the Carolingian empire. It is significant of the general disorganization that the German monarchs themselves, the true heirs of that empire and its ambitions, should have lacked either the authority or the intelligence necessary to secure the revival of an institution clearly so indispensable to the control of vast territories. Sovereigns, nobles, prelates were obliged to entrust their correspondence to special couriers, otherwise—as was usual among persons of lesser rank—the transport of letters was simply left to the kindness of passing travellers; as, for instance, the pilgrims on their way to St. James of Galicia.[1] The relative slowness of the messengers, the mishaps that at every stage threatened their progress, meant that the only effective authority was the one on the spot. Forced constantly to take the gravest steps—the history of the papal legates is in this respect very instructive—every local representative of a great potentate tended only too naturally to act for his personal advantage and thus finally to transform himself into an independent ruler.

As for knowledge of distant events, everyone, whatever his rank, was obliged to rely on chance encounters. The picture of the contemporary world which the best-informed men carried in their minds presented many lacunae; we can form an idea of them from the unavoidable omissions even from the best of those monastic annals which are as it were the written reports of medieval news-hawks. Moreover, it was seldom exact as to time. It is, for example, remarkable to find a person so well placed for acquiring information as Bishop Fulbert of Chartres showing astonishment on receiving gifts for his church from Cnut the Great: for he admits that he believed this prince to be still a heathen, although in fact he had been baptized in infancy.[2] The monk Lambert of Hersfeld is quite well-informed about German affairs, but when he goes on to describe the grave events which occurred in his time in Flanders (a region bordering on the Empire and in part an imperial fief), he soon makes a series of the strangest blunders. Such an imperfect state of knowledge was a poor foundation for any large political designs.

4 THE FIRST FEUDAL AGE: TRADE AND CURRENCY

The life of the Europe of the first feudal age was not entirely self-contained. There was more than one current of exchange between it and the neighbouring civilizations, and probably the most active was that which linked it to Moslem Spain, as witnessed by the numerous Arab gold pieces which, by this route, penetrated north of the Pyrenees and were there sufficiently sought after to become the object of frequent imitations. In the western Mediterranean, on the other hand, long-distance navigation was now practically unknown. The principal lines of communication with the East were elsewhere. One of them, a sea-route, passed through the

[1] Cf. E. Faral, in *Revue Critique*, 1933, p. 454.
[2] *Ep.*, no. 69, in Migne, *P. L.*, CXLI, col. 235.

Adriatic, at the head of which lay Venice, to all appearance a fragment of Byzantium, set in a world apart. On land the Danube route, for a long time severed by the Hungarians, was almost deserted. But farther north, on the trails which joined Bavaria to the great market of Prague and thence, by the terraces on the northern flank of the Carpathians, continued to the Dnieper, caravans passed back and forth, laden on the return journey with products of Constantinople or of Asia. At Kiev they met the great transversal which, running across the plains and from river to river, linked the riparian countries of the Baltic with the Black Sea, the Caspian or the oases of Turkestan. For the West had missed its chance of being the intermediary between the north or north-east of the continent and the eastern Mediterranean, and had nothing to offer on its own soil to compare with the mighty comings and goings of merchandise which made the prosperity of Kievian Russia.

Not only was this trade restricted to very few routes; it was also extremely small in volume. What is worse, the balance of trade seems to have been distinctly unfavourable—at any rate with the East. From the eastern countries the West received almost nothing except a few luxury articles whose value—very high in relation to their weight—was such as to take no account of the expense and risks of transport. In exchange it had scarcely anything to offer except slaves. Moreover, it seems that most of the human cattle rounded up on the Slav and Lettish territories beyond the Elbe or acquired from the slave-traders of Britain took the road to Islamic Spain; the eastern Mediterranean was too abundantly provided with this commodity from its own sources to have any need to import it on a large scale. The profits of the slave-trade, in general fairly small, were not sufficient to pay for the purchase of precious goods and spices in the markets of the Byzantine world, of Egypt or of nearer Asia. The result was a slow drain of silver and above all of gold. If a few merchants unquestionably owed their prosperity to these remote transactions, society as a whole owed scarcely anything to them except one more reason for being short of specie.

However, money was never wholly absent from business transactions in feudal Europe, even among the peasant classes, and it never ceased to be employed as a standard of exchange. Payments were often made in produce; but the produce was normally valued item by item in such a way that the total of these reckonings corresponded with a stipulated price in pounds, shillings and pence. Let us therefore avoid the expression 'natural economy', which is too summary and too vague. It is better to speak simply of shortage of currency. This shortage was further aggravated by the anarchic state of minting, another result of the subdivision of political authority and the difficulty of communication: for each important market, faced with the threat of shortage, had to have its local mint. Except for the imitation of exotic coinages and apart from certain insignificant little pieces, the only coins now produced were *denarii*, which were rather debased silver pieces. Gold circulated only in the shape of Arab and Byzantine coins or imitations of them. The *libra* and the *solidus* were only arithmetical multiples of the *denarius*, without a material basis of their own. But the various coins called *denarii* had a different metallic value according to their origin. Worse still, even in one and the same area almost every issue involved variations in the weight or the alloy. Not only was money generally scarce, and inconvenient on account of its unreliability, but it circulated too slowly and too irregularly for people ever to feel certain of being able to procure it in case of need. That was the situation, in the absence of a sufficiently active commerce.

But here again, let us beware of too facile a formula—the 'closed economy'. It would not even apply exactly to the small farming operations of the peasants. We know that markets existed where the rustics certainly sold some of the produce of their fields or their farmyards to the towns-folk, to the clergy, to the men-at-arms. It was thus that they procured the *denarii* to pay their dues. And poor indeed was the man who never bought a few ounces of salt or a bit of iron. As to the 'autarky' of the great manors, this would have meant that their masters had gone without arms or jewels, had never drunk wine (unless their estates produced it), and for clothes had been content with crude materials woven by the wives of tenants. Moreover, even the inadequacies of agricultural technique, the disturbed state of society, and finally the inclemency of the weather contributed to maintain a certain amount of internal commerce: for when the harvest failed, although many people literally died of starvation, the whole population was not reduced to this extremity, and we know that there was a traffic in corn from the more favoured districts to those afflicted by dearth, which lent itself readily to speculation. Trade, therefore, was not non-existent, but it was irregular in the extreme. The society of this age was certainly not unacquainted with either buying or selling. But it did not, like our own, live by buying and selling.

Moreover, commerce, even in the form of barter, was not the only or perhaps even the most important channel by which at that time goods circulated through the various classes of society. A great number of products passed from hand to hand as dues paid to a chief in return for his protection or simply in recognition of his power. It was the same in the case of that other commodity, human labour: the *corvée* furnished more labourers than hire. In short, exchange, in the strict sense, certainly played a smaller part in economic life than payment in kind; and because exchange was thus a rare thing, while at the same time only the poorest could resign themselves to living wholly on their own produce, wealth and well-being seemed inseparable from authority.

Nevertheless, in an economy so constituted the means of acquisition at the disposal even of the powerful were, on the whole, singularly restricted.

When we speak of money we mean the possibility of laying by reserves, the ability to wait, the 'anticipation of future values'—everything that, conversely, the shortage of money particularly impedes. It is true that people tried to hoard wealth in other forms. The nobles and kings accumulated in their coffers gold or silver vessels and precious stones; the churches amassed liturgical plate. Should the need arise for an unexpected disbursement, you sold or pawned the crown, the goblet or the crucifix; or you even sent them to be melted down at the local mint. But such liquidation of assets, from the very fact of the slowing down of exchange which made it necessary, was never easy nor was it always profitable; and the hoarded treasure itself did not after all constitute a very large amount. The great as well as the humble lived from hand to mouth, obliged to be content with the resources of the moment and mostly compelled to spend them at once.

The weakness of trade and of monetary circulation had a further consequence of the gravest kind. It reduced to insignificance the social function of wages. The latter requires that the employer should have at his disposal an adequate currency, the source of which is not in danger of drying up at any moment; on the side of the wage-earner it requires the certainty of being able to employ the money thus received in procuring for himself the necessities of life. Both these conditions were absent in the first feudal age. In all grades of the hierarchy, whether it was a question of the king's making sure of the services of a great official, or of the small landlord's retaining those of an armed follower or a farm-hand, it was necessary to have recourse to a method of remuneration which was not based on the periodic payment of a sum of money. Two alternatives offered: one was to take the man into one's household, to feed and clothe him, to provide him with 'prebend', as the phrase went; the other was to grant him in return for his services an estate which, if exploited directly or in the form of dues levied on the cultivators of the soil, would enable him to provide for himself.

Now both these methods tended, though in opposite ways, to create human ties very different from those based on wages. Between the prebend-holder and the master under whose roof he lived the bond must surely have been much more intimate than that between an employer and a wage-earner, who is free, once his job is finished, to go off with his money in his pocket. On the other hand, the bond was almost inevitably loosened as soon as the subordinate was settled on a piece of land, which by a natural process he tended increasingly to regard as his own, while trying to reduce the burden of service. Moreover, in a time when the inadequacy of communications and the insufficiency of trade rendered it difficult to maintain large households in relative abundance, the 'prebend' system was on the whole capable of a much smaller extension than the system of remuneration based on land. If feudal society perpetually oscillated between these two poles, the narrow relationship of man and man and the looser tie of land tenure, the responsibility for this belongs in large part to the economic regime which, to begin with at least, made wage-earning impracticable.

5 THE ECONOMIC REVOLUTION OF THE SECOND FEUDAL AGE

We shall endeavour, in another work, to describe the intensive movement of repopulation which, from approximately 1050 to 1250, transformed the face of Europe: on the confines of the Western world, the colonization of the Iberian plateaux and of the great plain beyond the Elbe; in the heart of the old territories, the incessant gnawing of the plough at forest and wasteland; in the glades opened amidst the trees or the brushwood, completely new villages clutching at the virgin soil; elsewhere, round sites inhabited for centuries, the extension of the agricultural lands through the exertions of the assarters. It will be advisable then to distinguish between the stages of the process and to describe the regional variations. For the moment, we are concerned only with the phenomenon itself and its principal effects.

The most immediately apparent of these was undoubtedly the closer association of the human groups. Between the different settlements, except in some particularly neglected regions, the vast empty spaces thenceforth disappeared. Such distances as still separated the settlements became, in any case, easier to traverse. For powers now arose or were consolidated —their rise being favoured by current demographic trends—whose enlarged horizons brought them new responsibilities. Such were the urban middle classes, which owed everything to trade. Such also were the kings and princes; they too were interested in the prosperity of commerce because they derived large sums of money from it in the form of duties and tolls; moreover they were aware—much more so than in the past—of the vital importance to them of the free transmission of orders and the free movement of armies. The activity of the Capetians towards that decisive turning-point marked by the reign of Louis VI, their aggressions, their domanial policy, their part in the organization of the movement of repopulation, were in large measure the reflection of considerations of this kind—the need to retain control of communications between the two capitals, Paris and Orleans, and beyond the Loire or the Seine to maintain contact with Berry or with the valleys of the Oise and the Aisne. It would seem that while the security of the roads had increased, there was no very notable improvement in their condition; but at least the provision of bridges had been carried much farther. In the course of the twelfth century, how many were thrown over all the rivers of Europe! Finally, a fortunate advance in harnessing methods had the effect, about the same time, of increasing very substantially the efficiency of horse-transport.

The links with neighbouring civilizations underwent a similar transformation. Ships in ever greater numbers ploughed the Tyrrhenian Sea, and its ports, from the rock of Amalfi to Catalonia, rose to the rank of great commercial centres; the sphere of Venetian trade continually expanded; the heavy wagons of the merchant caravans now followed the route of the Danubian plains. These advances were important enough. But relations with the East had not only become easier and more intimate. The most important fact is that they had changed their character. Formerly almost exclusively an importer, the West had become a great supplier of manufactured goods. The merchandise which it thus shipped in quantity to the Byzantine world, to the Latin or Islamic Levant and even—though in smaller amounts—to the Maghreb, belonged to very diverse categories. One commodity, however, easily dominated all the rest. In the expansion of the European economy in the Middle Ages, cloth played the same vital rôle as did metal and cotton goods in that of nineteenth-century England. If in Flanders, in Picardy, at Bourges, in Languedoc, in Lombardy, and yet other places—for the cloth centres were to be found almost everywhere—the noise of the looms and the throbbing of the fullers' mills resounded, it was at least as much for the sake of foreign markets as for local requirements. And undoubtedly this revolution, which saw our Western countries embarking on the economic conquest of the world by way of the East, is to be explained by a multiplicity of causes and by looking—as far as possible—towards the East as well as towards the West. It is none the less true that it could not have occurred without the demographic changes mentioned above. If the population had not been more numerous than before and the cultivated area more extensive; if the fields —their quality improved by augmented manpower and in particular by more intensive ploughing—had not become capable of yielding bigger and more frequent harvests, how could so many weavers, dyers or cloth-shearers have been brought together in the towns and provided with a livelihood?

The North was conquered, like the East. From the end of the eleventh century Flemish cloth was sold at Novgorod. Little by little, the route of the Russian plains became hazardous and was finally closed. Thenceforward Scandinavia and the Baltic countries turned towards the West. The process of change which was thus set in motion was completed when, in the course of the twelfth century, German merchants took over the Baltic. From that time onwards the ports of the Low Countries, especially Bruges, became the centres where northern products were exchanged not only for those of the West itself but also for merchandise from the East. Strong international links united the two frontiers of feudal Europe by way of Germany and especially through the fairs of Champagne.

Such a well-balanced external trade could not fail to bring a flow of coin and precious metals into Europe and so add substantially to its monetary resources. This relative easing of the currency situation was reinforced—and its effects multiplied—by the accelerated rhythm of circulation. For in the very heart of the West the progress of repopulation, the greater ease of communications, the cessation of the invasions which had spread such an atmosphere of confusion and panic over the Western world, and still other causes which it would take too long to examine here, had led to a revival of commerce.

Let us avoid exaggeration, however. The picture would have to be carefully shaded—by regions and by classes. To live on their own resources remained for long centuries the ideal—though one that was rarely attained—of many peasants and most villages. Moreover, the profound transformations of the economy took place only very gradually. It is significant that of the two essential developments in the sphere of currency, one, the minting of larger pieces of silver much heavier than the *denarius*, appeared only at the beginning of the thirteenth century (and even at that date in Italy alone) and the other, the resumption of the minting of gold coins of an indigenous type, was delayed till the second half of the same century. In many respects, what the second feudal age witnessed was less the disappearance of earlier conditions than their modification. This observation applies to the part played by distance as well as to commerce. But the fact that the kings, the great nobles, and the manorial lords should have been able to begin once more to amass substantial wealth, that wage-earning, sometimes under legal forms clumsily adapted from ancient practices, should have increasingly supplanted other methods of remunerating services—these signs of an economy in process of revival affected in their turn, from the twelfth century onwards, the whole fabric of human relations.

Furthermore, the evolution of the economy involved a genuine revision of social values. There had always been artisans and merchants; individuals belonging to the latter class had even been able, here and there, to play an important rôle, though collectively neither group counted for much. But from the end of the eleventh century the artisan class and the merchant class, having become much more numerous and much more indispensable to the life of the community, made themselves felt more and more vigorously in the urban setting. This applies especially to the merchant class, for the medieval economy, after the great revival of these decisive years, was always dominated, not by the producer, but by the trader. It was not for the latter class that the legal machinery of the previous age—founded on an economic system in which they occupied only an inferior place—had been set up. But now their practical needs and their mental attitude were bound to imbue it with a new spirit. Born in the midst of a very loosely-knit society, in which commerce was insignificant and money a rarity, European feudalism underwent a fundamental change as soon as the meshes of the human network had been drawn closer together and the circulation of goods and coin intensified.

71

V

MODES OF FEELING AND THOUGHT

1 MAN'S ATTITUDE TO NATURE AND TIME

THE men of the two feudal ages were close to nature—much closer than we are; and nature as they knew it was much less tamed and softened than we see it today. The rural landscape, of which the waste formed so large a part, bore fewer traces of human influence. The wild animals that now only haunt our nursery tales—bears and, above all, wolves—prowled in every wilderness, and even amongst the cultivated fields. So much was this the case that the sport of hunting was indispensable for ordinary security, and almost equally so as a method of supplementing the food supply. People continued to pick wild fruit and to gather honey as in the first ages of mankind. In the construction of implements and tools, wood played a predominant part. The nights, owing to the wretched lighting, were darker; the cold, even in the living quarters of the castles, was more intense. In short, behind all social life there was a background of the primitive, of submission to uncontrollable forces, of unrelieved physical contrasts. There is no means of measuring the influence which such an environment was capable of exerting on the minds of men, but it could hardly have failed to contribute to their uncouthness.

A history more worthy of the name than the diffident speculations to which we are reduced by the paucity of our material would give space to the vicissitudes of the human organism. It is very naive to claim to understand men without knowing what sort of health they enjoyed. But in this field the state of the evidence, and still more the inadequacy of our methods of research, are inhibitive. Infant mortality was undoubtedly very high in feudal Europe and tended to make people somewhat callous towards bereavements that were almost a normal occurrence. As to the life of adults, even apart from the hazards of war it was usually short by our standards, at least to judge from the records of princely personages which (inexact though they must often be) constitute our only source of information on this point. Robert the Pious died at about the age of 60; Henry I at 52; Philip I and Louis VI at 56. In Germany the first four emperors of the Saxon dynasty attained respectively the ages of 60 (or thereabouts), 28, 22 and 52. Old age seemed to begin very early, as early as mature adult life with us. This world, which, as we shall see, considered itself very old, was in fact governed by young men.

Among so many premature deaths, a large number were due to the great epidemics which descended frequently upon a humanity ill-equipped to combat them; among the poor another cause was famine. Added to the constant acts of violence these disasters gave life a quality of perpetual insecurity. This was probably one of the principal reasons for the emotional instability so characteristic of the feudal era, especially during its first age. A low standard of hygiene doubtless also contributed to this nervous sensibility. A great deal of effort has been expended, in our own day, in proving that baths were not unknown to seignorial society. It is rather puerile, for the sake of making this point, to overlook so many unhealthy conditions of life: notably under-nourishment among the poor and overeating among the rich. Finally, we must not leave out of account the effects of an astonishing sensibility to what were believed to be supernatural manifestations. It made people's minds constantly and almost morbidly attentive to all manner of signs, dreams, or hallucinations. This characteristic was especially marked in monastic circles where the influence of mortifications of the flesh and the repression of natural instincts was joined to that of a mental attitude vocationally centred on the problems of the unseen. No psychoanalyst has ever examined dreams more earnestly than the monks of the tenth or the eleventh century. Yet the laity also shared the emotionalism of a civilization in which moral or social convention did not yet require well-bred people to repress their tears and their raptures. The despairs, the rages, the impulsive acts, the sudden revulsions of feeling present great difficulties to historians, who are instinctively disposed to reconstruct the past in terms of the rational. But the irrational is an important element in all history and only a sort of false shame could allow its effects on the course of political events in feudal Europe to be passed over in silence.

These men, subjected both externally and internally to so many ungovernable forces, lived in a world in which the passage of time escaped their grasp all the more because they were so ill-equipped to measure it. Water-clocks, which were costly and cumbersome, were very rare. Hour-glasses were little used. The inadequacy of sundials, especially under skies quickly clouded over, was notorious. This resulted in the use of curious devices. In his concern to regulate the course of a notably nomadic life, King Alfred had conceived the idea of carrying with him everywhere a supply of candles of equal length, which he had lit in turn,[1] to mark the passing of the hours, but such concern for uniformity in the division of the day was exceptional in that age. Reckoning ordinarily—after the

---

[1] Asser, *Life of King Alfred*, ed. Stevenson, c. 104. According to L. Reverchon, *Petite histoire de l'horlogerie*, p. 55, a similar system was still employed by Charles V of France.

example of Antiquity—twelve hours of day and twelve of night, whatever the season, people of the highest education became used to seeing each of these fractions, taken one by one, grow and diminish incessantly, according to the annual revolution of the sun. This was to continue till the moment when—towards the beginnning of the fourteenth century—counterpoise clocks brought with them at last, not only the mechanization of the instrument, but, so to speak, of time itself.

An anecdote related in a chronicle of Hainault illustrates admirably the sort of perpetual fluctuation of time in those days. At Mons a judicial duel is due to take place. Only one champion puts in an appearance—at dawn; at the ninth hour, which marks the end of the waiting period prescribed by custom, he requests that the failure of his adversary be placed on record. On the point of law, there is no doubt. But has the specified period really elapsed? The county judges deliberate, look at the sun, and question the clerics in whom the practice of the liturgy has induced a more exact knowledge of the rhythm of the hours than their own, and by whose bells it is measured, more or less accurately, to the common benefit of men. Eventually the court pronounces firmly that the hour of 'none' is past.[1] To us, accustomed to live with our eyes turning constantly to the clock, how remote from our civilization seems this society in which a court of law could not ascertain the time of day without discussion and inquiry!

Now the imperfection of hourly reckoning was but one of the symptoms, among many others, of a vast indifference to time. Nothing would have been easier or more useful than to keep an accurate record of such important legal dates as those of the births of rulers; yet in 1284 a full investigation was necessary to determine, as far as possible, the age of one of the greatest heiresses of the Capetian realm, the young countess of Champagne.[2] In the tenth and eleventh centuries, innumerable charters and memoranda were undated, although their only purpose was to serve as records. There are exceptional documents which are better in this respect, yet the notary, who employed several systems of reference simultaneously, was often not successful in making his various calculations agree. What is more, it was not the notion of time only, it was the domain of number as a whole which suffered from this haziness. The extravagant figures of the chroniclers are not merely literary exaggeration; they are evidence of the lack of all awareness of statistical realities. Although William the Conqueror certainly did not establish in England more than 5,000 knights' fees, the historians of a somewhat later time, and even certain administrators (though it would certainly not have been very difficult for them to obtain the right information), did not hesitate to attribute to him the creation of from thirty-two to sixty thousand of these military tenements. The period had, especially from the end of the eleventh century, its

[1] Gislebert of Mons, ed. Pertz, pp. 188–9 (1188).
[2] *Les Établissements de Saint-Louis*, ed. P. Viollet, III, p. 165, n. 8.

mathematicians who groped their way courageously in the wake of the Greeks and Arabs; the architects and sculptors were capable of using a fairly simple geometry. But among the computations that have come down to us—and this was true till the end of the Middle Ages—there are scarcely any that do not reveal astonishing errors. The inconveniences of the Roman numerical system, ingeniously corrected as they were by the use of the abacus, do not suffice to explain these mistakes. The truth is that the regard for accuracy, with its firmest buttress, the respect for figures, remained profoundly alien to the minds even of the leading men of that age.

2 EXPRESSION

On the one hand, the language of the educated, which was almost uniformly Latin; on the other, the variety of tongues in everyday use: such is the singular dualism which prevailed almost throughout the feudal era. It was peculiar to Western civilization properly so called and helped to distinguish it sharply from its neighbours—from the Celtic and Scandinavian worlds with their rich poetic and didactic literatures in the national languages; from the Greek East; and, at least in the really Arabized zones, from the world of Islam.

In the West itself, it is true, one society long remained an exception. This was Anglo-Saxon Britain. Not that Latin was not written there and written very well, but it was by no means the only language written. The old English tongue was elevated at an early date to the dignity of a literary and legal language. It was King Alfred's wish that young people should learn it in the schools before the more gifted passed on to Latin.[1] The poets employed it in their songs, which were set down in writing as well as recited. It was also used by the kings in their laws; by the chanceries in the legal documents drawn up for kings or magnates; and even by the monks in their chronicles. This was something unique in that age, a culture that was able to keep in touch on its highest levels with the medium of expression employed by the mass of the population. The Norman Conquest cut short this development. Between William's letter to the people of London, written soon after the battle of Hastings, and a few occasional administrative instructions in the late twelfth century, there was not a single royal deed that was not drawn up in Latin. With virtually only one exception, the Anglo-Saxon chronicles are silent from the middle of the eleventh century. As for those writings which may, by stretching a point, be called 'literature', they were not to reappear till shortly before the year 1200 and then at first only in the form of a few minor works of edification.

On the continent the fine cultural effort of the Carolingian renaissance had not wholly neglected the national languages. True it occurred to no

[1] *Pastoral Care*, ed. Sweet, p. 6.

one in that age to consider the Romance tongues as worthy of being put into writing; they were regarded merely as a highly corrupt form of Latin. The German dialects, on the other hand, invited the attention of many men, at court or in the ranks of the higher clergy, whose mother-tongue they were. Old poems, hitherto purely oral, were transcribed and new ones, mainly on religious themes, were composed; manuscripts in *lingua theotisca* (Germanic) figured in the libraries of the great. But here again political events—this time the dismemberment of the Carolingian empire, with the troubles which followed—interrupted the trend. From the end of the ninth century to the end of the eleventh, a few pious poems and some translations comprise the meagre treasure which the historians of German literature must be content to record. In comparison with the Latin writings composed on the same soil and during the same period, we may as well admit that both in quantity and in intellectual quality it is negligible.

We must be careful, moreover, not to think of this Latin of the feudal era as a 'dead language', with all that the epithet implies of the stereotyped and uniform. In spite of the taste for correctness and purism re-established by the Carolingian renaissance, there was much which tended to produce to a greater or lesser extent, according to the environments and the persons concerned, new words and new turns of phrase. One of these circumstances was the need to describe facts unknown to the Ancients or to express thoughts which, in the sphere of religion especially, had been foreign to their ideas; another was the infectious influence of the logical process (very different from that embodied in the traditional grammar) to which people's minds grew accustomed through the use of the vernacular; finally, there were the effects of ignorance or half-knowledge. Moreover, if books tend to impede change, does not speech always favour it? Now men did not confine themselves to writing Latin. They sang it—witness the abandonment by poetry (at least in those forms of it most imbued with true feeling) of the classical prosody of long and short syllables in favour of accented rhythm, the only music henceforth perceptible to the ear. They also spoke it. It was for a solecism committed in conversation that a cultivated Italian, summoned to the court of Otto I, found himself cruelly mocked by a little monk of St. Gall.[1] In preaching, Bishop Notker of Liège, if he was addressing laymen, used Walloon; on the other hand, if he was preaching to his clergy he used Latin. Undoubtedly many ecclesiastics, especially among the parish priests, would have been incapable of imitating him, or even of understanding him. But for educated priests and monks the old κοινή of the Church retained its function for oral communication. Without Latin, how would it have been possible, at the Curia, in the great councils or in the course of their wanderings from abbey to abbey, for these men from different countries to communicate with each other?

Of course, in almost every society, the modes of expression vary, some-

[1] Gunzo Novariensis in Migne, *P. L.*, CXXXVI, col. 1286.

times very considerably, according to the use which it is desired to make of them or the class to which the people concerned belong. But the contrast is limited, as a rule, to slight variations in grammatical exactitude or quality of vocabulary. In feudal society it was incomparably more profound. In a great part of Europe, the common languages, which were connected with the Germanic group, belonged to quite another family from the language of the educated. The Romance tongues themselves were so far removed from their common ancestor that to pass from them to Latin involved long training at school.

Thus the linguistic separation was reduced, in the long run, to the division between two human groups. On the one hand there was the immense majority of uneducated people, each one imprisoned in his regional dialect, limited, so far as literary culture was concerned, to a few secular poems transmitted almost exclusively by word of mouth, and to those pious cantilenas which well-meaning clerics composed in the vulgar tongue for the benefit of simple folk and which they sometimes committed to parchment. On the other hand, there was the little handful of educated people who, constantly alternating between the local everyday speech and the universal language of learning, were in the true sense bilingual. To them belonged the works of theology and history, invariably written in Latin; the knowledge of the liturgy; even the understanding of business documents.

Latin was not only the language in which teaching was done, it was the only language taught. To be able to read was simply to be able to read Latin. Though there were exceptional cases, in legal documents, of a lapse into the vernacular, this anomaly, where it occurs, must be simply regarded as a sign of ignorance. If, from the tenth century, certain charters of southern Aquitaine are full of Provençal terms, in the midst of a more or less incorrect Latin, it is because the monasteries of Rouergue or Quercy, situated away from the great centres of the Carolingian renaissance, could count very few literate monks. Because Sardinia was a poor country whose inhabitants, after their flight from the coastal region ravaged by pirates, lived in quasi-isolation, the first documents written in Sardinian are much older than the earliest Italian texts of the Peninsula.

The most immediately perceptible result of this hierarchic division of languages is that the picture of itself left by the first feudal age is exasperatingly blurred. Acts of sale or donation, of bondage or enfranchisement, judgments of the courts, royal privileges, written records of homage— the legal documents of everyday life—are the most valuable sources for the historian of society. If they are not always honest, they have at least, unlike the narrative texts intended for posterity, the merit of having been at worst designed to deceive only contemporaries, whose credulity had other limits than ours. Now, with very few exceptions which have just been explained, they were, till the thirteenth century, invariably drawn up in Latin. But this was not the way in which the realities they were intended to record were first expressed. When two lords debated the price of an estate or the clauses of a contract of subjection they certainly did not talk to each other in the language of Cicero. It was the notary's business later to provide, as best he could, a classical vestment for their agreement. Thus every Latin charter or notarial record is the result of a work of translation, which the historian today, if he wishes to grasp the underlying truth, must put back, as it were, into the original.

This would be well enough if the process had always followed the same rules. But this was by no means the case. From the schoolboy exercise, clumsily reproducing an outline mentally projected in the vernacular, to the Latin oration, carefully polished by a learned clerk, all stages are to be found. Sometimes—and it is incontestably the most favourable case—the current word is simply disguised, as well as may be, by the addition of a pseudo-Latin termination: for example, *hommage* is scarcely concealed as *homagium*. In other cases, there was an endeavour to use only strictly classical terms, to the point of writing—by an almost blasphemous *jeu d'esprit* assimilating the priest of the Living God to the priest of Jupiter —*archiflamen* for archbishop. The worst of it was that, in the search for parallelisms, the purists did not hesitate to be guided by the analogy of sounds rather than of meanings. Because, in French, the nominative case of *comte* was *cuens*, it was translated as *consul*; or *fief* might be rendered as *fiscus*. It is true that general systems of translation were gradually established, some of which shared the universalist character of the learned language: *fief*, which was called *Lehn* in German, had as regular equivalents, in the Latin charters of Germany, words coined from French. But nothing was ever translated into notarial Latin, even when most skilfully handled, without being slightly deformed.

Thus, the technical language of law itself was handicapped by a vocabulary that was at once too archaic and too unstable to come really close to reality. As for the vulgar tongue, it had all the want of precision and the instability of a purely oral and popular vocabulary. As regards social institutions, confusion in words inevitably involved confusion of things. If only by reason of the imperfection of their terminology, a great uncertainty beset the classification of human relations. But this was not all. To whatever purposes it was applied, Latin had the advantage of providing the intellectuals of the age with an international medium of communication. On the other hand, to most of the men who made use of it, it presented the grave inconvenience of being radically divorced from the inner word— the term that stood naturally, in their minds, for the concept—so that they were forced to resort to perpetual approximations in the expression of their thoughts. Among the multiple causes that doubtless combine to explain the absence of mental precision, which was, as we have seen, one of the characteristics of those times, should we not include this incessant movement to and fro between the two planes of language?

3 CULTURE AND SOCIAL CLASSES

To what extent was the language of the educated, medieval Latin, also the language of the aristocracy? To what extent, in other words, can the group of *literati* be identified with the ruling class? So far as the Church is concerned, the answer is clear. It is of no great consequence that the pernicious system of nominations had resulted, here and there, in the appointment of ignorant men to the highest posts. The episcopal courts, the great monasteries, the chapels royal, in a word, all the headquarters of the ecclesiastical army, never lacked educated clergy who, while often of noble or knightly origin, had been brought up in the monastic and especially the cathedral schools. But as soon as we come to the lay world, the problem becomes more complex.

Let us not imagine that, even in the darkest times, this society was positively hostile to all learning. That it was commonly deemed proper that a leader of men should have access to the treasure-house of thoughts and memories to which the written word, that is to say Latin, alone provided the key is most clearly shown by the importance attached by many sovereigns to the education of their heirs. Robert the Pious, 'king learned in God', had been the pupil of the illustrious Gerbert at Rheims; William the Conqueror gave his son Robert a cleric as tutor. Among the great of the earth, there were to be found genuine book-lovers: Otto III, brought up, it is true, by his mother who, as a Byzantine princess, had brought from her native country the customs of a much more refined civilization, spoke Greek and Latin fluently; William III of Aquitaine had assembled a fine library where he was sometimes to be found reading far into the night.[1] To these examples may be added the cases, by no means exceptional, of those princes who, intended originally for the Church, had retained some of the learning and some of the tastes proper to the clerical world; such a one was Baldwin of Boulogne—a rough soldier, nevertheless—who became king of Jerusalem.

But an education of this type was possible only in the atmosphere of a great dynasty, already firmly based on their hereditary power. Nothing is more significant in this respect than the almost regular contrast in Germany between the founders of dynasties and their successors. Both Otto II, the third Saxon king, and Henry III, the second of the Salians, were carefully educated, in contrast with their fathers—Otto the Great, who learned to read at the age of thirty, and Conrad II, whose chaplain avows that he 'knew not his letters'. As often happened, both the fathers were thrown too young into a life of adventure and peril to have had time to prepare themselves, otherwise than by practical experience or oral tradition, for

---

[1] Adhemar of Chabannes, *Chronique*, ed. Chavanon, III, c. 54. The emperor Henry III, to whom reference is made below, had manuscripts copied for him by the monks: *Codex epistolarum Tegernseensium* (*M.G.H.*, *Ep. Selectae*, III), no. 122.

their profession as rulers. Still more was this true of the lower ranks of the nobility. The relatively brilliant culture of a few great royal or noble families should not deceive us; nor should the exceptional fidelity with which the knightly classes of Italy and Spain held to pedagogic traditions, somewhat rudimentary though these were: the Cid and Ximenes, if their knowledge perhaps did not extend much farther, at least knew how to sign their names.[1] But north of the Alps and the Pyrenees at least the majority of the small or medium lords who exercised most authority at this time were illiterates in the full sense of the word. So much was this the case that in the monasteries into which some of them precipitately retreated in the evening of their days, the terms *conversus*, that is to say one who comes late to the monk's vocation, and *idiota*, which designated the monk incapable of reading the Holy Scriptures, were treated as synonymous.

This neglect of education among the laity explains the rôle of the clergy both as interpreters of the ideas of the great and as depositaries of political traditions. The princes were obliged to rely on the clerical element among their servants for services that the rest of their entourage would have been incapable of rendering. About the middle of the eighth century the last lay referendaries of the Merovingian kings had disappeared; in April 1298, Philip the Fair handed over the seals to the knight Pierre Flotte. Between these two dates more than five centuries elapsed, during which the chancelleries of the sovereigns who reigned over France had at their head churchmen exclusively. It was the same elsewhere, on the whole. It is important to realize that the decisions of the powerful of this world were sometimes suggested and always expressed by men who, whatever their national or class allegiances, none the less belonged by their whole training to a society by nature universalist and founded on spiritual things. Beyond question they helped to maintain, above the confusion of petty local strife, a concern for certain wider issues. When required, however, to give written form to acts of policy, they felt impelled to justify them officially by reasons drawn from their own moral code. Thus there came to be diffused over the documents of almost the entire feudal era that veneer of disingenuousness the evidence of which is to be seen in particular in the preambles of so many enfranchisements masquerading as pure gifts, though they were in fact purchased for money, or in so many royal grants of privileges, invariably made to appear as inspired by simple piety. Since for a long period the writing of history itself, with accompanying value-judgments, was also in the hands of the clergy, the conventions of thought as much as the conventions of literature combined to hide the cynical reality of human motives behind a sort of veil which was only to be finally torn asunder, on the threshold of modern times, by the harsh hands of a Commynes and a Machiavelli.

The laity, however, remained in many respects the active element in

[1] Menendez Pidal, *La España del Cid*, II, pp. 590 and 619.

secular society. Undoubtedly the most illiterate of them were not on that account ignorant men. Apart from the fact that they were in a position, when necessary, to have translated for them what they could not read themselves, we shall see presently to what an extent tales told in the vernacular could transmit both memories and ideas. Still, we must never forget that the majority of lords and many great barons were administrators incapable of studying personally a report or an account, judges whose decisions were recorded (if at all) in a language unknown to the court. Is it surprising that these leaders, who were ordinarily obliged to reconstitute their past decisions from memory, should often have totally lacked the sense of continuity which, quite erroneously, some historians of today are at great pains to ascribe to them?

Almost strangers to writing, they tended to be indifferent to it. After Otto the Great had received the imperial crown in 962, he allowed a privilege to be issued in his name which was inspired by the 'pacts' of the Carolingian emperors and perhaps by certain historical writings; granting to the popes, 'till the end of time', the possession of an immense territory. By thus denuding himself of territory, the king-emperor would have abandoned to the Patrimony of St. Peter the greater part of Italy and even the control of some of the most important Alpine routes. Certainly Otto never dreamed for one moment that these dispositions, though very precise, would in fact be carried out. It would be less surprising if it were a question of one of those dishonest agreements which at all times, under pressure of circumstances, have been signed without the least intention of executing them. But absolutely nothing, save perhaps an imperfectly understood historical tradition, obliged the Saxon prince to make such a pretence. On the one hand, there is the parchment with the ink on it; on the other— quite unconnected with it—what was actually done; such was one particularly flagrant example of a typical dichotomy. A great many people in a position to direct human affairs did not understand the only language deemed worthy to record, not only the knowledge most useful to man and his salvation, but even the results of all social activity.

4 THE RELIGIOUS MENTALITY

'Ages of faith,' we say glibly, to describe the religious attitude of feudal Europe. If by that phrase we mean that any conception of the world from which the supernatural was excluded was profoundly alien to the minds of that age, that in fact the picture which they formed of the destinies of man and the universe was in almost every case a projection of the pattern traced by a Westernized Christian theology and eschatology, nothing could be more true. That here and there doubts might be expressed with regard to the 'fables' of Scripture is of small significance; lacking any rational basis, this crude scepticism, which was not a normal characteristic of educated people, melted in the face of danger like snow in the sun. It is even permissible to say that never was faith more completely worthy of its name. For the attempts of the learned to provide the Christian mysteries with the prop of logical speculation, which had been interrupted on the extinction of ancient Christian philosophy and revived only temporarily and with difficulty during the Carolingian renaissance, were not fully resumed before the end of the eleventh century. On the other hand, it would be wrong to ascribe to these believers a rigidly uniform creed.

Catholicism was still very far from having completely defined its dogmatic system, so that the strictest orthodoxy was then much more flexible than was to be the case later on, after scholastic philosophy and the Counter-Reformation had in turn exercised their influence. Moreover, in the ill-defined border land where Christian heresy degenerated into a religion actively opposed to Christianity, the old Manichaeanism retained a number of votaries in various places. Of these it is not precisely known whether they had inherited their religion from groups who had remained obstinately faithful to this persecuted sect since the first centuries of the Middle Ages, or had received it, after a long interval, from Eastern Europe. But the most notable fact was that Catholicism had incompletely penetrated among the common people. The parish clergy, taken as a whole, were intellectually as well as morally unfit for their task. Recruited with insufficient care, they were also inadequately trained; most commonly instruction consisted in casual lessons given by some priest, himself poorly educated, to a youth who was preparing himself for orders while serving the mass. Preaching, the only effective means of making accessible to the people the mysteries locked up in the Scriptures, was but irregularly practised. In 1031 the Council of Limoges was obliged to denounce the error which claimed that preaching was the prerogative of the bishops, for obviously no bishop would have been capable by himself of preaching the Gospel to the whole of his diocese.

The Catholic mass was recited more or less correctly in all parishes, though sometimes the standard was rather low. The frescoes and bas-reliefs on the walls or the capitals of the principal churches—'the books of the unlettered'—abounded in moving but inaccurate lessons. No doubt the faithful nearly all had a superficial acquaintance with the features most apt to strike the imagination in Christian representations of the past, the present, and the future of the world. But their religious life was also nourished on a multitude of beliefs and practices which, whether the legacy of age-old magic or the more recent products of a civilization still extremely fertile in myths, exerted a constant influence upon official doctrine. In stormy skies people still saw phantom armies passing by: armies of the dead, said the populace; armies of deceitful demons, declared the learned, much less inclined to deny these visions than to find for them a quasi-orthodox interpretation.[1] Innumerable nature-rites, among which

[1] Cf. O. Höfler, *Kultische Geheimbünde der Germanen*, I, 1934, p. 160.

poetry has especially familiarized us with the May-day festivals, were celebrated in country districts. In short, never was theology less identified with the popular religion as it was felt and lived.

Despite infinite variations according to environment and regional traditions, some common characteristics of this religious mentality can be discerned. Although it will mean passing over various deep and moving features and some fascinating problems of permanent human interest, we shall be obliged to confine ourselves here to recalling those trends in thought and feeling whose influence on social behaviour seems to have been particularly strong.

In the eyes of all who were capable of reflection the material world was scarcely more than a sort of mask, behind which took place all the really important things; it seemed to them also a language, intended to express by signs a more profound reality. Since a tissue of appearances can offer but little interest in itself, the result of this view was that observation was generally neglected in favour of interpretation. In a little treatise on the universe, which was written in the ninth century and enjoyed a very long popularity, Rabanus Maurus explained how he followed his plan: 'I conceived the idea of composing a little work . . . which should treat, not only of the nature of things and the properties of words . . . , but still more of their mystic meanings.'[1] This attitude explains, in large part, the inadequacy of men's knowledge of nature—of a nature which, after all, was not regarded as greatly deserving of attention. Technical progress—sometimes considerable—was mere empiricism.

Further, this discredited nature could scarcely have seemed fitted to provide its own interpretation, for in the infinite detail of its illusory manifestations it was conceived above all as the work of hidden wills—wills in the plural, in the opinion of simple folk and even of many of the learned. Below the One God and subordinated to his Almighty Power—though the exact significance of this subjection was not, as a rule, very clearly pictured —the generality of mankind imagined the opposing wills of a host of beings good and bad in a state of perpetual strife; saints, angels, and especially devils. 'Who does not know,' wrote the priest Helmold, 'that the wars, the mighty tempests, the pestilences, all the ills, indeed, which afflict the human race, occur through the agency of demons?'[2] Wars, we notice, are mentioned indiscriminately along with tempests; social catastrophes, therefore, are placed in the same class as those which we should nowadays describe as natural. The result was a mental attitude which the history of the invasions has already brought to notice: not exactly renunciation, but rather reliance upon means of action considered more efficacious than human effort. Though the instinctive reactions of a vigorous realism were never lacking, a Robert the Pious or an Otto III could nevertheless attach

---

[1] Rabanus Maurus, *De Universo libri XXII*, in Migne, *P.L.*, CXI, col. 12.
[2] Helmold, *Chronica Slavorum*, I, 55.

as much importance to a pilgrimage as to a battle or a law, and historians who are either scandalized by this fact or who persist in discovering subtle political manœuvres in these pious journeys merely prove thereby their own inability to lay aside the spectacles of men of the nineteenth and twentieth centuries. It was not merely the selfish quest of personal salvation that inspired these royal pilgrims. From the patron saints whose aid they went to invoke, they expected for their subjects as well as for themselves, not only the promise of rewards in heaven, but the riches of the earth as well. In the sanctuary, as much as on the field of battle or in the court of law, they were concerned to fulfil their function as leaders of their people.

The world of appearances was also a transitory world. Though in itself inseparable from any Christian representation of the Universe, the image of the final catastrophe had seldom impinged so strongly on the consciousness of men as at this time. They meditated on it; they assessed its premonitory signs. The chronicle of Bishop Otto of Freising, the most universal of all universal histories, began with Creation and ended with the picture of the Last Judgment. But, needless to say, it had an inevitable *lacuna*: from 1146—the date when the author ceased to write—to the day of the great catastrophe. Otto, certainly, expected this gap to be of short duration: 'We who have been placed at the end of time . . .' he remarks on several occasions. This was the general conviction among his contemporaries as it had been in earlier times, and it was by no means confined to the clergy; to suppose so would be to forget the profound interpenetration of the two groups, clerical and lay. Even among those who did not, like St. Norbert, go so far as to declare that the event was so close that the present generation would witness it no one doubted of its imminence. In every wicked prince, pious souls believed that they recognized the mark of Antichrist, whose dreadful empire would precede the coming of the Kingdom of God.

But when in fact would it strike—this hour so close at hand? The Apocalypse seemed to supply an answer: 'and when the thousand years are expired . . .' Was this to be taken as meaning a thousand years after the death of Christ? Some thought so, thus putting back the great day of reckoning—according to the normal calculation—to the year 1033. Or was it rather to be reckoned from his birth? This latter interpretation appears to have been the most general. It is certain at any rate that on the eve of the year one thousand a preacher in the churches of Paris announced this date for the End of Time. If, in spite of all this, the masses at that time were not visibly affected by the universal terror which historians of the romantic school have mistakenly depicted, the reason is above all that the people of that age, though mindful of the passage of the seasons and the annual cycle of the liturgy, did not think ordinarily in terms of the numbers of the years, still less in figures precisely computed on a uniform basis. How many charters lack any trace of a date! Even among the rest, what diversity there is in the systems of reference, which are mostly unconnected with the life of the Saviour—years of reigns or pontificates, astronomical indications of every kind, or even the fifteen-year cycle of the indiction, a relic of Roman fiscal practices! One entire country, Spain, while using more generally than elsewhere the concept of a definite era, assigned to it—for reasons that are somewhat obscure—an initial date absolutely unrelated to the Gospel, namely the year 38 B.C. It is true that legal documents occasionally and chronicles more frequently adhered to the era of the Incarnation; but it was still necessary to take into account the variations in the beginning of the year. For the Church excluded the first of January as a pagan festival. Thus, according to the province or the chancellery, the year designated the thousandth began at one or other of six or seven different dates, which ranged, according to our calendar, from 25th March 999 to 31st March 1000. What is worse, some of these initial dates, being essentially moveable since they were linked with a particular liturgical moment of the Easter period, could not be anticipated without tables, which only the learned possessed; they were also very apt to lead to permanent confusion in men's minds by making some years longer than others. Thus it was not unusual for the same day of the month, in March or April, or the feast of the same saint to occur twice in the same year. Indeed, for the majority of Western men this expression, 'the year 1000', which we have been led to believe was charged with anguish, could not be identified with any precise moment in the sequence of days.

Yet the notion of the shadow cast over men's minds at that time by the supposed imminence of the Day of Wrath is not altogether wrong. All Europe, it is true, did not tremble with fear towards the end of the first millennium, to compose itself suddenly as soon as this supposedly fateful date was past. But, what was even worse perhaps, waves of fear swept almost incessantly over this region or that, subsiding at one point only to rise again elsewhere. Sometimes a vision started the panic, or perhaps a great historic calamity like the destruction of the Holy Sepulchre in 1009, or again perhaps merely a violent tempest. Another time, it was caused by some computation of the liturgists, which spread from educated circles to the common people. 'The rumour spread through almost the whole world that the End would come when the Annunciation coincided with Good Friday,' wrote the abbot of Fleury a little before the year 1000.[1] Many theologians, however, remembering that St. Paul had said: 'the day of the Lord cometh like a thief in the night', condemned these indiscreet attempts to pierce the mystery in which the Divinity chose to veil his dread purpose. But is the period of waiting made less anxious by ignorance of when the blow will fall? In the prevailing disorders, which we should unhesitatingly describe as the ebullience of adolescence, contemporaries were unanimous in seeing only the last convulsions of an 'aged' humanity. In spite of

[1] *Apologeticus*, in Migne, *P.L.*, CXXXIX, col. 472.

everything, an irresistible vitality fermented in men, but as soon as they gave themselves up to meditation, nothing was farther from their thoughts than the prospect of a long future for a young and vigorous human race.

If humanity as a whole seemed to be moving rapidly towards its end, so much the more did this sensation of being 'on the way' apply to each individual life. According to the metaphor dear to so many religious writers, the true believer was in his earthly existence like a pilgrim, to whom the end of the road is naturally of more importance than the hazards of the journey. Of course, the thoughts of the majority of men did not dwell constantly on their salvation. But when they did, it was with deep intensity and above all with the aid of vivid and very concrete images, which were apt to come to them by fits and starts; for their fundamentally unstable minds were subject to sudden revulsions. Joined to the penitent mood of a world on the verge of dissolution, the desire for the eternal rewards cut short more than one leader's career by voluntary withdrawal to the cloister. And it ended for good and all the propagation of more than one noble line, as in the case of the six sons of the lord of Fontaines-lès-Dijon who eagerly embraced the monastic life under the leadership of the most illustrious of their number, Bernard of Clairvaux. Thus, in its way, the religious mentality favoured the mixing of the social classes.

Many Christians, nevertheless, could not bring themselves to submit to these austere practices. Moreover, they considered themselves (and perhaps not without reason) to be incapable of reaching heaven through their own merits. They therefore reposed their hopes in the prayers of pious souls, in the merits accumulated for the benefit of all the faithful by a few groups of ascetics, and in the intercession of the saints, materialized by means of their relics and represented by the monks, their servants. In this Christian society, no function exercised in the collective interest appeared more important than that of the spiritual organizations, precisely in so far—let us make no mistake about this—as they were spiritual. The charitable, cultural and economic rôle of the great cathedral chapters and of the monasteries may have been considerable: in the eyes of contemporaries it was merely accessory. The notion of a terrestrial world completely imbued with supernatural significance combined in this with the obsession of the beyond. The happiness of the king and the realm in the present; the salvation of the royal ancestors and of the king himself throughout Eternity: such was the double benefit which Louis the Fat declared that he expected from his foundation when he established a community of Canons Regular at the abbey of St. Victor in Paris. 'We believe', said Otto I, 'that the protection of our Empire is bound up with the rising fortunes of Christian worship.'[1] Thus we find a powerful and wealthy Church, capable of creating novel legal institutions, and a host of problems raised by the delicate

[1] Tardif, *Cartons des rois*, no. 357; *Diplom. regum et imperatorum Germaniae*, I, Otto I, no. 366.

task of relating this religious 'city' to the temporal 'city'; problems ardently debated and destined to influence profoundly the general evolution of the West. These features are an essential part of any accurate picture of the feudal world, and in face of them who can fail to recognize in the fear of hell one of the great social forces of the age?

VI

THE FOLK MEMORY

1 HISTORIOGRAPHY

IN feudal society many influences combined to encourage an interest in the past. Religion had books of history among its sacred writings; its feasts commemorated past events; in its most popular forms it drew sustenance from the stories that were told about the saints of long ago; finally, in affirming that mankind was soon to perish, it rejected the optimism which has caused other ages to be interested only in the present or the future. Canon law was founded on the ancient texts; secular law on precedents. The vacant hours of cloister or castle favoured the telling of long tales. History was not indeed taught *ex professo* in the schools, except through the medium of readings directed, in theory, to other ends: religious writings, which were read for the sake of theological or moral instruction, and works of classical antiquity, meant to serve as models of good style. In the common intellectual stock, history none the less occupied an almost predominant place.

What sources of information were accessible to people of education eager to learn about the past? Though known only through fragments of their writings, the historians of Latin antiquity had lost nothing of their prestige; though Livy was not by any means the one most often read, his name figures among the books distributed between 1039 and 1049 to the monks of Cluny for their Lenten readings.[1] Nor were the narrative works of the early Middle Ages forgotten: we possess, for example, several manuscripts of Gregory of Tours executed between the tenth and the twelfth century. But the most considerable influence belonged unquestionably to the writers who, about the decisive turning-point of the fourth and fifth centuries, had set themselves to combine in synthesis the two historical traditions, hitherto alien to each other, whose double legacy thrust itself upon the new world—that of the Bible and that of Greece and Rome. Moreover, there was no need to go directly to Eusebius of Caesarea, St. Jerome, or Paul Orosius to benefit from the work of reconciliation which these pioneers had undertaken. The substance of their works had passed and continued to pass unceasingly into numerous writings of more recent date.

So eager was the desire to reveal the impetuous flow of the great river of time beyond the present moment that many authors, even among those con-

[1] Wilmart, in *Revue Mabillon*, XI, 1921.

cerned primarily with the most recent events, nevertheless considered it useful to provide by way of a preamble a sort of rapid survey of universal
history. In the Annals which the monk Lambert composed in his cell at
Hersfeld about 1078 all that we look for is information on the clashes in the
Empire during the reign of Henry IV; the Annals, however, begin at the
Creation. Students who read the chronicle of Regino of Prüm on the
Frankish kingdoms after the collapse of the Carolingian power, the
chronicles of Worcester or Peterborough on the Anglo-Saxon societies, or
the Annals of Bèze for the minute details of Burgundian history, may
notice that these works outline the story of mankind from the Incarnation.
Even when the narrative does start from more recent times, it is common to
find it beginning at an epoch much anterior to the recollections of the
memorialist. Though the fruit of an often superficial and inaccurate reading of earlier works, and thus incapable of informing us correctly about the
extremely remote events which they profess to relate, these prolegomena
are still valuable for the information they furnish about the mentality of the
age in which they were written. They show us clearly the picture which
feudal Europe formed of its past; they prove emphatically that the com-
pilers of chronicles and annals did not deliberately limit their own horizons.
Unfortunately, once the writer left the safe shelter of literature and found
himself obliged to make his own investigations, the fragmentation of
society had the effect of limiting his knowledge; so that frequently, by a
singular contrast, the narrative as it progresses becomes both richer in
detail and, geographically, more restricted in scope. Thus the great history
of the French compiled in a monastery in Angoulême by Adhemar of
Chabannes gradually came to be scarcely more than a history of Aquitaine.
The very variety of the types of work produced by the writers of history
is evidence, moreover, of the universal pleasure then taken in telling or
listening to stories. Universal histories, or works regarded as universal
histories, histories of peoples, histories of churches, are ranged alongside
the simple compilations of news prepared from year to year. As soon as
great events made their impact on the minds of men, they were adopted as
themes by a whole series of chroniclers; as, for example, the struggle of the
Emperors and Popes, and especially the Crusades. Although the writers
were no more capable than the sculptors of portraying the distinctive
characteristics that make a human being an individual, biography was in
fashion, and not by any means exclusively in the form of lives of the saints.
William the Conqueror, Henry IV of Germany, Conrad II, monarchs for
whom the Church had certainly no great love, found clerics to narrate
their exploits. One great noble of the eleventh century, the count of Anjou,
Fulk le Réchin, went farther: he wrote himself, or had written in his name,
his own history and that of his line—so much importance did the great of
this world attach to memorials! True, certain regions seem relatively poor
in this type of literature, but these produced little writing of any kind.

Aquitaine and Provence, much poorer in chronicles or annals than the regions between the Seine and the Rhine, have also produced far fewer theological works. Amongst the preoccupations of feudal society history played a sufficiently large part to furnish, by its varying fortunes, a good barometer of the state of culture in general.

Let us not deceive ourselves on this point, however: this age, so interested in the past, could study it only in historical writings which were more copious than exact. The difficulty which men found in getting information even on the most recent events, as well as the general lack of precision in their thinking, meant that the majority of historical works had to be spun out with curious trash. A whole series of Italian narrative sources, beginning from the middle of the ninth century, by forgetting to record the coronation of the year 800 made Louis the Pious the first Carolingian emperor.[1] The criticism of evidence, almost inseparable from any form of study, was certainly not absolutely unknown—as is proved by the curious treatise of Guibert de Nogent on relics. But no one dreamed of applying it systematically to ancient documents—not, at least, before Abelard; and even with this great man it was still rather restricted in scope.[2] A bias towards the rhetorical and heroic—the unfortunate legacy of classical historiography—weighed heavily on these writers. If certain monastic chronicles abound in records, the reason is that almost their sole purpose was the modest one of justifying the right of the community to its possessions. A Gilles d'Orval, on the other hand, in a work written in a loftier strain, dedicates himself to the task of recounting the great deeds of the bishops of Liège, and when by chance he comes across one of the first charters of urban liberties, that of the town of Huy, he declines to give an analysis of it, for fear it should weary his readers. (One of the virtues of the Icelandic school, so superior in historical perception to the chroniclers of the Latin world, was that it avoided these pretensions.) The true comprehension of facts was further obscured by the symbolical interpretation placed upon them by another trend of thought. Were the books of the Bible to be regarded as books of history? Undoubtedly. But in one entire section of this history at least, namely the Old Testament, the interpretation imposed by exegesis was that it represented not so much a picture of events comprehensible in themselves as a prefigurement of what was to come: 'the shadow of the future', as St. Augustine expressed it.[3] Finally and above all, the representation of the past was distorted by an imperfect perception of differences in historical perspective.

It was not, as Gaston Paris maintained, that anyone clung obstinately to the belief in the 'immutability' of things. Such a tendency would scarcely

[1] Cf. E. Perels, 'Das Kaisertum Karls des Grossen in mittelalterlichen Geschichtsquellen' in *Sitzungsberichte der preussischen Akademie, phil.-hist. Klasse*, 1931.
[2] P. Fournier and G. Le Bras, *Histoire des collections canoniques*, II, 1932, p. 338.
[3] *De civ. Dei*, XVII, 1.

have been compatible with the idea of a mankind moving with rapid steps towards a predestined end. 'Of the Vicissitudes of Temporal Affairs': this was the title which Otto of Freising gave to his chronicle in accordance with the normal outlook of his day. Yet undeniably the poems in the vernacular invariably depicted the Carolingian paladins, the Huns of Attila, and the heroes of antiquity with the characteristics of knights of the eleventh and twelfth centuries, and no one was disturbed by the anachronism. The fact of eternal change, which men did not fail to perceive, they found quite impossible to grasp in its full implications. This was partly no doubt because of ignorance, but also and in particular because men thought of past and present as being so closely bound together that they were unable to perceive the contrasts between them and were unconscious even of the need to do so. How could people who believed that the Roman Empire was still in existence and that the Saxon and Salian princes were the direct successors of Caesar or Augustus resist the temptation to picture the emperors of old Rome as men exactly like the rulers of their own day? Every religious movement conceived of itself as a movement of reform, in the true sense of the word—meaning a return to original purity. In any case, is not the traditionalist attitude, which constantly draws the present towards the past and thereby tends naturally to blend the colours of the two, as far removed as possible from the historical spirit, of which the dominant characteristic is the sense of diversity?

Though as a rule unconscious, the illusion was sometimes deliberately contrived. The great forgeries which influenced civil or religious policy in the feudal era belong to a slightly earlier period: the so-called Donation of Constantine dated from the end of the eighth century, and the fabrications of the remarkable workshop whose principal productions were the Forged Decretals published under the name of Isidore of Seville and the False Capitularies of the deacon Benedict were among the fruits of the Carolingian renaissance in its heyday. But the example thus set was to be followed through the centuries. The collection of canons compiled between 1008 and 1012 by the saintly Bishop Burchard of Worms abounds in false attributions and almost cynical alterations. False documents were manufactured at the imperial court. A great many others were produced in the scriptoria of the churches, so notorious in this regard that the perversions of truth, known or conjectured, which were regularly practised there tended in no small measure to discredit all written evidence. 'Any pen will do to recount anything whatsoever,' a German nobleman remarked, in the course of a lawsuit.[1]

Undoubtedly if the trades of forgery and myth-making, which are practised in all ages, were exceptionally flourishing during these few centuries, the responsibility rests in large part both on the conditions of

[1] C. E. Perrin, *Recherches sur la seigneurie rurale en Lorraine d'après les plus anciens censiers*, p. 684.

legal practice, based as it was on precedent, and on the disorders of the times. More than one of these forged documents was fabricated purely for the purpose of making good the destruction of an authentic text. Nevertheless, that so many spurious productions should have been executed in those times and that so many pious and indisputably high-minded persons should have had a hand in such dealings, although they were expressly condemned by the law and morality of the age—the psychological implications of these things are well worth pondering. By a curious paradox, through the very fact of their respect for the past, people came to reconstruct it as they considered it ought to have been.

Numerous as they were, moreover, historical writings were accessible only to a small and select number, for except among the Anglo-Saxons they were in the Latin tongue. According to whether or not a leader of men belonged to the small circle of *literati*, the past—authentic or deformed—exercised a more or a less pervasive influence upon him. Witness, in Germany, after the realism of Otto I, the policy of Otto III, inspired by memories of the older Rome; after the illiterate Conrad II, prepared to abandon the Eternal City to the struggles of its aristocratic factions and its puppet popes, the highly-educated Henry III, 'patrician of the Romans' and reformer of the Papacy. Even the less cultivated among the leaders enjoyed their share of this hoard of memories, helped, no doubt, by their household clergy. Otto I, much less susceptible certainly than his grandson to the spell of Rome, had yet been the first of his line to claim the crown of the Caesars. Who can say from what teachers, translating or summarizing for him who knows what works, this almost illiterate king had imbibed the imperial tradition, before restoring it in his own person?

Above all, the epic tales in the vernacular were the history books of the people who could not read but loved to listen. The problems of the epic are among the most controversial in medieval studies, and a few pages would be insufficient for an examination of their complexities. However, it is appropriate to deal with them here from the point of view of the folk memory, for this approach is not only directly relevant to the history of the social structure, but, in a more general sense, is also perhaps the one most suited to open up promising perspectives.

2 THE EPIC

The history of the French epic, as we understand it, begins about the middle of the eleventh century, perhaps a little earlier. It is certain that from this time heroic *chansons* in the vernacular were in circulation in northern France. Unfortunately we possess only indirect information about these compositions of a relatively remote date: allusions in the chronicles, a fragment of an adaptation in Latin (the mysterious 'Hague fragment'). No epic manuscript is of earlier date than the second half of the following century, but from the age of a copy it is impossible to deduce the date of the text copied. There are clear indications that three poems at least were in existence, certainly not later than the year 1100, in a form very close to that in which we read them today. These are the *Chanson de Roland*; the *Chanson de Guillaume*, which itself mentions incidentally several other songs of which we no longer possess early versions; and finally—known to us both by a manuscript of the first portion and by abstracts the earliest of which dates from 1088—the tale generally known as *Gormont et Isembart*.

The plot of the *Chanson de Roland* is based on folklore rather than history—hatred between stepson and stepfather, envy and treason. This last *motif* reappears in *Gormont*. The plot of the *Chanson de Guillaume* is only a legend. In all three works, many of the characters, including some of the most important, seem to be pure inventions; as, for example, Oliver, Isembart and Vivien. Nevertheless, the embroideries of the tale are all worked upon a fabric of historical truth. It is a fact that, on the 15th August 778, Charlemagne's rear-guard was surprised by an enemy force while crossing the Pyrenees—history describes them as Basques, but legend called them Saracens—and that in this savage battle a count named Roland perished, along with many other leaders. The plains of the Vimeu, where the action of *Gormont* takes place, had witnessed in 881 the glorious triumph of a historical King Louis, the Carolingian Louis III, over actual pagans—they were Northmen, in this case—whom fiction again transmutes into soldiers of Islam. Count Guillaume, as well as his wife Guibourc, had lived under Charlemagne. A valiant slayer of Moslems as related in the *Chanson* which bears his name, he was sometimes, as in that poem, vanquished by the Infidels, but always after an heroic struggle. In all three works, in the middle distance and even in the teeming background of the picture, it is not difficult to recognize, side by side with dim imaginary figures, more than one personage who, though the poets do not always date him correctly, had none the less actually lived. Such were Archbishop Turpin; the pagan King Gormont, a celebrated Viking in real life; and even that obscure count of Bourges, Esturmi, whom the *Chanson de Guillaume* paints in such dark colours only through unconsciously echoing the contempt to which, in his own day, his servile birth had exposed him.

In the numerous poems on similar themes which were put into writing in the course of the twelfth and thirteenth centuries the same contrast appears. They abound in fables, which encroach more and more on reality as this class of literature, while growing richer, was obliged to resort increasingly to pure invention for its subject matter. Yet almost always, at least in the works of which the general outline, if not the version known today, clearly goes back to a fairly early time, we find some unquestionably historical *motif* at the very centre of the action and some surprisingly accurate detail—an episodic figure, perhaps, or a castle whose existence might well have been long forgotten. Thus the student is confronted with two insoluble problems. First, by what means was the knowledge of so remote a past transmitted to the poets across a gulf of many centuries? Between the tragedy of the 15th August 778, for example, and the *Chanson* of the last years of the eleventh century, what tradition wove its mysterious threads? And from whom had the twelfth-century *trouvère* of *Raoul de Cambrai* learned of the attack launched in 943 against the sons of Herbert de Vermandois by Raoul, son of Raoul of Gouy, of the death of the invader and (besides these central events) the names of several contemporaries of the hero—Ybert, lord of Ribémont, Bernard of Rethel, Ernaut of Douai? This is the first enigma. But here is the second, which is no less puzzling: how do these exact data come to be so strangely distorted? Or rather—for we could evidently not hold the latest authors solely responsible for the whole distortion—how does it happen that the good grain of truth should only have reached them mixed with the chaff of so many errors and inventions? The material is in part authentic, in part imaginary; and no attempt at interpretation can be acceptable which fails to give equal consideration to both elements.

The epic *gestes* were not, in theory, intended to be read. They were made to be declaimed or rather chanted, and they went the rounds from castle to castle or from public square to public square with professional reciters, called *jongleurs*. The humblest of these minstrels lived on the small pieces of money which each member of their audience drew 'from the lappet of his shirt',[1] and combined the profession of strolling story-teller with that of jester. Others, fortunate enough to have obtained the protection of some great nobleman, who attached them to his court, were thereby assured of a less precarious livelihood. These performers were sometimes also the authors of the poems. Thus some *jongleurs* performed the compositions of someone else; others recited poems of which they were themselves the original 'inventors' (*trouvères*). But between these extremes there were infinite shades of difference. Rarely did the 'inventor' devise the whole of his material; rarely did the interpreter refrain from some reshaping of it. The public for this literature was a very mixed one, for the most part illiterate, incapable as a rule of judging the authenticity of the facts, and much less interested in veracity than in being entertained and in hearing familiar sentiments exalted. Its authors were men accustomed to remodel incessantly the substance of their stories, yet dedicated to a life little favourable to study. They were in a position nevertheless to associate with the great from time to time and were anxious to please them. Such was the human background of this literature. To inquire by what means so many authentic memories have found their way into it is tantamount to asking by what channels the *jongleurs* could have become acquainted with the events or the names.

[1] *Huon de Bordeaux*, ed. Guessard and Grandmaison, p. 148.

It is almost superfluous to reiterate that every ounce of truth which, to our knowledge, the *chansons* contain was to be found again, in a different form, in the chronicles or charters; if it had been otherwise, how would it be possible for us today to sort it out? Whilst it would be blatant misrepresentation to depict the minstrels as so many rummagers in libraries, it is legitimate to ask if they may not have had indirect access to the subject matter of writings which they were scarcely in a position to consult in person. As intermediaries it is natural to think of those who ordinarily had charge of these documents, namely the clergy, and especially the monks. This theory is in no way inconsistent with the conditions of feudal society. The historians of the romantic school, obsessed with the idea of a complete contrast between the 'spontaneous' and the 'learned', were quite wrong in assuming that the exponents of the so-called popular poetry and those professional adepts in Latin literature, the learned clerics, were separated by some insurmountable barrier. In the absence of other evidence, the synopsis of the *chanson* of Gormont in the chronicle of the monk Hariulf, the 'Hague fragment', which is probably an academic exercise, and the Latin poem which a French cleric of the twelfth century composed on the treason of Ganelon would suffice to prove that in the shade of the cloisters the vernacular epic was neither unknown nor despised. Likewise in Germany *Waltharius*, whose Virgilian hexameters form so strange a vehicle for a Germanic legend, may well have originated as a school exercise, and we are told that later, in twelfth-century England, the moving accounts of the adventures of Arthur brought tears to the eyes of young monks as well as laymen.[1] What is more, despite the anathemas of some rigorists against the 'histrions', the monks in general, naturally glad to spread the fame of their houses and of the relics which constituted their most cherished possessions, could hardly fail to recognize in these minstrels, whose repertoire in the market-place ranged from the most profane songs to pious tales of the saints, an almost unrivalled medium of publicity.

In fact, as Joseph Bédier has shown in an unforgettable manner, the mark of the monk is clearly written on more than one epic legend. The insistence of the monks of Pothières, and still more of Vézelay, can alone explain the transferring to Burgundy of the story of Gérard de Roussillon, all the historical elements of which were associated with the banks of the Rhône. Without the abbey of Saint-Denis-de-France, its fair and its sacred remains, we should not have the poem of the *Voyage de Charlemagne*, a humorous embroidery on the history of relics, intended no doubt less for the pilgrims to the church than for the customers at the fair; or the *Floovant*, which treats a related subject in a more serious and tedious vein; or in all likelihood many another *chanson* wherein, against a backcloth on which the monastery is prominently displayed, there figure the Carolingian

[1] Ailred of Rievaulx, *Speculum charitatis*, II, 17, in Migne, *P.L.*, CXCV, *col.* 565.

princes whose memory was piously preserved within its walls. The last word has assuredly not yet been said on the subject of the part played in the elaboration of the Charlemagne theme by this great community, the allies and counsellors of the Capetian kings.

There are, however, many works, notably among the oldest ones, in which it would be difficult to discover a trace of monastic influence, at least in any concerted and sustained form. Examples of such works are the *Chanson de Guillaume, Raoul de Cambrai*, and the complete cycle of the *Lorrains*. In the *Chanson de Roland* itself, which has been thought by some to be connected with the pilgrimage to Compostela, is it not surprising, if this hypothesis be true, to find mention of so many saints and so many Spanish towns and yet to discover that St. James and the great Galician sanctuary are not among them? In a work supposedly inspired by the monks, how are we to explain the virulent contempt which the poet expresses for the life of the cloister?[1] Moreover, if it is beyond dispute that all the authentic details used by the *gestes* could, in theory, have been found by consulting the muniment chests and libraries, they only occur here and there in the documents, among many other features which have not been retained. To extract them from these texts, and to extract nothing else, would have required a major effort of comparison and selection, a labour of erudition, in short, quite out of keeping with the intellectual habits of the time. Lastly, and above all, to postulate as the source of every *chanson* this pedagogic pair—an educated cleric as teacher, with a minstrel as his apt pupil—is to abandon the attempt to explain the errors found in these works side by side with the truth.

For mediocre as was the annalistic literature, encumbered with legends and forgeries as the traditions of the religious communities are rightly judged to be—even allowing for what we know of the vagaries of minstrels' memories and their readiness to embroider any theme—the worst of the tales constructed by means of chronicles or charters could scarcely have perpetrated one quarter of the blunders of which the least untruthful of the *chansons* is guilty. In any case, we have further proof. About the middle of the twelfth century it happened that two clerics successively devoted themselves to putting into French verse, in a style closely modelled on the epic, an historical theme of which they had drawn the greater part from manuscripts. Now certainly neither the *Roman de Rou* of Wace, nor the *Histoire des ducs de Normandie* of Benoît de Sainte-Maure is free from legends or confusions; but, by comparison with the *Chanson de Roland*, they are masterpieces of accuracy.

It must therefore be considered improbable, at least in the majority of cases, that the *trouvères* of the late eleventh century and the early years of

---

[1] V. 1880–2. These remarks are the more striking because the *Chanson* puts them in the mouth of an archbishop. Clearly the Gregorian reform had not yet passed that way.

the twelfth had obtained the elements of their *gestes*, at the time of their composition, from chronicles or records, even indirectly.[1] We are in consequence obliged to admit that their stories are based on an older tradition. In point of fact this hypothesis, for long the classical theory, has become suspect only by reason of the forms in which it has too often been presented. To begin with (so runs the argument) there were some very short songs contemporaneous with the events; the *chansons* that we know were slowly and in general rather unskilfully put together from these primitive *cantilenae*, sewn end to end. At the beginning, in short, there was the spontaneity of the popular soul, at the end a literary effort. This conception, attractive though it is in the simplicity of its lines, scarcely stands up to serious scrutiny. Certainly all the *chansons* are not of homogeneous growth; there are some in which the traces of crude additions are not wanting. Yet who, reading the *Chanson de Roland* with an open mind, could fail to see in it the fruit of a single effort, the work of a man—and a great man —whose artistic standards, so far as they were not personal to him, expressed the conceptions of his time and not the pale reflection of lost songs? In this sense it is quite true to say that the *chansons de geste* were 'born' towards the end of the eleventh century. But even in the comparatively rare case where a poet has genius—we are apt to forget how exceptional is the beauty of the *Chanson de Roland*—does he as a rule do otherwise than use, as best he can, the themes of which the collective inheritance has been transmitted to him across the generations?

Indeed, when we realize the interest taken in the past by the men of the feudal age, and the pleasure they derived from hearing tales about it, can we be surprised that a tradition of story-telling should have threaded its way down through the ages? As its favourite centres it had all the places where wanderers were to be found—those places of pilgrimage and fairs, those routes of pilgrims and merchants whose memory has been imprinted on so many poems. We know, by a chance document, that the far-ranging German merchants brought to the knowledge of the Scandinavian world certain German legends.[2] Is there any reason to believe that Frenchmen did not, in the same way, transport along the familiar trade-routes, together with their bales of cloth or their sacks of spices, a good many heroic themes, or even just names? It was without doubt the tales of such travellers, as well as those of the pilgrims, that taught the *jongleurs* the geographical terminology of the East and acquainted these northern poets with the beauty of the Mediterranean olive-tree, which with a naive taste for the exotic and a fine contempt for local colour the *chansons* plant boldly on the hills of Burgundy or Picardy.

[1] There may be one exception. It is not impossible that in the *Couronnement de Louis* there is to be found some evidence of the use of chronicles. Cf. Schladko, in *Zeitschrift für die französische Sprache*, 1931, p. 428.

[2] Prologue of the *Thidreksaga;* cf. H. J. Seeger, *Westfalens Handel*, 1926, p. 4.

Though they may not ordinarily have inspired the legends, the monasteries none the less provided a soil in which they could grow and flourish. For one thing, they were much frequented by travellers. For another, they usually possessed monuments capable of evoking ancient memories. Finally, monks were always fond of telling stories—far too fond, in the opinion of rigorists like Peter Damiani.[1] The earliest anecdotes about Charlemagne were set down in writing in the ninth century, at St. Gall. The chronicle of the monastery of Novalesa on the Mont-Cenis route, compiled at the beginning of the eleventh century, abounds in legends relating to the great emperor.

It must not be imagined, however, that all historical lore came from the religious houses. The noble families had their own traditions from which more than one record of the past—accurate or distorted—must have been derived, and men loved to talk of their forefathers in the halls of castles, as well as under the arcades of the cloister. We happen to know that Duke Godfrey of Lorraine was in the habit of entertaining his guests with anecdotes about Charlemagne.[2] Must we assume that this taste was peculiar to him? In the epic poems, moreover, we find two portraits of the great Carolingian which are violently contradictory. In sharp contrast with the noble sovereign of the *Chanson de Roland*, portrayed with an almost religious veneration, is the covetous and besotted old man of so many other *chansons*. The first version was in accord with the canon of ecclesiastical historiography, as well as the needs of Capetian propaganda; in the second we can hardly fail to recognize the voice of the anti-monarchical feudal nobility.

It is quite possible for anecdotes to be transmitted in this way from generation to generation without necessarily taking shape as poems. But these poems did after all come into being. From what period? It is almost impossible to tell. For we are dealing with French, that is to say a language which, since it was regarded as merely a corrupt form of Latin, took several centuries to raise itself to literary dignity. Was some element of heroic poetry already seeping into the *chansons rustiques*—the songs in the vernacular, which as early as the end of the ninth century a bishop of Orleans deemed it necessary to forbid to his priests? We shall never know, because it all took place in a sphere very much beneath the notice of literary men. Nevertheless, without wishing to overstrain the argument *a silentio*, it must be affirmed that the first references to the epic songs appear only in the eleventh century; the sudden emergence of this evidence, after a long night, seems clearly to suggest that the versified *gestes* did not develop much earlier, or at least not in any abundance. It is very remarkable, moreover, that in the majority of the old poems, Laon figures as the usual residence of the Carolingian kings; the *Chanson de Roland* itself, which

---

[1] *De perfectione monachorum*, in Migne, *P.L.*, CXLV, col. 324.
[2] Peter Damiani, *De elemosina*, c. 7, in Migne, *P.L.*, CXLV, col. 220.

restored Aix-la-Chapelle to its true rank, nevertheless bears, as if inadvertently, some traces of the Laon tradition. Now this could have originated only in the tenth century, when 'Mont-Loon' was really playing the part which is thus assigned to it. At a later, as well as an earlier date it would be inexplicable.[1] It was therefore, according to all appearance, in this century that the principal themes of the epic were fixed, if not already in verse form, at least in a state fully ripe to receive it.

One of the essential characteristics of the *chansons*, moreover, was their reluctance to recount any but bygone events. The Crusades were almost alone in being thought immediately worthy of epic treatment. The reason is that they had everything needed to stimulate the imagination and that they transferred to the present a form of Christian heroism familiar in the poems since the eleventh century. These topical works provided the *jongleurs* with the opportunity to exert on their rich patrons a mild form of blackmail. For having refused to give one of them a pair of scarlet hose, Arnulf of Ardres had his name erased from the *Chanson d'Antioche*.[2] But whatever the pleasure that nobles must have experienced in hearing their exploits thus extolled, and however great the profit that poets might expect from such compositions, contemporary wars, unless their theatre was the Holy Land, did not as a rule find anyone to celebrate them in this manner. Does this mean that, as Gaston Paris has written, the 'epic fermentation' ceased at the moment when the French nation came definitely into being? This theory, in itself not very credible, is based on the assumption that the tales relating to the ninth and tenth centuries had immediately assumed a poetic form—which is anything but certain. The truth is no doubt that, imbued with respect for times gone by, the men of that age were unable to find inspiration save in memories already invested with the prestige proper to ancient things. In 1066 a minstrel accompanied the Norman warriors at Hastings. What did he sing? 'Of Karlemaigne and of Rollant.' Another, about 1100, preceded a band of Burgundian plunderers, in a little local war. What did he sing? 'The great deeds of forefathers.'[3] When the great sword-strokes of the eleventh and twelfth centuries had, in their turn, receded into the mists of time, the interest in the past still survived; but it found satisfaction in other ways. History, sometimes still versified, but based thenceforth on written records and consequently much less contaminated by legend, had replaced the epic.

The love of historical and legendary tales during the feudal age was not confined to France; it was common to the whole of Europe, but it expressed itself in different ways.

As far back as we are able to go in the history of the Germanic peoples,

[1] Cf. F. Lot in *Romania*, 1928, p. 375; and, on all the foregoing, the series of articles published by that scholar.

[2] Lambert of Ardre, *Chronique de Guines et d'Ardre*, c. CXXX, ed. Ménilglaise, p. 311.

[3] *Miracles de Saint Benoît*, ed. Certain, VIII, 36.

we find them in the habit of celebrating in verse the exploits of heroes. It appears moreover that among the Germans of the continent and of Britain, as among the Scandinavians, two types of warlike poetry existed side by side. One type was dedicated to various ancient and sometimes mythical personages; the other proclaimed the glory of leaders still alive or lately dead. Then in the tenth century a period began in which men hardly wrote at all and, with very few exceptions, only in Latin. During these obscure centuries the survival of the old legends on German soil is attested almost solely by a Latin version—the poem of *Waltharius*—and by the emigration of certain themes to the northern countries, where the spring of popular literature flowed ever fresh. They had not disappeared, however, or lost their spell. In preference to the works of St. Augustine or St. Gregory, Bishop Gunther, who from 1057 to 1065 occupied the see of Bamberg, chose—if we are to believe one of his canons—the stories of Attila and of the Amalings, the ancient Ostrogothic dynasty which came to an end in the sixth century. It is even possible—the text is obscure—that he himself 'poetized' on these profane subjects.[1] In his circle, therefore, men continued to recount the adventures of long-departed kings. They also doubtless continued to sing of them in the language of the people; but none of these songs have survived. The life of Archbishop Hanno, written in German verse shortly after 1077 by a cleric of the diocese of Cologne, belongs much more to hagiography than to a narrative literature intended for a wide circle of hearers.

The veil is only lifted at a date nearly a century later than the appearance of the French *gestes*, and by this time the imitation of those *gestes* or of more recent works from the same source had already for a generation accustomed the German public to appreciate the great poetic frescoes in the vernacular. The first heroic poems of native inspiration, in a form resembling that in which we know them today, were not composed before the end of the twelfth century. As in France, they sought their themes in adventures constantly re-told through the centuries: thenceforth the great deeds of contemporaries would be left to the chroniclers and the Latin versifiers. The curious thing is that the German poems relate to a much more distant past. The one exception is the *Lied* of Duke Ernst, which gives an oddly distorted account of an event belonging to the early eleventh century.

In the other heroic poems pure legend and a sense of the marvellous that is sometimes still completely pagan mingle with old memories of the time of the Invasions, though these are usually reduced from their exalted status as world catastrophes to the level of commonplace personal feuds. In the whole of this literature it is possible to name twenty-one principal heroes as identifiable historical figures. They range from a Gothic king who died in 375 to a Lombard king who died in 575. Does no personage of later date appear anywhere by chance? In the *Nibelungenlied* we do indeed find a

[1] C. Erdmann, in *Zeitschrift für deutsches Altertum*, 1936, p. 88, and 1937, p. 116.

tenth-century bishop insinuating himself into that already remarkably heterogeneous company in which Attila, Theodoric the Great, and the Burgundian kings of the Rhine consort with such shadowy, unhistorical figures as Siegfried and Brünhilde. But this intruder appears only in an episodic way, probably as a result of clerical or local influence. It would certainly not have been so, if the poets had received their subjects from clerics engaged in examining written documents. The German monasteries did not owe their foundations to barbarian chiefs, and if the chroniclers had a good deal to say of Attila and even of the 'tyrant' Theodoric, they painted them in colours decidedly darker than those in which the epic clothes them.

What could be more striking than this contrast? France, whose civilization had been profoundly refashioned in the crucible of the early Middle Ages, whose language, so far as it was a truly differentiated linguistic entity, was very young, found her remotest tradition no farther back than the Carolingians. (The Merovingian dynasty appears, so far as we know, only in a single *chanson*, the *Floovant*, a fairly late production which, as we have seen, probably formed part of a group of works directly inspired by the learned monks of Saint-Denis.) Germany, on the other hand, could draw upon an infinitely older fund of material for her tales; for, though flowing long underground, the stream of stories, and perhaps of songs, was never interrupted.

The example of Castile is equally instructive. The thirst for memories was there no less keen than elsewhere. But in that land of reconquest the oldest national memories were of quite recent events. The result was that the minstrels, in so far as they did not copy foreign models, drew their inspiration from events that were barely cold. The Cid died on the 10th July 1099; the *Poem of the Cid*, sole survivor of a whole family of *cantares* devoted to the heroes of the recent wars, dates from about 1150.

More remarkable is the case of Italy. She had no native epic, nor does she seem ever to have had one. What is the reason? It would be the height of temerity to pretend to solve so difficult a problem in a few words. One solution nevertheless deserves to be suggested. In the feudal period, Italy was one of the few countries where, among the nobility, as also no doubt among the merchants, a large number of persons were able to read. If the taste for the past did not express itself in songs, might it not be because it found satisfaction in reading the Latin chronicles?

The epic, where it was able to develop, exerted a strong influence on men's imaginations, because, unlike a written work, it was not addressed merely to the eyes, but had the advantage of all the warmth of human utterance and of that sort of impact upon the mind which results from the reiteration vocally of the same themes and even of the same couplets. Ask the governments of our own day if radio is not a more effective medium of propaganda than the newspaper. True, it was mainly from the end of the twelfth century that the upper classes began really to live their legends, in circles which by then were far more cultivated. A knight could find no more biting or apt form of mockery for a coward than an allusion borrowed from a romance; and somewhat later a group of Cypriot nobles played at impersonating the characters in the cycle of Reynard the Fox, just as, nearer to our own time, certain society circles amused themselves by aping the heroes of Balzac's novels.[1] Nevertheless, from the very earliest period of the French *gestes*—before 1110—noblemen took to giving their sons the names of Oliver and Roland, while that of Ganelon, branded with a mark of infamy, was never used again.[2] There were occasions when these tales were referred to as if they were authentic documents. Though the son of an epoch already much more familiar with books, the celebrated justiciar of Henry II Plantagenet, Ranulf Glanville, when questioned as to the reasons for the long weakness of the kings of France *vis-à-vis* the Norman dukes, ascribed it to the wars which formerly had 'almost destroyed' the chivalry of France; as proof, he said, take the stories of *Gormont* and of *Raoul de Cambrai*.[3] This great minister would certainly have learned to reflect on history from reading such poems. The conception of life to which the *gestes* gave expression was, in many respects, only the reflection of that of their public: in every literature a society contemplates its own image. Yet, along with the memory of old events, distorted and imperfect though it was, traditions genuinely derived from the past had filtered down; and the traces of these we shall encounter over and over again.

[1] *Histoire de Guillaume le Maréchal*, ed. P. Meyer, I, v. 8444 *et seq.*; Philip of Novara, *Mémoires*, ed. Ch. Kohler, c. LXXII; cf. c. CL *et seq.*

[2] It may be remarked in passing that the study of the disappearance of this name, apparently not so far undertaken, would provide a useful means of dating the popularity of the legend of Roland.

[3] Giraldus Cambrensis, *De principis instructione*, dist. III, c. XII (*Opera*, Rolls Series, VIII, p. 258).

VII

THE INTELLECTUAL RENAISSANCE
IN THE SECOND FEUDAL AGE

1 SOME CHARACTERISTICS OF THE NEW CULTURE

THE appearance of the great epic poems in eleventh-century France may be regarded as one of the signs that heralded the immense cultural development of the succeeding age. 'The twelfth-century renaissance' is the phrase frequently used to describe this movement; and with the necessary qualification that the word 'renaissance', literally interpreted, is apt to suggest a mere revival, rather than a new development, the formula is valid—provided that it is not understood in too exact a chronological sense. For though the movement only reached its full development in the course of the twelfth century, its earliest manifestations, like those of the demographic and economic changes that accompanied it, date from the two or three decades immediately preceding the year 1100. This was the really decisive period. To this time belong, to mention only a few examples, the philosophic work of Anselm of Canterbury; the legal work of the first Italian teachers of Roman law and that of their rivals, the canonists; and the beginning of the serious study of mathematics in the schools of Chartres. No more in the domain of the intellect than in any other field of human activity was the revolution a complete one. But the second feudal age, closely akin as it was to the first in many aspects of its mentality, was characterized by certain new intellectual features, the effects of which we must now try to define.

The development of intercommunication, so manifest on the economic map, was no less clearly marked on the map of culture. The abundance of translations of Greek and Arabic works, especially the latter (though these were for the most part mere interpretations of Hellenic thought), and the influence which they exercised upon Western science and philosophy bore witness to a civilization that was coming to be better equipped with antennae. It was no accident that among the translators were several members of the merchant colonies established at Constantinople. In the heart of Europe the old Celtic legends, borne eastwards from their original home, began to imbue with their strange magic the imagination of the French romancers, whilst the poems composed in France—old heroic tales or stories in a newer mode—were imitated in Germany, Italy, and Spain.

The centres of the new learning were the great international schools: Bologna, Chartres, and Paris, 'Jacob's ladder raised towards Heaven'.[1] Romanesque art, in so far as it possessed a universal quality over and above its innumerable regional varieties, expressed chiefly a certain community of civilization, the interaction of a multitude of small centres of influence. Gothic art, on the other hand, is one of those forms of art that lend themselves to export and which (subject, of course, to every sort of local adaptation) are not the less widely disseminated because issuing from a well-defined centre—France between the Seine and the Aisne, or the Cistercian monasteries of Burgundy.

In his *Confessions*, written about 1115, the abbot Guibert de Nogent, who was born in 1053, contrasts the conditions prevailing at the beginning and towards the end of his life. 'In the time just before my birth and during my childhood there was so great a dearth of teachers that it was practically impossible to find any in the small towns, and scarcely even in the cities. And supposing that by chance they were to be found? Their learning was so meagre that it could not be compared even with that of the little wandering scholars of today.'[2] During the twelfth century there was undoubtedly immense progress in education; it was both greatly improved in quality and much more widely diffused through the different social classes. More than ever before it was based on the imitation of ancient models, and though these were not more venerated perhaps, they were better understood, and more deeply felt—to such a degree that, among certain poets on the fringes of the clerical world, like the famous Rhenish *Archipoeta*, there emerged a kind of moral paganism quite alien to the spirit of the preceding period. But the new humanism was more often a Christian humanism. 'We are dwarfs perched on the shoulders of giants.' This oft-repeated saying of Bernard of Chartres illustrates the extent of the debt to classical culture acknowledged by the more serious minds of the age.

The new spirit had begun to pervade lay society. It was no longer exceptional to find a ruler like that count of Champagne, Henri le Liberal, who read Vegetius and Valerius Maximus in the original, or that count of Anjou, Geoffroi le Bel, who for advice on building a fortress also turned to the pages of Vegetius.[3] Most frequently, however, these interests were frustrated by an education that was still too primitive to penetrate the secrets of works written in the language of the learned; though this did not prevent them from seeking an outlet. Take for example Baldwin II, count of Guines (died 1205). Hunter, toper, and great wencher, this Picard noble was skilled in the minstrelsy of the *chansons de geste* and equally gifted in

[1] John of Salisbury in H. Denifle and E. Chatelain, *Chartularium universitatis Parisiensis*, I, pp. 18–19.

[2] *Histoire de sa vie*, I, 4; ed. G. Bourgin, pp. 12–13.

[3] D'Arbois de Jubainville, *Histoire des ducs et comtes de Champagne*, III, p. 189 *et seq.*, and *Chroniques des comtes d'Anjou*, ed. Halphen and Poupardin, pp. 217–19.

the recital of coarse *fabliaux*, but 'unlettered' though he was, he did not find his sole enjoyment in heroic tales or droll stories. He sought the conversation of the clergy, repaying them with 'godless' anecdotes; and he profited too well from these erudite discussions for the liking of at least one Picard priest, for he used the theological knowledge thus acquired to dispute with his masters. But he was not content merely to bandy words. He had several Latin works translated into French, so that they might be read aloud to him; among these, in addition to the *Song of Songs*, the Gospels and the *Life of St. Anthony*, were a large part of the *Physics* of Aristotle and the old *Geography* of the Roman grammarian, Solinus.[1] Thus, from these new needs, there came into being almost everywhere in Europe a vernacular literature which, though meant for men of the world, was not for their amusement only. If at the outset this literature consisted almost exclusively of paraphrases of Latin originals, it nevertheless opened wide the doors of a whole tradition; in particular, it gave access to a more faithful picture of the past.

It is true that for many years historical narrative in the vernacular languages retained the verse form and general style of the old *gestes*; it was not to be found in prose, the natural vehicle of a literature of fact, before the early decades of the thirteenth century, when two new types of historical writing made their appearance. On the one hand, there were the memoirs of two men who belonged neither to the world of minstrels nor to that of clerks, namely those of a great noble, Villehardouin, and those of a humble knight, Robert de Clary. On the other hand, there were compilations specifically intended for the enlightenment of the general public—the *Deeds of the Romans*, the compendium which called itself, without false modesty, *The Whole History of France*, and the Saxon production known as the *Universal Chronicle*. Nearly as many more years were to pass before, first in France, then in the Low Countries and Germany, a few charters began to appear—they were very rare at first—in the vernacular languages, thus making it possible at last for the parties to a contract to understand its meaning without an interpreter. The gulf between action and its expression in words was slowly narrowing.

Meanwhile the cultured courts of the great rulers—the Angevins, the counts of Champagne, the Welf princes of Germany—were coming under the spell of a whole new literature of myth and fantasy. The *chansons de geste*, more or less refashioned to the taste of the day and abounding with additional episodes, had assuredly not lost their popularity. But, as genuine history gradually replaced the epic in the folk memory, new poetic forms, originating in Provence or northern France, sprang into existence and were soon diffused over the whole of Europe.

One of these forms was the romance, a work of pure imagination, in which prodigious sword-strokes—the *grans borroflemens*—were given and

[1] Lambert of Ardre, *Chronique*, c. LXXX, LXXXI, LXXXVIII, LXXXIX.

taken, to the unfailing delight of what was still fundamentally a warlike society; but from this time on the normal background to these deeds would be the world of mystery and enchantment. The absence of any pretence to historical veracity and the flight into fairyland were the reflections of an age that was now sufficiently refined in its perceptions to separate the figments of the literary imagination from the description of real events.

Another poetic form that flourished at this time was the short lyric. The earliest examples are almost as old as the *chansons de geste*, but they were now being composed in ever-growing numbers and with ever-greater subtlety of contrivance. For a more developed aesthetic sense attached increasing importance to novelties of style, even when carried to the point of preciosity. To this period belongs the pleasant conceit with which one of the rivals of Chrétien de Troyes, regarded by twelfth-century France as its finest story-teller, sought to pay tribute to his memory; he could find no higher praise for him than to say: 'he took the French language by the handful.'

Particularly significant is the fact that the romancers and lyric poets were no longer content merely to recount men's deeds; they made a serious, if somewhat awkward, attempt to analyse their feelings. Even in the martial episodes the clash of armies, a favourite feature of the old epics, yielded place to the joust where only two combatants were engaged. The whole tendency of the new literature was towards the rehabilitation of the individual; it encouraged the growth of a more introspective habit of mind, reinforcing in this direction the influence of the religious practice of auricular confession which, after having been long confined to the monastic world, became widespread among laymen during the twelfth century. In many of his characteristics the man of A.D. 1200 or thereabouts, in the higher ranks of society, resembled his ancestor of earlier generations: he displayed the same spirit of violence, the same abrupt changes of mood, the same preoccupation with the supernatural; this last—where it took the form of an obsession with evil spirits—being perhaps even more pronounced as a result of the dualist influences with which the Manichaean heresies, then so flourishing, were infecting even the orthodox. But in two respects he differed profoundly from his predecessor. He was better educated. He was more self-conscious.

2 THE GROWTH OF SELF-CONSCIOUSNESS

This growth of self-consciousness indeed extended beyond the solitary human being to society itself. The impetus in this direction had been given, in the second half of the eleventh century, by the great religious 'awakening' which is usually called the Gregorian reform, after Pope Gregory VII, who was one of its leading figures. It was an extremely complex movement in which ideas thrown up from the depth of the popular soul were intermingled with the pious aspirations of clergy, particularly monks, brought up on the ancient texts. The idea that the priest guilty of unchastity becomes thereby incapable of administering the sacraments of the Church had champions just as uncompromising among the lay masses as among the monastic zealots, and much more so than in the ranks of the theologians. The Gregorian reform was an extraordinarily powerful movement from which, without exaggeration, may be dated the definite formation of Latin Christianity; and it was no mere coincidence that this was the very moment of the final separation between the eastern and western churches. Varied as were the manifestations of this spirit—a spirit more revolutionary than contemporaries realized—its essence may be summed up in a few words: in a world where hitherto the sacred and profane had been almost inextricably mingled, the Gregorian reform proclaimed both the unique character and the supreme importance of the spiritual mission with which the Church was entrusted; it strove to set the priest apart from and above the ordinary believer.

The strictest of the reformers, naturally, were hardly friends of the intellectual life. They distrusted philosophy. They despised rhetoric, though they themselves yielded often enough to its spell: 'My grammar is Christ,' said Peter Damiani, who nevertheless declined and conjugated very correctly. They considered that the monk's part was not to study, but to mourn. Since the time of St. Jerome, more than one Christian heart had been torn between admiration for the thought or art of antiquity and the jealous demands of an ascetic religion. In this drama of divided loyalties the zealots among the reformers ranged themselves on the side of that uncompromising group of churchmen who, far from sharing Abelard's view that the pagan philosophers were men 'inspired by God', held with Gerhoh of Reichersberg, that they were 'enemies of the cross of Christ'. But in their campaign for reform, and in the course of the struggle which they were compelled to wage against the temporal powers, especially the Empire, they were obliged to put their ideals in intellectual form; to reason, and invite others to do likewise. Now all at once problems which formerly had been discussed only by a handful of learned men became topics of the day. It was said that in Germany, even in the market-places and workshops, people read (or got others to read for them) works written in the heat of controversy by churchmen, wherein they freely debated such subjects as the ends of the State, and the rights of king, pope, and people.[1] Other countries had not been involved to the same degree in these polemics, but nowhere were they without effect. Human affairs were newly emerging as subjects for reflection.

There was yet another influence that contributed to this decisive change. In an age when every man of action had to be something of a lawyer, the

[1] Manegold of Lautenbach, *Ad Gebehardum liber* in *M.G.H., Libelli de lite*, I, pp. 311 and 420.

revival of jurisprudence (which will be surveyed in a later chapter) had wide repercussions; and it led to the recognition that the realities of social life were something that could be described methodically, and consciously worked out. Nevertheless the more positive results of the new legal education were manifested in another direction. First and foremost it inculcated the habit of reasoned argument no matter what the subject under discussion. In this way, it was associated with the progress of philosophical speculation, to which in other respects also it was closely allied. It is true that the logical work of a St. Anselm, an Abelard, or a Peter Lombard could only be followed by a few men, almost exclusively clergy. But these same clerks were often involved in the affairs of the world: it was a former student of the Paris schools, Reinald of Dassel, chancellor of the Empire, and later archbishop of Cologne, who for many years directed the policy of Germany; and it was the philosopher-prelate, Stephen Langton, who, in the reign of John Lackland, assumed the leadership of the English baronial revolt.

Moreover, it is surely possible to come under the influence of an intellectual movement without sharing in its highest manifestations. Place side by side two charters, one dating from about A.D. 1000, the other from the last years of the twelfth century: almost invariably you will find that the second is the more explicit, more accurate, and less ill-arranged. Naturally, there were very appreciable differences between documents of varying origin, even in the twelfth century. The urban charters, drawn up at the instance of burghers more shrewd than educated, were as a rule much inferior in their drafting to—let us say—the fine productions of the learned chancellery of a Barbarossa. Taken as a whole, however, the contrast between the two ages of feudalism is very marked. In the second there was no longer a divorce between the means of expression and the thought to be expressed. It is a significant fact in the history of the relation of thought and practice—still so obscure a subject—that towards the end of the twelfth century men of action had at their disposal a more efficient instrument of mental analysis than that which had been available to their predecessors.

VIII

THE FOUNDATIONS OF LAW

1 THE ASCENDANCY OF CUSTOM

IF a judge, in the pre-feudal Europe of the early ninth century, had to say what the law was, how did he proceed? His first task was to examine the texts. These consisted of the following: Roman compilations, if the case had to be decided according to the laws of Rome; customs of the Germanic peoples, almost all of which had been gradually committed to writing; and finally those legislative edicts which the sovereigns of the barbarian kingdoms had issued in great number. In cases where these authorities returned a clear answer, there was nothing to do but obey. But the task was not always so simple. Let us leave aside those cases, in practice no doubt quite frequent, in which, since the manuscript was lacking, or—as with the massive Roman collections—inconvenient to consult, the rule in question, although its source might have been the law-book, was in fact known only by usage. The most serious problem was that no book was capable of deciding everything. Whole aspects of social life—relations inside the manor, ties between man and man, in which feudalism was already foreshadowed—were only very imperfectly covered by the texts, and often not at all. Thus, by the side of the written law, there already existed a zone of purely oral tradition. One of the most important characteristics of the period that followed—the age in which the feudal regime was really established—was that this margin increased beyond all bounds, to the point where in certain countries it encroached on the whole domain of law.

In Germany and France this evolution reached its extreme limits. There was no more legislation. In France the last 'capitulary', a very unoriginal one moreover, dates from 884; in Germany, the spring seems to have run dry from the dismemberment of the Empire after the death of Louis the Pious. At most a few territorial princes—a duke of Normandy, a duke of Bavaria—promulgate here and there one or two measures of fairly general application. It has sometimes been supposed that this failure was an effect of the weakness into which the royal power had fallen. But this explanation, which we might be tempted to accept if only France were in question, would clearly not be valid for the much more powerful sovereigns of Germany. Moreover, these Saxon or Salian emperors who, north of the

109

Alps, never dealt in their charters with any but individual cases, set themselves up as legislators in their Italian States, though their power was certainly no greater there. If men north of the Alps no longer felt the need to add anything to the rules expressly formulated not so very long before, the real reason was that these rules themselves had passed quietly into oblivion. In the course of the tenth century the barbarian laws, like the Carolingian ordinances, gradually ceased to be transcribed or mentioned, except in passing allusions. If notaries still made a pretence of citing the Roman law, the reference in most cases was merely a commonplace or a misconstruction. How should it have been otherwise? The knowledge of Latin—the language in which all the old continental legal documents were written—was virtually the monopoly of the clergy. Now the ecclesiastical body had provided itself with a law of its own, which tended to become more and more exclusive. Based on the texts—so much so that the only Frankish capitularies which continued to be annotated were those which concerned the Church—this canon law was taught in the schools, which were completely in the hands of the clergy. Secular law was nowhere included in the curriculum. It is true that knowledge of the old law-books would not have been completely lost if a legal profession had existed. But the procedure did not call for advocates, and every chief was a judge. This meant in practice that the majority of judges were unable to read— a state of affairs unfavourable to the maintenance of a written law.

The close relation that thus existed in France and Germany between the decay of the old laws and the decline of education among the laity is thrown into clear relief by some examples of a contrary situation. In Italy, the connection between law and education was admirably expressed, as early as the eleventh century, by a foreign observer, the imperial chaplain Wipo. In this country, he said, where 'all the young men'—he was referring to those of the ruling classes—'were sent to the schools to work with the sweat of the brow',[1] the barbarian laws and the Carolingian capitularies, as well as the Roman law, continued to be studied, summarized and glossed. Similarly a series of acts, few and far between no doubt but displaying a visible continuity, attest the persistence in Italy of the practice of legislation. In Anglo-Saxon England, where the language of the laws was the common language, and where in consequence, as the biographer of King Alfred informs us, unlettered judges could have the manuscripts read to them and understand them,[2] the rulers, till Cnut, codified or completed the customs and even modified them specifically by their edicts. After the Norman Conquest, it seemed necessary to make available to the conquerors or at least to their clergy the substance of these texts whose language was unintelligible to them. Thus there developed in the island, from the beginning of the twelfth century, a thing unknown in the same

---

[1] *Tetralogus*, ed. Bresslau, v. 197 *et seq.*
[2] Asser, *Life of King Alfred*, ed. Stevenson, c. 106.

period on the other side of the Channel—a legal literature which, though written in Latin, was based essentially on Anglo-Saxon sources.[1]

Nevertheless, considerable as were the differences thus manifest among the various parts of feudal Europe, they did not affect its essential development. Where law was no longer based on the written word, many old rules of diverse origin had notwithstanding been preserved by oral transmission. Conversely, in the countries which continued to know and respect the old texts, social needs had brought with them a great number of new usages, some complementary to them, others superseding them. Everywhere, in short, it was custom that finally decided the fate of the legal heritage of the preceding age. Custom had become the sole living source of law, and princes, even in their legislation, scarcely claimed to do more than interpret it.

The progress of this customary law was accompanied by a profound reorganization of the legal structure. In the continental provinces of the ancient *Romania*, which the barbarians had occupied, and later in Frankish Germany, the presence side by side of men who belonged by birth to different peoples had at first resulted in the most singular medley that ever confronted a professor of law in his nightmares. In theory, and making due allowance for the difficulties in applying the law which inevitably arose between two litigants of completely different origin, the individual, wherever he lived, remained subject to the rules which had governed his ancestors. Hence the celebrated remark of an archbishop of Lyons, that when in Frankish Gaul five persons happened to be gathered together it was no occasion for surprise if each of them—a Roman perhaps, a Salian Frank, a Ripuarian Frank, a Visigoth and a Burgundian—obeyed a different law. No thoughtful observer from the ninth century onward could doubt that such a system, formerly imposed by imperious necessity, had become terribly cumbersome and more and more out of harmony with the conditions of a society in which the fusion of the ethnic elements was all but complete.

The Anglo-Saxons, who had scarcely had to reckon with native populations, had never known the system of the personality of law. The Visigothic monarchy, as early as 654, had deliberately got rid of it. But where these special codes existed in writing, their power of resistance was great. It is significant that the country where this multiplicity of legal codes continued longest—till the opening of the twelfth century—was that land of learning, Italy. But even there it only survived in a strangely altered form. For, as legal affiliations seemed less and less easy to determine, the practice was introduced of making each person, whenever he took part in a legal transaction, specify the law to which he considered himself subject; thus the law sometimes varied, at the will of the contracting party,

[1] Similarly in Spain, where, as we have seen, a certain level of education was maintained among the laity, the Visigothic codification continued to be copied and studied.

according to the nature of the case. In the rest of the continent, the oblivion which, from the tenth century, descended on the texts of the previous age permitted the advent of an entirely new order. This is sometimes called the system of territorial custom, but it would be more accurate to speak of group custom.

Each human group, great or small, whether or not it occupied a clearly defined area, tended to develop its own legal tradition. Thus, according to the different departments of their activity, men passed successively from one to the other of these zones of law. Let us take for example a rural agglomeration. The family law of the peasants normally followed much the same rules in the whole of the surrounding region. Their agrarian law, on the other hand, conformed to usages peculiar to their community. Among the obligations with which they were burdened, some, which they incurred as tenants, were fixed by the custom of the manor whose limits did not always coincide with those of the village's agricultural lands. Others, if the peasants were of servile status, touched their persons and were regulated by the law of the group, usually a more restricted entity, consisting of serfs of the same master living in the same place. All this, it goes without saying, was without prejudice to various contracts or precedents, some strictly personal, some capable of transmitting their effects from father to son through the whole length of a family line. Even where, in two small neighbouring societies similar in structure, the customary arrangements were originally constituted on roughly parallel lines, it was inevitable that, not being crystallized in writing, they should progressively diverge. Confronted with such a degree of subdivision, what historian does not sometimes feel tempted to endorse the disillusioned observations of the author of a *Treatise on the Laws of England*, compiled at the court of Henry II? 'To put in writing, in their entirety, the laws and customs of the realm,' he declared, 'would be utterly impossible today . . . such a confused mass are they.'[1]

The differences were most marked, however, in the details and in the way they were expressed. Among the rules observed inside the different groups in a given region there was a great family likeness. Often, the similarity extended even farther. A few powerful and simple ideas—some peculiar to particular European societies, some common to Europe as a whole—dominated the law of the feudal era. And though it is quite true that there was infinite variety in their application, does not this very variety serve as a prism which, by separating the multiple factors of the evolution, provides the historian with an exceptionally rich body of social material?

[1] Glanville, *De legibus et consuetudinibus regni Angliae*, ed. G. E. Woodbine, New Haven (U.S.A.), 1932 (Yale Historical Publications, Manuscripts, XIII), p. 24.

2 THE CHARACTERISTICS OF CUSTOMARY LAW

Fundamentally traditionalist, as was the whole of civilization in that period, the legal system of the first feudal age rested on the idea that what has been has *ipso facto* the right to be—though not indeed without some reservations inspired by a higher morality. Faced with a temporal society whose heritage was far from according completely with their ideals, the clergy in particular had good reasons for refusing to identify justice invariably with precedent. Already Hincmar of Rheims had declared that the king will not judge according to custom if this is seen to be more cruel than 'Christian righteousness'. Interpreting the Gregorian spirit, which among the zealots was inspired by a truly revolutionary fervour, and appropriating as a natural heritage a remark of Tertullian, who had also been in his day a breaker of traditions, Pope Urban II wrote in 1092 to the count of Flanders: 'Dost thou claim to have done hitherto only what is in conformity with the ancient custom of the land? Thou shouldst know, notwithstanding, thy Creator hath said: My name is Truth. He hath not said: My name is Custom.'[1] There could be, in consequence, 'bad customs'. In fact, the legal documents quite frequently use these words, but almost invariably they are applied to rules actually or supposedly of recent origin—'those detestable innovations', 'those unheard-of exactions', denounced by so many monastic texts. A custom, in other words, might seem especially to deserve condemnation when it was too new. Whether it was a question of Church reform or of a law-suit between two neighbouring lords, the prestige of the past could scarcely be contested save by setting against it a past more venerable still.

The strange thing is that this law in whose eyes any change seemed an evil, far from being unchangeable, was in fact one of the most flexible ever known. This was due above all to the fact that it was not firmly fixed in writing—either in legal documents or in the form of statutes. The majority of the courts contented themselves with purely oral decisions. What if it was desired to restate them later? Inquiry was made of the judges, if they were still alive. In contracts, the intentions of the parties were made binding by means of gestures and sometimes the repetition of conventional formulas, in fact by a whole series of formalities well calculated to impress imaginations little susceptible to the abstract. Italy was an exception in that writing played a part in the exchange of agreements and was itself a recognized element in the ritual. To indicate the cession of an estate, the deed was passed from hand to hand, as elsewhere a lump of earth or a straw would have been. North of the Alps, the parchment, even if it were produced, served as little more than a memento; it had no authentic value,

---

[1] Hincmar, *De ordine palatii*, c. 21; Migne, *P.L.*, CLI, col. 356 (1092, 2 Dec.). Cf. Tertullian, *De virginibus velandis*, c. 1.

and was intended chiefly to provide a list of witnesses. For in the last analysis everything depended on personal testimony—even if 'black ink' had been used, still more so in the undoubtedly more numerous cases where it had not. Since memory was obviously likely to be the more enduring the longer its possessors were destined to remain on this earth, the contracting parties often brought children with them. Did they fear the heedlessness of childhood? Various methods could be used to overcome it: a box on the ear, a trifling gift, or even an enforced bath.

Whether it was a question of particular transactions or of the general rules of customary law, memory was almost the sole guardian of tradition. Now the human memory, the fluid, the *escoulourjante* memory, as Beaumanoir calls it, is a marvellous instrument of elimination and transformation —especially what we call collective memory. Since this is in fact merely a transmission of material from generation to generation, it is not only liable, if not committed to writing, to the errors to which each individual brain is liable in the recording of facts but also suffers through misunderstandings of what is said. This would not have been serious had there existed in feudal Europe a class of professional keepers of the legal memory such as other societies—the Scandinavian, for example—employed. But, in feudal Europe and amongst the laity, few of the men to whom it fell to declare the law did so regularly. Not having undergone a systematic training, they were reduced more often than not, as one of them complained, to following 'any course that seemed open to them or was suggested by their whims'.[1] Jurisprudence, in short, was the expression of needs rather than of knowledge. Because its efforts to imitate the past were inevitably based only on an inaccurate picture of it, the first feudal age changed very quickly and very profoundly while believing itself to be unchanging.

In one sense, moreover, the very authority that was ascribed to tradition favoured the change. For every act, especially if it was repeated three or four times, was likely to be transformed into a precedent—even if in the first instance it had been exceptional or even frankly unlawful. In the ninth century, when one day there was a shortage of wine in the royal cellars at Ver, the monks of Saint-Denis were asked to supply the two hundred hogsheads required. This contribution was thenceforward claimed from them as of right every year, and it required an imperial charter to abolish it. At Ardres, we are told, there was once a bear, the property of the local lord. The inhabitants, who loved to watch it fight with dogs, undertook to feed it. The beast eventually died, but the lord continued to exact the loaves of bread.[2] The authenticity of this story may perhaps be disputed, but its symbolic significance is beyond doubt. Many dues originated in this way as bene-

---

[1] *Chron. Ebersp.*, in *M.G.H., SS.*, XX, p. 14; the whole passage is extremely curious.
[2] *Recueil des Historiens de France*, VI, p. 541; Lambert of Ardre, *Chronique*, c. CXXVIII.

I. A SCANDINAVIAN SHIP

From the Oseberg ship-burial, early 9th century. (Oslo, University Museum.)

II. HOMAGE

From the *Établissements de Saint-Louis*. MS. of the late 13th century. Bibl. Nat., MS. Fr. 5899, f. 83v.

III. HOMAGE TO THE DEVIL

Theophilus does homage to the Devil. From the *Psautier de la Reine Ingeburge* (about 1200). Musée Condé, Chantilly, MS. 9, f. 35v.

volent gifts and for a long time continued to be so described. Conversely a rent which ceased to be paid for a certain number of years, or a ceremony of submission once omitted, almost inevitably fell into desuetude by prescription. Thus the practice was introduced of drawing up, in growing numbers, those curious documents which students of diplomatic call 'charters of non-prejudice'. A baron or a bishop seeks lodgings from an abbot; a king, in need of money, appeals to the generosity of a subject. Agreed, replies the person thus approached, but on one condition: that it shall be specified, in black and white, that my compliance shall not create a right at my expense. These precautions, however, were seldom allowed except to men of a certain rank and were only effective when the balance of power was not too unequal. A too common consequence of the notion of custom was that brutality was legalized and encouraged by being made profitable. It was the practice in Catalonia, when an estate was alienated, to state, in a singularly cynical formula, that it was handed over with all the advantages that its possessor enjoyed 'by grace or by violence'.[1]

This respect for what had been done in the past operated with peculiar force on the system of real property rights. It is very rare, during the whole of the feudal era, for anyone to speak of ownership, either of an estate or of an office; much rarer still—never perhaps, except in Italy—for a lawsuit to turn on such ownership. What the parties claim is almost invariably 'seisin' (in German, *Gewere*). Even in the thirteenth century, the *Parlement* of the Capetian kings, responsive to Roman influences, vainly took the precaution, in every judgment on seisin, of reserving the 'petitory', that is to say the action claiming owners' p. It does not appear that in fact the procedure envisaged was ever employed. What then was this famous seisin? It was not exactly possession, which the mere seizure of the land or the right would have sufficed to create. It was possession made venerable by the lapse of time. Two litigants go to law about a field or a right to administer justice. No matter which of them is the present holder, that one will succeed who is able to prove that he ploughed the land or administered justice during previous years or, better still, that his ancestors before him did so. For this purpose, in so far as the case is not remitted to the ordeal or to trial by battle, he will invoke as a rule 'the memory of men, as far as it extends'. Title-deeds were hardly ever produced save to assist memory, and if they proved that a transfer had taken place it was merely a transfer of seisin. Once the proof of long usage had been adduced, no one considered it worth while to prove anything else.

Moreover, for yet other reasons, the word 'ownership', as applied to landed property, would have been almost meaningless. Or at least it would have been necessary to say—as was frequently done later on, when a more developed legal vocabulary was in use—ownership or seisin of

[1] E. de Hinojosa, *El regimen señorial y la cuestión agraria en Cataluña*, pp. 250–1.

such and such a right over the ground. For nearly all land and a great many human beings were burdened at this time with a multiplicity of obligations differing in their nature, but all apparently of equal importance. None implied that fixed proprietary exclusiveness which belonged to the conception of ownership in Roman law. The tenant who—from father to son, as a rule—ploughs the land and gathers in the crop; his immediate lord, to whom he pays dues and who, in certain circumstances, can resume possession of the land; the lord of the lord, and so on, right up the feudal scale—how many persons there are who can say, each with as much justification as the other, 'That is my field!' Even this is an understatement. For the ramifications extended horizontally as well as vertically and account should be taken of the village community, which normally recovered the use of the whole of its agricultural land as soon as it was cleared of crops; of the tenant's family, without whose consent the property could not be alienated; and of the families of the successive lords.

This hierarchical complex of bonds between the man and the soil derived its sanction, no doubt, from very remote origins. (In a great part of the Roman world itself, Quiritarian ownership had been little more than a façade.) In feudal times, however, the system blossomed out as never before. To minds not much alive to logical contradictions there was nothing disturbing in this interpenetration of 'seisins' on the same thing, and perhaps this attitude to legal rights could not be better defined than by borrowing a familiar formula from sociology and calling it the mentality of legal 'participation'.

3 THE REVIVAL OF WRITTEN LAWS

As we have noted, the study of Roman law had never ceased in the schools of Italy. But from about the end of the eleventh century, according to a monk of Marseilles, students were to be seen literally 'in crowds' attending the lectures given by teams of masters, now more numerous and better organized[1]—especially at Bologna, rendered illustrious by the great Irnerius, 'the torch of the law'. Simultaneously, the subject-matter of the teaching was undergoing profound changes. The original sources, in the past too often neglected in favour of poor summaries, once again took first place; the *Digest*, in particular, which had almost fallen into oblivion, thenceforward opened the way to Latin legal reflection in its most refined form. The links between this revival and the other intellectual movements of the age are obvious. The crisis of the Gregorian reform had inspired among all parties a speculative effort that was as much legal as political; it was no coincidence that the composition of the great canonical collections which it directly inspired was exactly contemporaneous with the appear-

---

[1] Martène and Durand, *Ampl. Collectio*, I, col. 470 (1065).

ance of the first works of the school of Bologna. In the latter we cannot fail to recognize the marks of that return to antiquity and that taste for logical analysis which were about to blossom in the new Latin literature, as well as in the revival of philosophy.

Similar developments were occurring at much the same time in the rest of Europe. There also, especially among the great nobles, there was a growing desire to secure the advice of professional jurists. After about 1096 there were to be found, among the assessors at the court of the count of Blois, persons who, not without pride, styled themselves 'learned in the laws'.[1] Possibly they had derived their education from some of the texts of ancient law that were still preserved in the monastic libraries north of the Alps. But these elements were too poor to furnish by themselves the material for an indigenous renaissance. The impulse came from Italy. Favoured by closer and more frequent social contacts than before, the influence of the Bolognese group was disseminated by its lectures (to which foreign students were admitted), by its writings, and finally by the emigration of several of its teachers. Frederick Barbarossa, ruler of the Italian kingdom as well as of the Germanies, welcomed Lombard legists into his retinue during his Italian expeditions. A former student of Bologna, Placentinus, established himself shortly after 1160 at Montpellier: another, Vacarius, had been called some years before to Canterbury. Everywhere, in the course of the twelfth century, Roman law penetrated into the schools. It was taught, for example, about 1170, side by side with canon law, in the shadow of the cathedral of Sens.[2]

Yet the revival of interest in Roman law provoked lively opposition. Fundamentally secular, it disturbed many churchmen by its latent paganism. The guardians of monastic virtue accused it of having turned the monks away from prayer. The theologians reproached it with supplanting the only forms of speculative activity that seemed to them worthy of clerics. The kings of France themselves or their counsellors, at least from Philip Augustus on, seem to have taken umbrage at the too easy justifications which it provided for the theorists of Imperial hegemony. Far from arresting the movement, however, this opposition did little more than attest its strength.

In the south of France, where customary law had retained a strongly Roman stamp, the work of the jurists, by providing access to the original texts, had the effect of elevating the 'written' law to the status of a sort of common law, which was applied in the absence of expressly contrary usages. It was thus too in Provence where, from the middle of the twelfth century, the knowledge of Justinian's Code seemed so important to the laity themselves that they were provided with a summary of it in the vernacular. Elsewhere the influence was less direct. Even where it found a

[1] E. Mabille, *Cartulaire de Marmoutier pour le Dunois*, 1874, nos. CLVI and LXXVIII.
[2] *Rev. histor. de Droit*, 1922, p. 301.

particularly favourable soil, the ancestral rules were too firmly rooted in the 'memory of men' and too closely bound up with a whole system of social organization very different from that of ancient Rome to be overthrown at the mere pleasure of a few teachers of law. But in all regions the hostility henceforth manifested to the old methods of proof, notably trial by battle, and the development, in public law, of the notion of treason owed something to the examples of the *Corpus Juris* and of the gloss. Here again the imitation of the ancient models received powerful support from quite other influences. There was the Church's horror of blood, as of every practice which might seem designed to 'tempt God'. There was the attraction—especially felt by the merchants—of more convenient and more rational procedures. And there was the renewed prestige of monarchy. If we find certain notaries of the twelfth and thirteenth centuries trying to express the realities of their age in the vocabulary of the Codes, these clumsy efforts scarcely affected fundamental human relations. It was by another route that Roman jurisprudence at that time exercised its true influence on living law, namely by teaching it to acquire a clearer conception of itself.

Looking with a new objectivity at the purely traditional precepts which had hitherto governed society after a fashion, men trained in the school of Roman law must inevitably have been inspired to remove their contradictions and uncertainties. It is in the nature of such attitudes to spread and it was not long before they passed beyond the relatively restricted circles which had a direct acquaintance with the marvellous instruments of intellectual analysis bequeathed by ancient jurisprudence. Here again, moreover, they were in harmony with more than one independent movement. Society was less uneducated than it had been and was filled with a great desire for the written word. More powerful groups—above all, the towns—demanded a more precise definition of rules whose uncertainty had lent itself to so much abuse. The consolidation of societies into great states or principalities favoured not only the revival of legislation but also the extension of a unifying jurisprudence over vast territories. It was not without justification that the author of the *Treatise on the Laws of England*, in the continuation of the passage cited above, emphasized the contrast between the discouraging multiplicity of local usages and the much more methodical practice of the royal court.[1] A characteristic feature of the Capetian kingdom is that about the year 1200, side by side with the old references to local custom in the narrowest sense of the word, there appear the names of much larger areas of customary law, such as France around Paris, Normandy, and Champagne. All these were signs that a work of crystallization was in progress, of which the closing years of the twelfth century witnessed at least the preliminaries, if not the completion.

In Italy, beginning with the charter of Pisa in 1142, the urban statutes

[1] See above, p. 112.

118

steadily increased in number. North of the Alps, the charters of enfranchisement granted to the townsmen tended more and more to become detailed statements of customs. In England, Henry II, the jurist king 'learned in the making and amending of laws, subtle inventor of unwonted judgments',[1] put out a mass of legislation. Under cover of the peace movement, the practice of legislation was reintroduced even in Germany. In France, Philip Augustus, prone in all things to imitate his English rivals, regulated a variety of feudal issues by ordinance.[2] Finally, we come across writers who, without official authorization and simply for the convenience of the practising lawyers, undertook the task of systematizing the rules in force around them. The initiative came, as was natural, from circles which had long ceased to rely upon a purely oral tradition. In northern Italy, for example, about 1150, a compiler brought together in a sort of *corpus* the opinions on the law of fiefs suggested to the lawyers of his country by the laws which the emperors had promulgated in their Lombard kingdom. In England, about 1187, in the circle of the justiciar Ranulf de Glanville, the *Treatise* to which we have already made several references was compiled. Next we have (*c.* 1200) the oldest Norman customary; and (*c.* 1221) the *Sachsenspiegel*, which was written in the vernacular[3] by a knight; double testimony to the far-reaching conquests of the new spirit.

The work was to be actively pursued during the following generations, and for this reason it is often necessary to make cautious use of relatively late works to understand a social structure which was never adequately described before the thirteenth century and which, in many of its features, survived into the Europe of the great monarchies. These later works reflect the organizing ability belonging to the great age of the cathedrals and the *Summae*. What historian of feudalism could ignore that admirable analyst of medieval society, Philippe de Beaumanoir, knightly poet and jurist, *bailli* to two kings of France (Philip III and Philip IV) and author, in 1283, of the *Coutumes* of Beauvaisis?

Since customary law was now taught and set down in writing and was in part fixed by legislation, it inevitably lost much of its variety and flexibility. There was certainly nothing to prevent it from developing, and it continued to do so, but change was less unconscious and consequently less frequent, for if one deliberates beforehand one may always decide not to make the contemplated change after all. A period of exceptional movement, an age of obscure and profound gestation, is therefore succeeded, from the second half of the twelfth century, by an era in which society tends to

---

[1] Walter Map, *De nugis curialium*, ed. M. R. James, p. 237.

[2] The kings of Jerusalem provide another and very early example of royal legislative activity. Cf. H. Mitteis, in *Beiträge zur Wirtschaftsrecht*, I, Marburg, 1931, and Grandclaude in *Mélanges Paul Fournier*, 1929. Another is that of the Norman kings of Sicily, though this was in part a continuation of traditions foreign to the West.

[3] At least in the only version which we possess; it was probably preceded by a Latin edition, now lost.

organize human relations more strictly, to establish more clear-cut divisions between the classes, to obliterate a great many local variations, and finally to allow change only at a slower rate. For this decisive metamorphosis of about the year 1200, the transformation of legal thought, closely linked as it was with other developments, was not solely responsible. There is no doubt, however, that it was a very important contributory factor.

PART III

The Ties between Man and Man: Kinship

IX

THE
SOLIDARITY OF THE KINDRED GROUP

1 THE 'FRIENDS BY BLOOD'

THE ties based on blood relationship existed long before, and were by their very nature foreign to, the human relations characteristic of feudalism; but they continued to exert such an important influence within the new structure that we cannot exclude them from our picture. Unfortunately this is not an easy subject for study. It was not without reason that in old France the family community of the country districts was commonly described as the 'silent' (*taisible*) community. Intercourse between close relatives naturally dispenses with writing. Though it was resorted to in exceptional cases, these specimens of family correspondence, which come almost exclusively from the upper classes, have for the most part perished —at least, those earlier than the thirteenth century. For the ecclesiastical archives are practically the only ones preserved up to that date. But that is not the only difficulty. A comprehensive picture of feudal institutions can be legitimately attempted because, originating at the very time when a real Europe was taking shape, they spread without fundamental differences to the whole European world. But the institutions of blood-relationship were, on the contrary, the legacy—and a singularly tenacious one—of the particular past of each of the groups of diverse origins whose destiny had brought them to live side by side. Compare for example the almost uniform character of the rules relating to the inheritance of the military fief with the almost infinite variety of those which regulated the transmission of other forms of property. In the following account, it will be more than ever necessary to concentrate upon a few major currents.

In the whole of feudal Europe, then, there existed groups founded on blood-relationship. The terms which served to describe them were rather indefinite—in France, most commonly, *parenté* or *lignage*. Yet the ties thus created were regarded as extremely strong. One word is characteristic. In France, in speaking of kinsfolk, one commonly called them simply 'friends' (*amis*) and in Germany, *Freunde*. A legal document of the eleventh century originating from the Île de France enumerates them thus: 'His friends, that is to say his mother, his brothers, his sisters and his other

123

relatives by blood or by marriage.'[1] Only with a regard for accuracy that was somewhat rare did people occasionally say expressly 'friends by blood' (*amis charnels*). The general assumption seems to have been that there was no real friendship save between persons united by blood.

The best-served hero was he whose warriors were all joined to him either by the new, feudal relationship of vassalage, or by the ancient tie of kinship—two equally binding ties which were ordinarily put on the same plane because they seemed to take precedence of all others. *Magen und mannen*—this alliteration is almost proverbial in the German epic. But poetry is not our only authority on the point, and the sagacious Joinville, even in the thirteenth century, knew well that if Guy de Mauvoisin's force did wonderfully well at Mansurah it was because it was composed entirely either of liegemen of the leader or of knights of his kin. Devotion reached its highest fervour when the two solidarities were mingled, as happened, according to the *geste*, to Duke Bègue whose thousand vassals were *trestous d'une parenté*—'everyone of the same kin'. Whence did a feudal noble, whether of Normandy or Flanders, derive his power, according to the chroniclers? From his castles, no doubt, from his handsome revenues in silver coin, and from the number of his vassals; but also from the number of his kinsmen. And the same thing was true at the lower levels, right down the social scale. It was true of merchants, as for example the burghers of Ghent of whom a writer who knew them well said that they possessed two great sources of strength: 'their towers'—patrician towers whose stone walls, in the towns, cast a huge shadow over the humble wooden dwellings of the people—and 'their kinsfolk'. It was true also of the members of those kindred groups—many of them peasants or at any rate simple freemen, with the modest wergild of 200 shillings—against whom, in the second half of the tenth century, the men of London were ready to go to war, 'if they prevent us from exercising our rights, by giving shelter to robbers'.[2]

The man who was brought before a court found in his kinsmen his natural helpers. Where the old Germanic procedure of compurgation or oath-helping remained in force, in which a collective oath sufficed to clear the accused of any charge or to confirm the complaint brought by a plaintiff, it was among the 'friends by blood' that either by law or by custom the oath-helpers must be found. A case in point was that of the four kinsmen who, at Usagre in Castile, were required to swear with a woman who

---

[1] *Cartulaire de Sainte Madeleine de Davron*: Bibl. Nat., MS. latin 5288. fol. 77 vo. This equivalence of the words 'friend' and 'relative' is found also in Welsh and Irish legal texts; cf. R. Thurneyssen, in *Zeitschr. der Savigny-Stiftung*, G.A., 1935, pp. 100–101.

[2] Joinville, ed., de Wailly (Soc. de l'histoire de France), p. 88; *Garin le Lorrain*, ed. P. Paris, I, p. 103; Robert of Torigny, ed. L. Delisle, pp. 224–5; Gislebert of Mons, ed. Pertz, pp. 235 and 258; Athelstan, *Laws*, VI, c. VIII, 2.

declared that she had been the victim of rape.[1] What if trial by battle were preferred, as a means of proof? In theory, Beaumanoir explains, it could be claimed only by one of the parties. There were, however, two exceptions to this rule: it was lawful for the liege vassal to demand battle on behalf of his lord, and any man could do so, if a member of his own kin was involved. Once more, the two relationships appear on the same footing. Thus we see, in the *Chanson de Roland*, Ganelon's kinsmen delegating one of their members to enter the lists against the traitor's accuser. In the *Chanson*, moreover, the solidarity of the kindred extends much farther still. After the defeat of their champion, the thirty kinsmen, who have 'stood surety' for him, are hanged all together on the tree of the Accursed Wood. A poet's exaggeration, beyond any doubt. The epic was a magnifying glass. But the poet's inventions could hope to find little response unless they conformed to the common sentiment. About 1200, the seneschal of Normandy, a representative of a more advanced stage of legal development, had difficulty in preventing his agents from including in the punishment of a criminal all his kinsfolk as well.[2] To such a degree did the individual and the group appear inseparable.

While the kinship group was a source of strength to the individual, it was also in its way a judge. To it, if we are to believe the *gestes*, the thoughts of the knight went out in the hour of peril. 'Come to my aid, that I may not play the poltroon and thereby bring shame upon my kindred'— was the simple prayer of Guillaume d'Orange to Our Lady;[3] and if Roland refuses to call to his aid the army of Charlemagne, it is for fear lest his kinsmen should incur reproach on his account. The honour or dishonour of one of the members of the little group reflected upon them all.

It was, however, especially in the vendetta that the ties of kinship showed themselves at their strongest.

2 THE VENDETTA

The Middle Ages, from beginning to end, and particularly the feudal era, lived under the sign of private vengeance. The onus, of course, lay above all on the wronged individual; vengeance was imposed on him as the most sacred of duties—to be pursued even beyond the grave. A rich Florentine, Velluto di Buonchristiano, was a member of one of those citizen communities whose very independence of the great states bred a deep-rooted regard for traditional points of honour. Having been mortally wounded by one of his enemies, in 1310 he made his will. Now a will, in the eyes of that age, was a work of piety as much as of wise provision and was intended above all to ensure the salvation of the soul by devout bequests.

[1] E. de Hinojosa, 'Das germanische Element im spanischen Rechte' in *Zeitschrift der Savigny-Stiftung*, G.A., 1910, p. 291, n. 2.
[2] J. Tardif, *Coutumiers de Normandie*, I, p. 52, c. LXI.
[3] *Le Couronnement de Louis*, ed. E. Langlois, vv. 787-9.

Yet even in such a document Velluto was not afraid to set down a legacy in favour of his avenger, if one were to be found.[1]

The solitary individual, however, could do but little. Moreover, it was most commonly a death that had to be avenged. In this case the family group went into action and the *faide* (feud) came into being, to use the old Germanic word which spread little by little through the whole of Europe —'the vengeance of the kinsmen which we call *faida*', as a German canonist expressed it.[2] No moral obligation seemed more sacred than this. In Flanders, about the end of the twelfth century, there lived a noble lady whose husband and two children had been killed by enemies; from that time, the blood-feud disturbed the surrounding countryside. A saintly man, Bishop Arnulf of Soissons, came to preach reconciliation, and to avoid listening to him the widow had the drawbridge raised. Among the Frisians, the very corpse cried out for vengeance; it hung withering in the house till the day when, the vengeance accomplished, the kinsmen had at last the right to bury it.[3] Even in the last decades of the thirteenth century, why did the wise Beaumanoir, the servant of French kings pre-eminent in the maintenance of peace, deem it desirable that everyone should be able to determine the degrees of relationship? In order, he says, that in private wars a man might be able to call upon 'the aid of his kinsman'.

The whole kindred, therefore, placed as a rule under the command of a 'chieftain', took up arms to punish the murder of one of its members or merely a wrong that he had suffered. But vengeance was not directed solely against the author of the wrong himself, for active solidarity was matched by a passive solidarity equally strong. In Frisia, the death of the murderer was not necessary in order that the corpse, its wrong requited, should be laid in the grave; the death of a member of the murderer's family was enough. And if, as we are told, twenty-four years after making his will Velluto found at last in one of his kinsmen the desired avenger, the vengeance, in its turn, fell not on the guilty man himself but on a kinsman. There is no better proof of the power and endurance of these ideas than a decree—a relatively late one—of the Parlement of Paris. In 1260, a knight, Louis Defeux, was wounded by a certain Thomas d'Ouzouer and proceeded against his assailant in court. The accused did not deny the fact, but he explained that he had himself been attacked some time before by a nephew of his victim. What offence, then, had he committed? Had he not, in conformity with the royal ordinances, waited forty days before taking his revenge—the time held to be necessary to warn one's kindred of the danger? Agreed, replied the knight; but what my nephew has done is no concern of mine. The argument availed him nothing, for the act of

---

[1] R. Davidsohn, *Geschichte von Florenz*, IV, 3, 1927, pp. 370 and 384–5.

[2] Regino of Prüm, *De synodalibus causis*, ed. Wasserschleben, II, 5.

[3] Hariulf, *Vita Arnulfi episcopi*, in *M.G.H., SS.*, XV, p. 889; Thomas de Cantimpré, *Bonum universale de apibus*, II, 1, 15.

an individual involved all his kinsfolk. Such, at any rate, was the decision of the judges of the pious and peace-loving St. Louis. Blood thus called for blood, and interminable quarrels arising from often futile causes set the hostile houses at each other's throats. In the eleventh century a dispute between two noble houses of Burgundy, begun one day during the vintage season, went on for thirty years, and in the course of it one of the parties had lost more than eleven men.[1]

Among these feuds, the chronicles have recorded especially the conflicts of the great noble families, as for example the 'perdurable hatred', mixed with abominable treacheries, which in twelfth-century Normandy embroiled the Giroys with the Talvas.[2] In the tales chanted by the minstrels, the nobility found the echo of their passions, elevated to epic grandeur. The blood-feuds of the *Lorrains* against the *Bordelais*, of the kindred of Raoul de Cambrai against those of Herbert de Vermandois, make up some of the finest of the *gestes*. The mortal blow dealt on a feast day by one of the children of Lara to one of the kinsmen of his aunt engendered the series of murders which, linked one to another, constitute the thread of a celebrated Spanish *cantar*. But at every level of society the same customs prevailed. It is true that when in the thirteenth century the nobility had finally become a hereditary body, it tended to reserve for itself as a mark of honour any form of recourse to arms. Legal doctrine and the public authorities—such as the count's court of Hainault in 1275[3]—readily followed suit, partly from sympathy with the prejudices of the noble class, but also partly from a more or less obscure desire on the part of princes or jurists preoccupied with keeping the peace, to prevent the fire from spreading. To impose on a military caste the renunciation of all private vengeance was neither possible in practice nor conceivable in principle; but at any rate a big step forward would have been taken if it could be imposed on the rest of the population. Thus violence became a class privilege—at least in theory. For even authors who, like Beaumanoir, consider that 'it is not permissible for others than noblemen to wage war' scarcely leave us in doubt as to the restricted implications of that rule. Arezzo was not the only city from which St. Francis could have exorcised the demons of discord, as in the paintings on the walls of the basilica at Assisi. The first urban constitutions had as their principal concern the maintenance of peace and appeared essentially—according to the very name they sometimes adopted—as acts of 'peace'. The main reason for this was that, among many other causes of strife, the rising bourgeoisie was torn, as again

[1] Ralph Glaber, ed. Prou, II, c. x.

[2] In the Vicomte de Motey's book, *Origines de la Normandie et du duché d'Alençon*, 1920, there is an account of this feud inspired by a candid partiality in favour of the Talvas.

[3] F. Cattier, *La Guerre privée dans le comté de Hainaut* in *Annales de la Faculté de philosophie de Bruxelles*, I, 1889–90. Cf. for Bavaria, Schnelbögl, *Die innere Entwicklung des bayerischen Landfriedens*, 1932, p. 312.

Beaumanoir says, 'by the strife and hatred which set one family against another'. The little that we know about the obscure life of the country districts shows that there too a similar state of things prevailed.

Such aggressive sentiments did not, however, hold undivided sway in men's minds. They were countered by other forces—the horror of bloodshed inculcated by the Church, the traditional notion of the public peace, and, above all, the need for that peace. The history of the painful efforts throughout the feudal era to establish internal order—of which more hereunder —provides striking evidence of the evils that it sought to combat.

The 'mortal hatreds'—the phrase had assumed an almost technical meaning—which the ties of kinship engendered ranked undoubtedly among the principal causes of the general disorder. But since they were an integral part of a moral code to which in their heart of hearts the most ardent champions of peace undoubtedly remained faithful, only a few utopians could believe it feasible to abolish them altogether. While fixing penalties, or naming places where violence of any sort was prohibited, many of the peace pacts still recognized the legality of the blood-feud. The authorities for the most part adopted a similar policy. They sought to protect innocent people against the most flagrant abuses of family solidarity, and they fixed the period of grace. They also strove to draw a distinction between lawful reprisals and plain brigandage carried out under the pretext of justifiable vengeance.[1] They tried sometimes to limit the number and nature of the wrongs which could be expiated in blood; in the Norman ordinances of William the Conqueror only the murder of a father or a son was so classified. They ventured increasingly, as they grew stronger, to forestall private vengeance by the repression of flagrant offences or of crimes which came under the heading of violations of the peace. Above all, they laboured to bring the hostile groups to reason, and sometimes to compel them to conclude treaties of armistice or reconciliation under the arbitration of the courts. In short, except in England where, after the Conquest, the disappearance of any legal right of vengeance was one of the aspects of the royal 'tyranny', they confined themselves to moderating the more extreme manifestations of practices which they were unable and perhaps unwilling to stop altogether. The judicial procedures themselves, when by chance the injured party preferred them to direct action, were hardly more than regularized vendettas. A significant illustration, in the case of wilful murder, is the allocation of rights and responsibilities laid down in 1232 by the municipal charter of Arques, in Artois. To the lord is assigned the property of the guilty man; to the kinsmen of his victim his person, so that they may put him to death.[2] The right of lodging a complaint belonged almost

[1] For example, in Flanders: Walterus, *Vita Karoli, c.* 19, in *M.G.H., SS.,* XII, p. 547.
[2] G. Espinas, *Recueil de documents relatifs à l'histoire du droit municipal, Artois,* I, p. 236, c. XXVIII. It is significant that this provision had disappeared from the *Keure* of 1469, p. 251, c. IV j.

invariably to the relatives alone;[1] and even in the thirteenth century in the best governed cities and principalities, in Flanders for example or in Normandy, the murderer could not receive his pardon from the sovereign or the judges unless he had first reached an agreement with the kinsmen of the victim.

For, important as might seem 'those old, well-nourished hatreds', of which the Spanish poets speak complacently, they could hardly be expected to go on for ever. Sooner or later, it was necessary to renounce—as the poet of *Girart de Roussillon* expressed it—'the vengeance of dead men'. According to a very ancient custom the reconciliation was normally effected by means of an indemnity. 'Buy off the spear aimed at your breast, if you do not wish to feel its point'—this old Anglo-Saxon saying was still wise counsel.[2]

The regular tariffs of composition which in the past the barbarian laws had set forth in such detail and, in particular, the meticulous gradation of wergilds now survived only in a few places—in Frisia, in Flanders, and in some regions of Spain—and then only in a much modified form. In Saxony, which was on the whole conservative, the system of tariffs was indeed mentioned in the *Sachsenspiegel*, compiled in the early thirteenth century; but it scarcely figures there save as a rather meaningless archaism. And the *relief de l'homme*, which under St. Louis certain texts from the Loire valley continued to fix at 100 *solidi*, was applied only in exceptional circumstances.[3] How should it have been otherwise? The old barbarian codes had been replaced by local customs which were thenceforth common to populations with very different penal traditions. The governing powers, which formerly took an interest in the strict payment of the prescribed sums because they obtained a share of them, had, during the anarchy of the tenth and eleventh centuries, lost the strength to claim anything at all. Finally and above all, the class distinctions on which the ancient assessments were based had been profoundly modified.

But the disappearance of the fixed scales did not affect the practice of compensation itself. This continued till the end of the Middle Ages to compete with the physical penalties advocated by the supporters of the peace movement as being more effective deterrents. But the compensation for injury or murder—to which was sometimes added a pious foundation on behalf of the departed soul—was henceforth determined in each particular case by agreement, arbitration, or judicial decision. Thus, to cite only two examples, taken from the two extremities of the social scale, about 1160 the bishop of Bayeux received a church from a kinsman of the nobleman

---

[1] It also belonged, as we shall see later, to the lord of the victim or to his vassal—though this was the result of a virtual assimilation of the tie of personal protection and dependence to that of kinship.

[2] *Girart de Roussillon*, trans. by P. Meyer, p. 104, no. 787; *Leges Edwardi Confessoris*, XII, 6.

[3] *Établissements de Saint Louis*, ed. P. Viollet, in table.

who had killed his niece; and in 1227 a peasant woman of Sens obtained a small sum of money from the murderer of her husband.[1]

Like the blood-feud itself, the payment which put an end to it concerned the whole group. Where a simple wrong was involved, it seems that the practice had been established at a very early date of limiting the compensation to the wronged individual. But suppose that, on the contrary, it was a case of murder or, as sometimes also happened, of mutilation. Then it was the kinsmen of the victim who received the wergild in whole or in part, and the kinsmen of the guilty person who contributed to the payment. In some regions set indemnities had been fixed by law, but elsewhere habit was the deciding factor, or perhaps a mere sense of fitness, both sufficiently compelling to be recognized by the authorities as having almost the force of law. The clerks of the chancery of Philip the Fair transcribed in their formulary, under the heading 'Of the finance of kinsmen', a royal decree requiring that the share of the payment due from the different kinsmen concerned be fixed according to ascertained custom. No doubt they expected to have to make frequent use of this model.[2]

The payment of an indemnity did not as a rule suffice to seal the agreement. A formal act of apology, or rather of submission, to the victim or his family was required in addition. Usually, at least among persons of relatively high rank, it assumed the form of the most gravely significant gesture of subordination known in that day—homage 'of mouth and hands'. Here again it was groups rather than individuals that confronted each other. When in 1208 the steward of the monks of Saint-Denis, at Argenteuil, made peace with the steward of the lord of Montmorency whom he had wounded, he was obliged to bring with him for the expiatory homage twenty-nine of his kinsmen. In March 1134, after the assassination of the sub-dean of Orleans, all the relatives of the dead man assembled to receive the homage not only of one of the murderers, of his accomplices and of his vassals, but also of the 'best of his kin'—in all, two hundred and forty persons.[3] In every way a man's action was propagated throughout the circle of his kinsfolk in successive waves.

3 ECONOMIC SOLIDARITY

The feudal West universally recognized the legality of individual possession, but in practice the solidarity of the kindred was frequently extended to community of goods. Throughout the country districts there were numerous 'brotherhoods'—groups consisting of several related households sharing the same hearth and the same board and cultivating the same common

---

[1] L. Delisle and E. Berger, *Recueil des actes de Henri II*, no. CLXII; cf. CXCIV; M. Quantin, *Recueil de pièces pour faire suite au cartulaire général de l' Yonne*, no. 349.

[2] Bibl. Nat., MS. latin 4763, fol. 47 ro.

[3] Félibien, *Histoire de l'abbaye royale de Saint Denys*, docs., no. CLV; A. Luchaire, *Louis VI*, no. 531.

IV. THE LOVER'S HOMAGE

From the seal of Raymond de Mondragon, 12th century. Cabinet des
Médailles, Bibliothéque Nationale, Paris.

V. INVESTITURE BY THE STANDARD

Charlemagne invests Roland with the Spanish March. From the *Rolandslied* of Konrad of Regensburg, 12th century. University Library, Heidelberg, MS. Palat. germ. 112.

fields. The lord frequently encouraged or even enforced these arrangements, for he considered it an advantage to hold the members of the 'communal households' jointly responsible, willy-nilly, for the payment of dues. In a great part of France the law of succession applicable to serfs knew no other system of devolution than the continuance of an already existing household community. Suppose that the natural heir, a son or sometimes a brother, had, before the succession took effect, abandoned the communal home. Then, but only then, were his rights completely extinguished in favour of those of the master.

Undoubtedly such arrangements were less common in the higher classes of society, partly because the division of property automatically becomes easier as wealth increases, but mainly, perhaps, because seignorial rights could not be clearly distinguished from political authority, which by its very nature was less easily exercised by a group. Many petty lords, however, particularly in central France and in Tuscany, practised parcenary just as the peasants did, exploiting their inheritance in common, living all together in the ancestral castle or at least sharing in its defence. These were the 'parceners of the ragged cloak', whom the troubadour, Bertrand de Born, himself one of their number, makes the very type of poor knights. To this category, as late as 1251, belonged the thirty-one co-possessors of a castle in the Gévaudan.[1] Suppose that by chance a stranger succeeded in joining the group. Whether it was a question of rustics or of persons of higher rank, the act of association was likely to take the form of a fictitious 'fraternity'—as if the only really solid social contract was one which, if not based on actual blood-relationship, at least imitated its ties. The great nobles themselves were not always strangers to these communitary practices. For several generations, the Boso family, who controlled the Provençal counties, while reserving to each branch of the family its particular zone of influence, regarded the general government of the fief as undivided, and all assumed the same title of 'count' or 'prince' of the whole of Provence.

Even when individual possession clearly prevailed, it was not on that account entirely free from family impediment. This age of legal 'participation' saw no contradiction between terms which we should probably consider conflicting. The deeds of sale or gift for the tenth, eleventh and twelfth centuries which the ecclesiastical muniment chests have preserved for us are instructive. Frequently, in a preamble written by the clerics, the alienator proclaims his right to dispose of his goods in complete freedom. Such was, in fact, the theory of the Church. Continually enriched by gifts, entrusted moreover with the guardianship of souls, it could scarcely have admitted that any obstacle stood in the way of the faithful desirous of

---

[1] B. de Born, ed. Appel, 19, vv. 16–17; C. Porée, 'Les Statuts de la communauté des seigneurs pariers de La Garde-Guérin (1238–1313)' in *Bibliothèque de l'École des Chartes*, 1907, and *Études historiques sur le Gévaudan*, 1919.

assuring their salvation or that of those dear to them. The interests of the greater nobility, whose patrimony was augmented by cessions of land agreed to more or less voluntarily by the small land-owners, pointed in the same direction. As early as the ninth century, the Saxon law enumerates the circumstances in which alienation—if it involves the disinheriting of the relatives—is permitted; and it is not by mere chance that among these cases, together with gifts to the churches and the king, it lists that of the poor devil who, 'compelled by hunger', has made it a condition that he be supported by the powerful man to whom he has made over his bit of ground.[1]

But loudly as these charters or deeds may proclaim the rights of the individual, they almost never fail to mention at a later stage the consent of the various relatives of the vendor or donor. Such consent seemed so far necessary that as a rule there was no hesitation in paying for it. But suppose that some relative, not having been consulted at the time, should claim (perhaps after many years) that the contract is null and void. The beneficiaries complain bitterly about the injustice and impiety of his action; sometimes they take the case to court and obtain judgment in their favour.[2] Nine times out of ten, however, despite protests and judgments, they are obliged after all to compound. Of course, there was no question of protection being given to heirs, in the restricted sense of the term, as in our legal system. No fixed principle limited the size of the group whose consent was considered necessary, and collaterals might intervene despite the presence of direct descendants; or in the same branch the different generations might be called on concurrently to give their approval. The ideal was to obtain, as a bailiff of Chartres undertook to do—even when wife, children and sisters had already given their consent—the favourable opinion of 'as many kinsmen and relatives as possible'.[3] The whole family felt that it had suffered damage when a property passed out of its grip.

Nevertheless, from the twelfth century onwards, customs which were often vague but which were governed by a few broad collective principles were gradually replaced by a system of law more devoted to precision and clarity, whilst changes in the economy rendered restrictions on buying and selling more and more irksome. Formerly, sales of landed property had been somewhat rare; their very legality seemed doubtful, in the eyes of public opinion, unless there was the excuse of great 'poverty'. Thus when the purchaser was a church, the sale was apt to be disguised under the name of a pious donation. Actually the vendor expected from his pretence, which was only half deception, a double gain. In this world he would receive the purchase-price (though a lower one perhaps than it would have been

---

[1] *Lex Saxonum*, c. LXII.

[2] See an example (judgment of the court of Blois), C. Métais, *Cartulaire de Notre-Dame de Josaphat*, I, no. CIII; cf. no. CII.

[3] B. Guérard, *Cartulaire de l'abbaye de Saint-Père de Chartres*, II, p. 278, no. XIX.

in the absence of any other remuneration); in the next, the salvation of his soul, obtained through the prayers of the servants of God.

From now on, however, genuine sale became a frequent operation, conducted without disguise. To be absolutely free it would have required what was to be found only in societies of an exceptional type—the commercial spirit and audacity of a few great burgher communities. Outside these circles the sale of land was governed by its own law, clearly distinguished from that relating to gifts—a law still subject to some limitations, though these were less strict than in the past and much better defined. The tendency at first was to require that before every alienation for value received the property should be offered first to one of the relatives, provided it had itself been acquired by inheritance—a significant restriction and one which was retained.[1] Finally, from about the beginning of the thirteenth century, family control was reduced to a simple recognition of the right of the relatives, within prescribed limits and according to a stipulated order, to take the place of the buyer once the sale had occurred, on repayment of the price already paid. In medieval society there was scarcely an institution more universal than this right of redemption enjoyed by relatives (*retrait lignager*). With the single exception of England[2]—and even there it is found in certain municipal customs—it prevailed everywhere from Sweden to Italy. Nor was there an institution more firmly rooted; in France, it was abolished only by the Revolution. Thus, through the centuries, in more precise though more attenuated forms, the economic influence of the family lived on.

[1] This restriction appears, as early as 1055–70, in a document of the *Livre Noir de Saint-Florent de Saumur: Bibl. Nat. nouv. acquis. lat. 1930, fol. 113 vo.

[2] As early as the Anglo-Saxon period, it should be added, there had been created in England a category of estates (not very numerous, it is true) which, under the name of 'bookland', were not subject to customary restrictions and could be alienated freely.

X

CHARACTER AND VICISSITUDES OF
THE TIE OF KINSHIP

1 THE REALITIES OF FAMILY LIFE

IN spite of the power of the family to give support to its members or impose restraints upon them, it would be a grave error to picture its internal life in uniformly idyllic colours. The fact that the family groups engaged readily in blood-feuds did not always prevent the most atrocious intestine quarrels. Though Beaumanoir finds wars between kinsmen distressing, he obviously does not regard them as exceptional or even, except when waged between full brothers, as actually unlawful. To understand the prevailing attitude it is enough to consult the history of the princely houses. If, for example, we were to follow from generation to generation the destiny of the Angevins, the true Atrides of the Middle Ages, we should read of the 'more than civil' war which for seven years embroiled the count Fulk Nerra with his son Geoffrey Martel; of how Fulk le Réchin, after having dispossessed his brother, threw him into prison—to release him only as a madman, at the end of eighteen years; of the furious hatred of the sons of Henry II for their father; and finally of the assassination of Arthur by his uncle, King John.

In the class immediately below, there are the bloody quarrels of so many middle and lesser lords over the family castle; as for example the case of that Flemish knight who, having been turned out of his home by his two brothers and having seen them massacre his wife and child, killed one of the murderers with his own hands.[1] More terrible still was the affair of the viscounts of Comborn, one of those tales for strong stomachs that lose nothing of their flavour through being set down by the tranquil pen of a monastic writer.[2] At the outset, we learn of the viscount Archambaud who, to avenge his deserted mother, kills one of his half-brothers and then, many years later, buys his father's pardon by the murder of a knight who had earlier inflicted an incurable wound on the old nobleman. The viscount leaves, in his turn, three sons. The eldest, who has inherited the viscounty, dies shortly afterwards, leaving a young boy as his only

---

[1] *Miracula S. Ursmari*, c. 6, in *M.G.H., SS.*, XV, 2, p. 839.
[2] Geoffroi de Vigeois, I, 25, in Labbé, *Bibliotheca nova*, II, p. 291.

descendant. Mistrustful of the second brother, it is to the youngest, Bernard, that he confides the protection of his estates during the minority of his son. Arrived at the age of knighthood, 'the child' Eble vainly claims the inheritance. Thanks to the mediation of friends, however, he obtains the castle of Comborn though nothing else. He resides there, with rage in his heart, till one day his aunt (Bernard's wife) accidentally falls into his hands. He violates her publicly, hoping in this way to compel the outraged husband to repudiate her. Bernard takes his wife back and prepares his revenge. One fine day, he rides past the walls of the castle with a small escort, as if out of bravado. Eble, just rising from table, his brain clouded by drink, sets out madly in pursuit. After having gone a little way, the pretended fugitives turn, set upon the youth and wound him mortally. This tragic end, the wrongs which the victim had suffered, and above all his youth, so moved the people that for several days offerings were laid on his temporary grave at the spot where he was killed, as if it were the shrine of a martyr. But the perjured and blood-stained uncle and his descendants after him remained in undisturbed possession of both the castle and the viscounty.

None of this need surprise us. In these centuries of violence and high-strung emotions social ties could easily seem very strong and even show themselves frequently to be so, and yet be ruptured by an outburst of passion. But even apart from these brutal quarrels, provoked as often by greed as by anger, the fact remains that in the most normal circumstances, a strong sense of community was quite compatible with a pretty callous attitude towards individuals. As was natural perhaps in a society in which kinship was above all regarded as a basis of mutual help, the group counted for much more than its members taken individually. It is to the official historian employed by a great baronial family that we owe the record of a characteristic remark made one day by the ancestor of the line. John, the marshal of England, had refused, in spite of his promises, to surrender one of his castles to King Stephen. His enemies therefore threatened to execute before his eyes his young son, whom he had a short while before handed over as a hostage. 'What recks it me of the child,' replied the good nobleman, 'have I not still the anvils and the hammers wherewith to forge finer ones?'[1] As for marriage, it was often quite frankly a mere combining of interests and, for women, a protective institution. Listen, in the *Poem of the Cid*, to the words of the hero's daughters, to whom their father has just announced that he has promised them to the sons of Carrion. The maidens who, needless to say, have never seen their prospective husbands express their thanks: 'When you have married us, we shall be rich ladies.' These conventions were so strong that among peoples who were yet profoundly Christian they led to a strange conflict between social habits and religious laws.

[1] *L'Histoire de Guillaume le Maréchal*, ed. P. Meyer, I, v. 399 *et seq.*

The Church had no love for second or third marriages, although it was not expressly opposed to them. Nevertheless, from top to bottom of the social scale remarriage was almost universal. This was partly no doubt from the desire to place the satisfaction of the flesh under the shelter of the sacrament; but another reason was that when the husband had died first, it seemed too dangerous for the wife to live alone. Moreover in every estate that fell to the distaff side the lord saw a threat to the proper performance of the services due from it. When in 1119, after the defeat of the chivalry of Antioch at the Field of Blood, King Baldwin II of Jerusalem undertook the reorganization of the principality, he made a point both of preserving their heritage for the orphans and of finding new husbands for the widows. And, of the death of six of his knights in Egypt, Joinville naively remarks: 'Wherefore the wives of all six of them had to remarry.'[1] Sometimes seignorial authority even went to the length of ordering that peasant women whom an untimely widowhood prevented from properly cultivating their fields or carrying out the prescribed labour services should be provided with husbands.

The Church proclaimed the indissolubility of the conjugal tie; but this did not prevent frequent repudiations, especially among the upper classes, often inspired by the most worldly considerations. Witness, among a great many others, the matrimonial adventures of John the Marshal, narrated, always in the same level tone, by the *trouvère* in the service of his grandsons. He had married a lady of high lineage, endowed—if we are to believe the poet—with all the highest qualities of body and mind: 'great joy had they together'. Unfortunately, John had also an 'over-mighty neighbour' whom prudence required him to conciliate. He got rid of his charming wife and married the sister of this dangerous personage.

But to place marriage at the centre of the family group would certainly be to distort the realities of the feudal era. The wife only half belonged to the family in which her destiny had placed her, perhaps not for very long. 'Be quiet,' says Garin le Lorrain roughly to the widow of his murdered brother who is weeping over the body and bemoaning her lot, 'a noble knight will take you up again . . . it is I who must continue in deep mourning.'[2] In the relatively late poem of the *Nibelungen*, Kriemhild avenges on her brothers the death of Siegfried, her first husband—although it must be admitted that the justice of her action seems by no means certain; but it appears that in the primitive version of the story she pursued the blood-feud of her brothers against Attila, her second husband and their murderer. Both in its emotional climate and in its size, the family of those days was quite a different thing from the small conjugal family of later times. What then, precisely, was its scope?

[1] William of Tyre, XII, 12; Joinville, ed. de Wailly (*Soc. de l'Hist. de France*), pp. 105–106.
[2] *Garin le Lorrain*, ed. P. Paris, II, p. 268.

2 THE STRUCTURE OF THE FAMILY

Vast *gentes* or clans, firmly defined and held together by a belief—whether true or false—in a common ancestry, were unknown to western Europe in the feudal period, save on its outer fringes, beyond the genuinely feudalized regions. On the shores of the North Sea there were the *Geschlechter* of Frisia or of Dithmarschen; in the west, Celtic tribes or clans. It seems certain that groups of this nature had still existed among the Germans in the period of the invasions. There were, for example, the Lombard and Frankish *farae* of which more than one Italian or French village continues today to bear the name; and there were also the *genealogiae* of the Alemans and Bavarians which certain texts show in possession of the soil. But these excessively large units gradually disintegrated.

The Roman *gens* had owed the exceptional firmness of its pattern to the absolute primacy of descent in the male line. Nothing like this was known in the feudal epoch. Already in ancient Germany each individual had two kinds of relative, those 'of the spear side', and those 'of the distaff side', and he was bound, though in different degrees, to the second as well as to the first. It was as though among the Germans the victory of the agnatic principle had never been sufficiently complete to extinguish all trace of a more ancient system of uterine filiation. Unfortunately we know almost nothing of the native family traditions of the countries conquered by Rome. But, whatever one is to think of these problems of origins, it is at all events certain that in the medieval West kinship had acquired or retained a distinctly dual character. The sentimental importance with which the epic invested the relations of the maternal uncle and his nephew is but one of the expressions of a system in which the ties of relationship through women were nearly as important as those of paternal consanguinity.[1] One proof of this is the clear evidence from the practices of name-giving.

The majority of Germanic personal names were formed by linking two elements, each of which had a meaning of its own. So long as people continued to be aware of the distinction between the two stems, it was the common custom, if not the rule, to mark the filiation by borrowing one of the components. This was true even in Romance-speaking regions where the prestige of the conquerors had led to the widespread imitation of their name system by the native peoples. Children took their names either from the father or the mother; there seems to have been no fixed rule. In the village of Palaiseau, for example, at the beginning of the ninth century, the peasant *Teud-ricus* and his wife *Ermen-berta* baptized one of their sons *Teut-hardus*, another *Erment-arius*, and the third, by way of a

[1] W. O. Farnsworth, *Uncle and Nephew in the Old French Chansons de Geste: a Study in the Survival of Matriarchy*, New York, 1913 (Columbia University: Studies in Romance Philology and Literature); C. H. Bell, *The Sister's Son in the Medieval German Epic: a Study in the Survival of Matriliny*, 1922 (University of California: Publications in Modern Philology, Vol. X, no. 2).

double memorial, *Teut-bertus*.[1] Then the practice developed of handing down the whole name from generation to generation. This was done again by taking the name from each side alternately. Thus of the two sons of Lisois, lord of Amboise, who died in 1065, one was named after his father but the other, who was the elder, was named Sulpice like his maternal grandfather and uncle. Still later, when people had begun to add patronymics to Christian names, they vacillated for a long time between the two modes of transmission. 'I am called sometimes Jeanne d'Arc and sometimes Jeanne Romée,' said the daughter of Jacques d'Arc and Isabelle Romée to her judges. History knows her only by the first of these names; but she pointed out that in her part of the country it was customary to give daughters the surname of their mother.

This double link had important consequences. Since each generation thus had its circle of relatives which was not the same as that of the previous generation, the area of the kindred's responsibilities continually changed its contours. The duties were rigorous; but the group was too unstable to serve as the basis of the whole social structure. Worse still, when two families clashed it might very well be that the same individual belonged to both—to one of them through his father and to the other through his mother. How was he to choose between them? Wisely, Beaumanoir's choice is to side with the nearest relative, and if the degrees are equal, to stand aloof. Doubtless in practice the decision was often dictated by personal preference. When we come to deal with feudal relations in the strict sense, we shall encounter aspects of this legal dilemma in the case of the vassal of two lords. The dilemma arose from a particular attitude of mind and in the long run it had the effect of loosening the tie. There was great internal weakness in a family system which compelled people to recognize, as they did in Beauvaisis in the thirteenth century, the legitimacy of a war between two brothers, sons of the same father (though by different marriages), who found themselves caught up in a vendetta between their maternal relatives.

How far along the lines of descent did the obligations towards 'friends by blood' extend? We do not find their limits defined with any precision save in the groups that maintained the regular scale of compensation, and even here the customs were set down in writing only at a relatively late date. All the more significant is the fact that the zones of active and passive solidarity which they fixed were surprisingly large, and that they were, moreover, graduated zones, in which the amount of the indemnity varied according to the closeness of the relationship. At Sepulveda in Castile in the thirteenth century it was sufficient, in order that the vengeance wreaked on the murderer of a relative should not be treated as a crime, for the

---

[1] *Polyptyque de l'abbé Irminon*, ed. A. Longnon, II, 87. The desire to mark the double filiation occasionally had oddly nonsensical results, as for example the Anglo-Saxon name Wigfrith which, literally translated, means 'war-peace'.

avenger to have the same great-great-grandfather as the original victim. The same degree of relationship entitled one to receive a part of the blood money according to the law of Oudenarde and, at Lille, made it obligatory to contribute to its payment. At Saint-Omer they went so far as to derive the obligation to contribute from a common founder of the line as remote as a grandfather of a great-grandfather.[1] Elsewhere, the outline was vaguer. But, as has already been pointed out, it was considered only prudent in the case of alienations to ask the consent of as many collaterals as possible. As for the 'silent' communities of the country districts, they long continued to gather together many individuals under one roof—we hear of as many as fifty in eleventh-century Bavaria and sixty-six in fifteenth-century Normandy.[2]

On close examination, however, it looks as if from the thirteenth century onwards a sort of contraction was in process. The vast kindreds of not so long before were slowly being replaced by groups much more like our small families of today. Towards the end of the century, Beaumanoir felt that the circle of people bound by the obligation of vengeance had been constantly dwindling—to the point where, in his day, in contrast with the previous age, only second cousins, or perhaps only first cousins (among whom the obligation continued to be very strongly felt), were included. From the latter years of the twelfth century we note in the French charters a tendency to restrict to the next of kin the request for family approval. Then came the system under which the relatives enjoyed the right of redemption. With the distinction which it established between acquired possessions and family possessions and, among the latter, between possessions subject, according to their origin, to the claims of either the paternal or the maternal line, it conformed much less than the earlier practice to the conception of an almost unlimited kinship. The rhythms of this evolution naturally varied greatly from place to place. It will suffice here to indicate very briefly the most general and most likely causes of a change which was pregnant with important consequences.

Undoubtedly the governmental authorities, through their activities as guardians of the peace, contributed to the weakening of the kinship bond. This they did in many ways and notably, like William the Conqueror, by limiting the sphere of lawful blood-feud; above all, perhaps, by encouraging refusal to take any part in the vendetta. Voluntary withdrawal from the kindred group was an ancient and general right; but whilst it enabled the individual to avoid many risks, it deprived him for the future of a form of protection long regarded as indispensable. Once the protection of the State

---

[1] *Livre Roisin*, ed. R. Monier, 1932, 143–4; A. Giry, *Histoire de la ville de Saint-Omer*, II, p. 578, c. 791. This explains why the canon law was able without too much presumption to extend the prohibition of consanguineous marriages to cousins of the seventh degree.

[2] *Annales Altahenses maiores*, 1037, in *M.G.H., SS.*, XX, p. 792. Jehan Masselin, *Journal des États Généraux*, ed, A. Bernier, pp. 582–4.

had become more effective, these 'forswearings' became less dangerous. The government sometimes did not hesitate to impose them. Thus, in 1181, the count of Hainault, after a murder had been perpetrated, forestalled the blood-feud by burning down the houses of all the relatives of the guilty man and extorting from them a promise not to give him succour. Nevertheless the disintegration and attenuation of the kindred group, both as an economic unit and as an instrument of the feud, seems to have been in the main the result of deeper social changes. The development of trade conduced to the limitation of family impediments to the sale of property; the progress of intercommunication led to the break-up of excessively large groups which, in the absence of any legal status, could scarcely preserve their sense of unity except by staying together in one place. The invasions had already dealt an almost mortal blow at the much more solidly constituted *Geschlechter* of ancient Germany. The rude shocks to which England was subjected—Scandinavian inroads and settlement, Norman conquest—were doubtless an important factor in the premature decay in that country of the old framework of the kindred. In practically the whole of Europe, at the time of the great movement of land reclamation, the attraction of the new urban centres and of the villages founded on the newly cleared lands undoubtedly broke up many peasant communities. It was no accident if, in France at least, these brotherhoods held together much longer in the poorest provinces.

It is a curious but not inexplicable fact that this period, in which the large kinship groups of earlier ages began to disintegrate in this way, was precisely that in which family names first appeared, though as yet in a very rudimentary form. Like the Roman *gentes*, the *Geschlechter* of Frisia and Dithmarschen both had their traditional labels. So too, in the Germanic period, had the dynasties of chiefs, invested with a sacred hereditary character. The families of the feudal era, on the contrary, remained for a long time strangely anonymous, partly no doubt on account of the vagueness of their outlines, but also because the genealogies were too well known for anyone to feel the need of a verbal reminder. Then, especially from the twelfth century onwards, it became a common practice to add to the original single name—the Christian or given name we should call it today—a nickname or perhaps a second Christian name. The disuse into which many old names had fallen, together with the growth of population, had the effect of increasing the number of homonyms in the most troublesome way. At the same time, the increased use of written legal material and a generally growing desire for clarity made the confusions arising from this poverty of names less and less tolerable, and impelled people to seek distinctive labels.

But these were still purely individual appellations. The decisive step was taken only when the second name, whatever its form, became hereditary and changed into a patronymic. It is characteristic that the use of

140

true family names first arose among the greater nobility, in which the individual was at once more mobile and more interested, when he went away from home, in retaining the support of his group. In twelfth-century Normandy people already spoke customarily of the Giroys and the Talvas; in the Latin East, about 1230, of 'those of the lineage surnamed d'Ibelin'.[1] Next the movement reached the urban bourgeoisie, who were also accustomed to moving about and who because of their commercial interests were anxious to avoid mistakes over the identity of persons and even of families, which were often identified with business associations. The development eventually spread through the whole of society.

But it must be clearly understood that the groups which thus acquired definite labels were neither very stable nor of a size at all comparable with the old kindreds. The transmission of names, which sometimes, as we have seen, alternated between the paternal and the maternal lines, suffered many interruptions. The branches, in separating, often became known by different names. Servants, on the other hand, readily adopted the names of their masters. In short, what was here involved was not so much the clan-names as—in conformity with the general evolution of blood-relationships—the nickname shared by the members of the same household, the continuity of which was at the mercy of the slightest accident in the history of the group or the individual. It was not till much later that strict heritability of names was imposed by the authorities—together with civil status—in order to facilitate the work of police and administration. Thus in Europe, long after the demise of feudal society, the permanent family name, which today is held in common by men often devoid of any feeling of solidarity, was the creation not of the spirit of kinship, but of the institution most fundamentally opposed to that spirit—the sovereign state.

3 TIES OF KINSHIP AND FEUDALISM

It must not be supposed that from the remote tribal ages there was steady progress towards emancipation of the individual. On the continent at least, it appears that at the time of the barbarian kingdoms alienations were much less dependent on the consent of the near relatives than they were to become during the first feudal age. The same was true of arrangements for the disposal of property after death. In the eighth and even in the ninth century, it was possible, sometimes by will as in Roman law, sometimes under various systems developed by the Germanic customary laws, for a man to make his own arrangements for the devolution of his property with some freedom. From the eleventh century, this power was virtually lost except in Italy and Spain which were both, as we know, exceptionally faithful to the teachings of the old written laws. Gifts that were intended

[1] Philip of Novara, *Mémoires*, ed. Kohler, pp. 17 and 56.

to take effect only after death thenceforward assumed exclusively the form of donations subject by the nature of the case to the approval of the relatives. This did not suit the Church, however, and under its influence the will properly so called was revived in the twelfth century. At first it dealt only with pious bequests; then, subject to certain restrictions for the benefit of the natural heirs, it was gradually extended. This was also the moment when the attenuated system of redemption (*retrait lignager*) replaced that of family consent. The blood-feud itself had been curtailed to some extent by the legislation of the states that sprang from the invasions. Once these barriers were removed, the feud took, or resumed, the foremost place in the penal law, till the time when it once more became the object of attack by the reconstituted royal or princely authorities. The parallelism, in short, appears in every respect complete. The period which saw the expansion of the relations of personal protection and subordination characteristic of the social conditions we call feudalism was also marked by a real tightening of the ties of kinship. Because the times were troubled and the public authority weak, the individual gained a more lively awareness of his links with the local groups, whatever they were, to which he could look for help. The centuries which later witnessed the progressive breakdown or metamorphosis of authentic feudalism also experienced—with the crumbling of the large kinship groups—the early symptoms of the slow decay of family solidarities.

Yet to the individual, threatened by the numerous dangers bred by an atmosphere of violence, the kinship group did not seem to offer adequate protection, even in the first feudal age. In the form in which it then existed, it was too vague and too variable in its outlines, too deeply undermined by the duality of descent by male and female lines. That is why men were obliged to seek or accept other ties. On this point history is decisive, for the only regions in which powerful agnatic groups survived—German lands on the shores of the North Sea, Celtic districts of the British Isles—knew nothing of vassalage, the fief and the manor. The tie of kinship was one of the essential elements of feudal society; its relative weakness explains why there was feudalism at all.

PART IV

The Ties between Man and Man: Vassalage and the Fief

XI

VASSAL HOMAGE

1 THE MAN OF ANOTHER MAN

TO be the 'man' of another man: in the vocabulary of feudalism, no combination of words was more widely used or more comprehensive in meaning. In both the Romance and the Germanic tongues it was used to express personal dependence *per se* and applied to persons of all social classes regardless of the precise legal nature of the bond. The count was the 'man' of the king, as the serf was the 'man' of his manorial lord. Sometimes even in the same text, within the space of a few lines, radically different social stations were thus evoked. An instance of this, dating from the end of the eleventh century, is a petition of Norman nuns, complaining that their 'men'—that is to say their peasants—were forced by a great baron to work at the castles of his 'men', meaning the knights who were his vassals.[1] The ambiguity disturbed no one, because, in spite of the gulf between the orders of society, the emphasis was on the fundamental element in common: the subordination of one individual to another.

If, however, the principle of this human nexus permeated the whole life of society, the forms which it assumed were none the less very diverse— with sometimes almost imperceptible transitions, from the highest to the humblest. Moreover there were many variations from country to country. It will be useful if we take as a guiding thread one of the most significant of these relationships of dependence, the tie of vassalage; studying it first in the most highly 'feudalized' zone of Europe, namely, the heart of the former Carolingian Empire, northern France, the German Rhineland and Swabia; and endeavouring, before we embark on any inquiries into its origins, to describe the most striking features of the institution at the period of its greatest expansion, that is to say, from the tenth to the twelfth century.

2 HOMAGE IN THE FEUDAL ERA

Imagine two men face to face; one wishing to serve, the other willing or anxious to be served. The former puts his hands together and places them, thus joined, between the hands of the other man—a plain symbol of

---

[1] C. H. Haskins, *Norman Institutions*, Cambridge (Mass.), 1918 (Harvard Historical Studies, XXIV), p. 63.

submission, the significance of which was sometimes further emphasized by a kneeling posture. At the same time, the person proffering his hands utters a few words—a very short declaration—by which he acknowledges himself to be the 'man' of the person facing him. Then chief and subordinate kiss each other on the mouth, symbolizing accord and friendship. Such were the gestures—very simple ones, eminently fitted to make an impression on minds so sensitive to visible things—which served to cement one of the strongest social bonds known in the feudal era. Described or mentioned in the texts a hundred times, reproduced on seals, miniatures, bas-reliefs, the ceremony was called 'homage' (in German, *Mannschaft*).[1] The superior party, whose position was created by this act, was described by no other term than the very general one of 'lord'.[2] Similarly, the subordinate was often simply called the 'man' of this lord; or sometimes, more precisely, his 'man of mouth and hands' (*homme de bouche et de mains*). But more specialized words were also employed, such as 'vassal' or, till the beginning of the twelfth century at least, 'commended man' (*commendé*).

In this form the rite bore no Christian imprint. Such an omission, probably explained by the remote Germanic origins of the symbolism, in due course ceased to be acceptable to a society which had come to regard a promise as scarcely valid unless God were guarantor. Homage itself, so far as its form was concerned, was never modified. But, apparently from the Carolingian period, a second rite—an essentially religious one—was superimposed on it; laying his hand on the Gospels or on relics, the new vassal swore to be faithful to his master. This was called fealty, *foi* in French (in German *Treue*, and, formerly, *Hulde*).

The ceremony therefore had two stages, but they were by no means of equal importance. For in the act of fealty there was nothing specific. In a disturbed society, where mistrust was the rule and the appeal to divine sanctions appeared to be one of the few restraints with any efficacy at all, there were a great many reasons why the oath of fealty should be exacted frequently. Royal or seignorial officials of every rank took it on assuming their duties; prelates often demanded it from their clergy; and manorial lords, occasionally, from their peasants. Unlike homage, which bound the whole man at a single stroke and was generally held to be incapable of renewal, this promise—almost a commonplace affair—could be repeated several times to the same person. There were therefore many acts of fealty without homage: we do not know of any acts of homage without fealty—

---

[1] See Plates II, III, IV.

[2] By a misconception, originating with the feudists of the Ancien Régime, 'suzerain' has sometimes been used in this sense. Its true meaning was very different. Suppose that Paul has done homage to Peter, who himself had done homage to James. James—and not Peter—will be the 'lord suzerain' or, briefly, the suzerain of Paul, that is to say the superior lord (the word seems to be derived from the adverb *sus*, by analogy with *souverain*). In other words, my suzerain is the lord of my lord, not my immediate lord. The expression appears in any case to belong to a late epoch (the fourteenth century?).

at least in the feudal period. Furthermore, when the two rites were combined, the pre-eminence of homage was shown by the fact that it was always
given first place in the ceremony. It was this alone that brought the two
men together in a close union; the fealty of the vassal was a unilateral
undertaking to which there was seldom a corresponding oath on the part of
the lord. In a word, it was the act of homage that really established the
relation of vassalage under its dual aspect of dependence and protection.

The tie thus formed lasted, in theory, as long as the two lives which it
bound together, but as soon as one or other of these was terminated by
death it was automatically dissolved. We shall see that in practice vassalage very soon became, in most cases, hereditary; but this *de facto* situation
allowed the legal rule to remain intact to the end. It mattered little that the
son of the deceased vassal usually performed this homage to the lord who
had accepted his father's, or that the heir of the previous lord almost
invariably received the homage of his father's vassals: the ceremony had
none the less to be repeated with every change of the individual persons
concerned. Similarly, homage could not be offered or accepted by proxy;
the examples to the contrary all date from a very late period, when the
significance of the old forms was already almost lost. In France, so far as it
applied to the king, this privilege was legalized only under Charles VII and
even then not without many misgivings.[1] The social bond seemed to be
truly inseparable from the almost physical contact which the formal act
created between the two men.

The general duty of aid and obedience incumbent on the vassal was an
obligation that was undertaken by anyone who became the 'man' of
another man. But it shaded off at this point into special obligations, which
we shall discuss in detail later on. The nature of these corresponded to conditions of rank and manner of life that were rather narrowly defined, for
despite great differences of wealth and prestige, vassals were not recruited
indiscriminately from all levels of society. Vassalage was the form of
dependence peculiar to the upper classes who were characterized above all
by the profession of arms and the exercise of command. At least, that is
what it had become. In order to obtain a clear idea of the nature of vassalage, it will be well at this point to inquire how it had progressively dis-
entangled itself from a whole complex of personal relationships.

3 THE ORIGINS OF TIES OF PERSONAL DEPENDENCE

To seek a protector, or to find satisfaction in being one—these things are
common to all ages. But we seldom find them giving rise to new legal

[1] L. Mirot, 'Les Ordonnances de Charles VII relatives à la prestation des hommages'
in *Mémoires de la Société pour l'Histoire du droit et des institutions des anciens pays
bourguignons*, fasc. 2, 1935; G. Dupont-Ferrier, *Les Origines et le premier siècle de la
Cour du Trésor*, 1936, p. 108; P. Dognon, *Les Institutions politiques et administratives
du pays de Languedoc*, 1895, p. 576 (1530).

institutions save in civilizations where the rest of the social framework is giving way. Such was the case in Gaul after the collapse of the Roman Empire.

Consider, for example, the society of the Merovingian period. Neither the State nor the family any longer provided adequate protection. The village community was barely strong enough to maintain order within its own boundaries; the urban community scarcely existed. Everywhere, the weak man felt the need to be sheltered by someone more powerful. The powerful man, in his turn, could not maintain his prestige or his fortune or even ensure his own safety except by securing for himself, by persuasion or coercion, the support of subordinates bound to his service. On the one hand, there was the urgent quest for a protector; on the other, there were usurpations of authority, often by violent means. And as notions of weakness and strength are always relative, in many cases the same man occupied a dual rôle—as a dependent of a more powerful man and a protector of humbler ones. Thus there began to be built up a vast system of personal relationships whose intersecting threads ran from one level of the social structure to another.

In yielding thus to the necessities of the moment these generations of men had no conscious desire to create new social forms, nor were they aware of doing so. Instinctively each strove to turn to account the resources provided by the existing social structure and if, unconsciously, something new was eventually created, it was in the process of trying to adapt the old. Moreover, the society that emerged from the invasions had inherited a strange medley of institutions and practices in which the traditions of the Germans were intermingled with the legacy of Rome, and with that of the peoples whom Rome had conquered without ever completely effacing their native customs. Let us not at this point fall into the error of seeking either in vassalage or, more generally, in feudal institutions a particular ethnological origin; let us not imprison ourselves once more in the famous dilemma: Rome or 'the forests of Germany'. Such phantasies must be left to those ages which—knowing less than we do of the creative power of evolution—could believe, with Boulainvilliers, that the nobility of the seventeenth century was descended almost entirely from Frankish warriors, or which, like the young Guizot, could interpret the French Revolution as a *revanche* of the Gallo-Romans. In the same way the old physiologists imagined in the sperm a fully formed *homunculus*. The lesson of the feudal vocabulary is nevertheless clear. This vocabulary is, as we shall see, full of elements of diverse origin subsisting side by side, some borrowed from the speech of the conquered people or that of the conquerors, or newly coined, like 'homage' itself. Such a vocabulary is surely a faithful reflection of a social régime which, though itself deeply moulded by a composite past, was above all the product of contemporary conditions. 'Men', says the Arab proverb, 'resemble their own times more than they do their fathers'.

Among the lowly people who sought a protector, the most unfortunate became simply slaves, thereby binding their descendants as well as themselves. Many others, however, even among the most humble, were anxious to maintain their status as free men; and the persons who received their allegiance had as a rule little reason to oppose such a wish. For in this age when personal ties had not yet strangled the institutions of government, to enjoy what was called 'freedom' meant essentially to belong by undisputed right to the people ruled by the Merovingian kings—to the *populus Francorum*, as contemporaries called it, lumping together under the same name the conquerors and the conquered. As a result, the two terms 'free' and 'frank' came to be regarded as synonymous and continued to be so regarded through the ages. To be surrounded with dependents who enjoyed the judicial and military privileges characteristic of free men was, for a chief, in many respects more advantageous than to command only a horde of slaves.

These dependent relationships 'befitting a freeman' (*ingenuili ordine*)—as they are called in a formula from Tours—were described by terms derived for the most part from classical Latin. For through all the vicissitudes of an eventful history the ancient practices of the patron–client relationship had never disappeared from the Roman or Romanised world. In Gaul especially they took root all the more easily since they were in keeping with the customs of these subject populations. Before the coming of the legions there was no Gaulish chieftain who was not surrounded by a group of retainers, either peasants or warriors. We are very ill informed as to how far these ancient native practices survived the Roman conquest and lived on under the veneer of an ecumenical civilization. Nevertheless, everything leads to the conclusion that, though profoundly modified by the pressure of a very different political régime, they continued to exist in one form or another. In any case, the troubles of later centuries in every part of the Empire made it more than ever necessary to look for aid to powers closer at hand and more effective than the institutions of public law. In the fourth or the fifth century, at all levels of society, if one wished to protect oneself from the harsh exactions of the tax-collector, to influence in one's own favour the decisions of the judges or merely to ensure for oneself an honourable career, one could do no better—even though free and perhaps a man of position—than attach oneself to someone more highly placed. Ignored or even prohibited by public law, these ties had no legal force. They constituted none the less one of the strongest of social bonds. In making increasing use of pacts of protection and obedience, the inhabitants of what had now become Frankish Gaul were therefore not aware that they were doing anything for which there was no ready term in the language of their ancestors.

The old word *clientela*, except as a literary anachronism, fell into disuse in the later centuries of the Empire. But in Merovingian Gaul, as at Rome, one continued to say of the chief that he 'took charge' (*suscipere*) of the subordinate whose 'patron' he thereby became; and of the subordinate that he 'commended' himself—that is to say 'entrusted' himself—to his protector. The obligations thus accepted were generally called 'service' (*servitium*). Not so long before, the word would have horrified a free man. In classical Latin it was used only in the sense of slavery; the only duties compatible with freedom were *officia*. But by the end of the fourth century *servitium* had lost this original taint.

Germania also made its contribution. The protection which the powerful man extended to his weaker neighbour was often termed *mundium*, *mundeburdum*—which became *maimbour* in medieval French—or again *mitium*, this latter term expressing more particularly the right and the duty of representing the dependent in judicial matters. All these were Germanic words ill-disguised by the Latin dress in which they appear in the charters.

These various expressions were almost interchangeable and were used regardless of whether the contracting parties were of Roman or of barbarian origin. The relationships of private dependence were not subject to the principle of the 'personality of laws', since they were still on the fringe of all legal systems. The fact that they were not officially controlled rendered them all the more capable of being adapted to an infinite variety of circumstances. The king himself, in his capacity as leader of his people, owed his support to all his subjects without discrimination and was entitled in turn to their allegiance as confirmed by the universal oath of free men; nevertheless he granted to a certain number of them his personal *maimbour*. A wrong done to persons thus placed 'within his word' was regarded as a offence against the king himself and was in consequence treated with exceptional severity. Within this rather ill-assorted group there arose a more restricted and more distinguished body of royal retainers who were called the *leudes* of the prince, that is to say his 'men'; in the anarchy of later Merovingian times they more than once controlled both king and state. As in Rome, a little earlier, the young man of good family who wished to get on in the world 'entrusted' himself to a powerful man—if his future had not already in his childhood been assured in this way by a far-sighted father. In spite of the prohibitions of councils, many ecclesiastics of every rank did not scruple to seek the protection of laymen. But it was apparently in the lower strata of society that the relationships of subordination were most widely diffused as well as most exacting. The only formula of 'commendation' that we possess shows us a poor devil who only accepts a master because 'he lacks the wherewithal to feed and clothe himself'. There was no distinction of words, however, and no difference—at least no very clear one—in conception between these diverse aspects of dependence, despite all differences of social status.

Whatever the status of the person who commended himself, he seems almost invariably to have taken an oath to his master. Was it also custom-

150

ary for him to make a formal act of submission? We do not know with any
certainty. The official legal systems, which are concerned only with the old
institutions regulating the affairs of the people and the family, are silent
on this point. As to the agreements themselves, they were hardly ever put
in writing, which alone provides definite evidence. From the second half
of the eighth century, however, the documents begin to mention the ceremony of the joined hands. The very first example shown to us is a case
where the persons involved are of the highest rank, the protégé being a
foreign prince, the protector the king of the Franks; but we must not be
deceived by this one-sidedness on the part of those who compiled the
records. The ceremony did not seem worth describing unless, being associated with matters of high policy, it was one of the features of an interview
between rulers; in the normal course of life it was regarded as a commonplace event and so was passed over in silence. Undoubtedly the ceremony
had been in use for a considerable time before it thus suddenly appeared in
the texts. The similarity of the custom among the Franks, the Anglo-
Saxons and the Scandinavians attests its Germanic origin. But the symbolism was too obvious for it not to be readily adopted by the whole population. In England and among the Scandinavians we find it being used
indiscriminately to express very different forms of subordination—that of
the slave to the master, that of the free companion to the warrior chieftain.
Everything points to the conclusion that this was also the case for a long
time in Frankish Gaul. The gesture served to conclude protective contracts
of various kinds; sometimes performed, sometimes omitted, it did not
seem indispensable to any of them. An institution requires a terminology
without too much ambiguity and a relatively stable ritual; but in the Merovingian world personal relationships remained on the level of customary
procedure.

4 THE HOUSEHOLD WARRIORS

There were already in existence, however, certain groups of dependants
permanently set apart from the rest of the population by the conditions
under which they lived. These were the groups of household warriors who
surrounded every powerful individual, including the king himself. For, of
all the problems besetting the governing classes in those days, the most
urgent by far was not that of administering the country or a private estate
in time of peace, but that of procuring the means to wage war. Whether
public or private, whether undertaken lightheartedly or in defence of life
and property, war was for many centuries to be regarded as the normal
thread of every leader's career and the *raison d'être* of every position of
authority.

When the Frankish kings had made themselves masters of Gaul, they
found that they had inherited two systems for the recruitment of armies,

both of which concerned the mass of the population. In Germania every free man was a warrior; Rome, in so far as she still used native troops, recruited them chiefly from the cultivators of the soil. The Frankish state, under its two successive dynasties, maintained the principle of the general levy, which indeed was destined to continue throughout the feudal age and to survive it. Royal ordinances attempted without success to regulate this obligation according to wealth, to form the poorest into small groups each of which had to provide one soldier. In practice these measures might vary with the needs of the moment, but the rule itself remained intact. In the same way, the great men in their quarrels did not scruple to involve their peasants in the fighting.

In the barbarian kingdoms, however, the recruiting machinery was a clumsy instrument in the hands of an increasingly incompetent officialdom. The conquest, moreover, had broken down the system created by the Germanic societies for war as well as for peace. The ordinary German, at the time of the invasion, was a soldier rather than a peasant, but in the end, preoccupied with the responsibilities of an increasingly stable agriculture, he became by degrees more peasant than soldier. It is true that the Roman *colonus* of an earlier day, when he was taken from his farm for military service, was equally ignorant of war. But he was enrolled in the ranks of organized legions and there he received his training as a soldier. In the Frankish state, by contrast, there was no standing army, apart from the guards whom the king and the magnates gathered about them, and consequently no regular training of conscripts. Lack of enthusiasm and experience among recruits, together with difficulties in arming them (under Charlemagne it was necessary to issue an order against joining the host armed only with a staff), were defects from which no doubt the Merovingian military system suffered from an early date. But they became more and more apparent as superiority on the field of battle passed from the foot soldier to the heavily armed horseman. For in order to possess a warhorse and to equip oneself from head to foot, it was necessary to be fairly well off or else to be assisted by someone richer than oneself. According to the Ripuarian Law a horse was worth six times as much as a cow; a *broigne*—a kind of cuirass of hide reinforced by metal plates—was worth the same; and even a helmet cost half that amount. In 761 a small landowner of Alemannia (the later Swabia) is recorded as having exchanged his ancestral fields and a slave for a horse and a sword.[1] Moreover, a long apprenticeship was necessary before a man could handle his charger effectively in battle and had mastered the difficulties of fighting with the sword while encumbered with heavy harness. 'You can make a horseman of a lad at puberty; later than that, never.' Under the early Carolingians this maxim had become a proverb.[2]

[1] H. Wartmann, *Urkundenbuch der Abtei Sankt-Gallen*, I, no. 31.
[2] Rabanus Maurus, in *Zeitschrift für deutsches Altertum*, XV, 1872, p. 444.

But what was the reason for this decline of the foot soldier, the social repercussions of which were to be so important? It has sometimes been interpreted as an effect of the Arab invasions. It is pointed out that in order to withstand the charge of the Saracen horsemen or to go in pursuit of them, Charles Martel put his Franks on horseback. Yet even supposing it were true—and it has been disputed—that cavalry played at that time so decisive a rôle in the armies of Islam, the Franks, who had always possessed mounted troops, had not waited till the battle of Poitiers before giving them prominence. When in 755 the annual gathering of the magnates and the host was transferred by King Pepin from the month of March to the month of May—the season of the first forage—this significant step marked only the concluding stage of an evolution which had been going on for several centuries. The reasons for it, though applying to most of the barbarian kingdoms and even to the Eastern Empire, have nevertheless not always been very well understood, partly because insufficient consideration has been given to certain technical factors and partly because in the specialized field of the history of war attention has been directed too exclusively to the tactics employed in battle, to the neglect of what determined them and what followed from them.

Unknown to the Mediterranean societies of classical times, the stirrup and the horse-shoe do not make their appearance in the illustrated documents of the West before the ninth century. But it is likely that representation lagged behind reality. The stirrup, which was probably invented by the Sarmatians, was a gift to western Europe from the nomads of the Eurasian steppes and the adoption of it was one of the results of the much closer contact which was established in the period of the invasions between the settled communities of the West and the equestrian peoples of the great plains. Sometimes this contact was direct, thanks to the migrations of the Alans, some of whom were swept along by the Germanic tide, from their earlier home in the region north of the Caucasus, till they eventually found a refuge in Gaul or Spain. More often contact was effected through the agency of those Germanic peoples who, like the Goths, had dwelt for some time on the shores of the Black Sea. The horse-shoe also apparently came from the East. Shoeing was an immense advantage in riding and charging over rough ground. And the stirrup not only saved the horseman from fatigue: by giving him a better seat it increased the effectiveness of his charge.

In the battle itself, the cavalry charge became a favourite method of attack, though not the only one. For when the terrain conditions required it the horsemen would dismount and attack on foot. The military history of the feudal era abounds in examples of these tactics. But in the absence of suitable roads or of troops trained in those skilfully co-ordinated manœuvres which had been the strength of the Roman legions, the horse alone made it possible to carry out either the long expeditions necessitated by wars between rulers or the swift guerilla operations favoured by most chiefs. It enabled one to arrive on the field of battle speedily and not too weary, after crossing ploughed fields and swamps, and to disconcert the enemy by unexpected manœuvres. If the day went ill, flight on horseback was the best means of escaping massacre. When the Saxons were defeated by Henry IV of Germany in 1075, the nobles owed it to the swiftness of their mounts that their losses were much less heavy than those of the slow peasant infantry.

In Frankish Gaul, everything conspired to make it more and more necessary to recruit professional warriors, men who had been trained by a group tradition and who were, first and foremost, horsemen. Although service on horseback for the king had continued almost to the end of the ninth century to be exacted in theory of all free men rich enough to be subject to it, the nucleus of these trained and well-equipped mounted troops—the only ones of whom a high standard of efficiency was expected —was naturally provided by the armed followers who had long been included in the retinue of kings and great personages.

Although in the ancient Germanic societies the affairs of the kindred group and the people offered sufficient scope for normal energies, they had never been able to satisfy the spirit of adventure and ambition. The chiefs, especially the young chiefs, surrounded themselves with 'companions' (in Old German *gisind*, meaning literally 'companion for an expedition'; Tacitus has rendered the word very accurately by the Latin *comes*). These companions they led in battle and on plundering expeditions, and in the intervals of rest gave them hospitality in their great wooden 'halls' where the atmosphere was congenial for long drinking-bouts. The little band was the mainstay of its captain in wars and vendettas; it supported his authority in the deliberations of the free men; and the generous gifts—of food and drink, of slaves, of gold rings—which he lavished upon these followers was an indispensable element of his prestige. Such, as Tacitus depicts it, is the 'companionage' (*comitatus*) in first-century Germania; such it is still, several centuries later, as it appears in the poem of Beowulf and (with some inevitable variants) in the old Scandinavian sagas.

Once settled in the wreckage of the Western Empire, the barbarian chiefs were the less inclined to give up these customs since, in the world into which they had penetrated, the practice of maintaining private bodies of armed retainers had long prevailed. In the later centuries of Rome there was scarcely a member of the high aristocracy who had not his own soldiers. They were often called *bucellarii*, from the name of the biscuit (*bucella*) which, being better than the ordinary ration bread, was generally distributed to these privileged soldiers. Hired soldiers rather than companions, these personal escorts were so numerous and so loyal that when their masters became generals of the Empire they were often given the foremost place among the fighting troops.

Amidst the troubles of the Merovingian epoch, the employment of such armed followings became more necessary than ever. The king had his guard which was called his *trustis* and which had always been, in great part at least, mounted. His principal subjects, whether Frankish or Roman by origin, also had their armed followers. Even the churches deemed it necessary to provide for their security in this way. These 'gladiators', as Gregory of Tours calls them, were a rather mixed company in which were to be found ruffians of the worst type. The masters did not hesitate to enrol their strongest slaves. Free men, however, clearly formed the largest element, though they themselves did not always belong by birth to the highest social class. No doubt such service admitted of varying degrees of prestige and reward. It is none the less significant that in the seventh century the same form of document could be used indifferently for the donation of 'a small property' in favour of a slave or of a *gasindus*.

In the last-mentioned term, we recognize the old name of the German war-companion. It seems in fact to have been in current use in Merovingian Gaul, as indeed in the whole of the barbarian world, as a name for the private fighting-man. Progressively, however, it yielded place to the indigenous word 'vassal' (*vassus, vassallus*) which was to have such a splendid future. This newcomer was not Roman by origin but Celtic.[1] Yet it had unquestionably penetrated into the spoken Latin of Gaul long before it occurs for the first time in writing, in the Salic Law; for the borrowing could only have taken place in the days—long before Clovis—when there still dwelt on French soil, side by side with the populations that had adopted the language of Rome, large groups which had remained faithful to their ancestral tongues. We may recognize therefore in this venerable relic one of those genuine survivals of ancient Gaul that live on at the deeper levels of the French language. But at the same time, we must beware of deducing from its incorporation in the feudal vocabulary some sort of distant ancestry of military vassalage. Undoubtedly Gaulish society before the Roman Conquest, like Celtic societies in general, had practised a system of 'companionage' in many respects akin to that of ancient Germany. But to whatever extent these customs may have survived under the Roman superstructure, one fact is certain: the names of the armed 'client', as given by Caesar—*ambacte* or, in Aquitania, *soldurius*—disappeared without trace.[2] The connotation of 'vassal', at the moment when it passed into spoken Latin, was very much more humble. It meant 'young boy'—this meaning was to persist throughout the Middle Ages in the form of the diminutive *valet, varlet* (page)—and also, by an imperceptible transition such as had occurred in the case of the Latin *puer*, domestic slave. It is

---

[1] G. Dottin, *La Langue gauloise*, 1920, p. 296.

[2] At least in this sense; but from *ambacte* is derived—by indirect routes that do not concern us here—the French word *ambassade* and its English derivatives 'embassy' and 'ambassador'.

155

natural for the master to call those whom he has constantly about him his 'boys'. This second sense is the one which continues to be given to the word in Frankish Gaul by a variety of texts ranging in date from the sixth to the eighth century. Then, by degrees, a new meaning emerges; in the eighth century, it competes with the previous one and in the following century replaces it. More than one household slave was 'honoured' by being admitted to the guard. The other members of this cohort, without being slaves, yet lived in the house of the master, pledged to serve him in a great variety of ways and to obey his orders. They also were his 'boys'. They were therefore included, together with their comrades of servile birth, in the category of vassal, which henceforth bore the specific meaning of armed follower. Finally, the label which had hitherto been common to them all, suggesting a praiseworthy familiarity, was reserved exclusively for the free men of the band.

Now this history of a word which emerged from the under-world of slavery to be promoted by degrees to a place of honour faithfully reflects the rise of the institution itself. Modest as was the original social status of many of the 'thugs' maintained by the magnates and even by the king, from now on it grew steadily in prestige. The ties which bound these war-companions to their chief represented one of those contracts of fidelity freely entered into which were compatible with the most respectable social position. The term which designates the royal guard is extremely significant: *trustis*, that is to say fealty. The new recruit enrolled in this body swore to be faithful; the king in return undertook to 'bear him succour'. These were the very principles of all 'commendation'. Doubtless the powerful men and their *gasindi* or vassals exchanged similar promises. To be protected by a person of rank offered, moreover, a guarantee not only of security but also of social standing. As the disintegration of the state proceeded, every person in power was obliged to look for support more and more to those directly attached to him; and, as the old forms of military service decayed, the recruitment of professional fighting-men became daily more necessary and the rôle of whoever bore arms more respected. In these conditions, there was a growing conviction that of all the forms of personal service the highest consisted in serving on horseback with sword and lance a master of whom one had solemnly declared oneself a faithful follower.

But already an influence was beginning to make itself felt which profoundly affected the development of the institution of vassalage and was destined in a large measure to deflect it from its original course. This was the intervention, in these human relationships hitherto unrecognized by the State, of a state which, if not a new one, was at least a renovated one, namely the Carolingian kingdom.

156

5 CAROLINGIAN VASSALAGE

The policy of the Carolingians—by which of course is meant not only the personal plans of the monarchs, some of whom were remarkable men, but also the views of their leading counsellors—may be said to have been dominated both by acquired habits and by principles. Members of the aristocracy who had attained power after a long struggle against the traditional royal house, they had gradually made themselves masters of the Frankish people by surrounding themselves with bands of armed dependants and by imposing their *maimbour* on other chiefs. Is it surprising that once they had reached the pinnacle of power they should continue to regard such ties as normal? On the other hand their ambition, from the time of Charles Martel, was to reconstitute the power of the central government which at the outset they, along with the rest of the aristocracy, had helped to destroy. They wanted to establish order and Christian peace throughout their realms. They wanted soldiers to spread their dominion far and wide and to carry on the holy war against the infidel, an enterprise both conducive to the growth of their own power and beneficial for souls.

The older institutions appeared inadequate for this task. The monarchy had at its disposal only a small number of officials: but these were in any case not very reliable men and—apart from a few churchmen—they lacked professional tradition and culture. Moreover, economic conditions precluded the institution of a vast system of salaried officials. Communications were slow, inconvenient and uncertain. The principal difficulty, therefore, which faced the central government was to reach individual subjects, in order to exact services and impose the necessary sanctions. Thus there arose the idea of utilizing for the purposes of government the firmly established network of protective relationships. The lord, at every level of the hierarchy, would be answerable for his 'man' and would be responsible for holding him to his duty. This idea was not peculiar to the Carolingians. It had already been the subject of legislation in Visigothic Spain; after the Arab invasion the many Spanish refugees at the Frankish court may have helped to make the principle known and appreciated there, and the very lively mistrust of the 'lordless man' which is reflected later in the Anglo-Saxon laws reflects a similar attitude. But hardly anywhere was the policy more consciously pursued and—one is tempted to add —the illusion more consistently maintained than in the Frankish kingdom about the year 800. 'Each chief must constrain his subordinates in order that the latter may with increasing willingness obey the Emperor's commands and instructions'[1]—these words from a capitulary of 810 sum up with expressive brevity one of the fundamental principles of the edifice constructed by Pepin and Charlemagne. In the same way, it is said that in

[1] *Capitularia*, I, no. 64, c. 17.

Russia in the days of serfdom the Tsar Nicholas I boasted that in his *pomeshchiks* (lords of villages) he had 'a hundred thousand police super-intendents'.

In the execution of this policy, the most urgent step was clearly to fit vassalage into the legal system and at the same time to give it the stability that alone could make it a firm bulwark of the royal power. At an early date, persons of humble status had commended themselves for life—like the starveling of the Tours formula. But though in practice (and this had no doubt long been the case) many war-companions had also continued to serve their masters to the end of their lives—whether as the result of an express undertaking or in obedience to the dictates of social convention or self-interest—nothing proves that under the Merovingians this had been the general rule. In Spain, Visigothic law had never ceased to recognize the right of private fighting-men to change their masters: for, as the law said, 'the free man always retains control of his person'. Under the Carolingians, on the other hand, various royal or imperial edicts were concerned with defining precisely the offences which, if committed by the lord, would justify the vassal in breaking the contract. This meant that, with the exception of such cases and apart from separations by mutual agreement, the tie lasted for life.

The lord, moreover, was made officially responsible for the appearance of the vassal in court and when required for his military service. If he himself took part in a campaign, his vassals fought under his orders. It was only in his absence that they came under the direct command of the king's representative, the count.

Yet what was the use of this scheme whereby the lords exacted loyalty from the vassals if these lords, in their turn, were not solidly attached to the sovereign? It was in trying to realize this indispensable condition of their great design that the Carolingians helped to push to the extreme limit the penetration of all social relations by the principle of vassalage.

Once in power, they had had to reward their 'men'. They distributed lands to them, by methods which we shall describe in detail later. Further-more, as mayors of the palace and then as kings they had to get supporters and above all create an army. So they attracted into their service—fre-quently in return for gifts of land—many men who were already of high rank. Former members of the military following, established on property granted by the ruler, did not cease to be regarded as his vassals; and his new followers were considered to be bound to him by the same tie, even if they had never been his companions-in-arms. Both groups served in his army, followed by their own vassals, if they had any. But, since most of their time was spent away from their master, the conditions under which they lived were very different from those of the household warriors of but a short time before. Each one of them was the centre of a more or less widely scattered group of dependants whom he was expected to keep in order; if necessary, he might even be required to exercise a similar super-vision over his neighbours. Thus, among the populations of the vast empire, there became distinguishable a relatively very numerous class of 'vassals of the Lord'—that is, 'of the Lord King' (*vassi dominici*). Enjoying the special protection of the sovereign and being responsible for furnishing a large part of his troops, they also formed, through the provinces, the links of a great chain of loyalty. When in 871 Charles the Bald, having triumphed over his son Carloman, wished to re-establish the allegiance of the young rebel's accomplices, he could conceive of no better way of doing it than by compelling each of them to select from among the royal vassals a lord of his own choosing.

There was another consideration. Experience had seemed to prove the strength of the tie of vassalage, and the Carolingians planned to extend its use to their officials, for the purpose of stabilizing their constantly waver-ing loyalty. The latter had always been regarded as being in the special *maimbour* of the sovereign; they had always taken an oath to him; and they were more and more frequently recruited from men who, before their appointment, had already served him as vassals. The practice gradually became more general. From the reign of Louis the Pious, at the latest, there was no office at court, no great command, no countship especially, whose holder had not been obliged, on assuming office, if not earlier, to bind himself in the most solemn fashion as vassal of the monarch. Even foreign rulers, if they recognized the Frankish protectorate, were required from the middle of the eighth century to submit to this ceremony and they also were called vassals of the king or emperor. Of course no one expected these distinguished personages to mount guard in the house of their master, like the followers of former days. In a manner, nevertheless, they belonged to his military household since they owed him first and foremost —along with their fealty—aid in war.

Now the magnates, for their part, had long been accustomed to see in the good companions of their household following men whom they could rely on, ready to carry out the most varied missions. What happened if a distant appointment, the gift of an estate or a heritage led one of these loyal fellows to withdraw from personal service? The chief none the less continued to regard him as his sworn follower. Here again, in short, vassalage by a spontaneous development tended to break out from the narrow circle of the lord's household. The example of the kings and the influence of the legal enactments they had promulgated gave stability to these changing customs. Lords as well as dependants could not fail to favour a form of contract which henceforth would be provided with legal sanctions. The counts bound to themselves by the ties of vassalage the officials of lower rank; the bishop or abbot similarly bound the laymen on whom they re-lied to assist them in administering justice or to lead their subjects when the latter were called up for service in the army. Powerful individuals, whoever they were, thus strove to draw into their orbit increasing numbers of petty lords and these in their turn acted in the same way towards those weaker than themselves. These private vassals formed a mixed society which still comprised elements of fairly humble status. Among those whom the counts, bishops, abbots and abbesses were authorized to leave in the district when the host was summoned, there were some to whom—like *vassi dominici* on a small scale—the noble task of maintaining the peace was entrusted. Others, again, had the more modest duty of guarding the house of the master, watching over the harvest and supervising the lord's domestic arrangements.[1] These were positions of authority and consequently positions worthy of respect. Around the chiefs of every rank, as around the kings, the purely household service of earlier times had provided the mould in which thenceforward every form of honourable dependence would be cast.

6 THE FORMATION OF THE CLASSICAL TYPE OF VASSALAGE

The collapse of the Carolingian state represented the swift and tragic defeat of a little group of men who, despite many archaisms and mis-calculations but with the best of intentions, had tried to preserve some of the values of an ordered and civilized life. After them came a long and troubled period which was at the same time a period of gestation, in which the characteristics of vassalage were to take definitive shape.

In the state of perpetual war—invasions as well as internal strife—in which Europe henceforth lived, men more than ever looked for chiefs, and chiefs for vassals. But the extension of these protective relationships no longer redounded to the benefit of the kings. Private ties now increased in number, especially in the neighbourhood of the castles. With the beginning of the Scandinavian and Hungarian invasions, more and more of these fortresses sprang up in the country districts, and the lords who commanded them—either in their own name or in that of some more powerful person-age—endeavoured to assemble bodies of vassals for their defence. 'The king has now nothing save his title and his crown . . . he is not capable of defending either his bishops or the rest of his subjects against the dangers that threaten them. Therefore we see them all betaking themselves with joined hands to serve the great. In this way they secure peace.' Such is the picture which, about 1016, a German prelate drew of the anarchy in the kingdom of Burgundy. In Artois, in the following century, a monk pertinently explains how among the 'nobility' only very few have been able to avoid the ties of seignorial domination and 'remain subject to the public authority alone'. Even here it is obviously necessary to understand by this term not so much the authority of the crown, which was much too remote, as that of the count, the repository, in place of the sovereign,

[1] *Capitularia*, I, no. 141, c. 27.

of all that remained of a power by its very nature superior to personal ties.

It goes without saying that these ties of dependence spread through all ranks of society and not only among those 'nobles' to whom our monk refers. But the lines of demarcation which the Carolingian age had begun to trace between the different kinds of relationships, characterized by different social atmospheres, were now more firmly drawn.

Certainly language and even manners for a long time preserved vestiges of the old confusion. Some groups of very modest manorial subjects, dedicated to the despised labours of the soil and tied to responsibilities which from now on were considered servile, continued till the twelfth century to bear that name of 'commended men' which the author of the *Chanson de Roland* applied to the greatest vassals. Because the serfs were the 'men' of their lord, it was often said of them that they lived in his 'homage'. Even the formal act by which an individual acknowledged himself the serf of another was sometimes described by this name and indeed at times, in its ritual, recalled the characteristic gestures of the homage 'of hands'.

This servile homage, however, where it was practised, was in sharp contrast with vassal homage; it did not have to be renewed from generation to generation. Two forms of attachment now began to be distinguished more and more clearly. One was hereditary. It was marked by all manner of obligations considered to be of a rather low order. Above all, it allowed of no choice on the part of the dependant, and so was regarded as the opposite of what was then called 'freedom'. It was in fact serfdom, into which most of those of inferior status who commended themselves descended imperceptibly, in spite of the 'free' character which had marked their original submission in a period when social classifications were based on different principles. The other relationship, which was called vassalage, terminated in law, if not in fact, on the day when one or other of the two lives thus bound together came to an end. By this very characteristic, which relieved it from the stigma of an hereditary restriction on the individual's liberty of action, it was well suited to the honourable service of the sword. And the form of aid which it involved was essentially warlike. By a characteristic synonymity the Latin charters from the end of the eleventh century speak almost indifferently of a man as being the vassal, or the *miles*, of his lord.

[1] Thietmar of Merseburg, *Chronicle*, VII, 30. *Miracula S. Bertini*, II, 8, in Mabillon, *AA. SS. ord. S. Benedicti, III, I, pp.* 133–4.

[2] The use of homage as an expiatory act, which has been mentioned above (p. 130), harks back to its rôle as a gesture of submission proper to persons of relatively high rank. Evidence adduced by G. Platon in an otherwise insufficiently critical article ('L'Hommage féodal comme moyen de contracter des obligations privées' in *Revue générale de droit*, XXVI, 1902) shows that this rite was, in addition, a means of confirming various contractual obligations of private law. The reference, however, is to a deviant practice, restricted to a few regions (Catalonia, perhaps Castile) and of late date.

Literally, the second term should be translated by 'soldier'. But the French texts, from the moment of their appearance, rendered it by 'knight' and it was certainly this vernacular expression which the notaries of an earlier day had had in mind. The soldier was typically a man who served on horseback in heavy armour, and the function of the vassal consisted above all in fighting in this manner for his lord. So that, by another avatar of the old word which not long before had been so humble, 'vassalage' in popular speech came into common use as a name for the finest of the virtues known to a society perpetually at war—to wit, bravery. The relation of dependence thus defined was formally sealed by homage with joined hands, which was henceforth almost entirely restricted to this use. But, from the tenth century, this rite of profound dedication seems generally to have been completed by the addition of the kiss which, by placing the two individuals on the same plane of friendship, lent dignity to the type of subordination known as vassalage. In fact, this relationship was now confined to persons of high—sometimes even of very high—social status. Military vassalage had emerged by a slow process of differentiation from the ancient and disparate practice of commendation, and had come in the end to represent its highest form.

XII

THE FIEF

1 'BENEFIT' AND FIEF: STIPENDIARY TENEMENT

IN the Frankish period, the majority of those who commended themselves
sought from their new master something more than protection. Since this
powerful man was at the same time a wealthy man, they also expected him
to contribute to their support. From St. Augustine, who in the closing
decades of the Western Empire describes the poor in search of a patron
who would provide them with 'the wherewithal to eat', to the Merovingian
formula which we have more than once cited, we hear the same importunate
cry—that of the empty stomach. The lord, for his part, was not influenced
solely by the ambition to exercise authority over men; through their agency
he often sought to lay hold of property. From the outset, in short, protective
relationships had their economic aspect—vassalage as well as the others.
The liberality of the chief towards his war-companions seemed so essential
a part of the bond between them that frequently, in the Carolingian age,
the bestowal of a few gifts—a horse, arms, jewels—was an almost invariable
complement to the gesture of personal submission. One of the capitularies
forbids the breaking of the tie by the vassal if he has already received from
his lord the value of a golden *solidus*. The only true master was he who had
given presents to his dependants.

Now the chief of a group of vassals, like every employer, was more or
less restricted by the general economic conditions of the time. He had to
choose between two methods of rewarding services. Either he could keep
the vassal in his own house and feed, clothe and equip him at his own
expense, or he could endow him with an estate or a regular income derived
from land and leave him to provide for his own maintenance. In French-
speaking districts the latter method was called 'housing' (*chaser*) the vassal,
meaning literally to give him a house of his own (*casa*). By what means was
this concession put into effect?

In early times the simple gift, free from any restrictions on its heritability, was widely resorted to. This is the form employed in a formula of the
seventh century, whereby a chief grants a small estate to his 'companion'.
Later, we find it used on many occasions by the sons of Louis the Pious,
when they wished to display their generosity towards their vassals, with
the express object of holding them to their duty; and in some cases it was

163

accompanied by the stipulation that the gift might be revoked if it did not have the desired effect. Nevertheless, since the estates regularly distributed by the lord to his followers were much more in the nature of pay than of reward, it was essential that they should revert to him without difficulty as soon as the service ceased to be rendered; at the latest, therefore, when the tie was broken by death. In other words, since vassalage was not transmitted by inheritance, the remuneration of the vassal could not, logically, take on a hereditary character.

For such grants of land, by definition temporary and, originally at least, devoid of any 'warranty', neither the official Roman law nor Germanic custom, with their rigid systems of bilateral contracts, afforded any precedents. Nevertheless in the Empire, under the influence of powerful individuals, there had already come into existence as a matter of private arrangement a great many pacts of this kind, which were naturally associated with the patron–client relationship, since they involved the maintenance of the client by the master. The terminology of these contracts was rather vague, as was only to be expected in the case of institutions on the margin of legality. One of the words used to describe them was *precarium*, by reason of the prayer (*preces*) which came or was supposed to come from the recipient of the grant; another name was 'benefit' (*beneficium*). Although the law, which did not recognize such contracts, did not provide the grantor with the means of enforcing in the courts the obligations which he ordinarily imposed on the estate, this mattered little to him, since he always had the right to take back what was in theory a gift made out of pure benevolence.

Both these terms continued to be used in Frankish Gaul, though in the case of *precarium* at the cost of a metamorphosis which has given historians much food for thought. From the neuter it passed to the feminine as *precaria*—simply a special case, it would seem, of a linguistic phenomenon very widely current in low Latin. This was produced by a contamination to which neuter words with plurals ending in *a* were susceptible; among other examples, the French *feuille* was derived in this way from *folium*. The change was facilitated, in the case we are considering, by the attraction exercised by the very name of the request framed by the suppliant— 'praying letter', [*epistola*] *precaria*.

Precaria, beneficium—the two terms appear to have been used almost indifferently at first. But as the *precaria*, which embodied elements borrowed from the law of letting and hiring, gradually assumed the form of a fairly specific contract, this name tended to be reserved for grants which involved the payment of rent. On the other hand the term 'benefit'—at once more vague and more honourable, since it did not suggest the idea of supplication—was applied by preference to temporary grants, made in return for service, to persons attached to seignorial households and especially to vassals. An event of some importance helped to establish the distinction. In order to obtain the estates with which they planned to enlist the support of a great number of sworn followers, the Carolingians shamelessly helped themselves to the immense wealth of the clergy. The first spoliation, under Charles Martel, had been ruthless. His successors did not abandon these levies; but they regularized them—dealing at one and the same time with the sequestrations that had taken place already as well as those that might occur in the future—and they were concerned to safeguard in some measure the rights of the legitimate owners. The bishop or the monastery required to surrender an estate to one of the king's vassals —in theory for life only—was henceforth paid a certain rent; the vassal's service belonged to the king. In relation to the Church, therefore, the estate was in law a *precaria*; but the vassal held it of the king 'in benefit'.

The use of the word 'benefit' to describe the lands granted in exchange for service, and in particular vassal service, was to continue in the Latin of the chancelleries and the chroniclers till well into the twelfth century. *Beneficium*, however, in contrast with really living legal terms, provided no derivative (such as *commendé*) in the Romance tongues; when at length it emerged in French, as *bénéfice*, it was a word steeped in associations dear to the clergy. Quite clearly, its function in the spoken language had long since been taken over by another term. During the feudal ages, perhaps as early as the ninth century, when the French scribes wrote *beneficium*, what they had in mind was 'fief'.

Despite some phonetic difficulties which, in any case, affect the Romance forms less than their Latin transliterations, the history of this famous word is clear.[1] The ancient Germanic languages all possessed a word distantly related to the Latin *pecus*. In some it was used indifferently to describe either movable property in general or the form of it which was then most common and most valuable, namely cattle; in others, it was restricted to one or other of these meanings. The German language has preserved the second of them and writes the word today as *Vieh*. The Gallo-Romans, borrowing it from the German invaders, reproduced it as *fief* (in Provençal *feu*). In this form it retained at first at least one of its traditional meanings— the wider sense of movable property. That it was still so used up to the beginning of the tenth century is attested by various Burgundian charters. An individual, we are told, has purchased a piece of land. The price has been fixed in terms of the ordinary monetary standard, but the purchaser has not got this sum in cash. He therefore pays, according to a practice then current, in objects of equivalent value. The texts express the transaction thus: 'We have received from thee the agreed price, in *feos* valued at so many pounds, shillings or pence.'[2] Comparison with other documents

---

[1] The best account, from the linguistic point of view, is to be found in W. von Wartburg, *Französisches etymologisches Wörterbuch*, III (it should be pointed out, however, that the charter of Charles the Fat, dated 884, is a forgery).

[2] *Recueil des chartes de l'abbaye de Cluny*, ed. Bruel et Bernard, I, nos. 24, 39, 50, 54 68, 84, 103, 236, 243.

proves that what were normally involved were arms, clothing, horses, and sometimes food. These were very much the same commodities as were distributed to the followers maintained in the lord's household or equipped at his expense. In those circles also, no doubt, they spoke of *feos.*

But this word was derived from languages which no one in Romance-speaking Gaul any longer understood, and being in consequence deprived of the support of the entire vocabulary of which it had originally formed part, it naturally lost much of its etymological content. In the seignorial households where it was in daily use, it came to be associated exclusively with the idea of remuneration *per se*, regardless of whether the gifts were in the form of movable or landed property. What happened if a companion received a piece of land from a chief who had originally maintained him in his household? This in its turn was called the vassal's *feus*. Then, since land had become little by little the normal remuneration of the vassal, it was for this form of payment alone that the old word whose original meaning had been quite the reverse was finally reserved. As has happened more than once, semantic evolution ended in mistranslation. Of fiefs in the sense of landed estates held by vassals the earliest example to find its way into the written documents belongs to the end of the ninth century.[1] It appears in one of those southern charters which, having been drawn up by poorly educated clerks, made more than normal use of the spoken vocabulary. In the following century the term appeared in several other texts, also from Languedoc. In spite of their greater concern for linguistic purity, the chancelleries of Brittany, of northern France, and of Burgundy in about the year 1000 began to give way on this point to the pressure of popular speech. Even so this often meant at first that the vernacular expression was reduced to the rank of a gloss designed to make the meaning of the classical term clear to all. 'A benefit (*beneficium*) which in vulgar parlance is called fief,' is the way it is put in 1087 in a document from Hainault.[2]

In the countries where the Germanic tongues were spoken, however, *Vieh* kept its meaning of cattle, to the exclusion of nobler connotations. There was nothing to prevent the language of the charters from borrowing from the notaries of Gaul one or other of the Latin equivalents which they had ingeniously devised for the Romance expression *fief*; the most widely disseminated of them, *feodum*, was familiar to the German chancelleries as well as to those of the Capetian kingdom. But, in order to express something which was so much a part of everyday life as this, the vernacular had

---

[1] *Cartulaire de Maguelonne*, ed. J. Rouquette and A. Villemagne, no. III (different text in C. de Vic and J. Vaissète, *Histoire générale de Languedoc*, V. no. 48). Date: 23rd January 893–27th January 894, or (more probably) 1st January–31st December 898. It is not possible for me here to cite my references for the later examples. The Provençal form *feuz* is in evidence as early as 9th June 956 (*Histoire générale de Languedoc*, V, no. 100).

[2] A. Miraeus, *Donationes belgicae*, II, XXVII.

to have a word of its own. Since the grants of land made to vassals were in theory temporary, the habit developed of describing them by a substantive derived from a verb in common use whose meaning was 'to hand over temporarily, to lend'. The fief was a loan—*Lehn*.[1] Nevertheless, since the connection between this term and its verbal root (which continued to be widely used in current German) always remained perceptible, it never became so specialized as its French equivalent. In popular usage, at least, it continued to be applied to all manner of grants involving land. All of which illustrates the fact that borrowed words adapt themselves more easily than any others to a new and precise technical meaning.

'Benefit', fief, *Lehn*—the concept which these various synonyms sought to express was, on the whole, a very clear one. It was—let us make no mistake about this—basically an economic concept. By fief was meant a property granted not against an obligation to pay something—when this entered into the matter, it was only in a secondary way—but against an obligation to do something. More precisely, a fief involved not only an obligation of service but also a very definite element of professional specialization and of individual action. The villein tenement, which the charters of the eleventh century, anticipating the jurists of the thirteenth, already expressly distinguished from the fief, was burdened with labour services as well as with rents in kind. But the services which it entailed— work in the fields, cartage, even the provision of small products of domestic industry—were considered tasks that anyone could perform. Furthermore, they were regulated by the customs of the village community. But suppose that land had been granted to a lord's 'serjeant' on condition that he should exercise faithful supervision over the other tenants; or to a painter in return for decorating the church of the monks whom he served; or to a carpenter or a goldsmith on the understanding that he would henceforth place his skill at the disposal of the lord; or to a parish priest as payment for exercising the cure of souls; or finally to a vassal, the armed companion of his lord and a warrior by profession. The tenement thus charged with services of a very special nature, which were in each case governed by a different convention or tradition, was distinguished primarily by the fact that it was a form of remuneration; in short, it was a stipendiary tenement. It was called a fief.[2] This was so, regardless of any consideration of rank, and of course, where a humble workman was concerned, without the requirement of homage. The lord's steward was frequently a serf; and

[1] In the poem *Heliand* (822–40), the two subjects to which the word 'fief' and the German *Lehn* relate are found curiously associated in the expression *Lehni feho* = borrowed property (v. 1548).

[2] The examples of serjeant's fiefs (the *fevum sirventale* of southern France, cf. de Vic and Vaissète, *Histoire générale de Languedoc*, V, no. 1037) are well known, as are also those of the *feudum presbyterale*. On the artisans' fiefs, see my references in 'Un Problème d'histoire comparée: la ministerialité en France et en Allemagne', *Revue historique de droit*, 1928, pp. 54–5.

probably neither the cooks of the Benedictines of Maillezais or of the count of Poitou, nor the wielder of the lancet whose duty it was periodically to bleed the monks of Trier, acquired any very great prestige from these occupations. Nevertheless, as they had all been endowed with tenements, instead of merely living on the victuals distributed in the lord's house, these professionally-qualified servants were legitimately numbered among the enfeoffed dependants.

Certain historians, noting some examples of these humble fiefs, have believed them to be a late deviation. But they are wrong. The surveys of the ninth century are already acquainted with 'benefits' held by manorial stewards, artisans and grooms. Einhard, in the reign of Louis the Pious, mentions the 'benefit' of a painter. When for the first time in the Rhineland, between 1008 and 1016, the new name fief appears, disguised in its Latin form, it is used to describe the tenement of a blacksmith. The history of the fief (as well as of vassalage and of many other legal forms in the feudal ages) was that of an institution, originally of a very comprehensive character, which was gradually transformed into one pertaining to a particular social class. Such was the course of its evolution, and not in the reverse direction.

For people undoubtedly found it inconvenient to be obliged to describe by the same name properties which, besides differing greatly in nature and extent, were held by men of such varied status as a petty manorial official, a cook, a warrior (himself the lord of many peasants), a count, or a duke. (Even in our relatively democratic societies, do we not feel the need of words that preserve class distinctions? Do we not speak of the wages of the manual worker, the salary of the official, and the fees of the professional man?) The ambiguity nevertheless persisted for a long time. In thirteenth-century France they continued to speak of fiefs of manorial officials and of artisans; so that the jurists, concerned to segregate the fiefs of vassals, were apt to characterize them by the epithet 'free' (*francs*), that is to say, subject only to obligations befitting a full free man. In other languages, which had borrowed the word fief from French usage, it continued even longer to be used in the general sense of remuneration, even apart from any grant of land. In Italy, in the thirteenth century, the salaries paid in money to certain magistrates or civic officials were termed *fio*; in English-speaking countries today the remuneration of the doctor or the lawyer is still called a 'fee'. Increasingly, however, when the word was used without special qualification, it tended to be understood as applying to the fiefs (at once more numerous and socially more important) with regard to which a true 'feudal' law had developed; namely, the tenements charged with the services of vassalage in the distinctly specialized sense which that term had acquired even earlier. Finally, in the fourteenth century, the *Gloss* of the *Sachsenspiegel* defined it thus: 'The fief (*Lehn*) is the pay of the knight.'

2 THE 'HOUSING' OF VASSALS

The two methods of paying the vassal for his services—by the fief and by maintaining him in the household—were not absolutely incompatible. Once established on his tenement, the vassal did not on that account relinquish his claim to other marks of the lord's generosity—in particular to the gifts of horses and arms, and especially of robes and mantles of 'vair and gris', which came to be expressly provided for in many 'customs' and which even the greatest personages—such as a count of Hainault, vassal of the bishop of Liége—did not disdain to accept. Sometimes we find, as in England in 1166, among the followers of a great baron, certain knights who, though duly provided with lands, none the less live with him and receive from him the 'necessaries of life'.[1]

Nevertheless, apart from some exceptional cases, 'household' vassals and beneficed vassals in reality represented two very well-marked types, serving—from the lord's point of view—different purposes; and as early as Charlemagne's time it was considered abnormal for a royal vassal attached to the palace to hold a benefice 'notwithstanding'. Whatever, in fact, might be required of the feudatories in the way of military service or counsel, or of administrative duties in peace-time, it was only the household vassals, able to be constantly in attendance, who could be expected to perform the innumerable escort duties or higher household services. Since the two categories were not interchangeable, the contrast between them was not, in the strict sense, the contrast between successive stages of development. Undoubtedly the companion maintained in the house of the master represented an older type of relationship. But he continued for a long time to exist side by side with the more recent type—the enfeoffed dependant. What happened if a vassal, after spending some time in the lord's immediate following, obtained a fief? Another person—it might be a youth awaiting his inheritance, or a younger son—took the vacant place at the lord's table; and security of board and lodging, thus guaranteed, seemed so desirable that knightly families of middle rank sometimes solicited the promise of it for their younger members.[2] At the beginning of the reign of Philip Augustus, landless vassals were still so numerous that, in his ordinance concerning the 'tenth' for the Crusade, the king, unwilling to allow any class of contributors to escape the net, considered it necessary to place them in a special category.

There can be no doubt, however, that, as early as the Carolingian epoch, there was a marked disparity in numbers between the two groups of vassals, in favour of the holders of fiefs; and this disparity increased as time went on. Regarding this process and some at least of its causes, we possess unusually striking evidence. Though it relates to an episode which took

---

[1] Gislebert of Mons, *Chronique*, ed. Pertz, p. 35; *Red Book of the Exchequer*, ed. H. Hall, I, p. 283.   [2] *Cartulaire de Saint-Sernin de Toulouse*, ed. Douais, no. 155.

place outside France, it is nevertheless relevant to our subject, since the institutions involved were essentially French in origin.

When William the Bastard had conquered England, his first concern was to introduce into his new kingdom the remarkable system of feudal military service which prevailed in his Norman duchy. He therefore imposed on his principal vassals the obligation of holding constantly at his disposal a prescribed number of knights, the number being fixed once and for all, barony by barony. Thus each of the great nobles immediately dependent on the king was obliged, in his turn, to attach to himself a certain number of military vassals. But he remained free, of course, to decide by what means he would provide for their upkeep. Many bishops and abbots preferred, at first, to give them board and lodging 'on the demesne', without enfeoffing them. This was naturally, in every country, the most attractive solution from the point of view of the princes of the Church, since it seemed to keep intact the inalienable patrimony of landed estates which had been entrusted to their care. About a century later, the biographer of Archbishop Conrad I of Salzburg could still congratulate his hero on having been able to conduct his wars 'without enlisting the support of his knights otherwise than by gifts of movables'. With very few exceptions, however, the English prelates were fairly soon obliged to abandon this system, which suited them so well, and thereafter to place the responsibility for service with the royal army on fiefs carved out of the ecclesiastical estates.[1] The Ely chronicler relates that the vassals, at the time when they were directly maintained by the monastery, made an intolerable nuisance of themselves by their noisy complaints to the cellarer. It may easily be believed that a boisterous body of men-at-arms with undisciplined appetites was a disturbing factor in the peace of the cloister. It seems certain that in Gaul itself such annoyances were partly responsible for the early and rapid reduction in the numbers of those household vassals of churches, who, about the beginning of the ninth century, had been still so numerous in the great religious houses that, at Corbie for example, the monks had been accustomed to reserve for them a special bread of better quality than that provided for other dependants. But, in addition to this inconvenience, peculiar to feudal lordships of a particular kind, there was a more serious difficulty which, if it did not completely put a stop to the practice of domestic maintenance, at least greatly restricted it. During the first feudal age, the regular provisioning of a fairly large group was a big undertaking. More than one monastic annalist speaks of famine in the refectory. Therefore in many cases it was found best, for the master as well as for the armed follower, to make the latter responsible for providing for his own subsistence while giving him the means to do so.

<hr>

[1] J. H. Round, *Feudal England*, London, 1907; H. M. Chew, *The English Ecclesiastical Tenants-in-Chief and Knight-Service, especially in the Thirteenth and Fourteenth Centuries*, Oxford, 1932. For Salzburg, *M.G.H., SS.*, XI, c. 25, p. 46.

The disadvantages of the system of household maintenance were still more evident when the vassals whose fealty had to be paid for were of too high a rank to be content to live perpetually under their master's wing. These men had need of independent revenues which, associated with the political authority they already exercised, would enable them to live in conditions consistent with their prestige. Sometimes, moreover, this was necessary in the interests of vassal service itself. The rôle of a *vassus dominicus* presupposed that a man should pass the greater part of his time in his province, exercising his supervisory functions. Thus it was that in the Carolingian period the extension of vassal relationships, not only in number but also, so to speak, in height, was accompanied by an immense distribution of 'benefits'.

It would be a misconception to suppose that all fiefs were in fact created by a grant made by the lord to the vassal. Paradoxical as it may seem, many actually originated in a gift by the vassal to the lord; for the man who sought a protector had frequently to pay for the privilege. The powerful individual who forced his weaker neighbour to submit to him was apt to require the surrender of his property as well as his person. The lesser men, therefore, in offering themselves to the chief, also offered their lands. The lord, once the bond of personal subordination had been sealed, restored to his new dependant the property thus temporarily surrendered, but subject now to his superior right, expressed by the various obligations imposed upon it. This great movement of land surrender went on at every social level during the Frankish period and the first feudal age. But it assumed very different forms according to the rank and the manner of life of the man who commended himself. The lands of the peasant were returned to him charged with rents in money or in kind and with agricultural labour services. The person of higher social status and warlike habits, after having done homage, received back his former possessions as the honourable fief of a vassal. Thus the distinction between the two great classes of real property rights was finally drawn. On the one hand, there were the modest villein tenements, regulated by the common custom of the manor, and the fiefs; on the other, there were the 'allods', which had remained completely independent.

Like the word fief, but of much more straightforward etymological descent (*od*, 'property', and perhaps *al*, 'whole'), 'allod' was of Germanic origin; like fief, it was adopted by the Romance languages—as *alleu*—and was destined to live only in the company of such borrowed words. The German equivalent was *eigen* ('own'). In spite of some inevitable distortions here and there, the meaning of those two synonymous words remained perfectly stable from the Frankish period to the end of the feudal age and even later. It has sometimes been defined as 'freehold'; but this is to forget that this term can never be applied with strict accuracy to medieval law. Even apart from the universal kinship impediments, the possessor of an allod, if he were himself a lord, might very well have under him tenants, even feudatories, whose rights over the soil—in most cases hereditary in practice—constituted a severe limitation on his own. In other words, the allod was not necessarily an absolute right at the lower end of the scale. At the upper end, however, it was. 'Fief of the sun'—that is to say, without human lord—was the happy description applied to it by the German jurists towards the end of the Middle Ages.

Naturally this privilege could apply to any kind of landed property or revenue from land, whatever the nature of the estate—from the small peasant farm to the largest complex of rents or powers—and whatever the social rank of the holder. There was therefore a contrast between the allod and the villein tenement as well as between the allod and the fief. Only the second of these need concern us at present. In this respect, French and Rhenish development was marked by two stages, of unequal duration.

The anarchy which accompanied and followed the disintegration of the Carolingian state at first gave a good many vassals the opportunity to appropriate outright the lands which they had received as temporary grants. This was especially the case when the grant was made by a church or by the king. Let us compare two charters from Limoges, separated by an interval of thirty-eight years. In the first, dated 876, Charles the Bald hands over to the vassal Aldebert, for his own lifetime and that of his sons, the estate of *Cavaliacus* to be held 'as a usufruct, in benefit'. In the later one, which bears the date 914, Alger, son of Aldebert, makes a gift to the canons of Limoges of 'my allod called *Cavaliacus*, which I got from my parents'.[1]

Nevertheless, unless they fell into the hands of the clergy, as this one did, neither the allods which were the fruits of usurpation nor those of ancient and authentic origin were usually destined to preserve their character for long. Once upon a time, a chronicler tells us, there were two brothers named Herroi and Hacket, who, after the death of their father, a wealthy lord at Poperinghe, shared his allodial estates between them. But the count of Boulogne and the count of Guines were tireless in their efforts to compel them to do homage for these lands. Hacket, 'fearing men more than God', yielded to the demands of the count of Guines. Herroi, on the other hand, being unwilling to submit to either of his two persecutors, took his share of the heritage to the bishop of Thérouanne and received it back from him as a fief.[2] Told at a later date and as mere hearsay, the story is perhaps not very reliable in its details. In its essentials, however, it certainly provides a faithful picture of what could happen to these petty allodial lords, caught up in the rival ambitions of powerful neighbours. Similarly the accurate chronicle of Gilbert of Mons shows us the castles built on the allodial estates of the Hainault region being gradually re-

[1] *S. Stephani Lemovic. Cartul.*, ed. Font-Réaulx, nos. XCI and XVIII.
[2] Lambert of Ardre, *Chronique de Guines*, ed. Menilglaise, c. CI.

duced to the status of fiefs by the counts of Hainault or Flanders. Since the feudal régime, which may be defined essentially as a kind of network of dependent ties, never became a perfect system even in the countries which gave it birth, allodial estates continued to exist. They were still very numerous under the first Carolingians; indeed, the possession of one—and it had to be in the county concerned—was then the necessary condition for appointment as lay representative (*avoué*) of a church. But from the tenth century onwards they were rapidly disappearing, while the number of fiefs was constantly growing. The soil passed into subjection along with the men.

Whatever the real origin of the vassal's fief—whether an estate carved out of the possessions of the lord or a *fief de reprise*, that is to say, a former allod surrendered by its original owner and then 'taken back' by him on feudal terms—it appeared officially as the substance of a grant made by the lord. This explains the adoption of a ceremonial act in keeping with the forms usual at that time for all transfers of real property rights. Such symbolic acts were known as investitures. To the vassal the lord handed an object which symbolized the property. For this purpose a small stick often sufficed, but sometimes a more eloquent token was preferred—a clod of earth, representing the soil conceded; a lance to evoke the idea of military service; a banner, if the vassal was not only a warrior but also a chieftain, with other knights at his call. Into this originally rather indefinite picture custom and the genius of the jurists introduced a host of embellishments, varying according to the region. When a fief was granted to a new vassal, investiture took place immediately after homage and fealty—never before them.[1] The ceremony which created the bond of fealty was a necessary preliminary to its remuneration.

In theory, any form of property could be a fief. In practice, however, where vassals' fiefs were concerned, the social status of the beneficiaries imposed certain limitations—at least after the establishment of a clear-cut distinction between the different forms of commendation. The formula of the grant made to a 'companion', as it has come down to us in a document of the seventh century, appears to provide that agricultural labour services could be demanded. But the vassal of later times no longer condescended to work with his hands. He was therefore obliged to live on the labour of someone else. When he received an estate, he would expect to find on it tenants who were subject, on the one hand, to the payment of rents and, on the other, to labour services which would permit the cultivation of the portion of land generally reserved for direct farming by the master. In short, the majority of the fiefs of vassals were manors of varying size. Others, however, consisted of revenues and, while these also ensured for their possessors a life of aristocratic ease, they did not carry with them

---

[1] At least in the highly feudalized countries, like most of France. Italy was an exception. (For the ceremony of investiture, see Plate V.)

authority over other dependants, except in a subsidiary capacity. They included tithes, churches with their perquisites, markets, and tolls.

As a matter of fact, even revenues of this type, being in some measure attached to the soil, were, in accordance with the medieval classification, placed in the category of landed property. Only later, when the development of an exchange economy and administrative organization had enabled kingdoms and large principalities to accumulate considerable stocks of currency, did the kings and great nobles begin to distribute revenues pure and simple as fiefs. Although they were not based on land, these 'money fiefs' (*fiefs de chambre*) none the less involved homage, and had many advantages from the lord's point of view. In their case there was no risk of the alienation of estates. Largely unaffected by the deformation which, as we shall see, transformed the majority of territorial fiefs into hereditary properties, these grants conferred a life-interest at most and kept the beneficiary in much stricter subordination to the grantor. To the rulers they afforded the means of securing distant vassals, even outside the territories under their immediate control. The kings of England, who early became rich, seem to have been among the first to resort to this method; as early as the end of the eleventh century, they granted money fiefs to Flemish nobles (the count of Flanders above all) in order to enlist their military support. Then Philip Augustus, always ready to imitate his rivals, the Plantagenets, tried to compete with them by using the same method in the same region. Again, by similar means, in the thirteenth century the Hohenstaufen won over the counsellors of the Capetians and the Capetians those of the Hohenstaufen. In this way Saint Louis formed a direct tie with Joinville, who hitherto had been only his sub-vassal.[1] But what if the vassals concerned were armed retainers of the household type? In that case, the money payments obviated the inconvenience of feeding them. If, in the course of the thirteenth century, the number of household vassals diminished very rapidly, this was certainly due in most cases to the fact that the system of maintenance pure and simple had been replaced by the grant—in the form of a fief—of a fixed salary in money.

Was it certain, however, that a revenue of an exclusively movable type could legitimately be the subject of an enfeoffment? The problem was not solely a verbal one; it resolved itself into the question how far the very distinctive legal rules that had gradually been developed round the concept of the vassal's fief should be extended. That is why, in Italy and Germany —the countries where, in the special conditions which will be described later, this feudal law proper was most successful in constituting itself an autonomous system—legal doctrine and court practice refused in the end to recognize money incomes as fiefs. In France, on the other hand, the

[1] G. G. Dept, *Les Influences anglaise et française dans le comté de Flandre*, 1928; Kienast, *Die deutschen Fürsten im Dienste der Westmächte*, I, 1924, p. 159; II, pp. 76, n. 2; 105, n. 2; 112; H. F. Delaborde, *Jean de Joinville*, no. 341.

difficulty seems hardly to have troubled the jurists. Under the old name of military tenure, the great baronial and princely families were able to pass imperceptibly to what was to all intents and purposes a system of cash remuneration, characteristic of a new economy founded on buying and selling.

Since the grant of a fief was the pay of a commended individual, its natural duration was that of the human bond which constituted its *raison d'être*. From about the ninth century onwards, vassalage was regarded as uniting two lives, and consequently it was considered that the 'benefit' or fief was held by the vassal till either his own death or that of his lord, and only till then. This remained to the end the letter of the law. Just as the vassal relationship between the survivor of the original pair and his partner's successor continued only if the act of homage was repeated, so the renewal of the enfeoffment to the vassal's heir or to the vassal himself by the grantor's heir necessitated a repetition of the rite of investiture. How flagrant was the contradiction that soon manifested itself between facts and theories we shall have shortly to consider. But since in this respect the course of evolution was common to the whole of feudal Europe, it will be well first of all to attempt to sketch the development of institutions either similar or analogous to those just described, in countries which so far have remained outside our purview.

XIII

GENERAL SURVEY OF EUROPE

1 FRENCH DIVERSITY: THE SOUTH-WEST AND NORMANDY

IT has been France's lot, since the Middle Ages, to bind together by ever-closer ties of national unity—like the Rhône receiving the Durance, as Mistral finely says—a cluster of societies originally separated by strong contrasts. Everyone knows or is instinctively aware of this; yet no study has been more neglected than that of this social geography. It is therefore only possible here to offer a little guidance to students.

Let us take first the Aquitanian south—the Toulouse region, Gascony, Guienne. In these regions, whose social structure was in every respect very distinctive and which had been influenced only slightly by Frankish institutions, the spread of protective relationships seems to have encountered many obstacles. The allods—small peasant holdings as well as manorial lordships—remained very numerous to the end. Though the concept of the fief was introduced in spite of obstacles, its outlines soon became blurred. As early as the twelfth century, 'fief' was the term applied, in the neighbourhood of Bordeaux or Toulouse, to all sorts of tenements, including those charged with humble rents in kind or agricultural labour services. A similar development occurred in the case of the term 'honour', which had become in the north (as a result of a semantic process which will be described later) almost synonymous with 'fief'. Undoubtedly the two names, when first adopted, had been used in their normal, highly specialized sense. The deviation in meaning, which did not occur at all in the thoroughly feudalized countries, took place subsequently. The truth is that the legal concepts themselves had been imperfectly understood by a regional society familiar with quite different practices.

On the other hand, the Scandinavian followers of Rollo, accustomed to a system of companionage akin to the primitive usages of the Franks, found at the time of their settlement in Neustria nothing in their native traditions which resembled the institutions of the fief and vassalage, as they were already developed in Gaul. Their chiefs nevertheless adapted themselves to these practices with remarkable flexibility. Nowhere better than on this conquered soil were the princes able to use the network of feudal relationships in the interest of their authority. Nevertheless, at the lower levels of society, certain imported characteristics continued in evi-

176

dence. In Normandy, as on the banks of the Garonne, the word fief rapidly acquired the sense of a tenement in general; but not for quite the same reasons. For what seems to have been lacking here was the feeling, elsewhere so powerful, of the differentiation of classes, and consequently of estates, by the kind of life a man led. Witness the special position of the 'vavasours'. There was nothing unusual about the word itself. Throughout the Romance-speaking world, it designated the lowest grade among the holders of military fiefs—those who, in relation to kings and great nobles, were only vassals of vassals (*vassus vassorum*). But the original feature of the Norman vavasour consisted in the singular medley of responsibilities with which his property was burdened. Apart from the obligations of armed service, sometimes on horseback, sometimes on foot, the holding of the vavasour (*vavassorerie*) was subject to rents, and even occasionally to labour services; it was, in fact, half fief, half villein tenement. It seems that this anomaly was a vestige of Viking days; and this is borne out by a glance at the English 'Normandy'—that is at the counties of the north and northeast, known as the 'Danelaw'. The same duality of obligations was there imposed on the holdings of a class of dependants called 'drengs'—the term dreng having originally the same meaning as vassal, i.e. 'boys', though it was frankly Nordic and, as we have seen, apparently already in use, immediately after the invasions, on the banks of the Seine.[1] In the course of the following centuries both vavasour and dreng were to give a great deal of trouble to the jurists, who could not escape from classifications that had become progressively more crystallized. In a world which set the profession of arms above and apart from all other secular activities, they were a constant and embarrassing reminder of the time when, among the Northmen (as is still seen so clearly in the Icelandic sagas), there was no gulf between the life of the peasant and that of the warrior.

2 ITALY

Lombard Italy had witnessed the spontaneous development of ties of personal dependence similar in almost every respect to the various forms of commendation known to Gaul—from the simple delivery of one's own person into servitude to the institution of military companionage. The war-companions, at least those surrounding the kings, dukes and principal chiefs, bore the common Germanic name of *gasindi*. Many of them received estates, though as a rule they had to hand them back to the chief if they withdrew their allegiance. For, in conformity with the customs which we find everywhere at the root of this kind of relationship, the tie at that

[1] The best account of the English 'drengs' is that by G. Lapsley in the *Victoria County History: Durham*, I, p. 284. Cf. J. E. A. Jolliffe, 'Northumbrian Institutions' in *English Historical Review*, XLI (1926).

period was not yet indissoluble: to the free Lombard, provided that he did not leave the kingdom, the law expressly recognized the right to 'go with his kindred whither he would'.

Nevertheless the notion of a legal category of estates specifically devoted to the remuneration of services does not seem to have emerged clearly before the absorption of the Lombard state in the Carolingian. In Italy, the 'benefit' was a Frankish importation; and soon, as in the land of its origin, it came to be called by preference a 'fief'. This word was to be found in the Lombard tongue with the old meaning of movable property. But its use, as early as the end of the ninth century, in the new sense of military tenement is attested by documents from the neighbourhood of Lucca.[1] At the same time, the Gallo-Frankish word 'vassal' gradually replaced *gasindus*, which was relegated to the more restricted meaning of unenfeoffed armed retainer. Foreign domination had placed its imprint on the institutions themselves. As a result partly of the social crisis provoked by the wars of conquest (on this subject a Carolingian capitulary provides curious evidence),[2] and partly of the ambitions of the immigrant aristocracy which had taken over the higher offices, there had been an increase of every type of patronage. What is more, Carolingian policy simultaneously regularized and extended, on this side of the Alps as on the other, what had been originally a rather loose system of personal and territorial dependence. If, in the whole of Europe, northern Italy was unquestionably the region where the system of vassalage and the fief most nearly resembled that prevailing in France proper, the reason was that in both countries the basic conditions were much the same. In both countries there was a similar foundation to the system—a social substratum where the practices of Roman clientage were blended with the traditions of Germany; and in both a cohesive force was provided by the organizing work of the first Carolingians.

But, in this land where neither legislative activity nor the teaching of law was ever interrupted, feudal custom ceased at a very early date to consist exclusively, as for so long in France, of a rather vague and almost purely oral collection of traditional or jurisprudential precepts. The ordinances on this subject promulgated from 1037 onwards by the rulers of the Italian kingdom—who were in fact the German kings—gave rise to a whole technical literature which, besides providing a commentary on the laws themselves, set out to describe 'the good customs of the courts'. The principal chapters of this literature were brought together, as we know, in the famous compilation of the *Libri Feudorum*. Now one thing is unique about the law of vassalage as set forth in these texts. Homage of mouth and hands is never mentioned; the oath of fealty appears to suffice as the basis

---

[1] P. Guidi and E. Pelegrinetti, 'Inventari del vescovato, della cattedrale e di altre chiese di Lucca' in *Studi e Testi pubblicati per cura degli scrittori della Biblioteca Vaticana*, XXXIV, 1921, no. 1.　　　　　[2] *Capitularia*, I, no. 88.

of allegiance. In this, it is true, there was a measure of systematization and artificiality, in harmony with the spirit of almost all the didactic writings of that period. The ordinary legal documents show that in Italy, in feudal times, homage after the Frankish fashion was sometimes performed; but not invariably, nor even perhaps usually. It was not considered necessary to the creation of the bond. An imported rite, it had undoubtedly never been completely accepted by legal opinion, which here much more than beyond the Alps was ready to recognize obligations contracted without any formal act.

A vivid light is thrown on the intrinsic conception of the vassal's fief by its history in another part of Italy—the Patrimony of St. Peter. In 999, the favour of the Emperor Otto III placed on the papal throne a man who had been born in the heart of Aquitaine and who in the course of his brilliant and restless career had gained experience of the monarchies and great ecclesiastical principalities of the old Frankish countries, as well as of Lombard Italy. This man was Gerbert of Aurillac, who became Pope Sylvester II. He found that his predecessors had known nothing of the fief. Certainly the Roman Church had its vassals, and it was accustomed to provide them with estates; but it still employed for this purpose the old Roman forms, especially *emphyteusis*, and these contracts, adapted to the needs of societies of quite another type, were ill-suited to the necessities of the time. They did not in themselves carry any obligations of service; the grants were temporary, though they might embrace several lives, but they did not embody the salutary principle of reversion to the grantor from generation to generation. Gerbert wished to replace them by genuine enfeoffments, and he explained why.[1] Though he was apparently not very successful in this first effort, fief and homage after his time gradually penetrated into the practice of the papal government—a proof that this dual institution was henceforth deemed indispensable to any sound organization of ties of dependence within the military class.

3 GERMANY

In addition to the provinces of the Meuse and the Rhine, which were from the first integral parts of the kingdom founded by Clovis and centres of Carolingian power, the German state, as it took definite shape towards the beginning of the tenth century, included vast territories which had remained outside the great heterogeneous mass of men and institutions which constituted Gallo-Frankish society. Of these regions the most important was the Saxon plain between the Rhine and the Elbe, which had been brought into the Western orbit only from the time of Charlemagne. The

---

[1] In the bull relating to Terracina, dated December 26 in the year 1000. Cf. Karl Jordan, 'Das Eindringen des Lehnwesens in das Rechtsleben der Römischen Kurie' in *Archiv für Urkundenforschung*, 1931.

institutions of the fief and vassalage nevertheless spread throughout trans-Rhenish Germany, but—and this was particularly true of the North—without ever penetrating the social body as profoundly as they had done in the old Frankish territories. Homage had been adopted by the upper classes, less completely than in France, as the human relationship appropriate to their rank, and in consequence it retained more of its primitive character as a rite of pure subordination. Only very exceptionally was the joining of hands accompanied by that kiss of friendship which placed lord and vassal almost on an equal level. It is possible that at the outset members of the great families of chiefs had felt some reluctance to submit to ties still regarded as half-servile. In the twelfth century, the story was told in Welf circles that one of the ancestors of the house, having heard of the homage done by his son to the king, had been so incensed by this act, which he regarded as a blemish on the 'nobility' and 'freedom' of his line, that he retired into a monastery and refused to his dying day to see the offender again. The story, which contains genealogical errors, is not of established authenticity. It is none the less symptomatic; nothing like the attitude it reflects is to be found elsewhere in the feudal world.

Moreover the distinction between military service and the cultivation of the soil, the real foundation elsewhere of the cleavage between classes, here took longer to establish itself. When, in the early years of the tenth century, King Henry I, himself a Saxon, set up fortified bases on the eastern frontier of Saxony, which was constantly threatened by Slavs and Hungarians, he entrusted their defence to warriors who are said to have been divided normally into groups of nine. Eight of them were settled in the neighbourhood of the fortress and came in to man it only in face of a threatened attack. The ninth lived there permanently in order to look after the houses and provisions reserved for his companions. At first sight, the system is not unlike that adopted at the same period for the defence of various French castles. On closer scrutiny, however, an extremely important difference is apparent. Unlike the Western vassals engaged in 'castle-guard', who depended for their subsistence either on distributions made by the master or on the rents of the fiefs with which he had provided them, these defenders of the Saxon borders were themselves genuine peasants, cultivating the soil with their own hands—*agrarii milites*.

Till the close of the Middle Ages, two characteristics continued to bear witness to this less developed feudalization of German society. First, there was the number and extent of the allodial estates, especially those belonging to the great men. When the Welf Henry the Lion, duke of Bavaria and Saxony, had in 1180 been deprived by a legal judgment of the fiefs that he held of the Empire, his allodial estates, which remained in the hands of his descendants, proved large enough to constitute a veritable principality; this was transformed in its turn seventy-five years later into

180

an imperial fief and, under the name of the duchy of Brunswick and Lüneburg, was to form the basis of the states of Brunswick and Hanover in the
future German Confederation.[1] Secondly, in Germany the law of the
fief and vassalage, instead of being, as in France, inextricably woven into
the whole legal fabric, was at an early date treated as a separate system,
whose rules were applicable only to certain estates or certain persons and
were administered by special courts—much in the same way as in France
today the law regulating commercial transactions and merchants is
separate from the civil law. *Lehnrecht*, the law of fiefs; *Landrecht*, the
general law of the country—the great legal manuals of the thirteenth
century are almost entirely based on this dualism, of which the Frenchman
Beaumanoir would never have dreamed. Its sole justification was that
many legal ties, even among the upper classes, failed to come under the
feudal heading.

4 OUTSIDE THE CAROLINGIAN EMPIRE: ANGLO-SAXON ENGLAND AND NORTH-WESTERN SPAIN

Across the Channel, which even in the worst periods of disorder was still
traversed by small craft, the barbarian kingdoms of Britain were not
beyond the reach of Frankish influences. The admiration which the Carolingian state, especially, inspired in the island monarchies seems at times
to have expressed itself in genuine attempts at imitation; witness, among
other instances, the appearance in a few charters and narrative texts of
the word vassal, an obvious borrowing. But these foreign influences remained wholly on the surface. Anglo-Saxon England affords the historian
of feudalism the most precious of examples—that of a society of Germanic
structure which, till the end of the eleventh century, pursued an almost
completely spontaneous course of evolution.

No more than any of their contemporaries did the Anglo-Saxons find
in the ties of the folk or the kindred the means to satisfy fully either the
weak man's need for protection or the strong man's desire for power.
From the beginning of the seventh century, when we begin to penetrate the
obscurity of a history hitherto devoid of written records, we find in process
of formation a system of protective relationships whose development was
completed two centuries later under the pressure of the Danish invasion.
From the outset the laws recognized and regulated these relationships,
which, here also, when the emphasis was on the submission of the inferior,
bore the Latin name of *commendatio*. If, on the other hand, the emphasis
was on the protection accorded by the master, the Germanic word *mund*
was used. These practices were favoured by the kings, at least from the
tenth century onwards, as being conducive to public order. A law of

---

[1] Cf. L. Hüttebräuker, 'Das Erbe Heinrichs des Löwen' in *Studien und Vorarbeiten
zum historischen Atlas Niedersachsens*, H. 9, Göttingen, 1927.

Aethelstan, between 925 and 935, deals with the case of the lordless man. If this situation is found to be an impediment to the exercise of legal sanctions, his kinsmen must name a lord for him in the folk-moot. What if they are unwilling or unable to do so? He becomes an outlaw and whoever encounters him is entitled to kill him, like any robber. The rule clearly did not touch persons of sufficiently high rank to be subject to the immediate authority of the sovereign; these were their own warrantors. But such as it was—and we do not know to what extent it was enforced in practice—it went farther, in intention at least, than anything Charlemagne or his successors had ever dared to attempt.[1] Moreover, the kings themselves did not hesitate to use these ties to their own advantage. Their military dependants, who were called 'thegns', were dispersed—like so many *vassi dominici*—throughout the realm, protected by special scales of *wergild* and entrusted with genuine public duties. If nevertheless, by one of the typical time-lags of history, protective relationships in England before the Norman Conquest never went beyond the still indeterminate state which had been more or less the stage reached by Merovingian Gaul, the reason must be sought less in the weakness of a monarchy profoundly affected by the Danish wars than in the persistence of an original social structure.

In England, as elsewhere, the armed followers with whom the kings and nobles surrounded themselves had at an early date become conspicuous among the crowd of dependants. Various names with nothing in common but a rather humble and domestic ring were used concurrently or successively to describe these household warriors. Among them we find, naturally, *gesith*, already familiar in the Latinized form *gasindus*; *gesella* signifying 'hall-companion'; *geneat*, 'table-companion'; *thegn*, a word distantly related to the Greek τέκνον and having, like vassal, the original meaning of 'young boy'; and 'knight', which is the same word as the German *Knecht*, i.e. servant or slave. From the time of Cnut, the term *housecarl*—'houseboy', borrowed from the Scandinavian—was frequently applied to the armed followers of the king or the magnates. The lord—of the military retainer as well as of the humblest commended man and even of the slave —was called *hlaford* (whence was derived the modern English word 'lord'), meaning literally 'loaf-giver', just as the men gathered in his house were 'loaf-eaters' (*hlafoetan*). He was indeed a foster-father as well as a protector. A curious poem brings before us the plaint of one of these war-companions, compelled after the death of his lord to roam the highways in search of a new 'distributor of treasure'. It is the poignant lament of a sort of social

---

[1] Aethelstan, II, 2.—Among the agreements concluded at Mersen in 847 by the three sons of Louis the Pious, the proclamation of Charles the Bald contains the following phrase: 'Volumus etiam ut unusquisque liber homo in nostro regno seniorem, qualem voluerit, in nobis et in nostris fidelibus accipiat.' But examination of the similar dispositions included in the various partitions of the Empire shows that 'volumus' means here 'we permit', not 'we ordain'.

outcast, deprived at one and the same time of protection, kindness, and the pleasures most necessary to life. 'He dreams at times that he embraces and kisses his lord, and lays hands and head upon his knees, as he did in days gone by at the high seat whence bounty flowed; then the friendless man awakes and sees before him now only the dark waves. . . . Where are the joys of the great hall? Where, alas, the bright cup?'

Alcuin, describing in 801 one of these armed bands, which was attached to the household of the archbishop of York, mentioned that it included both 'noble warriors' and 'non-noble warriors'—a proof at once of the mixing of classes that originally characterized all groups of this sort and of the distinctions which nevertheless already tended to prevail amongst them. One of the services rendered by the Anglo-Saxon documents is that on this point they underline a causal relation which is scarcely revealed in the deplorably scanty Merovingian sources. The differentiation was a natural development; but it was clearly hastened by the practice, which spread progressively, of providing these fighting-men with lands. The extent and nature of the grant, varying in accordance with the man's rank, had the effect of sharpening these distinctions. Nothing is more revealing than the changes in terminology. Among the words which have just been listed, some eventually fell into disuse. Others acquired a more specialized meaning, moving either up or down the social scale. At the beginning of the seventh century, the *geneat* was a real warrior and a person of fairly high rank; in the eleventh, he was a modest tenant-farmer, almost the only difference between him and the other peasants being that he was required to perform guard duties for his master and carry his messages. *Thegn*, on the contrary, remained the label of a much more highly regarded class of military dependants. But, since the majority of these had been gradually provided with tenements, the need soon arose for a new term with which to describe the domestic fighting-men who had replaced them in the military service of the household. The name adopted was 'knight', which had now lost its servile taint. Nevertheless the movement making for the institution of a stipendiary form of land tenure was so irresistible that on the eve of the Norman Conquest there were instances of 'knights' who had also been provided with estates.

The fluidity of these verbal distinctions demonstrates the continued absence of any clear differentiation among the classes. Another piece of evidence is furnished by the very form of the acts of submission. To the end the ceremony of the joined hands was included or omitted at will, whatever the social ranks involved. In Frankish Gaul the extremely clear-cut separation which finally appeared between vassalage and the lower forms of commendation was based on a twofold principle. On the one hand there was the incompatibility between two kinds of life and therefore of obligations—the way of the warrior and the way of the peasant; on the other, there was the wide gulf between a voluntary life commitment and an hereditary tie. Neither of these factors was operative to the same degree in Anglo-Saxon society.

Agrarii milites, 'peasant warriors'—this phrase, which we have already encountered in Germany, was also used by an Anglo-Norman chronicler, in 1159, to characterize certain traditional elements of the military forces which England (whose organization had not been completely upset by the Conquest) continued to place at the disposal of its foreign king.[1] Although they were mere survivals at this period, the elements referred to were related to what had been very general practices a century earlier. Those *geneats* and those *radmen*, whose holdings, so numerous in the tenth century, were burdened with escort or message duties as well as rents and agricultural services, were in fact fighting-men and peasants combined. Was not this equally true of certain of the thegns themselves, who were also subject, by virtue of their estates, to humble *corvées* along with military service? Everything conspired to maintain this sort of confusion of classes. In the first place, Britain lacked that substratum of Gallo-Roman society which in Gaul—though its influence cannot be precisely appraised—seems clearly to have contributed to the development of class distinctions. Then there was the influence of the Nordic civilizations. It was in the northern counties, which had been profoundly affected by Scandinavian influences, that peasant thegns were especially to be found, alongside the drengs with whom we are already acquainted. Another factor was the minor rôle assigned to the horse. Many of the Anglo-Saxon retainers did indeed possess mounts; but they normally fought on foot. The battle of Hastings was essentially the defeat of a body of infantry by a mixed force in which the foot-soldiers were supported by the manœuvres of the cavalry. In pre-Conquest England, 'vassal' and 'horseman' were never identified, as they normally were on the continent; and if, after the arrival of the Normans, the word 'knight' came eventually—though hesitatingly—to be employed as a translation of the second of these terms it was undoubtedly because the horsemen originally brought over by the invaders were for the most part, like the majority of 'knights', landless warriors. The apprenticeship and the constant training which were required to manage a charger in the mêlée and fight from the saddle with heavy weapons were scarcely necessary to enable a peasant to ride as far as the field of battle.

As for the contrasts which arose elsewhere from the varying duration of the tie, they had little opportunity to manifest themselves very strongly in England. For—with the obvious exception of slavery pure and simple—the protective relationships at all levels could be terminated without much difficulty. The laws, it is true, forbade a man to abandon his lord without the latter's consent, but this permission could not be refused provided that the property granted in return for services was restored and that no obligation incurred in the past remained unfulfilled. The 'quest for a lord'—a

---

[1] Robert of Torigny, ed. L. Delisle, I, p. 320.

search which might be perpetually renewed—was regarded as an impre-
scriptible privilege of the free man. 'Let no lord obstruct it,' says Aethelstan,
'once he has received what is due to him.' Undoubtedly special agreements,
local or family customs, or even force were sometimes more powerful than
legal rules. More than one subordination of man to lord was in practice
transformed into a life-long or even an hereditary tie; but even so a great
many dependants, sometimes of very humble status, retained the right,
as *Domesday Book* puts it, 'to betake themselves to another lord'. Furthermore, there was no rigid classification of territorial relationships to provide
a framework for a system of personal relationships. If among the estates
which the lords granted to their retainers many—as on the continent in the
days of early vassalage—were ceded in full ownership, there is no doubt
that others were to be held only so long as the fealty itself endured. These
temporary concessions frequently bore, as in Germany, the name of loan
(*laen*, in Latin *praestitum*). But the idea of a stipendiary property, with
obligatory reversion to the grantor at each death, does not seem to have
been clearly developed. When, in the late tenth century, the bishop of
Worcester granted land in this way in return for the promise of obedience,
the payment of rents and military service, he adopted the old ecclesiastical
system of granting a lease for three generations. It sometimes happened
that the two ties—of the man and of the land—did not coincide. Under
Edward the Confessor a person who obtained the grant of a holding from
an ecclesiastical lord (also for three generations) received at the same time
the authorization 'to go with it, during this term, to whatsoever lord he
would'—that is to say, to commend himself, both his person and his land,
to a master other than the grantor. It was a dualism which would have been
quite inconceivable in France at the same period, among the upper classes
at least.

Moreover, important as the protective relationships had become in
Anglo-Saxon England as a means of social cohesion, they had by no means
extinguished every other tie. The lord was responsible publicly for his men,
but alongside this solidarity of master and subordinate, there subsisted
—in full vigour and carefully organized by the law—the old collective
solidarities of families and groups of neighbours. In the same way, the
military obligation of every member of the folk survived, more or less in
proportion to his wealth. As a result a confusion occurred here, which is
immensely instructive. Two types of fully equipped warrior served the king
—his thegn, who was more or less equivalent to the Frankish vassal, and
the ordinary free man, provided that he had means. Naturally, the two
categories partly overlapped, since the thegn was not as a rule a poor man.
It became customary therefore, towards the tenth century, to describe as
thegns (meaning king's thegns), and to credit with the privileges of thegn-
hood, all free subjects of the king who possessed sufficiently extensive
estates, even though they might not be placed under his special protection.

This status might even be accorded to those who had successfully engaged in the highly-regarded occupation of overseas trading. Thus the same word was used indifferently to express either the status gained by an act of personal submission, or membership of an economic class—an ambiguity which (even when allowance is made for the fact that the minds of that age were remarkably impervious to contradictions in ideas) could only have come about because in pre-Conquest England the tie between man and man was not regarded as incomparably the strongest of social bonds. Perhaps it would not be wholly incorrect to interpret the collapse of Anglo-Saxon civilization as the calamity of a society which, when its old social categories disintegrated, proved incapable of replacing them by a system of clearly defined protective relationships, organized on hierarchical principles.

The historian of feudalism searching for a really distinctive field of comparisons in the Iberian peninsula should not direct his attention to north-eastern Spain. Catalonia, originally a march of the Carolingian Empire, had been profoundly influenced by Frankish institutions. The same was true, though more indirectly, of the neighbouring kingdom of Aragon. Nothing was more original, on the other hand, than the structure of the societies of the north-western Iberian group—Asturias, Leon, Castile, Galicia and, later, Portugal. Unfortunately, the study of it has not been carried very far. Here, briefly, is what research has so far yielded.

The heritage of Visigothic society transmitted by the early kings and the nobility, and the conditions of life common to the entire West at that period, favoured, there as elsewhere, the development of personal dependence. The chiefs in particular had their household warriors whom they usually called their *criados*, that is to say, their 'fosterlings'. The texts sometimes describe them as 'vassals'; but this was a borrowed word, and the very rare instances of its use are chiefly interesting as recalling that even this exceptionally independent region of the Iberian peninsula was nevertheless subject—apparently increasingly so—to the influence of the feudal societies beyond the Pyrenees. How could it have been otherwise, when so many French knights and clerics were constantly going to and fro over the passes? Similarly, the word homage is occasionally found and, with it, the rite. But the native gesture of submission was different. It consisted in the kissing of hands, and was conducted with a much less rigorous formality. It might be repeated fairly frequently, as an act of ordinary courtesy. Although the name *criados* seems above all to imply household retainers and though the *Poem of the Cid* can still describe the followers of the hero as 'those who eat his bread', the tendency here, as everywhere, was to replace the distribution of food and gifts by endowments of land; but in this case the process was somewhat retarded by the exceptional amount of booty brought back from expeditions into Moorish territory by kings and nobles. There emerged nevertheless a fairly clear notion of a tenement charged with services and revocable in case of failure to perform them. A few documents, inspired by foreign terminology, and in some cases drafted by clerks from France, call it 'fief' (using its Latin equivalents). The vernacular had evolved, quite independently, a term of its own, *prestamo*, meaning literally—by a curious parallelism of ideas with the German or Anglo-Saxon *Lehn*—'loan'.

These practices, however, never gave rise, as in France, to a strong and well-ordered network of feudal relationships penetrating the whole of society. Two great events stamp the history of the societies of north-western Spain with a character of their own—the reconquest and the re-settlement. In the vast areas wrested from the grasp of the Moors, peasants were established as small-holders. These settlers escaped at least the most oppressive forms of seignorial subjection, while maintaining of necessity the warlike aptitudes of a sort of border militia. The result was that far fewer vassals than in France could be provided with revenues derived from the rents and forced labour of unfree tenants; and a further result was that though the armed retainer was the fighting-man *par excellence*, he was not the only fighting-man, or even the only one to be mounted. By the side of the knighthood of the *criados* there existed a 'peasant knighthood', composed of the richest of the free tenants. More-over, the power of the king, the war-leader, remained much more effective than it was north of the Pyrenees; and since the kingdoms were far less extensive, their rulers experienced much less difficulty in keeping in direct touch with the mass of their subjects. Hence, there was no confusion be-tween the homage of the vassal and the subordination of the official, between the office and the fief. Neither was there a regular gradation of vassal engagements, rising step by step—save where interrupted by an allodial property—from the humblest knight to the king. There were, here and there, groups of retainers, many of them provided with estates as remuneration for their services; but they were imperfectly linked together and were far from constituting, as in France, the main framework of society and the State. Two factors, indeed, appear to have been indispensable to any fully developed feudal régime: the enjoyment by the vassal-knight of a virtual monopoly of the profession of arms and the more or less volun-tary abandonment, in favour of the tie of vassalage, of other means of government.

5 THE IMPORTED FEUDAL SYSTEMS

The establishment of the dukes of Normandy in England was one among a remarkable series of examples of the migration of legal institutions—the transmission to a conquered country of French feudal practices. This phenomenon occurred three times in the course of the same century: across the Channel, after 1066; in southern Italy where, from about 1030, other Norman adventurers began to carve out for themselves principalities which were destined, a century later, to be united to form the kingdom of Sicily; and lastly in Syria, in the states founded from 1099 onwards by the Crusaders. On English soil the existence among the conquered population of practices already closely resembling vassalage facilitated the adaptation of the foreign institutions. Latin Syria presented a *tabula rasa*. As for southern Italy, it had been partitioned, before the arrival of the Normans, among three different powers. In the Lombard principalities of Benevento, Capua, and Salerno the practices of personal dependence were very widespread, though they had not been developed into a well-organized hierarchic system. In the Byzantine provinces, oligarchies of landowners, warriors, and often merchants also, dominated the mass of the humble folk who were sometimes bound to them by a sort of patron–client relationship. Finally, in the regions ruled by the Arab emirs there was nothing even remotely akin to vassalage. But, however great the contrasts may have been, the transplantation of feudal and vassal relationships was made easy by the fact that they were class institutions. Above the peasant class, and in some cases the burgher class, both of hereditary type, the ruling groups, composed essentially of invaders (to whom in England and especially in Italy were joined some elements of the native aristocracy), formed so many colonial societies governed by usages which, like the rulers themselves, came from abroad.

In the countries where feudalism was an importation it was much more systematically organized than in those where its development had been purely spontaneous. It is true that in southern Italy allodial estates continued to exist; for in these territories, which had been conquered gradually (as a result of agreements as much as of wars), the upper classes and their traditions had not completely disappeared. Many of these allods—and this was a characteristic feature—were in the hands of the old urban aristocracies. On the other hand, neither in Syria nor in England—if we disregard certain fluctuations of terminology—was the allod permitted. All land was held of a lord and this chain, which was nowhere broken, led link by link to the king. Every vassal, in consequence, was bound to the sovereign not only as his subject, but also by a tie which ascended from man to man. Thus the old Carolingian principle of 'coercion' by the lord was applied, in these lands which had never known the Carolingian Empire, with almost ideal precision.

In England, ruled by a powerful monarchy which had introduced the strong administrative practices of the Norman duchy, these imported institutions not only formed a more strictly regulated system than in any other country; by a sort of contagion, which spread from top to bottom, they penetrated virtually the whole of society. In Normandy, as we know, the word fief underwent a profound change of meaning—to the extent of being applied to any form of tenement. The deviation had probably begun before 1066, though at that date the change was not yet complete. But if the lines of development on both sides of the Channel were parallel, they were not exactly the same. English law, in the second half of the twelfth century, came to distinguish clearly two great categories of tenements. Some (and these no doubt comprised the majority of the small peasant holdings), since they were regarded as both of uncertain duration and subject to dishonourable services, were described as unfree. Others, the possession of which was protected by the royal courts, formed the group of free holdings. It was to this group that the name fief (fee) was now applied. The knight's fees were included in this category along with lands held in free socage or in burgage. We must not think of the assimilation as a purely verbal one. In the whole of Europe, in the eleventh and twelfth centuries, the military fief, as we shall see shortly, was transformed into what was to all intents and purposes an hereditary estate. Furthermore, being regarded as indivisible, it was in many countries transmitted only from eldest son to eldest son. Such was the case in England, in particular. But here primogeniture gradually permeated a large part of the social structure. It was applied to all the estates described as fees, and sometimes to humbler holdings. Thus this privilege of birthright, which was to become one of the most important and distinctive features of English social custom, was fundamentally an expression of the process by which the fief became, as it were, transmuted into the characteristic tenure of free men. Among feudal societies, England is in a sense at the opposite pole from Germany. It was not enough for her merely to refrain, like France, from erecting the 'custom' of the feudal classes into a separate body of law; in England, a considerable part of the *Landrecht*—that relating to real property rights—was *Lehnrecht*.

XIV

THE FIEF BECOMES
THE PATRIMONY OF THE VASSAL

1 THE PROBLEM OF INHERITANCE: 'HONOURS' AND ORDINARY FIEFS

THE establishment of the heritability of fiefs was numbered by Montesquieu among the constituents of 'feudal government' as opposed to the 'political government' of Carolingian times. This classification is correct, though it should be borne in mind that, in the literal sense, the term 'heritability' is inexact. Possession of the fief was never transmitted automatically by the death of the previous holder. But, except in certain rigorously prescribed circumstances, the lord had no power to refuse investiture to the natural heir, provided the latter did homage beforehand. The triumph of heritability in this sense was the triumph of social forces over an obsolescent right. In order to understand the reasons for this it is essential to form an idea of the attitude of the parties concerned. We shall confine our enquiry to the simplest case: that in which the vassal left only one son.

Even in the absence of any grant of an estate, the bond of fealty tended to unite not so much two individuals as two families, one of them pledged to exercise authority, the other to submit to it. Could it have been otherwise in a society in which the ties of kinship were so strong? Throughout the Middle Ages great sentimental value was attached to the expression 'natural lord'—meaning lord by birth. But as soon as enfeoffment took place the claim of the son to succeed his father in the vassal relationship became almost irresistible. To refuse homage, or not to have it accepted, was not only to lose the fief but to lose a considerable part, perhaps even the whole, of the paternal inheritance as well. The loss must have seemed even harder when it was a *fief de reprise*, that is to say when it represented in reality an old family allod. Stipendiary tenure, by attaching the vassal relationship to the soil, inevitably attached it to the family group.

The lord had less freedom of action. It was of the greatest importance to him that the 'forsworn' vassal should be punished and that the fief, if the obligations failed to be discharged, should be available for a better

190

servant. His interest, in short, led him to insist strongly on the principle of revocability. On the other hand, he was not necessarily opposed to hereditary succession. For above everything he needed men, and where better could he recruit them than among the descendants of those who had already served him? Furthermore, in refusing the father's fief to the son he not only ran the risk of discouraging new commendations; he was in danger—and this was an even more serious matter—of alarming his other vassals, understandably apprehensive as to the treatment in store for their own descendants. In the words of the monk Richer, who wrote in the reign of Hugh Capet, to rob the child was to drive all 'good men' to despair. But the lord who was temporarily disseised of a part of his patrimony might also desire urgently to resume possession of the estate and the castle as well as the political authority exercised by the vassal; even when he decided on a new enfeoffment, he might prefer another commended man, considered to be more reliable or more useful than the heir of the previous vassal. Finally, the churches, guardians of a theoretically inalienable fortune, were particularly disinclined to recognize the permanent character of enfeoffments to which, in most cases, they had originally agreed only with reluctance.

The complex interplay of these different factors never appeared more clearly than under the first Carolingians. From that time 'benefits' were frequently transmitted to descendants. A case in point was the estate of Folembray, which was a royal 'benefit' as well as a *precaria* of the Church of Rheims; from the reign of Charlemagne to that of Charles the Bald it was handed down through four successive generations.[1] Even the consideration due to the vassal while alive, by a curious roundabout process, sometimes helped to make a fief hereditary. Suppose, says Archbishop Hincmar, that a vassal, enfeebled by age or sickness, becomes incapable of carrying out his duties. If he is able to substitute a son for this purpose, the lord will not be allowed to dispossess him.[2] It was no great step to recognize in advance this heir's right to succeed to a position whose responsibilities he had assumed during the lifetime of the holder. Already, indeed, it was deemed a very cruel act to deprive an orphan of his father's 'benefit', even if he were too young to perform his military duties. In a case of this sort we find Louis the Pious allowing himself to be moved by a mother's prayers, and the abbot of Ferrières, Servatus Lupus, appealing to the kind-heartedness of a bishop. That in strict law, however, the 'benefit' was purely a life grant was not yet disputed. In 843 a certain Adalard gave to the monastery of Saint-Gall extensive estates of which a part had been distributed to vassals. The latter, having passed under the domination of the Church, were to retain their 'benefits' for life, as were their sons after

[1] E. Lesne, *Histoire de la propriété ecclésiastique en France*, Lille, 1910–36, II, 2, pp. 251–2.
[2] *Pro ecclesiae libertatum defensione*, in Migne, *P.L.*, CXXV, col. 1050.

them should they be willing to serve. After this the abbot was free to dispose of the estates as he would: evidently it would have been considered contrary to recognized practice to tie his hands indefinitely.[1] Moreover Adalard may have been interested only in the children whom he knew personally. Homage, still close to its source, engendered only narrowly personal feelings.

On this first basis of convenience and expediency true heritability gradually established itself in that troubled period, prolific in innovations, which opened with the disintegration of the Carolingian Empire. The course of evolution everywhere tended in this direction. But the problem did not present itself in the same terms for every type of fief. One category must be treated separately—those fiefs which later the feudists called *fiefs de dignité*—that is, fiefs created from public offices delegated by the king.

From the time of the early Carolingians, as we have seen, the king bound to himself by the ties of vassalage those to whom he entrusted the chief responsibilities of government and, particularly, the great territorial commands—counties, marches or duchies. But these functions, which retained the old Latin name of 'honours', were at that time carefully distinguished from 'benefits'. They differed from them, among other things, by one particularly striking feature: they were not granted for life. Their occupants could always be removed from office even without any fault on their part and sometimes in their own interest. For a change of post might be a promotion—as it was in the case of the petty count from the banks of the Elbe who, in 817, was placed at the head of the important march of Friuli. 'Honours', 'benefits'—in enumerating the favours which the sovereign has bestowed on one or other of his vassals, the texts of the first half of the ninth century never fail to list them under these two headings.

Nevertheless, since economic conditions precluded cash remuneration, an office was its own salary. The count not only took a third of the fines in his own area; he received (among others) certain estates belonging to the fisc, which were specially set aside for his maintenance. Even the authority exercised over the inhabitants—apart from the opportunity it too often furnished for illegal gain—was bound to appear, in itself, a legitimate source of profit, in that age when true wealth consisted in being the master. In more senses than one, therefore, the grant of a county was one of the finest gifts with which it was possible to reward a vassal. That the beneficiary was thereby made judge and chieftain did not differentiate him at all—except in the relative extent of his authority—from many holders of ordinary 'benefits'; for the latter carried with them, for the most part, the exercise of seignorial rights. There remained the factor of revocability. As the crown, from Louis the Pious onwards, became progressively weaker, this principle—the safeguard of the central authority—

[1] *M.G.H., EE.*, V, p. 290, no. 20; Loup de Ferrières, ed. Levillain, II, no. 122; Wartmann, *Urkundenbuch der Abtei Sankt-Gallen*, II, no. 386.

became in practice more and more difficult to apply. For the counts, reverting to the practices which had characterized the aristocracy in the decline of the Merovingian dynasty, strove with growing success to transform themselves into territorial potentates, firmly rooted in the soil. Had not Charles the Bald, in 867, tried in vain to snatch the county of Bourges from a rebellious vassal? There was thenceforth no obstacle to an assimilation for which the way had in fact been prepared by undeniable similarities. In the heyday of the Carolingian Empire it had begun to be customary to treat as 'honours' all 'benefits' of the royal vassals, whose rôle in the state so closely resembled that of officials properly so called. The word finally became merely a synonym of fief, though in certain countries at least, such as Norman England, there was a tendency to restrict its use to the largest fiefs, which enjoyed a substantial measure of administrative autonomy. By a parallel development the estates allocated to the remuneration of an office, and then—by a much more serious deviation —the office itself, came to be described as a 'benefit' or 'fief'. In Germany, where the traditions of Carolingian policy preserved an exceptional vitality, the bishop and chronicler Thietmar, faithful to the first of these two rôles, distinguishes very clearly, about the year 1015, the county of Merseburg from the 'benefit' attached to that county. But current speech had long ceased to trouble itself with these subtleties: what it described as a 'benefit' or fief was actually the office in its entirety, the indivisible source of power and wealth. As early as 881, the *Annals of Fulda* recorded that Charles the Fat in that year gave to Hugh, his relative, 'in order to ensure his fealty, divers counties in benefit'.

Now those whom ecclesiastical writers were fond of calling the new 'satraps' of the provinces might derive from royal delegation the essential basis of the powers which they meant henceforward to use to their own profit. But in order to hold a district firmly they needed also to acquire new estates here and there; to build castles at the junctions of roads; to constitute themselves interested protectors of the principal churches; and above all, to provide themselves with local vassals. This was a long and difficult task which required the patient work of generations occupying the same estates in succession. In short, the movement towards heritability arose naturally out of the needs of territorial power. It would therefore be a grave error to regard it simply as an effect of the assimilation of honours to fiefs. It was as indispensable to the Anglo-Saxon 'earls', whose vast commands were never regarded as feudal tenements, and to the *gastaldi* of the Lombard principalities, who were not vassals, as it was to the French counts. But in the states originating from the Frankish Empire, the duchies, marches, and counties early ranked as feudal grants, and the history of their transformation into family properties was in consequence inextricably bound up with that of the growth of hereditary fiefs in general; though it always had the appearance of a special case. Not only was the rhythm of evolution everywhere different for ordinary fiefs and for *fiefs de dignité*, but when we pass from one state to another, we find that the contrast assumes a different character.

2 THE EVOLUTION OF INHERITANCE: THE CASE OF FRANCE

In western France and in Burgundy, as a result of the early weakening of the crown, the 'benefits' formed out of public offices were among the first to become hereditary. Nothing is more instructive, in this respect, than the arrangements made by Charles the Bald in 877, in the famous *placitum* of Quierzy. On the eve of his departure for Italy he was concerned to provide for the government of the kingdom in his absence. What was to be done if a count should happen to die while he was away? First of all, the king must be informed, for he reserved for himself the right to make any permanent appointment. To his son Louis, whom he left as regent, he accorded only the power to designate provisional administrators. In this general form the measure reflected the spirit of jealous authority of which the rest of the capitulary provides so many proofs. Nevertheless, that it was also inspired at least as much by the desire to humour the family ambitions of the magnates is proved by the specific mention of two particular eventualities. The count might die leaving a son who had gone with the army to Italy. By refusing the regent power to fill the vacant office, Charles intended above all to assure his comrades in arms that their loyalty would not deprive them of the hope of succeeding to a long-coveted office. Another possibility was that the count might die leaving the infant son in France. In that case, until such time as the royal decision was known, the county was to be administered in the name of this child by his father's officials. The edict goes no farther than this. Clearly, it seemed preferable, in a law, not to expatiate at length on the principle of hereditary devolution. This reticence, on the other hand, is no longer found in the proclamation which the emperor made his chancellor read to the assembly. There he promised unequivocally to hand over to the son—whether he had gone to fight in Italy or was still a minor—the honours that had belonged to his father. To be sure, these were emergency measures, dictated by the necessities of an ambitious policy. They did not expressly bind the future. But still less did they break with the past. They gave official recognition, for a certain period, to what was already a customary privilege.

Moreover, we have merely to follow—wherever possible—the chief families of counts down the generations in order to perceive the trend towards hereditary succession. Let us consider, for example, the ancestors of the third dynasty of French kings. In 864, Charles the Bald could still take away from Robert the Strong his Neustrian honours in order to employ him elsewhere. The deprivation was not lasting, however, for when Robert fell at Brissarthe in 866, he was once more in command of the region between the Seine and the Loire. But, although he left two sons —both very young, it is true—neither of them inherited his counties, which the king granted to another magnate. It was not till the death of this intruder in 886 that the elder son, Odo, was able to recover Anjou, Touraine, and possibly the county of Blois. Thenceforward, these territories remained part of the family patrimony—at least till the day when the Robertians were driven out of them by their own officials, transformed in their turn into hereditary potentates. In the sequence of counts, all of the same descent, who from about 885 till the extinction of the line in 1136 succeeded each other at Poitiers, there was only one break. It was, moreover, a very short one (from 890 to 902) and was caused by a minority, rendered more serious by a suspicion of illegitimacy. It is typical, too, that this dispossession, decreed by the king, should ultimately benefit—in defiance of his orders—one who, as the son of an earlier count, could also claim hereditary rights. Centuries later, a Charles V and even a Joseph II held Flanders only because, by marriage after marriage, there had come down to them a little of the blood of that Baldwin Iron Arm who, in the year 862, had so boldly abducted the daughter of the king of the Franks. All this, as we see, takes us back to the same period: beyond question the decisive stage was reached towards the second half of the ninth century.

What happened, however, in the case of ordinary fiefs? The arrangements of Quierzy applied expressly not only to the counties, but also to the 'benefits' held by royal vassals, which were also 'honours' of a sort. But edict and proclamation did not stop there. Charles required that the benefit of the rules by which he was committed in favour of his vassals should in turn be extended by the latter to their own men. It was an order dictated once again, it would seem, by the exigencies of the Italian expedition: it was advisable to offer a sop to the mass of the troops, consisting of the vassals of vassals, as well as to a few great chiefs. Yet we encounter something here that goes deeper than a mere measure of expediency. In a society in which so many individuals were at one and the same time commended men and masters, there was a reluctance to admit that if one of them, as a vassal, had secured some advantage for himself he could, as a lord, refuse it to those who were bound to his person by a similar form of dependence. From the old Carolingian capitulary to the Great Charter, the classic foundation of English 'liberties', this sort of equality in privilege, descending smoothly from top to bottom of the scale, was to remain one of the most fertile sources of feudal custom.

The influence of this idea and still more the very strong sense of what may be called family reversion—the feeling that the services rendered by the father created a right for his descendants—governed public opinion; and, in a civilization which had neither written codes nor organized jurisprudence, public opinion came very near to being identical with law. It found a faithful echo in the French epic. Not that the picture drawn by the poets can be accepted without some retouching. The historical frame-work which tradition imposed on them led them to state the problem only in connection with the great royal fiefs. Furthermore, since they gave the leading rôles to the first Carolingian emperors, they represented them, not without justification, as much more powerful than the kings of the eleventh and twelfth centuries; still strong enough in fact to be able to dispose freely of the honours of the realm, even at the expense of the natural heirs. Of this the Capetian monarchy had become quite incapable, so that the testimony of the poets on that subject has no value save as a reconstruction —and a fairly accurate one—of an age by then long past. What is really of their time, on the other hand, is the judgment—meant no doubt to apply to all types of fiefs—which they pass on these practices. They do not hold them to be exactly contrary to law; but they consider them morally reprehensible: in the epics these acts lead to disaster, as if by divine justice. A double spoliation of this sort is at the root of the unheard-of misfortunes which fill the *geste* of Raoul de Cambrai. The good master is he who keeps in mind that maxim which one of the *chansons* numbers among Charlemagne's lessons to his successor: 'Take care not to deprive the orphan child of his fief.'[1]

But how many lords were—or had to be—good masters? To write the history of feudal inheritance would involve compiling statistics, period by period, of the fiefs which were inherited and those which were not—a task which, in view of the meagreness of the source material, can never be performed. Undoubtedly the solution in each particular case depended for a long time on the balance of forces. The churches, which were weaker than the lay magnates and often badly administered, appear for the most part to have been yielding to the pressure of their vassals from the begin-ning of the tenth century. In the great lay principalities, on the other hand, we gain an impression of a remarkable instability of practice, persisting till about the middle of the following century. We can follow the history of an Angevin fief—that of Saint-Saturnin—under the counts Fulk Nerra and Geoffrey Martel (987–1060).[2] The count resumes possession of it, not only at the first sign of a breach of fealty, but even when the departure of the vassal for a neighbouring province seems likely to interfere with the performance of his services. There is no sign that the count considers himself in any way obliged to respect family rights. Among the five holders who succeeded each other during a period of some fifty years, two only—two brothers—appear to have been blood relations; and even between them a stranger interposed. Although two knights are deemed worthy of keeping Saint-Saturnin for life, after their death the estate passed out of their succession. There is admittedly no positive evidence that they left

---

[1] *Le Couronnement de Louis*, ed. E. Langlois, v. 83.
[2] Métais, *Cartulaire de l'abbaye cardinale de 'La Trinite' de Vendôme*, I, Nos. LXVI and LXVII.

sons. But, even assuming the absence of any male posterity in both cases, nothing could be more significant than the silence preserved on this point by the very detailed record to which we owe our information. This document was designed to establish the title of the monks of Vendôme, who eventually succeeded to the estate. If it neglects to cite the extinction of various lines in justification of the successive transfers of which the abbey was to reap the ultimate benefit, the reason obviously is that the dispossession of an heir did not at that time seem in any way unlawful.

Such lack of stability was nevertheless, from that time on, abnormal. In Anjou itself the foundation of the principal feudal dynasties dated from about the year 1000. Furthermore, in Normandy the fief must have been generally regarded as transmissible to heirs by the year 1066, when it was exported to England, for its hereditary character was virtually never disputed in that country. In the tenth century, on the rare occasions when a lord agreed to recognize the hereditary devolution of a fief, he would have this concession set down specifically in the deed of grant. From the middle of the twelfth century the situation was reversed; the only stipulations which were henceforth considered necessary were those which, by a rare but always permissible exception, restricted the enjoyment of the fief to the lifetime of the first beneficiary. The presumption was now in favour of hereditary succession. In France, as in England at this period, the word fief by itself meant a heritable estate and when, for example, ecclesiastical communities declared that this term must not be used to describe the services of their officials, as had been the earlier fashion, their sole intention in so doing was to repudiate any obligation to accept the services of the son after those of the father. As early as the Carolingian age custom favoured the claims of descendants, and this tendency was reinforced by the existence of numerous *fiefs de reprise*, which had acquired an almost inevitably patrimonial character from the very circumstances of their origin. Under the later Carolingians and the early Capetians, the investiture of the son in succession to the father had already become an almost universal practice. During the second feudal age, which was everywhere marked by a sort of legal awakening, it became law.

3 THE EVOLUTION OF INHERITANCE: IN THE EMPIRE

The conflict of social forces underlying the evolution of the fief is nowhere to be seen more clearly than in northern Italy. Let us consider the society of the Lombard kingdom in its feudal gradations. At the summit was the king who after 951, except for brief intermissions, was at the same time king of Germany and (when he had been crowned by the pope) emperor; immediately below him were his tenants-in-chief, great ecclesiastical or lay nobles; lower still was the modest crowd of these nobles' vassals, who were in consequence sub-vassals of the crown and for this reason commonly called 'vavasours'. At the beginning of the eleventh century a serious quarrel arose between the two last-named groups. The vavasours claimed the right to treat their fiefs as family property, but the tenants-in-chief insisted on the life character of the grant and its constant revocability. In 1035, these conflicts at last gave rise to an actual class war. Leagued together by oath, the vavasours of Milan and the surrounding territory inflicted a resounding defeat on the army of the great nobles. The news of these troubles brought the King-Emperor Conrad II from distant Germany. Breaking with the policy of his Ottonian predecessors, who had before all else respected the inalienability of ecclesiastical property, he took the side of the vassals of lesser rank and, since Italy was still the country of laws—it had, he said, a 'hunger for legislation'—he proceeded to settle the law in favour of such vassals by a formal legislative decree dated 28th May 1037. He laid it down that thenceforward all 'benefits' of which the lord was a lay tenant-in-chief, a bishop, an abbot, or an abbess, were to be regarded as hereditable by the son, the grandson, or the brother of the vassal; and the same rule was to apply to the sub-fiefs formed from such 'benefits'. No mention was made of enfeoffments accepted by allodial proprietors. Conrad clearly conceived of himself as legislating less in his capacity as sovereign than as head of the feudal hierarchy, but he none the less affected the immense majority of the small and medium-sized knights' fees. Though certain special motives may have influenced his attitude— notably the personal enmity he felt towards the principal adversary of the vavasours, Archbishop Aribert of Milan—he certainly seems to have looked beyond his momentary interests and rancours. Against the great feudatories, always a danger to monarchies, he sought a kind of alliance with their own followers. The proof of this is that in Germany, where the weapon of legislation was not available to him, he tried to attain the same end by other means—probably by influencing the jurisprudence of the royal court in the desired direction. There also, according to his chaplain, he 'won the hearts of the knights by not allowing the benefits granted to the fathers to be taken away from their descendants'.

This intervention of the imperial monarchy in favour of the hereditary principle was a stage in a process of evolution which was already more than half complete. As early as the beginning of the eleventh century, there was in Germany a growing number of private agreements which recognized the rights of descendants over particular fiefs. In 1069 Duke Godfrey of Lorraine still believed that he could dispose freely of the 'stipendiary tenements' of his knights in order to give them to a church, but the 'murmurs' of the wronged vassals were so loud that after his death his successor was obliged to change this form of gift for another.[1] In law-making Italy, in Germany ruled by relatively powerful kings, and in France, without statute laws and in practice almost without a king, parallel developments

---

[1] *Cantatorium S. Huberti*, in *M.G.H., SS.*, VII, pp. 581–2.

proclaimed the influence of forces deeper than political interests. This at least was true so far as ordinary fiefs were concerned. It is in what happened to the *fiefs de dignité* that we must look for the distinctive character imparted to the history of German and Italian feudalism by a central authority more powerful than elsewhere.

Since these fiefs were held directly of the Empire the law of Conrad II was, by definition, irrelevant to them. But the common prejudice in favour of the rights of kinsmen existed here also, and did not fail of its effect. From the ninth century onward it was only in exceptional cases that the sovereign could bring himself to disregard a tradition so worthy of respect. If he did so nevertheless, public opinion (of which the chroniclers bring us the echo) cried out against such arbitrary action. However, when it was a question either of rewarding a good servant or of excluding a young child or a man who was considered unreliable, this serious step was often taken—even if the heir thus wronged had to be compensated by the grant of some other similar office. For counties, in particular, seldom changed hands save within a fairly restricted group of families and the career of count was, in a sense, hereditary long before the individual counties became so themselves. The greatest territorial commands, marches and duchies, were also those which remained subject longest to these acts of authority. Twice, in the tenth century, the duchy of Bavaria failed to pass to the son of the previous holder; the same thing happened in 935 to the march of Misnia (Meissen) and in 1075 to that of Lusatia (Lausitz). By one of those archaisms which were so common in medieval Germany, the practice regarding the principal honours of the Empire remained, till the end of the eleventh century, much what it had been in France under Charles the Bald.

After that date a change took place. In the course of the century the movement had been rapidly gathering strength. We possess a grant of a county with hereditary rights made by Conrad II himself. His grandson Henry IV and his great-grandson Henry V accorded the same privilege to the duchies of Carinthia and Swabia and to the county of Holland. In the twelfth century the principle was no longer disputed. In the Empire, as elsewhere, the rights of the lord, even if he were the king, had had to give way, little by little, before those of the vassal dynasties.

4 THE TRANSFORMATIONS OF THE FIEF AS REFLECTED IN ITS LAW OF SUCCESSION

The case of an only son, qualified to succeed immediately, served to provide a convenient starting point for our analysis, but the reality was often less simple. As soon as opinion began to recognize the rights of kinship, it was faced with a variety of family situations, each of which raised problems of its own. A brief survey of the solutions which various societies

199

found for these difficulties will contribute to a realistic understanding of the metamorphoses of the fief and of the tie of vassalage.

The son or, where there was no son, the grandson seemed the natural successor of the father or grandfather in those services which in the lifetime of the one or the other he would often have helped to perform. A brother or a cousin, on the other hand, had usually already made his career elsewhere. This is why the recognition of collateral succession affords, in the simplest terms, a true measure of the extent to which the old 'benefit' was being transformed into a patrimony.[1] Opposition was strong, especially in Germany. In 1196, the Emperor Henry VI, who was trying to obtain the consent of his nobles to another kind of heritability—that of the German crown—could still offer them, in return for this splendid gift, official recognition of collateral succession to fiefs; but the project came to naught. With the exception of specific provisions inserted in the original grant, or special 'customs', like that which in the thirteenth century governed the fiefs of imperial *ministeriales*, German lords in the Middle Ages were never obliged to grant investiture to heirs other than descendants, though this did not in fact prevent them from conceding the favour fairly frequently. Elsewhere, it seemed logical to draw a distinction: the fief was transmissible in all directions within the posterity of the first beneficiary, but not outside those limits. Such was the solution devised by Lombard law. From the twelfth century onwards, the same principle was adopted, in France and England, in the charters of a considerable number of newly-created fiefs; though here it represented a deviation from the common law. For in the kingdoms of the West the movement towards the hereditary principle had been sufficiently strong to work in favour of almost the whole group of relatives. One reservation continued in those countries to recall the fact that feudal custom had developed in relation to the idea of service. For a long time there was a reluctance to admit that a dead vassal might be succeeded by his father. In England this never was admitted. In particular it would have seemed absurd that a military tenement should pass from a young man to an old one.

Nothing appeared more contrary to the nature of the fief than to allow it to be inherited by women. Not that the Middle Ages had ever deemed them incapable of exercising authority. No one was disturbed by the spectacle of the great lady presiding over the baronial court when her husband was away. But women were held incapable of bearing arms. It is symptomatic that in Normandy towards the end of the twelfth century, where custom already allowed the hereditary succession of daughters, the rule should have been deliberately abrogated by Richard Cœur-de-Lion

---

[1] Brothers, however, were at an early date the subject of special privileges (see the Law of Conrad II), which sometimes, in conformity with the prejudice of certain popular rights in favour of the elder generation, went so far as to give them the advantage over sons. Cf. M. Garaud in *Bullet. Soc. Antiquaires Ouest*, 1921.

as soon as the relentless war with the Capetian king broke out. Those legal systems which endeavoured most jealously to preserve the original character of the institution—the juridical doctrine of Lombard Italy, the customaries of Latin Syria, the jurisdiction of the German royal court —always in theory withheld from the heiress what they accorded to the heir. That Henry VI, as a concession to his great vassals, should have offered to remove this disability, along with that which affected collateral inheritance, proves how tenacious the rule still was in Germany. It also tells us a great deal about baronial aspirations. The concession which the Hohenstaufen monarch offered to his vassals was one which the founders of the Latin Empire of Constantinople were a little later to demand of their future sovereign.

In fact, even where the exclusion of women continued in theory, it was soon subject in practice to many exceptions. Apart from the fact that the lord always had the right to disregard it, the principle might be overridden by particular customs or expressly waived by the deed of grant itself. This was the case in 1156 with the duchy of Austria. In France and in Norman England it had been decided long before this time to accord to daughters (in default of sons) and sometimes even to ordinary female relatives (if there were no male relatives of equal degree) the same rights over fiefs as over other forms of property. For it was very quickly appreciated that if a woman was incapable of carrying out the services of the fief, her husband could do so in her stead. By a characteristic parallelism, the earliest examples of such deviation from the primitive rules of vassalage, for the benefit of the daughter or son-in-law, all relate to those great French principalities which were also the first to acquire heritability in the ordinary sense, and which, moreover, no longer to any extent involved personal services. As husband of the daughter of the 'principal count of Burgundy', the Robertian Otto owed to this union, as early as 956, the possession of the Burgundian counties, which formed the main basis of his future ducal title. In this way—and especially because the succession rights of descendants in the female line had been admitted at almost the same time as those of immediate heiresses—feudal families of every rank found themselves in a position to embark on a policy of marriage alliances.

The presence of an heir who was a minor undoubtedly presented the most delicate of the problems which feudal custom had to resolve from the outset. It was no wonder that the poets always preferred to look at the great debate about heritability from this angle. How illogical to hand over a military tenement to a child! Yet how cruel to dispossess the little fellow! A solution for this dilemma had been evolved as long ago as the ninth century. The minor was recognized as heir; but until such time as he should be in a position to perform his duties as a vassal a temporary administrator held the fief in his behalf, did homage, and carried out the services. It would be incorrect to call this man a guardian; for as *baillistre*, who thus assumed the responsibilities of the fief, he also pocketed its revenues, without any other obligation towards the minor than to provide for his maintenance. Although the creation of this sort of temporary vassal struck a serious blow at the very nature of the tie of vassalage, which was conceived of as a bond which endured till death, it reconciled the needs of vassal service so well with family feeling that it was very widely adopted wherever the system of fiefs that originated in the Frankish Empire prevailed. Italy alone, where there was little inclination to multiply exceptional arrangements in favour of feudal interests, preferred to retain the system of simple guardianship.

Nevertheless a curious deviation soon appeared. It seemed the most natural procedure to choose a member of the family to take the place of the child as the head of the fief. This, to all appearance, was the general rule at first, and in many regions it remained so to the end. Although the lord himself also had duties towards the orphan, duties which proceeded from the oath of fealty but lately taken by the dead man, the idea that during the minority he might himself seek to replace his own vassal at the expense of the relatives would originally have been regarded as absurd; what he needed was a man, not an estate. But theories were very soon contradicted by actual practice. It is significant that one of the earliest examples of the supplanting—at least the attempted supplanting —of a kinsman by the lord as *baillistre*, should have brought face to face the king of France, Louis IV, and the young heir to one of the great 'honours' of the realm—Normandy. To exercise authority in person at Bayeux or Rouen was undoubtedly more satisfactory than to rely on the uncertain aid of a regent for the duchy. The introduction in various countries of the system of seignorial wardship marks the moment when the value of the fief as a property to be exploited seemed generally to exceed that of the services which could be expected from it.

Nowhere did the practice take root more firmly than in Normandy and England where the system of vassalage was organized in every way to the advantage of the feudal superior. The English barons suffered from it when the lord was the king. They benefited from it, on the other hand, when they were able to exercise this right in regard to their dependants; so much so that, having in 1100 secured a return to the system of family wardship, they were unable or unwilling to prevent this concession from becoming a dead letter. In England, moreover, the original significance of the institution was soon so far lost sight of that the lords—the king in particular —regularly ceded or sold the wardship of the child along with the administration of his fiefs. At the court of the Plantagenets a gift of this nature was one of the most coveted of rewards. As a matter of fact, however desirable it might be to be able, by virtue of so honourable a duty, to garrison the castles, collect the dues, hunt in the forests or empty the fish-ponds, the estates in such cases were not the most important part of the gift. The person of the heir or heiress was worth even more: for in the guardian lord or his representative was vested, as we shall see, the responsibility for arranging the marriage of his ward; and from this right also he did not fail to derive financial profit.

In theory the fief must be indivisible; so much was clear. If a public office were involved, the superior authority, by allowing it to be divided, would run the risk at once of weakening the executive power exercised in its name and of making control more difficult. If it were an ordinary knight's fee, its dismemberment would create confusion over the performance of services, which were very difficult to apportion satisfactorily between the different copartners. Furthermore, the original grant having been so calculated as to provide for the pay of a single vassal with his followers, there was a danger that if it were broken up the fragments would not suffice to maintain the new holders, with the result that they would be ill-armed or perhaps forced to seek their fortunes elsewhere. It was therefore important that the tenement, having become hereditary, should at any rate pass to a single heir. But on this point the requirements of the feudal organization came into conflict with the ordinary rules of the law of succession, which in the greater part of Europe favoured the equality of heirs of the same degree. Under the influence of opposing forces this grave legal problem was resolved in different ways according to the place and the time.

An initial difficulty presented itself: between candidates related to the deceased in equal degree, between his sons, for example, what criterion would determine the choice of heir? Centuries of feudal law and dynastic law have accustomed us to accord a certain prior right to primogeniture as such. In reality it is no more 'natural' than so many other myths on which our society rests today—the majority fiction, for example, which makes the will of the greatest number the lawful interpreter even of that of their opponents. In the Middle Ages primogeniture, even in royal houses, was not accepted without much opposition. In certain country districts, customs persisting from time immemorial did indeed favour one of the sons at the expense of the others, but what happened in the case of a fief? The primitive usage seems to have recognized the lord's right to grant it to the son whom he considered best fitted to hold it. This was still the rule in Catalonia about 1060. Sometimes also the father himself named his successor for the lord's approval, after having during his lifetime more or less associated this chosen son with himself in the duties of the fief. Or yet again, where the system of joint heirship prevailed, a collective investiture would take place.

Nowhere did these archaic practices persist more stubbornly than in Germany, where they continued till well into the twelfth century. Concurrently, in Saxony at least, another usage prevailed which revealed the depth of family feeling: the sons themselves decided which of them was to succeed to the inheritance. Naturally it might happen, indeed it often did happen, that the choice would fall on the eldest whatever the method adopted. But German law was reluctant to concede binding force to this preference. It was, as a poet said, an 'outlandish' custom, an 'alien trick'.[1] Had not the emperor himself, Frederick Barbarossa, in 1169, arranged for the crown to pass to a younger son? Now the absence of any clearly established principle of discrimination between heirs made it singularly difficult in practice to maintain the indivisibility of the fief. Moreover, within the Empire the influence of the old social groups, traditionally opposed to inequalities between men of the same kin, was not so effectively counterbalanced as in other countries by the feudal policy of kings or princes. Since the kings and territorial chiefs of Germany had been left by the Carolingian state with a system which had long served as an adequate basis for their authority, they were less dependent than the rulers of France on the services of their vassals, and they naturally devoted less attention to the system of fiefs. The kings, in particular, concerned themselves almost exclusively—as did Frederick Barbarossa in 1158—with prohibiting the dismemberment of the 'counties, margravates and duchies'. Nevertheless, at this date, the fragmentation of the counties at least had already begun. In 1255, a ducal title, that of Bavaria, was for the first time divided, along with the territory itself. As to ordinary fiefs, the law of 1158 had been obliged to recognize that the partitioning of these was legal. *Landrecht*, in short, had finally triumphed over *Lehnrecht*. The reaction did not come till much later—towards the end of the Middle Ages in fact, and under the pressure of different forces. In the great principalities it was the princes themselves who, by appropriate succession laws, strove to prevent the disintegration of the power they had acquired at the cost of so much effort. As regards fiefs in general, one of the means adopted was the introduction of primogeniture, by the roundabout route of entail. Thus dynastic anxieties and class interests accomplished, rather late in the day, what the feudal law could not.

In the greater part of France the course of evolution was very different. The kings did not feel impelled to forbid the breaking up of the great principalities that had been formed by the agglomeration of several counties, except where they could use these concentrations of power in the defence of the country. But before long the provincial chiefs had become adversaries rather than servants of the crown. Individual counties were rarely divided; but the aggregations were carved up to give each of the sons his share of the inheritance, with the result that in each generation they were in danger of disintegration. The princely houses were not slow to recognize the threat and—in some places sooner than in others—applied the remedy of primogeniture. In the twelfth century it was almost every-

[1] Wolfram von Eschenbach, *Parzival*, I, verses 4–5.

where established. As in Germany, but at a considerably earlier date, the great principalities of former days reverted to indivisibility, though as states of a new type rather than as fiefs.

As for the fiefs of lesser importance, the interests of vassal service (to which much more regard was paid on this favourite soil of feudalism) had at an early date, after a little uncertainty, brought them under the precise and clear rule of primogeniture. Nevertheless, as the former tenement was transformed into a patrimonial property, it seemed harder to exclude the younger brothers from the succession. Only a few exceptional customs, like that of the Caux district, preserved the principle in all its rigour to the end. Elsewhere it was admitted that the eldest son, who was under a moral obligation not to leave his brothers without support, could and indeed must make some provision for them from their father's estate. Thus there developed in many provinces the system generally known as 'parage'. The eldest brother alone did homage to the lord and in consequence alone assumed responsibility for the services due from the fief. The younger brothers held their portions from him and sometimes, as in the Île-de-France, they did homage to him in their turn. Sometimes, as in Normandy and Anjou, the strength of the family bond seemed to make any other form of tie, within this group of relatives, superfluous. This view at least prevailed for some time; but after the principal fief and the subordinate fiefs had descended through several generations, the degrees of relationship between the successors of the original co-heirs became eventually so distant that it appeared unwise to rely solely on the solidarity of kinship.

This system, in spite of everything, by no means obviated all the disadvantages of partition. That is why in England, where it had first been introduced after the Conquest, it was abandoned towards the middle of the twelfth century in favour of strict primogeniture. Even in Normandy the dukes, who succeeded in turning feudal obligations to such good account in the recruitment of their armies, had never admitted the system of 'parage' save when the succession involved several knights' fees which could be distributed separately among the heirs. If there was only one fief it passed undivided to the eldest. But so strict a delimitation of the unit of service was only possible under the influence of a territorial authority of exceptional strength and organizing capacity. In the rest of France customary theory might seek to exclude at least the greater fiefs, usually described as baronies, from the process of dismemberment; in practice, the heirs almost invariably divided the whole inheritance between them, without distinguishing between its various components. The only thing that preserved some measure of the former indivisibility was the homage done to the eldest son and his descendants in order of primogeniture. In the end this safeguard, too, disappeared, in conditions which throw a vivid light on the later transformations of feudalism.

Hereditary succession, before it became a right, had long been regarded as a favour. It therefore seemed only proper that the new vassal should show his gratitude to the lord by a gift; there is evidence of this practice as early as the ninth century. And in this society, which was essentially based on custom, every voluntary gift, if it became at all habitual, was eventually transformed into an obligation. The practice in this case the more easily acquired the force of law because precedents were not far to seek. From what must have been a very early period, no one could enter into possession of a peasant holding, burdened with rents and services owed to the lord, without having first of all obtained from the latter an investiture, which was not, as a rule, accorded for nothing. Now, in spite of the fact that the military fief was a tenement of a very special type, it none the less became embodied in the intricate system of real property rights characteristic of the medieval world. 'Relief', *rachat*, sometimes *mainmorte*—in parts of France the words used were the same, whether the succession tax fell on the property of a vassal, of a villein, or even of a serf.

Feudal relief proper was nevertheless distinguished by the methods of paying it. Like the majority of similar taxes, till the thirteenth century it was generally paid, at least partly, in kind. But whereas the heir of the peasant would hand over, for example, a head of cattle, the heir of the military vassal would be obliged to offer a war 'harness', that is to say either a horse or arms, or both together. In this way, quite naturally, the lord would adapt his requirements to the form of the services with which the land was burdened.[1] Sometimes only the harness was required of the newly-invested vassal, and even this liability could be compounded, by mutual agreement, for an equivalent sum of money. Sometimes, in addition to the charger or farm-horse (*roncin*) a money payment was exacted. Where the other methods of payment had fallen into disuse, settlement might even be made entirely in money. In the details of these practices there was, in short, an almost infinite variety, since the effect of custom had been to crystallize by region, by vassal group, or even fief by fief, usages that had often originated in an entirely fortuitous way. Fundamental divergences alone have value as symptoms.

Germany, at a very early date, restricted the obligation of relief almost exclusively to the less important fiefs held by seignorial officials, who were often of servile origin. This was no doubt one of the symptoms of the hierarchical arrangement of classes and holdings so characteristic of the

---

[1] Certain historians explain this exaction by the practice whereby originally the lords themselves furnished the equipment for their vassals; the harness thus provided, it is maintained, had to be returned after the vassal's death. But from the moment when the son in his turn was accepted as a vassal, what was the good of such restitution? The interpretation suggested here has the advantage of taking account of the evident resemblance between feudal relief and other similar taxes; for example, the rights of entry into certain crafts, also payable to the lord in the form of objects connected with the craft in question.

social structure of medieval Germany. It was destined to have important repercussions. When, towards the thirteenth century, as a result of the decay of vassal services, it had become practically impossible for the German lord to obtain fighting-men from the fief, he could no longer obtain anything at all from it. This was a serious situation, especially from the point of view of the princely states, since naturally the majority of fiefs and the richest ones were held from the princes and kings.

The kingdoms of the West, on the other hand, passed through an intermediate stage in which the fief, reduced to insignificance as a source of services, remained a lucrative source of profits, thanks primarily to the system of reliefs which was here in very general use. The kings of England in the twelfth century derived enormous sums from it. In France, it was by virtue of this practice that Philip Augustus obtained the cession of the stronghold of Gien, which gave him control of a crossing over the Loire. So far as the majority of petty fiefs were concerned, the lords generally came to interest themselves only in these succession taxes. In the fourteenth century, it was at length officially admitted in the Paris region that the exaction of a farm-horse exonerated the vassal from any personal obligation other than the purely negative one of doing no injury to his lord. Nevertheless, as fiefs became increasingly part and parcel of patrimonies, the heirs grew more and more impatient of a situation in which they could only obtain the investiture they had come to regard as a right by opening their purses. Though they were unable to get rid of the burden altogether, they did at length succeed in reducing it substantially. In certain 'customs' it was retained only for collaterals, whose hereditary title was less apparent. Above all, in conformity with a movement which developed from the twelfth century onwards in all classes of society, there was a tendency to substitute a fixed scale of tariffs for variable payments, the amount of which was arbitrarily fixed in each case or decided after difficult negotiations. The next step was taken when—following a practice common in France—the value of the annual revenue brought in by the estate was adopted as the norm; such a basis of evaluation was uninfluenced by monetary fluctuations. Where, on the contrary, the rates were fixed once and for all in terms of cash—the most celebrated example of this is provided by England's Great Charter—the tax was eventually subjected to that progressive devaluation which, from the twelfth century to modern times, inevitably affected all payments that were permanently fixed.

Meanwhile, however, the attention paid to these contingent rights had drastically modified the terms of the succession problem. The institution of 'parage', while it safeguarded the services due from the fief, reduced the profits from relief, which it restricted to changes of ownership in the senior branch—the only one directly bound to the lord of the original fief. This failure to reap financial benefit was not resented so long as services were more important than anything else, but it became intolerable after their value had declined. The first law affecting the feudal system to be promulgated by a Capetian king—a law demanded by the barons of France and obtained apparently without difficulty, in 1209, from a sovereign who was himself the greatest feudal lord in the kingdom—had as its specific object the abolition of 'parage'. There was no question of prohibiting partition, which had definitely become part of accepted usage. But henceforth the portions were to be held directly from the original lord. In point of fact the 'establishment' of Philip Augustus does not appear to have been very faithfully observed. Once more the old traditions of family custom were in conflict with feudal principles proper; having brought about the dismemberment of the fief, they were working now to prevent the effects of that fragmentation from impairing the solidarities of kinship. We know that parage was slow to disappear. Nevertheless, the changed attitude of the French nobility clearly marks the moment when, in France, the fief, which had once been the pay of the armed retainer, sank to the status of a tenement characterized chiefly by the payment of rent.[1]

5 FEALTY FOR SALE

Under the first Carolingians the idea that the vassal could alienate the fief at will would have seemed doubly absurd; for the property did not belong to him, and it was only entrusted to him in return for strictly personal services. Nevertheless, as the effects of the originally precarious nature of the grant ceased to be felt, the vassals, either from need of money or out of generosity, were increasingly inclined to dispose freely of what they came to regard as their own property. In this they were encouraged by the Church which, during the Middle Ages, assisted in every way in the breakdown of the old seignorial or customary impediments which had obstructed individual possession. If the many lords whose sole wealth consisted of their fiefs had been prevented from taking something from their patrimony for the benefit of God and his saints, alms-giving would have become impossible, the fire of Hell which it extinguished 'like water' would have burned unquenchably, and the religious communities would have been in danger of dying of inanition. The truth is that the alienation of the fief assumed two very different aspects according to the nature of the case.

Sometimes only a fraction of the property was alienated. The traditional obligations, which had formerly rested on the whole of it, were now concentrated, as it were, on the portion which remained in the hands of the vassal. Leaving aside the possibility, increasingly remote, of a confiscation or an escheat, the lord therefore lost nothing of material value. He might

[1] In England in 1290 the same considerations brought about (by the Statute of *Quia Emptores*) the prohibition of the practice of selling fiefs in the form of subinfeudation. The purchaser was thereafter obliged to hold the estate directly from the lord of the vendor.

nevertheless be afraid that the fief, thus diminished, would be insufficient to support a dependant capable of carrying out his duties; thus partial alienation, together with such practices as the exemption from rents of the inhabitants of the estate, came under the heading of what French law called 'abridgment' of the fief, that is to say diminution of its value. Towards alienation, as towards abridgment in general, the attitude of the 'customs' differed. Some in the end allowed it, subject to restrictions. Others persisted in requiring the approval of the immediate lord, and sometimes even of the whole hierarchy of superior lords. Naturally this consent was as a rule purchased and, because it was a source of lucrative exactions, there was a tendency to think of it more and more as something which could not be refused. Once more, the eagerness for gain ran counter to the requirements of feudal service.

Alienation of the whole fief was still more opposed to the spirit of vassalage. Not that there was any risk, in that case either, that the obligations would thus be extinguished, since they went with the fief; it was only that they devolved upon a different person. This was carrying to the limit the paradox which already resulted from the practice of hereditary transmission. For how could one expect of an unknown person, whose sole title to the vassalage of which he thus assumed the duties consisted in the possession of a full purse at the right moment, that innate loyalty which (with a little optimism) one could hope to receive from successive generations of the same lineage? It is true that the risk was removed if the consent of the lord was required; and this it was, for a long time. To put it more precisely, the lord first of all had the fief restored to him; then, if he so desired, he reinvested the new tenant with it, after having received his homage. In almost every case, it goes without saying, a preliminary agreement allowed the seller or donor to defer the surrender of the property until he had obtained the lord's approval of his successor. In this form the practice of alienation was almost as old as the institution of the fief or 'benefit' itself. As in the case of hereditary succession, the crucial change occurred when the lord lost, first in the eyes of feudal society, then in those of the law, the right to refuse the new investiture.

It would be a mistake to imagine an unbroken course of degeneration. In the anarchy of the tenth and eleventh centuries the rights of the lords of fiefs had often lapsed. Their revival in the following centuries was due partly to the progress of legal logic and partly to the pressure of certain governments desirous of establishing a well-ordered system of feudal relationships—like that prevailing in Plantagenet England, for example. On one point indeed this reinforcement of the ancient principle was almost universal. It was admitted in the thirteenth century much more generally and unreservedly than in the past that the lord could absolutely prohibit the transfer of a fief to a church. The very success of the clergy's struggle to disentangle itself from feudal society appeared to justify more than ever a rule which was founded on the incapacity of clerics for military service. Kings and princes insisted on its being observed, since they saw in it both a safeguard against formidable monopolies and a means of fiscal extortion.

With this exception, the principle of the lord's consent soon became subject to the usual process of deterioration; it ended simply as the legalization of a tax on change of tenancy. Another resource, it is true, was generally open to the lord: to retain the fief himself in the course of transfer, while compensating the purchaser. Thus the weakening of the lord's supremacy expressed itself through precisely the same institution as the decay of the family—a parallelism all the more striking in that where the *retrait lignager* did not exist, as in England, the *retrait féodal* was also absent. Moreover nothing shows more clearly than this last privilege accorded to the lords how firmly the fief was now rooted in the patrimony of the vassal, since a lord had henceforth to pay the same price as any other purchaser in order to recover what was legally his own property. In practice, from the twelfth century at least, fiefs were sold or granted almost without restriction. Fealty had become an object of trade. The result was not to make it stronger.

XV

THE MAN OF SEVERAL MASTERS

1 THE PLURALITY OF HOMAGE

'A samurai does not have two masters.' This old Japanese maxim, which as late as 1912 was invoked by Marshal Nogi to justify his refusal to survive his emperor, expresses the ineluctable law of any system of personal allegiance, strictly conceived. This was, beyond doubt, the rule of Frankish vassalage at the outset. Although not expressly formulated in the Carolingian capitularies, probably because it seemed self-evident, it is taken for granted in all their provisions. The commended man could change his lord, if the person to whom he had first sworn fealty agreed to release him from his oath. To pledge himself to a second master while remaining the man of the first was strictly forbidden. Regularly, in the partitions of the Empire, the necessary measures were taken to prevent any overlapping of vassal engagements, and the memory of this original strictness was preserved for a long time. About 1160, a monk of Reichenau, having set down in writing the rule regarding military service as required by the emperors of his time for their Roman expeditions, conceived the idea of falsely placing this text under the venerable name of Charlemagne. 'If by chance,' he says, in terms which no doubt he believed to be in conformity with the spirit of ancient custom, 'it happens that the same knight is bound to several lords, by reason of different "benefits", a thing which is not pleasing to God.' .'[1]

But by this time it had long been usual for members of the knightly class to be the vassals at one and the same time of two masters or even more. The oldest example which has so far been brought to light belongs to the year 895 and comes from Tours.[2] Everywhere cases multiply in the following centuries—so much so that in the eleventh a Bavarian poet, and towards the end of the twelfth a Lombard jurist, treat this situation as perfectly normal. The number of these successive acts of homage was sometimes

---

[1] *M.G.H.*, *Constitutiones*, I, no. 447, c. 5.

[2] H. Mitteis (*Lehnrecht und Staatsgewalt*, Weimar, 1933, p. 103) and W. Kienast (*Historische Zeitschrift*, CXLI, 1929–30) point to what they believe to be earlier examples. But the only one which really appears to represent a double fealty relates to the division of authority at Rome between pope and emperor—a dualism of sovereignty, not of fealty. The charter of Saint-Gall, which neither Professor Ganshof nor Professor Mitteis has been able to find, and which in fact bears the number 440 in the *Urkundenbuch*, refers to a grant of land charged with rent.

very great. In the last years of the thirteenth century, one German baron became in this way the enfeoffed vassal of twenty different lords; another of forty-three.[1]

Such a multiplicity of vassal engagements was the very negation of that dedication of the whole being to the service of a freely chosen chief which the contract of vassalage had originally implied. The most thoughtful contemporaries were as well aware of this as we are. From time to time a jurist, a chronicler, and even a king like St. Louis, would sadly recall to the vassals the saying of Christ: 'No man can serve two masters.' Towards the end of the eleventh century a good canonist, Bishop Ivo of Chartres, judged it necessary to release a knight from his oath of fealty—to all appearance an engagement of vassalage—to William the Conqueror; for, the prelate said, 'such engagements are contrary to those which this man has previously contracted towards his lawful lords by right of birth, from whom he has already received his hereditary benefits'. The surprising thing is that this striking deviation should manifest itself so soon and so widely.

Historians are inclined to lay the blame for it on the practice, which grew up at an early date, of paying vassals for their services by the grant of fiefs. There can indeed be no doubt that the prospect of obtaining a fine and well-stocked manor induced many a warrior to do homage to more than one lord. In the reign of Hugh Capet, a direct vassal of the king refused to go to the aid of a certain count until the latter had also formally accepted him as his man. The reason, he says, is that 'it is not customary among the Franks for a man to fight otherwise than in the presence or on the orders of his lord'. The sentiment was excellent; the reality was less so. For we learn that a village of the Île-de-France was the price of this new fealty.[2] It nevertheless remains to be explained why the lords so readily accepted, and even sometimes solicited, these halves, thirds or quarters of a man's loyalty, and also how the vassals were able, without scandal, to make so many contradictory promises. Perhaps we ought to seek the explanation, not in the institution of the military tenement as such, but rather in the process of evolution which transformed what was formerly a personal grant into a patrimonial property and an article of commerce. Certainly it is difficult to believe that a knight, who, after swearing fealty to one master, found himself as a result of inheritance or purchase in possession of a fief dependent on a different lord, would ordinarily refuse to enter into a new contract of vassalage and thereby renounce this providential accession of property. Let us not jump to hasty conclusions, however. Double homage was not the sequel, in point of time, to heritability; the earliest examples of it seem, on the contrary, to have been

[1] *Ruodlieb*, ed. F. Seiler, I, v. 3; E. Mayer, *Mittelalterliche Verfassungsgeschichte: deutsche und französische Geschichte vom 9. bis zum 14. Jahrhundert*, Leipzig, 1899, II, 2, 3; W. Lippert, *Die deutschen Lehnsbücher*, Leipzig, 1903, p. 2.
[2] *Vita Burchardi*, ed. de la Roncière, p. 19; cf. p. xvii.

almost exactly contemporaneous with the hereditary principle when it was still only an occasional practice. Nor was it, logically, the necessary consequence. Japan, which never knew multiple fealties except as a rare abuse, had its hereditary and even its alienable fiefs. But as each vassal held them of a single lord, their transmission from generation to generation had the result of implanting in a line of dependants a permanent attachment to a line of chiefs. As to the alienation of fiefs, it was allowed only within the group of vassals dependent upon a common master. In the medieval West the second of these very simple rules was frequently imposed on dependants of lower status—the tenants of rural manors. It could conceivably have become the guardian principle of vassalage, but no one seems to have thought of it.

In point of fact, though destined to become incontestably one of the principal solvents of vassal society, the profusion of acts of homage done by one man to several lords had itself been at first only one symptom among others of the almost congenital weakness which—for reasons we shall have to examine—beset a relationship which was nevertheless held to be extremely binding. The diversity of ties was embarrassing at any time. In moments of crisis the problems it engendered became so urgent that both the theory and the practice of feudalism were obliged to look for a solution. When two of his lords were at war with each other, where did the duty of the good vassal lie? To stand aside would simply have meant committing a double 'felony'. It was therefore necessary to choose. But how? A whole body of casuistry developed, which was not confined to the works of the jurists but was also expressed, in the form of carefully balanced stipulations, in the charters which—as written documents came into use again—generally accompanied the oaths of fealty. Opinion seems to have fluctuated between three principal criteria. First, the acts of homage might be classified in order of date, the oldest one taking precedence over the most recent; often, in the very formula by which the vassal acknowledged himself to be the man of a new lord, the vassal expressly reserved the fealty promised to an earlier master. Another criterion which was adopted in some places throws a curious light on the circumstances under which many protestations of loyalty were made. The lord most deserving of respect, it was argued, was the one who had given the richest fief. Already in 895 the count of Le Mans, when the canons of Saint-Martin begged him to bring one of his vassals to order, had replied that this person was 'much more' the vassal of the count-abbot Robert, 'since he held of the latter a more important benefit', and such was the rule followed, even at the end of the eleventh century, by the court of the count of Catalonia, in the case of conflicting acts of homage. Finally attention might be directed to the other side of the question, and the cause of the conflict

[1] F. L. Ganshof, 'Depuis quand a-t-on pu en France être vassal de plusieurs seigneurs?' in *Mélanges Paul Fournier*, 1929; *Us. Barc.*, c. 25.

itself be taken into account. Towards a lord who had taken up arms in his own defence, the obligation seemed more compelling than towards one who was merely going to the help of kinsmen.

None of these solutions, however, resolved the problem. That a vassal should have to fight his lord was already bad enough; even more intolerable was the prospect of his using for that purpose the resources of the fiefs which had been entrusted to him for quite another. One way of getting round the difficulty was to authorize the lord to confiscate provisionally—till peace was made—the estates with which he had not long before invested the vassal, now for the moment guilty of a technical breach of his oath. Or else the more paradoxical situation was envisaged in which a vassal, finding his two lords at war with each other and being constrained to serve in person the one with the strongest claim on his fealty, would be required to levy—on the estates held from the other antagonist—troops composed principally of his own vassals, in order to place them at the disposal of this second master. Thus, by a sort of extension of the original abuse, the man with two chiefs ran the risk, in his turn, of encountering his own subjects on the field of battle.

Yet despite these subtleties, which were complicated even more by frequent efforts to reconcile the various systems, the vassal was in practice usually left to make his own decision, often after prolonged bargaining. When, in 1184, war broke out between the counts of Hainault and Flanders, the lord of Avesnes, a vassal of both nobles, first of all obtained from the court of Hainault a judgment which learnedly defined his obligations. He then proceeded to throw all his forces on the Flemish side. Did fealty so unstable still deserve the name?

2 HEYDAY AND DECLINE OF LIEGE HOMAGE

Nevertheless, in this society, where neither the state nor even the family provided an adequate bond of unity, the need to attach the subordinates firmly to the chief was so acute that, since ordinary homage had notoriously failed in its purpose, an attempt was made to raise above it a sort of super-homage. This was known as 'liege' homage.

In spite of some phonetic difficulties, which are a common feature of the history of legal terms in the Middle Ages—probably because, being at once learned and popular, they passed perpetually from one level of speech to another—there is hardly any room for doubt that this famous adjective *lige* was derived from a Frankish word, of which the corresponding term in modern German is *ledig*, free, pure. The Rhenish scribes who in the thirteenth century translated *homme lige* by *ledichman* were already conscious of the parallelism, But however complicated this problem of origins may be—and it is of secondary importance, after all—the actual meaning of the epithet, as employed in medieval French, was in no wise

obscure. The notaries of the Rhineland were also right in translating it—
this time into Latin—by *absolutus*. And 'absolute' would be the nearest
translation today. Of the 'residence' at their churches required of certain
clerics it was said that it must be 'personal and liege'. More often the term
was used to describe the exercise of a right. At the market of Auxerre the
'weight', a monopoly of the count, was 'liege of the count'. A widow,
freed by death from the legal control of a husband, extended over her own
property her 'liege widowhood'. In Hainault the demesne exploited
directly by the lord constituted, in contrast with the tenements, his 'liege
lands'. Two monasteries of the Île-de-France, let us say, divide up between
them a manor which has hitherto remained intact. Each share passes into
the 'liegeance' (*ligesse*) of the house which will henceforth be its sole owner.
Similar expressions were used when this exclusive authority was exercised,
not over things, but over men. The abbot of Morigny, having no canonical
superior other than his archbishop, declared himself 'liege of My Lord of
Sens'. In many regions, the serf, bound to his master by the strictest ties of
all, was called his 'liegeman' (the Germans occasionally used *ledig* in the
same context).[1] Very naturally, when it was desired to single out from
among the acts of homage done by the same vassal to several lords one
which carried a fealty ranking above all other engagements, it became
customary to speak of 'liege homage', 'liege lords' and also—with that
admirable indifference to ambiguity which we have already encountered—
'liegemen', the latter being in this case vassals and not serfs.

The development began with engagements which still lacked any specific
terminology. The lord receiving the homage of a vassal merely made him
swear to observe the fealty thus contracted in preference to all other
obligations. But, with the exception of a few regions where the vocabulary
of 'liegeance' penetrated only later, this phase of anonymous growth
lost to sight in the obscurity of ages when even the most sacred under-
takings were not set down in writing. For throughout a vast area the
emergence of the word 'liege', like the relationship it described, followed
very closely on the general growth of multiple fealties. The rise in the
number of acts of homage described as 'liege' may be traced (according to
the surviving texts) in Anjou from about 1046, in the Namur region only a
little later, and, from the second half of the century, in Normandy,
Picardy, and the county of Burgundy. Liegeance was already sufficiently
widespread in 1095 to attract the attention of the Council of Clermont. At
about the same time it had appeared under another name, in the county of
Barcelona; instead of 'liegeman', the Catalans said—in pure Romanic
—*soliu* ('solid man'). By the end of the twelfth century the practice had

[1] For the references, see the works cited in the bibliography. To these should be added:
for the two monasteries, Arch. Nat. LL 1450 A, fol. 68, ro and vo (1200–1209); for
Morigny, Bibl. Nat. lat. 5648, fol. 110 ro (1224, Dec.); for the serfs, Marc Bloch, *Rois
et serfs*, 1920, p. 23 n. 2.

almost reached the limits of its expansion—at least in so far as the word liege corresponded to a living reality. Later on, its original meaning became, as we shall see, greatly attenuated and it came to be used in the chancelleries almost as a matter of convention. If we confine ourselves to documents earlier than about 1250, the map—indefinite as its outlines remain in the absence of systematic information—nevertheless offers fairly clear indications. Gaul between Meuse and Loire, Burgundy, and Catalonia —a sort of highly feudalized colonial march—together constituted the true homeland of the new type of feudal relationship. Thence it emigrated to the countries of imported feudalism: England, Norman Italy, and Syria. Around its original home, the practice spread southwards as far as Langue-doc, though rather sporadically, it seems; and north-eastwards as far as the Rhine valley. Neither trans-Rhenish Germany, nor northern Italy, where the Lombard *Book of Fiefs* adhered to the system of classification by dates, ever knew it in its full strength. This second wave of vassalage—a reinforcing wave, we might say—sprang from the same countries as the first. But it did not carry so far.

'However many lords a man may acknowledge,' says an Anglo-Norman customary of about 1115, 'it is to the one whose liegeman he is that his chief duty lies.' And it goes on to say: 'A man must observe fealty to all his lords, saving always his fealty to the earlier lord. But his strongest fealty is owed to that lord whose liegeman he is.' Similarly in Catalonia the 'Usages' of the count's court ordain: 'The lord of a liegeman (*home soliu*) is entitled to his aid against all and sundry; no man may use it against him.'[1] Liege homage therefore takes precedence of all other acts of homage, irrespective of dates. It is really in a class by itself. In every way this 'pure' bond renewed the original human tie in all its completeness. A vassal is killed, let us say. Among all his lords, it is the 'liege lord' who collects the blood-money, if any has to be paid. Or it may be a question, as in the reign of Philip Augustus, of raising the 'tenth' for the crusade. In that case each lord takes the share due from the fiefs held of him; but the liege lord takes the tax on movable property, which the Middle Ages always regarded as peculiarly personal. In the intelligent analysis of vassal relationships given by the canonist William Durand shortly after the death of St. Louis, emphasis is placed, with good reason, on the 'mainly personal' character of liege homage. It would be impossible to express better the return to the living source of Frankish commendation.

But precisely because liege homage was merely the resurrection of the primitive form of homage, it was bound in its turn to be affected by the same causes of decline. It became subject to them all the more easily because nothing but a fragile oral or written agreement distinguished it from ordinary homage whose ceremonies it reproduced without modifica-tion—as though, after the ninth century, the power of inventing a new

[1] *Leges Henrici*, 43, 6, and 82, 5; 55, 2 and 3; *Us. Barc.*, c. 36.

216

symbolism had suddenly been lost. Many liegemen, at an early date, had received investiture of estates, positions of authority, and castles. It would have been impossible for a lord to withhold this reward or these recognized instruments of power from the followers on whose fealty he proposed mainly to depend. The introduction of the fief was therefore followed, in that case also, by the usual consequences. The subordinate was separated from his chief; obligations were detached from the person and laid on the estate instead—to the extent that the term 'liege fief' began to be employed; and, finally, liegeance became hereditary and, what was worse, an article of commerce. The practice of doing homage to several lords, the true scourge of vassalage, in its turn exercised its baneful influence. Yet it was to combat this evil that liegeance had been brought into being. As early as the last years of the eleventh century, however, the 'Usages' of Barcelona made provision for a disturbing exception. 'No one', they declare, 'may become the *soliu* of more than one lord, save with the consent of him to whom he first did homage of this sort.' A century later, this development had occurred almost everywhere. It was henceforth a common thing for one man to acknowledge two or more liege lords. These engagements continued to take precedence over all others, yet it remained necessary to discriminate between different liege engagements and to grade the obligations by means of the same deplorably inaccurate tests which had already been used to decide between ordinary acts of homage. This was so in theory at least. In practice it meant that the door was again open to 'felony' (the breach of feudal obligations), which might indeed in some circumstances be almost necessary. The result, in short, had been merely to create two degrees of vassalage.

Moreover, it was not very long before this hierarchical arrangement itself took on the appearance of an empty archaism. For liege homage tended very quickly to become the normal name for every kind of homage. Two degrees of attachment between lord and vassal had been devised—one stronger, the other weaker. What lord was sufficiently modest to be content with the second? About 1260, of forty-eight vassals of the count of Forez, in the Roannais, four at the most did ordinary homage.[1] As an exceptional practice, the engagement might perhaps have retained some effectiveness; once it had become a commonplace affair it meant very little. Nothing was more significant than the case of the Capetians. In persuading the greatest nobles of the realm to acknowledge themselves their liegemen, what else were they doing but obtaining from these territorial chiefs, whose situation was incompatible with the complete devotion of the armed retainer, a facile acquiescence in a formula that was hopelessly unreal? It was a revival—on the higher plane of 'liegeance'—of the illusion of the Carolingians, who believed that they could ensure the loyalty of their officials by homage alone.

[1] *Chartes du Forez*, no. 467.

In two states where feudalism was an importation, however, the Anglo-Norman kingdom after the Conquest, and the kingdom of Jerusalem, the course of evolution was diverted by the influence of better-organized monarchies. Deeming that 'liege' fealty alone—that is to say, the fealty that came before all others—was what they were entitled to, the kings endeavoured first of all, and not unsuccessfully, to secure for themselves the monopoly of this type of homage. But they had no intention of limiting their authority to their own vassals. Any subject of theirs, even if he did not hold his land directly from the crown, owed them obedience. Gradually, therefore, it became customary in these countries to reserve the term 'liegeance' for the fealty to the king, often confirmed by oath, which was demanded of the whole body of free men whatever their place in the feudal hierarchy. Thus the concept of this 'absolute' bond retained something of its original value only where it had been detached from the system of vassal ceremonies and identified with the subject's special act of submission to the Crown; in this way it contributed to the consolidation of power within the framework of the State. But as a means of revitalizing the old personal bond, which had fallen into irremediable decay, it was obviously ineffective.

XVI

VASSAL AND LORD

1 AID AND PROTECTION

'TO serve' or (as it was sometimes put) 'to aid', and 'to protect'—it was in these very simple terms that the oldest texts summed up the mutual obligations of the armed retainer and his lord. Never was the bond felt to be stronger than in the period when its effects were thus stated in the vaguest and, consequently, the most comprehensive fashion. When we define something, do we not always impose limitations on it? It was inevitable, nevertheless, that the need to define the legal consequences of the contract of homage should be felt with increasing urgency, especially in so far as they affected the obligations of the subordinate. Once vassalage had emerged from the humble sphere of domestic loyalty, what vassal thenceforth would have regarded it as compatible with his dignity if it had been frankly stated, as in early times, that he was compelled 'to serve the lord in all manner of tasks which may be required of him'?[1] Furthermore, could the lord continue to expect to have always at his beck and call persons who thenceforward—since they were for the most part settled on fiefs—lived at a distance from their master?

In the gradual work of definition professional jurists played only a belated and, on the whole, insignificant part. It is true that, as early as about 1020, Bishop Fulbert of Chartres, whose study of the canon law had trained him in the methods of legal reflection, attempted an analysis of homage and its effects. But interesting though it was as a symptom of the penetration of jurisprudence into a sphere which had hitherto been alien to it, this endeavour scarcely succeeded in rising above the level of a rather barren scholastic exercise. The decisive influence, here as elsewhere, was that of custom, formed by precedents and progressively crystallized by the legal practice of courts attended by many vassals. More and more frequently, the practice was adopted of having these stipulations, which but a short while before had been purely traditional, included in the agreement itself. The oath of fealty, since it could be expanded at will, formed a better vehicle for the details of these conditions than the few words that accompanied the act of homage. Thus a detailed contract, carefully drawn up, replaced an unqualified submission. As a further precaution, which clearly

[1] *M.G.H., EE.*, V., p. 127, no. 34.

testifies to the weakening of the tie, the vassal as a rule no longer promised merely to render aid to his lord. He was now required in addition to undertake not to injure him. In Flanders, from the beginning of the twelfth century, these negative clauses had assumed sufficient importance to give rise to a separate oath of 'security' which was sworn after fealty and apparently authorized the lord, in the event of the vassal's failure to observe it, to distrain on certain specified pledges. It goes without saying, however, that for a long time it was the positive obligations which continued to hold first place.

The primary duty was, by definition, military service. The 'man of mouth and hands' was bound, first and foremost, to serve in person, on horseback and with full equipment. Nevertheless he rarely appeared alone. Apart from the fact that his own vassals, if he had any, would naturally gather under his banner and share his privileges and his prestige, custom sometimes required him to be attended by at least one or two squires. On the other hand there were as a rule no foot-soldiers in his contingent. Their rôle in battle was considered so unimportant and the difficulty of feeding fairly large bodies of men was so great that the leader of the feudal host contented himself with the peasant infantry furnished by his own estates or those of the churches of which he had officially constituted himself the protector. Frequently the vassal was also required to garrison the lord's castle, either during hostilities only, or—for a fortress could not remain unguarded—at any time, in rotation with his fellow-vassals. If he had a fortified house of his own, he was obliged to throw it open to his lord.

Gradually differences in rank and power, the development of inevitably divergent traditions, special agreements, and even abuses transformed into rights introduced innumerable variations into these obligations. This, in the long run, almost invariably tended to lighten them.

A serious problem arose from the hierarchical organization of vassalage. Since the vassal was at once subject and master, he would often have vassals of his own. The duty which required him to render aid to his lord to the utmost of his ability might be thought to oblige him to join the lord's army, together with the entire body of his dependants. Custom, however, at an early date authorized him to bring with him only a stated number of followers; the figure was fixed once and for all, and might be much less than the number he employed in his own wars. Take the case, towards the end of the eleventh century, of the bishop of Bayeux. More than a hundred knights owed him military service, but he was bound to provide only twenty of them for the duke of Normandy, his immediate lord. Moreover, if the duke demanded the help of the prelate in the name of the king of France (of whom Normandy was held as a fief) the number was reduced to ten. This fining down of the military obligation towards the summit, which the Plantagenet kings of England in the twelfth century tried without much success to arrest, was undoubtedly one of the principal causes of the final failure of vassalage as a means of defence or conquest in the hands of governments.[1]

It was the chief desire of vassals both great and small not to be held to an indefinite period of military service. But neither the traditions of the Carolingian state nor the earliest usages of vassalage offered direct precedents for limiting its duration. Both the subject and the household warrior remained under arms as long as their presence seemed necessary to king or chief. The old Germanic customs, on the other hand, had widely employed a sort of standard period fixed at forty days or, as they said earlier, forty nights. This not only regulated many forms of procedure; Frankish military legislation itself had adopted forty days as the period of rest to which the levies were entitled between two mobilizations. This traditional period, which came naturally to mind, provided from the end of the eleventh century the normal standard for the obligation imposed on the vassals; on the expiration of forty days they were free to return home, usually for the rest of the year. It is true that they fairly frequently remained with the army, and certain 'customs' even sought to make this prolongation of the period of service compulsory, though only on condition that the lord bore the expense and paid wages to the vassal. The fief, once the stipend of the armed 'satellite', had so far ceased to fulfil its original purpose that it was necessary to supplement it by other remuneration.

It was not only for war that the lord summoned his vassals. In peacetime, they constituted his 'court', which he convoked in solemn session at more or less regular intervals, coinciding as a rule with the principal liturgical feasts. It was by turns a court of law, a council which the master was required by the political conceptions of the time to consult on all serious matters, and a ceremonial parade of rank and power. Could a chief have a more striking manifestation of his prestige or a more delightful way of reminding himself of it than to appear in public surrounded by a multitude of dependants, some of whom were themselves men of high rank, and to get them to perform publicly those gestures of deference—by acting as squire, cup-bearer or steward—to which an age susceptible to visible things attached great symbolic value?

The splendour of these courts, 'full, marvellous and great', has been naïvely exaggerated by the epic poems, in which they are frequent backgrounds to the action. While the glories of the ceremonial gatherings graced by the presence of crowned kings were greatly magnified, the poets even added gratuitous splendours to the modest courts convoked by

[1] C. H. Haskins, *Norman Institutions*, 1918, p. 15; Round, *Family Origins*, 1930, p. 208; H. M. Chew, *The English Ecclesiastical Tenants-in-Chief and Knight-Service*, Oxford, 1932; Gleason, *An Ecclesiastical Barony of the Middle Ages*, 1936; H. Navel, *L'Enquête de 1133*, 1935, p. 71.

barons of medium or lesser rank. Nevertheless, we know from the most reliable sources that much legal business was dealt with in these assemblies; that the most brilliant of them were marked by much ceremonial display and attracted—in addition to those who normally attended—a mixed crowd of adventurers, mountebanks and even pick-pockets; and that the lord was required by usage as well as by his acknowledged interest, to distribute to his men on these occasions those gifts of horses, arms, and vestments which were at once the guarantee of their fealty and the symbol of their subordination. We know, moreover, that the presence of the vassals —each, as the abbot of Saint-Riquier prescribed, 'carefully arrayed in accordance with his rank'—was always expressly required. According to the *Usages of Barcelona*, the count, when he holds court, must 'render justice . . . give help to the oppressed . . . announce mealtimes with trumpets so that nobles and others of lesser rank may participate; he must distribute cloaks to his chief vassals; make arrangements for the expedition which will harry the lands of Spain; and create new knights'. At a lower level of the social hierarchy, a petty knight of Picardy, acknowledging himself in 1210 the liegeman of the vidame of Amiens, promised him, in the same breath, military aid for a period of six months and 'to come, when I am required to do so, to the feast given by the said vidame, staying there, with my wife, at my own expense, for eight days'.[1]

This last example (together with many others) shows how court service, like military service, was gradually regulated and limited—though it is true that the attitude of the vassals towards the two obligations was not altogether the same. Military service was an obligation and little else, but attendance at court carried with it many advantages: gifts from one's lord, a groaning board and a share in the exercise of authority. The vassals were, therefore, much less eager to be relieved of court service than of military service. Till the end of the feudal era these assemblies compensated in some measure for the separation of lord and vassal resulting from the grant of a fief; they helped to maintain the personal contact without which a human tie can scarcely exist.

The vassal was bound by his fealty to 'render aid' to his lord in all things, and it was taken for granted that this meant placing his sword and his counsel at his lord's disposal. But there came a time when he was expected to make his purse available as well. No institution reveals better than this financial obligation the deep-seated unity of the system of dependence on which feudal society was built. Whoever owed obedience was obliged to give financial help to his chief or master in case of need: the serf, the so-called 'free' tenant of a manor, the subject of a king, and finally the vassal. The very terms applied to the contributions which the lord was thus authorized to demand from his men were, at least in French feudal law,

---

[1] Hariulf, *Chronique*, III, 3, ed. Lot, p. 97.; *Us. Barc.*, c. CXXIV.; Du Cange, *Dissertations sur l'hist. de Saint Louis*, V, ed. Henschel, VII, p. 23.

identical regardless of who paid them. People spoke simply of 'aid'; or again of *taille* (tallage), a vivid expression which was derived from the verb *tailler*, meaning literally to take from someone a part of his substance and, consequently, to tax him.[1] Naturally, in spite of this similarity of principle, the history of the obligation followed very different lines in different social groups. For the moment we are concerned only with the 'aid' or *taille* payable by vassals.

In its primitive form this tax appears simply as an occasional and more or less voluntary gift. In Germany and Lombardy it seems never to have passed beyond this stage; a significant passage of the *Sachsenspiegel* shows the vassal still 'bringing gifts to his lord'. In these countries the bond of vassalage was not strong enough to enable the lord who wanted additional help after the primary service had been duly performed, to demand it of right. It was otherwise in France. There, towards the end of the eleventh century or the beginning of the twelfth, conditions favoured the development of the *taille* as a feudal exaction. This was the moment when it was becoming more widespread in the form applied to the poor and when, altogether, the increasing circulation of money was tending to make the needs of the chiefs more urgent and the means of the taxpayers less limited. Custom was making the payments compulsory; but, by way of compensation, it also specified the occasions when they could be demanded. Thus in 1111 an Angevin fief was already subject to the 'four standard *tailles*': for the lord's ransom, if he were taken prisoner; for the knighting of his eldest son; for the marriage of his eldest daughter; and to enable the lord himself to make a purchase of land.[2] The last case was too arbitrary in its application and it quickly disappeared from most of the customs. The first three, on the other hand, were recognized almost everywhere. Others were sometimes added—the 'aid' for the crusade, in particular, or that which the lord levied when his superiors demanded one from him. Thus the money element, which we have already noted as present in the case of relief, gradually insinuated itself among the old relationships based on fealty and service.

It was to enter by yet another channel. Inevitably it happened from time to time that the obligation of military service was not carried out. The lord thereupon claimed a fine or compensation; occasionally the vassal offered it in advance. This was called 'service', in conformity with the linguistic convention whereby the payment of compensation was frequently given the name of the obligation which it extinguished; in France it was sometimes

---

[1] In England, however, these terms were eventually assigned to different social levels. 'Aid' was reserved for vassals and 'tallage' for the more humble classes of dependants.

[2] First cartulary of Saint-Serge (Marchegay's restoration). Arch. Maine-et-Loire, H., fol. 293. Naturally, the occasions were different on ecclesiastical fiefs; on those held of the bishop of Bayeux, for example, they were the bishop's journey to Rome, repairs to the cathedral, a fire at the bishop's palace (Gleason, *An Ecclesiastical Barony*, p. 50).

known as *taille de l'ost*. These dispensations for a cash payment were not in fact widely practised except in the case of two categories of fiefs: those which had fallen into the hands of religious communities, who were unable to bear arms; and those held directly of the great monarchies, which were adept at turning to their own financial profit the inadequacies of the system of vassal recruitment. For the majority of feudal tenements, the duty of military service from the thirteenth century onward merely became less and less exacting, without any tax being imposed in its place. Even the pecuniary aids frequently fell into desuetude in the end. The fief had ceased to procure good servants: neither did it long remain a fruitful source of revenue.

Custom in most cases did not require of the lord any verbal or written agreement corresponding to the oath of the vassal. Such pledges on the lord's part appeared only at a later date and always remained exceptional. There was no opportunity, therefore, to define the obligations of the chief in as much detail as those of the subordinate. A duty of protection, moreover, did not lend itself so well as services to such precise definition. The vassal was to be defended by his lord 'towards and against all men who may live and die'; first and foremost in his person, but also in his property and more especially in his fiefs. Furthermore he expected from this protector—who had become, as we shall see, a judge—good and speedy justice. In addition, there were the imponderable but nevertheless precious advantages which accrued, rightly or wrongly, from the patronage of a powerful man in a highly anarchic society. All these advantages were prized; nevertheless in the long run the vassal's obligations outweighed the benefits he received. As remuneration for service, the fief had originally redressed the balance, but when by reason of its transformation into a patrimonial property its original function was lost sight of, the inequality of the obligations seemed all the more flagrant, and those who suffered from it were all the more anxious to limit their burden.

2 VASSALAGE AS A SUBSTITUTE FOR THE KINSHIP TIE

Nevertheless, were we to concern ourselves only with this debit and credit balance we should gain but an emasculated impression of the essential nature of the tie of vassalage. The relationships of personal dependence had made their entry into history as a sort of substitute for, or complement to, the solidarity of the family, which had ceased to be fully effective. In the eyes of tenth-century Anglo-Saxon law, the lordless man is an outlaw unless his relatives are prepared to assume responsibility for him.[1] In relation to the lord, the vassal long remained a sort of supplementary relative, his duties as well as his rights being the same as those of relatives by blood. If an incendiary, declares Frederick Barbarossa in one of his

[1] Cf. above, p. 182.

peace ordinances, shall have sought asylum in a castle, the master of the fortress shall be compelled, if he does not wish to be regarded as an accomplice, to hand over the fugitive, 'provided, however, that the latter be not his lord, his vassal or his kinsman'. And it was no accident that the oldest Norman customary, in treating of the murder of a vassal by his lord or of a lord by his vassal, grouped these crimes indiscriminately in the same chapter with the most atrocious homicides committed within the family group. This quasi-family character of vassalage was responsible for several enduring features, in the legal rules as well as in the habits of feudal society.

The primary duty of the kinsman was vengeance. The same was true of the man who had done homage or received it. Was not the Latin *ultor*—avenger—simply translated, in an ancient German gloss, by the Old High German word *mundporo*, patron?[1] This equality of function between the kinship group and the tie of vassalage, which began in the blood-feud, continued to manifest itself in the courts of law. No one, declares a twelfth-century English customary, if he has not himself been present at the crime, may bring an accusation in a case of murder, unless he is a kinsman of the dead man, his lord, or his vassal. The obligation was equally binding on the lord in relation to his vassal and on the vassal in relation to his lord. A difference of degree was nevertheless noticeable, very much in conformity with the spirit of this relationship of subordination. If we are to believe the poem of *Beowulf*, the companions of the slain chieftain in ancient Germania were entitled to a share of the *wergild*. It was no longer so in Norman England. The lord shared in the compensation paid for the murder of the vassal; of that which was due for the murder of the lord the vassal received nothing. The loss of a servant was paid for; that of a master was not.

Only in rare instances was the knight's son brought up in his father's house. Custom decreed—and was obeyed so long as feudal *mores* retained some vitality—that his father entrust him, while still a child, to his lord or one of his lords. In the household of this chief the boy, while performing the duties of a page, received instruction in the arts of hunting and of war, and later in courtly manners. An historical example of this tradition was the young Arnulf of Guines in the household of Count Philip of Flanders; in legend, there was little Garnier of Nanteuil, who served Charlemagne so well:

> When to the woods the king repairs, the child goes too;
> Sometimes his bow he bears, sometimes his stirrup holds.
> If wildfowl lure the king, Garnier is by his side.
> Oft on his wrist the hawk or keen-eyed falcon sits.
> And when to rest the king retires, Garnier is there, ·
> Beguiling him with song and old heroic lays.

In other medieval European societies similar practices prevailed, and

[1] Steinmeyer and Sievers, *Althochdeutsche Glossen*, I, p. 268, 23.

there also they served to reinforce, through the agency of the young, ties which the physical separation of lord and vassal constantly threatened to stretch to breaking point. But the system of 'fosterage' practised in Ireland seems to have been used above all to strengthen the link between the child and the maternal clan, and occasionally to establish the pedagogic prestige of a body of learned priests. Among the Scandinavians, it was the dependant's duty to bring up his master's children. So much was this the case that, when Harald of Norway wished to demonstrate to the world at large the overlordship which he claimed over King Aethelstan of England, he found no better means to this end, the Saga tells us, than to have his son set down unexpectedly on the knees of this involuntary foster-father. The feudal world reversed the obligation, and the vassal's son was brought up by the lord. The ties of respect and gratitude thus created were held to be very strong. All his life the little boy of earlier days remembered that he had been the *nourri* of the lord—the word, with what it stood for, dates in Gaul from the Frankish period and still recurs in the pages of Commynes.[1] Doubtless, in this case as in others, the facts were often at variance with the rules of honour. Nevertheless, this practice certainly served a purpose; for, while placing a precious hostage in the lord's hands, it enabled each generation of vassals to enjoy anew something of that participation in the overlord's intimate domestic life whence early vassalage had derived its deepest human value.

In a society where the individual was so little his own master, marriage (which, as we know already, was bound up with a great variety of interests) was very far from being considered an act of personal choice. The decision was first and foremost a matter for the father. 'He wishes to see his son take a wife while he is still alive; he therefore buys for him the daughter of a nobleman'—that is how the old *Poem of St. Alexis* puts it, with no beating about the bush. The relatives intervened in these matters, sometimes in association with the father, but especially when he was no longer alive. So too did the lord, when the orphan was the son of a vassal; and the vassals also occasionally had a say when the marriage of their lord was at issue. In this latter case, it is true, the rule never amounted to more than a mere formality; on all important matters the baron was bound to consult his men and hence in this. On the other side, the lord's rights in regard to the personal affairs of his vassal were much more clearly defined. The tradition went back to the remotest origins of vassalage. 'If a private warrior (*bucellarius*) leaves only a daughter,' declares a Visigothic law of the fifth century, 'she shall remain under the control of the master, who will find her a husband of the same social status. If, however, she herself shall choose a husband, against the wishes of the master, she shall be obliged to restore

[1] Flodoard, *Hist. Remensis eccl.*, III, 26 in *M.G.H., SS.*, XIII, p. 540; cf. already *Actus pontificum Cenomannensium*, pp. 134 and 135 (616: 'nutritura'); Commynes, VI, 6 (ed. Mandrot, II, p. 50).

to the latter all the gifts which her father has received from him' [1] The heritability of fiefs, already present in this text in a rudimentary form, furnished the lords with one more reason, and a very cogent one, for keeping a close eye on marriages which, when the estate had passed to the distaff side, resulted in their acquiring a vassal who did not belong to the original line. Their control over marriages became absolute, however, only in France and Lotharingia, the true homelands of the system of vassalage, and in the countries of imported feudalism. It is true that families of knightly rank were not the only ones which had to submit to such interference in their personal affairs; for many others were subjected, through various ties, to an authority of seignorial character, and kings, in their capacity as sovereign, sometimes considered that they were entitled to dispose of the hands of their female subjects. But as applied to vassals—as sometimes to serfs, who also were personal dependants—a practice which was regarded as an abuse of power when applied to other types of subordinates was almost universally held to be lawful. 'We will not marry widows and daughters against their will,' Philip Augustus promises the people of Falaise and Caen, 'unless they hold of us, in whole or in part, a *fief de haubert*'—that is to say, a military fief characterized by service with coat of mail.[2]

The ideal procedure was that the lord should come to an agreement with the kinsfolk. Such collaboration was provided for in the thirteenth century, for example, by an Orleans 'custom', and the arrangement is given prominence in a curious charter of Henry I of England.[3] When the lord was strong, however, he could overrule all opposition. In Plantagenet England this institution, derived from the principles of guardianship, degenerated in the end into blatant commercialism. Kings and barons—kings especially—vied with each other in giving or selling the hands of orphan sons or daughters. Sometimes, threatened with the prospect of an unwelcome husband, a widow would pay in hard cash for permission to refuse him. Despite the progressive loosening of the tie, it is clear that vassalage did not always avoid the other danger which threatens almost every system of personal protection—that of degenerating into a device for the exploitation of the weak by the strong.

3 RECIPROCITY AND BREACH OF ENGAGEMENTS

The contract of vassalage bound together two men who were, by definition, on different social levels. Nothing shows this more strikingly than one of

---

[1] *Codex Euricianus*, c. 310. The vassal mentioned by the synod of Compiègne of 757, whose marriages were arranged by his two successive masters, is—in conformity with the original meaning of the word vassal—a mere slave, and we are not concerned with such cases here. [2] *Ordonnances*, XII, p. 275.

[3] *Ét. de Saint Louis*, I, c. 67; F. M. Stenton, *The First Century of English Feudalism* (1066–1166), 1932, pp. 33–34.

the provisions of the old Norman law. Both the lord who has killed his vassal and the vassal who has killed his lord are punished by death, but only the crime against the chief involves the dishonourable penalty of hanging.[1] Yet, whatever the inequalities between the obligations of the respective parties, those obligations were none the less mutual: the obedience of the vassal was conditional upon the scrupulous fulfilment of his engagements by the lord. This reciprocity in unequal obligations, which was emphasized by Fulbert of Chartres as early as the eleventh century and which was very strongly felt to the end, was the really distinctive feature of European vassalage. This characteristic distinguished it not only from ancient slavery but also, and very profoundly, from the forms of free dependence known to other civilizations, like that of Japan, and even to certain societies bordering on the feudal zone proper. The very ceremonies perfectly express the contrast. The 'prostration' of the Russian 'men of service' and the kissing of hands practised by the warriors of Castile contrast with the French form of homage which, by the gesture of hands closing upon hands and by the kiss on the mouth, made the lord no mere master with the sole function of receiving whatever was due to him, but a partner in a genuine contract. 'As much', writes Beaumanoir, 'as the vassal owes his lord of fealty and loyalty by reason of his homage, so much the lord owes his vassal.'

The solemn act which had created the contract seemed so binding that even in face of the worst breaches its final rupture seemed to demand a sort of cancellation ceremony. Such at least was the practice in the old Frankish regions. In Lotharingia and northern France, a ceremony of breach of homage took shape, in which perhaps was revived the memory of the gestures used by the Salian Frank, in times gone by, to renounce his kindred. The procedure was adopted occasionally by the lord, but more often by the vassal. Declaring his intention to cast away from him (*rejeter*) the 'felon' partner, with a violent gesture he hurled to the ground a twig—sometimes breaking it beforehand—or a thread from his cloak. But, in order that the ceremony should seem as decisive as the one whose effects it was to destroy, it was necessary that it should follow the pattern of homage by bringing the two individuals face to face. This proceeding was not without its dangers. Consequently, in preference to the gesture of throwing down the 'straw' (which before reaching the stage at which a usage becomes a rule fell into disuse) the practice developed of making a simple 'defiance' (*défi*)—in the etymological sense of the word, that is to say a renunciation of faith—by letters or by herald. The less scrupulous, who were not the least numerous, naturally began hostilities without any preliminary declaration.

But in the great majority of cases the personal tie had its counterpart in a real property tie. So once the vassalage was broken, what happened to the

[1] *Très ancien Coutumier*, XXXV, 5.

fief? When the fault lay with the vassal, there was no difficulty: the property reverted to the injured lord. This was what was called the *commise*, confiscation, of the fief. The 'disinheritance' of Duke Henry the Lion by Frederick Barbarossa and that of John Lackland by Philip Augustus are the most celebrated examples of this procedure. When the responsibility for the breach appeared to be the lord's the problem was more delicate. The fief, as the remuneration for services which were no longer to be rendered, would lose its *raison d'être*. Yet it would be unfair that an innocent man should be thus dispossessed. The hierarchical arrangement of fealties permitted escape from this quandary. The rights of the unworthy lord passed to his own lord—just as if a chain should be re-united after the removal of a broken link. It is true that when the fief had been held directly of the king, the highest link, this solution was not feasible. But it seems to have been admitted that in relation to the king no renunciation of homage could be lasting. Italy alone steered a separate course. There, the vassal who had suffered from a seignorial felony merely had his fief changed into an allodial property—a feature symptomatic (among many others) of the weakness of the more strictly feudal conceptions south of the Alps.

Carolingian legislation had defined the felonies which were held to justify the abandonment of the lord by the vassal, and its principles were never quite forgotten. In the poem of *Raoul de Cambrai*, the 'foster-child' Bernier, despite many grounds for hatred, repudiates Raoul only when struck by him. Now the Carolingian capitulary had said: 'No one shall quit his lord after having received a shilling's worth from him . . . unless this lord has beaten him with a stick.' A little later this motive for the breach was invoked by a court romance, in the course of a curious discussion of feudal casuistry; it was still expressly retained in the thirteenth century by various French customaries, and at the beginning of the following century by the *Parlement* of the first Valois king.[1] Nevertheless, even the soundest of the legal rules of former days survived, in feudal times, only as parts of an indeterminate tradition. The arbitrary conduct which resulted from this transformation of a legal code into a vague collection of moral laws could have been combated by the influence of courts capable of establishing a standard of judicial practice and giving it authority. Indeed, certain tribunals were in theory available for such cases. There was in the first place the lord's court, composed in reality of the vassals themselves, who were considered the natural judges of law-suits between the lord, their master, and his man, their peer; next, at the level above, there was the court of the chief of more exalted rank to whom the lord in his turn had done homage. Also certain 'customs', committed to writing at an early date,

---

[1] *Le Roman de Thèbes*, ed. L. Constans, I, v. 8041 *et seq.*—Arch. Nat. X Iᴀ, 6, fol. 185; cf. Olivier-Martin, *Histoire de la coutume de la prévôté et vicomté de Paris*, 1922–30, I, p. 257, n. 7.

like those of Bigorre, endeavoured to outline a procedure to which the vassal must conform before his 'departure' should be lawful.[1] But the great weakness of feudalism was precisely its inability to construct a really coherent and efficient judicial system. In practice, the individual who sustained what he considered or professed to consider an infringement of his rights would decide to break his engagement and the issue of the struggle would depend on the relative strength of the parties. It was as though a marriage were to be terminated by divorce, without the petitioner's case having been proved and without there being a judge to pronounce the decree.

[1] J. Fourgous and G. de Bezin, *Les Fors de Bigorre*, Bagnères, 1901 (*Travaux sur l'histoire du droit méridional*, fasc. 1), c. 6.

XVII

THE PARADOX OF VASSALAGE

1 THE CONTRADICTIONS OF THE EVIDENCE

BEYOND the numerous particular problems raised by the history of European vassalage there is one great human problem which dominates them all. What was it in the actions and the hearts of men that constituted the real strength of vassalage as a social cement? The first impression conveyed by the documents is of a strange contradiction, which must be squarely faced.

No protracted study of the texts is necessary in order to cull from them an eloquent anthology in praise of vassalage. First of all, it is extolled as the most cherished of bonds. A common synonym for 'vassal' was 'friend' (*ami*), and commoner still was the old word *dru* (probably of Celtic origin) which had almost the same meaning, but with a more definite suggestion of choice; for if it was sometimes applied to amorous relationships, it seems never (unlike *ami*) to have been extended to those of the family. Moreover, it was a term common to the Gallo-Roman and the German languages. 'In the last hour', said the bishops of Gaul to Lewis the German in 858, 'there will be neither wife nor son to aid thee; nor companionship of *drus* and vassals to bring thee succour.' Needless to say, as affection flows upward from the vassal to the lord, so it descends from the lord to the vassal. 'Girart', says a character in the French epic, 'became the liege-man of Charlemagne, from whom he then received friendship and a lord's protection.' 'Mere fiction!' those historians who only accept the testimony of dry documents will perhaps exclaim. But this is not the final word. 'I am the lord of this estate,' a landowner of Anjou is reported by the monks of Saint-Serge to have said: 'for Geoffrey' (who was in possession of it) 'had it from me as a fief, in friendship.' And how can we ignore the evidence of the following lines from *Doon de Mayence* which express with such frank simplicity that true union of hearts in which life is inconceivable for one without the other?

> Se me sire est ochis, je voeil estre tués,
> Et se il est pendu, avec li me pendés;
> Se il est ars en feu, je voeil estre bruslés,
> Et se il est noié, avec li me getés.

If my dear lord is slain, his fate I'll share.
If he is hanged, then hang me by his side.
If to the stake he goes, with him I'll burn;
And if he's drowned, then let me drown with him.[1]

It was a bond which called for an unfaltering devotion and for the sake of which a vassal was required, in the words of the *Chanson de Roland*, to endure 'both heat and cold'. 'I will love what thou lovest: I will hate what thou hatest,' so ran the Anglo-Saxon oath of commendation. For the continent we have other texts: 'Thy friends will be my friends, thy enemies my enemies.' The first and obvious duty of the good vassal is to know how to die for his chief, sword in hand—a fate to be envied above all others, for it is that of a martyr and it leads to Paradise. Is this what the poets say? Undoubtedly: but it is also what the Church says. A knight, provoked by threats, had killed his lord. 'Thou shouldst have accepted death for his sake,' declared a bishop, speaking in the name of the council of Limoges in 1031; 'thy fidelity would have made thee a martyr of God.'[2]

Finally, it was a bond of such a nature that to disregard it was the most terrible of sins. When the peoples of England had received the faith of Christ, wrote King Alfred, of their Christian charity they fixed scales of compensation for most offences 'save that of treason against one's lord, not daring to extend this mercy to such a crime . . . no more than Christ had accorded it to him who gave him over to death'. After an interval of more than two centuries, in an England already feudalized on the continental model, the principle is reaffirmed in the law-book known as the *Laws of Henry I*: 'No redemption for the man who has killed his lord; let him perish by the most atrocious tortures.' The story was told in Hainault that a knight, having killed in a fight the young count of Flanders, his liege lord, had gone to seek absolution of the pope—like the Tannhaüser of legend. The pope ordered that his hands be cut off. But because his hands did not tremble, the pope remitted the punishment; though on condition of bewailing his sin in a monastery for the rest of his life. 'He is my lord,' was the reply of the sire d'Ibelin in the thirteenth century to those who suggested that he should assassinate the Emperor, who had become his worst enemy; 'whatever he may do, I shall keep my faith to him.'[3]

This bond was felt to be so strong that the idea of it dominated all other human ties—even those which were older and which might have appeared more worthy of respect. Thus vassalage came to permeate family relationships. 'In law-suits brought by parents against sons or by sons against

---

[1] *Girart de Roussillon*, trans. P. Meyer, p. 100 (ed. Foerster, *Romanische Studien*, V, v. 3054); first cartulary of Saint-Serge, Marchegay's restoration, Arch. Maine-et-Loire, H., fol. 88; *Doon de Mayence*, ed. Guessard, p. 276.

[2] For example, *Girart de Roussillon*, trans. P. Meyer, p. 83; *Garin le Lorrain*, ed. P. Paris, II, p. 88. For the council, see Migne, *P.L.*, CXLII, col. 1400.

[3] Alfred in F. Liebermann, *Die Gesetze der Angelsachsen*, I, p. 47 (49, 7); *Leges Henrici*, 75, 1.; Gislebert de Mons, ed. Pertz, p. 30; Philip of Novara, ed. Kohler, p. 20.

parents, the parents shall be treated for purposes of the judgment as if they were the lords and the sons their men, bound to them by the rite of homage.' Such was the decision of the court of the count of Barcelona. When the Provençal poets invented courtly love, the devotion of the vassal to his lord was the model on which they based their conception of the fealty of the perfect lover. This fitted the fact that the lover was often of lower social rank than the lady of his dreams. The assimilation was carried so far that by a strange turn of speech, the name or surname of the beloved was apt to be assigned to the masculine gender, as is appropriate to the name of a chief. *Bel Senhor*, 'my beautiful lord'—one of the ladies to whom Bertrand de Born pledged his fickle heart is known to us only by this pseudonym. Occasionally a knight would have engraved on his shield the clasped hands of his Dulcinea with his own between them. Moreover, does not the memory of this symbolism, so typically feudal in its tenderness— a symbolism which doubtless owed its resuscitation in the early days of the romantic revival to antiquarian interests—still survive in our own day in the rules of politeness which, in French, enjoin a virtually one-sided use of the sadly-faded word *hommages*? Even religious symbolism took on these borrowed tints. To give oneself to the Devil was to become his vassal; the scenes of men surrendering themselves to the Evil One rank—along with the lovers' seals—among the best representations of the act of homage which we possess.[1] For the Anglo-Saxon Cynewulf, the angels are the 'thegns' of God; for Bishop Eberhard of Bamberg, Christ is the vassal of the Father. But beyond doubt the most eloquent testimony to the universal prevalence of the spirit of vassalage is to be found in the transformations of religious ritual itself. The ancient attitude of prayer, with hands outstretched, was replaced by the gesture of the joined hands, borrowed from 'commendation', and this became throughout Catholic Christendom the characteristic praying posture.[2] Before God, the good Christian in his inmost soul saw himself as a vassal bending the knee before his lord.

It was nevertheless inevitable that the vassal's obligation should from time to time come into conflict with other obligations—those of the subject, for example, or of the kinsman. In the event, it almost invariably triumphed over these rivals; not only in practice, but also in the eyes of the law. When Hugh Capet retook Melun in 991, the viscount, who had defended the fortress against him, was hanged together with his wife, and this was certainly not so much because he had rebelled against his king as because he had at the same time committed the atrocious crime of breaking his fealty to the count, his immediate lord, who was in the royal camp. On the other hand, Hugh's own followers demanded that he should pardon

[1] Cf. Plates III and IV.
[2] *The Christ of Cynewulf*, ed. A. S. Cook, v. 457; Migne, *P.L.*, CXCIII, cols. 523 and 524; L. Gougaud, *Dévotions et pratiques du moyen âge*, 1925, p. 20 *et seq.*

the knights who had defended the castle. As vassals of the viscount, had they by taking part in his revolt done otherwise than display their 'virtue', as the chronicler puts it—meaning their loyalty to their feudal obligations, which took precedence over their loyalty to the state?[1] The very ties of kinship, which were certainly regarded as more sacred than those of public law, yielded place to the obligations of personal dependence. 'It is permissible', declare the laws of Alfred, in England, 'to take up arms in defence of a kinsman wrongfully attacked; but not against one's lord—that we do not allow.' The Anglo-Saxon Chronicle in a famous passage brings before us the members of a family embroiled with each other as a result of the vendetta of the two different lords between whom their obedience is divided. They accept their unhappy situation: 'No relative is dearer to us than our lord,' they declare. This is a grave utterance; it finds an echo, well on in the twelfth century and in (of all places) Italy with its respect for public law, in the *Book of Fiefs*: 'Vassals must help their lord against everyone—against their brothers, against their sons, against their fathers.'[2]

At this point, however, an Anglo-Norman law-book issues a sharp reminder: 'Against the commands of God and the Catholic faith no order is valid.' Such was the opinion of the clergy. Knightly opinion demanded a more unqualified surrender. 'Raoul, my lord, may be a greater criminal than Judas; he is, nevertheless, my lord'—on this theme the *chansons* composed innumerable variations, and it sometimes found an echo in legal agreements as well. 'If the abbot has any suit in the king's court,' says an English charter of enfeoffment, 'the vassal shall support him, save against the king himself.' Let us disregard the final qualification: it was symptomatic of the exceptional respect which a monarchy created by conquest was able to command. Only the first part of the clause, in its cynical candour, has a general significance; clearly the obligation of fealty was too overriding for it to be permissible to ask oneself which of the parties had the better case. Moreover, why be so scrupulous? 'It matters little if my lord is in the wrong,' thinks Renaud of Montauban; 'he will bear the blame'. He who surrenders himself completely *ipso facto* relieves himself of personal responsibility.[3]

In this summary it has been necessary to cite pieces of evidence of different kinds and from different periods, and some readers may doubt whether this evidence taken from old texts, legal literature, and poetry reflects the actualities of the case. To set these misgivings at rest it will suffice to appeal finally to Joinville, a dispassionate observer, if ever there

[1] Richer, IV, 78. For other examples (up to the thirteenth century), see Jolliffe, *The Constitutional History of Medieval England*, p. 164.

[2] *Alfred*, XLII, 6; *Two of the Saxon Chronicles*, ed. Plummer, vol. I, 48–9 (755); Karl Lehmann, *Das Langobardische Lehnrecht* (*Handschriften, Textentwicklung, ältester Text und Vulgattext nebst den capitula extraordinaria*), *Vulgata*, II, 28, 4, Göttingen, 1896.

[3] *Leges Henrici*, 55, 3.; *Raoul de Cambrai*, V. 1381.; *Chron. mon. de Abingdon* (R.S.), II, p. 133 (1100–35).; *Renaus de Montauban*, ed. Michelant, p. 373, v. 16.

was one, who wrote in the reign of Philip the Fair. I have already quoted the passage. One contingent particularly distinguished itself in battle. Could it have been otherwise? That contingent consisted almost entirely of warriors who were either kinsmen or liegemen of the leader.

Now let us look at the reverse of the medal. The very epics which set such great store by the 'virtue' of the vassal are nothing but one long recital of the wars launched by vassals against their lords. Occasionally the poet adopts a censorious attitude; more often he indulges in a rather charming casuistry. What he knows beyond question is that it is from these revolts that daily life received its tragic colouring. Yet in this respect the *chansons* were little more than a pale reflection of reality. Struggles of the great feudatories against the kings; rebellions against the former by their own vassals; derelictions of feudal duty; the weakness of vassal armies, incapable from the earliest times of halting invaders—these features are to be read on every page of the history of feudalism. A charter of the end of the eleventh century shows us the monks of Saint-Martin-des-Champs concerned to determine what is to happen to a rent levied on a mill, in the event of its being pillaged during a war waged by the two petty lords to whom the sum is due. This situation is expressed in the following words: 'in the event of their making war on their lords or other men'.[1] Thus, of all the occasions for going to war, the first that came to mind was to take up arms against one's lord. Towards these so-called crimes life was very much more indulgent than fiction. Legend recounts that Herbert de Vermandois, who so vilely betrayed Charles the Simple, his lord and king, perished by hanging—the death of Judas; but history informs us that he died the most natural of deaths in his old age.

It was, of course, inevitable that there should be bad vassals as well as good ones; and also that many of them should oscillate between loyalty and faithlessness according to the interests or the mood of the moment. In face of so much seemingly contradictory evidence, is it not enough to repeat the words of the poet of the *Couronnement de Louis*?

> Là tous jurèrent le serment.
> Tel le jura, qui le tint bravement;
> Tel aussi, qui ne le tint point du tout.

> There, all did swear a solemn oath;
> And some there were who kept that bond,
> And some who kept it not at all.

There is certainly much in that. Deeply attached to tradition, but of violent manners and unstable temperament, the men of the feudal ages were in every way much more disposed to show formal respect for rules

---

[1] J. Depoin, *Recueil de Chartes et documents de Saint-Martin-des-Champs*, I, no. 47, and *Liber Testamentorum S. Martini*, no. XVIII.

than to obey them consistently in practice. We have already noted such contradictions in connection with the ties of kinship. Nevertheless it is fairly clear that in this case the root of the inconsistency must be sought elsewhere—in the institution of vassalage itself, in its changes and variations.

2 LEGAL TIES AND HUMAN CONTACT

About early vassalage, based on the group of armed followers gathered round the chief, there was a sort of cosy domestic flavour, which was expressed in its very vocabulary. The master was 'the old man' (*senior, herr*) or the giver of loaves (lord); the men were his companions (*gasindi*), his boys (*vassi*, thegns, knights), his bread-eaters (*buccellarii, hlafoetan*). Fealty, in short, was based at that time on personal contact and subjection shaded off into comradeship.

In the course of time, however, this bond, which was originally restricted to the household, was greatly extended. This was partly because there was a continued desire on the part of the master to retain the loyalty of those who, after living for a time in his house, departed to fend for themselves, often on estates which he had given them. But the chief reason was that, in face of the growing anarchy, the great men, and still more the kings, hoped to find in this extremely strong tie, or in the imitation of it, a remedy for failing loyalties while, conversely, many persons whose existence was threatened saw in it the means of obtaining a protector. Anyone above a certain social rank who wished, or was bound, to serve was treated as a companion-in-arms.

But it was futile to attempt to impose in this way a quasi-domestic loyalty on persons who no longer shared either the board or the fortunes of the chief, persons whose interests frequently ran counter to his and who sometimes even, far from having been enriched by his gifts, had been obliged to surrender their own patrimony to him, in order to take it back burdened with new obligations. Eventually this fealty, so much sought after, became completely meaningless, and the dependence of one man upon another was soon no more than the concomitant of the dependence of one estate upon another.

Inheritance itself, instead of cementing the solidarity of two families, tended only to loosen the tie, since it was concerned above all with territorial interests: the heir did homage only for the purpose of keeping the fief. The problem arose in the case of the humble fiefs of artisans as well as honourable and knightly ones. It seems to have been resolved, in both cases, in much the same way. The son of the painter or the carpenter succeeded to his father's property only if he had also inherited his craft.[1] Similarly the son of the knight received investiture only if he undertook to

---

[1] See, for example, the reference to a painter's fief in B. de Broussillon, *Cartulaire de l'abbaye de Saint Aubin d'Angers*, II, no. CCCCVIII.

continue his father's services. But the skill of a qualified craftsman was a much more dependable factor than the devotion of a warrior, which might be easier to promise than to fulfil. By a very significant ruling an ordinance of 1291, in enumerating the grounds of objection which might be raised against the judges of the French royal court, holds that a vassal of one of the litigants may be suspected of partiality only if he holds a life fief. So feeble at that time did the hereditary bond appear![1]

The sense of free choice was so far lost that it was no uncommon thing for a vassal to alienate the duties of vassalage along with the fief, and for the lord to give or sell the loyalty of his men along with his fields, his woods, and his castles. It is true that the fief could not, in theory, be transferred without the lord's permission. It is true that the vassals, for their part, were likely to claim that they could not be handed over without their own consent: official recognition of the right was, indeed, one of the favours granted in 1037 by the Emperor Conrad to the vavasours of Italy. Practice, however, soon overthrew these feeble impediments. Except in Germany—virtually preserved from this abuse, as we shall see, by an exceptionally strong sense of rank and status—the commercialization of feudal relations had, in addition, the absurd result that often a powerful individual was induced to become the man 'of mouth and hands' of some- one much weaker than himself. Are we to believe that the great count who had acquired a fief in the *mouvance* of a petty lord ever took very seriously the rite of submission which an empty custom still required him to perform? Finally, despite the attempt to salvage the institution by means of liegeance, the plurality of vassal engagements—itself a consequence of the weakening of the bond—ended by depriving it of any possibility of working effectively. From a comrade-in-arms whose devotion was sustained by constant gifts and personal contact, the vassal had degenerated into a sort of leaseholder, not over-eager to pay his rent of services and obedience. One restraining influence remained—the respect for the vassal's oath—and it was not without effect. But when the promptings of self-interest or passion were insistent this abstract impediment too often gave way.

Such at least was the case where vassalage lost its primitive character. There had been many stages in this process. It would be a mistake to regard as typical of vassal sentiment the often disturbed relations of the great or medial barons with the kings or territorial princes who were their lords. It is true that chronicles and *chansons de geste* seem to invite us to do so. For the resounding breaches of faith committed by these magnates attracted the attention of writers of history as well as of fiction; they were dramas played out in the foreground of the political stage. What do they prove, however, except that in thinking to attach their principal officials to themselves by a tie borrowed from quite a different sphere the Caro- lingians and their imitators had made a serious blunder?

[1] C. V. Langlois, *Textes relatifs à l'histoire du Parlement*, no. CXI, c. 5 bis.

Lower down in the social scale, the texts afford a glimpse of groups much more closely ranged round chiefs who were better known to their vassals and better served. There were in the first place those landless knights, those 'bachelors' of the *mesnie*—in other words, the household (*maisonnée*)—whose condition for long centuries throughout the West continued to reproduce in its every feature the life of the early vassals.[1] The French epic did not misrepresent the position. Its great rebels—an Ogier, a Girart, a Renaud—are mighty feudatories. But what if it is a question of portraying a good vassal? There is Bernier in *Raoul de Cambrai*; Bernier, faithful despite the unjust war carried on against his family by his lord, faithful still after having seen his mother perish in the conflagration started by this 'Judas' and who, even when an atrocious insult has at last decided him to forsake the most deplorable of masters, seems never to know—any more than does the poet—whether he did right or wrong in committing this breach of fealty; Bernier, a simple squire, whose loyalty to his lord is reinforced by the memory, not of an estate received, but of a horse and clothing freely bestowed. These loyal servants were also recruited from among the more numerous body of modest vavasours whose petty fiefs were often grouped in the neighbourhood of the castle where they performed in rotation their tour of garrison duty. This group consisted of men too poor, as a rule, to hold their lands by virtue of more than one act of homage, or at least of more than one act of liege homage;[2] too weak not to attach a high value to the protection which alone could enable them to fulfil their duties. Since they were little involved in the great affairs of the time they were ready to focus both their interests and their feelings on the lord who summoned them regularly to his court, supplemented the scanty revenues of their fields or tenements with welcome gifts, received their sons as 'nurslings', and, finally, led them forth to joyous and profitable war.

Such were the circles in which, in spite of inevitable outbursts of resentment, the fealty of the vassal long survived in all its freshness, and in which also, when the old rites were finally outmoded, it was replaced, as we shall see, by other forms of personal dependence. To have been founded originally on affectionate comradeship at home and in arms; then, having forsaken the domestic circle, to have preserved something of its human value only where the degree of personal separation was least—this was the destiny of European vassalage and in this lies the explanation of its apparent paradoxes.

---

[1] To the French examples may be added, e.g., F. Chalandon, *Histoire de la domination normande en Italie*, II, p. 565; C. G. Homeyer, *System des Lehnrechts der sächsischen Rechtsbücher* in *Sachsenspiegel*, ed. Homeyer, II, 2, p. 273; W. Kienast, *Die deutschen Fürsten im Dienste der Westmächte bis zum Tode Philipps des Schönen von Frankreich*, II, p. 44.

[2] The point has not perhaps received sufficient attention: the French ordinance of 1188, on the 'tenth' for the crusade, which brings to mind these petty vassals, takes it for granted that they have a single liege lord.

PART V

Ties of Dependence among the Lower Orders of Society

XVIII

THE MANOR

1 THE LORD'S ESTATE

THE relatively high social circles of which military homage was a characteristic feature were not the only ones where 'men' of other men were to
be found. But at the lower level relationships of dependence found their
natural setting in an arrangement which was much older than vassalage
and which was for a long time to survive it. This was the manor (*seigneurie*).
Neither the origins of the manorial régime nor its rôle in the economy fall
within the scope of the present work: we are here concerned solely with its
place in feudal society.

Whereas the authority deriving from vassal homage became a source of
profit only belatedly and by an undoubted deviation from its original form,
in the manor the economic aspect was of primary importance. There, from
the beginning, the object—if not the exclusive, at least the principal object
—of the powers enjoyed by the chief was to provide him with revenues
by securing for him a portion of the produce of the soil. A manor was
therefore first and foremost an estate (*terre*)—there was hardly any other
word for it in spoken French—but an estate inhabited by the lord's subjects.
As a rule the area thus delimited was in its turn divided into two closely
interdependent parts. On the one hand there was the 'demesne', known
also to historians as the 'reserve', all the produce of which was taken
directly by the lord; on the other there were the tenements (*tenures*), small
or medium-sized peasant holdings, which, in varying numbers, were
grouped round the lord's 'court'. The superior real property right which the
lord claimed over the cottage, the arable, and the meadow of the villein
was expressed by his demand for a new investiture (rarely granted free of
charge) every time they changed hands; by the right to appropriate them
in case of default of heirs or by lawful confiscation; finally and above all,
by the right to impose taxes and demand services. The latter consisted for
the most part in agricultural labour services performed on the demesne.
Thus, at least at the beginning of the feudal era, when these compulsory
labour services were particularly heavy, the tenements not only added
their contribution in produce or money to the revenues of the fields
directly exploited by the master; they were in addition a source of manpower in the absence of which those fields must have lain fallow.

241

Needless to say, all manors were not of the same size. The largest, in the regions of nucleated settlements, covered the whole of the village territory. From the ninth century onward, however, this was probably not the most usual case; and in spite of some examples of successful concentration here and there it became in the course of time increasingly rare throughout Europe. No doubt this was a result of partitions amongst heirs; but it was also a result of the creation of fiefs. In order to pay his vassals for their services more than one chief had to parcel out his estates. Moreover, since it happened fairly often that—whether by gift or sale or as a result of one of those acts of territorial subjection, of which the mechanism will be described later—a powerful individual asserted his authority over a number of fairly widely-dispersed peasant farms, there were many manors which spread their tentacles over the lands of several villages at once, without coinciding exactly with any. In the twelfth century, manor and village were seldom any longer coterminous, except in the zones of recently cleared land where manors and villages had been founded together on virgin territory. The majority of peasants belonged therefore at one and the same time to two groups constantly out of step with each other; one of them composed of subjects of the same master, the other of members of the same village community. For the cultivators whose houses stood side by side and whose holdings were interspersed were perforce united—although they might be subject to different lords—by all manner of bonds of common interest, and indeed by submission to common agricultural practices.

This dualism was eventually to bring about a serious weakening of the lord's authority. As for the regions where families of patriarchal type lived either independently or two or three together in tiny hamlets, the manor there comprised as a rule a larger or smaller number of these little establishments; and this dispersion must have meant an appreciably looser structure.

2 THE EXTENSION OF THE MANORIAL SYSTEM

How extensive was the manorial régime? And if it is true that small islands of independence always existed, what was the proportion of these to the manors at different times and places? These are extremely difficult problems. For only the manors kept archives (those of the Church at least did so), and fields without lords are fields without a history. If an independent field by chance figures in the texts, it is only at the moment of its disappearance, so to speak—at the moment when a written document records its final absorption in the complex of manorial rights. Therefore the more lasting the independence of such lands, the more irremediable our ignorance of them is likely to be. In order to clear up a little of this obscurity, we ought at least to distinguish carefully two forms of subjection: that which affected a man in his person, and that which affected him only as the

242

holder of a certain piece of land. Undoubtedly, the two forms were closely related; so much so that one of them frequently involved the other. In the lower classes, however—in contrast with the world of vassalage and the fief—they were far from identical. Let us begin with dependence on the land or through the land, leaving for the next chapter the discussion of personal conditions.

In the countries where Roman institutions, themselves superimposed on ancient Italic or Celtic traditions, had left a deep impress on rural society, the manor had already under the early Carolingians assumed a very definite shape. For all that, it is not difficult to find evidence in the *villae* of Frankish Gaul or Italy of the various elements from which they had been formed. Among the tenements or—to employ the name given to the most important of them, which were characterized by their indivisibility —the *mansi*, a certain number were described as 'servile'. This epithet, like the heavier and more arbitrary obligations to which they were subjected, recalled the time when the masters had created them by allotting to their slaves, whom they were transforming into farmers, vast portions of their former *latifundia*, which had ceased to be profitable under direct exploitation. This process of parcelling out estates, having also attracted free cultivators, had given rise simultaneously to other types of grant destined to be placed in the general category of 'free' tenements, which term recalled the condition of personal freedom enjoyed by their original tenants. But among the very considerable number of tenements so described the majority were of very different origin. Far from originating in grants made in the process of whittling down a great estate, they had always been peasant farms, as old as agriculture itself. The rents and compulsory services with which they were burdened had been originally only the mark of the subordination of the occupants to a village chief, or the head of a tribe or clan, or a patron—masters who had been gradually transformed into lords in the true sense. Finally—just as in Mexico in recent times groups of peasant proprietors were to be found side by side with the *haciendas*—there still subsisted a substantial number of genuine rural allods, exempt from seignorial rule.

As for the truly Germanic regions—of which the purest type was unquestionably the Saxon plain between Rhine and Elbe—in these areas also many slaves, freedmen, and doubtless even free farmers were established on the estates of the powerful, in return for rents and services. But among the peasant body the distinction between manorial dependants and allodialists was much less clearly drawn because only the first indications of the manorial system itself had so far appeared. The stage had still hardly been passed in which a chief of a village or part of a village was in process of becoming a lord; the gifts he traditionally received—as Tacitus bears witness in the case of the German chiefs—were only beginning to be transmuted imperceptibly into rents.

Now, during the first feudal age, the evolution of the two sections of the Frankish empire followed the same course. There was a uniform tendency towards increasing manorialization. A more or less complete fusion of different kinds of tenure; the acquisition of new powers by the manors; above all the transference of many allods to the control of a powerful individual—this happened everywhere or almost everywhere. Furthermore, where at the outset the only relationships of territorial dependence that existed were still somewhat loose and unstable, these were gradually regularized, giving rise to genuine manors. Let us not imagine that these developments were uniformly spontaneous. They were subject to the play of particular influences, favoured by the circumstances of immigration or conquest. This was seen in Germany where, in the south, from before the Carolingian age, and then, during that period, in Saxony itself, the bishops, the abbots, and the other great men who had come from the Frankish kingdom helped to spread the social habits of their country among a native aristocracy ready to imitate them. It was seen still more clearly in England. So long as Anglo-Saxon or Scandinavian traditions predominated there, the network of territorial dependence remained singularly tangled and unstable; the demesne and the tenements were but imperfectly linked together. It was not till after 1066, under the brutal compulsion of foreign masters, that a manorial régime of exceptional rigour made its appearance.

In this triumphant progress of the manor the abuse of force had nowhere been a negligible factor. With good reason the official texts of the Carolingian period were already deploring the oppression of the 'poor' by the 'powerful'. The latter, as a rule, had little desire to deprive men of their land; for the soil without labour to till it was of little value. What they wanted was to assert their authority over the small cultivators along with their fields.

In the achievement of this object many of them found a valuable weapon in the administrative structure of the Frankish state. Whoever still enjoyed complete freedom from any seignorial authority was, in theory, directly dependent on the king; which meant, in practice, on his officials. The count or his representatives conducted these people to the king's army, presided over the courts which tried them, and levied on them such public taxes as remained—all this, of course, in the king's name. But was the distinction clearly appreciated by those who were subject to these obligations? At all events, it is certain that the royal officials were not slow to exact taxes or labour services, for their own benefit, from the free subjects thus committed to their care. This, admittedly, was done under the honourable name of a voluntary gift or service. But soon, as one capitulary declares, the abuse became 'custom'.[1] In Germany, where the old Carolingian edifice took a long time to disintegrate, at least the new rights sprung from this usurpation remained, in a considerable number of cases,

[1] *Cap.*, I, no. 132, c. 5.

linked to the office; and the count exercised them, as such, over men whose property had not been annexed to his manorial estates. Elsewhere, as a result of the dividing-up of the count's authority—amongst the heirs of the first holder of the office, or the count's subordinates or vassals—the former allodialist, henceforth subject to rents and labour services, ended by being merged completely in the mass of manorial subjects and his fields became tenements.

Moreover, it was not necessary to hold an office in order to exercise legitimately a portion of the public authority. By the operation of the Frankish 'immunity', which will be studied later, the majority of ecclesiastical lords and a great number of lay potentates had acquired by delegation a fraction at least of the judicial powers of the State as well as the right to collect for their own profit certain of its revenues. This, of course, applied only to the estates which were already dependent on them or were to become so in the future. The immunity strengthened the lord's authority; it did not—at least in theory—create it. But these manors were only rarely all in one piece. Small allodial estates were often to be found in their midst, and to make contact with these became extremely inconvenient for the royal officials. Sometimes, it appears, the judicial and fiscal rights over them were abandoned to the holder of the immunity by the express decision of the sovereign. Much more often and much more quickly, the allods succumbed of their own accord to this inevitable attraction.

Finally, and this was not the least frequent case, downright violence was employed. About the beginning of the eleventh century, there was in Lorraine a widow living on her allodial estate. Since the death of her husband had left her without a protector, the agents of a neighbouring lord attempted to extort from her the payment of a quit-rent, as a sign of the dependent character of the estate. The attempt in this case failed because the woman placed herself under the protection of the monks.[1] How many similar claims, with no better foundation in law, were more successful! *Domesday Book*, which offers us two successive cross-sections, as it were, of English agrarian history, one immediately before the Norman Conquest, the other eight to ten years later, shows how during the intervening period many little independent estates had been unceremoniously 'attached' to the adjacent manors. A German or French *Domesday Book* of the tenth century, if there were one, would certainly record many plain 'attachments' of this sort.

Nevertheless manors expanded by another method, too, which, in appearance at least, was much less open to criticism—namely, by virtue of contracts. This was perhaps the most common method. The petty allodialist surrendered his land—sometimes, as we shall see, together with his person—to take it back subsequently in the form of a tenement, just like the knight who converted his allod into a fief, and with the same ostensible

[1] A. Lesort, *Chroniques et chartes . . . de Saint-Mihiel*, no. 33.

purpose of securing a protector. These agreements were invariably represented as being entirely voluntary. Were they so, in fact, everywhere and
at all times? The adjective could be employed only with strong reservations.
There were undoubtedly many ways of imposing one's protection on
someone weaker than oneself; one would only need to begin by dunning
him. Add to this the fact that the first agreement was not always respected.
When the people of Wolen, in Alemannia, took a local landowner as their
protector they promised him only a quit-rent; but soon, by assimilation
to other tenants of the same powerful man, they were forced to perform
labour services and denied the use of the neighbouring forest except on
payment of rents.[1] Once get a finger trapped in the machine and your whole
body may be drawn into it. Let us not imagine, however, that the situation
of the lordless man appeared uniformly enviable. The peasant of Forez
who, as late as 1280, transformed his allod into a villein tenement on
condition of being henceforth 'protected, defended and warranted' (*gardé,
défendu et garanti*) by the Hospitallers of Montbrison, his new lords, 'as
are the other dependants of that house', doubtless thought he was doing
something to his advantage.[2] And yet this was a less troubled period than
the first feudal age. Sometimes a whole village submitted itself in this way
to a powerful man. It was an especially frequent occurrence in Germany,
where, at the beginning of the evolution, there were still a large number of
rural communities enjoying complete freedom from seignorial authority.
In France and in Italy where, from the ninth century, the lord's power was
much more developed, deeds of conveyance assumed as a rule an individual
character. They were no less numerous on that account. About the year
900, as many as fourteen free men had burdened their own property with
labour services in this way, in favour of an abbey at Brescia.[3]

Indeed, the most flagrant brutalities as well as the most genuinely spontaneous contracts proclaimed the influence of the same fundamental cause,
namely, the weakness of the independent peasants. Let us not attempt to
explain it as the result of economic adversity. That would be to forget
that the expansion of the manorial régime was not confined to the country
districts: even in a good many of the cities, few of which had known
anything of the kind in Roman times, the system of the tenement, with
its normal obligations, was introduced on the same lines as in the ancient
rural *villa*. What is more, such an explanation would assume a contrast
between farming methods in large and small landholdings respectively;
a contrast which may hold good of other societies, but certainly not of
this one. For the manor was first and foremost an agglomeration of small
dependent farms; and on becoming a tenant the allodialist, though assuming new obligations, in no way changed his farming methods. He sought

[1] *Acta Murensia*, in *Quellen zur Schweizer Geschichte*, III, 2, p. 68, c. 22.
[2] *Chartes du Forez antérieures au XIVe siècle*, no. 500 (t. IV).
[3] *Monumenta Historiae Patriae*, XIII, col. 711.

or submitted to a master only on account of the inadequacy of the other social arrangements—the kinship groups or the authority of the State. The case of the men of Wolen is significant. Victims of the most flagrant tyranny, they tried to make their complaint to the king, but finding themselves in the midst of a great court in full session they failed, with their rustic speech, even to make themselves understood. It is true that the lack of an effective government was partly due to the sluggishness of trade and monetary circulation. It is also true that the same factors, by depriving the cultivators of any reserve of cash, helped to undermine their capacity for resistance. But it was only in such indirect ways as this that economic conditions contributed to the social crisis of the peasantry. In the humble drama of rural life we recognize an aspect of the same development which, at a higher social level, impelled so many men to submit themselves to the ties of vassalage.

Moreover, in this connection it is enough to refer to the diversity of examples with which Europe presents us. The Middle Ages knew one extensively manorialized, but not feudalized, society—Sardinia. It is not surprising that, in this land long isolated from the great currents which swept the continent, an ancient system of rural chiefdoms, regularized during the Roman period, could be maintained without the power of the local aristocracies assuming the specific form of Frankish commendation. On the other hand, there were no countries without manors which were not at the same time countries without vassalage, as witness most of the Celtic societies of the British Isles; the Scandinavian peninsula; and finally, in Germania itself, the low-lying regions along the shores of the North Sea—Dithmarschen, beyond the estuary of the Elbe, and Frisia, from the Elbe to the Zuiderzee. This applies to the last-named country till the fourteenth or fifteenth century, when certain dynasties of 'chiefs'—the word is an exact translation of the Frisian *hoveling*—raised themselves above the mass of free peasants. Strong in the possession of landed wealth accumulated from generation to generation, in the armed bands which they maintained and by their seizure of certain judicial functions, these petty village tyrants succeeded late in the day in creating for themselves what was really a manorial system in embryo. The fact was that at this time the old framework of Frisian society, based essentially on the ties of kinship, was beginning to crack. In the period when feudal institutions were at their height, these non-feudal societies on the fringes of the West were certainly not unfamiliar with the dependence of the small farmer (whether slave, freedman or free man) upon a richer man than himself, or the devotion of the companion to the prince or the leader of the war-band. But they had nothing which recalled the vast, hierarchically-organized system of peasant subjection and military vassalage to which we give the name of feudalism.

Shall we attribute the sole responsibility for this to the absence of any enduring Frankish influence—seeing that in Frisia itself the administrative

247

organization which the Carolingians had for a time imposed collapsed at an early date? This factor is undoubtedly important; but it chiefly applies to the inability of companionage to transform itself into vassalage. The dominant facts went beyond questions of influence. Where every free man remained a warrior, liable to be constantly called to service and distinguished from the pick of the fighting-men by nothing essential in his equipment, the peasant had no difficulty in avoiding subjection to the manorial régime, while the groups of armed retainers failed to develop into a clearly specialized knightly class with a legal structure of its own. Where men of all ranks were able to rely for support on other forms of strength and solidarity than personal protection—kindred groups especially among the Frisians, the people of Dithmarschen and the Celts, kindred groups again among the Scandinavians, but also institutions of public law of the type common to the Germanic peoples—neither the relationships of dependence peculiar to territorial lordship, nor vassalage and the fief invaded the whole of social life.

Furthermore, just as was the case with the feudal system proper, the manorial régime was destined to reach a state of perfection only in the countries where it had been imported bag and baggage. In the England of the Norman kings there were no peasant allods any more than there were knightly ones. On the continent the peasant allod was much harder to eliminate. It is true that in France between the Meuse and the Loire, and in Burgundy, it had become extremely rare in the twelfth and thirteenth centuries; over wide areas it seems to have disappeared altogether. But there were peasant allods, in varying but always appreciable numbers, in south-western France, in certain provinces of central France like Forez, in Tuscany, and above all in Germany, where Saxony was their favourite soil. These were the very regions where, by a striking parallelism, the allodial estates of the nobility survived—agglomerations of tenements, demesnes and political authority owing homage to no one. The manor was something much older than the institutions truly characteristic of the first feudal age. But its progress during this period, like its partial setbacks, is explained—everything points to this conclusion—by the same causes which contributed to, or militated against, the success of vassalage and the fief.

3 LORD AND TENANTS

Apart from contracts of individual subjection—and these were generally imprecise in their terms and quickly forgotten—the relations of the lord with the tenants were regulated only by 'the custom of the manor'. So true was this that in France the ordinary name for rents was simply 'customs' and that of the person who owed them 'customary man'. From the first appearance of a rudimentary form of manorial system—as far back as the Roman Empire, for example, or Anglo-Saxon England—it was this peculiar tradition which really defined each manor, as a human group, by distinguishing it from its neighbours. The precedents which thus governed the life of the community were themselves necessarily of a communal kind. That a tax has ceased to be paid by a particular holding almost since time immemorial makes no difference, says in effect a judgment of the Parlement of Paris in the reign of St. Louis; if the other holdings have paid it regularly all this time, it is compulsory also for the one which has so long evaded it.[1] This at least was the opinion of the jurists. Actual practice must often have been more elastic. In theory, everyone was required to observe these ancestral rules—the master as well as the dependants; but this professed respect for what had been done before was characteristically deceptive. For although they were linked together through the ages by a supposedly unchanging custom nothing was less like the manor of the ninth century than the manor of the thirteenth.

The responsibility for this state of things cannot be ascribed to the defects of oral transmission. In the time of the Carolingians, many lords, after inquiry, had had the customs of their estates set down in writing, in the form of those detailed descriptions which were later called 'surveys' (*censiers*) or 'terriers'. But the pressure of local social conditions was stronger than respect for the past.

Through the innumerable conflicts of daily life legal memory was unceasingly stocked with new precedents. Above all, a custom could only be really binding where there was an impartial and effective judicial authority to enforce it. In the ninth century, in the Frankish state, the royal courts came to assume this rôle; and if the only decisions of these courts which are known to us are invariably unfavourable to the tenants the reason is perhaps simply that the ecclesiastical archives were not greatly concerned to preserve the others. Subsequently, the appropriation of judicial authority by the lords ruled out the possibility of recourse to the royal courts. The most scrupulous of lords did not hesitate to defy tradition when it interfered with their own interests or with those entrusted to them. Thus we find Abbot Suger, in his memoirs, congratulating himself on having been able to force the peasants of one of his estates to replace the quit-rent in money, which within living memory they had always paid, by a rent proportional to the harvest, from which more profit could be expected.[2] Almost the only forces that were now capable of counterbalancing (often very effectively, it is true) the abuses of power by the masters were the peasantry's remarkable capacity for passive resistance and, on the negative side, the inefficient management of the manors.

Nothing varied more from manor to manor according to locality, nothing exhibited more diversity, than the burdens of tenancy in the first

---

[1] *Olim.*, I, p. 661, no. III.
[2] Suger, *De Rebus*, ed. Lecoy de la Marche, c.X., p. 167.

feudal age. On certain days, the tenant brings the lord's steward perhaps a few small silver coins or, more often, sheaves of corn harvested on his fields, chickens from his farmyard, cakes of wax from his beehives or from the swarms of the neighbouring forest. At other times, he works on the arable or the meadows of the demesne. Or else we find him carting casks of wine or sacks of corn on behalf of the master to distant residences. His is the labour which repairs the walls or moats of the castle. If the master has guests the peasant strips his own bed to provide the necessary extra bed-clothes. When the hunting season comes round, he feeds the pack. If war breaks out he does duty as foot-soldier or orderly, under the leadership of the reeve of the village. The detailed study of these obligations belongs primarily to the study of the manor as an economic 'enterprise' and source of revenue. We shall confine ourselves here to stressing the facts of the evolution which most profoundly affected the human tie proper.

The dependence of the peasant farms on a common master was expressed by the payment of a sort of land rent. In this respect the work of the first feudal age was above all one of simplification. A fairly large number of dues which were paid separately in the Frankish period ended by being combined in a single quit-rent; and this in France, when it was paid in money, was generally known by the name *cens*. Now, among the earliest taxes, there were some which the manorial administrations had originally, in theory, levied only on behalf of the State. (An example is the purveyance formerly due to the royal army, or the payment which was substituted for it.) Their embodiment in an obligation which benefited only the lord and was conceived of as the expression of his superior rights over the soil attests with a peculiar clarity the preponderance acquired by the local power of the little chief of a group, at the expense of any higher social bond.

The problem of inheritance, one of the most delicate which the institution of the military fief had set, had almost no place in the history of rural tenements—at least during the feudal era. Almost universally, the peasants succeeded each other from generation to generation on the same fields. Occasionally, as will be explained later, collaterals were excluded when the tenant was of servile status; but the right of descendants was always respected, provided that they had not already deserted the family circle. The rules of succession were fixed by the old regional usages, without any interference from the lords, save for their efforts, at certain periods and in certain districts, to ensure the indivisibility of the property, which was considered necessary for the accurate levying of taxes. What is more, the hereditary succession of tenants seemed so much a matter of course that as a rule the texts, taking the principle as already established, did not trouble to mention it, except incidentally. Doubtless one reason for this was that with the majority of peasant farms, before the village chiefdoms transformed themselves into lordships, hereditary succession had been the immemorial custom; and it had gradually been extended to the holdings more recently carved out of the demesne. Moreover it was not in the interest of the lords to break with this practice. At this period, when land was more plentiful than men, when moreover economic conditions precluded the exploitation of excessively large demesnes with the help of hired labour or workers maintained in the lord's household, it was better for the lord instead of keeping all the plots of land in his own hands to have permanently at his disposal the labour and resources of dependants who were in a position to maintain themselves.

Of all the new 'exactions' imposed on the tenants, the most characteristic were the monopolies of many different kinds which the lord arrogated to himself at their expense. Sometimes he reserved for himself the right to sell wine or beer at certain times of year. Sometimes he claimed the sole right to provide, in return for payment, the services of bull or boar for stud purposes, or again to supply the horses which, in certain regions of southern France, were used to tread out the corn on the threshing-floor. More often he forced the peasants to grind their corn at his mill, to bake their bread in his oven, to make their wine in his wine-press. The very name of these exactions was significant. They were normally called *banalités*. Unknown in the Frankish period, their sole foundation was the lord's acknowledged power to give orders, signified by the old Germanic word *ban*. This was a power obviously inseparable from any authority exercised by a chief and therefore in itself, as a part of the lord's authority, of great antiquity; in the hands of petty local potentates, however, it had been greatly reinforced by their rôle as judges. The distribution of these *banalités*, by area, is no less instructive. France, where the weakening of governmental authority and the usurpation of judicial rights had been carried farthest, was their favourite soil. Yet even there they were chiefly exercised by those of the lords who held the highest form of judicial rights, known as *haute justice*. In Germany, where they did not extend to such a large number of activities, they seem frequently to have been retained by the direct heirs of the counts, those judges *par excellence* of the Frankish state. In England, they were introduced only by the Norman Conquest, and even then in-completely. Evidently the less effective the competition from the other *ban*—that of the king or his representatives—the more pervasive and profitable was the lord's authority.

The parish church was dependent almost everywhere on the local lord, or if there were several in the same parish, on one of them. Usually the church would have been built not long before by one of his predecessors on the demesne. But that condition was not necessary in order to justify an appropriation of this kind; for the idea prevailed at that time that the place of public worship belonged to the worshippers. Where, as in Frisia, the manor did not exist, the church belonged to the village community itself;

in the rest of Europe the peasant group, having no legal existence, could be represented only by its chief or one of its chiefs. This right of ownership, as it was called before the Gregorian reform, or of 'patronage', as it was later more modestly labelled, consisted primarily in the power to nominate or 'present' the priest in charge. But the lords also claimed to derive from it the right to take for their own benefit a part at least of the parish revenues. Of the latter the fees, though not negligible, scarcely amounted to a large sum. Tithe brought in much more. After having long been considered a purely moral duty, the payment of tithe had been rigorously imposed on all the faithful—in the Frankish state by the first Carolingians and in Britain, about the same time, by the Anglo-Saxon kings, their imitators. It was, in theory, a tax of one-tenth, collected in kind and levied on all forms of income, without exception. Actually it came very soon to be applied almost exclusively to agricultural produce. The appropriation of tithe by the lords was by no means complete. England was to a large extent free from this abuse owing to the tardy development there of the manorial system. Even on the continent the parish priest frequently, and the bishop occasionally, retained a certain proportion. Moreover, the religious revival born of the Gregorian reform quickly brought about the 'restitution' to the clergy (which in practice meant to the monasteries in most cases) of many tithes— together with a still greater number of churches—which had earlier fallen into lay hands. Nevertheless, the appropriation of this revenue of spiritual origin by eminently temporal masters, in the first feudal age, had been one of the most striking as well as one of the most profitable achievements of a power which certainly appeared to repudiate the right of anyone else to demand anything from its subjects.

The pecuniary aid or tallage (*taille*) required of the rural tenants arose, like the tallage of vassals and at about the same time, out of the general duty incumbent on every subordinate to give succour to his chief. Like the vassals' tallage it tended at first to masquerade as a gift, and this fiction was till the end commemorated in some of the names which it bore: in France, *demande* or *queste*, in Germany *Bede*, which means prayer. But it was also called, more frankly, *toulte* from the verb *tolir*, 'to take'. Its history, though it began at a later date, was not unlike that of the manorial monopolies. It was very widespread in France, and it was imported into England by the Norman conquerors; but in Germany it remained the privilege of a smaller number of lords—those who exercised the higher judicial powers, which were less divided up in that country than in France. (In the feudal era the most powerful individual was always the judge.) No more than the tallage of the vassals did the tallage of the peasants escape the regularizing influence of custom, though the results were perceptibly different. Since the peasant taxpayers were not as a rule strong enough to secure a strict definition of their obligations, the tax, which had at first been exceptional, was levied at more and more frequent intervals as the circulation of money increased.

This process, moreover, was marked by great variations from manor to manor. In the Île-de-France, about the year 1200, estates where tallage was collected annually or even biennially adjoined others where it was collected only at irregular intervals. The law almost everywhere was uncertain. This newest of manorial burdens was not only too recent to be incorporated easily in the fabric of 'good customs'; the irregularity with which it was collected and, even where its recurrence had been regularized, the uncertainty of the sum exacted on each occasion caused it to retain an arbitrary character. In Church circles, 'worthy people', as a Parisian text says, questioned the legality of tallage, and it was particularly hateful to the peasants whom it frequently drove to active revolt. Half-crystallized in an age of monetary scarcity, the tradition of the manor did not lend itself easily to the needs of a new economy.

Thus the tenant at the end of the twelfth century paid tithe, tallage and the multifarious dues of the *banalités*—all exactions which, even in the countries where the manor had been in existence longest, his ancestor of the eighth century, for example, had not known. Unquestionably compulsory payments had become heavier, though not without—in certain regions, at least—some compensating reduction of compulsory labour services.

For—by a sort of prolongation of the process of dismemberment from which the Roman *latifundium* had formerly suffered—the lords in a great part of Europe began to parcel out vast portions of their demesnes. Sometimes they distributed them piecemeal to their old tenants; sometimes they carved them up into new tenements; occasionally they even formed them into little vassal fiefs, soon in their turn to be broken up into peasant holdings. Provoked mainly by economic causes which it is impossible for us to examine here, the movement seems to have started as early as the tenth and eleventh centuries in France and Lotharingia, as well as in Italy; it had reached trans-Rhenish Germany a little later and—more slowly still and not without some capricious regressions—England, where the manorial system itself was of more recent origin. Now a decline in the size of the demesne meant also, of necessity, abolition or reduction of compulsory labour services. Where the tenant under Charlemagne owed several days a week, in the France of Philip Augustus or St. Louis he no longer worked in the fields or meadows of the demesne more than a few days a year. The development of new 'exactions' not only varied from country to country, according to the extent to which the right to issue orders had been taken over; it operated also in direct ratio to the lord's abandonment of personal exploitation of the estate. Having both more time and more land, the peasant could pay more. And the master, naturally, sought to recover on one side what he lost on the other. If in France the mill had not been the monopoly of the lord, how could it have continued to function once the supply of corn from the demesne had ceased? Nevertheless, by ceasing to exact labour from his subjects throughout the year, by transforming them into producers, heavily taxed certainly, but economically autonomous, by himself becoming a landed proprietor pure and simple, the lord, where this evolution was fully accomplished, inevitably allowed some small relaxation of the bond of human domination. Like the history of the fief, the history of the peasant holding was, in the long run, that of the transition from a social structure founded on service to a system of land rent.

XIX

SERVITUDE AND FREEDOM

1 THE STARTING POINT: PERSONAL STATUS IN THE FRANKISH PERIOD

IMAGINE the problem confronting a man in the early ninth century, trying to determine the differences in legal status among a group of assorted
human beings in, say, the Frankish state. He might be a high official of the
Palace on a mission in the provinces, a bishop counting his flock, a lord
taking a census of his subjects. There is nothing fanciful in the situation;
we know of more than one actual attempt of this kind, and the impression
conveyed is that there was much hesitation and disagreement. In the same
region, at more or less the same date, we almost never find two manorial
surveys (*censiers*) employing the same criteria. Evidently, to contemporaries the structure of the society in which they lived did not possess
clear-cut contours. The fact was that very different systems of classification
cut across each other. Some, borrowing their terminology indifferently
from Roman or from Germanic traditions—traditions that were themselves in conflict—were now very imperfectly adapted to the present;
others tried their best to express the reality but did it clumsily.

One fundamental and very simple contrast prevailed; on one side were
free men, on the other slaves (in Latin *servi*). If we allow for the way in
which the harshness of theory was mitigated by whatever still survived of
the humanitarian legislation of the Roman emperors, by the spirit of
Christianity, and by the inevitable compromises of everyday life, the *servus*
remained, in law, the chattel of the master, who had the unrestricted disposal of his person, his labour, and his property. In consequence, having
no legal personality of his own, he appeared as an alien being, outside the
ranks of the community. He was not summoned to the royal host. He did
not sit in the judicial assemblies, could not bring an action there in his own
right, and was not justiciable by them unless, having committed a grave
offence against a third party, he found himself handed over by his master
to the justice of the State. That the *populus Francorum* was composed only
of free men, independently of any ethnic distinction, is proved by the fact
that the national name and the legal status came in the end to be synonymous. *Libre* or *franc*—the two words became interchangeable.

On closer examination, however, this apparently sharp antithesis gives

255

a very inaccurate picture of the real diversity of conditions. Among the slaves themselves—and they were relatively few in number—their diverse ways of life had led to profound differences. A certain number of them, employed partly in the lower forms of domestic service, partly in agricultural labour, were maintained in the master's house or on his farms. These continued to be regarded as human cattle, officially classified as movable property. The tenant-slave, on the other hand, had his own dwelling; he subsisted on the produce of his own labour; nothing prevented him from selling for his own benefit the surplus of his harvest, if there chanced to be any; he was no longer directly dependent on his master for support and the latter seldom interfered with him. Undoubtedly he remained subject to terribly heavy burdens imposed by the possessor of the domanial 'court'. But at least the burdens were limited; sometimes in law, invariably in fact. Certain surveys, indeed, may tell us that a man 'must serve at all times when he shall be ordered to do so'; in practice, the acknowledged interest of the master induced him to leave each small peasant the workdays necessary to cultivate his holding—otherwise the very substance of the revenues would have disappeared. Leading a life very like that of the 'free' tenants, with whose families they often intermarried, the 'domiciled' *servi* were drawing near to them through an all-important feature of their legal status. The royal courts recognized that even the serf's duties were fixed by the custom of the manor—a stability absolutely contrary to the very conception of slavery, of which the arbitrary authority of the master was an essential element. Finally, certain slaves figured, as we know, in the bodies of armed retainers who surrounded the great. The prestige of arms, the confidence they inspired, in short (to borrow the words of one capitulary) 'the honour of vassalage' ensured for them in society a rank and possibilities of influence so far outweighing any social stigma attaching to their condition that the kings thought it advisable, as an exceptional measure, to require of them that oath of fealty which in theory was taken only by the true 'Franks'.

As regards the free men, the confusion seemed even greater. Distinctions of wealth, which were considerable, did not fail to be reflected in distinctions of law. The person, however well-born he might be, who could not be summoned to the army because he was too poor to equip himself, or simply because he could not afford to come—should he still be regarded as a true member of the Frankish people? He was, at most, as one capitulary declares, only a 'free man of the second order'; another capitulary, more brutal in its frankness, contrasts 'the poor' with the 'free'.[1] Above all, the majority of those who were in theory free men, besides being subjects of the king, were also dependants of this or that particular chief, and it was the almost infinite gradations of this subordination which mainly determined the condition of the individual in each case.

[1] *Cap.*, I, no. 162, c. 3, no. 50, c. 2.

The tenants of the manors, when they were not of servile status, generally appeared, in the official Latin documents, under the name of *coloni*. Many of them, in the parts of the Frankish state which had formerly been Roman, were in fact undoubtedly descended from ancestors who had been subject to the laws of the colonate. But bondage to the soil, which had formerly been the essential characteristic of this status, had almost fallen into desuetude. Several centuries before, under the Later Empire, the idea had been conceived of binding practically every man to his hereditary task as well as to his share of taxation—the soldier to the army, the artisan to his craft, the decurion to the municipal senate, and the farmer to his land, which he was not to quit and from which the owner could not remove him; and the power of a government ruling over vast areas had at that time almost brought about the realization of this dream. The barbarian kingdoms, on the contrary, did not possess—any more than did the majority of the medieval states which succeeded them—the strength to pursue the runaway peasant or prevent a new master from receiving him. Moreover, the decay of the land tax in the hands of inexpert governments had removed almost all incentive to such efforts. It is significant that in the ninth century we find many *coloni* established on servile tenements (tenements, that is to say, which had formerly been allotted to slaves), and many slaves on 'free' tenements, originally assigned to *coloni*. This lack of accord between the status of the man and the status of the land—of which the specific obligations continued to recall the past—not only increased the confusion of classes; it showed to what an extent the rule of perpetual succession on the same tract of land had ceased to be observed.

Furthermore, the abstract concept in Roman law which made the *colonus* (a free man by personal status) 'the slave of the estate on which he was born', in short the dependant not of an individual but of a thing, became meaningless in an age too realistic not to reduce all social relationships to an exchange of obedience and protection between beings of flesh and blood. Whereas an imperial edict had said 'the *colonus* must be returned to the estate whence he came', the manual of Roman law compiled at the beginning of the sixth century for the needs of the Visigothic state was already decreeing 'that he be returned to his master'.[1] There can be no doubt that the *colonus* of the ninth century remained, like his distant predecessor, a free man in the eyes of the law. He took the oath of fealty to the sovereign. He occasionally attended the judicial assemblies. Nevertheless he had only very rare and very indirect contacts with the governmental authorities. If he went to the royal army, it was under the banner of the chief from whom he held his tenement. If he had to go to court, the effect of the immunities and, still more, of the usages which those privileges as a rule merely confirmed, was to impose this lord on him once again as his normal judge. Increasingly, in short, his place in society was defined by his

[1] *Lex Romana Visigothorum*, ed. Haenel, *Cod. Theod.*, V, 10, 1, and *Interpretatio*.

subjection to another man, a subjection so strict, indeed, that it was a matter of course to regulate his family status by forbidding him to marry outside the manor. His union with a fully free woman was treated as an 'unequal marriage'; the canon law sought to refuse him entry into holy orders, while the secular law inflicted on him corporal punishments formerly reserved for slaves; finally, when his lord released him from his burdens, this act was often called enfranchisement. Not without reason, in contrast with so many terms from the vocabulary of legal Latin, the word *colonus* in the end bequeathed no derivatives to the Gallo-Romanic tongues. The survival of other words which also described status was naturally subject to many distortions of meaning; but the fact that they survived at all bears witness to the feeling, or the illusion, of continuity. From the Carolingian age the *colonus*, on the other hand, began to be merged in the uniform crowd of manorial dependants, whom the charters lumped together under the name of *mancipia* (formerly the synonym, in classical Latin, for slaves) and the vernacular under the still vaguer designation of 'men' of the master. While very close to the class of 'domiciled' slaves in one respect he was, in another, virtually identified (to such a degree that there is sometimes no difference in the names employed) with those clients properly so-called who were not fighting-men.

For, as we know, the practice of commendation was not confined to the upper classes. Many free men of modest rank sought a protector, without on that account being prepared to become his slaves. As they handed over their land to him, to take it back subsequently as a tenement, a relationship of a more personal character was formed between the two individuals, which for a long time remained ill-defined. Gradually it acquired a more precise character by borrowing some features from another form of dependence, which was very widespread and for that reason predestined, as it were, to serve as a model for all ties of subjection of the humbler sort. This was the status of freedman *cum obsequio*, 'owing obedience'.

In the countries which made up the Frankish state, innumerable enfranchisements of slaves had taken place since the later centuries of the Roman Empire. In the time of the Carolingians, many others had been granted every year. From the masters' point of view there was everything to be said for this policy. The transformations of the economy favoured the dissolution of the great teams which but a little while before had served to cultivate the now sub-divided *latifundia*. Just as men recognized that in future this wealth would have to be based on the exaction of rents and services rather than on the direct exploitation of vast estates, so the desire for power, in its turn, found in the protection extended over free men— members of the people—a much more effective instrument than the possession of human cattle with no legal rights of their own. Finally, concern for their own salvation, especially acute as death drew near, disposed people to pay heed to the voice of the Church which, if it was not opposed to slavery as such, none the less made the liberation of the Christian slave an act of especial piety. Moreover the attainment of freedom had been at all times, at Rome as well as in Germania, a normal culmination in the lives of many slaves; and in the barbarian kingdoms it seems probable that the process had been gradually accelerated.

But it would seem that the masters only showed themselves so generous because they were far from being obliged to surrender everything. Nothing is more intricate, at the first approach, than the legal system of enfranchisement in the Frankish state of the ninth century. The traditions of the Roman world on the one hand, and a variety of Germanic laws on the other, furnished a multitude of different ways of carrying out the act of enfranchisement and fixed the status of those who benefited by it in a bewildering variety of terms. To mention only practical effects, however, they all agreed in offering the choice between two main types of procedure. Sometimes the freedman was no longer subject to any private authority save that of those whose support he might later seek of his own free will. Sometimes, on the contrary, he remained liable, in his new status, to certain duties of submission, either towards his former master or towards a new one—a church, for example—to whom that master agreed to surrender him. Since these obligations were generally regarded as transmissible from generation to generation, their effect was to create a true hereditary clientage. The first type of 'manumission'—to employ the language of the time—was rare; the second (*cum obsequio*) was very frequent, since it alone corresponded to prevailing needs. The 'manumitter' might agree to give up a slave, but he was determined to keep a dependant. The 'manumitted' one himself, being afraid to live without a protector, thus found there and then the desired protection. The contract of this subordination was considered so binding that the Church, which preferred full independence for its priests, was reluctant to grant ordination to these new free men who, in spite of their name, remained subject to what it regarded as too rigorous a bondage. Usually the freedman was at the same time the tenant of his patron, either because he had been 'domiciled' (*chasé*) by him before getting rid of the servile stigma, or because the grant of freedom was accompanied by a gift of land. Furthermore, it frequently happened that the subjection was emphasized by obligations of a more personal nature. In some cases the lord took a part of the heritage at each death. Still more often, a poll-tax was imposed which fell on the freedman from year to year, and on each of his descendants after him. While providing a regular revenue of which the total amount was not negligible, this 'chevage', thanks to the frequent intervals at which it was levied, obviated any risk that through the ill will of the subordinate or the negligence of the superior the bond should fall into oblivion. The model for this bond had been furnished by certain

259

methods of Germanic enfranchisement. It was soon imitated in almost all the manumissions which entailed 'obedience'.

Succession tax and chevage: these two tokens of subjection were destined to have a long career in the societies of the Middle Ages. The second at least had at an early date ceased to be restricted to the small group of people freed from slavery. As is shown in specific terms in certain deeds of manumission, the few pennies or cakes of wax offered every year were considered to represent the price of the protection extended over his former slave by the master who had now become the patron. Now the freedmen were not the only men described as free who willy-nilly had placed themselves under the *maimbour* of a powerful individual. As early as the ninth century chevage, spreading everywhere, appeared as the specific 'sign' of a whole group of relationships of personal dependence which—regardless of all the caprices of terminology—had as their common characteristics a rigorous subjection on the subordinate's part, and on that of the protector a virtually uninhibited authority, productive of lucrative revenues. Thus amidst the persisting confusion of relationships between man and man there began to emerge a few firm features around which the institutions of the succeeding age were gradually to crystallize.

2 FRENCH SERFDOM

In France proper and in Burgundy, a series of converging influences during the feudal age resulted in a virtual sweeping away of the old social nomenclature. Written laws were forgotten. Of the surveys of the Frankish period a certain number had perished and others, as a result both of changes in the vocabulary and of the confusion into which the arrangement of many of the estates had been thrown, could now be consulted only with difficulty. Finally, the lords and the judges were generally too ignorant to be encumbered with legal memories. Nevertheless, in the new classification of social ranks which was worked out at that time an important part was once more assigned to a concept familiar to the minds of men since time immemorial—the contrast between freedom and servitude. But this was at the cost of a profound change of meaning.

Is it surprising that the old implications of the contrast should have ceased to make sense? For in France there were almost no remaining slaves properly so called. Soon there would be none at all. The kind of life lived by the tenant-slaves had nothing in common with slavery. As for the little groups of slaves who had lived and been fed in the household of the master, the gaps constantly made in their ranks by death and enfranchisement were irremediable. Religious sentiment forbade the enslavement of Christian prisoners of war. True, there remained the slave trade, supplied by raids into the lands of the heathen. But its main currents either did not reach north-western Europe or else—no doubt because sufficiently wealthy buyers were not to be found there—merely passed through it on the way to Moslem Spain or the East. What is more, the weakening of the State deprived of any concrete meaning the ancient distinction between the free man, a subject in full right, and the slave, a being outside the scope of public institutions. Yet people did not lose the habit of thinking of society as composed partly of the free and partly of the unfree; they preserved for these latter their old Latin name of *servi*, which became *serfs* in French. It was the line of cleavage between the two groups that was imperceptibly changed.

To have a lord seemed in no way inconsistent with freedom. Who was without one? But the notion arose that freedom was lost when free choice could not be exercised at least once in a lifetime. In other words, every hereditary tie was regarded as being marked by a servile character. The inescapable bond that claimed the child 'while still in its mother's womb' had been one of the greatest hardships of traditional slavery. The feeling of this almost physical compulsion is expressed to perfection in the phrase *homme de corps*, forged by common speech as a synonym for serf. The vassal whose homage was not inherited was, as we have seen, essentially 'free'. On the other hand, almost inevitably the label of a common servitude came to be applied both to the small number of descendants of tenant slaves and to the much more numerous crowd of dependants—heirs of freedmen or humble commended men—whose ancestors had engaged not only their own persons but their posterity as well. The same was true, by a significant assimilation, in the case of bastards, strangers or 'foreigners', and sometimes Jews. Deprived of all natural support in the family or the people, they had been automatically entrusted by the old rules to the protection of the prince or of the chief of the place where they resided; the feudal era made them serfs, subject as such to the lord of the estate on which they lived, or at least to him who possessed the superior powers of justice in that place. In the Carolingian age a growing number of clients had paid chevage, though on condition of keeping or receiving the status of free men. For the slave had a master who could take everything from him; not a defender to whom payment was due for the protection given. Gradually, nevertheless, this obligation of chevage, once considered perfectly honourable, came to be associated with baseness, and eventually to be counted by the courts among the characteristic features of serfdom. It continued to be exacted from the same families as in the past and for reasons fundamentally the same; all that had changed was the place allotted, in the current classification, to the bond of which this tax seemed to be the symbol.

Almost imperceptible to contemporaries, like all natural changes in the meanings of words, this great revolution in the index of social values had been heralded by a lax use of the vocabulary of servitude, which from the late Frankish period began to fluctuate between the old acceptations and

261

the new. These fumblings went on for a long time; the terms employed varied from region to region and with the clerks whose duty it was to draw up the charters. In several provinces certain groups, descended from slaves earlier set free on condition of 'obedience', retained till the beginning of the twelfth century, as a mark of their origin, their special designation of *culverts*, derived from the Latin *collibertus*, 'freedman'. In disregard of the manumission granted earlier, they were considered henceforth as being unfree in the new sense of the word. But they were regarded as forming a class superior to the ordinary 'serfs'. Other families here and there, despite a *de facto* assimilation to all the obligations characteristic of servile status, long continued to be known as 'commended persons' or *gens d'avouerie* (which may be freely translated as 'protected people'). What was the procedure when a man placed both himself and his posterity in dependence on a master, to whom—among other obligations—he promised chevage? Sometimes the deed was expressly described as one of voluntary entry into servitude. Sometimes, on the contrary, a clause safeguarding his freedom was inserted in it, as in the ancient Frankish formula of commendation. Or else the document was so drafted as to avoid any compromising expressions. Nevertheless, when the records cover several centuries, like those of the abbey of Saint-Pierre at Ghent, it is easy to see, with the passage of time, the evolution of a more and more purely servile phraseology.

But however numerous these deeds of voluntary submission may have been—and it is surprising how many have survived considering the paucity of our documents in general—it goes without saying that they were not the only factor contributing to the growth of serfdom. Without any special agreements, the majority of manorial subjects, whether recent or of long standing, slid gradually, through the agency of prescription, of violence, and of the changes that had come about in legal opinion, into this condition, of which the name was old but the criteria more or less new. In the village of Thiais in the Parisis, at the beginning of the ninth century, out of 146 heads of families there were only 11 slaves, as against 130 *coloni*; in addition, there were 19 'protected' persons paying chevage. In the reign of St. Louis, almost the entire population consisted of persons whose status was described as servile.

To the end there existed individuals and even whole communities not susceptible of any exact classification. The peasants of Rosny-sous-Bois—were they or were they not serfs of Sainte-Geneviève? Were the people of Lagny serfs of their abbey? These problems occupied the attention of popes and kings from the time of Louis VII to that of Philip III. Subject for generations to chevage and to several other 'customs' which were generally held to be inconsistent with freedom, the members of several burgher communities of northern France in the thirteenth century refused nevertheless to allow themselves to be treated as serfs. Uncertainties and anomalies, however, did not alter essential facts. From the first half of the twelfth century, at the latest—the *colliberti* having by then ceased to exist as a class and their name having become purely a synonym for serf—a single category of humble personal dependants was constituted, bound to a master by their birth and therefore marked by the servile 'taint'.

But the question at issue was by no means merely one of words: certain disabilities which were traditionally held to be inseparable from servitude almost inevitably attached to these unfree men whose bondage was of an essentially new type, though its novelty was not very clearly appreciated. Such disabilities were the refusal of admission to holy orders, the loss of the right to bear witness against free men (though this was accorded by special privileges to the royal serfs and to those of a few churches), and in a general way, a very painful note of inferiority and contempt. Furthermore, a genuine status was evolved, defined by a whole set of specific obligations. Though infinitely varied in their details according to the customs of the group, they were at one in their broad lines, which were everywhere almost alike—a contrast incessantly repeated in this society at once divided and fundamentally one. First, there was chevage (head-tax). Then there was the ban upon marriage with a person not of the same status or a dependant of the same lord—except with special permission, which was expensive. Finally, there was a sort of inheritance tax. In Picardy and Flanders, this *mainmorte* normally took the form of a regular succession tax; on the death of each tenant the lord exacted either a small sum of money or, more frequently, the best piece of furniture or the best head of cattle. Elsewhere *mainmorte* rested on the recognition of the family community: if the deceased left sons (sometimes it might be brothers) who had shared his hearth, the lord received nothing; in the contrary case, he took everything.

Now, heavy as these obligations might seem, they were, in one sense, at the opposite pole from slavery, since they were based on the assumption that the person liable to them possessed a genuine patrimony. As a tenant the serf had exactly the same duties and the same rights as anyone else; his possession of his holding was no longer precarious, and his labour, once rents and services had been paid, was his own. No longer should we picture him as a *colonus* 'bound to the soil'. Of course the lords sought to retain their peasants. What was the estate worth without labour to work it? But it was difficult to prevent desertions because, on the one hand, the fragmentation of authority was more than ever inimical to any effective police control and, on the other, the great abundance of virgin soil made it useless to threaten with confiscation a fugitive who was almost always certain of finding a new place for himself elsewhere. Moreover, what the masters tried with varying success to prevent was the abandonment of the holding itself; the particular status of the cultivator mattered little. In cases where two persons made an agreement that neither would receive the subjects of the other, no distinction was drawn as a rule between servile and free among those whose migrations it was thus agreed to prevent.

It was moreover by no means necessary that the soil should have followed the same path to subjection as the man. Nothing, in theory, prevented the serf from keeping in his own possession even allodial lands free from any territorial supremacy. As a matter of fact it was generally admitted in any such case—we find examples of this even in the thirteenth century—that while remaining exempt from the obligations characteristic of the villein holding, the land nevertheless could not be alienated without the authorization of the lord who disposed of the person of the serf—a condition which, in practice, somewhat impaired its allodial character. Much more frequently it happened that the serf, possessing only tenements, did not hold them, or held only some of them, from the lord to whom he was bound by the ties peculiar to his status; and it might even happen that while the serf of one master he lived on the estate of another. Did the men of the feudal age ever feel revulsion at this tangled network of powers? 'I give to the church of St. Peter of Cluny this farm, with these appurtenances' —meaning 'I surrender the eminent right over the soil'—'except the villein who cultivates it, his wife, his sons and his daughters, for they do not belong to me'—so ran a Burgundian charter of about the end of the eleventh century.[1] From the first this dualism had been inherent in the situation of certain dependants and the movement of population gradually made it less exceptional. Naturally, it was bound to raise delicate problems of partition and more than one master ended by losing his right over a tenement or a man. On one point, however—and a very significant one— the tie between man and man was almost unanimously accorded a sort of primacy. It was considered that the serf who committed a crime, at least a crime involving a 'judgment of blood', ought not to have any other judge than the lord of his body—regardless both of the lord's normal judicial powers and the domicile of the accused. In short, bondage to the soil was in no sense characteristic of the serf; his distinguishing feature, on the contrary, was that he was so strictly dependent on another human being that wherever he went this tie followed him and clung to his descendants.

Thus, just as the serfs for the most part were not the descendants of ancient slaves, so their status did not represent merely a more or less improved version of the ancient slavery or colonate of Rome. Under old names, with features borrowed from different periods, the institution reflected the needs and the collective ideas of the society that had witnessed its formation. Undoubtedly the lot of the serf was very hard. Behind the bare texts, we must envisage a crude and primitive world with its moments of tragedy. A genealogy of a family of serfs, prepared in eleventh-century Anjou for the purpose of a trial, ends with this item: 'Nive, who had his throat cut by Vial, his lord.' The lord was apt to lay claim, even in defiance

[1] A. Bernard and A. Bruel, *Rec. des chartes de . . . Cluny*, IV. no. 3024.

of custom, to the exercise of an arbitrary authority: 'he is mine from the soles of his feet to the crown of his head,' an abbot of Vézelay said of one of his serfs. More than one *homme de corps* tried by trickery or by flight to escape the yoke. Doubtless, however, there is some truth in the remark of the monk of Arras who portrays the serfs of his abbey as being no less eager to advertise the bond, as soon as a pressing danger prompted them to look for a protector, than they were to repudiate it when life was peaceful.[1] Protection, oppression—between these two poles every system of clientage almost inevitably oscillates; and it was as one of the principal elements in a system of this sort that serfdom was originally constituted.

But not all the peasants had passed into servitude—even when their land itself had fallen into subjection or had remained in that state. Among the tenants of the manors the existence, side by side with the serfs, of groups expressly described as 'free' is attested by an uninterrupted succession of texts throughout the feudal era.

Above all, let us not conceive of the free peasants as mere farmers, maintaining with the supreme master of the soil only the cold relationships of debtor and creditor. Steeped in a social atmosphere in which every relationship of inferior and superior took on a directly human colour, these people were not only obliged to render to the lord the multifarious rents or services with which the house and field were burdened; they owed him in addition aid and obedience. And they counted on his protection. The solidarity thus established was so strong that the lord had the right to an indemnity if his 'free' dependant was wounded; and, reciprocally, in the event of a vendetta, or even of simply reprisals directed against him, it was thought legitimate to take measures against the whole group of his subjects without distinction of status. The relationship seemed sufficiently worthy of respect, moreover, to take precedence over what might have been thought duties of a higher order. They were not serfs, those burghers of a new town owned jointly by Louis VI and the sire de Montfort, who were authorized by their charter to preserve neutrality in case of war between their two lords, in spite of the fact that one of these was at the same time their king.[2] Nevertheless, this tie, tenacious as it was, remained strictly fortuitous. Consider moreover the terms employed. *Vilain* (villein), that is to say, inhabitant of the manor, in Latin *villa; hôte; manant; couchant et levant*—these terms, which suggested simply the idea of residence, applied to all tenants as such, even if they were serfs. But the 'free' tenant had no other name since he was an 'inhabitant' pure and simple. If he sold, gave away, or abandoned his land to go and live elsewhere, nothing any longer tied him to the lord from whom this plot was held. That is why this *vilain*,

[1] Bibl. de Tours, MS. 2041, fly-leaf; *Historiens de France*, XII, p. 340; *Cartulaire de Saint-Vaast*, p. 177.

[2] 'Coutumes de Montchauvet' (granted originally about 1101–1137) in *Mém. Soc. archéolog. Rambouillet*, XXI, 1910, p. 301; Cf. also *Ordonn.*, XI, p. 286 (Saint-Germain-des-Bois).

this *manant* was regarded as endowed with freedom and—making allowance here and there for a period of growth and uncertainty—as exempt, in consequence, from those restrictions on matrimonial and succession rights which, in the case of the *homme de corps*, marked the rigorous subjection of the family as well as the individual.

What a lot one could learn from a map of peasant freedom and servitude! Unfortunately, only some rough approximations are possible. We know already the reasons why Normandy would show as a large blank space on this imaginary sketch. Other areas equally free from serfdom would appear here and there, though they would be less extensive and more difficult to explain—as, for example, Forez. In the rest of the country, we should see a vast majority of serfs; but side by side with them a sprinkling, as it were, of free villeins, in groups of greatly varying density. Sometimes we see them closely intermixed with the servile population, house to house, on the same manor. Sometimes, on the contrary, there are villages which seem to have almost entirely escaped servitude. Even if we were better informed as to the operation of the causes which in one place precipitated a family into hereditary subjection and elsewhere kept another from making the same descent, some situations would always defy analysis. Conflicts of forces infinitely difficult to weigh, and sometimes pure chance, were decisive, perhaps after a series of fluctuations, and the very persistence of these chaotic conditions constitutes perhaps the most instructive phenomenon of all. In a perfect feudal régime, just as all land would have been held in fee or in villeinage, so every man would have been either vassal or serf. But it is well that the facts are there to remind us that a society is not a geometrical figure.

3 THE CASE OF GERMANY

Were we to make a complete study of the European manor in the feudal age we should now have to move to the south of France, where we should point to the existence (concurrently with personal serfdom) of a sort of territorial serfdom, which passed from the land to the man and attached him to it—an institution which is the more mysterious because its emergence is extremely difficult to date. Then it would be necessary to depict the development in Italy of a conception of servitude closely akin to that created by French law, but apparently less widespread and more blurred in outline. Finally, Spain would offer the sort of contrast we should expect: on the one hand, Catalonia with its French type of serfdom; on the other, the lands of the reconquest, Asturias, Leon, Castile—regions where, as in the whole peninsula, slavery persisted by reason of the flow of prisoners from the holy war, but where, among the native population, the relationships of personal dependence were not particularly exacting at this social level (any more than at the higher ones) and almost free from servile taint. However, rather than attempt a review of this kind, which would be too long and beset with too many uncertainties, it will be better to concentrate on the particularly instructive examples of Germany and England.

Only in a very artificial sense can the rural areas of Germany be treated as a unity. The study of the regions of colonization to the east of the Elbe scarcely comes within our period. But in the very heart of the old Germany, Swabia, Bavaria, Franconia, and the left bank of the Rhine, where the manorial system was relatively old and deep-rooted, presented an immense contrast with Saxony, which by the number of its free peasants—free both as to their lands and as to their persons—seemed to represent a transitional stage from that of Frisia, which had no manorial system and consequently no serfs. If, however, we concentrate on fundamentals, certain genuinely national characteristics emerge clearly.

As in France and by a similar process, a wide dissemination of the relationships of hereditary submission occurred. The deeds of voluntary surrender are as numerous in the German cartularies as in those of France. As in France, the condition of these dependants of recent origin tended to be assimilated to that of the old subjects of manors, and the model of the status thus developed borrowed many features from the type of subordination represented by enfranchisement 'with obedience'—a filiation which the language here underlined with a particularly neat stroke. The name of *Laten*, whose etymology evokes the idea of liberation, had but lately stood in German law for a legally well-defined class which (together with some foreign residents and, occasionally, the members of conquered populations) comprised the freedmen still bound to their old masters by the ties of a sort of clientage. In northern Germany in the twelfth century there were included under the name of *Laten* large groups of dependants, among whom the sons of slaves recently transformed into clients were certainly no more than a minority. Chevage, succession taxes—most frequently in the form of a piece of movable property collected in each generation—had become burdens characteristic of personal subordination; and so too had the prohibition of marriage outside the manor (*formariage*). Finally, as in France, by a distortion of the original meaning of the notions of freedom and non-freedom, there was a tendency henceforth to attach the stigma of servitude to every heritable tie. On the estates of the Alsatian abbey of Marmoutier, the free and servile tenements of the ninth century were in the twelfth reduced to a single category, which was described as servile. In spite of their name, the *Laten* of the feudal era—just like their brothers across the frontier, the French *culverts*—generally ceased to be regarded as free men. So much was this the case that paradoxically enough the lord, if he renounced his rights over them, was said to set free these ex-freedmen. On the other hand, 'freedom' was universally attributed to the *Landsassen* ('people settled on the land'), known also—by a further analogy with French conditions—as 'guests' (*Gäste*). These men were true *manants*, free from all ties other than the obligations arising from residence.

Nevertheless, various distinctively German conditions interfered with this development. In France, so profound a transformation of the original conceptions of freedom had been made possible only by the atrophy of the State, especially in the sphere of justice. But in Germany and especially in the north, during the whole of the feudal era, public tribunals (*placita*) of the early type subsisted in places, in competition with the seignorial courts. Is it surprising then that the idea should more or less obscurely have survived that those men were free—and those alone—who sat in these public courts and were subject to their jurisdiction? Where peasant allods were numerous as in Saxony, another cause of complications arose. For between the allodialist and the tenant, even when both were equally free from any personal and hereditary bond, no one could fail to perceive a difference of social level. The freedom of the allodialist, since it also extended to the land, seemed more complete. He alone therefore had the right—at least when his allod was of a certain size—to take part in the tribunal as judge or, in the old Frankish terminology, as *échevin* (*scabinus*); he was 'the free man eligible to serve as échevin' (*Schöffenbarfrei*).

Finally, there were economic factors. In feudal Germany slavery proper, without being as negligible as in France—for the proximity of the Slav was a perpetual incitement to raids which helped to maintain the slave trade—nevertheless did not play a very important part. On the other hand the former *servi*, resident on the demesne, had not been transformed into tenants so generally as in France, since the demesnes themselves in many cases remained extensive. Most of the *servi* had indeed been 'domiciled' (*casati*) after a fashion, but only to the extent of receiving insignificant bits of land. Subject to daily labour services these *Tageschalken*—they were in fact compulsory day-labourers, a species completely unknown in France—lived in a state of profound subjection which it would have been impossible not to regard as servile to the last degree.

Certain historians, having forgotten that a social classification exists, in the last analysis, only by virtue of the ideas which men form of it—and that these are not necessarily free of inconsistencies—have gone to the length of introducing forcibly into the law of persons as it functioned in feudal Germany a clarity and a uniformity which were altogether alien to it. The jurists of the Middle Ages had shown them the way, and with no better results. We must recognize the fact that the systems presented to us by the great authors of customaries, like Eike von Repgow in his *Sachsenspiegel*, are not only somewhat disjointed in themselves, but in addition agree but poorly with the language of the charters. There is nothing comparable here with the relative simplicity of French serfdom. In practice the hereditary dependants within each manor hardly ever formed a single class, subject to uniform obligations. Moreover, from manor to manor, the lines of demarcation between the groups and their designations varied greatly.

One of the most common criteria was furnished by chevage, which still retained a little of its former value as a symbol of a protection that was not dishonourable. Those liable to forced day labour—people so poor that it was frequently necessary to dispense them even from the payment of succession taxes—naturally did not pay chevage. But it was also absent from the traditional mass of obligations—very heavy ones all the same—which weighed on a whole section of the servile tenants. Thus, the families distinguished by liability to this tax, with its suggestions of a once voluntary submission—although often themselves, on account of the hereditary nature of the bond, considered as 'unfree'—were generally held to be of a higher rank than the rest of those so described. Elsewhere the descendants of the former clients continued to be designated by the old word *Muntmen*, derived from the Germanic term *Munt*, a word which from the earliest times had signified the authority exercised by a protector. In a Romance-speaking country they would have been called commended men. But while in the French countryside the commended peasants of the twelfth century (who were very few) retained only an empty name as a reminder of their origin, having in fact been merged with the servile class, many among their German fellows had managed to preserve their existence, and sometimes even their fundamental freedom, as members of a special class. The prohibition of intermarriage, or at least the lowering of status which, in law, any union with a person of lower rank involved, helped to maintain firm barriers between these different strata of the subject population.

Perhaps in the long run the most original feature of German manorial evolution was its failure to synchronize with developments elsewhere. With its indivisible tenements, frequently arranged in several legal categories, and the numerous layers in which it endeavoured to classify status, the German manor, about the year 1200, remained on the whole closely akin to the Carolingian type—much more so, certainly, than the French manor of the same period—though it was destined to depart from it more and more during the next two centuries. In particular, the fusion of the hereditary dependants under a common legal heading began towards the end of the thirteenth century—two or three hundred years later, that is, than in France. In Germany also the new terminology proceeded by means of borrowings from a vocabulary which smacked of slavery. The term *homo proprius* (*homme propre*) or, as they said in German, *eigen*, used at first mainly to describe the unfree persons maintained as farm-hands on the demesne, was extended gradually to many tenants, however weak their hereditary tie with the master. Next it became customary to complete the phrase by the addition of another word, which emphasized the personal nature of the bond. By a curious parallelism with one of the most widely-disseminated of the names of the French serf, people said henceforth more and more frequently: *homme propre de son corps, eigen von dem lipe, leibeigen*. Naturally, between this late *Leibeigenschaft*, the study of which does not fall within the feudal era, and the French serfdom of the twelfth century, there were many contrasts due to differences of period and environment. It is none the less true that here once again we appear to be confronted with that singular quality of archaism, which through almost the entire feudal era seems the distinctive mark of German society.

4 ENGLAND: THE VICISSITUDES OF VILLEINAGE

Though something like two centuries divide them, the state of the peasant classes in England about the middle of the eleventh century irresistibly reminds one of the picture presented by the old Carolingian surveys. It is true that there was a less solid organization of the territorial manor, but the system of personal dependence was quite as complicated. This confusion, to which they were not accustomed, proved very troublesome to many of the continental clerks entrusted by William the Conqueror with the task of making a cadastral survey of his new kingdom. Their terminology, borrowed as a rule from western France, was not really suited to express the facts. A few general features, nevertheless, stand out clearly. There are genuine slaves (*theow*), of whom some are 'domiciled' (*casati*); there are tenants who, though charged with rent and services, are regarded as free. There are 'commended' persons, subject to a protector who is not necessarily identical with the lord from whom they hold their tenements, if they have any. Sometimes this subordination of man to man is still sufficiently loose to be broken at the will of the inferior. Sometimes it is on the contrary indissoluble and hereditary. Finally, there are genuine peasant allodialists —though they are not so described. Moreover, two other criteria coexisted with the foregoing ones, without necessarily overlapping with them. One was derived from the varying extent of the holdings; the other from submission to one or other of the manorial courts that were coming into being.

The Norman Conquest, which brought about an almost complete change in the ownership of manors, upset these arrangements and simplified them. It is true that many traces of former conditions survived—particularly in the North, where we have seen how the peasant warriors raised problems for jurists accustomed to quite different social classifications. On the whole, however, a century or so after Hastings the situation had become very like that prevailing in France. As distinct from the tenants who were dependent on a lord merely because they held their houses and their fields from him, there was constituted a class of bondmen, i.e. 'bound men', 'men by birth' (*nativi, niefs*), personal and hereditary subjects who were regarded as thereby debarred from 'freedom'. They were subject to obligations and incapacities whose pattern scarcely ever varied and with which we are already familiar—the prohibitions against entry into orders and against *formariage*; the exaction of the best article of movable property at every death; and the tax called chevage (though this last, following a usage to which Germany offers a parallel on certain points, was as a rule levied only if the individual dwelt outside his master's estate). Add to these an exaction conducing in a curious way to the maintenance of good morals and whose equivalent—so fundamentally uniform was this feudal society—was to be found in distant Catalonia: the serf's daughter guilty of unchastity paid a fine to her lord. Much more numerous than the slaves of former days, these unfree persons resembled them neither by the sort of life they lived, nor by the law which governed them. A significant feature was that in the event of one of them being murdered their families, unlike those of the *theow* of the Anglo-Saxon period, were entitled to a share of the *wergild* along with the lord. The solidarity of the family was non-existent for the slave; it was never so for the serf of a later day.

On one point, however, there was a really profound contrast with France. The English lord was much more successful than his continental neighbour in retaining his serfs and even his ordinary tenants on his estate. One reason for this was that in this remarkably centralized country the royal authority was sufficiently strong to have the runaway *niefs* tracked down and to punish those who had harboured them. Another was that within the manor itself the lord had at his disposal, for the purpose of maintaining a grip on his subjects, an institution whose antecedents were undoubtedly Anglo-Saxon, but which the early Normans, in their concern for efficient police arrangements, had regularized and developed. It was called 'frankpledge', which means suretyship—mutual suretyship, that is —of free men. Its object was to establish a vast social network for the purpose of repressing crime. By this plan, the population throughout almost the whole of England was divided into groups of ten. Each 'tithing' was responsible, as a group, for the appearance of its members in court. At fixed intervals its head had to present the guilty or the suspect to the representative of the crown, who at the same time made sure that everyone was a member of a tithing. Originally all free men were supposed to be included in this system, the only exceptions being the upper classes, the servants or men-at-arms maintained in the household (for whom their chief served as natural warrantor), and lastly the clergy. Then an important and very rapid change took place; and the only people who remained subject to frankpledge were the dependants of manors, irrespective of their status. Hence the very name of the institution came to be misleading, since many of the dependants were no longer considered free—a paradoxical but typical example of those changes of meaning which we have noticed already on many occasions. Moreover, the right to hold a judicial inspection of this kind ('view of frankpledge', it was called), since there were not enough officials to exercise it, was increasingly entrusted to the lords themselves, or at least to a considerable number of them. In their hands it was destined to be a powerful instrument of coercion.

But the Conquest, which had so greatly strengthened the manorial structure, had also favoured the establishment of an exceptionally strong monarchy. A kind of boundary agreement concluded between the two powers explains the final transformation which the classification of social groups and even the very notion of freedom underwent in medieval England. From the middle of the twelfth century, under the influence of the Norman and then of the Angevin dynasty, the judicial powers of the crown had developed to an extraordinary degree. But this unusually rapid growth had to be paid for. Obliged to accept limitations which, later on, states like France, which were slower in their development, did not find it so difficult to overstep, the judges of the Plantagenets, after some hesitations, abandoned the attempt to intervene between the lord of the manor and his men. It was not that the latter were deprived of all access to the royal courts, for only the cases which concerned their relations with their lord were reserved exclusively for hearing by the latter or his court. The cases thus defined, however, affected these humble folk in their most vital interests, such as the burden of their liabilities and the possession or transmission of their holdings. Moreover, the number of persons involved was considerable: it included, along with the bondmen, the majority of the ordinary tenants who were usually described—by a borrowing from the French—as villeins (*vilains*). Thus a new dividing-line whose practical importance was evident to all was drawn through English society. On the one hand, there were the true subjects of the king to whom was extended, at all times, the protection of his courts; on the other, there was the mass of the peasantry, largely abandoned to the jurisdiction of the lord of the manor.

Now the idea had probably never altogether disappeared that to be free was first and foremost to have the right to be tried in the public courts: the slave was subject to correction only by his master. The jurists therefore made the subtle distinction that in relation to his lord, but to him alone (since against third parties recourse to the ordinary tribunals was not prohibited), the villein was an unfree person. Common opinion and even the courts themselves took a broader and simpler view. From the thirteenth century, the two words 'villein' and 'serf', which were formerly, as in France, almost antithetic, were normally regarded as synonymous—an assimilation fraught with serious consequences, since it was not confined to language, which in reality merely expressed current social conceptions. Villeinage itself was henceforth considered hereditary; and, though among villeins a certain stamp of inferiority continued as a rule to segregate the descendants of the old bondmen (who apparently were always less numerous than the French serfs), there was a growing tendency—favoured by the omnipotence of the manorial courts—to subject all the members of the new servile class to the obligations and the social stigma which had formerly rested on the 'bound men' alone.

Nevertheless, to define the villein as the man who in his relations with

272

his lord was subject to the jurisdiction of that lord alone and then (as the status of the man and the soil more and more frequently ceased to coincide, owing to the instability of landed wealth) to define tenure in villeinage as that form of tenure which was unprotected by the royal courts—this was no doubt a definition of the characteristics of a class of men and of a species of landed property, but it left open the question of what these categories did or did not include. For it was still necessary to find a means of deciding which persons or which lands were to be subjected to this disability, whence all the rest proceeded. No one would have dreamed of ranging under the contemptuous headings of villein and villein tenure all the individuals who had a lord or all the landed property dependent on a lord. It was not even enough to exclude knights' fees and those who held them. Among the possessors of the villein tenements included in a manor there were many persons of too high a rank, and even many peasants whose freedom was too long and too well attested, for it to be possible to lump them all together arbitrarily in one servile mass. Jurisprudence therefore had recourse to a criterion provided, in this case also, by the heritage of ideas or prejudices deeply rooted in the mind of the community. The slave had owed all his labour to his master; consequently, for a man to owe much of his time to a lord seemed a serious curtailment of freedom —especially when the tasks thus exacted belonged to an order of manual toil considered somewhat degrading and described throughout Europe by the significant name of 'servile' labour. Tenure in villeinage was therefore that which was charged with heavy agricultural labour services—heavy at times to the point of being virtually at the discretion of the lord—together with other services regarded as not particularly honourable; and the men who in the thirteenth century happened to hold these lands formed the main body of the villein class. In particular cases, the distinction was often capricious; from some regions villeinage was almost absent. But the principle prevailed all the same.

The concrete problem which the coexistence of a precociously developed royal justice and a powerful landed aristocracy presented for the lawyers of the Plantagenet rulers was, like the facts themselves, specifically English; so too was the distinction of classes—a distinction destined to have important and revolutionary consequences in later times beyond our period. On the other hand, the conceptions evolved by juridical opinion to develop the new idea of servitude belonged to the common heritage of feudal Europe. That the villein—even the free villein—ought not to have any other judge than his lord was still maintained by a French jurist of the court of St. Louis, and we know to what an extent the equation of freedom with the right to public justice remained an active principle in Germany. The opinion that the obligation to perform certain services regarded as dishonourable or too rigorous was a badge of serfdom added fuel to certain village feuds in the Île-de-France about the year 1200, although such a criterion was contrary to strict law and was opposed by the courts.[1] But the evolution of the French state, slow, insidious, and sure, prevented the establishment of a sharp dividing line between the judicial powers of the king and those of the lords. As for the idea of dishonourable forms of work, if it played its part in the delimitation of the noble class in France, it never succeeded there in supplanting the old criteria of servitude, since nothing occurred to necessitate a new classification of status. Thus the case of England shows with unusual clarity how in the midst of what was in many respects a homogeneous civilization certain creative ideas, taking shape under the influence of a given environment, could result in the creation of a completely original legal system, while elsewhere surrounding conditions kept those ideas in a more or less permanently embryonic state. In this way English feudalism has something of the value of an object-lesson in social organization.

[1] *Le Conseil de Pierre de Fontaines*, ed. A. J. Marnier, 1886, XXI, 8. p. 225; Marc Bloch, 'Les transformations du servage' in *Mélanges d'histoire du moyen âge offerts à M. F. Lot*, 1925, p. 55 *et seq.*

XX

TOWARDS NEW FORMS
OF MANORIALISM

1 THE STABILIZATION OF OBLIGATIONS

THE profound changes which from the twelfth century onwards began to transform the relations of subject and lord were to extend over several centuries. It will suffice to indicate here how the institution of the manor emerged from feudalism.

After the Carolingian surveys had fallen into disuse, as being no longer practicable, and increasingly difficult to interpret, there was a danger that the internal life of the manors, even of the largest and least ill-administered, would henceforth be regulated only by purely oral rules. There was indeed nothing to prevent the drawing up of statements of property and of rights better adapted to the conditions of the time. This is, in fact, what was done by certain churches in regions like Lorraine where the Carolingian tradition had remained particularly vigorous; the practice of compiling these inventories was never lost. At an early date, nevertheless, attention was directed to another type of document which, in concentrating on questions of human relations rather than on the description of the land, seemed to correspond more exactly to the needs of a time when the manor had become above all a community subject to a lord. This was a charter defining the customs peculiar to such and such an estate. Granted in theory by the lord, little local constitutions of this sort were yet as a rule the outcome of preliminary negotiations with the subjects, and such an agreement seemed all the more necessary because the text did not usually confine itself to recording ancient practice but frequently modified it on certain points. An example of this was the charter by which, as early as 967, the abbot of St. Arnulf of Metz lightened the services of the men of Morville-sur-Nied; another, pointing in the opposite direction, was the 'pact' whose somewhat harsh terms the monks of Bèze in Burgundy, about 1100, imposed on the inhabitants of a village destroyed by fire, before they would sanction its rebuilding.[1] But till the beginning of the twelfth century these documents remained very rare.

[1] C. E. Perrin, *Recherches sur la seigneurie rurale en Lorraine d'après les plus anciens censiers*, p. 225 et seq; *Chronique de l'abbaye de Saint-Bénigne . . .* ed. E. Bougaud and J. Garnier, pp. 396–7 (1088–1119).

From that date onwards, however, various causes helped to multiply them. Among the lords, a new taste for legal clarity put a premium on written documents; even among the poor, as a result of the progress of education, more value was attached to them than hitherto. Not that many of them could read; but no doubt the reason why so many illiterate rural communities found it worth while to demand charters and preserve them was the presence in their immediate neighbourhood of clergy, merchants, and jurists who were prepared to interpret these documents for them.

Above all, changes in social life prompted the stabilization of obligations and their progressive alleviation. In practically the whole of Europe, a great movement of land clearance was proceeding. He who wished to attract pioneers to his estate was obliged to promise them favourable conditions; the least they could demand was the assurance in advance that they would not be subject to the arbitrary authority of the lord. In the surrounding districts the example thus given soon had to be followed by the lords of the older villages, if they did not wish to see their subjects yield to the attraction of land less heavily burdened. It was certainly no accident that the two constitutions of customary rights and obligations which were to serve as models for so many similar texts—namely the charters of Beaumont-en-Argonne and of Lorris, near the Forest of Orleans (one of which was granted to a settlement of recent foundation, and the other, by contrast, to a very old establishment)—had the common feature that, since they both originated on the verge of great woodland areas, they were first promulgated amidst the sound of the assarters' axes. No less significant is the fact that in Lorraine the name *villeneuve* was applied to every place which had received a charter, however old it might be. The example of the urban communities had a similar effect. Though they also were subject to the manorial régime, many of them had been successful as early as the end of the eleventh century in securing substantial advantages which had been recorded in writing. The story of their triumphs encouraged the peasant masses, and the attraction which the privileged towns might exercise gave the masters cause for concern. In the end, the growth of economic exchange inclined the lords to wish for certain modifications in the distribution of obligations and by causing some cash to flow even into the coffers of the peasants opened up new possibilities for the latter. Less poor and consequently less helpless and resigned, they could either buy what would not have been given to them or take it by force; for by no means all seignorial concessions were given free of charge or voluntarily. Thus the number of these little village codes everywhere increased. They were called in France charters of 'customs' or of 'franchises'. Sometimes the two words were linked together. The second, without necessarily signifying the abolition of serfdom, suggested the mitigations now introduced into the traditional practices.

The charter of customs was a very general institution in the Europe of later feudal times and the period that followed. We come across a great many examples of it throughout the kingdom of France, in Lotharingia and the kingdom of Arles, in Rhenish Germany, in practically the whole of Italy, including the Norman kingdom, and lastly through the length and breadth of the Iberian peninsula. It is true that the *poblaciones* or the *fueros* of Spain and the Italian *statuti* differed in nature as well as in name from the French charters, while these, in their turn, were by no means all cast in the same mould. There were also great differences between one country or province and another, in the number of charters granted; and others no less pronounced in the chronology of the movement. The oldest *poblaciones* of Spain, which were contemporaneous with the efforts of the Christians to repopulate the conquered territories, go back to the tenth century. On the middle Rhine the first charters of villages, imitated apparently from models further west, date from not much earlier than the year 1300.

Nevertheless, despite the extent of these divergences the problems they raise are trifling compared with that set by the presence on the map of rural 'franchises' of two enormous blanks—England on the one hand, trans-Rhenish Germany on the other. In both cases, a fairly large number of communities received charters from their lords, but these were almost exclusively towns. No doubt in almost every medieval town, with the exception of the great commercial centres, a rural element survived: the community had its communal pastures, individual inhabitants had their fields, which the poorest cultivated themselves. The majority of the German or English places with charters were simple 'burgs' rather than towns in the modern sense. It is none the less true that what in every case determined the grant of such favours was the existence of a market, a merchant class, and an artisan class, whereas in other countries the movement had affected ordinary villages.

In the case of England, the absence of charters of rural customs can probably be explained by the strength of the manorial structure and its evolution in a direction entirely favourable to the arbitrary authority of the lord. For written record, the lords had their surveys and the rolls recording the judgments of their courts: they would hardly have felt the need for further codification of usages whose very instability enabled them to render the possession of tenements progressively more precarious. Furthermore, since land clearance in England appears to have been relatively limited while the lords for their part possessed very effective means of retaining their subjects, one of the causes which on the continent had most powerfully conduced to the concessions was not operative here.

The case of Germany was very different. The charter of customs was exceptional there simply because another method of fixing obligations was preferred—the *Weistum* which Professor Perrin has ingeniously proposed to call in French *rapport de droits*, 'statement of rights'. In the German

277

manors it had continued to be the practice to summon the dependants to periodic assemblies, relics of the judicial *placita* of the Carolingians. This provided a convenient opportunity for the lord to read out the traditional rules by which they were governed and to which they seemed to acknowledge their submission by their very attendance at this proclamation. This sort of inquest on customs, which was constantly repeated, closely resembled in principle those on which the surveys of former times had been based. Texts were thus established, to which additions were made from time to time. Germany beyond the Rhine was the true home of the *Weistum*; on the left bank and extending even into French-speaking territory there was a zone of transition where it was to be found side by side with the charter of customs. More detailed as a rule than the latter, it was on the other hand more susceptible of modification. But the fundamental result in both cases was the same. Though there were everywhere many villages without *Weistum* or charter, and though neither of these methods of fixing obligations, where it did exist, had any inordinate power to preserve the *status quo*, it was in fact this tendency towards an increasing stabilization of relations between masters and subjects which opened a new phase in the history of the European manor. 'No quit-rent must be levied unless it is in writing'—this phrase from a Roussillon charter proclaims an attitude and a legal structure remote from the ethos of the first feudal age.[1]

2 THE TRANSFORMATION OF HUMAN RELATIONSHIPS

The stabilization of obligations was accompanied by certain drastic modifications in the internal structure of the manor. There was a general reduction of compulsory labour services; sometimes they were replaced by money payments, which were also occasionally substituted for rents in kind; finally there was a progressive elimination of those parts of the system of obligations which had remained uncertain and fortuitous. These changes were henceforth inscribed on every page of the cartularies. Tallage, in particular, which until lately had been 'arbitrary', was in France very widely 'regularized', that is to say transformed into a tax of which both the amount and the periodicity were fixed. In the same way, the right of purveyance (*fournitures*) exercised by the lord on the occasion of visits— necessarily of varying duration—was often commuted for a lump sum. In spite of many variations, regional or local, it was clear that the subject was tending more and more to be transformed into a taxpayer whose assessment varied little from year to year.

Meanwhile the form of dependence in which the subordination of man to man had found its most complete expression either disappeared or changed its character. From the thirteenth century onwards, repeated

[1] Charter of Codalet in Conflent, 1142, in B. Alart, *Privilèges et titres relatifs aux franchises . . . de Roussillon*, I, p. 40.

enfranchisements which sometimes applied to whole villages considerably reduced the number of French and Italian serfs. Other groups slipped into freedom through mere desuetude. Moreover, where serfdom survived in France it progressively deviated from the old form of personal bondage (*hommage de corps*). It was conceived of less as a personal tie and more as an inferiority of class which by a sort of contagion could pass from the soil to the man. There would henceforth be servile tenements, the possession of which made a man a serf, and the abandonment of which sometimes set him free. In more than one province, the body of specific obligations itself was broken up. New criteria appeared. Formerly innumerable tenants had been tallageable at will; but some serfs, while remaining serfs, had got their obligations placed on a contractual basis. Henceforth, to pay at the will of the lord established at least a presumption of serfdom. Such changes were almost universal. Was English villeinage, in spite of its highly original characteristics, anything other than a definition of status by uncertainty of obligations (compulsory labour services here being taken as the standard) and of obligations essentially attaching to a piece of land? Formerly, in the days when as yet the only unfree persons were the bondmen, the 'bond of the man' had been regarded as a mark of servitude; in future, this stigma attached to a man in his capacity as a *manant*, a villein. And the villein *par excellence* was he who was subject to irregular services and 'did not know in the evening what he would have to do the next morning'. In Germany, where the class of *Leibeigene* was not unified till very late, the evolution was slower; it none the less in the end followed much the same course.

The manor in itself has no claim to a place among the institutions which we call feudal. It had coexisted (as it did again later on) with a stronger State, with less numerous and less solid relationships of clientage, and with a much freer circulation of money. Nevertheless, in the new conditions of life which arose from approximately the ninth century onwards, this ancient method of social organization was destined not only to extend its grip over a much larger proportion of the population, but also to consolidate to a remarkable degree its own internal structure. Like the family it was profoundly influenced by surrounding conditions. In the days when vassalage was developing, or when it was in its prime, the manor was first and foremost a community of dependants who were by turns protected, commanded, and oppressed by their lord to whom many of them were bound by a sort of hereditary link, unconnected with possession of the soil or place of abode. When the relationships truly characteristic of feudalism fell into decay the manor lived on, but with different characteristics; it became more territorial, more purely economic.

Thus feudalism, a type of social organization marked by a special quality in human relationships, expressed itself not only in the creation of new institutions; it imparted its own colouring to what it received from the past, as if passing it through a prism, and transmitted it to succeeding ages.

279

BOOK TWO: SOCIAL CLASSES AND POLITICAL ORGANIZATION

PART VI

Social Classes

INTRODUCTORY NOTE

THE most characteristic feature of the civilization of feudal Europe was the network of ties of dependence, extending from top to bottom of the social scale. (How such a distinctive structure arose and developed, what were the events and the mental climate that influenced its growth, what it owed to borrowings from a remoter past, we have endeavoured to show in Book I.) In the societies to which the epithet 'feudal' is traditionally applied, however, the lives of individuals were never regulated exclusively by these relationships of strict subjection or direct authority. Men were also divided into groups, ranged one above the other, according to occupation, degree of power or prestige. Moreover, above the confused mass of petty chiefdoms of every kind, there always existed authorities of more far-reaching influence and of a different character. From the second feudal age onwards, not only were the orders of society more and more strictly differentiated; there was also an increasing concentration of forces round a few great authorities and a few great causes. We must now direct our attention to the study of this second aspect of social organization; then we shall at last be in a position to attempt to answer the question which it has been the main purpose of our inquiry to elucidate, namely: by what fundamental characteristics, whether or not peculiar to one phase of Western evolution, have these few centuries deserved the name which thus sets them apart from the rest of European history? What portion of their heritage has been transmitted to later times?

XXI

THE NOBLES AS A *DE FACTO* CLASS

1 THE DISAPPEARANCE OF THE ANCIENT ARISTOCRACIES OF BIRTH

FOR the writers who first gave feudalism its name, for the men of the French Revolution, who worked to destroy it, the idea of nobility seemed inseparably linked with it. It would scarcely be possible, however, to find an association of ideas more palpably false—at least if we set any store by the exact use of historical terms. Certainly there was nothing egalitarian about the societies of the feudal era; but not every dominant class is a nobility. To deserve this name such a class must evidently combine two characteristics. First, it must have a legal status of its own, which confirms and makes effectual the superiority to which it lays claim. In the second place, this status must be hereditary—with the qualification, however, that a limited number of new families may be admitted to it, in accordance with formally established rules. In other words, actual power is not enough, nor is even that form of inheritance (effective though it is in practice) which consists as much in the advantages children enjoy through having parents of high status as in the wealth they may inherit; it is necessary, in addition, that social privileges as well as hereditary succession should be recognized by law. If in France we speak today of the upper middle classes as a capitalist aristocracy, it is only in irony. Even where, as in our modern democratic societies, the legal privileges of the nobility have disappeared, the memory of them keeps class consciousness alive; no one is accepted as a genuine nobleman unless he can prove that they were exercised by his ancestors. In this sense—and it is the only legitimate one—nobility made its appearance relatively late in western Europe. The first lineaments of the institution did not begin to emerge before the twelfth century, and it took definite shape only in the following century when the fief and vassalage were already in decline. Throughout the first feudal age, and in the period immediately preceding it, it was unknown.

In this respect the first feudal age differed from the earlier civilizations whose legacy it had received. The Later Empire had had the senatorial order, from which, under the first Merovingians, despite the disappearance of the legal privileges of former days, the leading Roman subjects of the Frankish king still proudly claimed descent. Among many German peoples

283

there had existed certain families officially described as 'noble'—in the vulgar tongue *edelinge*, which term the Latin texts render as *nobiles* and which, in Franco-Burgundian, long survived in the form *adelenc*. Their status allowed them specific advantages, notably a higher *wergild*; their members, as the Anglo-Saxon documents put it, were 'born dearer' than other men. Descended, so far as we know, from ancient dynasties of local chiefs—the 'chiefs of cantons' mentioned by Tacitus—the majority of them, where the monarchic form of government prevailed, had been gradually dispossessed of their political power in favour of the royal house, which itself was sprung originally from their ranks. They none the less retained some of their original prestige as sacred families.

But these distinctions did not survive the age of the barbarian kingdoms. Many of the *edeling* dynasties no doubt became extinct at an early date. Their very greatness made them the favourite target of private vengeance, proscriptions, and wars. Save in Saxony, very few outlasted the period immediately following the invasions—there were only four, for example, among the Bavarians in the seventh century. Among the Franks, assuming —and this is something that cannot be proved—that they also had known a hereditary aristocracy in former times, it had disappeared before the earliest written records. Similarly, the senatorial order constituted only an unstable and scattered oligarchy. Those families whose pride was founded on ancient memories naturally disappeared in the new kingdoms, where the effective bases of superiority among free men were of quite another type: wealth, with its corollary, power; and the king's service. Both these qualifications, though in practice they often passed from father to son, none the less left the way open for sudden rises and equally sudden falls. By a highly significant restriction of meaning, in England from the ninth or tenth century onwards only the relatives of the king retained the right to the name of *aetheling*.

The most striking feature of the history of the dominant families in the first feudal age is the shortness of their pedigrees—at least if we agree to reject not only the fables invented by the Middle Ages themselves, but also the ingenious though improbable conjectures which in our own day various scholars have founded on very hypothetical principles for the transmission of proper names. The earliest known ancestor of the Welfs, a family who after playing a considerable rôle in West Francia wore the crown of Burgundy from 888 to 1032, was a Bavarian count whose daughter married Louis the Pious. The line of the counts of Toulouse arose under Louis the Pious; that of the marquises of Ivrea, who were later kings of Italy, under Charles the Bald; and that of the Ludolfings, dukes of Saxony, then kings of East Francia and emperors, under Lewis the German. The Bourbons, descended from the Capetians, are probably today the oldest dynasty in Europe. Yet what do we know of the origins of their ancestor, Robert the Strong, who was killed in 866 and who already counted among the magnates of Gaul? Simply the name of his father and the possibility that he may have had Saxon blood.[1] It seems as if inevitably, once this crucial turning-point of the year 800 is reached, obscurity prevails. Moreover, these were particularly ancient houses more or less closely connected with those dynasties—sprung for the most part from Austrasia or the regions beyond the Rhine—to whom the first Carolingians had entrusted the chief positions of authority throughout the Empire. In northern Italy, in the eleventh century, the Attoni were masters of hill and plain over a large area; they were descended from a certain Siegfried, the owner of large estates in the county of Lucca, who died shortly before 950; beyond that date, nothing more can be ascertained. The middle of the tenth century also saw the sudden emergence of the Swabian Zähringen, the Babenbergs (the real founders of Austria), the lords of Amboise. . . . If we turn to feudal lineages of lower rank we lose the trail at a much more recent date.

Now, it is not enough in this case to lay the blame on the poverty of our sources. Undoubtedly, if the charters of the ninth and tenth centuries were less scarce we should discover a few more ancestral links. But the surprising thing is that we should need such chance records at all. In the days of their greatness the Ludolfings, the Attoni, the lords of Amboise, among others, all had their historians. How did it happen that those learned men were unable or unwilling to tell us anything about the ancestors of their masters? It is a fact that the genealogies of Icelandic peasants, transmitted for centuries by a purely oral tradition, are much better known to us than those of our medieval barons. So far as the latter were concerned, it seems evident that no interest was taken in their ancestry till the moment—relatively recent, as a rule—when for the first time one of them attained a really exalted rank. No doubt there were good reasons for thinking that before the chosen date the family history would have offered nothing of special interest; either because in fact it began at a rather humble social level—the celebrated Norman house of Bellême seems to have been descended from an ordinary cross-bowman of Louis d'Outre-Mer[2]—or (a more frequent case) because it had long remained half-concealed in the mass of those petty manorial lords whose origin as a group raises, as we shall see later, such difficult problems. But the chief reason for what appears to be so strange a silence was that these powerful individuals did not constitute a noble class, in the full sense of the word. To speak of nobility is to speak of pedigrees: in the case in point, pedigrees did not matter because there was no nobility.

[1] See the latest account of the problem by J. Calmette, in *Annales du Midi*, 1928.

[2] H. Prentout, 'Les origines de la maison de Bellême' in *Études sur quelques points d'histoire de Normandie*, 1926.

2 DIFFERENT MEANINGS OF THE WORD 'NOBLE'
IN THE FIRST FEUDAL AGE

This is not to say, however, that from the ninth to the eleventh century the word 'noble' (in Latin *nobilis*) was not to be found fairly frequently in the documents. But it had no precise legal meaning and simply indicated an actual or an accepted pre-eminence, in accordance with a variety of different criteria. Almost invariably it involved the idea of a certain distinction of birth; but it also implied a measure of wealth. Thus we find Paul the Deacon (an eighth-century writer who is usually more lucid than in this case), in a commentary on a passage of the *Rule* of St. Benedict, hesitating between, and confusing, these two interpretations.[1] From the beginning of the feudal era these uses of the word 'noble', though too fluctuating to admit of precise definition, at least reflected some major trends, and their very vicissitudes are instructive.

In days when so many men had to agree to hold their lands of a lord, the mere fact of escaping such subjection was a sign of superiority. It is not surprising therefore that the possession of an allod (even if this was no more than a peasant property) should have been sometimes considered a sufficient title to the name 'noble' or *edel*. It is also worth noticing that in the majority of the texts in which petty allodialists appear with this designation, we see them parading it only to surrender it immediately by becoming the tenants or serfs of a more powerful man.

If from the end of the eleventh century onwards we come across scarcely any more 'nobles' of this sort—in reality rather humble folk—the crystallization of the idea of nobility which was then taking place on altogether different lines was not the only reason. In a great part of the West practically the whole social class had disappeared; it had become extinct.

In the Frankish period a great number of slaves had received their freedom. Naturally these intruders were not readily accepted as equals by families which had never been sullied by the servile taint. With the 'free man' (*liber*), who might be a former slave set free or the recent descendant of a freedman, the Romans had not so long before contrasted the pure *ingenuus*; but in the Latin of the decadence the two words had become almost synonymous. An unblemished line was nevertheless genuine nobility in the vague sense in which that word was ordinarily employed. 'To be noble is to count among one's ancestors no one who has been subjected to slavery.' Such was the definition still given, towards the beginning of the eleventh century, by an Italian gloss, systematizing a usage of which we find more than one trace elsewhere.[2] But this use of the term did not survive the changes in social classifications either; as we have seen,

---

[1] *Bibliotheca Casinensis*, vol. IV, p. 151.
[2] *M.G.H., LL*, vol. IV, p. 557, col. 2, l. 6.

it was not long before the descendants of the former freedmen became for the most part quite simply serfs.

Nevertheless, even among the humble folk there were individuals who, while subjects of a lord as to their land, had none the less managed to retain their personal 'freedom'. Naturally a condition which had become so rare was invested with a particularly honourable character, which it was not contrary to the practices of the time to call 'nobility'. Even a few texts here and there seem to favour this equivalence; but freedom and nobility could never really be regarded as identical. To describe as nobles the mass of so-called free men, many of whom, as tenants, were subject to heavy and humiliating labour services—this idea was too repugnant to the common conception of social values to find general acceptance, and the temporary identification of the words 'noble' and 'free' was destined to leave no enduring traces save in the vocabulary of a special form of subordination —military vassalage.

Unlike the ties of many dependants, rural or domestic, the fealty of vassals was not heritable and their services were in a high degree compatible with the most exacting definition of freedom. Among all the lord's 'men' they were in a special sense his 'free men' (*francs hommes*); more than other fiefs, their tenements had, as we know, a claim to be called *francs-fiefs*. And since, in the motley crowd of the lord's dependants, their rôle as armed retainers and counsellors gave them the semblance of aristocracy, they were also distinguished from that crowd by the fine-sounding name of nobility. The little church which the monks of Saint-Riquier, about the middle of the ninth century, reserved for the devotions of the vassals maintained at the abbot's court bore the name of 'the nobles' chapel', in contrast with that of the 'common people', where the artisans and minor officials of the monastery heard mass. When Louis the Pious exempted the tenants of the monks of Kempten from military service, he specified that this exemption did not apply to the 'more noble persons' provided with 'benefits' by the abbey.[1] Of all the senses of the word, this one, which tended to confound the two ideas of vassalage and nobility, was destined to enjoy the longest life.

Finally, at a higher level, among those men who were neither of servile birth nor in a condition of humble dependence, this magic word might serve to segregate the most powerful, the oldest, and the most highly regarded families. 'Are there no more nobles in the kingdom?' asked the 'magnates' of West Francia, according to the chronicler, when they saw Charles the Simple relying wholly on the counsels of his favourite Hagano.[2] Now this upstart, humble as was his origin in comparison with the great dynasties of counts, was certainly not of lower social rank than the

[1] Hariulf, *Chronique*, ed. Lot, p. 308; cf. p. 300; *Monumenta boica*, vol. XXVIII, 2, p. 27, no. XVII.
[2] Richer, *Histoires*, I, c. 15.

household warriors to whom Saint-Riquier opened its *capella nobilium*. But did the epithet at that time ever suggest anything other than a relative superiority? It is significant that it is frequently to be found employed in the comparative: *nobilior*, 'more noble' than one's neighbour.

Nevertheless, in the course of the first feudal age, the word gradually lost its humbler uses and tended more and more to be reserved for those groups of powerful men who had been able to acquire a growing dominance in society as a result of the breakdown of government and the general extension of protective ties. In this sense the word was still loosely used, without any precise definition of status or caste; but not without a very strong sense of the supremacy of the rank so described. Certainly the strong sense of a hierarchic order was present in the minds of those parties to a peace pact in 1023 who swore to refrain from attacking 'noble-women' —no others were mentioned.[1] In short, if the concept of nobility as a legal class remained unknown, it is quite permissible from this period, by a slight simplification of terminology, to speak of a social class of nobles and especially, perhaps, of a noble way of life. For it was principally by the nature of its wealth, by its exercise of authority, and by its social habits that this group was defined.

3 THE NOBLE CLASS A CLASS OF LORDS

This dominant class has sometimes been described as a landed class, and if by that is meant that fundamentally its members derived their revenues from their control of the soil, we may agree. From what other source could they have looked for them? Yet it must be added that, when available, tolls, market fees, and fines levied on a local trade were not the least coveted of properties. The characteristic feature was some form of exploitation. Whatever the sources of the noble's income—agricultural land or, as was much more rarely the case, shops or workshops—he always lived on the labour of other men. In other words, he was above all a manorial lord; or to put it in another way, if not every man whose way of life could be described as noble was lucky enough to possess manors—he might be a vassal maintained in the chief's household or a younger son who had adopted the wandering life of a soldier of fortune—at least all who did belonged *ipso facto* to the upper ranks of society.

Now a problem arises here—among the most difficult of all those presented by the genesis of our civilization. A certain number of seignorial families were doubtless descended from adventurers who had risen from nothing; men-at-arms who, having received a share of the chief's property, had become his enfeoffed vassals. The ancestors of others, perhaps, were among those rich peasants of whose transformation into landlords, each

---

[1] Peace oath of Beauvais in C. Pfister, *Études sur le règne de Robert le Pieux*, 1885, p. lxi.

288

with a group of tenements, we catch a glimpse in certain documents of the tenth century. But such assuredly was not the most common case. Over a large part of the West the manor, in forms originally more or less rudimentary, was very ancient, and the class of lords, however much mixed and intermixed, cannot well have been less so. Certainly we shall never know how many of the persons to whom the villeins of feudal times owed rents and labour services would have been entitled, had they been aware of it, to include in their pedigrees the shadowy figures from whom so many European villages derive their names—the Brennos of Bernay, the Cornelius of Cornigliano, the Gundolf of Gundolfsheim, the Aelfred of Alversham—or else some of those local chiefs of Germania whom Tacitus depicts as grown rich through the 'gifts' of the peasants. The link is completely missing. But it is not impossible that with the fundamental contrast between the lords of manors and the immense multitude of tenants we are in the presence of one of the most ancient lines of cleavage in Western society.

4 THE PROFESSION OF ARMS

If the possession of manors was the mark of a genuinely noble status and, along with treasure in money or jewels, the only form of wealth which seemed compatible with high rank, this was due in the first place to the authority over other men which it implied. (Could there ever be a surer basis of prestige than to be able to say: 'It is my will'?) But another reason was that the very vocation of the noble prevented him from engaging in any direct economic activity. He was committed body and soul to his particular function—that of the warrior. This fact, which is of fundamental importance, explains the rôle of the military vassals in the formation of medieval aristocracy. They did not constitute the whole of it; the owners of allodial manors, quickly assimilated by social habits to the enfeoffed vassals and sometimes more powerful than they, could hardly have been excluded. The vassal groups, nevertheless, formed the basic element in it. Here again the evolution of the Anglo-Saxon vocabulary illustrates admirably the transition from the old conception of nobility as a sacred race to the new conception of it as consisting in a mode of life. Whereas the ancient laws contrasted *eorl* and *ceorl*—the noble, in the Germanic sense of the word, and the ordinary free man—the later laws, while retaining the second of these contrasted terms, replaced the first by words such as *thegn, thegnborn, gesithcund,* meaning a companion or vassal (especially a royal vassal) or else a descendant of vassals.

It was not only vassals, of course, who had the capacity or the duty to fight; nor were they the only ones with a love of fighting in that first feudal age, when society from top to bottom was imbued with the taste for violence or the fear of it. The laws which attempted to restrict or prohibit the bearing of arms by members of the lower classes did not make their appearance before the second half of the twelfth century, and they coincided both with the progress of legal differentiation between classes and with a relative abatement of disorder. The merchant—as he appears in an ordinance of Frederick Barbarossa—was a traveller who journeyed 'with sword on saddle'; and once back at his counter he retained the habits contracted in the course of the life of adventure that was inseparable from trading in that age. At the time of the turbulent revival of urban life it could be said of many burghers, as Gilbert of Mons said of those of Saint-Trond, that they were 'right puissant in arms'. (In so far as he is not purely legendary, the traditional type of shopkeeper with his aversion to fighting belongs to the period of settled commerce, as opposed to the old nomadism of the 'dusty-footed' merchants; he dates from the thirteenth century, at the earliest.) Furthermore, small as medieval armies were, they were never recruited from the nobility alone. The lord raised his foot-soldiers among his villeins. And though from the twelfth century onwards the military obligations of the latter were increasingly curtailed, and though, in particular, the very common limitation of the duration of service to one day had the effect of restricting the employment of the rural contingents to ordinary police operations, these changes were exactly contemporaneous with the attenuation of feudal service itself. The peasant pikemen or archers were not superseded by vassals; they were rendered superfluous by the introduction of mercenaries who served at the same time to make good the deficiency of enfeoffed knights. But whether he was a vassal or even—where such still existed—an allodial lord, the 'noble' of early feudal times, in contrast with all the temporary soldiers, had the special characteristic of being a better armed warrior and a professional warrior.

He fought on horseback; and though he might on occasion dismount during the battle, he always moved about on horseback. Moreover, he fought fully equipped; his offensive weapons were the lance and the sword, occasionally the mace, while for defence he wore a helmet and a garment made wholly or partly of metal, and he carried a round or triangular shield. Strictly speaking, it was not the horse alone which made the knight; his humbler companion, the squire, whose duty it was to look after the horses and arrange the change of mounts along the road, was also mounted. Sometimes in addition to the heavy cavalry of the knights, armies included the more lightly equipped horsemen usually known as 'serjeants'. The distinguishing mark of the highest class of fighting-man was the combination of horse and complete equipment.

The improvements introduced in the warrior's equipment from the Frankish period onwards had made it more costly (and also more difficult to handle), with the result that it became less and less possible for anyone who was not a rich man—or the vassal of a rich man—to take part in this form of warfare. As the logical consequence of the adoption, about the tenth century, of the stirrup, the short spear of former days, brandished at arm's length like a javelin, was abandoned and replaced by the long and heavy lance which the warrior, in close combat, held under his armpit and, when at rest, supported on the stirrup itself.[1] To the helmet was added the nasal and later the visor. Finally, the *broigne,* a sort of garment of leather or cloth, on which were sewn iron rings or plates, gave place to the hauberk, perhaps copied from the Arabs; completely woven of metal rings, it was of much more delicate workmanship, and might have to be imported. By degrees moreover, the class monopoly, which had at first been imposed by mere practical necessity, began to pass into law. In their effort to keep their manorial officials in a state of relative inferiority, the monks of Beaulieu, shortly after 970, forbade them to carry the shield and sword; those of St. Gall, at about the same time, reproached the stewards of their estates with possessing arms of excessively fine quality.[2]

Imagine a military force of the period. It presents a dual aspect. On the one hand there is a body of infantry as ill-equipped for attack as for defence, slow in advancing to the assault and slow in flight, and quickly exhausted by long marches on wretched tracks or across-country. On the other hand, looking down from their chargers on the poor wretches who, 'shamefully' as one court romance puts it, drag their feet in the dust and mire, are stalwart soldiers, proud of being able to fight and manœuvre swiftly, skilfully, effectively—the only force, indeed, in the opinion of the Cid's biographer, which it is worth the trouble of counting when assessing the numerical strength of an army.[3] In a civilization where war was an everyday matter, there was no more vital contrast than this. The word 'knight', which had become almost synonymous with vassal, became also the equivalent of 'noble'. Conversely, more than one text in applying to the lower orders the contemptuous designation of *pedones,* 'foot-soldiers'—or rather perhaps 'foot-sloggers'—raised it almost to the status of a legal term. Among the Franks, said the Arab emir Ousâma, 'all pre-eminence belongs to the horsemen. They are in truth the only men who count. Theirs it is to give counsel; theirs to render justice.'[4]

Now is it surprising that in the eyes of generations which had good reasons for exalting force in its crudest form the fighting-man *par excellence* should have been the most feared, the most sought-after and the most respected of men? A theory at that time very widely current represented the human community as being divided into three 'orders': those who prayed, those who fought, and those who worked. It was unanimously

[1] See Plates VI and VII.

[2] Deloche, *Cartulaire de l'abbaye de Beaulieu,* no. L; *Casus S. Galli,* c. 48.

[3] Fritz Meyer, *Die Stände . . . dargestellt nach den altfr. Artus- und Abenteurromanen,* 1892, p. 115; *Poema del mio Cid,* ed. Menendez Pidal, v. 918.

[4] H. Derenbourg, *Ousâma Ibn Mounkidh,* I (*Publications École Langues Orientales,* 2ᵉ série, T. XII, 1), p. 476.

agreed that the second should be placed much higher than the third. But the evidence of the epic goes farther still, showing that the soldier had little hesitation in rating his mission even higher than that of the specialist in prayer. Pride is one of the essential ingredients of all class-consciousness. That of the 'nobles' of the feudal era was, above all, the pride of the warrior.

Moreover, fighting was for them not merely an occasional duty to be performed for the sake of their lord, or king, or family. It represented much more—their whole purpose in life.

XXII

THE LIFE OF THE NOBILITY

1 WAR

'I LOVE the gay Eastertide, which brings forth leaves and flowers; and I love the joyous songs of the birds, re-echoing through the copse. But also I love to see, amidst the meadows, tents and pavilions spread; and it gives me great joy to see, drawn up on the field, knights and horses in battle array; and it delights me when the scouts scatter people and herds in their path; and I love to see them followed by a great body of men-at-arms; and my heart is filled with gladness when I see strong castles besieged, and the stockades broken and overwhelmed, and the warriors on the bank, girt about by fosses, with a line of strong stakes, interlaced. . . . Maces, swords, helms of different hues, shields that will be riven and shattered as soon as the fight begins; and many vassals struck down together; and the horses of the dead and the wounded roving at random. And when battle is joined, let all men of good lineage think of naught but the breaking of heads and arms; for it is better to die than to be vanquished and live. I tell you, I find no such savour in food, or in wine, or in sleep, as in hearing the shout "On! On!" from both sides, and the neighing of steeds that have lost their riders, and the cries of "Help! Help!"; in seeing men great and small go down on the grass beyond the fosses; in seeing at last the dead, with the pennoned stumps of lances still in their sides.'

Thus sang, in the second half of the twelfth century, a troubadour who is probably to be identified with the petty nobleman from Périgord, Bertrand de Born.[1] The accurate observation and the fine verve, in contrast with the insipidity of what is usually a more conventional type of poetry, are the marks of an uncommon talent. The sentiment, on the other hand, is in no way extraordinary; as is shown in many another piece from the same social world, in which it is expressed, no doubt with less gusto, but with equal spontaneity. In war—'fresh and joyful war', as it has been called in our own day by someone who was not destined to see it at such close quarters—the noble loved first and foremost the display of physical strength, the strength of a splendid animal, deliberately maintained by constant exercises, begun in childhood. 'He who has stayed at school till the age of

[1] Ed. Appel, no. 40; compare, for example, *Girart de Vienne*, ed. Yeandle, v. 2108 *et seq.*

293

twelve,' says a German poet, repeating the old Carolingian proverb, 'and never ridden a horse, is only fit to be a priest.'[1] The interminable accounts of single combats which fill the epics are eloquent psychological documents. The reader of today, bored by their monotony, finds it difficult to believe that they could have afforded so much pleasure—as clearly they did—to those who listened to them in days of old; theirs was the attitude of the sedentary enthusiast to reports of sporting events. In works of imagination as well as in the chronicles, the portrait of the good knight emphasizes above all his athletic build: he is 'big-boned', 'large of limb', the body 'well-proportioned' and pitted with honourable scars; the shoulders are broad, and so is the 'fork'—as becomes a horseman. And since this strength must be sustained, the valiant knight is known for his mighty appetite. In the old *Chanson de Guillaume*, so barbarous in its tone, listen to Dame Guibourc who, after having served at the great table of the castle the young Girart, her husband's nephew, remarks to her spouse:

> *Par Deu, bel sire, cist est de de vostre lin,*
> *Et si mangue un grant braun porcin,*
> *Et a dous traitz beit un cester de vin.*
> *Ben dure guere deit il rendre a sun veisin.*[2]

> By God! fair sire! he's of your line indeed,
> Who thus devours a mighty haunch of boar
> And drinks of wine a gallon at two gulps;
> Pity the man on whom he wages war!

A supple and muscular body, however, it is almost superfluous to say, was not enough to make the ideal knight. To these qualities he must add courage as well. And it was also because it gave scope for the exercise of this virtue that war created such joy in the hearts of men for whom daring and the contempt for death were, in a sense, professional assets. It is true that this valour did not always prevent mad panics (we have seen examples of them in face of the Vikings), nor was it above resorting to crude stratagems. Nevertheless the knightly class knew how to fight—on this point, history agrees with legend. Its unquestionable heroism was nurtured by many elements: the simple physical reaction of a healthy human being; the rage of despair—it is when he feels himself 'wounded unto death' that the 'cautious' Oliver strikes such terrible blows, in order 'to avenge himself all he could'; the devotion to a chief or, in the case of the holy war, to a cause; the passionate desire for glory, personal or collective; the fatalistic acquiescence in face of ineluctable destiny, of which literature offers no more

[1] Hartmann von Aue, *Gregorius*, v, 1547–53.
[2] *La Chanson de Guillaume*, ed. D. McMillan (*Soc. des Anc. Textes Francais*), V. 1054 *et seq.*

poignant examples than some of the last cantos of the *Nibelungenlied*; finally, the hope of reward in another world, promised not only to him who died for his God, but also to him who died for his master.

Accustomed to danger, the knight found in war yet another attraction: if offered a remedy for boredom. For these men whose culture long remained rudimentary and who—apart from a few great barons and their counsellors—were seldom occupied by very heavy administrative cares, everyday life easily slipped into a grey monotony. Thus was born an appetite for diversions which, when one's native soil failed to afford the means to gratify it, sought satisfaction in distant lands. William the Conqueror, bent on exacting due service from his vassals, said of one of them, whose fiefs he had just confiscated as a punishment for his having dared to depart for the crusade in Spain without permission: 'I do not believe it would be possible to find a better knight in arms; but he is unstable and extravagant, and he spends his time gadding about from place to place.'[1] Of how many others could the same have been said! The roving disposition was especially widespread among the French. The fact was that their own country did not offer them, as did half-Moslem Spain, or, to a less degree, Germany with its Slav frontier, an arena for conquests or swift forays; nor, like Germany again, the hardships and the pleasures of the great imperial expeditions. It is also probable that the knightly class was more numerous there than elsewhere, and therefore cramped for room. In France itself it has often been observed that Normandy was of all the provinces the richest in bold adventurers. Already the German Otto of Freising spoke of the 'very restless race of the Normans'. Could it have been the legacy of Viking blood? Possibly. But it was above all the effect of the state of relative peace which, in that remarkably centralized principality, the dukes established at an early date; so that those who craved the opportunity for fighting had to seek it abroad. Flanders, where political conditions were not very different, furnished an almost equally large contingent of roving warriors.

These knights-errant—the term is a contemporary one[2]—helped the native Christians in Spain to reconquer the northern part of the peninsula from Islam; they set up the Norman states in southern Italy; even before the First Crusade they enlisted as mercenaries in the service of Byzantium and fought against its eastern foes; finally, they found in the conquest and defence of the Tomb of Christ their chosen field of action. Whether in Spain or in Syria, the holy war offered the dual attraction of an adventure and a work of piety. 'No need is there now to endure the monk's hard life in the strictest of the orders . . .' sang one of the troubadours; 'to accomplish honourable deeds and thereby at the same time to save oneself from

[1] Ordericus Vitalis, *Histoire ecclésiastique*, ed. Le Prevost, III, p. 248.
[2] *Guillaume le Maréchal*, ed. P. Meyer, vv. 2777 and 2782 (it referred to knights who frequented tournaments).

hell—what more could one wish?'[1] These migrations helped to maintain relations between societies separated from each other by great distances and sharp contrasts; they disseminated Western and especially French culture beyond its own frontiers. A case to strike the imagination is that of one Hervé 'the Francopol' who was taken prisoner by an emir in 1057 when in command on the shores of Lake Van. At the same time the blood-letting thus practised abroad by the most turbulent groups in the West saved its civilization from being extinguished by guerilla warfare. The chroniclers were well aware that at the start of a crusade the people at home in the old countries always breathed more freely, because now they could once more enjoy a little peace.[2]

Fighting, which was sometimes a legal obligation and frequently a pleasure, might also be required of the knight as a matter of honour: in the twelfth century, Périgord ran with blood because a certain lord thought that one of his noble neighbours looked like a blacksmith and had the bad taste to say so.[3] But fighting was also, and perhaps above all, a source of profit—in fact, the nobleman's chief industry.

The lyrical effusions of Bertrand de Born have been mentioned above. He himself made no secret of the less creditable reasons which above all disposed him 'to find no pleasure in peace'. 'Why', he asks, 'do I want rich men to hate each other?' 'Because a rich man is much more noble, generous and affable in war than in peace.' And more crudely: 'We are going to have some fun. For the barons will make much of us . . . and if they want us to remain with them, they will give us *barbarins*' (i.e. coin of Limoges). And again: 'Trumpet, drums, flags and pennons, standards and horses white and black—that is what we shall shortly see. And it will be a happy day; for we shall seize the usurers' goods, and no more shall beasts of burden pass along the highways by day in complete safety; nor shall the burgess journey without fear, nor the merchant on his way to France; but the man who is full of courage shall be rich.' The poet belonged to that class of petty holders of fiefs, the 'vavasours'—he so described himself—for whom life in the ancestral manor-house lacked both gaiety and comforts. War made up for these deficiencies by stimulating the liberality of the great and providing prizes worth having.

The baron, of course, out of regard for his prestige as well as his interest, could not afford to be niggardly in the matter of presents, even towards vassals summoned to his side by the strictest conventions of feudal duty. If it was desired to retain them beyond the stipulated time, to take them farther or call on them more often than an increasingly rigorous custom appeared to permit, it was necessary to give them more. Finally, in face of

---

[1] Pons de Capdeuil, in Raynouard, *Choix*, IV, pp. 89 and 92.

[2] C. Erdmann, *Die Entstehung des Kreuzzugsgedankens*, Stuttgart, 1935 (*Forschungen zur Kirchen- und Geistesgeschichte*, VI), pp. 312–13.

[3] Geoffroi de Vigeois, I, 6, in Labbé, *Bibliotheca*, II, 281.

the growing inadequacy of the vassal contingents, there was soon no army which could dispense with the assistance of that wandering body of warriors to whom adventure made so strong an appeal, provided that there was a prospect of gain as well as of mighty combats. Thus cynically, our Bertrand offered his services to the count of Poitiers: 'I can help you. I have already a shield at my neck and a helm on my head. . . . Nevertheless, how can I put myself in the field without money?'[1]

But it was undoubtedly considered that the finest gift the chief could bestow was the right to a share of the plunder. This was also the principal profit which the knight who fought on his own account in little local wars expected from his efforts. It was a double prize, moreover: men and things. It is true that the Christian code no longer allowed captives to be reduced to slavery and at most permitted a few peasants or artisans to be forcibly removed from one place to another. But the ransoming of prisoners was a general practice. A ruler as firm and prudent as William the Conqueror might indeed never release alive the enemies who fell into his hands; but most warriors were not so far-sighted. The ransoming of prisoners occasionally had more dreadful consequences than the ancient practice of enslavement. The author of the *chanson* of Girart de Roussillon, who certainly wrote from personal observation, tells us that in the evening after a battle Girart and his followers put to the sword all the humble prisoners and wounded, sparing only the 'owners of castles', who alone were in a position to buy their freedom with hard cash.[2] As to plunder, it was traditionally so regular a source of profit that in the ages accustomed to written documents the legal texts treat it as a matter of course—on this point, the barbarian codes, at the beginning of the Middle Ages, and the thirteenth-century contracts of enlistment at the end, speak with the same voice. Heavy wagons followed the armies, for the purpose of collecting the spoils of war. Most serious of all, by a series of transitions almost unnoticed by the rather simple minds of the time, forms of violent action which were sometimes legitimate—requisitions indispensable to armies without commissariat, reprisals exacted against the enemy or his subjects —degenerated into pure brigandage, brutal and mean. Merchants were robbed on the highway; sheep, cheeses, chickens were stolen from pens and farmsteads—as was done, typically, by a small Catalan landowner of the early thirteenth century bent on annoying his neighbours of the abbey of Canigou. The best of men contracted strange habits. William Marshal was certainly a valiant knight. Nevertheless when, as a young and landless man travelling through France from tourney to tourney, he encountered on the road a monk who was running away with a girl of noble family and who candidly avowed his intention of putting out to usury the money he

---

[1] Bertrand de Born, ed. Appel, 10, 2; 35, 2; 37, 3; 28, 3.
[2] Guibert de Nogent, *De vita*, ed. Bourgin, I, c. 13, p. 43; *Girart de Roussillon*, translated by P. Meyer, p. 42.

was carrying, William did not scruple to rob the poor devil of his cash, under the pretext of punishing him for his evil designs. One of his companions even reproached him for not having seized the horse as well.[1]

Such practices reveal a signal indifference to human life and suffering. War in the feudal age was in no sense war in kid gloves. It was accompanied by actions which seem to us today anything but chivalrous; as for instance—a frequent occurrence, sometimes even in disregard of a solemn oath—the massacre or mutilation of garrisons which had held out 'too long'. It involved, as a natural concomitant, the devastation of the enemy's estates. Here and there a poet, like the author of *Huon of Bordeaux*, and later a pious king like St. Louis protested in vain against this 'wasting' of the countryside which brought such appalling miseries upon the innocent. The epics, the German as well as the French, are faithful interpreters of real life, and they show us a whole succession of 'smoking' villages. 'There can be no real war without fire and blood,' said the plain-spoken Bertrand de Born.[2]

In two passages exhibiting striking parallels, the poet of *Girart de Roussillon* and the anonymous biographer of the Emperor Henry IV show us what the return of peace meant for the 'poor knights': the disdainful indifference of the great, who would have no more need of them; the importunities of money-lenders; the heavy plough-horse instead of the mettlesome charger; iron spurs instead of gold—in short an economic crisis as well as a disastrous loss of prestige.[3] For the merchant and the peasant, on the contrary, peace meant that it was possible once again to work, to gain a livelihood—in short, to live. Let us appeal once more to the evidence of the observant *trouvère* of *Girart de Roussillon*. Outlawed and repentant, Girart with his wife wanders through the countryside. They meet some merchants, and the duchess thinks it prudent to make them believe that the exile whose features they think they recognize is no more. 'Girart is dead; I saw him buried.' 'God be praised,' the merchants reply, 'for he was always making war and through him we have suffered many ills.' At these words, Girart's brow darkened; if he had had his sword 'he would have smitten one of them'. It is a story based on actual experience and illustrates the fundamental hostility which separated the classes. It cuts both ways. For the knight, proud of his courage and skill, despised the unwarlike (*imbellis*) people—the villeins who in face of the armies scampered away 'like deer', and later on the townsmen, whose economic power

---

[1] For booty, see for example *Codex Euricianus*, c. 323; Marlot, *Histoire de l'église de Reims*, III (documents), no. LXVII (1127); For the wagons, *Garin le Lorrain*, ed. P. Paris, I, pp. 195 and 197; For the complaints of the monks of Canigou, Luchaire, *La société française au temps de Philippe Auguste*, 1909, p. 265.

[2] *Huon de Bordeaux*, ed. F. Guessard, p. 41, vv. 1353–4; Louis IX, *Enseignemens*, c. 23, in C. V. Langlois, *La vie spirituelle*, p. 40; Bertrand de Born, 26, v. 15.

[3] *Girart de Roussillon*, translated P. Meyer, §§ 633 and 637; *Vita Heinrici*, ed. W. Eberhard, c. 8.

seemed to him so much the more hateful in that it was obtained by means which were at once mysterious and directly opposed to his own activities. If the propensity to bloody deeds was prevalent everywhere—more than one abbot indeed met his death as the victim of a cloister feud—it was the conception of the necessity of war, as a source of honour and as a means of livelihood, that set apart the little group of 'noble' folk from the rest of society.

2 THE NOBLE AT HOME

Favourite sport though it was, war had its dead seasons; but at these times the knightly class was distinguished from its neighbours by a manner of life which was essentially that of a nobility.

We should not think of this mode of existence as having invariably a rural setting. Italy, Provence and Languedoc still bore the age-old imprint of the Mediterranean civilizations whose structure had been systematized by Rome. In those regions, each small community was traditionally grouped round a town or large village which was at one and the same time an administrative centre, a market, and a place of refuge; and consequently the normal place of residence of the powerful. These people continued as much as ever to inhabit the old urban centres; and they took part in all their revolutions. In the thirteenth century, this civic character was regarded as one of the distinctive traits of the southern nobility. In contrast with Italy, said the Franciscan Salimbene, a native of Parma, who visited the kingdom of St. Louis, the towns of France are inhabited only by burgesses; the nobility live on their estates. But, though true in general of the period in which the good friar was writing, the contrast would not have been equally true of the first feudal age. Undoubtedly in the purely merchant cities which, especially in the Low Countries and trans-Rhenish Germany, came into being almost entirely from the tenth or the eleventh century onwards—Ghent, Bruges, Soest, Lübeck and so many others— the dominant caste was almost invariably composed of men grown rich through trade; though where there was a governor of princely rank a small body of vassals was sometimes maintained, consisting of unenfeoffed knights or those who came regularly to perform their turn of duty. In the old Roman cities such as Rheims or Tournai, on the other hand, groups of knights seem to have resided over a long period, many of them no doubt attached to the courts of bishops or abbots. It was only gradually and in consequence of a more pronounced differentiation of classes that knightly society, outside Italy and southern France, became almost entirely divorced from the urban populations properly so called. Although the noble certainly did not cease altogether to visit the town, he henceforth went there only occasionally, in pursuit of pleasure or for the exercise of certain functions.

Everything tended to induce him to live in the country. First, there was the habit, which was becoming more and more widespread, of remunerating vassals by means of fiefs, consisting in the vast majority of cases of rural manors; then there was the weakening of feudal obligations, which favoured the tendency among the retainers who had now been provided with fiefs to live each in his own home, far from the kings, the great barons, and the bishops, who controlled the towns; finally, a taste for the open air, natural to these sportsmen, played its part. There is a moving story, told by a German monk, of a count's son who had been dedicated by his family to the monastic life; on the day when he was first subjected to the harsh rule of claustration, he climbed up to the highest tower of the monastery, in order 'at least to feast his vagrant soul on the spectacle of the hills and fields where he might no longer roam'.[1] The pressure of the burghers, who had very little desire to admit into their communities elements indifferent to their activities and their interests, accelerated the movement.

Thus whatever modifications it may be necessary to introduce into the picture of a nobility exclusively rural from the outset, it remains true that, ever since knights existed, a growing majority of them in the North and many even in the coastal regions of the Mediterranean ordinarily resided in a country mansion.

The manor-house usually stood in the midst of a cluster of dwellings, or nearby; sometimes there were several in the same village. The manor-house was sharply distinguished from the surrounding cottages, just as it was in the towns from the habitations of the poor—not only because it was better built, but above all because it was almost invariably designed for defence. The desire of the rich to protect their dwellings from attack was naturally as old as the social disorders themselves; witness those fortified *villae* whose appearance about the fourth century bears witness to the decline of the Roman peace. The tradition may have continued here and there in the Frankish period, but most of the 'courts' inhabited by rich proprietors and even royal palaces themselves long remained almost without permanent means of defence. It was the invasions of the Northmen or the Hungarians which, from the Adriatic to the plains of northern England, led not only to the repair or rebuilding of town ramparts, but also to the erection on every hand of the rural strongholds (*fertés*) which were destined to cast a perpetual shadow over the fields of Europe. Internal wars soon added to their number. The rôle of the great potentates, kings or princes, in this prolific building of castles, and their efforts to control it, will be dealt with later; for the present they need not detain us. For the fortified houses of the petty lords, scattered over hill and dale, had almost always been constructed without any authorization from above. They answered elementary needs, spontaneously felt and satisfied. A hagiographer has given a very exact account of them, although in an unsympathetic spirit: 'their purpose was to enable these men, constantly occupied with quarrels

[1] *Casus S. Galli*, c. 43.

and massacres, to protect themselves from their enemies, to triumph over their equals, to oppress their inferiors';[1] in short, to defend themselves and dominate others.

These edifices were generally of a very simple type. For a long time the most common, at least outside the Mediterranean regions, was the wooden tower. A curious passage of the *Miracles of St. Benedict* describes, towards the end of the eleventh century, the extremely primitive arrangement of one of these castles. On the first floor there was a large room where the 'powerful man . . . together with his household, lived, conversed, ate, slept'; on the ground floor there was a storeroom for provisions.[2] Normally, a ditch was dug at the foot. Sometimes, at a little distance from the tower, there was a stockade or a rampart of beaten earth, surrounded in its turn by another ditch. This enclosure provided a place of safety for various domestic buildings and for the cook-house, which it was considered wise to place away from the tower on account of the risk of fire; it served at need as a refuge for the dependants; it prevented an immediate assault on the main building and obstructed the most effective method of attack, which was to set fire to it.[3] Tower and stockade frequently stood on a mound (*motte*), sometimes natural, sometimes—at least in part—man-made. Its purpose was twofold: to confront the attackers with the obstacle of the slope and to gain a better view of the surrounding country. But to garrison even one of these primitive wooden castles required more armed retainers than the ordinary run of knights could maintain. It was the great men who first had recourse to stone as a building-material; those 'rich men that build in stone', whom Bertrand de Born depicts amusing themselves by making 'from lime, sand and freestone . . . gateways and turrets, vaults and spiral staircases'.[4] It was adopted only slowly, in the course of the twelfth century or even the thirteenth, for the houses of knights of lesser and middle rank. Before the completion of the great clearings, the forests seem to have been easier and less expensive to exploit than the quarries; and while masonry called for specialist workers, the tenants, a permanent source of compulsory labour, were almost all to some extent carpenters as well as wood-cutters.

There is no doubt that for the peasant his lord's little fortress sometimes provided a defence and a refuge. Contemporary opinion had nevertheless good reasons for regarding it as, above all, a dangerous haunt. For those concerned to keep the peace, for the townsmen, interested in preserving freedom of communications, for the kings or princes, there was to be no more urgent task than that of razing to the ground the countless castles with which so many petty local tyrants had covered the plains. And,

[1] *Vita Johannis ep. Teruanensis*, c. 12, in *M.G.H.*, *Scriptores*, vol. XIV, 2, p. 1146.
[2] *Miracula S. Benedicti*, ed. Certain, VIII, c. 16.
[3] See Plate VIII.
[4] See Plate IX.

whatever may have been said on this subject, it was not only in the novels of Mrs. Radcliffe that castles, whether large or small, had their *oubliettes*. Lambert of Ardres, describing the fortress of Tournehem, rebuilt in the twelfth century, did not forget the deep dungeons 'where the prisoners, amidst darkness, vermin and ordure, ate the bread of sorrow'.

As is indicated by the very nature of his dwelling, the knight lived in a state of perpetual watchfulness. A lookout man, a familiar figure in the epic as well as in lyric poetry, kept his nightly watch on the summit of the tower. Lower down, in the two or three rooms of the cramped fortress, a whole little world of permanent residents, with an admixture of transient guests, lived together in conditions that admitted of no privacy. Partly, no doubt, this was due to lack of space, but it was also the result of habits which in that age seemed inseparable from the position of a chief. Day and night, the baron was surrounded by retainers—men-at-arms, menials, household vassals, young nobles committed to his care as 'nurslings'—who served him, guarded him, conversed with him and who, when the hour of sleep at last arrived, continued to keep faithful watch over him even when he was in bed with his wife. 'It is not seemly that a lord should eat alone' was an opinion still held in thirteenth-century England.[1] In the great hall the tables were long and most of the seats were benches on which the diners sat side by side. Poor persons took up their lodging under the stair-case—where two illustrious penitents died: St. Alexis, in legend, and Count Simon de Crépy, in fact. This way of living, incompatible with any sort of private meditation, was general at this time; the monks themselves slept in dormitories, not in cells. It explains why some people chose to take refuge in the only ways of life which at that time were compatible with the enjoyment of solitude—those of the hermit, the recluse, and the wanderer. On the cultural side, it meant that among the nobles knowledge was transmitted much less by books and study than by reading aloud, the reciting of verse, and personal contacts.

3 OCCUPATIONS AND DISTRACTIONS

Though usually a countryman in the sense that his home was in the country, the noble was nevertheless no agriculturalist. To put his hand to the hoe or the plough would have been an indication that he had come down in the world—as happened to a poor knight whose history is known to us through a collection of anecdotes. And if he sometimes liked to contemplate the workers in the fields or the yellowing harvest on his estates, it does not appear that as a rule he took a very direct part in the management of the farm.[2] The manuals of estate management, when they came to be written, were intended not for the master, but for his stewards; the 'country

[1] Robert Grosseteste's *Rules* in Walter of Henley's *Husbandry*, ed. E. Lamond.
[2] Marc Bloch, *Les caractères originaux de l'histoire rurale française*, 1931, p. 148.

gentleman' belongs to quite another age—after the economic revolution in the sixteenth century. Although the rights of jurisdiction which he possessed over his tenants constituted one of the essential sources of his power, the lord of the village as a rule exercised them much less frequently in person than through the agency of bailiffs, themselves of peasant extraction. Nevertheless the exercise of judicial functions was certainly one of the few peaceful occupations of the knight. As a rule he only concerned himself with judicial duties within the framework of his class, which meant that he either settled the law-suits of his own vassals or sat as judge of his peers in the court to which he had been summoned by his feudal lord; but where public justice survived, as in England and Germany, he took his place in the court of the county or the hundred. There was enough of this activity to make the legal spirit one of the earliest cultural influences to be diffused in knightly circles.

The favourite amusements of the nobility bore the imprint of a warlike temper.

First, there was hunting. As has already been said, it was more than a sport. The people of western Europe were not yet living in surroundings from which the menace of wild beasts had been finally removed. Moreover, at a time when the flesh of cattle, inadequately fed and of poor stock, furnished only indifferent meat, much venison was eaten, especially in the homes of the rich. Since hunting thus remained an almost necessary activity, it was not altogether a class monopoly. The case of Bigorre, where it was forbidden to peasants as early as the beginning of the twelfth century, appears to be an exception.[1] Nevertheless kings, princes, and lords, each within the limits of his own authority, everywhere tended to monopolize the pursuit of game in certain reserved areas: large animals in the 'forests' (which term, originally, denoted every area thus reserved, whether wooded or not), rabbits and hares in the 'warrens'. The legal foundation of these claims is obscure; it seems as though they seldom had any save the decree of the master, and very naturally it was in a conquered country—the England of the Norman kings—that the creation of royal forests, too often at the expense of arable land, was most extensive, and their protection most stringent. Such abuses attest the strength of a taste which was very much a class characteristic; and so do the requisitions imposed on the tenants—the obligation to lodge and feed the lord's pack of hounds, and to construct hunting-boxes in the woods, at the season of the great meets. The monks of St. Gall made it a primary cause of complaint against their stewards, whom they accused of seeking to raise themselves to the ranks of nobles, that they bred dogs to pursue hares and, worse still, wolves, bears, and boars. Moreover, in order to practise the favourite sports of coursing with greyhounds and hawking, which—among other contributions—had been transmitted to the West by the equestrian societies of the Asiatic plains,

[1] *Fors de Bigorre*, c. XIII.

303

wealth, leisure and dependants were necessary. Of more than one knight it could have been said, as was said of a count of Guines by the biographer of his house, that 'he set greater store by a goshawk beating the air with its wings than by a preaching priest', or, in the naive and charming words which a minstrel puts into the mouth of one of his characters, as he sees the murdered hero surrounded by the howling pack: 'A nobleman he was; greatly did his hounds love him.'[1] By bringing these warriors closer to nature, the chase awakened in them a form of sensibility which otherwise they would doubtless have lacked. If they had not been brought up by the tradition of their class 'to know the wood and the river's edge', would the poets of knightly rank, who were to contribute so much to the French lyric and the German *Minnesang*, have found notes so true to sing the dawn or the joys of the month of May?

Then there were the tournaments. In the Middle Ages the tournament was generally thought to be of relatively recent origin, and the name of its supposed inventor was even mentioned—a certain Geoffroy de Preuilly, said to have died in 1066. In reality the practice of these make-believe combats undoubtedly dates back to the remotest times: witness the 'pagan games', sometimes fatal, mentioned in 895 by the council of Tribur. The custom was continued, among the people, at certain feasts—Christianized rather than Christian—as for example those other 'pagan games' (the recurrence of the word is significant) in 1077, during which the son of a cobbler of Vendôme, who was taking part in them with other young people, was mortally wounded.[2] The contests of young men are an almost universal feature of folklore. In the armies, moreover, the imitation of war at all times provided a training for troops as well as a pastime. During the celebrated interview which the 'Oaths of Strasbourg' made famous, Charles the Bald and Lewis the German diverted themselves with a spectacle of this kind, and did not disdain to participate actively. The distinctive contribution of the feudal age was to evolve from these contests, whether military or popular, a type of mock battle at which prizes were generally offered, confined to mounted combatants equipped with knightly arms; and hence to create a distinctive class amusement, which the nobility found more exciting than any other.

Since these meetings, which could not be organized without considerable expense, usually took place on the occasion of the great 'courts' held from time to time by kings or barons, enthusiasts roamed the world from tournament to tournament. These were not only poor knights, sometimes grouped in 'companies', but also very great lords, such as the count of Hainault, Baldwin IV, or among the English princes, Henry, the 'Young King', who however scarcely distinguished himself in the lists. As in our

---

[1] Lambert of Ardres, *Chronique*, c. LXXXVIII; *Garin le Lorrain*, ed. P. Paris, II, p. 244.

[2] C. Métais, *Cartulaire de l'abbaye . . . de la Trinité de Vendôme*, I, no. CCLXI.

present-day sporting events, the opponents were normally grouped by regions; a great scandal arose one day at a tournament near Gournay when the men of Hainault took the side of the men of France proper, instead of joining the Flemings and the men of Vermandois, who were, in this sphere at least, their normal allies. There can be no doubt that these games helped to establish provincial solidarities. So much was this the case that it was not always a question of make-believe battle: far from it. Wounds were not uncommon, nor even mortal blows when—to borrow the words of the poet of *Raoul de Cambrai*—the jousting 'took an ill turn'. This explains why the wisest sovereigns frowned upon these frolics, in which the blood of vassals was drained away. The Plantagenet Henry II formally prohibited them in England. For the same reason—and also on account of their connection with the revels at popular feasts, which savoured of 'paganism' —the Church rigorously forbade them, going to the length of refusing burial in consecrated ground to the knight who had met his death in this way, even if he had repented. The fact that, in spite of legislation by lay and ecclesiastical authorities, the practice could not be eradicated shows how deep was the need that it satisfied.

Nevertheless, the passion for tournaments, as for genuine warfare, was not always disinterested. Since the victor frequently took possession of the equipment and horses of the vanquished and sometimes even of his person, releasing him only on payment of a ransom, skill and strength were profitable assets. More than one jousting knight made a profession, and a very lucrative one, out of his skill in combat. Thus the love of arms inextricably combined the ingredients of 'joy' and the appetite for gain.[1]

4 RULES OF CONDUCT

It was natural that a class so clearly defined by its mode of life and its social supremacy should eventually devise a code of conduct peculiar to itself. But it was only during the second feudal age, which was in every sense the age of awakening self-consciousness, that these rules assumed a precise form and, along with it, a more refined character.

The term which, from about the year 1100, commonly served to describe the sum of noble qualities was the characteristic word 'courtesy' (*courtoisie*), which is derived from *cour* (at that time written and pronounced, as in English today, with a final 't'). It was in fact in the assemblies, temporary or permanent, which were formed round the principal barons and the kings, that these laws of conduct came to be evolved; the isolation of the knight in his 'tower' would not have permitted their development. Emulation and social contacts were necessary, and that is why this advance in moral

[1] On tournaments, in addition to the works listed in the Bibliography, see Waitz, *Deutsche Verfassungsgeschichte*, V, 2nd ed., p. 456; *Guillaume le Maréchal*, ed. P. Meyer, III, p. xxxvi *et seq*; Gislebert of Mons, *Chronique*, ed. Pertz, pp. 92–3; 96; 102; 109–10; 128–30; 144; *Raoul de Cambrai*, v. 547.

sensibility was bound up both with the consolidation of the great principalities or monarchies and with the restoration of a greater degree of
intercommunication. Another term was *prudhomme*, and as 'courteous'
(*courtois*) gradually acquired a more commonplace meaning, this word was
used more and more frequently to denote something higher: a name so
great and so good that merely to pronounce it 'fills the mouth', declared
St. Louis, intending thereby to vindicate the secular virtues as against
those of the monk. Here again the semantic evolution is extremely instructive. For *prudhomme* is in fact the same word as *preux* which, having
departed from its first rather vague sense of 'useful' or 'excellent', was later
applied above all to warlike valour. The two terms diverged—*preux* keeping its traditional meaning—when it began to be felt that strength and
courage were not enough to make the perfect knight. 'There is a great
difference between the *homme preux* and the *prudhomme*,' Philip Augustus
is said to have remarked one day; he regarded the second as much the
superior of the two.[1] This might seem like hair-splitting; but if we go to the
root of the matter it is a precious piece of evidence on the evolution of the
knightly ideal.

Whether it was a question of ordinary usages of decorum or of moral
precepts properly so called, of *courtoisie* in the strict sense, or of *prudhommie*, the new code was unquestionably born in the courts of France and
in those of the Meuse region, which were completely French in language
and manners. As early as the eleventh century French manners were being
imitated in Italy.[2] In the next two centuries, these influences became still
more pronounced; witness the vocabulary of the German knightly class,
full of 'alien' words, which had come in as a rule via Hainault, Brabant or
Flanders. *Höflich* itself is only an imitation of *courtois*, courteous. More
than one young German-speaking noble came to learn the rules, as well as
the language, of good taste at the courts of the French princes. Does not the
poet Wolfram von Eschenbach call France 'the land of well-conducted
chivalry'? This dissemination of an aristocratic form of culture was only
one feature of the influence exercised at that time throughout Europe—
chiefly, it goes without saying, among the upper classes—by French
culture as a whole; others were the propagation of artistic and literary
ideals; the prestige of the schools of Chartres, and later of Paris; and the
virtually international use of the French language. And doubtless it is not
impossible to find reasons for this: the long expeditions through the West
carried out by the most adventurous chivalry in Europe; the relative
prosperity of a country affected much earlier than Germany (though not,
indeed, than Italy) by the development of trade; the distinction, emphasized
at a very early date, between the knightly class and the unwarlike rabble;
the absence, despite so many local wars, of any internal conflicts com-

[1] Joinville, c. CIX.
[2] Rangerius, *Vita Anselmi* in *M.G.H.*, *Scriptores*, XXX, 2, p. 1252, v. 1451.

VI. FIGHTING WITH THE LANCE: THE OLD STYLE AND THE NEW

The Battle of Hastings: the Norman knights advance to the attack, some using the lance as a javelin, others handling it in the new manner. Bayeux Tapestry, end of the 11th century.

VII. FIGHTING WITH THE LANCE: THE NEW STYLE

Frieze of west façade of Angoulême Cathedral, first third of the 12th century.

parable with those which resulted within the Empire from the great quarrels of emperors and popes. But this having been said, we may well ask ourselves if it is not futile to attempt to explain something which, in the present state of our knowledge of man, seems to be beyond our understanding—the ethos of a civilization and its power of attraction.

'We shall yet talk of this day in ladies' chambers,' said the count of Soissons, at the battle of Mansurah.[1] This remark, the equivalent of which it would be impossible to find in the *chansons de geste*, but which might have been heard on the lips of more than one hero of courtly romance as early as the twelfth century, is characteristic of a society in which sophistication has made its appearance and, with it, the influence of women. The noblewoman had never been confined within her own secluded quarters. Surrounded with servants, she ruled her household, and she might also rule the fief—perhaps with a rod of iron. It was nevertheless reserved for the twelfth century to create the type of the cultivated great lady who holds a salon. This marks a profound change, when we consider the extraordinary coarseness of the attitude usually ascribed by the old epic poets to their heroes in their relations with women, even with queens —not stopping at the grossest insults, which the lady requites with blows. One can hear the guffaws of the audience. The courtly public had not lost their taste for this heavy humour; but they now allowed it only—as in the *fabliaux*—at the expense of the peasants or the bourgeoisie. For courtesy was essentially an affair of class. The boudoir of the high-born lady and, more generally, the court, was henceforth the place where the knight sought to outshine and to eclipse his rivals not only by his reputation for great deeds of valour, but also by his regard for good manners and by his literary talents.

As we have seen, the nobility had never been completely illiterate; still less had it been impervious to the influence of literature, though this was listened to rather than read. But a great step forward was taken when knights themselves became literary men. It is significant that the *genre* to which they devoted themselves almost exclusively up to the thirteenth century was lyric poetry. The earliest of the troubadours known to us—it should be added that he was certainly not the first—ranked among the most powerful princes in France. This was William IX of Aquitaine (d. 1127). In the list of Provençal singers who followed him, as also a little later among their rivals, the lyric poets of the North, all ranks of the knighthood were abundantly represented—leaving aside, of course, the professional minstrels kept by the great. These short pieces, which were generally characterized by an intricate technique—sometimes amounting to deliberate hermeticism, the famous 'close' style (*trobar clus*)—were admirably suited for recital in aristocratic gatherings. The fact that the nobility was thus able to savour and to find genuine enjoyment in pleasures

---

[1] Joinville, c. XLIX.

too refined to be appreciated by villeins naturally reinforced its sense of superiority. As the poems were usually set off by singing and instrumental accompaniment the charm of music was wedded to the charm of words, and exercised an equally potent influence. William Marshal, who had been so tough a fighter, on his deathbed, longing, but not daring, to sing himself, would not say farewell to his daughters till they had allowed him to hear for the last time the 'sweet sound' of some *rotrouenges*.[1] And it was while listening to Volker's fiddle in the calm night, that the Burgundian heroes of the *Nibelungenlied* fell into what was to be their last sleep.

Towards the pleasures of the flesh the attitude of the knightly class appears to have been frankly realistic. It was the attitude of the age as a whole. The Church imposed ascetic standards on its members and required laymen to restrict sexual intercourse to marriage and the purpose of procreation. But it did not practise its own precepts very effectively, and this was especially true of the secular clergy, among whom even the Gregorian reform purified the lives of few but the episcopate. Significantly, we are told with admiration of pious persons, parish priests, nay even abbots, of whom 'it is said' that they died virgins. The example of the clergy proves how repugnant continence was to the majority of men: it was certainly not calculated to inspire it in the faithful. As a matter of fact—if we exclude such intentionally comic episodes as Oliver's boasting about his virility in the *Pèlerinage de Charlemagne*—the tone of the epics is fairly chaste. This was because their authors did not attach great importance to describing goings-on which had in fact no epic quality. Even in the less reticent narratives of the age of 'courtesy', libertinism is commonly represented as something for which the womenfolk rather than the heroes are responsible. Here and there nevertheless a characteristic touch gives a hint of the truth —as in the old poem of *Girart de Roussillon* where we find a vassal, who is required to give hospitality to a messenger, providing him with a beautiful girl for the night. And doubtless those 'delightsome' encounters were not wholly fictitious which, according to the romances, the castles so happily facilitated.[2]

The evidence of history is clearer still. The noble's marriage, as we know, was often an ordinary business transaction, and the houses of the nobility swarmed with bastards. At first sight, the advent of 'courtesy' does not seem to have effected any great change in these morals. Certain of the songs of William of Aquitaine sing the praises of sensual pleasure in barrack-room style and this attitude was to find more than one imitator among the poets who succeeded him. Nevertheless, with William, who was apparently the heir of a tradition whose origins elude us, another conception of love

---

[1] [A *rotrouenge* was a type of song with a refrain, composed by the *trouvères*.]

[2] *Girart de Roussillon*, translated P. Meyer, S. 257 and 299. Cf. *La Mort de Garin*, ed. E. du Méril, p. xl. And see, among others, the delicately voluptuous scene in *Lancelot*, ed. Sommer, *The Vulgate Version of the Arthurian Romances*, III, p. 383.

was already emerging—that 'courtly' love, which was certainly one of the most curious products of the moral code of chivalry. Can we conceive of Don Quixote without Dulcinea?

The characteristic features of courtly love can be summarized fairly simply. It had nothing to do with marriage, or rather it was directly opposed to the legal state of marriage, since the beloved was as a rule a married woman and the lover was never her husband. This love was often bestowed upon a lady of higher rank, but in any case it always involved a strong emphasis on the man's adoration of the woman. It professed to be an all-engrossing passion, constantly frustrated, easily jealous, and nourished by its own difficulties; but its stereotyped development early acquired something of a ritual character. It was not averse to casuistry. Finally, as the troubadour Geoffrey Rudel said, in a poem which, wrongly interpreted, gave rise to the famous legend of Princess Far-away, it was, ideally, a 'distant' love. It did not indeed reject carnal intercourse on principle, nor according to Andrew the Chaplain, who discoursed on the subject, did it despise minor physical gratifications if obliged to renounce 'the ultimate solace'. But absence or obstacles, instead of destroying it, only enriched it with a poetic melancholy. If possession, always to be desired, was seen to be quite out of the question, the sentiment none the less endured as an exciting emotion and a poignant joy.

Such is the picture drawn for us by the poets. For courtly love is only known to us through literature and for that reason it is very difficult to determine to what extent it was merely a fashionable fiction. It is certain that, though tending in some measure to dissociate sentiment from sensuality, it by no means prevented the flesh from seeking satisfaction in a more direct way; for we know that with the majority of men emotional sincerity exists on several planes. In any case we may be sure that such an idea of amorous relationships, in which today we recognize many elements with which we have now become familiar, was at first a strikingly original conception. It owed little to the ancient arts of love, or even—although they were perhaps nearer to it—to the always rather equivocal treatises which Graeco-Roman civilization devoted to the analysis of masculine friendship. In particular the humble attitude of the lover was a new thing. We have seen that it was apt to express itself in terms borrowed from the vocabulary of vassal homage; and this was not merely a matter of words. The identification of the loved one and the lord corresponded to an aspect of social morality entirely characteristic of feudal society.

Still less, in spite of what has sometimes been said, was this code dependent on religious ideas.[1] If we leave out of account a few superficial

[1] In connection with courtly love and the lyric poetry which served as its expression, the question of Arab influence has also been raised by some scholars. No conclusive proof seems so far to have been adduced. Cf. in addition to A. Jeanroy, *La poésie lyrique des troubadours*, 1934, II, p. 366, a review by G. Appel in *Zeitschrift für romanische Philologie*, LII, 1932, p. 770 (on A. R. Nykl).

analogies, which are at the most only the result of environment, we must in fact recognize that it was directly opposed to them, although its adherents had no clear consciousness of this antithesis. It made the love of man and woman almost one of the cardinal virtues, and certainly the supreme form of pleasure. Above all, even when it renounced physical satisfaction, it sublimated—to the point of making it the be-all and end-all of existence—an emotional impulse derived essentially from those carnal appetites whose legitimacy Christianity only admits in order to curb them by marriage (profoundly despised by courtly love), in order to justify them by the propagation of the species (to which courtly love gave but little thought), and in order, finally, to confine them to a secondary plane of moral experience. It is not in the knightly lyrics that we can hope to find the authentic echo of the attitude of contemporary Christianity towards sexual relations. This is expressed, quite uncompromisingly, in that passage of the pious and clerical *Queste du Saint-Graal* where Adam and Eve, before they lie together under the Tree to beget 'Abel the Just', beg the Lord to bring down upon them a great darkness to 'comfort' their shame.

The contrast between the two moralities in their treatment of this subject perhaps provides us with the key to the problem of social geography presented by these new preoccupations with romantic love. Like the lyrical poetry which has preserved them for us, they arose as early as the end of the eleventh century in the courtly circles of southern France. It was only a reflection of them which appeared a little later in the North—still in the lyrical form or through the medium of the romances—and which subsequently passed into the German *Minnesang*.

Now, it would be absurd to attempt to explain this fact by attributing some indefinable superiority to the civilization of Languedoc. Whether relating to the artistic, the intellectual or the economic sphere, the claim would be equally untenable. It would mean ignoring the French epic, Gothic art, the first efforts of philosophy in the schools between Loire and Meuse, the fairs of Champagne, and the teeming cities of Flanders. It is beyond dispute, on the other hand, that in the South the Church, especially during the first feudal age, was less rich, less cultivated, less active than in the northern provinces. No great works of clerical literature, no great movements of monastic reform emanated from that region. This relative weakness of the religious centres alone can explain the extraordinary successes achieved, from Provence to the region of Toulouse, by heresies fundamentally international; and it was also no doubt the reason why the higher ranks of the laity, being less subject to clerical influence, were relatively free to develop their own secular morality. Moreover, the fact that these precepts of courtly love were subsequently so easily propagated shows how well they served the new requirements of a class. They helped it to become aware of itself. To love in a different way from the generality of men must inevitably make one feel different from them.

That a knight should carefully calculate his booty or his ransoms and, on returning home, impose a heavy 'tallage' on his peasants provoked little or no criticism. Gain was legitimate; but on one condition—that it should be promptly and liberally expended. 'I can assure you,' said a troubadour when he was reproached for his brigandage, 'if I robbed, it was to give, not to hoard.'[1] No doubt we are entitled to regard as a little suspect the insistence with which the minstrels, those professional parasites, extolled above all other duties that of generosity, *largesse*, 'lady and queen in whose light all virtues shine'. No doubt also, among the nobles of middle or lesser rank and still more perhaps among the great barons, there were always miserly or merely prudent individuals, more inclined to amass scarce coin or jewels in their coffers than to distribute them. It is none the less true that, in squandering a fortune that was easily gained and easily lost, the noble thought to affirm his superiority over classes less confident in the future or more careful in providing for it. This praiseworthy prodigality might not always stop at generosity or even luxury. A chronicler has preserved for us the record of the remarkable competition in wasteful expenditure witnessed one day at a great 'court' held in Limousin. One knight had a plot of ground ploughed up and sown with small pieces of silver; another burned wax candles for his cooking; a third, 'through boastfulness', ordered thirty of his horses to be burnt alive.[2] What must a merchant have thought of this struggle for prestige through extravagance— which reminds us of the practices of certain primitive races? Here again different notions of honour marked the line of separation between the social groups.

Thus set apart by its power, by the nature of its wealth and its mode of life, by its very morals, the social class of nobles was toward the middle of the twelfth century quite ready to solidify into a legal and hereditary class. The ever more frequent use which from that time onwards seems to have been made of the word *gentilhomme*—man of good *gent* or lineage—to describe the members of this class is an indication of the growing importance attributed to qualities of birth. With the wide adoption of the ceremony of 'dubbing' or formal arming of the knight the legal class of nobility took definite shape.

[1] Albert de Malaspina, in C. Appel, *Provenzalische Chrestomathie*, 3rd ed., no. 90, v 19 *et seq.*
[2] Geoffroi de Vigeois, I, 69 in Labbe, *Bibliotheca*, II, p. 322.

XXIII

CHIVALRY

1 DUBBING TO KNIGHTHOOD

FROM the second half of the eleventh century, various texts, soon to become more numerous, begin to mention that here and there a ceremony has taken place for the purpose of 'making a knight'. The ritual consisted of several acts. To the candidate, who as a rule was scarcely more than a boy, an older knight first of all handed over the arms symbolic of his future status; in particular, he girded on his sword.[1] Then, almost invariably, this sponsor administered a heavy blow with the flat of his hand on the young man's neck or cheek—the *paumée* or *colée*, as the French documents term it. Was it a test of strength? Or was it—as was held by some rather late medieval interpreters—a method of making an impression on the memory, so that, in the words of Ramon Lull, the young man would remember his 'promise' for the rest of his life? The poems do indeed often show the hero trying not to give way under this rude buffet—the only one, as a chronicler remarks, which a knight must always receive and not return;[2] on the other hand, as we have seen, a box on the ear was one of the commonest methods, sanctioned by the legal customs of the time, of ensuring the recollection of certain legal acts—though it is true that it was inflicted on the witnesses and not on the parties themselves. But a very different and much less purely rational meaning seems at first to have attached to the gesture of 'dubbing' (the word was derived from an old Germanic verb meaning 'to strike'), originally considered so essential to the making of a knight that the term came to be used habitually to describe the whole ceremony. The contact thus established between the hand of the one who struck the blow and the body of the one who received it transmitted a sort of impulse—in exactly the same way as the blow bestowed by the bishop on the clerk whom he is ordaining priest. The ceremony often ended with an athletic display. The new knight leapt on his horse and proceeded to transfix or demolish with a stroke of his lance a suit of armour attached to a post; this was known as the *quintaine*.

[1] See Plate X.
[2] Raimon Lull, *Libro de la orden de Caballeria*, ed. J. R. de Luanco, Barcelona, R. Academia de Buenos Letras, 1901, **IV**, 11. English translation: *The Book of the Ordre of Chivalry trans. and printed by W. Caxton*, ed. Byles, 1926 (Early English Text Society).

By its origins and by its nature dubbing to knighthood is clearly connected with those initiation ceremonies of which primitive societies, as
well as those of the ancient world, furnish many examples—practices
which, under different forms, all had the common object of admitting the
young man to full membership of the group, from which his youth had
hitherto excluded him. Among the Germans they reflected a warlike
society. Without prejudice to certain other features—such as the cutting
of the hair, which was sometimes found later, in England, in association
with dubbing—they consisted essentially in a delivery of arms. This is
described by Tacitus and its persistence at the period of the invasion is
attested by many texts. There can be no doubt as to the continuity between
the Germanic ritual and the ritual of chivalry. But in changing its setting
the act had also changed its social significance.

Among the Germans all free men were warriors. All had therefore the
right to initiation by arms wherever this practice was an essential part of
the tradition of the folk (we do not know if it was universal). On the other
hand, one of the characteristics of feudal society was, as we know, the
formation of a group of professional fighting-men, consisting primarily of
the military vassals and their chiefs. The performance of the ancient
ceremony naturally became restricted to this military class; and in consequence it came near to losing any kind of permanent social foundation.
It had been the rite which admitted a man to membership of the people.
But the people in the ancient sense—the small *civitas* of free men—no
longer existed; and the ceremony began to be used as the rite which admitted a man to membership of a class, although this class still lacked any
clear outline. In some places the usage simply disappeared; such seems to
have been the case among the Anglo-Saxons. But in the countries where
Frankish custom prevailed it survived, though for a long time it was not
in general use or in any way obligatory.

Later, as knightly society became more clearly aware of what separated
it from the unwarlike multitude and raised it above them, there developed
a more urgent sense of the need for a formal act to mark the individual's
entry into the society so defined, whether the new member was a young
man of 'noble' birth who was being admitted into adult society, or—as
happened much more rarely—some fortunate upstart placed on a level
with men of ancient lineage by recently acquired power, or merely by
his own strength or skill. In Normandy, as early as the end of the eleventh
century, to say of the son of a great vassal: 'He is not a knight', was tantamount to implying that he was still a child or an adolescent.[1]

Undoubtedly the concern thus to symbolize every change of legal status
as well as every contract by a visible gesture conformed to characteristic
tendencies in medieval society—as witness the frequently picturesque ritual
of entry into the craft gilds. It was necessary, however, that the change of

[1] Haskins, *Norman Institutions*, 1918, p. 282, c. 5.

status thus symbolized should be clearly recognized as such, which is why the general adoption of the ceremony of dubbing really reflected a profound modification in the idea of knighthood.

During the first feudal age, what was implied by the term *chevalier*, knight, was primarily a status determined either by a *de facto* situation or by a legal tie, the criterion being purely personal. A man was called *chevalier* because he fought *à cheval*, on horseback, with full equipment; he was called the *chevalier* of someone when he held a fief of that person, on condition of serving him armed in this fashion. The time came, however, when neither the possession of a fief nor the criterion—necessarily a somewhat vague one—of mode of life was any longer sufficient to earn the title; a sort of consecration was necessary as well. The transformation was completed towards the middle of the twelfth century. A turn of phrase in use even before 1100 will help us to grasp its significance. A knight was not merely 'made'; he was 'ordained'. This was how it was put, for example, in 1098 by the count of Ponthieu as he was about to arm the future Louis VI.[1] The whole body of dubbed knights constituted an 'order', *ordo*. These are learned words, ecclesiastical words, but we find them from the beginning on the lips of laymen. They were by no means intended—at least when they were first used—to suggest an assimilation with holy orders. In the vocabulary which Christian writers had borrowed from Roman antiquity, an *ordo* was a division of society, temporal as well as ecclesiastical. But it was a regular, clearly defined division, conformable to the divine plan,—an institution, really, and not merely a plain fact.

Nevertheless, in a society accustomed to live under the sign of the supernatural, the rite of the delivery of arms, at first purely secular, could scarcely have failed to acquire a sacred character and two usages, both of them very old, gave openings for the intervention of the Church.

In the first place there was the blessing of the sword. Originally it had had no specific connection with the dubbing. Everything in the service of man seemed in that age to call for this protection from the snares of the Devil. The peasant obtained a blessing for his crops, his herd, his well; the bridegroom, for the marriage bed; the pilgrim, for his staff. The warrior naturally did the same for the tools of his profession. The oath 'on consecrated arms' was already known to the old Lombard law.[2] But most of all the arms with which the young warrior was equipped for the first time seemed to call for such sanctification. The essential feature was a rite of contact. The future knight laid his sword for a moment on the altar. This gesture was accompanied or followed by prayers, and though these were inspired

---

[1] *Rec. des Histor. de France*, XV, p. 187.

[2] *Ed. Rothari*, c. 359. Insufficient research has hitherto been devoted to the liturgy of dubbing to knighthood. In the bibliography will be found an indication of the works and collections which I have consulted. This first attempt at classification, rudimentary though it is, was only made possible for me by the kind assistance of my Strasbourg colleague, Abbé Michel Andrieu.

by the general form of benediction, they early took on a form specially appropriate to an investiture. In this form they appeared already, shortly after 950, in a pontifical compiled in the abbey of St. Alban of Mainz. This compilation, a substantial part of which was doubtless based on borrowings from older sources, was soon in use throughout Germany, as well as in northern France, England, and even Rome itself, where it was imposed by the influence of the Ottonian court. It diffused far and wide the model of benediction for the 'newly-girt' sword. It should be understood, however, that this consecration at first constituted only a sort of preface to the ceremony. The dubbing proceeded afterwards according to its peculiar forms.

Here again, however, the Church was able to play its part. Originally the task of arming the adolescent could as a rule be performed only by a knight already confirmed in that status—his father, for example, or his lord; but it might also be entrusted to a prelate. As early as 846, Pope Sergius had girded the baldric on the Carolingian Louis II. Similarly, William the Conqueror later had one of his sons dubbed by the archbishop of Canterbury. No doubt this compliment was paid less to the priest as such than to the prince of the Church, chief of many vassals. Nevertheless, a pope or a bishop could scarcely dispense with religious ceremonial. In this way, the liturgy was enabled to permeate the whole ceremony of dubbing.

This process was completed by the eleventh century. It is true that a pontifical of Besançon composed at this time contains only two benedictions of the sword, both of them very simple. But from the second of these it emerges very clearly that the officiating priest was supposed to do the arming himself. Nevertheless, to find a genuine religious ritual of dubbing, we must look farther north, towards the region between Seine and Meuse which was the true cradle of most authentic feudal institutions. Our oldest piece of evidence here is a pontifical of the province of Rheims, compiled towards the beginning of the century by a cleric who, while taking the Mainz collection as his model, none the less drew abundantly on local usages. Together with a benediction of the sword, which reproduces that in the Rhenish original, the liturgy comprises similar prayers for the other arms or insignia—banner, lance, shield, with the single exception of the spurs, the delivery of which was to the end reserved for laymen. Next follows a benediction upon the future knight himself, and finally it is expressly mentioned that the sword will be girded on by the bishop. After an interval of nearly two centuries, the ceremonial appears in a fully developed form, once again in France, in the pontifical of the bishop of Mende, William Durand, which was compiled about 1295, though its essential elements apparently date from the reign of St. Louis. Here the consecratory rôle of the prelate is carried to the ultimate limit. He now not only girds on the sword; he also gives the *paumée*; in the words of the text, he 'marks' the aspirant 'with the character of knighthood'. Adopted in the fourteenth century by the Roman pontifical, this form was destined to become the official rite of Christendom. As to the accessory practices—the purifying bath, imitated from that taken by catechumens, and the vigil of arms—these do not appear to have been introduced before the twelfth century or ever to have been anything but exceptional. Moreover, the vigil was not always devoted entirely to pious meditations. If we are to believe a poem of Beaumanoir, it was not unknown for it to be whiled away to the sound of fiddles.[1]

Nevertheless, it would be a mistake to suppose that any of this religious symbolism was ever indispensable to the making of a knight, if only because circumstances would often have prevented it from being carried out. At all times knights might be made on the field, before or after the battle; witness the accolade (*colée*)—performed with the sword, according to late medieval practice—which Bayard bestowed on his king after Marignano. In 1213, Simon de Montfort had surrounded with a religious pomp worthy of a crusading hero the dubbing of his son, whom two bishops, to the strains of *Veni Creator*, armed as a knight for the service of Christ. From the monk Pierre des Vaux-de-Cernay, who took part in it, this ceremony drew a characteristic exclamation: 'O new fashion of chivalry! Fashion unheard of till then!' The less ostentatious blessing of the sword itself, according to the evidence of John of Salisbury,[2] was not general before the middle of the twelfth century. It seems, however, to have been very widely adopted at that time. The Church, in short, had tried to transform the ancient delivery of arms into a 'sacrament'—the word, which is found in the writings of clerics, gave no offence in an age when theology was still far from having assumed a scholastic rigidity and people continued freely to lump together under the name of sacrament every kind of act of con-secration. It had not been wholly successful in this; but it had carved out a share for itself, larger in some places, more restricted in others. Its efforts, by emphasizing the importance of the rite of ordination, did much to kindle the feeling that the order of chivalry was a society of initiates. And since every Christian institution needed the sanction of a legendary calendar, hagiography came to its aid. 'When at mass the epistles of St. Paul are read,' says one liturgist, 'the knights remain standing, to do him honour, for he was a knight.'[3]

2 THE CODE OF CHIVALRY

Once the religious element had been introduced, its effects were not con-fined to strengthening the *esprit de corps* of the knightly world. It also exercised a potent influence on the moral law of the group. Before the

---

[1] *Jehan et Blonde*, ed. H. Suchier (*Oeuvres poétiques de Ph. de Rémi*, II, v. 5916 *et seq.*).
[2] *Polycraticus*, VI, 10 (ed. Webb, II, p. 25).   [3] Guillaume Durand, *Rationale*, IV, 16.

future knight took back his sword from the altar he was generally required to take an oath defining his obligations.[1] It was not taken by all dubbed knights, since not all of them had their arms blessed; but, many ecclesiastical writers considered, with John of Salisbury, that by a sort of quasi-contract even those who had not pronounced it with their lips were 'tacitly' bound by the oath through the mere fact of having accepted knighthood. Little by little the rules thus formulated found their way into other texts: first into the prayers, often very beautiful ones, which punctuated the course of the ceremony; later, with inevitable variations, into various writings in the vulgar tongue. One of these, composed shortly after 1180, was a celebrated passage from the *Perceval* of Chrétien de Troyes. In the following century these rules were set forth in some pages of the prose romance of *Lancelot*; in the German *Minnesang*, in a fragment of the 'Meissner'; finally and above all, in the short French didactic poem entitled *L'Ordene de Chevalerie*. This little work had a great success. Paraphrased before long in a cycle of Italian sonnets, imitated in Catalonia by Ramon Lull, it opened the way to the abounding literature which, during the last centuries of the Middle Ages, drained to the lees the symbolic significance of the dubbing ceremony and, by its final extravagances, proclaimed the decadence of an institution which had become more a matter of etiquette than of law, and the impoverishment of the very ideal which men professed to rate so high.

Originally this ideal had not lacked genuine vitality. It was super-imposed on rules of conduct evolved at an earlier date as the spontaneous expression of class consciousness; rules that pertained to the fealty of vassals (the transition appears clearly, towards the end of the eleventh century, in the *Book of the Christian Life* by Bishop Bonizo of Sutri, for whom the knight is, first and foremost, an enfeoffed vassal) and constituted above all a class code of noble and 'courteous' people. From these secular moral precepts the new decalogue borrowed the principles most acceptable to the religious mind: generosity; the pursuit of glory or 'praise' (*los*); contempt for fatigue, pain and death—'he has no desire to embrace the knight's profession,' says the German poet Thomasin, 'whose sole desire is to live in comfort'.[2] But this reorientation was effected by imparting to these same rules a Christian colouring; and, still more, by cleansing the knightly tradition of those profane elements which had occupied, and in practice continued to occupy, so large a place in it—that dross which had brought to the lips of so many rigorists, from St. Anselm to St. Bernard, the old play on words so charged with the cleric's contempt for the world: *non militia, sed malitia*:[3] 'Chivalry is tantamount to wickedness.' But after the Church had finally appropriated the feudal virtues, what writer would

---

[1] Peter of Blois, ep. XCIV.   [2] *Der Wälsche Gast*, ed. Rückert, vv. 7791–2.
[3] Anselm, *Ep.*, I (*P.L.*, CLVIII, col. 1147); St. Bernard, *De laude novae militiae*, 77, c. 2.

thenceforth have dared to repeat this equation? Lastly, to the old precepts which had undergone this process of refinement, others were added of an exclusively spiritual character.

The clergy and the laity were therefore united in demanding of the knight that piety without which Philip Augustus himself considered that he was no true *prudhomme*. He must go to mass 'every day' or at least 'frequently'; he must fast on Friday. Nevertheless this Christian hero remained by nature a warrior. What he looked for most from the benediction upon his arms was that it would make them effective, as is clearly shown in the wording of the prayers themselves. But the sword thus consecrated, though it might still as a matter of course be drawn at need against his personal enemies or those of his lord, had been given to the knight first of all that he might place it at the service of good causes. The old benedictions of the end of the tenth century already lay emphasis on this theme, which is greatly expanded in the later liturgies. Thus a modification of vital importance was introduced into the old ideal of war for war's sake, or for the sake of gain. With this sword, the dubbed knight will defend Holy Church, particularly against the infidel. He will protect the widow, the orphan, and the poor. He will pursue the malefactor. To these general precepts the lay texts frequently add a few more special recommendations concerning behaviour in battle (not to slay a vanquished and defenceless adversary); the practice of the courts of law and of public life (not to take part in a false judgment or an act of treason—if they cannot be prevented, the *Ordene de Chevalerie* modestly adds, one must withdraw); and lastly, the incidents of everyday life (not to give evil counsel to a lady; to give help, 'if possible', to a fellow-being in distress).

It is hardly surprising that the realities of knightly life, with its frequent trickery and deeds of violence, should have been far from conforming always to these aspirations. One might also be inclined to observe that, from the point of view either of a 'socially' inspired ethic or of a more purely Christian code, such a list of moral precepts seems a little short. But this would be to pass judgment, whereas the historian's sole duty is to understand. It is more important to note that in passing from the ecclesiastical theorists or liturgists to the lay popularizers the list of knightly virtues appears very often to have undergone a rather disturbing attenuation. 'The highest order that God has made and willed is the order of chivalry,' says Chrétien de Troyes, in his characteristically sweeping manner. But it must be confessed that after this high-sounding preamble the instructions which his *prudhomme* gives to the young man he is knighting seem disconcertingly meagre. It may well be that Chrétien represents the 'courtesy' of the great princely courts of the twelfth century rather than the *prudhommie*, inspired by religious sentiments, which was in vogue in the following century in the circle of Louis IX. It is doubtless no accident that the same epoch and the same environment in which this knightly saint lived

318

should have given birth to the noble prayer (included in the *Pontifical* of William Durand) which may be regarded as a kind of liturgical commentary on the knights carved in stone on the porch of Chartres and the inner wall of the façade of Rheims: 'Most Holy Lord, Almighty Father ... thou who hast permitted on earth the use of the sword to repress the malice of the wicked and defend justice; who for the protection of thy people hast thought fit to institute the order of chivalry ... cause thy servant here before thee, by disposing his heart to goodness, never to use this sword or another to injure anyone unjustly; but let him use it always to defend the Just and the Right.'

Thus the Church, by assigning to it an ideal task, finally and formally approved the existence of this 'order' of warriors which, conceived as one of the necessary divisions of a well-ordered society, was increasingly identified with the whole body of dubbed knights. 'O God, who after the Fall, didst constitute in all nature three ranks among men,' we read in one of the prayers in the Besançon liturgy. At the same time it provided this class with a religious justification of a social supremacy which had long been a recognized fact. The very orthodox *Ordene de Chevalerie* says that knights should be honoured above all other men, save priests. More crudely, the romance of *Lancelot,* after having explained how they were instituted 'to protect the weak and the peaceful', proceeds—in conformity with the emphasis on symbols common to all this literature—to discover in the horses which they ride the peculiar symbol of the 'people' whom they hold 'in right subjection'. 'For above the people must sit the knight. And just as one controls a horse and he who sits above leads it where he will, so the knight must lead the people at his will.' Later, Ramon Lull did not think he offended Christian sentiment by saying that it was conformable to good order that the knight should 'draw his well-being' from the things that were provided for him 'by the weariness and toil' of his men.[1] This epitomizes the attitude of a dominant class: an attitude eminently favourable to the development of a nobility in the strictest sense of the term.

[1] *Libro de la orden de Caballeria,* I, 9. The whole passage has a remarkable flavour.

XXIV

TRANSFORMATION OF THE NOBILITY INTO A LEGAL CLASS

1 THE INHERITANCE OF KNIGHTHOOD AND NOBILITY

ABOUT 1119, the Order of the Temple was founded for the protection of the settlements in the Holy Land. It consisted of two categories of fighting-men, distinguished from each other by their dress, their arms and their rank. In the higher category were the 'knights'; in the lower, the ordinary 'serjeants'—white mantles contrasted with brown. There can be no doubt that from the first the contrast corresponded to a difference of social origin among the recruits. Nevertheless, the earliest *Rule*, drawn up in 1130, does not contain any precise provisions on this subject. What might be called the consensus of opinion evidently decided into which of the two grades a man was to be admitted. A little more than a century later (*c.* 1250) the second *Rule*, by contrast, displays an uncompromising legalism. To be entitled to wear the white mantle, it was first of all necessary that the candidate should have been knighted before his entry into the Order. But even that was not enough. He had to be in addition 'a knight's son or a descendant of knights on his father's side'; in other words, as it is expressed in another passage, he had to be a 'nobleman' (*gentilhomme*). For, as the *Rule* again prescribes, it is only on this condition that a man 'must and can' receive knighthood. This is not all. What happens if a newcomer chooses to conceal his knightly rank and slip in among the serjeants? Once the truth is known, he is to be put in irons.[1] Even among the soldier-monks in this mid-thirteenth century, pride of class, which regarded any voluntary forfeiture of rank as a crime, counted for more than Christian humility. Between 1130 and about 1250, therefore, an important development had taken place: the right to be made a knight had been transformed into a hereditary privilege.

In the countries where the legislative tradition had never been lost, or had lapsed and been revived, the new law was defined by various edicts.

---

[1] For the old rule, see G. Schnürer, *Die ursprüngliche Templerregel*, 1903. For a French text of the rule: H. de Curzon, *La règle du Temple* (Soc. de l'hist. de France), c. 431; 445; 446; 448. For similar provisions among the Hospitallers, in the general chapter of 19th September, 1262, Delaville Le Roulx, *Cartulaire général*, III, p. 47, c. 19.

In 1152, a peace ordinance of Frederick Barbarossa at one and the same time forbade 'peasants' to carry the lance and the sword—knightly weapons—and recognized as 'lawful knights' only men whose ancestors had been knights before them; another, in 1187, expressly forbade the sons of peasants to get themselves knighted. As early as 1140, Roger II of Sicily decreed that only the descendants of knights be admitted to knighthood; and in this he was followed in 1234 by King James I of Aragon and in 1294 by Count Charles II of Provence. In France there was at that time almost no statute law. But the judgments of the royal court under St. Louis were explicit on this point, and so were the customaries. Except by a special dispensation from the king, no knighthood could lawfully be conferred unless the father of the recipient or his grandfather, in the male line, had been a knight (perhaps as early as this period, in any case not much later, the provincial customs of at least a part of Champagne agreed that this 'nobility' could be transmitted through the mother). The same conception seems also to form the basis of a passage, admittedly less clear, in the great treatise on Castilian law, the *Siete Partidas*, compiled about 1260 on the orders of King Alfonso the Wise. It is a striking fact that these various texts were almost contemporaneous and in perfect accord not only with each other, but also with the rule of the Temple, an international Order. On the continent at least—the case in England, as we shall see, was otherwise—the evolution of the upper classes followed a fundamentally uniform pattern.[1]

It is true that when they expressly imposed the hereditary rule sovereigns and courts of law were hardly aware that they were doing anything new, since at all times the great majority of those who were knighted were descendants of knights. In the eyes of an increasingly exclusive group opinion, only high birth—'guarantee of the continuation of ancient honour', as it was called by Ramon Lull—enabled a man to observe the code of behaviour to which he was committed by the delivery of arms. 'Ah, God! how badly is the good warrior rewarded who makes the son of a villein a knight!' exclaims the poet of *Girart de Roussillon*, about 1160;[2] which, however, testifies to the fact that these intruders were by no means rare. No law, no custom, could altogether exclude them. Moreover, they appeared at times to be almost necessary for the recruitment of armies; for that same class prejudice produced a strong conviction that only knights had the right to fight on horseback fully armed. In 1302, on the eve of the battle of Courtrai, the Flemish princes, desiring to have a cavalry force,

---

[1] *M.G.H., Constitutiones*, I, p. 197, c. 10; p. 451, c. 20; H. Niese, *Die Gesetzgebung der norm. Dynastie*, p. 67; P. de Marca, *Marca Hisp.*, col. 1430, c. 12; Papon, *Histoire Genérále de Provence*, III, p. 423; *Siete Partidas*, Part II., XXI, I, 2. Cf. for Portugal, E. Prestage, *Chivalry*, p. 143. For France, the references are too numerous to be listed here; cf. Petit-Dutaillis, *L'Essor des États d'Occident*, p. 22 *et seq.*

[2] Raimon Lull, *Libro de la orden de Caballeria*, ed. I, R. de Luanco, III, 8; *Girart de Roussillon*, trans. P. Meyer, p. 28 (cf. ed. Foerster, *Roman.Studien*, vol. V, v. 940 *et seq.*).

knighted a number of rich burghers whose wealth enabled them to provide themselves with the necessary horses and equipment.[1] The transformation of what had long been by mere convention a hereditary vocation, liable to many setbacks, into a legalized and jealously-guarded privilege was therefore of capital importance, even if contemporaries had no clear awareness of this development. The profound social changes which were in progress at that time on the fringes of the knightly world had certainly done much to inspire these Draconian measures.

In the twelfth century a new power was born—the urban patriciate. In these rich merchants who frequently acquired manors and many of whom had aspired to 'the baldric of knighthood', for themselves or their sons, the hereditary warriors could not fail to recognize elements much more foreign to their own mentality and way of life—much more disturbing also on account of their number—than the soldiers of fortune or the manorial officials who had hitherto provided most of the non-noble candidates for knighthood. We know, through Bishop Otto of Freising, the reactions of the German barons to the knighthoods which they considered were too freely distributed, in northern Italy, to 'men in trades and crafts'; Beaumanoir, in France, has very clearly explained how the pressure of the new social classes, eager to invest their capital in land, led the kings to take the precautions necessary to prevent the purchase of a fief from making every *nouveau riche* the equal of a descendant of knights. When a class feels itself threatened it tends to close its ranks.

It would be a mistake, however, to imagine that there was, in theory, any insuperable obstacle. A class of powerful individuals could not transform itself completely into a hereditary caste without being compelled to exclude from its ranks the new forces whose inevitable emergence is the very law of life, thereby condemning itself, as a social group, to permanent enfeeblement. Thus the evolution of legal opinion during the feudal period tended much less to impose a strict ban on new admissions than to subject them to rigorous control. Formerly every knight could make a knight. Such was still the opinion of three resourceful persons of whom Beaumanoir writes towards the end of the thirteenth century. All three were knights themselves, but they needed, as a mere lay-figure, a fourth person of the same rank whose presence was required by custom for a particular legal transaction. So on their way they laid hold of a peasant and gave him the accolade, saying: 'Be thou a knight!' By that date, however, such action had become illegal, and a heavy fine was the just punishment for this anachronism. For a member of the knightly order no longer had the right to confer membership on others unless the aspirant was already of knightly lineage. When such was not the case he might indeed be knighted, but only by special permission from the sole authority who, according to contemporary notions, was entitled to exercise the extraordinary power of

[1] P. Thomas, *Textes historiques sur Lille*, II, 1936, p. 237.

VIII. SETTING FIRE TO A WOODEN CASTLE

Capture of Dinan. Bayeux Tapestry, end of the 11th century.

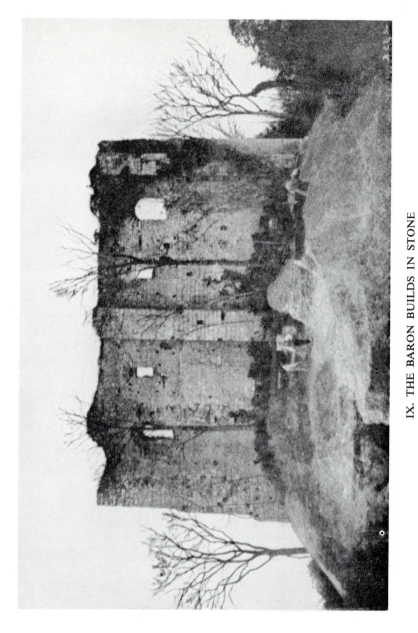

IX. THE BARON BUILDS IN STONE

The keep of Langeais, built in 994-995 by Fulk Nerra, Count of Anjou.

dispensing from customary rules: namely the king, the sole bestower, as Beaumanoir says, of 'novelties'.

We have already seen that this was the ruling of the French royal judges as early as St. Louis. Soon, at the Capetian court, the practice arose of giving these authorizations the form of 'letters of chancery', described almost from the first as 'letters of nobility'—for to be qualified to receive knighthood was to succeed in being assimilated to the 'nobles' by birth. The first examples we possess of documents of this kind, which had a great future before them, date from Philip III or Philip IV. Occasionally the king, in accordance with ancient practice, made use of his prerogative to reward with the accolade some act of gallantry on the field of battle—as did Philip the Fair, who knighted a butcher after the battle of Mons-en-Pevèle.[1] Most frequently, however, it was received in recognition of long services or of a pre-eminent social position. 'Letters of nobility' not only permitted a new knight to be created: since the capacity to receive knighthood was transmitted from generation to generation, they in effect brought into being each time a whole new line of knights.

Sicilian legislation and practice were based on exactly the same principles as those just described; and this was also true of Spain. In the Empire—though the decrees of Barbarossa did not actually provide for this—we know that the Emperor considered that he had a right to confer knighthood on ordinary soldiers;[2] thus showing that he did not regard himself as being personally bound by the seemingly absolute prohibitions of his own laws. Moreover, from the following reign onwards the example of Sicily exercised an influence over sovereigns who, for more than half a century, were to unite both crowns. From the time of Conrad IV, who began to reign independently in 1250, we find the German monarchs granting, by letters, permission to receive the 'baldric of knighthood' to persons who had no claim to it by birth.

Certainly the monarchies did not succeed without difficulty in establishing this monopoly. Roger II of Sicily himself made an exception in favour of the abbot of La Cava. In France the nobles and prelates of the *sénéchaussée* of Beaucaire still claimed in 1298—with what success we do not know—the unrestricted right to create knights among the townsmen.[3] Resistance was strong, especially on the part of the great feudatories. Under Philip III, the king's court had to institute proceedings against the counts of Flanders and Nevers, who were guilty of illegally knighting 'villeins'. (The latter were in fact wealthy persons.) Later, in the disorders of the time of the Valois, the great princes of the royal houses had less difficulty in arrogating this privilege to themselves. It was naturally in the Empire that the right to admit newcomers to knighthood in this way was most widely exercised: by territorial princes like the bishop of

[1] *Rec. des Hist. de France*, XXII, p. 18.   [2] Otto of Freising, *Gesta*, II, 23.
[3] *Hist. de Languedoc*, 2nd ed., VIII, col. 1747.

Strasbourg,[1] from 1281; and even occasionally, in Italy, by urban communes such as Florence, which possessed the right as early as 1260. But this represented simply the dismemberment of regalian rights: the principle that the sovereign alone had the right to remove the impediment was preserved. More serious was the case of the interlopers—and there were certainly a good many of them—who took advantage of the actual situation to insinuate themselves illicitly into the ranks of knighthood. Since the nobility remained in large measure a class distinguished by its power and its mode of life, common opinion, in spite of laws, seldom refused to the possessor of a military fief, to the lord of a manor, or to the veteran warrior whatever his origin, the name of noble and the right, accordingly, to receive knighthood. Since in most cases the title derived from long usage after some generations, no one dreamed of disputing the family's right to it; and in this situation the governments' usual course was merely to exact a little money from those concerned by ratifying the abuse. It is none the less true that the transformation of *de facto* inheritance into legal inheritance, in the course of a long process of spontaneous development, had been made possible only by the strengthening of the royal or princely authority which alone was capable both of instituting a stricter control of society and of regularizing the inevitable and salutary transitions from class to class by making them legal. If the Parlement of Paris had not existed or had lacked the strength needed to execute its judgments, there would not have been a petty lord in the kingdom who would not have contrived to make knights as he thought fit.

There was at that time scarcely an institution which, in the hands of perpetually needy governments, was not more or less transformed into a money-making machine. The authorizations to create knights were no exceptions to the rule. Like other documents issued by the chancelleries, royal letters, with very rare exceptions, were not granted free of charge. There were also cases where people paid in order not to have to prove their origin.[2] But Philip the Fair seems to have been the first sovereign openly to make knighthood a saleable commodity. In 1302, after the defeat of Courtrai, commissioners scoured the provinces in order to canvass people prepared to pay for ennoblement, and at the same time to sell the royal serfs their freedom. It does not appear, however, that this practice was very general at that time either in Europe or in France itself, or that the returns were large. At a later date the kings learned to make the *savonette à vilains*—'peasants' toilet soap'—one of their regular sources of revenue and for the rich taxpayers it afforded a means of escaping, by a single payment, the taxes from which the nobility were exempted. But until about the middle of the fourteenth century, the fiscal privilege of the nobles

[1] *Annal. Colmar.* in *M.G.H.* SS, XVII, p. 208, l. 15; cf. p. 244, l. 31.
[2] A. de Barthélemy, 'De la qualification de chevalier' in *Revue nobiliaire*, 1868, p. 123, and 'Études sur les lettres d'anoblissement' in *Revue nobiliaire*, 1869, p. 205.

remained as ill-defined as State taxation itself; and *esprit de corps*, very strong in knightly society—to which the princes themselves were conscious of belonging—would doubtless scarcely have permitted the multiplication of favours which were felt to be so many insults to men of noble birth.

If access to the circle of knights by birth was not absolutely closed, the door was nevertheless only very slightly ajar. It was certainly very much less easy to enter than it had been before or would be in the future; hence the violent reaction against the nobility which, in France at least, broke out in the fourteenth century. What more striking proof can be found of the solidarity and exclusive spirit of a class than the fierceness of the attacks to which it is subjected? 'Revolt of the non-nobles against the nobles'— the expression, which was virtually in official use at the time of the Jacquerie, is revealing; and not less so is the list of combatants. Étienne Marcel, a rich burgess and the first magistrate of the first of cities, deliberately set himself up as the enemy of the nobles. Under Louis XI or Louis XIV he would have been one of them himself. In truth, the period from about 1250 to about 1400 was, on the continent, the period which witnessed the most rigid stratification of social classes.

2 THE DESCENDANTS OF KNIGHTS BECOME A PRIVILEGED CLASS

By itself, however, the restriction of knighthood to members of families already confirmed in that status or to the recipients of exceptional favours would not have sufficed to form a genuine nobility. For this would have meant that the privileges which according to the conception of nobility were inseparable from noble birth would have been made dependent on a ceremony which might or might not be carried out. It was not just a question of prestige. Increasingly the pre-eminent position which it was agreed to accord to knights, both as 'ordained' warriors and as vassals charged with the highest responsibilities in war and counsel, tended to take concrete shape in a precise legal code. Now, from the end of the eleventh century to the first years of the thirteenth, the same rules were reproduced throughout feudal Europe. In order to enjoy these advantages it was necessary in the first place that a man should efficiently perform his duties as a vassal, 'that he have arms and horses, that, unless prevented by age, he take part in the host and in the expeditions, in the assemblies and in the courts', say the *Usages* of Catalonia. It was also necessary that he should have been knighted. The general weakening of vassal services had the result that gradually the first condition ceased to be insisted on; the later texts pass it over in silence. The second, on the other hand, remained for a long time very much in force. As late as 1238, a private family regulation, the statute of the parceners who possessed in common the castle of La Garde-Guérin in the Gévaudan, gives priority to a younger son over the eldest, if the former has received knighthood and the latter has not. Suppose it happened

325

nevertheless—no matter where—that a knight's son failed to be knighted in his turn and remained a simple 'squire' (the traditional title of the noble youth in the service of his elders), then once he had passed the age after which such neglect was deemed no longer permissible—twenty-five in Flanders and Hainault, thirty in Catalonia—he was numbered among the 'clod-hoppers'.[1]

But pride of birth had become too potent for these requirements to be maintained for ever. Their disappearance was effected by stages. In Provence in 1235, and in Normandy about the same time, it was still only the son who was recognized as having a right to the benefits of the father's rank, without any obligation to get himself knighted, and if he in his turn had a son the latter, according to the conditions laid down in the Provençal text, must personally receive knighthood if he wished to share those privileges. More significant still is the series of charters granted by the German kings to the men of Oppenheim: the same rights are granted in 1226 to knights, from 1269 to 'knights and sons of knights', and in 1275 to 'knights, their sons and their grandsons'.[2] People must at times have grown weary of counting the generations. In any case the formal reception of arms continued to be regarded as a duty which the noble youth could not evade without in some degree losing caste. In the family of the counts of Provence, of the house of Barcelona, however, it was delayed as long as possible owing to an extraordinary superstition that it was a presage of approaching death.[3] Since to be knighted involved by convention the assembling of the complete equipment necessary to effective service in the field, the kings of France, from Philip Augustus to Philip the Fair, tried to make the ceremony obligatory for those of their subjects who belonged to knightly families. So little did they succeed in this, however, that the royal administration, powerless even to obtain a lucrative financial yield from the collection of fines or the sale of dispensations, had in the end to content itself merely with ordering this class, as soon as war threatened, to be in possession of arms.

In the last years of the thirteenth century, the evolution was almost everywhere complete. What henceforth made the noble was not the old rite of initiation, now reduced to the status of a polite formality and neglected by the majority because as a rule it involved great expense; it was the hereditary right to be knighted, whether or not that right was exercised. One calls a nobleman, writes Beaumanoir, whoever is 'of knightly lineage'. And shortly after 1284 the earliest authorization of knighthood granted by the chancellery of the kings of France to a person not of noble

---

[1] *Usatici Barcin.*, c. 9 and 8; C. Porrée, *Études historiques sur le Gévaudan*, 1919 (and *Bibl. Éc. Chartes*, 1907), p. 62, c. 1; Peace Charter of Hainault (1200), in *M.G.H.*, SS. XXI, p. 619.

[2] *Summa de legibus*, in Tardif, vol. II, XIV, 2; F. Benoit, *Recueil des actes des comtes de Provence*, II, no. 246, c; ixa, 275, c; va, 277; 278 (1235–1238). P. Guilhiermoz, *Essai sur les origines de la noblesse en France au moyen-âge*, 1902, p. 481.

[3] 'Annales Colonienses max.' in *M.G.H.*, SS. XVII, p. 845.

birth raised at one stroke, without imposing any conditions at all, the entire posterity of the recipient 'to the privileges, rights and franchises which the nobles are accustomed to enjoy by virtue of the two lines of descent'.[1]

3 THE LAW OF THE NOBLES

This body of private law (which with certain necessary modifications applied to women of noble birth as well as to men) varied considerably in its details from one region to another. Moreover it evolved only slowly, and in the course of time underwent important modifications. We shall confine ourselves here to noting the most general characteristics as they emerged in the course of the thirteenth century.

Traditionally, the ties of vassalage were the form of dependence peculiar to the upper classes. But here, as elsewhere, a *de facto* situation was replaced by a legal monopoly. Formerly a man had been regarded as noble because he was a vassal. Henceforth, by a veritable reversal of the order of the terms, it was impossible, in theory, to be a vassal—in other words to hold a military fief or 'free' fief—if one did not already rank among the nobles by birth. This was commonly admitted almost everywhere towards the middle of the thirteenth century. Nevertheless, the rise of burgher wealth as well as the need of money by which the old families were so often harassed did not allow the rule to be maintained in all its rigour. Not only was it in practice very far from being constantly observed—which opened the way to many usurpations of nobility—but even in law it was necessary to make provision for exemptions. Sometimes these were general in scope, as for example those in favour of persons born of a noble mother and a non-noble father;[2] more often, they were in favour of individuals. The latter sort, once again, redounded to the profit of the monarchs who alone were capable of legitimatizing such anomalies in the social order, and were not in the habit of distributing these favours free. Since the fief was most frequently a manor, political authority over the common people tended as a result of these practices to be detached from noble rank. But what if the fief involved the submission of sub-vassals? If the latter were noblemen the right of the non-noble purchaser to require homage from them was not ordinarily recognized; he had to be content with taxes and services, without gestures of fealty. There was even reluctance to admit that he could himself, as a vassal, do homage to his superior lord. The ceremony was reduced to an oath of fealty or, at any rate, the kiss was omitted from it, as being too egalitarian. Even in the manner of soliciting or contracting obedience there were forms that were forbidden to the man of low birth.

Military vassals had for a long time been governed by a law which

---

[1] A. de Barthélemy, 'De la qualification de chevalier', in *Revue nobiliaire*, 1869, p. 198.
[2] Beaumanoir, II, § 1434.

differed from the common rules. They were not tried by the same courts as other dependants; their fiefs were not inherited in the same way as other properties. Their family status itself bore the marks of their rank. When the nobility arose from among the possessors of military fiefs, the customary law formerly attached to the exercise of a function tended to become the customary law of a group of families. On this point, a change in terminology is instructive: whereas formerly people had spoken of *bail féodal*, 'feudal wardship' (the institution has been defined in an earlier chapter),[1] henceforth they began to say in France *garde noble*, 'noble wardship'. As was natural for a class which derived its distinctive character from very ancient institutions, the private law of the nobles retained in many respects an archaic cast.

A number of other features underlined still more emphatically the social supremacy of the class as well as its character as a fighting order. If it was a question of maintaining purity of blood, there was obviously no more effective means than the complete prohibition of marriages with persons of inferior status. Only in the imported feudalism of Cyprus and the hierarchic society of Germany, however, did it come to that; and in the latter country, which was characterized, as we shall see, by a highly-developed system of gradations within the nobility itself, it was only the higher ranks and not the petty knights, sprung from former manorial officials, who were restricted in this way. Elsewhere the memory of the ancient equality of free men continued, so far as marriage was concerned, to be reflected in law, if not in practice. Everywhere, however, certain great religious communities, which hitherto had displayed their aristocratic spirit only in rejecting postulants of servile origin, decided now to admit them only if they were descended from the nobility.[2] Everywhere also—earlier in one place, later in another—we find evidence that the noble was specially protected in his person against the non-noble; that he was subject to an exceptional penal law, with heavier fines, as a rule, than those exacted from the common people; that recourse to private vengeance, regarded as inseparable from the bearing of arms, tended to be reserved for him; that the sumptuary laws assigned to him a place apart. The importance attached to birth as the source of privilege was expressed in the transformation of the old individual signs of 'recognition', painted on the knight's shield or engraved on his seal, into the armorial bearings, sometimes transmitted with the fief but more often handed down, even without the property,

---

[1] pp. 201–3.

[2] The works of A. Schulte, *Der Adel und die deutsche Kirche im Mittelalter*, 2nd ed., Stuttgart, and of Dom Ursmér Berlière, *Le recrutement dans les monastères bénédictins aux XIIIᵉ et XIVᵉ siècles* (*Mém. Acad. royale Belgique* in-8, 2ᵉ série, XVIII), provide a great deal of information on this subject, though with an insufficiency of exact chronological and critical data. Whatever Schulte thinks, it follows from the texts cited that —allowing for the very loose sense in which the words *nobiles* and *ignobiles* were used in early times—the monopoly of the nobles, in the exact sense of the term, was everywhere a relatively late phenomenon. The admission of the unfree sets quite another problem.

from generation to generation. The use of these symbols of continuity, first seen in the royal and princely dynasties, where pride of birth was particularly strong, and soon adopted by houses of lesser rank, was regarded henceforth as the monopoly of the families classed as noble. Finally, although tax exemptions were still far from being strictly defined, the military obligation—formerly the characteristic duty of the vassal, now the noble's duty *par excellence*—had henceforth the effect of relieving the nobleman of the usual pecuniary burdens; these being in his case replaced by warlike services.

However strong the rights acquired by birth, they were not so strong that they might not be lost by the exercise of certain occupations deemed to be incompatible with high rank. It is true that the conception of derogation (*dérogeance*) was as yet far from being fully developed.[1] The rule which forbade nobles to engage in trade seems at that time to have been imposed on them above all by certain urban statutes, which were intended to protect the virtual monopoly of the merchant communities rather than to serve the pride of a hostile caste. But by universal consent agricultural labour was regarded as contrary to the honour of the military class. Even with his own compliance—so the Parlement of Paris decided—a knight who had acquired a tenement in villeinage could not perform rural labour services. 'To plough, to dig, to carry a load of wood or manure'—these were actions which, according to a Provençal ordinance, automatically involved deprivation of knightly privileges. It was also in Provence that a noblewoman was characterized as one who goes 'neither to the oven, nor to the wash-house, nor to the mill'.[2] The nobility had ceased to be defined by the exercise of a function—that of the armed retainer. It was no longer a class of initiates. It remained, however, a class distinguished by its mode of life.

4 THE EXCEPTIONAL CASE OF ENGLAND

In England, where the institutions of vassalage and knighthood were all imported, the evolution of the *de facto* nobility at first followed almost the same lines as on the continent—only to take a very different direction in the thirteenth century.

As the very powerful masters of an island kingdom whose primary purpose, in their eyes, was to provide them with the means to pursue truly imperial ambitions, the Norman and later the Angevin kings set themselves to stretch to the limit the scope of military obligation. To this end they made use of two principles belonging to different ages: the general levy of all free men; and the specialized service required of vassals. As early as

---

[1] [*Dérogeance* was an act on the part of a nobleman which constituted an impairment of his rank and led to its forfeiture.]

[2] *Olim*, I, p. 427, no. XVII (Chandeleur, 1255); F. Benoit, *Recueil des actes*, passages cited above, p. 326, n.1; M. Z. Isnard, *Livre des privilèges de Manosque*, 1894, no. XLVII, p. 154.

1180 and 1181 we find Henry II, first in his continental dominions, then in England, compelling his subjects to provide themselves with arms, each man according to his rank. The English 'assize' specifies, among others, those required of the holder of a knight's fee. It does not mention dubbing to knighthood. Nevertheless, this ceremony, as we know, was regarded as a certain guarantee that the warrior would be properly equipped. Therefore in 1224 and 1234 Henry III judged it wise to compel every possessor of such a fief to undergo this initiation without delay, at least—the qualification was introduced by the second ordinance—if homage was done directly to the king.

So far, there was nothing in these measures which greatly differed from the Capetian legislation of the same period. Yet the English government, with its strong administrative traditions, could hardly have been unaware of the increasing ineffectiveness of the old system of feudal service. Many fiefs had been parcelled out; others underwent continual and always imperfect reassessments; finally, when all was said and done, their number was necessarily limited. Was it not more reasonable firmly to base the vassal's duty to serve, and consequently to equip himself, on a much more tangible reality—on landed wealth, whatever its nature? This, moreover, was the principle which already, in 1180, Henry II had striven to apply to his continental states, where the feudal organization was not nearly so regular as in England or the duchy of Normandy. The same thing was done in England, from 1254 onwards, by using varying economic criteria, the details of which need not concern us here. But, whereas Henry II had confined himself to the question of equipment, henceforth, in conformity with practices which had already taken root, the formal assumption of knighthood was required of all free possessors of a certain quantity of free land. The rule was doubtless imposed the more readily because the royal treasury could look forward to a welcome crop of fines from the expected contraventions.

Even in England, however, the machinery of government was not at that time sufficiently well organized to ensure the strict observance of such measures. As early as the end of the century, apparently, and certainly in the following century, they had become practically inoperative. They had to be abandoned; and the knighting ceremony, less and less regularly practised, was finally, as on the continent, relegated to a place among the accessories of a social code that was becoming more and more outmoded. But the policy of the crown, with its inevitable corollary, the absence of any attempt to stop the buying and selling of fiefs, had a very important result. In England knighthood, transformed into a fiscal institution, could not serve as the focal point for the formation of a class founded on the hereditary principle.

Such a class in fact never came into being across the Channel. In the French or German sense of the word, medieval England had no nobility;

that is to say that among the free men there was no intrinsically superior class enjoying a privileged legal status of its own, transmitted by descent. In appearance English society was an astonishingly egalitarian structure. Essentially, nevertheless, it was based on the existence of an extremely rigid hierarchic division, though the line was drawn at a lower level than elsewhere. In fact at a time when everywhere else the caste of nobles was being established above the growing mass of a population described as 'free', in England, the conception of serfdom had been extended to the point where the majority of peasants were branded with this stigma. On English soil the ordinary free man was in law scarcely distinguishable from the nobleman. But the free men themselves were an oligarchy.

Yet England had an aristocracy as powerful as any in Europe—more powerful perhaps, because the land of the peasants was still more at its mercy. It was a class of manorial lords, of warriors or chieftains, of royal officials and of 'knights of the shire'—all of them men whose mode of life differed greatly and consciously from that of the common run of free men. At the top was the narrow circle of earls and 'barons'. During the thirteenth century this highest group had begun to be endowed with fairly definite privileges, but these were of an almost exclusively political and honorific nature; and above all, being attached to the *fief de dignité*, to the 'honour', they were transmissible only to the eldest son. In short, the class of noblemen in England remained, as a whole, more a 'social' than a 'legal' class. Although, naturally, power and revenues were as a rule inherited, and although, as on the continent, the prestige of birth was greatly prized, this group was too ill-defined not to remain largely open. In the thirteenth century, the possession of landed wealth had been sufficient to authorize the assumption of knighthood, in fact to make it obligatory. Something like a century and a half later it officially conferred the right (always restricted by a characteristic rule to free tenure) to elect, in the shires, the representatives of the 'Commons of the Land'. And although in theory these same representatives—they were known by the significant name of 'knights of the shire' and had originally, in fact, to be chosen from among the dubbed knights—were required to furnish proof of hereditary armorial bearings, it does not appear that, in practice, any family of solid wealth and social distinction ever encountered much difficulty in obtaining permission to use such emblems.[1] There were no 'letters of nobility' among the English at this period (the creation of baronets by the needy House of Stuart was only a belated imitation of French practices). There was no need for them. The actual situation was enough.

It was mainly by keeping close to the practical things which give real power over men and avoiding the paralysis that overtakes social classes which are too sharply defined and too dependent on birth that the English aristocracy acquired the dominant position it retained for centuries.

[1] Cf. E. and A. G. Porritt, *The Unreformed House of Commons*, 2nd ed., 1909, I, p. 122.

XXV

CLASS DISTINCTIONS WITHIN THE NOBILITY

1 GRADATIONS OF POWER AND RANK

DESPITE the common characteristics of their military calling and their mode of life, the group of nobles *de facto*, and later *de jure*, was never in any sense a society of equals. Profound differences of wealth and power, and consequently of prestige, established a hierarchy among them, which was first tacitly recognized, and later confirmed by custom or statute.

At a time when the obligations of vassalage still retained their full force, the principle of this classification was sought by preference in the gradations of acts of homage themselves. At the lower end of the scale we have first of all the vavasour, the 'vassal of vassals' (*vassus vassorum*), who was not himself the lord of any other warrior—not, at least, when the term vavasour, which was common to all the Romance languages, was under-stood in its strict sense. Not to exercise authority or to exercise it only over rustics was to be entitled to but small consideration. In practice this status usually went with an extremely modest fortune and the needy life of a petty country nobleman, given up to adventure. Consider the portrait of the heroine's father in the *Erec* of Chrétien de Troyes—'very poor was his house'—or, in the poem of *Gaydon*, that of the great-hearted vavasour with his rude armour. Outside the realm of fiction we learn of the impover-ished household from which Robert Guiscard escaped in search of war and plunder; the begging habits of Bertrand de Born; or again those knights depicted in various charters of a Provençal cartulary whose sole fief was a *mansus*, that is to say the equivalent of a peasant tenement. Sometimes the term 'bachelor', literally 'young man', was used in almost the same sense, for such was naturally the condition of many young men not yet enfeoffed or still insufficiently endowed, though it might be prolonged[1] till much later in life.

As soon as the noble became the chief of other nobles he increased in dignity. After having enumerated the various indemnities due to the knight

---

[1] For Provence, F. Kiener, *Verfassungsgeschichte der Provence seit der Ostgothenherr-schaft bis zur Errichtung der Konsulate* (510–1200), Leipzig, 1900, p. 107. On the 'bachelors', cf. E. F. Jacob, *Studies in the Period of Baronial Reform*, 1925 (*Oxford Studies in Social and Legal History*, VIII), p. 127 *et seq.*

who had been struck, imprisoned, or in any way maltreated, the *Usages of Barcelona* continue: 'but if he has himself two other knights established on the lands of his fief and maintains another in his household, the compensation shall be doubled'.[1] Such a person might assemble under his banner a considerable body of armed retainers; in which case he was called a banneret. If no further step separated him from the king or territorial prince to whom he did homage directly, he was also called tenant-in-chief, *capital* or baron.

Borrowed from the Germanic languages, the term 'baron' first of all passed from its original meaning of 'man' to that of 'vassal': in swearing fealty to a lord, one acknowledged oneself his 'man'. Then the habit arose of applying it more particularly to the principal vassals of the great chiefs. In this sense it expressed what was only a relative superiority of status compared with other sworn retainers of the same group. The bishop of Chester or the lord of Bellême had his barons, just as the kings had. But even the most important feudatories of the crown—the mightiest among the mighty—were in common parlance simply 'barons'.

Almost synonymous with 'baron'—in fact, employed by certain texts as its exact equivalent—the term 'peer', though possessing from the outset a more precise legal significance, belonged properly speaking to the vocabulary of judicial institutions. One of the most cherished privileges of the vassal was that of being tried in his lord's court by the latter's other vassals. The common tie of vassalage made for equality, and 'peer' thus decided the fate of 'peer'. But among the persons who held their fiefs directly of the same master there were wide differences of power and prestige. Must the rich banneret be compelled to accept the judgments of the humblest nobleman, merely by virtue of an alleged similarity in their relationship to their lord? Once again the consequences of a legal situation conflicted with the sense of more concrete realities. At an early date, therefore, it became customary in many places to reserve for the leading vassals the right to sit in judgment in cases which concerned those who were genuinely their equals in rank, as well as to offer their counsel on serious issues. The circle of 'peers' *par excellence* was thus restricted, often by recourse to a traditional or mystical number—seven, like the assessors (*scabini*) in the public tribunals of the Carolingian epoch; twelve, like the Apostles. Such bodies were to be found in lordships of moderate size like that of the monks of Mont-Saint-Michel, as well as in the great principalities such as Flanders; and the epics pictured the peers of France gathered round Charlemagne in apostolic number.

There were also other names, merely expressive of power and wealth, which readily occurred to the chroniclers or the poets when they evoked the figures of the great aristocrats. 'Magnates', *poestatz*, *demeines* seemed to them to dominate the mass of knights from a high eminence. For

---

[1] *Us. Barc.*, c. 6.

contrasts of rank were, in truth, extremely sharp within the nobility. When a knight has wronged another knight, the Catalan *Usages* explain, if the guilty party is 'superior' to the victim, it will not be possible to exact expiatory homage from him personally.[1] In the *Poem of the Cid*, the sons-in-law of the hero, descended from a line of counts, regard their marriage with the daughters of an ordinary vassal as a *mésalliance*. 'We should not have taken them even as concubines, without being begged to do so. They were not our equals—to sleep in our arms.' From the other side, the memoirs of the 'poor knight' from Picardy, Robert de Clary, relating to the Fourth Crusade, have preserved for us the sharp echo of the grievances long cherished by the rank and file (*commun de l'ost*) against 'the great men', 'the rich men', 'the barons'.

It was reserved for the thirteenth century, an age of definition and hierarchy, to try to create a rigidly organized system from these social distinctions, which hitherto had been not so much defined as acutely felt. In carrying on this task the jurists displayed a zeal for mathematical precision ill-adapted to realities which continued to be much more subtle. Moreover, the course of evolution was very different from one country to another. We shall confine ourselves here, as usual, to the most characteristic examples.

In England, where the aristocracy had been able to fashion an instrument of government from the old feudal obligation of court service, the word 'baron' continued to be used to describe the principal feudatories of the king, summoned to his 'Great Council' by virtue of a *de facto* monopoly which was gradually transformed into a strictly hereditary right. These persons also liked to flatter themselves with the name of 'peers of the realm' and eventually succeeded in getting it adopted officially.[2]

In France, by contrast, the two terms diverged widely. There people still spoke of 'vavasours' and 'barons' but as a rule the distinction implied nothing more than a simple difference of wealth and prestige: the decay of the tie of vassalage rendered meaningless the criteria derived from the gradations of acts of homage. But in order to draw a clearer line of division between the two ranks the feudal lawyers devised a criterion based on the gradations of judicial authority: the exercise of 'high justice' was a distinguishing feature of the barony, while the fief of the vavasour was restricted to 'low' or 'middle' justice. In this sense—it was never unreservedly adopted in everyday speech—there were a great many French barons. On the other hand, there were very few peers of France. For since epic legend favoured the number twelve, the six most important vassals of the Capetian monarch succeeded—along with the six most powerful bishops or archbishops whose churches were directly dependent on the crown—in acquiring for themselves the exclusive right to the title of peer. They

[1] *Us. Barc.*, c. 6.
[2] Cf. T. F. Tout, *Chapters in Administrative History*, III, p. 136 *et seq.*

were much less successful, however, in their efforts to derive practical privileges from it; they even had to submit to the curtailment of their right to be tried by their own members by accepting the presence of royal officials in court. There were too few of them, their interests as great territorial princes were too remote from those of the greater nobility as a whole, and lay too far outside the kingdom itself, for them to be able to assert their primacy in the sphere of political realities; such pre-eminence as they enjoyed was destined to remain purely honorary. Moreover, as three of the six original lay peerages became extinct in the course of the century, as a result of the reversion to the crown of the fiefs on which they had been based, the kings began, from 1297 onwards, to create new ones on their own account.[1] The age of the spontaneous formation of the nobility was followed by one in which, from top to bottom of the social scale, the crown would henceforth have the power to determine and modify the status of its subjects.

A similar trend, so far as France is concerned, may be observed in the history of the old official titles (*titres de dignités*). At all times the counts —along with the dukes and marquises, each of them the head of several counties—had figured in the first rank of magnates, as. did also their descendants, known in the south of France as *comtors*. But these terms, derived from Frankish nomenclature, originally expressed a well-defined type of authority. They were applied exclusively to the heirs of the great 'honours' of the Carolingian epoch, formerly public offices, now fiefs. If some usurpations had taken place at an early date, they had affected in the first place the nature of the power itself: and the name had gone with the power. Gradually, however, as we shall see, the body of rights appertaining to the counts was broken up and ceased to have any specific meaning. The holders of the different counties might continue to possess a great many rights which they had in fact inherited from ancestors who had been officials; but since the list of these rights varied greatly from one county to another and the counts seldom had the absolute monopoly of them, their exercise was no longer related to the notion of a count's authority as something universal in character. The title of count, in short, merely signified, in each case, a great deal of power and prestige. There was therefore now no valid reason for limiting its use to the successors of the provincial governors of long ago. From 1338, at the latest, the kings began to create counts.[2] In this way there came into existence a formal classification of the nobility, archaic in its terminology, but new in spirit, and becoming more and more complicated as time went on.

Yet among the French nobility these degrees of honour and sometimes

---

[1] In favour of the duke of Brittany: Dom Morice, *Histoire de Bretagne*, I, col. 1122. On the claims of the peers, cf. Petit-Dutaillis, *L'Essor des États d'Occident*, pp. 266-7.
[2] Borrelli de Serres, *Recherches sur divers services publics*, III, 1909, p. 276.

of privilege did not produce any profound breach in the unity of class consciousness. If, by contrast with England, where there existed no law of the nobles as distinct from that common to all free men, France in the thirteenth century gives the effect of a hierarchical society, at least in that country these specific rights were, in their essentials, common to all persons entitled to knighthood. Developments in Germany took a very different direction.

At the outset we encounter a rule peculiar to German feudalism. It appears that at an early date the view prevailed that, on pain of forfeiture of rank, a person of a given social level could not hold a fief of one who was considered his inferior. In other words, whereas in other countries gradations of acts of homage determined a man's rank, here the scale had to be modelled on pre-existing class distinctions. Although it was not always strictly respected in practice, this rigid ordering of the 'shields of knighthood' (*Heerschilde*) expressed very strongly the spirit of a society which, having accepted the ties of vassalage only with some reluctance, refused to let them interfere with a firmly rooted hierarchic sentiment. It remained to establish the degrees of nobility. At the summit of the lay aristocracy it was agreed to place those who were known as 'the first men', *Fürsten*. The Latin texts translated the word by *principes*, and in French it became customary to say *princes*. Here again it is characteristic that the criterion should not have depended originally on feudal relationships properly so called. For the earliest usage was to include under this name all who held the office of count, even when, having received investiture from a duke or a bishop, they did not figure among the immediate vassals of the king. In the Empire, where the Carolingian imprint remained so strong, the count was always regarded as exercising his office in the name of the crown, no matter what lord had enfeoffed him with it. All princes, so defined, sat in the great courts where the kings were elected.

Nevertheless, towards the middle of the twelfth century, the growing power of the great territorial lords, together with the increasingly marked permeation of German institutions with a genuinely feudal spirit, brought about a very pronounced shift of the dividing-lines between the social ranks. By a doubly significant restriction, it became customary henceforth to reserve the title of prince for the direct feudatories of the king; and, within that group itself, to those whose authority extended over several counties. Furthermore these magnates, together with their ecclesiastical colleagues, were the only ones empowered to elect the sovereign. This at least was so until by a second segregation which took place very shortly afterwards there was constituted above them a still more restricted group of hereditary Electors. Eventually the new class of lay princes, including the Electors, formed the third rank of 'shields', after the king and the princes of the Church (i.e. the bishops and the greater abbots directly dependent on the crown). But not even in Germany was inequality carried

336

far enough to prevent the continuance, for a long time, of a sort of internal unity within the nobility, reinforced in particular by freedom of inter-marriage. An exception was the lowest grade of knights which as a legal group, if not as a social class, was highly characteristic of the stratification peculiar at that time to German society. This was the class of *Ministeriales*, or servile knights.

2 SERJEANTS AND SERF-KNIGHTS

A powerful man does not live without servants, nor does he exercise authority without assistance. Even on the smallest manor a representative of the master was needed to direct the cultivation of the estate, to call for the labour services and see that they were properly carried out, to levy taxes, and to keep good order among the tenants. Frequently this *maire*, *bayle*, *Bauermeister* or 'reeve' (as he was variously called according to the country) had assistance in his turn. It might be thought that such elemen-tary duties would quite simply be exercised in rotation by the tenants, or even that the latter would be required to appoint temporary officials from among their own ranks. This was in fact a very common practice in England, but on the continent, as a rule, these functions—though also performed, as was natural, by the peasants—none the less constituted genuine offices, permanent and paid, and filled by men appointed by the lord alone. Then again, in his house itself, the petty nobleman, like the baron, was sur-rounded by a little world of retainers—varying greatly in number according to his wealth or rank. These comprised domestic servants, artisans attached to the workshops of the 'court', and officials who helped in the control of the men or in running the household. Language failed to make any clear distinction between these forms of service, so long as they were not in-cluded in the honourable category of knightly obligations. Artisans, domestic servants, messengers, estate officials, bailiffs in the lord's im-mediate circle—these were all comprised under a single head. The Latin of the charters (an international language) usually called them *ministeriales*; in French, they were known as *sergents*; in German, as *Dienstmänner*.[1]

As usual, there were two alternative methods of remunerating these various services: maintenance in the master's household ('prebend') or the grant of a tenement which, being burdened with professional duties, was called a fief. The rural serjeants, since they were peasants separated by their very functions from their much more nomadic lord, were by definition tenants; their 'fiefs', originally at least, were scarcely distinguishable from the surrounding villein tenements except for certain exemptions from taxes

---

[1] Since the references for this paragraph are easy to find among the various works listed in Section No. X, 8 of the bibliography, I have kept my notes to a bare minimum. To these works, however, should be added K. H. Roth von Schreckenstein, *Die Ritter-würde und der Ritterstand. Historisch-politische Studien über deutsch-mittelalterliche Standesverhältnisse auf dem Lande und in der Stadt*, Freiburg im Breisgau, 1886.

and labour services, a natural counterpart to the special obligations to which the man himself was subject. A certain percentage deducted from the taxes which it was their duty to collect completed their remuneration. The system of 'prebend' was undoubtedly much the best suited to the conditions of life of both the domestic craftsmen and the household officials. Nevertheless, the evolution which had led to the enfeoffment of so many vassals was paralleled at the lower level of service. A great number of *ministeriales* of this type were also enfeoffed at an early date; but they nevertheless continued to look to the customary distribution of food and clothing for a considerable part of their remuneration.

Many of the serjeants of every class were of servile status. The tradition went back a long way; in every period there had been slaves to whom positions of trust in the household of their masters had been confided, and we know that in the Frankish period some of these had found their way into the ranks of the early vassals. With the development of the relationships of personal and hereditary subjection, thenceforth described as serfdom, it was very naturally to dependants of this sort that the lord by preference assigned the offices which he did not reserve exclusively for his vassals. By their lowly status and the strictness of their hereditary bond, from which there was no escape, they seemed to offer a more certain guarantee of prompt and strict obedience than did the free man. Although the servile *ministeriales* never constituted the whole of the ministerial class—remember that there was nothing of mathematical precision about this society— their growing importance in the first feudal age cannot be doubted.

Of one person who was at first employed as a furrier by the monks of Saint-Père of Chartres and afterwards got himself put in charge of their store-room, the contemporary record says: he had wished 'to rise higher'. In its naivety, the remark is extremely significant. Although they were united by the idea of a common service, expressed by a common name, and were stamped, for the most part, with the same servile 'stigma', the serjeants formed a heterogeneous group and one that was becoming ever more hierarchic in structure. The duties were too diverse not to produce great inequalities in mode of life and prestige. It is true that the level to which a man might rise largely depended on the particular usages of his group, and on his opportunities or his skill. In a general way, nevertheless, three features—wealth, a share of authority, and the bearing of arms—raised the majority of the manorial stewards, on the one hand, and the principal court officials, on the other, well above the small fry of the petty rural serjeants, the servants properly so called and the domestic craftsmen.

Could the *maire*, the lord's steward, be described as a peasant? Undoubtedly he could—at the outset, at least, and sometimes to the end; but he was from the first a rich peasant who became progessively richer through his functions. For the lawful profits were already appreciable and still more so, doubtless, were the illicit ones. In this period, when the only

X. ARMING A NEW KNIGHT

The young Offa receives his arms from King Wermund; a pen-and-ink sketch in Matthew Paris, *Historia de Offa Rege*, perhaps by the author himself (about 1250), British Museum, Cotton MS., Nero D1, f. 3.

XI. THE ANOINTING OF A KING

Ordo of the Coronation Ceremony of the Kings of France. MS. dating from the beginning of the 14th century; the miniatures perhaps copied from models of slightly earlier date. Bibl. Nat., MS. Lat. 1246, f. 17.

effective authority was the one close at hand, it was only to be expected that the usurpations of rights which in practice made so many great royal officials sovereigns on their own account, would be repeated at the lower end of the scale in the humble setting of the village. Charlemagne himself had shown a well-founded mistrust of the stewards of his *villae* and had recommended that they should not be selected from among men who were too powerful. But although a few unscrupulous men might succeed here and there in completely usurping their lords' authority, such flagrant self-aggrandizement was always exceptional. On the other hand, how much produce was improperly retained, with a resulting loss to the lord's store-house or his pocket? 'An estate abandoned to serjeants, an estate lost,' was a maxim of the wise Suger. How many taxes and labour services were extorted from the villeins for his own benefit by this petty rural tyrant; how many chickens taken from their poultry-yards; how many casks of wine claimed from their cellars, or cuts of bacon from their storehouses; how much weaving imposed on their wives! All these were often, in origin, simple gifts; but gifts which could scarcely be refused, and which custom as a rule very soon changed into obligations. What is more, this man of peasant birth was, in his own sphere, a master. In theory, no doubt, his orders were given in the name of one more powerful than himself; they were orders none the less. What is more, he was a judge. He presided, alone, over the peasant courts; and occasionally he sat on more serious cases by the side of the abbot or the baron. Among his other duties was that of marking out the boundaries of the fields in cases of dispute. What function was more calculated to inspire respect in peasant minds? Finally, in the hour of peril, it was he who rode at the head of the contingent of villeins. By the side of Duke Garin, stricken unto death, the poet could place no better servant than a faithful steward.

There was, of course, immense variation in the steps that marked the social rise of this official. Nevertheless, we can hardly doubt the evidence of the many charters and monastic chronicles whose complaints, in exactly the same strain, echo from Swabia to Limousin; not to mention the testimony of the *fabliaux* themselves. From these sources a portrait emerges whose vivid colours may not have been true everywhere, but were so in many cases. It is the portrait, if you will, of the successful *maire*. He is not only very well off; his wealth, as such, has nothing in common with that of a peasant. He possesses tithes and mills. He has established tenants on his own lands, and in some cases even vassals. His dwelling is a fortified house. He dresses 'like a nobleman'. He keeps war-horses in his stables and hounds in his kennels. He is armed with sword, shield and lance.

The principal serjeants who, at the courts of the counts, formed as it were the general staff of the ministeriality were also rich men by virtue of their fiefs and the gifts they constantly received; they were raised still higher in dignity by their proximity to the master, by the important missions which the latter inevitably confided to them, by their military rôle when they were required to serve as a mounted escort and even as commanders of small contingents. Of this class, for example, were those 'non-noble knights' at the court of the lord of Talmont, whom a charter of the eleventh century mentions along with the 'noble knights'. They sat in law-courts and in councils; they served as witnesses to the most solemn legal acts. All this was true, occasionally, even of persons whose humble duties might have been expected to confine them to the class of menial servants. We find, for example, the 'kitchen-serjeants' of the monks of Arras taking part in judgments, and the locksmith of the monks of Saint-Trond (who was at the same time their glazier and their surgeon) trying to transform his tenement into a 'free military fief'. But it applied more frequently and in much greater degree to those whom we may call the head-servants: the seneschal, who in theory was responsible for the catering, the marshal, who had charge of the stables, the butler, and the chamberlain.

Originally most of these domestic offices had been filled by vassals, usually unenfeoffed ones. To the end the dividing line between the functions which were reserved for vassals and those which were not remained very vague. But as vassalage grew in honour and lost more and more of its primitive character, while the institution of the fief became more general, with a resulting dispersal of the old household group of knights, lords of every rank became accustomed to assign the duties of their courts to dependants of humbler birth—men who were closer to them, whom they regarded as easier to control. A charter of the Emperor Lothar for the abbey of St. Michael of Lüneburg, in 1135, prescribes that henceforward the abbot shall cease to distribute 'benefits' to free men and shall no longer grant them to any save *ministeriales* of the church. In this society, which had at first expected so much from the fealty of the vassal, the progress of the institution of court ministeriality was a symptom of disillusionment. Between the two types of service and the two classes of servants, a genuine rivalry thus developed, the echo of which has been preserved in epic and courtly literature. We find the poet Wace, for instance, congratulating one of his heroes on never having given the 'occupations of his household' to any but 'noblemen'. But in another poem we have the following portrait, also devised for the delectation of a castle audience (since its subject will finally be unmasked as a traitor) but certainly based on a familiar reality. 'A baron was seen there whom Girart thought the most faithful of his men. He was his serf and his seneschal for many a castle.'[1]

Everything contributed to make the highest class of serjeants a sharply defined social group, at least as to its lower boundary. In the first place, there was the factor of heritability; for, in spite of efforts to oppose it, notably on the part of the Church, the majority of the fiefs of serjeanty had rapidly become—frequently in law and generally in practice—transmissible

[1] *Girart de Roussillon*, trans. P. Meyer, § 620 (ed. Foerster, v. 9139).

from generation to generation. The son succeeded simultaneously to the estate and the office. Secondly, there was the practice of intermarriage, the evidence for which is to be found, from the twelfth century, in the agreements concluded between lords for the exchange of serfs. The son or daughter of a *maire* who could not find in his own village a partner of equal rank was obliged to look for one in the neighbouring manor. There could hardly be a more eloquent expression of class-consciousness than this refusal to marry outside one's own circle.

Nevertheless, this group, apparently so firmly constituted, suffered from a curious internal contradiction. In many features, it was similar to the 'nobility' of the vassals—authority, social habits, type of wealth, the military calling. As soldiers its members were naturally required to go through certain legal formalities. Homage 'of mouth and hands' was not required for all ministerial fiefs, but for many of the most important this characteristic rite of military vassals was regarded as indispensable. Then there was initiation into knighthood: more than one dubbed knight was to be found among the *maires* and court officials. But these knights, these powerful individuals whose mode of life was that of the nobility, were in most cases serfs at the same time, and as such subject to *mainmorte* and the prohibition against *formariage* (except where exemption was purchased, always at considerable cost); unless enfranchised, they were excluded from holy orders; they were deprived of the right to bear witness in court against free men; above all, they bore the humiliating stigma of a subordination which was not of their own choosing. In short, their *de jure* status was in stark contrast with their *de facto* status; and the remedies for these inconsistencies that were finally evolved differed widely from country to country.

In England serjeanty was of least importance, even as a mere social factor. The village serjeants, as we have seen, were not as a rule specialists. The court officials were not ordinarily recruited from the bondmen, originally too poor and too few; later on, as serjeants were specifically exempted from rural labour services, there could be no question of ranking them among the villeins. Thus for the most part they escaped both the old form of servitude and the new. As free men they were subject only to the common law of free men; as knights—if they were admitted to knighthood—they enjoyed the prestige peculiar to knights. Legal doctrine was content to elaborate the rules proper to the fiefs of serjeanty, as distinct from the exclusively military fiefs, and above all strove to establish among the former an ever clearer line of demarcation between the 'grand' and most honourable serjeanties which *ipso facto* entailed homage, and the 'petty' serjeanties, which were virtually assimilated to 'free' peasant tenements.

In France a cleavage occurred. The less powerful or less fortunate of the *maires* remained simply rich peasants; sometimes they became farmers of the demesne and the seignorial rights, and sometimes also they became gradually detached from any administrative rôle. For when economic conditions once more made possible the payment of money wages many of the lords bought back the offices from their holders, in order to entrust the management of their estates to genuine salaried officials. Of the officials of baronial courts a certain number, who had been for a long time concerned in the administration of urban lordships, finally took their place among the town patriciate. Many others, however, together with the most favoured of the rural serjeants, found their way into the nobility at the time when it was being formed into a legal class. The preliminary phases of this fusion appeared at an early date, notably in the form of ever more frequent marriages between the families of *ministeriales* and those of the knightly vassals. The chroniclers as well as the anecdotists of the thirteenth century found a frequent theme in the misadventures of the knight of servile birth who sought to live down this taint, only to fall back after all into the hard grip of his master.

Serfdom in fact was the only effective barrier to an assimilation favoured by so many common characteristics. In one sense, the obstacle might seem to have been more impassable than ever from the thirteenth century onwards. For, from that period, by a significant break with almost immemorial usage, jurisprudence decided to regard knighthood as incompatible with serfdom—so much stronger had the sense of hierarchy now become. But this was also the period of the great movement of enfranchisement. Better provided with money than the common run of serfs, the serjeants everywhere were among the first to purchase their freedom. There was therefore nothing now—since the law proved adaptable—to debar those of them who were nearest to a knightly mode of life, and who perhaps already counted knights among their ancestors, from admission to the order of persons whose birth entitled them to knighthood. Nor, since they entered it completely free from any stigma, was there anything to distinguish them from the rest of the nobility. They were destined to be the progenitors of a considerable section of the petty nobility of the countryside, and they did not always remain confined to it. The dukes of Saulx-Tavannes, who ranked towards the end of the Ancien Régime among the greatest members of the military aristocracy, were descended from a provost (*prévôt*) of the lord of Saulx, enfranchised by the latter in 1284.[1]

In Germany, the group of court *Dienstmänner*, together with some rural serjeants, early assumed an exceptional importance. Vassalage had never figured as largely in German society as in northern France and Lorraine. The decay of the tie had been rapid and no one had been much concerned to find a remedy, as is clearly proved by the absence of any effort such as was represented elsewhere by the practice of liege homage. More than in any other country, therefore, it seemed desirable in Germany to entrust

[1] *Sur les routes de l'émigration. Mémoires de la duchesse de Saulx-Tavannes*, ed. de Valous, 1934, Introduction, p. 10.

the duties of seignorial households to unfree dependants. As early as the beginning of the eleventh century these 'serfs living as knights' (as they are called in a Swabian text) were so numerous at the courts of the principal magnates, and the spirit of solidarity which animated their turbulent little communities was so active, that a whole series of group 'customs' was created in which their privileges were defined. Soon these customs were set down in writing and fused into the common law of a class. The lot of the *ministeriales* seemed so enviable that in the following century more than one free man of honourable rank entered into servitude in order to join their number. They played a rôle of the first importance in military expeditions. They made up the bulk of the judiciary, for by a decision of the diet of the Empire they were allowed to form the courts of the princes, provided that at least two 'noblemen' sat with them. They held such a high place in the counsels of the great that the sole condition laid down by an imperial decision of 1216 for the alienation, by the emperor, of the homage of a principality was—in addition to the consent of the prince himself—the approval of the *ministeriales*. In the ecclesiastical lordships they occasionally took part in the election of the bishop or the abbot, and when the latter was away they tyrannized over the monks.

In the first rank were the *Dienstmänner* of the sovereign; for the high offices of the court, which the Capetians entrusted to the members of the vassal dynasties, were committed by their German neighbours to simple serjeants, born into servitude. Philip I of France, it is true, had taken a serf as chamberlain.[1] But the office was a relatively modest one and the case, it seems, remained exceptional. As seneschal the French king occasionally employed a great baron; as marshals he regularly employed petty nobles from the region between Loire and Somme. In Germany—where the changes of dynasty, and as we shall see, certain peculiarities in the structure of the State, prevented the kings from ever creating an Île-de-France, reservoir of a faithful and stable nobility—neither seneschals nor marshals of the Empire were normally chosen from any but men of servile condition. Undoubtedly there was opposition to this policy among the aristocracy; and this opposition (which is constantly reflected in the literature of the courts) seems to have been at the root of certain rebellions. But in spite of everything the *ministeriales* continued to form the normal *entourage* of the Salian and Hohenstaufen monarchs. To them were entrusted the education of the young princes, the custody of the most important castles, and sometimes, in Italy, the great administrative offices; to them also belonged the purest tradition of imperial policy. In the history of Barbarossa and his first successors, few men stand out so prominently as the uncouth figure of the seneschal Markward of Anweiler, who died regent of Sicily; he had

[1] The servile status of this person—as W. M. Newman has rightly perceived (*Le Domaine royal sous les premiers Capétiens*, 1937, p. 24, n. 7)—may be deduced from the fact that after his death the king received his *mainmorte*.

only been enfranchised in 1197, on the day when his master invested him with the duchy of Ravenna and the marquisate of Ancona.

It goes without saying that nowhere did these *parvenus*, by virtue of their power and mode of life, approach nearer to the world of vassals than in Germany; yet they were not absorbed into it almost imperceptibly as in France. There were too many of them for that; they had been too long segregated from other classes by their special customs; too much importance was still attached in Germany to the old concept of freedom in public law; lastly, the German legal mind was too fond of hierarchic distinctions. Knighthood was not forbidden to serfs; but the serf-knights (sometimes themselves divided, by a further refinement, into an upper and a lower group) formed in the general class of nobles a rank apart—the lowest. And no problem was more troublesome to the legal theorists or to the courts than that of deciding the exact status in relation to ordinary free men which was to be accorded to these persons, so powerful and yet branded with the stigma of serfdom. For after all, even burghers and simple peasants, though lacking so many of the things that gave prestige to the *ministeriales*, were none the less their superiors by purity of birth. This was a serious difficulty, particularly when it was a question of the composition of courts of justice. 'That no men of servile status be in future set up to judge you': this promise is still to be read in the charter which Rudolf of Habsburg granted to the peasants of the original cantons of Switzerland.[1]

Nevertheless the inevitable development came about eventually, as in France; but, with the usual lack of synchronism between the two evolutions, a century or a century and a half later. The less fortunate of the families of *Dienstmänner* remained among the rich peasantry or infiltrated into the bourgeoisie of the towns. Those who had been admitted to the knightly dignity, though they might still be excluded from the highest nobility (for the German nobiliary law to the end remained imbued with the spirit of caste), were henceforth at least no longer separated by any peculiar distinguishing mark from the knighthood of free birth. So here again—and this is no doubt the most important lesson provided by the history of the ministeriality—legal tradition had finally yielded to facts.

[1] *Quellenwerk zur Entstehung der schweizerischen Eidgenossenschaft*, no. 1650.

XXVI

CLERGY AND BURGESSES

1 THE ECCLESIASTICAL SOCIETY WITHIN THE FEUDAL WORLD

IN the feudal period the dividing-line between the clergy and lay society was not so clear and firm as that which the Catholic reform movement endeavoured to draw about the time of the Council of Trent. A whole population of 'tonsured persons', whose status remained ill-defined, formed an indeterminate borderland on the frontiers of the two great groups. Nevertheless the clergy constituted in a high degree a legal class; for, as a body, it was characterized by its own peculiar law and jealously-guarded rights of jurisdiction. On the other hand, it was in no sense a social class; within its ranks coexisted human types differing widely in mode of life, power and prestige.

First of all we have the multitude of monks, all 'sons of St. Benedict', but subject in fact to increasingly varied versions of the primitive Benedictine Rule—a divided and pulsating world, ceaselessly tossed to and fro between pure asceticism and the more mundane cares inseparable from the administration of great wealth, or even from the humble business of gaining a livelihood. Moreover, we must not picture this body as separated from the laity by impassable barriers. Even those Rules which embodied the most uncompromising principles of reclusion had in the last resort to yield to practical necessity. Monks had the cure of souls in parishes. Monasteries opened their schools to pupils who would never assume the cowl; especially after the Gregorian reform they became a nursery of bishops and popes.

Socially in the lowest category of the secular clergy, the priests of country parishes, poorly educated and badly paid, led a life which differed little if at all from that of their flocks. Before Gregory VII they had almost all been married. Even after the great ascetic campaign instigated—in the words of one monastic text—by 'that teacher of impossible things',[1] the 'priestess', the priest's wife in fact and sometimes in law, long continued to figure among the familiar personages of village folklore. So much was this the case that here the word class could almost have been taken in its strictest sense: in the England of Thomas Becket, dynasties of priests do not

[1] K. Rost, *Die Historia pontificum Romanorum aus Zwettl*, Greifswald, 1932, p. 177, n. 4.

appear to have been much more uncommon than descendants of 'popes' are today in the Orthodox countries, nor as a general rule less respectable.[1] Then, higher up the scale there was the wealthier and more refined circle of the town priests, the canons attached to a cathedral, the clerks or dignitaries of episcopal courts.

Finally, at the summit, forming to some extent the link between the two hierarchies, the regular and the secular, stood the prelates: abbots, bishops, and archbishops. In wealth, power, and aptitude for command these great lords of the Church were the equals of the greatest military barons.

Now the sole problem with which we need to concern ourselves here is a social one. This body of servants of God, whose mission, inherited from what was already an old tradition, remained in theory remote from all temporal concerns, was nevertheless obliged to find a place for itself in the characteristic structure of feudal society. In what degree was it influenced by surrounding institutions, while influencing them in its turn? In other words, since historians are accustomed to speak of the 'feudalization' of the Church, what concrete meaning are we to attach to this phrase?

For the clergy, preoccupied with liturgical duties or the demands of the ascetic life, with the cure of souls or with study, it was impossible to seek a livelihood through directly productive forms of labour. The monastic reformers attempted at various times to induce the monks to live on the produce of fields cultivated by their own hands. But they invariably ran up against the same fundamental difficulty: time devoted to these material tasks was time taken from meditation or divine service. As for hired labour, we know very well that it was out of the question. It was therefore necessary that the monk and the priest should live—as Ramon Lull said of the knight[2]—by the 'weariness' of other men. The country parson himself, though no doubt he did not disdain on occasion to handle the plough or the spade, derived the best part of his meagre income from the share of fees or tithe which the lord of the village had agreed to allot to him.

Formed by the accumulated alms of the faithful, augmented by purchases, often at a price which took into account the benefit of the prayers promised for the soul of the vendor, the patrimony of the great churches, or rather the patrimony of the 'saints' (for this, so far from being a mere legal fiction, was then the prevailing notion), was essentially of a seignorial nature. Immense fortunes were amassed by monastic communities or prelates, sometimes amounting to those almost princely agglomerations of estates and varied rights whose rôle in the establishment of territorial lordships we shall consider later. Now, lordship meant not only rents, but also authority. The heads of the clergy had therefore under their orders a great many lay dependants of every rank, from military vassals, indispensable

[1] See, especially, Z. N. Brooke in *Cambridge Historical Journal*, II, p. 222.
[2] See above, p. 319.

for the protection of such great properties, to villeins and 'commended men' of inferior degree.

The latter group, in particular, gravitated to the church estates in large numbers. Was it really because to live 'under the cross', rather than the sword, seemed an enviable lot? The controversy went back a long way: as early as the twelfth century, we find the critical Abelard opposing the views of the abbot of Cluny, eager to extol the mildness of the monastic régime.[1] In so far as it is permissible to leave the individual factor out of account, what it amounts to, after all, is the question whether a strict master (such as the clergy generally were) is better than an unreliable one. The problem is really insoluble; but two things are certain. The perennial character of ecclesiastical establishments and the respect which surrounded them caused them to be much sought after as protectors by the poor. Moreover, he who gave himself to a saint gained both protection against earthly perils and the no less precious benefits of an act of piety. It was a double advantage which the charters, drawn up in the monasteries, frequently expressed by asserting that the man who became the serf of a church was in reality entering into true freedom. By this was meant—though the distinction between the two ideas was not always very clearly drawn—that in this world he would share in the immunities of a privileged corporation, and in the next be guaranteed 'the eternal freedom which is in Christ'.[2] There are cases on record of grateful pilgrims earnestly seeking permission from their original lord to subject themselves and their posterity to the representatives of the powerful intercessor who had healed them.[3] Thus, in the formation of the network of personal subjections so characteristic of the age, the houses of prayer were among the most powerful centres of attraction.

Nevertheless, by thus transforming itself into a great earthly power, the Church of the feudal era exposed itself to two risks of which contemporaries were fully aware. In the first place, it was in danger of being too readily forgetful of its proper function. 'What a fine thing it would be to be archbishop of Rheims, if only one did not have to sing mass!' Public rumour attributed this remark to Archbishop Manasses, deposed in 1080 by the papal legates. Whether true or slanderous, the anecdote is symbolic of the period when the recruitment of the French episcopate was more scandalous than at any other time in its history. After the Gregorian reform, such cynicism would have made the story incredible. But the type of warrior prelate—those 'good knights of the clergy', as one German bishop called them—was to be found in all periods. Moreover, the spectacle of so much wealth amassed by churchmen, the resentment awakened in the hearts of 'impoverished' heirs at the thought of so many fine estates but

[1] Migne, *P.L.*, CLXXXIX, col. 146; P. Abaelardi, *Opera*, ed. V. Cousin, I, p. 572.
[2] A. Wauters, *Les Libertés communales. Preuves*, Brussels, 1869, p. 83 (1221, April). Cf. Marc Bloch, in *Anuario de historia del derecho español*, 1933, p. 79 *et seq.*
[3] L. Raynal, *Histoire du Berry*, I, 1845, p. 477, no. XI (23rd April 1071—22nd April 1093. Saint-Silvain de Levroux).

lately surrendered by their ancestors to monks skilled in making capital out of the fear of hell, together with the contempt of the warrior for so sheltered a mode of life, produced that brand of anticlericalism which found such forthright expression in many passages of the epics.[1] Though quite compatible with the renewal of generous alms-giving in moments of remorse, or in the anguish of death, these sentiments none the less underlay certain political attitudes as well as some genuinely religious movements.

In a world which was inclined to conceive of all ties between one man and another in terms of the most binding of them, it was almost inevitable that in the very heart of ecclesiastical society the practices of vassalage should impregnate relationships of subordination of a much older and essentially very different kind. The bishop demanded homage from the dignitaries of his chapter or the abbots of his diocese; the canons who held the largest prebends required it from their less well-provided colleagues; and the parish priests had to do homage to the head of the religious community on which their parishes were dependent.[2] The introduction into the spiritual citadel of customs so plainly borrowed from the secular world could not fail to arouse the protests of the rigorists. But the evil became much graver when the hands in which those of the priest, sanctified by the consecrated oil of ordination and the contact of the Eucharist, were placed for the rite of submission were the hands of a layman. The problem here is inseparable from another and much vaster one—one of the most anxious, certainly, which ever confronted the Church: the problem of appointments to the various posts in the ecclesiastical hierarchy.

It was not the feudal era which originated the practice of handing over to the temporal powers the responsibility for choosing the shepherds of souls. In the case of the village cures, of which the lords disposed more or less freely, the practice went back to the very origins of the parochial system. What of the bishops or abbots? The sole procedure conformable to the canonical rule was unquestionably election: by the clergy and people of the city, in the case of the former; by the monks, in the case of the latter. But as far back as the last days of the Roman Empire, the emperors had not hesitated to impose their will on the electors in the cities and even occasionally to appoint bishops directly. The sovereigns of the barbarian kingdoms followed suit, and the bishops were appointed by the rulers much more generally than hitherto. Abbots of monasteries which were not also directly

---

[1] Guibert de Nogent, *Histoire de sa vie*, I, 11 (ed. Bourgin, p. 31); Thietmar of Merseburg, *Chronicon*, II, 27 (ed. Holtzmann, pp. 72–3). For a characteristic reference in the epics, see *Garin le Lorrain*, ed. P. Paris, I, p. 2.

[2] The popes of the great Gregorian period have sometimes been credited with the design of making themselves the feudal lords of certain kings. It appears, in fact, that they confined themselves to claiming and sometimes obtaining an oath of fealty and a tribute—forms of subjection, undoubtedly, but with nothing peculiarly feudal about them. Homage was at that time demanded only of territorial princes (such as Norman leaders in southern Italy and the count of Substantion in Languedoc). John Lackland performed it, it is true; but at a much later date (1213).

348

dependent on the king were frequently appointed by the founder of the house or his heirs. The truth was that no serious government could afford to leave outside its control the assignment of offices which—apart from a heavy religious responsibility, from which no ruler solicitous for the welfare of his people had the right to dissociate himself—involved so great a measure of purely secular authority. Confirmed by Carolingian practice, the idea that it was for the kings to 'designate' the bishops ended by becoming a recognized principle. In the tenth century and the beginning of the eleventh, popes and prelates unanimously concurred in it.[1]

Nevertheless, in this sphere as in others, the institutions and practices inherited from the past were to come under the influence of a new social atmosphere.

In the feudal era every transfer of property—an estate, a right, or an office—was effected by the handing over of a material object which represented the subject of the grant. The cleric appointed by a layman to take charge of a parish, a diocese, or a monastery therefore received from this collator an 'investiture' in the usual forms. For the bishop the favourite symbol, from the time of the first Carolingians, was very naturally a crosier:[2] to this was later added a pastoral ring. It goes without saying that this delivery of insignia by a temporal chief by no means dispensed with the liturgical consecration; in this sense, it was powerless to create a bishop. But we should be gravely mistaken were we to imagine that its rôle was limited to marking the transfer to the prelate of the property attached to his new dignity. Both the right to the office and the right to the stipend that went with it—though no one felt the need to distinguish between two indissoluble elements—were thereby simultaneously conveyed. Moreover this ceremony, if it underlined somewhat crudely the preponderant part claimed by the secular authorities in ecclesiastical appointments, in itself added almost nothing to a state of things that had long been recognized. It was otherwise with another gesture charged with much deeper human significance.

From the cleric to whom he had just confided an ecclesiastical office, the local potentate or the sovereign expected in return an unwavering loyalty. Now, since the formation of Carolingian vassalage, no engagement of this nature—at least among the upper classes—was considered really binding unless it was contracted according to the forms developed by the Frankish practice of commendation. The kings and the princes were therefore accustomed to require from the bishops or abbots nominated by them an act of homage; and the lords of villages sometimes required the same of their parish priests. But homage, in the strict sense, was a rite of subjection;

---

[1] Jaffé-Wattenbach, *Regesta pontificum*, I, no. 3564; Rathier of Verona, in Migne' *P.L.*, CXXXVI, col. 249; Thietmar, *Chronicon*, I, 26 (pp. 34-5).

[2] For one of the earliest examples, often overlooked, see G. Busson and Ledru, *Actus pontificum Cenomannensium*, p. 299 (832).

and a much respected rite, moreover. By its means the subordination of the representatives of the spiritual power to the lay power was not only strikingly displayed; it was also reinforced, inasmuch as the combination of the two formal acts—homage and investiture—fostered a dangerous assimilation of the office of the prelate to the fief of the vassal.

The right to appoint the bishops and greater abbots, essentially a regalian attribute, was necessarily involved in the subdivision of sovereign rights in general, characteristic of feudal societies. But this fragmentation did not take place everywhere in equal degree, so that the effects on the recruitment of ecclesiastical officials varied widely. In regions where, as in France—especially in the South and Centre—many bishoprics fell under the control of the great barons and even of those of middle rank, the worst abuses found their favourite soil: from the hereditary succession of the father by the son to the open sale of the episcopal office. Note the contrast with Germany, where the kings were able to retain their grip on almost all the episcopal sees. Certainly their choice of bishops was not inspired by exclusively spiritual motives. Before all else, they needed prelates capable of governing, and even on occasion of fighting. Bruno of Toul, who under the name of Leo IX was to become a very saintly pope, owed his episcopal see primarily to qualities of which he had given proof as a military commander. To poor churches the sovereign by preference appointed rich bishops, nor was he himself above accepting the gifts which custom tended to make obligatory for newly invested persons, whether the object of the investiture was a military fief or a religious office. There is no doubt, however, that taken as a whole the imperial episcopate, under the Saxons and the first Salians, was far superior in education and moral tone to that of neighbouring countries. Once it became necessary for the Church to submit to a lay ruler it was evidently better for it to depend on one of higher rank, which tended to produce a broader outlook.

And now the Gregorian impulse began to be felt. There is no need here to recount the vicissitudes of this impassioned attempt to wrest the spiritual forces from the grip of the world and reduce the secular powers to the discreetly subordinate function of auxiliaries enrolled in the great work of salvation. The final balance-sheet, if we leave out of account many slight variations in the different countries, can be summarized in a few words.

It was not towards the parochial system that the principal effort of the reformers was directed. In the legal control of the parishes few changes were in fact made. A more respectable name, 'patronage', was finally substituted for the crude expression 'property', and there was a stricter control by the episcopal authority over the selection of priests; but these modest innovations did not count for much as against the right of nomination, which in practice was retained by the lords. The only new feature of any significance belonged to the domain of fact rather than of law: by gift or by sale, a great number of village churches had passed from the hands of laymen into those of ecclesiastical establishments, especially monasteries. The seignorial supremacy continued, even though it was now exercised by masters who ranked among the soldiers of the Church. It was one more proof that the manor, though essentially older than the rest of the social structure of feudalism, was one of its most indestructible parts.

So far as the great offices of the Church were concerned the most scandalous forms of subjection to the temporal power had been eliminated. There were no more monasteries openly 'appropriated' by local dynasts; no more military barons constituting themselves abbots or 'arch-abbots' of religious houses; no more investitures by the distinctive insignia of the spiritual power. The sceptre replaced the crosier and the ring, and the canonists laid it down in principle that the sole object of the ceremony was to grant the enjoyment of the material rights attached to the exercise of a religious function independently conferred. Election was universally recognized as the rule and laymen, even in the capacity of simple electors, were finally excluded from all regular participation in the choice of the bishop. The latter, as a consequence of a revolution which occupied the whole of the twelfth century, was henceforth designated by a college restricted to the canons of the cathedral church—a new feature, absolutely contrary to the primitive law and one which, more than any other, reveals the growing schism between the priesthood and the lay multitude.

Nevertheless, the elective principle functioned with difficulty, because of a reluctance merely to count votes. The decision was considered to belong, not to the majority pure and simple, but, according to the traditional formula, to the fraction which was at once 'the most numerous and the most sound'. It is doubtful if any minority resisted the temptation of denying to its adversaries, victorious according to the rule of number, the less ponderable of these two qualities. Hence the frequency of disputed elections, which favoured the intervention of authorities of higher rank—popes, assuredly, but also kings. Add to this that no one could cherish any illusions about the bias of very restricted electoral colleges, often closely subject to the influence of the least reputable local interests. The most intelligent canonists scarcely denied that a control exercised over a wider field would be in their view beneficial; and here the supreme head of the Church and the heads of state were in agreement. Under cover of a general reorganization of political forces the small fry among the barons in the greater part of the West were in fact gradually eliminated to the advantage of the king or a few particularly powerful princes; but the sovereigns who thus remained sole masters of the field were all the more capable of handling effectively the various means at their disposal for exerting pressure on the ecclesiastical bodies. One method of intimidation, the presence of the sovereign at the election, had been recognized as legal in 1122 by the Concordat concluded between the Pope and the Emperor. The monarchs most sure of their strength did not hesitate to resort occasionally to direct appointment. The history of the second feudal age, as of the centuries which followed, reverberated with the sound of the innumerable quarrels provoked, from one end of the Catholic world to the other, by appointments to bishoprics or abbacies. All in all, the Gregorian reform had shown itself powerless to wrest from the great temporal powers this means of control—in truth almost indispensable to their very existence—which consisted in the right to choose the principal dignitaries of the Church or, at the very least, to supervise the choice.

The bishop or abbot of the new age was endowed with vast manorial estates which imposed on him the normal obligations of every great baron to the king or prince, and which even involved services of more than ordinary importance; for ecclesiastical estates were, as we shall see, considered to be attached to the royal domain by a particularly close tie. Thus the ecclesiastical dignitary remained bound to his sovereign by duties of fidelity whose legitimate force could not be denied, and the reformers confined themselves to stipulating that these be expressed in a manner consistent with the high office of the churchman. That the prelate should pronounce the oath of fealty, well and good; but for him there must be no homage. Such was the theory—very logical and clear-cut— which, from the end of the eleventh century, councils, popes and theologians vied with each other in developing. For a long time it was disregarded in practice; but little by little it gained ground, and towards the middle of the thirteenth century, it had triumphed almost everywhere— with one important exception. France, the chosen home of vassalage, had remained on this point obstinately devoted to the traditional practices, and apart from a few special privileges, it remained attached to them till the sixteenth century. That St. Louis, calling one of his bishops to order, should not have hesitated to say to him 'you are my man, of your hands' is eloquent testimony to the persistence of the most characteristic concepts of feudalism, even when extended to an essentially spiritual society.[1]

2 THE BURGESSES

Beneath the noble and the churchman the literature of knightly inspiration affected to see only a uniform population of 'rustics' or 'villeins'. But really this vast multitude was deeply divided by various social distinctions. Even among the 'rustics', in the exact and restricted sense of the term, such distinctions prevailed. Not only did the different degrees of subjection create within their ranks fluctuating legal divisions, gradually reduced to the antithesis between 'servitude' and 'freedom'; side by side with those differences of status and unconnected with them, substantial economic inequalities also divided the small rural communities. To mention only the

[1] Joinville, c. CXXXVI.

simplest and most readily formulated contrast, what plough-owning peasant, proud of his draught animals, would have accepted as his equals the poor cultivators of his village who had to rely on their muscles to exploit their meagre plots?

Above all, apart from both the peasant population and the groups engaged in the honourable tasks connected with the exercise of authority, there had always existed isolated nuclei of merchants and craftsmen. From these beginnings, fostered by the economic revolution in the second feudal age, there arose the powerful and well-differentiated social group of the urban classes, swollen with innumerable additional elements. The study of a class so distinctively professional in character could not be undertaken without an intensive examination of its economics. A rapid sketch will be sufficient here to indicate its position against the backcloth of feudalism.

None of the languages spoken in feudal Europe possessed terms which allowed a clear distinction to be made between the town and the village. *Ville*, town, *Stadt* applied indifferently to both types of community. *Burg* designated any fortified area. *Cité* was reserved for the diocesan centres or, by extension, to some other centres of exceptional importance. On the other hand, as early as the eleventh century the name *bourgeois*, burgess, French by origin, but quickly adopted by international usage, was employed in unequivocal opposition to the words knight, cleric, villein. If the agglomeration as such remained anonymous, the most active of its denizens, those whose occupations as merchants and craftsmen were most typically urban, came to be recognized as a distinctive group in society, with a distinctive name. It was perceived that the dominant characteristic of the town was that it was inhabited by a special type of human being.

Of course it would be easy to exaggerate the contrast. The burgess of the early phases of town life shared with the knight a warlike disposition and the practice of bearing arms. For a long time he might be seen, like a peasant, attending to the cultivation of fields whose furrows were sometimes prolonged even inside the fortified enclosure, or one might find him outside the walls, driving his herds to graze on the jealously guarded common pastures. If he became rich he acquired rural manors in his turn. But for the burgess the activities which thus seemed to approximate him to the other classes were in fact only secondary and, most often, the survivals, as it were, of former modes of existence which he had gradually discarded.

Essentially the burgess lived by commerce. He derived his subsistence from the difference between the price at which he bought and the price at which he sold; or between the capital lent and the amount of repayment. And since the legality of such intermediate profit—unless it were merely a question of the wages of a workman or a carrier—was denied by the theologians and its nature ill-understood by knightly society, his code of conduct was in flagrant conflict with prevailing moral notions. For his part, as a speculator in real estate he found the feudal restrictions on his landed property intolerable. Because his business had to be handled rapidly and, as it grew, continued to set new legal problems, the delays, the complications, the archaism of the traditional judicial procedures exasperated him. The multiplicity of authorities governing the town itself offended him as obstacles to the proper control of business transactions and as an insult to the solidarity of his class. The diverse immunities enjoyed by his ecclesiastical or knightly neighbours seemed to him so many hindrances to the free pursuit of profit. On the roads which he ceaselessly traversed, he regarded with equal abhorrence rapacious toll-collectors and the predatory nobles who swooped down from their castles on the merchant caravans. In short he was harassed or annoyed by almost everything in the institutions created by a society in which he as yet had only a very small place. With franchises won by violence or purchased with hard cash, organized and equipped for economic expansion as well as for the necessary reprisals, the town which it was his ambition to build would be as it were a foreign body in feudal society.

In the last resort the collective independence which was the ideal of so many eager communities rarely went beyond varying degrees of limited administrative autonomy; but in order to escape the unintelligent restrictions of local tyrannies another course was available to the burgesses which, although it might seem little more than a desperate remedy, was often proved by experience to be the most effective. This was to place themselves under the protection of the great royal or princely governments, guardians of law and order over vast areas. Their very concern for their finances gave these authorities—as they came to appreciate more and more—an interest in the prosperity of rich taxpayers. In this way again, and perhaps more decisively, the increasing power of the burgesses tended to undermine one of the most characteristic features of feudalism—the subdivision of authority.

One act of outstanding significance generally marked the entry on the scene of the new urban community, whether in a mood of revolt or for peaceful organization. This was the communal oath of the burgesses. Hitherto they had been only isolated individuals: henceforth they had a collective being. It was the sworn association thus created which in France was given the literal name of *commune*. No word ever evoked more passionate emotions. The rallying cry of the bourgeoisies in the hour of revolt, the call for help of the burgess in peril, it awakened in what were previously the only ruling classes prolonged echoes of hatred. Why was there so much hostility towards 'this new and detestable name', as Guibert de Nogent called it? Many feelings no doubt contributed to it: the apprehensions of the powerful, directly threatened in their authority, their revenues, their prestige; the fears, not wholly groundless, aroused in the heads of the Church by the ambitions of groups with little respect for ecclesiastical 'liberties', which stood in their way; the contempt or ill-will

XII. The Land of the Slavs, Germania, Gaul (i.e. the Imperial Territories on the left bank of the Rhine) and Rome do obeisance to the Emperor Otto III. From Otto III's Gospelbook, School of Reichenau, end of the 10th century. Munich, Staatsbibliothek, Latin 4453.

XIII. THE LORD OF THE HILLS BECOMES THE LORD OF THE PLAIN

The Castle of Canossa in the Emilian Apennines.

of the knight for the trader; the virtuous indignation provoked in the heart of the cleric by the audacity of these 'usurers', of these 'engrossers' whose gains seemed to spring from tainted sources.[1] There was, however, another, and a deeper cause.

In feudal society the oath of aid and 'friendship' had figured from the beginning as one of the main elements of the system. But it was an engagement between inferior and superior, which made the one the subject of the other. The distinctive feature of the communal oath, on the other hand, was that it united *equals*. Certainly engagements of this type were not absolutely unknown. Of this nature, as we shall see, were the oaths taken 'one to another' by the fellow-members of those popular 'gilds' which Charlemagne prohibited; and later by the members of the peace associations of whom, in more ways than one, the urban communes were the heirs. Such again were the oaths which, before the first efforts of the towns to achieve autonomy, bound together the merchants in little societies, also sometimes called 'gilds'. These, although formed simply to serve the needs of commercial enterprise, constituted one of the earliest manifestations of burgess solidarity. But never, before the communal movement, had the practice of these mutual fealties been so widespread or displayed such strength. The 'conspiracies' which had arisen on every hand were truly like so many 'bundles of thorns intertwined', as one writer of sermons expressed it.[2] It was there, in the commune, that the really revolutionary ferment was to be seen, with its violent hostility to a stratified society. Certainly these primitive urban groups were in no sense democratic. The 'greater bourgeois', who were their real founders and whom the lesser bourgeois were not always eager to follow, were often in their treatment of the poor hard masters and merciless creditors. But by substituting for the promise of obedience, paid for by protection, the promise of mutual aid, they contributed to the social life of Europe a new element, profoundly alien to the feudal spirit properly so called.

[1] Cf. the synod of Paris, 1212: Mansi, *Concilia*, XXII, col. 851, c. 8 (*feneratoribus et exactoribus*).

[2] A. Giry, *Documents sur les relations de la royauté avec les villes*, 1885, no. XX, p. 58.

PART VII
Political Organization

XXVII

JUDICIAL INSTITUTIONS

1 GENERAL CHARACTERISTICS OF THE JUDICIAL SYSTEM

HOW were men tried? There is no better touchstone for a social system than this question. Let us therefore see how matters stood in this respect in the Europe of about the year 1000; on a first scrutiny, a few dominant features stand out in strong relief from the mass of legal detail. First, we may note the tremendous fragmentation of judicial powers; next, their tangled interconnections; and lastly, their ineffectiveness. The most serious cases could be heard in many different courts exercising parallel jurisdiction. Undoubtedly there were certain rules which, in theory, determined the limits of competence of the various courts; but in spite of them uncertainty persisted. The feudal records that have come down to us abound in charters relating to disputes between rival jurisdictions. Despairing of knowing before which authority to bring their suits, litigants often agreed to set up arbitrators of their own or else, instead of seeking a court judgment, they preferred to come to a private agreement—even at the risk that subsequently it might not be respected. Uncertain of its competence and doubtful of its strength, the court sometimes did not disdain to ask the parties to accept its judgment, either in advance or after it had been pronounced. Even if one had obtained a favourable decision there was often no other way to get it executed than to come to terms with a recalcitrant opponent. Nothing reminds us more forcibly than these conflicts that disorder can be a most important historic fact: a fact which nevertheless needs to be explained. In the present case it was clearly due in large part to the coexistence of contradictory principles which, being derived from diverse traditions and compelled to adapt themselves in a somewhat rough and ready fashion to the needs of a highly unstable society, were incessantly in conflict with each other. But it also had its source in the actual conditions imposed on the exercise of justice by the human environment.

In this society, in which protective relationships had multiplied, every chief—and there were certainly enough of them—desired to be a judge. One reason was that the right to sit in judgment on his subordinates, to the exclusion of other courts, alone enabled a lord both to protect them and to maintain effective control over them. Another was that this right was also

359

essentially lucrative. Not only did it carry with it the proceeds of judicial fines and costs, it also favoured, more than any other right, that transformation of usages into legal obligations which the lords found so profitable. It was no accident that the meaning of the word *justitia* was sometimes extended so as to describe a lord's powers as a whole. It is true that this was merely the recognition of a necessity common to almost all group activity: even in our own day, is not every employer in his business, every military commander, a judge after his fashion? But his powers in this capacity are limited to a well-defined sphere of activity. He must confine himself to judging the workman or the soldier as such. The chief of feudal times had greater scope, because the ties of subjection tended at that time to fetter the whole man.

Moreover, in feudal times the administration of justice was not a very complicated task, though it naturally called for a modicum of legal knowledge. Where written codes existed this amounted to knowing their rules more or less by heart or having them read to one; though often numerous and detailed, these rules were too rigid to require in most cases any personal effort of thought. If, on the other hand, written law had been superseded by oral custom, it sufficed to have some acquaintance with this diffuse tradition. Finally, it was important to know the prescribed gestures and the necessary phrases, which imposed a rigid formality on procedure. In short, it was all a matter of memory and practice. The means of proof were rudimentary and easily applied. The court seldom heard evidence, and when it did, confined itself to recording the statements of witnesses rather than examining them. To take cognizance of the contents of a legal document (which for a long time was rarely necessary), to receive the oath of one of the parties or of the oath-helpers, to declare the result of an ordeal or a trial by battle (the latter was increasingly favoured at the expense of other forms of 'judgment of God')—such duties required but little technical training. The matters with which the actions themselves were concerned were few and simple. The anaemic condition of commerce greatly reduced the number of cases relating to contracts. When in certain quarters, a more active economy of exchange once more developed, the inefficiency of the common law and the ordinary courts in dealing with such disputes early led the merchant groups to settle these among themselves, at first by unofficial arbitration, later by means of their own courts. Seisin (that is to say, possession sanctioned by long usage), powers over things and men—such were the constant subjects of almost all litigation. In addition, of course, there were crimes and civil wrongs to be dealt with; but here the action of the courts was, in practice, greatly restricted by private vengeance. In short, there was no intellectual obstacle to prevent anyone who had the necessary power from setting up himself or his representative as a judge.

Side by side with the ordinary courts, however, there existed a system of special courts—those of the Church. (We refer to the courts of the Church in the exercise of its proper function; for the judicial powers which bishops and monasteries exercised over their dependants, on the same basis as so many lay lords, naturally did not come under the heading of ecclesiastical jurisdiction in the true sense of the word.) These courts had a twofold sphere of action. They sought to embrace under their jurisdiction all tonsured persons, clerics and monks alike. In addition, they had more or less completely appropriated certain cases which, even when they concerned laymen exclusively, were considered to be of a religious nature— from heresy to the swearing of oaths and marriage. The growth of this jurisdiction during the feudal era not only reveals the weakness of the great temporal powers (the Carolingian monarchy had allowed much less independence to its clergy); it also bears witness to the tendency of the ecclesiastical world increasingly to widen the gulf between the small body of God's servants and the profane multitude. Here again the question of competence provoked lively quarrels about the limits of jurisdictions, which became especially fierce from the time when genuine state governments once again began to oppose the encroachments of the spiritual power.

Among the institutions peculiar to feudalism, both the judicial system of the Church and its law were thus a sort of empire within an empire, and for this reason it is logical that, having briefly recalled their rôle and their importance, we should exclude them from our review.

2 THE DISINTEGRATION OF JUDICIAL AUTHORITY

Like the law of persons, the judicial system in barbarian Europe had been dominated by the traditional antithesis between free men and slaves. The former were in theory tried by courts composed of other free men and the trials were conducted by a representative of the king. Over the slaves the master exercised a power of decision (in disputes among themselves) and a power of correction, which were too exclusively dependent on his personal discretion to be fitly described as justice. There were, it is true, exceptional cases of slaves being brought before the public courts, either because their owner voluntarily chose this method of relieving himself of responsibility, or even in certain cases because the law in the interests of good order compelled him to do so. But even then it was by superiors and not by equals that their fate was decided. Nothing was clearer than this contrast. Yet, at an early date, it had to give way before the irresistible pressure of circumstances.

In practice, as we know, the gulf between the two legal categories tended gradually to lessen. Many slaves had become tenants, as had many free men. Numbers of free men lived under the authority of a lord and held their fields from him; thus it is not surprising that the master frequently came to extend his right of correction uniformly over this mixed body of humble folk, and also appointed himself judge in the lawsuits which arose within the group. As early as the end of the Roman period, these private jurisdictions of the 'powerful', often with their own prisons, were springing up on the margin of the law. When the biographer of Caesarius of Arles, who died in 542, praises his hero for never having allotted more than twenty-nine strokes with a stick to any of his dependants (at least not at one time), he makes it clear that the saint showed this mildness not only towards his slaves but also towards 'the free men of his obedience'. It was left to the barbarian monarchies to give legal recognition to this *de facto* situation.

This from the outset was one of the principal objects of the Frankish 'immunity', and soon became its real *raison d'être*. Of great antiquity in Gaul, this institution was disseminated by the efforts of the Carolingians throughout their vast empire. The term designated the combination of two privileges: exemption from certain fiscal burdens; and the immunity of a territory from visitation by the royal officials, for any reason whatsoever. It thus almost necessarily involved the delegation to the lord of certain judicial powers over the population.

It is true that the grant of immunities by specific charter appears to have been strictly limited to ecclesiastical authorities, and the rare examples to the contrary which one might be tempted to cite are not only of late date, but are clearly accounted for by wholly exceptional circumstances. Moreover, even if the silence of the cartularies, always suspect, does not carry conviction, that of the formularies employed by the Frankish chancellery should do so; and there we should look in vain for a form of document of this type in favour of laymen. In practice, nevertheless, a large number of the latter had attained the same advantages by other means. Traditionally, the royal estates were also classed as 'immunities'; in other words, being run directly for the benefit of the prince and administered by a special body of agents, they were outside the control of the ordinary royal officials. The count and his subordinates were forbidden to levy any taxes on them and even to enter them. Now, when the king, in return for services rendered or to be rendered, granted away one of these estates, he ordinarily allowed it to retain the privilege of exemption previously enjoyed. In theory the 'benefit', as a temporary grant, continued to form part of the domain of the crown, so that the powerful men, whose wealth was in very large part derived from these liberalities, enjoyed on many of their manors exactly the same legal privileges as the ecclesiastical immunists. Moreover, there can be no doubt that they often succeeded, less legitimately, in extending them to their patrimonial possessions, which they had so long been accustomed to rule as masters.

These grants continued to be made throughout the first feudal age, and till a much later date the chancelleries still handed down their formulas, which by that time had become rather meaningless. The sovereigns had been led to resort to them for various reasons all equally cogent. In the case of the churches, to load them with favours was a pious duty which came near to being identified with a duty of good government, since the prince thereby called down upon his peoples the dew of heavenly blessings. As for the magnates and the vassals, these gifts were considered the necessary price of their fickle loyalty. Moreover, there was something to be said for restricting the scope of the royal officials. Harsh in their treatment of their master's subjects, and often not particularly submissive to the master himself, their conduct gave only too much ground for mistrust. Henceforth, it was on the chiefs of the little groups into which the mass of its subjects was divided, as much as on the royal officials, that the crown laid the responsibility for ensuring order and obedience; by strengthening their authority it hoped to consolidate its own police system. Finally, the encroachments of private jurisdictions had been growing for a long time, and since they arose from the mere exercise of force, it was force alone which determined their limits. By legalizing them they could be brought within proper bounds. This concern, very evident in the Carolingian immunity, was bound up with the general reform of the judicial system undertaken by Charlemagne, which was destined to exercise a strong influence on all subsequent developments.

In the Merovingian state the fundamental judicial division had been a comparatively small territory: allowing, needless to say, for innumerable local variations, it was more or less the equivalent in size of the smallest of the *arrondissements*, the districts into which the French departments were divided by Napoleon. It was generally known by Romance or Germanic names signifying 'a hundred'—a designation of rather mysterious origin, which went back to the old institutions of the Germanic peoples and perhaps to a numerical system different from ours (the earliest meaning of the word which in modern German is written as *hundert* seems to have been 'one hundred and twenty'). In Romance-speaking regions, the terms *voirie* or *viguerie* (Latin, *vicaria*) were also used. The count, in the course of his circuit through the various hundreds placed under his authority, summoned all the free men to his court. There judgment was rendered by a small group of 'jurors' taken from the assembly; the rôle of the royal official was confined to presiding over the proceedings and getting the sentences carried out.

In practice, however, this system seemed to suffer from a double drawback: for the local inhabitants it involved too frequent summonses, and on the count it imposed a responsibility too heavy for him to fulfil satisfactorily. Charlemagne therefore substituted for it a system in which there were two courts at different levels, each enjoying full powers within its own sphere. The count continued to visit the hundred regularly to hold his court, and this, as in the past, the whole population was obliged to attend.

But these plenary sessions of the count's court now took place only three times a year—an arrangement which made possible a limitation of competence. For henceforward the only cases brought before these general assemblies were those turning on the most important matters—the 'major causes'. As for the 'minor causes', they were reserved for less infrequent and more restricted sittings, which only the jurors were obliged to attend and which were presided over by a simple subordinate of the count—his representative in the district, the 'hundred-man', known in France as the *centenier* or *voyer*.

Now, despite the appalling vagueness of our documents, there can be scarcely any doubt that in the reign of Charlemagne and his immediate successors the extent of the jurisdiction conceded to the immunists over the free men of their territories coincided generally with the 'minor causes'. In other words, the lord enjoying this privilege acted within his own territory in the capacity of *centenier*. What happened if a 'major' cause were in question? The immunity stood in the way of any attempt by the count himself to seize the accused, the defendant, or the oath-helpers in exempt territory. But the lord was obliged on his own responsibility to deliver the persons summoned to the count's court. Thus, cutting his losses, the sovereign hoped at least to preserve the most serious decisions for the public law courts.

The distinction between major and minor causes was to have prolonged repercussions. It is this distinction, in fact, which we find persisting throughout the feudal era and much later still under the new names of 'high' and 'low' justice. This fundamental antithesis, common to all the countries which had been subject to Carolingian domination and to those alone, continued to distinguish between two degrees of competence which, within the same territory, were not necessarily united in the same hands. But neither the limits of the judicial powers thus superimposed, nor their distribution, remained at all as they had been when first established.

In criminal justice, the Carolingians had, after some uncertainty, established a criterion for 'major causes' based on the nature of the punishment: the count's court alone could pronounce sentence of death or reduction to slavery. This principle, a very clear one, passed down through the ages. As a result of changes in the conception of freedom, penal enslavement proper rapidly disappeared (where we find the murderer of a serf being enslaved to the lord of his victim the case comes under quite a different heading—it is classed as compensation). Crimes 'of blood', however—that is, crimes punishable by death—always remained within the normal jurisdiction of those who exercised 'high justice'. But these 'pleas of the sword', as they were called in Norman law, ceased to be the privilege of a few great counts. One of the most striking features of the first feudal age everywhere, but particularly in France—and one most decisive for the future—was the multitude of petty chiefs thus provided with powers of life and death. What then had happened? It is clear that neither the fragmentation of certain powers of the count by inheritance or gift, nor even usurpations pure and simple, can suffice to explain the phenomemon. What is more, there are various indications which clearly point to an actual change in juridical values. All the great ecclesiastical authorities exercised judgment of blood, either on their own account or through their representatives; this right had in fact become a natural consequence of the privilege of immunity, in defiance of the ancient rules. It was sometimes called *centaine* or *voirie*—a sort of official recognition that it was henceforth regarded as being within the competence of the lower courts. In other words, the barrier raised not so long before by the Carolingians had on this point given way. And this development can without doubt be explained.

It would indeed be a mistake to imagine that these death sentences, formerly reserved for the count's courts—or, at a higher level still, for the king's court or the assizes held by the *missi*—had ever been very numerous in the Frankish period. Only crimes considered particularly heinous from the point of view of the public peace were at that time visited with such punishments. Much more often, the rôle of the judges was confined to proposing or imposing a settlement, and then ordering the payment, in accordance with the legal tariff, of an indemnity, of which the judicial authority took a share. But in the period when governments were at their weakest, there were continual vendettas and acts of violence, and it was not long before a reaction set in against the old system of criminal justice, whose dangerous inefficiency seemed to be demonstrated by events. This reaction was closely bound up with the movement which gave rise to the peace associations. It found its most characteristic expression in the entirely new attitude adopted by the most influential ecclesiastical circles. Not so long before, through their horror of bloodshed and feuds, they had favoured the practice of pecuniary settlements. But now they began to insist that these too lenient measures should be replaced by afflictive penalties, which in their view were alone capable of frightening evil-doers. It was in this period—about the tenth century—that the European penal code began to assume that aspect of extreme harshness which it was destined to retain until the humanitarian movement of comparatively recent times. This grim development, which was to result in increased indifference to human suffering, had nevertheless been originally inspired by the desire to alleviate it.

Now in all criminal cases, however serious, in which the executioner had no part the inferior jurisdictions, courts of hundreds or immunity, had always been competent. When money compensation gradually gave way to punishment, the judges remained the same; the only change was in the nature of the sentences pronounced, and the death penalty ceased to be the monopoly of the counts. The transition, moreover, was facilitated by two features of the earlier system. The hundred courts had always possessed the right to punish with death criminals caught *in flagrante delicto*. So much concern for public order had seemed to require. This same concern now induced these courts to pass beyond the limit previously fixed. As for the immunists, they had always had the power of life and death over their slaves. Where henceforth, among dependants, was the dividing line between freedom and slavery?

Apart from crimes, the count's courts had had exclusive jurisdiction over two classes of cases: those which turned on the status, free or unfree, of one of the parties, or which concerned the possession of slaves; and those which related to the possession of allodial lands. This double heritage was not to pass intact to the much greater number of courts exercising high justice in the succeeding age. Lawsuits relating to allods—which were becoming increasingly rare—often remained the monopoly of the real heirs of the count's rights; this was the case until the twelfth century at Laon, where the count was the bishop.[1] As for questions relating to servile status or slaves, the virtual disappearance of household slavery, as well as the emergence of a new conception of freedom, led to their being merged in the mass of disputes on property in general and personal dependence—a type of dispute which had never been included among 'major causes'. Despoiled, as it were, at the lower end as well as the upper, it might be thought that 'high justice' was now confined to the rôle of a purely criminal jurisdiction; but the 'civil' side—in the modern sense of the word—returned to it through the medium of procedure. In the feudal era a very great number of disputes of every kind were decided by single combat. Now, by a natural association of ideas, it was admitted—not invariably, but very frequently —that this sanguinary solution could only be effected before courts having jurisdiction in the case of crimes punishable by death.

In feudal times everyone who exercised the rights of 'high justice' also possessed those of 'low justice' over the territories under his direct control. But the converse was not true, except in certain regions and only there at a later stage—as in Beauvaisis in the thirteenth century, if Beaumanoir is to be believed. Thus it was for a long time not exceptional for men subject to the jurisdiction of their local lord in minor cases to take their more serious actions to a neighbouring court. Extensive as had been the subdivision of judicial powers, it had not done away with the system whereby two degrees of competence, a higher and a lower, reposed in different hands; though it had moved it one step down all along the line. Just as the successors of the *voyers* or *centeniers* and the immunists (not to mention a great many powerful men, with no official position) had taken from the count—save in matters relating to allods—the monopoly of major causes and thus come to exercise 'high justice', so in their turn they lost the monopoly of minor causes, to the advantage of the great body of manorial lords. Whoever

---

[1] For the peace institution of Laon (26th August, 1128), see Warnkoenig and Stein, *Französische Staats- und Rechtsgeschichte*, I, *Urkundenbuch*, p. 31, c. 2.

found himself the master of a small group of humble dependants, whoever derived rents and services from a small group of rural tenements, henceforth possessed at least the right of 'low justice'. In this right many elements of different date and different kinds were mingled.

It included in the first place the trial of all disputes between the lord himself and his tenants—particularly as regards the obligations of the latter. It is useless to try to explain this right as a legacy of official judicial systems. Its real source was in an ancient yet increasingly prevalent conception of the powers proper to the chief, or rather to the person, whoever he might be, who was in a position to exact from another man an obligation which savoured of inferiority. In France in the twelfth century we find the holder of a modest tenement in villeinage, which he in turn had rented to a cultivator, getting his own lord to grant him, in the event of the rent not being paid, 'the exercise of jurisdiction in this matter only and in none other'.[1] From jurisdiction properly so called to distraint carried out personally by the creditor—so frequently practised at that time and often legally recognized—the transitions were not always very perceptible and most people no doubt failed to make any very clear distinction between the two ideas. This jurisdiction over tenants' obligations—called *justice foncière* by French jurists of a later age—did not, however, constitute the whole of 'low justice'. He who exercised the latter was, for the men who lived on his land, the normal judge of practically all the civil actions which they could institute among themselves (unless there was recourse to trial by battle), as well as of all except the most serious of their offences. His function was thus a mixture of the legacy of 'minor causes' and that of the rights of decision and correction which had for so long been exercised in fact by the masters.

Both high justice and low justice were essentially territorial: he who resided within their boundaries was subject to them; he who lived outside was not. But, in a society in which the ties between man and man were so strong, this territorial principle had constantly to compete with a personal principle. Whoever in the Frankish period extended his *maimbour* over someone weaker than himself assumed both the right and the duty of accompanying his protégé to court, of defending him there and of standing surety for him. From this to claiming the power of pronouncing sentence upon him was an easy step; and it was in fact taken at all levels of the hierarchy.

Among the personal dependants, the humblest and most subordinate were those who, on account of the hereditary character of the bond, it had become customary to describe as unfree. It was in general considered that they could only be tried, at any rate for crimes punishable by death, by the lord to whom they were personally bound—this even when they did not live on his land, or when the lord did not exercise high justice over his

---

[1] *Cartulaire du prieuré de Notre-Dame de Longpont*, ed. Marion, no. 25.

other tenants. It was often sought to apply similar principles to other types
of humble dependant who, though not in hereditary bondage to the master,
were none the less considered to be very close to his person: servants of
both sexes, for example, or again the merchants who, in the cities, acted as
buying and selling agents for ecclesiastical lords. These claims, of which it
was difficult to obtain practical recognition, were a constant source of
uncertainty and conflict.

In so far as the new form of servitude had retained the imprint of the
old, the exclusive jurisdiction of the lord over his serfs might be regarded
as the natural consequence of the old right of correction—such, moreover, is the idea which seems still to be expressed in one German text of
the twelfth century.[1] The military vassals, on the other hand, as free men,
were in the Carolingian epoch subject only to the jurisdiction of the public
courts. This at least was their position in law. Can it be doubted that in
fact the lord himself tried to settle the differences which threatened to sow
discord among his vassals, or that persons injured by the henchmen of a
powerful man ordinarily considered that they were more sure of obtaining
redress by going to him? From the tenth century onwards, these practices
gave rise to a genuine right of jurisdiction. The change, moreover, had
been favoured and sometimes rendered almost imperceptible by the way in
which the general evolution of powers had affected the public tribunals. In
the form of 'honours', and later as patrimonial fiefs, these courts had for
the most part fallen into the hands of the magnates, who filled them with
their retainers; and in certain principalities we can follow clearly the
process by which the count's court, thus composed, was gradually transformed into a really feudal court, in which it was the vassals themselves
who decided the cases of other vassals.

3 TRIAL BY PEERS OR TRIAL BY THE LORD

The free man tried by an assembly of free men, the slave punished by his
master alone—this division could scarcely survive the drastic changes in
social classifications nor, in particular, the entry into servitude of so many
men formerly free who in their new bonds still retained many of the
features of their original status. The right to be tried by their 'peers' was
never disputed in the case of persons of even the most modest rank—
despite the introduction of hierarchic distinctions which seriously impaired the old principle of judicial equality, born simply of a common
freedom. What is more, in many places customary law extended to
dependants and even to serfs the right of trial, if not always by exact
equals, at least by bodies composed of subjects of the same master. In the
regions between Seine and Loire, high justice continued ordinarily to be
dispensed in general assemblies (*plaids généraux*), which the entire popula-

[1] Ortlieb of Zwiefalten, *Chronicon*, I, c. 9, in *M.G.H.*, SS. X, p. 78.

tion of the territory was required to attend. As for the jurors, they were still frequently appointed for life by the holder of the judicial rights, in conformity with the purest Carolingian tradition, and were still known as *échevins* (*scabini*); in other cases, as a result of the feudalization of offices, the hereditary obligation to sit in the court was finally attached to certain tenements. Elsewhere, the lord or his representative appears to have been content to surround himself, in a somewhat haphazard way, with the chief personages, the 'good men and true' of the locality. Over and above these divergences, a central fact remains. To speak of royal, baronial, or seignorial justice may be convenient. But it is only legitimate provided that we do not forget that the king or the great baron almost never decided a case personally and that the same was true even of many manorial lords or stewards. Convoked by the chief, who frequently presided over it, it was his court which 'declared' or 'found' the law; that is, it recalled the rules and incorporated them in its judgment. 'The court passes judgment; not the lord', one English text declares, in so many words.[1] And no doubt it would be as unwise to exaggerate as to deny altogether the protection thus afforded to the litigants. 'Quick, quick, hasten ye to get me a judgment'—thus spoke the impatient Henry Plantagenet, demanding of his vassals the condemnation of Thomas Becket.[2] The command neatly reflects the limitations—varying immensely from case to case—imposed by the power of the chief on the impartiality of the judges; at the same time it shows that even the most imperious of tyrants found it impossible to dispense with a collective judgment.

But the idea that the unfree and, by a natural assimilation, the humblest dependants should have no other judge than their master was too deeply rooted in men's minds to be easily obliterated. In the countries that were formerly Romanized, moreover, it found support in what had remained of the imprint or the memories of Roman organization; there the magistrates had been the superiors, not the equals, of those subject to their jurisdiction. Once more the existence of contrary principles, between which it was necessary to choose, produced a diversity of customs. According to the region or even the village, the peasants were tried sometimes by the whole body of the court, sometimes by the lord or his steward alone. The latter system does not appear to have been the most usual at first, though during the second feudal age the course of development turned clearly in its favour. 'Court baron', composed of free tenants who decided the fate of other free tenants; 'customary court', in which the villein, henceforth regarded as unfree, submitted to the judgment of the lord's steward—such was the distinction, pregnant with consequences, which in the thirteenth century English jurists strove to introduce into the hitherto much simpler judicial structure of the English manor. Similarly in

---

[1] *Monumenta Gildhallae Londoniensis* (Rolls Series), 1, p. 66.
[2] Roger of Hoveden, *Chronica* (Rolls Series), Vol. I, p. 228.

France, in defiance of what was still a widespread practice, legal doctrine as interpreted by Beaumanoir chose to regard trial by peers as the monopoly of noblemen. The hierarchization, which was one of the marks of the period, forced even the judicial system to subserve its ends.

4 ON THE EDGE OF DISINTEGRATION:
SURVIVALS AND NEW FACTORS

Subdivided and manorialized though judicial authority was, it would be a grave mistake to imagine that in the feudal world nothing survived of the old courts of popular or public law, though their power of resistance to change, nowhere negligible, varied greatly from country to country. The time has therefore come to emphasize national contrasts more clearly than has been done so far.

Despite its distinctive features, the course of development in England presented some obvious analogies with that in the Frankish state. Here again we find, at the base of the organization, the hundred with its court of free men. Above the hundreds, and comprising a varying number of them, were the counties (called in the native speech 'shires'). In the south they corresponded to actual ethnic divisions, ancient kingdoms such as Kent or Sussex which had gradually been absorbed in larger monarchies, or else groups spontaneously formed within a people in the course of settlement, like Suffolk and Norfolk ('southern folk' and 'northern folk') which represented the two halves of the original East Anglia. In the centre and north, on the other hand, the counties were at the outset only administrative and military districts created more recently and more arbitrarily at the time of the struggle with the Danes, each with a citadel as its centre, which explains why in this part of the country they mostly bear the name of the county town. Henceforth, the shire also had its court of free men; but the division of competence between county and hundred was here much less clearly marked than in the Carolingian Empire. Despite some efforts to reserve for the county court the trial of certain crimes particularly inimical to the public peace, it appears to have intervened mainly in cases where the lower court had proved powerless to act. This explains why the distinction between high and low justice always remained foreign to the English system.

As on the continent, these public tribunals had to compete with the courts of the chiefs. At an early date we find mention of sessions held by the lord in his house, his 'hall'. Later the kings legalized this *de facto* situation, and from the tenth century onwards we find them granting rights of jurisdiction known as 'sake and soke' (*sake*, which corresponds to the German noun *Sache*, signified 'case' or 'action'; *soke*, which is to be compared with the German verb *suchen*, meant seeking a judge, that is, having recourse to his judgment). The powers thus granted, which applied

370

sometimes to a particular territory, sometimes to a group of persons, coincided more or less with what we know to have been the very wide competence of the Anglo-Saxon hundred. This gave them, from the beginning, a larger sphere of application than that which, in theory, went with the Carolingian immunity, though it was approximately equal to the rights which the immunists had contrived to appropriate in the tenth century. The influence of these rights upon social ties was such that the free tenant derived from his submission to the master's court his ordinary title of sokeman, literally 'suitor'. Sometimes certain churches or certain magnates received as a gift in perpetuity the right to hold a hundred court; and a few monasteries—though very few—were even accorded the right to try all crimes, including those normally reserved for the king.

Nevertheless, these grants, important as they were, never completely superseded the old communal courts of public law. Even where the hundred court was in the hands of a baron it continued to meet, as in the days when it had been presided over by a representative of the king. As for the county court, it continued to function without interruption according to the ancient forms. It is true that the great men, too exalted in rank to submit to the judgments of these tribunals, and the peasants—even the free ones—who had been snapped up by the manorial courts, ceased generally to appear at these assemblies (though for the humble folk of the villages it was still obligatory, in theory, to be represented by the priest, the reeve, and four men). But all who occupied an intermediate position in power and freedom were still required to attend. Stifled between the lords' courts and—after the Norman Conquest—the encroachments of royal justice, the old courts were progressively reduced to relative insignificance. Nevertheless it was there—within the framework of the county, mainly, but also in the more restricted sphere of the hundred—that the most vital elements in the nation preserved the habit of meeting to determine the customary law of the territorial group, reply in its name to all manner of inquiries and even, if the need arose, bear the responsibility for its collective offences. And so it continued till the time when, summoned to meet as one body, the representatives of the shire courts formed the earliest nucleus of what was later to be the House of Commons. Assuredly the English parliamentary system was not cradled in 'the forests of Germania'. It bore the deep imprint of the feudal environment from which it sprang. But the peculiar quality which distinguished it so sharply from the continental systems of 'Estates', and, more generally, that collaboration of the well-to-do classes in power, so characteristic of the English political structure as long ago as the Middle Ages—the origin of these is surely to be found in the firm establishment on English soil of the system of assemblies composed of the free men of the territory, in accordance with the ancient practice of the barbarian epoch.

Over and above the infinite variety of local or regional customs, two great facts dominated the evolution of the German judicial system. First, since the 'law of fiefs' remained distinct from the 'law of the land', the feudal courts developed side by side with the ancient tribunals, without absorbing them. Secondly, the maintenance of a more stratified social hierarchy, and more especially, the long survival of the idea that to enjoy freedom was to be subject directly to the authority of the State, preserved for the ancient courts of county and hundred (whose respective jurisdictions were somewhat imperfectly delimited) a very extensive sphere of action. This was especially the case in the Swabian Alps and in Saxony, regions of many allods and of incomplete feudalization. It was nevertheless customary, as a general rule, to require the jurors or *scabini* (German, *Schöffen*) to be possessed of a certain amount of landed wealth. Sometimes, in accordance with what was then an almost universal tendency, their offices were even regarded as hereditary; so that the very respect for the old principle that a free man should be tried by a court of free men often resulted in the long run in the composition of the courts being more oligarchic than elsewhere.

France (along with northern Italy, of course) was the land of feudalized justice in its purest form. It is true that the Carolingian system left deep and lasting traces, especially in the northern parts of the country, but their influence was chiefly felt in the hierarchization of the seignorial courts—in terms of high and low justice—and their internal organization. The hundred or district courts disappeared very rapidly and very completely. It is characteristic that the jurisdiction of the lord who exercised high justice ordinarily acquired the name of 'castellany'—as if the only source of judicial rights that common opinion now recognized was the possession of a fortified dwelling, at once the origin and the symbol of actual power. This is not to say, however, that nothing survived of the old jurisdictions of the counts. In the great territorial principalities the prince was sometimes able to reserve for himself the monopoly of cases where the death penalty was involved—as in Flanders, Normandy, Béarn. Frequently, as we have seen, the count had jurisdiction over allodial estates; he decided lawsuits in which the churches, imperfectly incorporated in the feudal hierarchy, figured as parties; and, in theory, he possessed jurisdiction over markets and public highways, except where these rights had been granted away or usurped. Here already, at least in embryo, was a powerful antidote to the dispersal of judicial powers.

Furthermore, two great forces throughout Europe were working to limit or counteract the disintegration of judicial powers; both for a long time had only a modest success, but both were rich in promise.

First, there were the monarchies. That the king was by his very nature the supreme judge of his people—on this point all were agreed. It remained to deduce the practical consequences of this principle; and here it became a question of action and effective power. In the eleventh century the functions of the Capetian royal court were largely confined to trying cases

372

involving the ruler's immediate dependants and his churches, or (on exceptional occasions and much less effectively) acting as a feudal court with jurisdiction, in theory, over the great feudatories of the crown. On the other hand the tribunal of the German king, conceived on the Carolingian model, still attracted a large number of important cases. But even when relatively active, these courts attached to the person of the sovereign obviously remained inaccessible to the mass of his subjects. It was not enough that, as in Germany, wherever the king passed in the course of his official visitations his jurisdiction should supersede all others. The power of the monarchy could become a decisive element in the judicial system only by extending its grip over the entire realm by means of a complete network of itinerant justices or permanent representatives. This was achieved at the time of the general reconcentration of authority during the second feudal age, first by the Norman and Angevin kings of England, later and much more slowly by the Capetians. In both countries, but in France especially, the monarchy was to find a valuable buttress in the system of vassalage itself. For feudalism, which had had the effect of dividing judicial authority among so many hands, nevertheless provided a remedy for this process in the practice of appeals.

At this period, no lawsuit, once decided, could be begun again between the same adversaries in a different court, since it was held that for a genuine error, committed in good faith, there was no redress. Suppose, however, that one of the litigants believed that the court had deliberately rendered false judgment, or else that he charged it with having bluntly refused to try the action at all. There was nothing to prevent him from proceeding against the members of this court in a higher one. If, in this action, absolutely distinct from the previous one, he won his case, the bad judges were generally punished and their judgment was in any case annulled. This form of appeal—we should today call it 'suing the judge'—existed as early as the era of the barbarian kingdoms. But at that time it could only be brought before the sole tribunal which stood above the assemblies of free men—namely the royal court. Thus the procedure was an unusual and a difficult one. The system of vassalage opened up new possibilities; every vassal's feudal lord was henceforth his normal judge; and the denial of justice was a crime, like other crimes. Quite naturally, the common rule was applied to it and appeals ascended, step by step, through the gradations of homage. The procedure continued to require delicate handling; above all it was dangerous, for the customary mode of proof was trial by battle. However, the feudal court, recourse to which was henceforth necessary, proved much more accessible than that of a king too far removed from his subjects; if a case eventually reached the sovereign's court it did so by successive stages. In the legal affairs of the upper classes appeals became less and less exceptional. Because it involved a hierarchy of ties of dependence and established a series of direct contacts between chiefs ranged one above the other, the system of vassalage and the fief permitted the reintroduction into the judicial organization of an element of unity which monarchies of the earlier type, out of touch with the mass of their nominal subjects, had shown themselves powerless to safeguard.

XXVIII

THE TRADITIONAL POWERS:
KINGDOMS AND EMPIRE

1 GEOGRAPHICAL DISTRIBUTION OF THE MONARCHIES

ABOVE the profusion of manors, family or village communities, and vassal groups, there were in feudal Europe various powers whose wider range was for a long time counter-balanced by much less effective action; it was nevertheless their destiny to maintain in this divided society certain principles of order and unity. At the summit, kingdoms and Empire derived their strength and their ambitions from a long past. Lower down, younger powers were ranged one above another, by an almost imperceptible gradation, from the territorial principality to the simple barony or castellany. We must first consider the position of the powers with a long history behind them.

After the fall of the Roman Empire, the West had been divided up into kingdoms ruled by Germanic dynasties. It was from these 'barbarian' monarchies that almost all those of feudal Europe were more or less directly descended. The line of descent was particularly clear in Anglo-Saxon England, which towards the first half of the ninth century was still divided into five or six kingdoms; genuine heirs—although their number was much smaller—of the states founded not so long before by the invaders. We have seen how the Scandinavian invasions left in the end only Wessex, enlarged at the expense of its neighbours. In the tenth century its sovereign took to calling himself either king of all Britain, or more frequently and with more lasting effect, king of the Angles or English. On the frontiers of this *regnum Anglorum* there nevertheless subsisted, at the time of the Norman Conquest, a Celtic fringe. The Britons of Wales were divided among several little principalities. Towards the north a family of Scottish —that is to say, Irish—chiefs, conquering in turn the other Celtic tribes of the Highlands and the Germanic or Germanized populations of Lothian, had bit by bit established a large realm, which took from the conquerors the name of Scotland.

In the Iberian peninsula a number of Gothic nobles, who had taken refuge in Asturias after the Moslem invasion, had set up a king. Several times partitioned among the heirs of the founder, but considerably enlarged by the Reconquest, the state thus formed had its capital transferred, about the beginning of the tenth century, to Leon, on the plateau to the south of the mountains. In the course of the same century a military command which had been established to the east in Castile, and which had at first been dependent on the kingdoms of Asturias and Leon, gradually made itself autonomous and its chief, in 1035, took the title of king. Then a century or so later a similar secession in the west gave birth to Portugal. Meanwhile, the Basques of the Central Pyrenees, who were known as the Navarrese, were living apart in their valleys. They also finally formed themselves into a kingdom which emerged clearly about the year 900 and from which, in 1037, another tiny monarchy detached itself, taking the name of 'Aragon' from the torrent which watered its territory. Finally, to the north of the lower course of the Ebro was a 'march' created by the Franks, which under the name of the county of Barcelona was considered, until the time of St. Louis, to be legally a fief of the king of France. These were the political formations—with fluctuating frontiers and subject to all the vicissitudes of partitions, conquests and political marriages—from which 'the Spains' were born.

To the north of the Pyrenees the barbarian kingdom of the Franks had been vastly enlarged by the Carolingians. The deposition of Charles the Fat in November 887, shortly followed by his death on 13th January of the following year, marked the failure of the final effort to restore the unity of the Empire. It was not through a mere whim that the new king of the East Franks, Arnulf, declined to take over the rule of the western kingdom, offered to him by the archbishop of Rheims. Plainly, the heritage of Charlemagne seemed too great a burden. Broadly speaking, the division followed the lines laid down by the first partition, that of Verdun, in 843. The kingdom of Lewis the German, formed at that date by the union of three dioceses on the left bank of the Rhine—Mainz, Worms and Speyer —with the vast Germanic territories on the east bank subdued not long before by the two Frankish dynasties, was in 888 re-established for the benefit of his only surviving descendant, Arnulf of Carinthia. This formed 'East Francia' which, by an anachronism that is harmless provided we are conscious of it, we may here and now call 'Germany'.

In the former kingdom of Charles the Bald, 'West Francia', or simply France as we call it today, two great lords were proclaimed king almost at the same time—Guy of Spoleto, an Italian duke of Frankish ancestry, and Odo, a Neustrian count, probably of Saxon origin. The latter, who commanded a much larger following and had distinguished himself in the war against the Northmen, was successful in securing recognition. Here again the frontier was approximately that of Verdun. Based on a juxtaposition of county boundaries, it crossed and recrossed the Scheldt several times and reached the Meuse a little downstream from its junction with the Semois; after which it ran almost parallel with the river, a few miles distant from the left bank. It then reached the Saône, below Port-sur-

Saône, and followed its course for a fairly long distance, hardly leaving it save for a sharp bend towards the east, opposite Châlon. Finally, to the south of the Mâconnais, it abandoned the line Saône-Rhône, in such a way as to leave to the neighbouring power all the riparian counties on the western bank and only rejoined the stream at the delta, to skirt the Petit Rhône as far as the sea. There remained the intermediate strip which, to the north of the Alps, was wedged between the states of Lewis the German and Charles the Bald, and then extended down the Italian peninsula as far as Rome. This territory had in 843 formed the ill-balanced kingdom of Lothar; but no descendant of that prince in the male line now survived, and the whole of his heritage was eventually annexed to East Francia, though the annexation took place piecemeal.

The kingdom of Italy, the successor of the former Lombard state, covered the north and centre of the peninsula with the exception of the Byzantine Venice, and for nearly a century it had a very stormy history. Several dynasties disputed the crown: dukes of Spoleto in the south and, above all, the masters of those Alpine passes towards the north whence it was so easy and so tempting to swoop down upon the plain—marquises of Friuli or Ivrea, kings of Burgundy, who held the passes of the Pennine Alps, kings or counts of Provence, and dukes of Bavaria. Several of these claimants, in addition, got themselves crowned emperor by the pope; for after the first partition of the Empire in the reign of Louis the Pious, the possession of Italy, on account of the rights of protection and domination which it conveyed over Rome and the Roman Church, seemed at once the necessary condition of this august office and the best title to it. Nevertheless, unlike the kings of West Francia, who were kept by their very remoteness from cherishing Italian or imperial ambitions, the sovereigns of East Francia were also among the near neighbours of the beautiful neglected realm. Already, in 894 and 896, Arnulf, strong in his Carolingian ancestry, had descended into Italy, secured his recognition as king and received the imperial crown. In 951 one of his successors, Otto I, a Saxon whose grandfather had perhaps accompanied Arnulf across the Alps, once more took the same road. He was acclaimed king of the Lombards in the old capital of Pavia; then—having been obliged in the meantime to turn his attention to other tasks—he returned ten years later, subjugated the country more thoroughly and finally pressed on to Rome, where the pope crowned him 'Imperator Augustus' (2nd February 962). Henceforth, except for short periods of crisis, Italy as such had no other lawful monarch than the German king right down to modern times.

In 888 a very great personage of Bavarian origin, the Welf Rudolf, was at the head of the great military command which the Carolingians, in the course of the preceding years, had established between the Jura and the Alps and which was ordinarily called the duchy of Transjurania—a position of first importance, since it commanded some of the principal internal routes of the Empire. Rudolf also hoped to find a crown by fishing in troubled waters and, to this end, chose the 'no man's land' between West Francia and East Francia formed by the regions which were later to be called, so appropriately, *Entre Deux*. The fact that he was crowned at Toul is a sufficient indication of the direction of his hopes. Nevertheless, at such a distance from his own duchy, he lacked followers. Beaten by Arnulf, he was obliged, while retaining the royal title, to content himself with joining to Transjurania the greater part of the ecclesiastical province of Besançon.

To the north of this territory a whole portion of the heritage of Lothar therefore remained vacant. This was the region which, for the lack of an appropriate geographical term, was frequently called 'Lotharingia' from a second Lothar, the son of the first, who had ruled it for some time. It was a large territory bounded on the west by the frontiers of West Francia, as they have already been defined, and on the east by the course of the Rhine, except for about 125 miles, where the boundary left the river to allow East Francia its three left-bank dioceses; a country of great abbeys and rich bishoprics, of fine rivers, alive with merchant craft; a venerable land, moreover, for it had been the cradle of the Carolingian house and the very heart of the great empire. Its vivid memories of the legitimate lines were probably the obstacle which prevented any native sovereigns from establishing themselves in this region. Since, however, ambitious men were present here as elsewhere, their game was to play off one neighbouring monarchy against the other. Nominally subject at first to Arnulf, who in 888 was the only one of Charlemagne's descendants to wear the crown, and subsequently very refractory towards the king whom Arnulf soon created for it in the person of one of his bastards, Lotharingia, after the extinction of the German branch of the Carolingians in 911, was for a long time disputed by the neighbouring princes. Although different blood flowed in their veins, the kings of East Francia regarded themselves as the heirs of Arnulf. As for the sovereigns of West Francia—so long, at least, as they belonged to the Carolingian line, which was the case from 898 to 923, and from 936 till 987—it is hardly surprising that they should have claimed the inheritance of their ancestors on the Meuse and the Rhine. Nevertheless, East Francia was plainly the stronger; so that when in 987 the Capetians, in their turn, took the place of the ancient race in the opposing kingdom, they quite naturally abandoned the prosecution of a design that was alien to their own family traditions and for which, moreover, they would no longer have found ready support in the territory itself. For long centuries—indeed permanently as regards the north-eastern part, Aachen and Cologne, Trier and Coblenz—Lotharingia was incorporated in the German political constellation.[1]

On the borders of Transjurania, an extensive area—Lyonnais and

[1] See Plate XII.

Viennois together with Provence and the Alpine dioceses—recognized no king for nearly two years. In these regions, however, there survived the memory and the retainers of an ambitious person called Boso who, before 887, in disregard of the legitimate claims of the Carolingians, had succeeded in carving out a kingdom for himself—the kingdom of Provence. His son Louis (who, moreover, was descended through his mother from the Emperor Lothar) was able at length to get himself crowned at Valence towards the end of 890. But the kingship thus founded proved ephemeral. Neither Louis, who in 905 had his eyes put out at Verona by Berengar of Friuli, nor his kinsman Hugh of Arles, who after this tragedy ruled for a long time in the name of the unfortunate victim, seems ever to have seen in their lands between the Rhône and the mountains anything but a convenient starting point for the fascinating project of Italian conquest. Hence after the death of Louis in 928, Hugh, proclaimed king in Lombardy, left the Welfs virtually free to extend their dominion to the sea. From about the middle of the tenth century therefore the kingdom of Burgundy—as the state founded by Rudolph was generally called—stretched from Basle to the Mediterranean. Nevertheless from this time on its weak kings figured as little more than vassals of the German kings or emperors. Finally— though not without much reluctance and vacillation—the last of the line, who died in 1032, recognized the sovereign of Germany as his successor. Moreover, unlike Lotharingia, but like Italy, 'Burgundy'—usually known from the thirteenth century onwards as the kingdom of Arles—was not exactly absorbed in the former East Francia. The union was conceived of rather as that of three distinct kingdoms indissolubly united in the same hands.

Thus the feudal era witnessed the emergence of the first lineaments of a political map of Europe, certain features of which are still perceptible; it also saw debated those problems of frontier zones which were destined till our own day to be responsible for the spilling of both ink and blood. But perhaps, all things considered, the most characteristic feature of this geography of kingdoms was that though their territorial limits were so fluctuating, their number varied remarkably little. Although in the former Carolingian Empire a crowd of virtually independent powers arose, only to fall into decay one after another, not even the most powerful of these local tyrants—after Rudolf and Louis the Blind—dared to assume the royal title or to deny that he was legally the subject or the vassal of a king. There could be no more eloquent testimony to the continued strength of the monarchic tradition, much older than feudalism and destined long to survive it.

2 TRADITIONS AND NATURE OF THE ROYAL POWER

The kings of ancient Germania liked to claim descent from the gods. Themselves like 'Aesir or demi-gods', in the words of Jordanes, it was from the mystic virtue with which their persons were imbued that their peoples looked for victory in battle, and in time of peace fertility for their fields. The Roman emperors had also worn the halo of divinity, and from this double heritage, but especially from the Germanic element, the kingships of the feudal age derived their sacred character. Christianity had sanctioned it, while borrowing from the Bible an old Hebraic or Syriac accession rite. In the states which had succeeded the Carolingian Empire, in England and in Asturias, the kings on their accession received from the hands of prelates the traditional insignia of their office, including the crown which was thereafter worn formally at the courts held on the occasion of the great feasts—the 'crowned courts' which are called to mind by a charter of Louis VI of France.[1] Moreover, it was a bishop, a new Samuel, who anointed these new Davids on various parts of the body with a consecrated oil—a rite whose universal significance in the Catholic liturgy is that it invests with a sacred character the person or object so anointed.[2] This rite was to prove a double-edged weapon. 'He that blesseth is superior to him that is blessed,' St. Paul had said, and thus it might be argued that the consecration of the king by the priests clearly signified the supremacy of the spiritual power. Such at least, almost from the beginning, was the view of some ecclesiastical writers. Awareness of the dangers inherent in this interpretation doubtless explains the fact that among the first sovereigns of East Francia several neglected, or refused, to have themselves anointed. Their successors, however, were not slow to make amends, for they were naturally loath to abandon to their rivals of the West the sole privilege of this wondrous chrism. The ecclesiastical ceremony of the delivery of the insignia—ring, sword, standard, crown itself—was imitated, somewhat tardily, in various principalities: Aquitaine, Normandy, the duchies of Burgundy and Brittany. It is characteristic, on the other hand, that no great feudatory, however powerful he might be, ever dared to demand the most sacred part of the ceremony, the anointing. Apart from priests, the 'Lord's anointed' were to be found only among kings.

This supernatural quality, of which the anointing was the confirmation rather than the origin, was deeply felt in an age accustomed to associate the influences of the Beyond with everyday life; yet a genuinely sacerdotal kingship would have been incompatible with the religion which prevailed throughout western Europe. The powers of the Catholic priest are perfectly defined; he and he alone can transform the bread and wine into the body and blood of Christ. Not having been ordained, the kings were incapable of celebrating the Blessed Sacrament, and were not therefore in the strict sense priests. But still less were they pure laymen. It is difficult to express clearly conceptions by their very nature opposed to logic. One may nevertheless give an approximate idea of them by saying that, although not

---

[1] Warnkoenig and Stein, *Französische Staats- und Rechtsgeschichte*, vol. I, *Urkundenbuch*, p. 34, c. 22.
[2] See Plate XI.

invested with the priesthood, the kings, in the phrase of an eleventh-century writer, 'participated' in its ministry. The consequence of this—and an extremely serious one—was that in their efforts to govern the Church they believed, and others believed, that they acted as members of it, though this view never found general acceptance in ecclesiastical circles. In the eleventh century the Gregorian reformers attacked it with great vigour and perspicacity. They argued for that distinction between the spiritual and the temporal which Rousseau and Renan have taught us to recognize as one of the greatest innovations introduced by Christianity. Moreover their purpose in separating the two powers so completely was to humble the rulers of men's bodies before the rulers of their souls—'the moon', which is only bright through reflection, before 'the sun', the source of all light. But in this they had little success. Many centuries were to elapse before kingship was reduced in the eyes of the people to the rôle of an ordinary human power.

In the popular mind the sacred character of kingship was expressed not only by the abstract notion of a right to govern the Church but also by a whole cycle of legends and superstitions about kingship in general and the various individual monarchies. It is true that it only attained its full expansion in the period when the majority of monarchical powers had grown actually stronger—that is, about the twelfth and thirteenth centuries—but its origins went back to the first feudal age. From the end of the ninth century the archbishops of Rheims claimed to have the custody of a miraculous oil, brought down to Clovis of old by a dove from the vault of heaven—a wonderful privilege which at once enabled these prelates to claim the monopoly of the coronation and their kings to declare and to believe that they had been consecrated by God himself. The kings of France, certainly from Philip I and probably from Robert the Pious, and the kings of England, from Henry I, were believed to possess the power to cure certain sicknesses by the touch of their hands. When in 1081 the excommunicated Emperor Henry IV passed through Tuscany, the peasants crowded the route and strove to touch his garments, convinced that by so doing they were making sure of good harvests.[1]

It would be easy to cast doubt on the effectiveness of this popular conception of kingship by contrasting the marvellous aura which surrounded the persons of kings with the scant respect which was often paid to the royal authority. But this would be to misinterpret the evidence. The examples of kings whose vassals disobeyed them, fought against or flouted them, and even held them prisoner, are indeed numberless. But of kings who died a violent death at the hands of their subjects in the period we are considering there are, unless I am mistaken, exactly three cases: in England, Edward the Martyr, the victim of a palace revolution fomented on behalf of his own brother; in France, Robert I, a usurper slain in

[1] Rangerius, *Vita Anselmi*, in *M.G.H.*, SS. XXX, 2, p. 1256, v. 4777 *et seq.*

combat by a partisan of the legitimate king; and in Italy, the scene of so many dynastic struggles, Berengar I. By comparison with the hecatombs of Islamic history, or with what the West itself could show in the number of great vassals murdered, and considering the general moral outlook of this age of violence, this number seems small indeed.

These religious or magical ideas of kingship were only the expression, on the plane of the supernatural, of the political mission recognized as belonging peculiarly to kings—the king as 'head of the people', *thiudans*, to use the old Germanic term. In the proliferation of lordships character-istic of the feudal world, the kingdoms, as Guizot rightly said, constituted a unique type of authority—not only superior, theoretically, to all others, but also of a genuinely different order. It was a significant feature that, while the other powers were for the most part mere agglomerations of various rights so intertwined that any attempt to delineate on the map the extent of these 'fiefs', great or small, is bound to be inaccurate, the king-doms, on the contrary, were separated by what might legitimately be called frontiers. Not indeed that these boundaries could be, or needed to be, drawn with rigorous exactitude, for the soil was still too loosely occupied. To separate France from the Empire in the marches of the Meuse, what more was needed than the uninhabited thickets of the Argonne? But at least, no town or village, however much its ownership might occasionally be disputed, ever appeared to be legally dependent on more than one of the contiguous kingdoms, whereas one might very well find in the same place one potentate exercising high justice, another possessing serfs, a third having quit-rents with the jurisdiction which went with them, and a fourth with the right to tithe. In other words, for a piece of land, as for a man, to have several lords was almost a normal thing; to have several kings was impossible.

Outside Europe, in distant Japan, it so happened that a system of personal and territorial subordination, very similar to Western feudalism, was gradually formed over against a monarchy which, as in the West, was much older than itself. But there the two institutions coexisted without interpenetration. In the land of the Rising Sun the emperor—like the kings of Europe a sacred personage, but much nearer to divinity—remained legally the sovereign of the whole people. Below him the hierarchy of vassals culminated in the shogun, their supreme head. The result was that for long centuries the shogun monopolized all real power. In Europe, on the contrary, the monarchies, though older than the system of vassalage and by their nature foreign to it, none the less took their place at its summit. Yet they were able to avoid being themselves enveloped in the network of dependence. What happened when an estate previously held from a private lord or a church became, by inheritance, part of the royal domain? The invariable rule was that the king, though he might succeed to certain obligations, was nevertheless dispensed from doing homage;

for he could not acknowledge himself the vassal of one of his subjects. On the other hand, nothing ever prevented him from choosing among his subjects (who, as such, were all his *protégés*) certain privileged persons over whom he extended a special protection in accordance with the rite of homage.

Now from the ninth century onwards, as we have seen, there figured among these royal *commendati*, alongside a crowd of petty 'satellites', all the great men of the realm, soon to be transformed into regional princes; so that the monarch was not only the ruler of the whole people, but also, by a series of ascending steps, the ultimate lord of an immense number of vassals and, through them, of a still greater multitude of humble dependants. In the countries where an exceptionally close feudal structure excluded allodial estates—as in England after the Norman Conquest—there was no poor wretch so far down the ladder of subjection that he could not perceive, on looking upwards, the king on the topmost rung. Elsewhere, before reaching this height, the continuity was sometimes broken. But even so this feudalization of the monarchies contributed everywhere to their preservation. Wherever he was unable to exercise authority as head of the state the king could at least use to his own advantage the weapons of the law of vassalage, sustained by the sentiment of the strongest human tie known to that age. In the *Chanson de Roland*, is it for his sovereign or for the lord to whom he has done homage that Roland fights? Doubtless he does not know himself; but he fights with such selfless devotion for his sovereign only because the latter is at the same time his lord. Later, when Philip Augustus disputed the pope's right to dispose of the property of a heretic count, he could still say quite naturally, 'this county is held of me as a fief'; not, 'it is part of my realm'. In this sense the policy of the Carolingians, who had dreamed of building their government on vassalage, did not perhaps, on a long view, prove so vain as its early failures would lead one to believe. We have already noted (and we shall return to the point later) that many factors conspired during the first feudal age to reduce to insignificance the really effective action of the royal power. But at least it had at its disposal two great latent forces, all ready to expand under more favourable conditions—the inviolate heritage of its ancient prestige, and the rejuvenation which it enjoyed through adapting itself to the new social system.

3 THE TRANSMISSION OF THE ROYAL POWER: DYNASTIC PROBLEMS

How was this monarchical office, with its weight of mixed traditions, handed on—by hereditary succession or by election? Today we are apt to regard the two methods as strictly incompatible; but we have the evidence of innumerable texts that they did not appear so to the same degree in the Middle Ages. 'We have obtained the unanimous election of the peoples and the princes and the hereditary succession to the undivided realm'—declared Henry II of Germany in 1003. And in France, according to that excellent canonist Ivo of Chartres: 'That man was rightly crowned king, to whom the kingdom fell by hereditary right and who was designated by the unanimous consent of the bishops and great men.'[1] The fact is that neither of the two principles was interpreted in an absolute sense. It is true that pure election, regarded less as the exercise of free choice than as obedience to a sort of private revelation which led to the discovery of the true chief, had its champions among the churchmen. Not only were they hostile to the quasi-pagan idea of a sacred virtue residing in a particular family; they were also inclined to see the legitimate source of all power in a method of appointment which the Church, for its own part, maintained was the only one consistent with its law: must not the abbot be chosen by his monks, the bishop by the clergy and people of the cathedral city? On this point, these theologians were of the same mind as the great feudatories, who desired nothing so much as to see the monarchy come under their control. But the prevailing opinion, dictated by a whole world of ideas which the Middle Ages had received principally from Germania, was altogether different. Men believed in the hereditary vocation not of an individual but of a dynasty; this alone they thought capable of producing able leaders.

The logical conclusion would doubtless have been the exercise of authority in common by all the sons of the dead king, or the division of the realm among them. These practices, as we know, had been familiar to the barbarian world, and they have sometimes been interpreted, quite wrongly, as proving the hereditary character of kingship, whereas they really only embodied the principle of the participation of all descendants in the same dynastic privilege. They were continued for a long time in the feudal period by the Anglo-Saxon and Spanish states. Nevertheless, they seemed injurious to the public welfare. They ran counter to that concept of an indivisible monarchy which Henry II very consciously emphasized and which corresponded with the survival, amidst all the disorders, of a feeling for the State which was still very much alive. Another solution therefore gained general acceptance; one which, moreover, had always worked on more or less parallel lines to the first. Within the predestinate family—and occasionally, if the male line was extinct, in families allied to it by marriage—the principal personages of the realm, the natural representatives of the whole body of subjects, named the new king. 'The usage of the Franks', wrote Archbishop Fulk of Rheims, very pertinently in 893 (the year in which he crowned Charles the Simple), 'was always on the death of their king to elect another within the royal house.'[2]

[1] *M.G.H.*, *Diplom. regum et imp.*, III, no. 34; *Histor. de France*, XV, p. 144, no. CXIV.

[2] Flodoard, *Historia Remensis ecclesiae*, IV, 5, in *M.G.H.*, SS. XIII, p. 563.

This collective heritability, moreover, tended almost inevitably to result in individual heritability in the direct line. Did not the sons of the late king share in a high degree the virtues of his blood? The decisive factor here, however, was another usage, which the Church employed in its own affairs as a useful corrective to the hazards of election. An abbot would induce his monks to recognize, during his own lifetime, the person designated by him as his successor: this was the procedure followed by the first heads of the great monastery of Cluny. Similarly the king or the prince got his vassals to agree that one of his sons should be associated in his office during his lifetime, and even—if it were a question of a king—crowned there and then. This was a very general practice during the feudal era and one which was followed by the doges of Venice and the 'consuls' of Gaeta in common with all the Western monarchs. Again there might be several sons. How was one to choose from among them the fortunate beneficiary of this advance election? The law of monarchy did not at first recognize primogeniture, any more than did the feudal law. Frequently it conflicted with the rights of the child 'born in the purple'—born, that is to say, when his father was already king; or else more personal reasons might tip the scale. Nevertheless, the right of primogeniture was a convenient fiction; moreover, it was gradually imposed by the example of the fief itself, and in France, in spite of some opposition, it became the rule almost from the outset. Germany, more faithful to the spirit of the old Germanic customs, never admitted it without reservation. Even in the middle of the twelfth century Frederick Barbarossa appointed his second son as his successor.

This, moreover, was only the symptom of more profound divergences. For, starting from similar conceptions, involving the two principles of election and dynastic right, monarchic custom in the various states evolved in very different directions. It will suffice here to recall two typical cases: that of France, on the one hand, and that of Germany, on the other.

The history of West Francia was inaugurated in 888 by a startling break with dynastic tradition. In the person of King Odo the magnates had chosen a new man, in the fullest sense of the term; for the only remaining descendant of Charles the Bald at that date was a child of eight who on account of his youth had already been twice passed over for the throne. Scarcely, however, had this youngster—he also was called Charles and nicknamed by uncharitable historians 'the Simple'—reached the age of twelve (the age of majority as fixed by the Salian Franks) than he was crowned at Rheims, on 28th January 893. War between the two kings continued for a long time. But shortly before his death on 1st January 898, Odo, in accordance, it seems, with an agreement concluded a few months earlier, urged his supporters to rally, when he had gone, to the Carolingian. It was twenty-four years before Charles was again faced with a rival; but then, provoked by the favour he showed to a petty knight, and naturally inclined to rebelliousness, a number of the greatest personages in the land began to look for another king. Since Odo had left no son, his brother Robert had inherited his family honours and his following, and he was elected by the rebels on 29th June 922. Having already occupied the throne, this family was considered half-sacred. When the following year Robert was killed on the field of battle, his son-in-law Raoul, duke of Burgundy, was crowned in his turn; and when a little later Charles was ambushed by one of the principal rebels and afterwards imprisoned for the rest of his life, the victory of the usurper was assured. Nevertheless the death of Raoul, who also left no male descendants, was the signal for a Carolingian restoration. The son of Charles the Simple, Louis IV, was recalled from England where he had taken refuge (June 936), and his son, and subsequently his grandson, succeeded him without serious opposition; so that towards the end of the tenth century everything seemed to point to the final re-establishment of legitimacy.

It needed the chance factor of the death in the hunting-field of the young king Louis V to raise the question of the succession once more. On 1st June 987 the grandson of King Robert, Hugh Capet, was proclaimed king by the assembly of Noyon. However, there was still living a son of Louis IV named Charles, whom the Emperor had made duke of Lower Lorraine, and he was not slow to take up arms in prosecution of his claim. Many people doubtless saw in Hugh only a king *ad interim*, as Gerbert expressed it. A successful surprise attack decided otherwise, and betrayed by the bishop of Laon, Charles was captured in that city on Palm Sunday, 991, to die eventually in captivity like his grandfather before him. Thenceforth all France's kings till the day when she no longer acknowledged any at all were of the Capetian line.

From this long tragedy, brought to an end by chance, it seems clear that the sentiment in favour of legitimacy remained fairly strong over a considerable period. The Aquitanian charters of the reigns of Raoul and Hugh Capet display in their system of dating an unwillingness to recognize the usurpers; but then the regions south of the Loire had always led a life apart and the baronage there was naturally hostile to chiefs sprung from Burgundy or France proper. More important than this—or the conventional or partisan indignation of certain chroniclers—is the evidence on this point of the facts themselves. The experiences of Odo, of Robert, and of Raoul may well have discouraged others from running the risk of repeating them. Though Robert's son, Hugh the Great, had no scruples about keeping Louis IV a prisoner for more than a year, it is significant that he did not dare to assume the crown himself.

The accession of Hugh Capet in 987 was brought about by an utterly unforeseen death and was not, whatever may have been said about it, 'primarily the work of the Church'. Though the archbishop of Rheims, Adalbero, was unquestionably its chief contriver, he did not have the whole of the Church behind him. To all appearance the threads of intrigue led back to the imperial court of Germany, to which the archbishop and his counsellor, Gerbert, were bound by both personal interest and political convictions. For in the eyes of these learned priests Empire was synonymous with Christian unity. The Saxon monarchs, who at that time reigned over Germany and Italy, were afraid of the Carolingians of France as representing the dynasty of Charlemagne, whose august heritage they had acquired, though they were not descended from him. More particularly, they expected with good reason that a change of dynasty would give them the peaceful possession of Lorraine, which the Carolingians, who looked on it as their homeland, had never ceased to dispute with them. Their success was assisted by the balance of power within France itself. Not only was Charles of Lorraine obliged to seek his fortune outside his native land, where he had almost no personal followers; in a more general way, the Carolingian cause suffered from the inability of the last kings to retain the direct control of enough lands or churches to guarantee them the hereditary support of a great body of vassals, constantly kept faithful by the promise of new rewards. In this sense the triumph of the Capetians represented the victory of a young power—that of a territorial prince, the lord and distributor of many fiefs—over the traditional authority of kingship pure and simple.

The surprising thing, moreover, is not so much their initial success as the cessation, from as early as 991, of all dynastic strife. The Carolingian line did not become extinct with Charles of Lorraine. He left sons who, sooner or later, escaped from captivity. But they seem never to have attempted any move against the Capetians; nor, despite their turbulence, did the counts of Vermandois whose house, which was descended from a son of Charlemagne, came to an end only in the second half of the eleventh century. Perhaps by a sort of contraction of loyalty to the crown, there was a reluctance to extend hereditary rights to these collaterals who, if it had been the case of a fief, would at that time have been generally considered to be excluded from the succession. The argument seems to have been employed in 987 against Charles, though at that date and in the mouth of adversaries it is suspect. It may nevertheless account in some measure for the abstention of the Vermandois branch, as early as 888. And who knows what would have been the fate of the Capetians without the remarkable good fortune which they enjoyed from 987 to 1316, in that each king had a son to succeed him? Above all, the respect for Carolingian legitimacy, overshadowed among the great by their own ambitions and deprived of the support which a large body of personal followers could have given it, could scarcely have been maintained save in those clerical circles which, alone or almost alone at that time, had intellectual horizons wide enough to see beyond the petty intrigues of everyday life. That the most energetic and intelligent of the leaders of the Church, an Adalbero and a Gerbert, through their devotion to the imperial idea deemed it necessary to support the current representatives of that idea at the expense of the dynasty of Charlemagne—this was undoubtedly the decisive factor in a balance of forces no longer material but moral.

How are we to explain nevertheless that, even apart from the last representatives of the Carolingians, no rival ever raised his head against the Capetians? The principle of election did not disappear for a long time. Consider the testimony of Ivo of Chartres, mentioned above; it relates to Louis VI, who was crowned in 1108. A solemn court assembled and proclaimed a king; then on the day of the coronation the prelate, before proceeding to the anointing, once more asked the consent of those present. But such ostensibly free choice invariably fell on the son of the previous sovereign, generally in the latter's lifetime, thanks to the practice of association. It sometimes happened that this or that great feudatory was by no means eager to do homage, and rebellions were frequent; but no anti-king was set up.

It is significant that the new dynasty at once showed its desire—as Pepin and his successors had done in regard to the Merovingians—to link itself with the tradition of the line which it had supplanted. The kings spoke of the Carolingians as their predecessors, and at an early date they appeared to have prided themselves on being descended from them through a female line—a claim that was no doubt correct, since a little of the blood of Charlemagne probably flowed in the veins of Hugh Capet's wife. Then from the time of Louis VI at the latest, we find the entourage of the reigning family seeking to exploit for the latter's benefit the legend of the great Emperor which, thanks to the epics, flourished in France at that time; they may even have contributed to its diffusion. From this heritage, the Capetians derived above all the high prestige of sacred kingship. They were not long in adding to it a particularly impressive miracle of their own devising—the power of healing. Respect for an anointed king did not prevent revolts, but it prevented usurpation. Almost unknown to the Roman world, the sense of the mysterious virtue residing in a predestined royal race had reached the West, via Germania, from remote primitive ages. It continued to exercise such an influence that when, after the accession of the Capetians, it was reinforced by an uninterrupted succession of male births and fostered by the presence of numerous vassals around the royal house, it enabled a completely new form of legitimacy to be built on the ruins of the old.

In Germany, the history of succession to the crown was at the outset much less complicated. When in 911 the German branch of the Carolingian dynasty came to an end, the choice of the magnates fell on a great Frankish lord, Conrad I, who was related by marriage to the extinct line. Unable to command much obedience, though no other claimant ever rose against him, this prince himself designated Henry, duke of Saxony, to reign

388

after his death. Despite the rival claims of the duke of Bavaria, Henry was elected and recognized without much trouble, and while the western kingdom was engaged in a long dynastic struggle the sovereigns of this Saxon family succeeded each other for more than a century (919–1024), from father to son and even, in one case, from cousin to cousin. Election, which continued to take place in accordance with the proper forms, seemed merely to confirm hereditary succession. If we now jump forward about a century and a half, we find that the contrast between the two countries persists, but in inverse sense. In Europe it came to be one of the common-places of political discussion to contrast France, where the monarchy was now entirely hereditary, with Germany, where it was—at least in principle —elective.

Three main causes had brought about the change in Germany. The accidents of procreation, so favourable to the Capetians, here proved detrimental to dynastic continuity. Successively there died, without male issue or descendants in the male line, the fifth of the Saxon kings, then the fourth of the 'Salian' (Frankish) dynasty, which had succeeded them. Furthermore, the German monarchy since Otto I seemed tied to the imperial office; and whereas the monarchies were based on the funda-mentally Germanic tradition of hereditary succession—if not by an individual, at least by a family—the Empire was based on the Roman tradition, which had never fully recognized the hereditary right of par-ticular families. That tradition was moreover supported by a body of historical or pseudo-historical literature which became increasingly influential from the end of the eleventh century onwards. 'It is the army which makes the Emperor' was an oft-repeated saying; and the great barons were naturally quite ready to assume the rôle of the legions or even, as they were also fond of saying, of the 'Senate'. Finally, the violent struggle which at the time of the Gregorian movement broke out between the sovereigns of Germany and the papacy, recently reformed by their efforts, led the popes to use the principle of election, so conformable to the sentiment of the Church, as a weapon against the enemy monarch whose deposition they wished to bring about. The first anti-king whom Germany had known since 888 was elected against the Salian Henry IV on 15th March 1077, in the presence of the papal legates. He was not by any means to be the last; and though it is doubtless untrue that this assembly pro-nounced expressly in favour of the permanent adoption of the elective principle, the rumour to this effect which at once swept through the monas-teries might at least be called prophetic. But the very bitterness of the quarrel which thus divided the German kings and the Curia can, in its turn, only be explained by the fact that those kings were also emperors. While the popes could reproach other sovereigns only with the oppression of partic-ular churches, they found in the successors of Augustus and Charlemagne rivals for the mastery of Rome, of the Holy See, and of Christendom.

4 THE EMPIRE

The collapse of the Carolingian state had had the effect of handing over to local factions the two universal offices of Western Christendom: the papacy to the clans of the Roman aristocracy; the Empire to the parties that were ceaselessly being formed and dissolved within the Italian nobility. For as we have already seen, the imperial title seemed associated with the possession of the kingdom of Italy. It was only after its appropriation (from 962 onwards) by the German sovereigns, whose claims could be backed by what was, for those times, considerable strength, that it once again acquired some meaning.

Not that the two titles, royal and imperial, were ever confused. The period from Louis the Pious to Otto I had witnessed the definitive affirmation of the dual character—at once Roman and pontifical—of the Western Empire. To call oneself emperor, it was therefore not enough to have been acknowledged and crowned in Germany. It was absolutely necessary to have received, at Rome itself, a specific consecration from the hands of the pope through a second anointing, and investiture with the imperial insignia. The new development was that henceforth the choice of the German magnates was regarded as the sole legitimate candidate for this august rite. In the words of a monk of Alsace, writing towards the end of the twelfth century, 'whichever prince Germany has chosen as her chief, before him gilded Rome bows the head and adopts him as her master'. Soon it was even considered that from the moment of his accession to the German throne the monarch *ipso facto* succeeded immediately to the government not only of East Francia and Lotharingia, but also of all the imperial territories—Italy, and later the kingdom of Burgundy. In other words, being, as Gregory VII put it, the 'future Emperor', he already exercised command within the Empire—a provisional status expressed from the end of the eleventh century by the title 'king of the Romans'. This title was borne by the German sovereign from the day of his election on the banks of the Rhine and exchanged for a more splendid one only when, having at last undertaken the classic 'Roman expedition', the traditional *Römerzug*, he was able, on the banks of the Tiber, to put on the crown of the Caesars; and if circumstances prevented him from making the long and difficult journey he was obliged to content himself for the rest of his life with being only the king of an empire. However, all the monarchs called to reign over Germany were made emperor, prior to Conrad III (1138–52).

What was the significance of this coveted title? There is no doubt that it was considered to express a superiority over the common run of kings— the 'kinglets' (*reguli*), as they were fond of saying at the imperial court, in the twelfth century. For this reason the title of emperor was occasionally assumed, outside the limits of the old Carolingian Empire, by various sovereigns who thereby intended to mark both their independence of

any so-called universal monarchy and their own hegemony over neighbouring kingdoms or former kingdoms. This was done, in England, by
certain kings of Mercia or Wessex, and (more frequently) in Spain, by the
kings of Leon. But, there was no authentic emperor in the West, except the
emperor 'of the Romans'—this was the formula which, from 982 on, the
Ottonian chancery had resumed, in opposition to Byzantium. The memory
of the Caesars nourished the myth of the Empire; and especially the
memory of the Christian Caesars. Rome was not only 'the head of the
world'; it was also the city of the apostles, 'renewed' by the precious blood
of the martyrs. Mingled with the echoes of Roman universalism and
strengthening them with the memory of things less remote was the image
of Charlemagne also, in the words of an imperialist bishop, a 'conqueror
of the World'.[1] Otto III inscribed on his seal the motto 'Renewal of the
Roman Empire', already employed by Charlemagne himself; what is more,
he had a search made at Aachen for the tomb of the great Carolingian,
which had been neglected by generations more indifferent to history, and
while providing for these glorious bones a sepulchre worthy of their
renown kept for his own use as relics a jewel and some fragments of
clothing from the corpse. These gestures expressed his fidelity to a dual
and indissoluble tradition.

These were, of course, above all clerical ideas—at least in origin—and it
is not at all certain that rather uneducated warriors like an Otto I or a
Conrad II were ever completely receptive to them. But the clerics who
surrounded and counselled the kings and had sometimes been their tutors
were not without influence on their actions. Otto III, because he was
young, educated, and of a mystical temperament, and because he had been
born in the purple and brought up by a Byzantine princess, his mother,
was completely intoxicated by the imperial dream. 'Roman, Saxon and
Italian victor (*triumphator*), slave of the Apostles, by the gift of God
august emperor of the World'—the notary who rolled off this list of titles
at the beginning of one of his diplomas surely must have been certain in
advance of his master's concurrence. Like a refrain, the expressions 'ruler
of the World', 'lord of the lords of the World' are repeated, a little more
than a century later, by the official historiographer of the first of the
Salians.[2]

Yet this ideology was in reality a tissue of contradictions. Nothing was
more attractive, at first sight, than to allow oneself (like Otto I) to be
described as the successor of the great Constantine. But the forged
'Donation', which the Curia had attributed to the maker of the Peace of
the Church and by which he was supposed to have granted Italy and even
the whole of the West to the pope, proved such an embarrassment to the
imperial power that at the court of Otto III its authenticity began to be

[1] Liutprand, *Antapodosis*, II, c. 26.
[2] Wipo *Opera*, ed. Bresslau, pp. 3 (5) and 106 (11).

called in question; partisan sentiments had awakened the critical sense. The German kings from Otto I onwards, in having themselves crowned by preference at Aachen, indicated that they regarded themselves as the legitimate heirs of Charlemagne; yet we know from the chroniclers that in Saxony, whence the reigning dynasty had sprung, the memory of the terrible war waged there by the conqueror had left an abiding bitterness. The view that the Roman Empire was still in existence found much support among the clergy, especially since the usual interpretation of the Apocalypse required them to see in it the last of the four Empires, preceding the End of the World. Other writers, however, questioned its survival; according to them, the partition of Verdun marked the beginning of an entirely new era. Finally, these Saxons, Franks, Bavarians or Swabians—emperors or great lords of the Empire—who wished to march in the steps of the Romans of old felt themselves to be in reality strangers and conquerors where the Romans of their own day were concerned. They neither liked nor respected them, and were detested by them in return. The case of Otto III, truly Roman at heart, was exceptional, and his reign ended in the tragedy of a shattered dream. He did not die at Rome, for he had been driven from the city by a revolt of the citizens; and the Germans, for their part, accused him of having neglected for the sake of Italy 'the land of his birth, delectable Germania'.

As for the claims to universal monarchy, they obviously lacked all material support from sovereigns whose effective control of their own territories was often imperilled by—not to mention more serious difficulties —a revolt of the Romans or the people of Tivoli, the fact that a castle at a point of transit was held by a rebel lord, or even the recalcitrance of their own troops. In fact till the time of Frederick Barbarossa (whose accession took place in 1152), these claims do not seem to have gone beyond the sphere of chancery formulas. They do not appear ever to have been advanced in the course of the numerous interventions of the first Saxon emperors in the West Frankish kingdom. If these vast ambitions manifested themselves at all at that time, it was in an indirect way. As the supreme master of Rome, and consequently *advocatus* (that is defender) of St. Peter, above all heir to all the traditional rights which the Roman emperors and the first Carolingians had exercised over the papacy, and finally guardian of the Christian faith wherever he exercised (or claimed to exercise) dominion, the Saxon or Salian emperor had in his own eyes no higher mission nor one more closely attached to his office than to protect, reform and direct the Roman Church. As a bishop of Vercelli expressed it, 'it is in the shadow of Caesar's power' that 'the pope washes away the sins of the ages'.[1] More precisely, this 'Caesar' regards himself as having the right to appoint the sovereign pontiff, or at least to require that he be appointed only with his consent. 'For love of St. Peter we have chosen as

[1] Hermann Bloch, in *Neues Archiv*, 1897, p. 115.

pope our teacher, the lord Sylvester, and with the approbation of God, we have ordained and established him as pope'—thus Otto III in one of his diplomas. In this way, since the pope was not only bishop of Rome but also and above all head of the Church Universal—*Universalis papa* is the phrase used on two occasions in the privilege accorded by Otto the Great to the Holy See—the Emperor reserved for himself over the whole of Christendom a sort of right of control which, if it could have been made effective, would have made him much more than a king. In this way, too, the germ of discord between the spiritual and the temporal was introduced into the Empire—a lethal germ, as it proved.

XXIX

FROM TERRITORIAL PRINCIPALITIES TO CASTELLANIES

1 THE TERRITORIAL PRINCIPALITIES

THERE had long been a tendency in the West for the greater states to split up into smaller political formations. The insubordination of the city aristocracies, sometimes organized in regional leagues, had constituted almost as great a threat to the unity of the Roman Empire in its last days as the ambitions of military commanders. In certain parts of feudal Europe some of these little oligarchic *Romaniae* still survived as witnesses of an age that had elsewhere come to an end. One of these was the 'community of the Venetians', an association of townships founded in the lagoons by refugees from the mainland, and whose collective name, borrowed from the province where they originated, only tardily became attached to the island of Rialto, our Venice, which was gradually promoted to the rank of capital. Other such survivals, in southern Italy, were Naples and Gaeta. In Sardinia, dynasties of native chiefs had divided the island into 'judicatures'. Elsewhere the establishment of the barbarian monarchies had prevented this fragmentation, though not without some concessions having to be made to the irresistible pressure of local forces. The Merovingian kings had been obliged at various times to grant to the aristocracy of a particular county the right to elect the count, and to the great men of Burgundy the privilege of appointing their own mayor of the palace. Thus the establishment of provincial governments, which occurred all over the continent at the time of the collapse of the Carolingian Empire, and which had its counterpart among the Anglo-Saxons a little later, might appear in one sense simply a reversion to earlier practice. But in this age the influence of the very strong public institutions of the period immediately preceding it gave the phenomenon an original cast.

Throughout the Frankish Empire we regularly find that the territorial principalities are based on agglomerations of counties. Thus, since the Carolingian count was a genuine official, it would hardly be anachronistic to picture the men into whose hands the new powers had fallen as a kind of super-prefects each of whom (supposing that such officials existed in modern France), in addition to exercising the military command, would be responsible for the administration of several *départements*. Charlemagne is said to have made it a principle never to entrust several districts at the same time to the same count; but we cannot be sure that even during his lifetime this wise precaution was always observed. It is certain that under his successors and particularly after the death of Louis the Pious the rule ceased altogether to be followed. Not only was it opposed by the greed of the magnates but circumstances made it difficult to apply. The invasions, together with the quarrels of rival kings, had carried war to the heart of the Frankish world, and it therefore became necessary nearly everywhere to set up great military commands similar to those which had always existed on its borders. Sometimes they owed their origin to one of those tours of inspection instituted by Charlemagne; the temporary inspector, the *missus*, would transform himself into a permanent governor—as did for example Robert the Strong, between Seine and Loire, or farther south, the ancestor of the counts of Toulouse.

The grant of a county was as a rule supplemented by the grant of the principal royal monasteries of the region. Having become their protector, perhaps even their 'lay abbot', the great chief derived substantial resources from them in property and men. Often he already had possessions of his own in the province; to these he added new fiefs or new allods; and he built up for himself locally—particularly by usurping the homage of the royal vassals—a large body of followers. Incapable of exercising direct control over the territories legally subject to his authority and consequently forced to instal or at least to accept in some of them either subordinate counts or simply viscounts (literally delegates of the count), he at any rate bound those subordinates to him by ties of homage. To describe those who controlled several counties, ancient usage provided no precise label. They were called and they called themselves, more or less indiscriminately, 'arch-counts', 'principal counts', 'marquises' (that is to say, commanders of a march, by analogy with the governments of frontier regions which had provided the model for those of the interior), and finally 'dukes', a borrowing from Merovingian and Roman terminology. But this last term was seldom used except where an old provincial or ethnic unity served as a basis for the new power. Force of habit slowly led to the adoption in this place or that of one or other of these titles; or else, as at Toulouse and in Flanders, the simple title of count was retained.

Needless to say, these clusters of powers only acquired a real stability from the time—very early, as we know, in West Francia, appreciably later in the Empire—when the heritability of 'honours' in general was introduced. Till then an untimely death, the changing designs of a king capable perhaps of effectively asserting his authority, or the hostility of powerful or crafty neighbours might at any moment ruin the edifice. In the north of France at least two attempts were made by two different dynasties to effect a union of counties, before the 'marquises of Flanders' brought their effort to a successful conclusion from their citadel of Bruges. In short, chance certainly played a great part in the success or failure of such efforts. Nevertheless it does not explain everything.

The founders of principalities were doubtless not very subtle geographers. But their work was only effective where geography did not run counter to their ambitions; where they were able to join together territories between which communications were sufficiently easy and of established frequency; and where, above all, they could make themselves masters of those points of transit whose importance the study of the monarchies has already shown us, both as vital military positions and as sources of handsome revenues from tolls. Threatened as it was by many unfavourable circumstances, the Burgundian princedom could hardly have survived and prospered if the dukes had not held the routes through the bleak upland solitudes of the Côte d'Or—from Autun to the valley of the Ouche—which joined France proper to the Rhône basin. 'He longed to possess the citadel of Dijon,' said the monk Richer of one claimant, 'thinking that, as soon as this place was in his hands, he could bring the greater part of Burgundy under his sway.' The lords of Canossa, in the Apennines, were not slow to extend their power from the mountain-tops over the neighbouring lowlands, towards the Arno as well as the Po.[1]

In many cases also the way was prepared by the ancient traditions of a common way of life among the people. This explains why old national names reappeared in the titles of many new chiefs; though in fact, where the group so designated was too widely scattered, nothing more of it survived in the long run than a label somewhat arbitrarily applied to a fragment of the whole.

Of the great traditional subdivisions of the Frankish state, which more than once had formed separate kingdoms, almost the whole of Austrasia had been absorbed by Lorraine. But the memory of the three others—Aquitaine, Burgundy, Neustria, the last of which it gradually became customary to call simply 'France'—had not yet, about the year 900, been effaced from the minds of men. Consequently various persons placed at the head of vast regional commands styled themselves dukes of the Aquitanians, of the Burgundians, or of the Franks. Because the union of those three principalities seemed to cover the whole realm, the king himself was sometimes called 'king of the Franks, of the Aquitanians and of the Burgundians', and Robert I's son Hugh the Great, aspiring to rule the whole, believed that there was no surer means of achieving this end than to unite the duchies of Burgundy and Aquitaine to that of France, in which he had succeeded his father. But this was a concentration too vast to endure.[2]

---

[1] See Plate XIII.
[2] It has sometimes been held that the title of duke of France, borne by the Robertians from the time of Robert I, expressed a sort of viceroyalty over the whole kingdom. It is possible that certain contemporaries may have held this view, though nowhere in

In point of fact the dukes of France, when later they became the Capetian kings, never exercised real authority except over the counties which they kept in their own hands and which—those of the Lower Loire having been usurped by their own viscounts—were reduced, about 987, to some six or eight districts in the neighbourhood of Paris and Orleans. As for the ancient land of the Burgundians, its name was finally divided in the feudal period between the kingdom of Rudolf's heirs, a great fief held of those kings (the 'county' of Burgundy, later known as Franche-Comté), and a French duchy. Moreover, the last-named territory, which extended from the Saône to the regions of Autun and Avallon, was far from including all the regions—those of Sens and Troyes, for example—which in West Francia itself continued to be spoken of as 'in Burgundy'. The kingdom of Aquitaine had been extended to the north as far as the Loire and for a long time the centre of gravity of the duchy which succeeded it remained near that river. It was from Bourges, in 910, that Duke William the Pious dated the foundation charter of Cluny. Nevertheless, after the title had been disputed by several rival houses, the one which retained it found its effective power limited at first to the plains of Poitou and the western parts of the Massif Central. Then about 1060 a fortunate inheritance enabled it to join to its original patrimony the principality founded between Bordeaux and the Pyrenees by a family of native rulers, who—since this region had not long before been occupied in part by invaders of Eskuaran speech— were called dukes of the Basques or Gascons. The feudal state born of this fusion was certainly large, but a great part of the original Aquitaine remained outside its frontiers.

Elsewhere the ethnic basis was more definite. By this is meant—leaving out of account all so-called racial factors—the presence, as substratum, of a group possessing a certain traditional unity of civilization. Amidst many setbacks the duchy of Brittany had inherited the 'kingdom' which Celtic chiefs of Armorica, profiting by the troubles of the Carolingian Empire, had created by uniting—like the Scottish kings, far away in the North— the areas of Celtic population with their border regions, where another language was spoken; these were the old Romance-speaking marches of Rennes and Nantes. Normandy owed its origin to the Scandinavian

---

the texts do I find any very clear expression of it (the term *dux Galliarum* employed by Richer, II, 2, is only a pedantic translation of *dux Franciae*; 11, 39, *omnium Galliarum ducem constituit* refers to the investiture of Hugh the Great with the duchy of Burgundy, in addition to the duchy of France). But there is no doubt that the original meaning was territorial. It is surely impossible, on the contrary hypothesis, to understand Hugh's attempt to unite the three duchies. Perhaps the office of count of the palace (i.e. the royal palace) had also been divided, as in Germany, on the same lines, each duchy having henceforth its own count of the palace; this would explain the title of count palatine which was claimed, in 'France' by the count of Flanders, in Burgundy by the count of Troyes (later described as 'of Champagne'), and in Aquitaine by the count of Toulouse. For the tripartite royal title, see *Rec. des Hist. de France*, IX, pp. 578 and 580 (933 and 935).

'pirates'. In England, the ancient divisions of the island resulting from the settlement of the various Germanic peoples served approximately as limits for the great administrative districts which, from the tenth century onwards, the kings were accustomed to set up for the benefit of a few great men. But nowhere was this character more pronounced than in the German duchies.

We find that these duchies originated in the same way as the principalities of West Francia or Italy: through the union of several counties in military commands; and here too names were at first indefinite, though in this case the nomenclature was much more quickly decided and with much greater uniformity. In a remarkably short interval of time—roughly between 905 and 915—there arose the duchies of Alemannia or Swabia, of Bavaria, of Saxony, and of Franconia (the riparian dioceses on the left bank of the Rhine and the lands of Frankish colonization on the Lower Main), without counting that of Lorraine, where the duke was nothing but the diminished successor of a king. These names are significant. In East Francia, which had not, like the old Romania, gone through the melting-pot of the invasions, the ancient divisions of the Germanic peoples persisted beneath the theoretical unity of a very recently founded state. Magnates taking part in the election of the king—or abstaining from it—were grouped in accordance with these ethnic affinities. Particularist sentiment, maintained by the use of codified customs peculiar to each people and, in practice, to its territory, was fostered by memories derived from a recent past. Alemannia, Bavaria, and Saxony had been successively annexed to the Carolingian state in the second half of the eighth century, and the title of duke itself, revived by the feudal princes, reproduced that which had long been borne, under an intermittent Frankish hegemony, by the hereditary sovereigns of the first two of the above-mentioned countries. Thuringia provides by contrast the perfect negative example: since the collapse of the native monarchy, as early as 534, it had had no independent national existence, and no stable ducal power succeeded in establishing itself there.

To such an extent was the duke regarded as the head of a people, rather than the mere administrator of a provincial area, that the aristocracy of the duchy frequently claimed the right to elect him, and in Bavaria it sometimes got the kings to recognize its right to share in the appointment at least to the extent of approving it. Nevertheless, the tradition of the Carolingian state was still too much a living thing in Germany for the kings to cease treating the persons vested with these great governmental powers as being, above all, their representatives, and for a long time, as we have seen, they refused to recognize their right to hereditary succession.

Now this character of a public office, which the ducal power had thus preserved, combined with the persistence of ethnic particularism to make the German duchy of the tenth century something very different from a French principality: something, so to speak, much less feudal and consequently very typical of a country which had not, to the same degree as France, reached the stage where the vassal relationship constituted among the powerful almost the only effective organization of command and obedience. In France (despite the efforts of the first dukes of the Franks, of the Aquitanians and the Burgundians) dukes, marquises and arch-counts very soon came to exercise real power only over the counties which belonged to them personally or were held of them in fee. The German duke, on the other hand, while evidently drawing a great part of his power from his own 'honours', nevertheless remained the supreme head of a much larger territory. It might very well be that among the counts whose districts were situated within the frontiers of the ducal territory there were some who owed homage directly to the king. They were none the less in some measure subordinated to the duke, rather in the way that—if I may venture to employ such a comparison—in France today a sub-prefect, in spite of being appointed by the central government, remains the subordinate of the prefect. The duke summoned to his formal courts all the great men of the duchy, commanded its army, and being responsible for the maintenance of peace within its boundaries, extended over it a right of jurisdiction, somewhat ill-defined in scope, but not incapable of being enforced.

Nevertheless, these great 'ethnic' duchies—the *Stammesherzogtümer* of the German historians—were threatened from above by the king, whose power was greatly limited by them, and from below by all the forces of disintegration, increasingly active in a society which was moving away from its origins, as well as from the memory of the primitive peoples, in the direction of a progressive feudalization. Sometimes they were simply suppressed by the kings as in the case of Franconia in 939; more often they were broken up and, deprived of all authority over the principal churches and over the counties which had been attached to these, they progressively lost their original characteristics. After the ducal title of Lower Lorraine or 'Lothier' had passed in 1106 to the House of Louvain, the holder of this dignity tried, forty-five years later, to establish his rights throughout the former extent of the duchy. The reply of the imperial court was that according to usage duly ascertained 'he had ducal authority only in the counties which he held himself or which were held of him'. This a contemporary chronicler translated by saying that the dukes of that line 'had never exercised jurisdiction outside the limits of their own estates'.[1] It would be impossible to express better the new direction of development. Of the duchies of the earlier type there subsisted a few titles and sometimes more than a title. But the few principalities so described could now scarcely be distinguished from the crowd of 'territorial' powers which, taking

[1] Gislebert of Mons, ed. Pertz, pp. 223–4 and 58.

advantage of the growing weakness of the monarchy, firmly established themselves in Germany at the end of the twelfth century, and above all in the thirteenth, to give rise finally to the federated states which survived into the present century. As political organisms they were much nearer to the French type, since they too were merely conglomerations of the rights of counts and various other powers. By one of those time-lags in evolution with which we are already familiar, Germany, after an interval of something like two centuries, entered on the same course from which her western neighbour seemed already to be emerging.

2 COUNTIES AND CASTELLANIES

In the states born of the Carolingian Empire the counties, which had sooner or later become hereditary, had not all been absorbed by the great principalities. Some long continued to lead an independent existence—as did for example Maine until 1110, although perpetually menaced by its Angevin and Norman neighbours. But as a result of partitions and the establishment of many immunities, not to mention plain usurpation, the counts' rights disintegrated; so that the difference between the legitimate heirs of the Frankish officials and the ordinary 'powerful men', lucky enough or clever enough to have gathered into their hands a great number of lordships and judicial rights, came more and more to be merely a question of whether or not they used the title of count; which title itself was sometimes usurped by certain lay representatives of churches (as, for example, the *advocati* of Saint-Riquier, who became counts of Ponthieu), and even, in Germany, by a few rich allodialists. Thus did the idea of the public office yield to the undisguised realities of power.

In the establishment and strengthening of these lordships of varying title and extent, a common feature is to be observed—the part played by the castles as focal points. 'He was powerful,' said Ordericus Vitalis of the sire de Montfort, 'like a man who possessed strong castles, guarded by strong garrisons.' These castles were not the mere fortified houses such as the common run of knights, as we have seen, were content to live in. The fortresses of the magnates were virtually small entrenched camps. There was indeed a tower which served both as the lord's living quarters and the defenders' last redoubt; but around it were one or more *enceintes*, enclosing a fairly large area where stood buildings reserved as quarters for troops, servants and craftsmen, or as storehouses for provisions and the produce contributed by the peasants. The count's *castrum* at Warcq-sur-Meuse seems, as early as the tenth century, to have been a fortress of this type, as also two centuries later those of Bruges and Ardres, though these latter were much better constructed.

The first of these citadels had been built at the time of the invasions of the Northmen and the Hungarians by the kings or the heads of the great military commands, and the idea that the right to build fortifications belonged essentially to the State never completely disappeared. For generations the castles built without the permission of the king or prince were described as unlawful or, according to the Anglo-Norman expression, 'adulterine'. But the ban had no sanction save the physical power of the authority concerned to see that it was observed, and in most countries it only became effective as a result of the consolidation of monarchic and territorial powers, from the twelfth century onwards. More serious still, the kings and princes, powerless to prevent the erection of new fortresses, were hardly more successful in keeping the control of those which they had built themselves and subsequently handed over as fiefs to the care of vassals; the dukes and greater counts even found themselves defied by their own castellans, who were also officials or vassals ambitious to transform themselves into dynasts.

Now these castles were not only a safe refuge for the master and sometimes for his subjects; they also constituted, for the whole of the surrounding district, an administrative capital and the centre of a network of dependencies. There the peasants carried out the compulsory labour of fortress-building and deposited their contributions in kind; there the vassals of the neighbourhood performed their garrison duties, and their fiefs were often said to be held of the fortress itself—as, for example, in Berry, from the 'great tower' of Issoudun. The castle was the seat of justice, and the source of all visible authority. So much was this so that in Germany, from the end of the eleventh century, many counts who had become incapable of controlling the whole of an irremediably subdivided territory, became accustomed to substitute in their title the name of their principal patrimonial fortress for that of the district or *Gau*. This practice sometimes extended to persons of still higher rank: for instance Frederick I, duke of Swabia, called himself duke of Staufen.[1] In France at about the same time it became customary to give the name of *châtellenie* to the territory over which high justice was exercised. An outstanding example was the castle of Bourbon-l'Archambault in Aquitaine. Although its possessors were not of the rank of counts, it gave rise in the end to an actual territorial principality, whose name survives in one of the French provinces, the Bourbonnais, as well as in the patronymic of an illustrious family. The towers and the walls which were the visible source of the power also gave it its name.

3 THE ECCLESIASTICAL LORDSHIPS

Following the Merovingian and Roman tradition, the Carolingians had always regarded as normal and desirable the participation of the bishop

---

[1] *Monumenta Boica*, XXIX, 1, No. CCCCXCI: *Würtemberger Urkundenbuch*, II, No. CCCLXXXIII.

in the temporal administration of his diocese, but only as a colleague or, occasionally, as a sort of supervisor of the representative of the crown, i.e. of the count. The monarchies of the first feudal age went farther; they sometimes made the bishop the count as well.

This development took place in two phases. More than the rest of the diocese, the city where the cathedral church stood was considered to be under the special protection and authority of its pastor. Whereas the count had innumerable occasions to roam about the country districts, the bishop by preference resided in his *cité*. In the hour of danger, while his followers helped to man the ramparts—which were often built or repaired at his expense—and while his granaries were opened to provide food for the besieged, he himself often assumed the command. By recognizing the bishop's right to exercise the powers of a count over this urban fortress and its immediate approaches (together with other rights such as that of mintage, or even the possession of the fortified enclosure), the kings sanctioned a *de facto* situation considered favourable to defence. Such was the case at Langres as early as 887; at Bergamo, certainly, in 904; at Toul in 927: at Speyer in 946—to mention only the earliest known example in each country. To the count was reserved the government of the surrounding territory. This division was sometimes permanent. For centuries, the city of Tournai had its bishop or its cathedral chapter as count, while the count of Flanders was the count of the surrounding territory. Elsewhere the whole territory was eventually granted to the bishop. Thus, after an interval of sixty years, the grant of the county of Langres followed that of the countship *in* Langres. Once the practice of these gifts of whole counties had been introduced, it became customary to speed up the process: without apparently ever having been counts of the city of Rheims, the archbishops became in 940 counts of Rheims and the surrounding territory.

The motives which drove the kings to make these grants are obvious. They were hoping to have the best of both worlds. In heaven, the saints would certainly rejoice to see their servants not only provided with lucrative revenues but also relieved of inconvenient neighbours. On earth, to give the county to the bishop was to place the command in the most reliable hands. The prelate was not likely to transform his office into a hereditary patrimony; his appointment was subject to the approval of the king (when indeed it was not made by the latter directly); and both his culture and his interests tended to make him side with the monarchic party. Amidst the disorder of the feudal states, he proved to be, all things considered, the least insubordinate of the officials. It is significant that the first counties entrusted to the episcopate by the German kings should have been certain Alpine districts—far from cathedral cities—whose loss, by closing the mountain passes, would have gravely jeopardized imperial policy. Nevertheless, originating from needs which were the same everywhere, the institution evolved in very different directions in different countries.

In the French kingdom many bishoprics as early as the tenth century had fallen under the domination of territorial princes, and even of ordinary counts. The result was that the number of bishops who themselves obtained the powers of counts was fairly small; they were concentrated above all in France proper and Burgundy. Two of them at least, at Rheims and at Langres, appeared at one time to be on the point of forming genuine principalities, by assembling round the central district which they governed themselves a cluster of vassal counties. In the records of the wars of the tenth century no military force is mentioned more often or with more respect than the 'knights of the church of Rheims'. But, subjected to pressure from the neighbouring lay principalities, and victims of the faithlessness of their feudatories, these vast ecclesiastical lordships seem to have rapidly decayed. From the eleventh century onwards, none of these bishop-counts had any resource against the power of their enemies but to attach themselves more and more closely to the crown.

Faithful to the Frankish tradition, the German sovereigns seem to have long hesitated to touch the old county organization. Nevertheless, towards the end of the tenth century we find frequent grants of entire counties, and even groups of counties, in favour of bishops; so that, since these gifts were supplemented by grants of immunity and a whole variety of concessions, substantial territorial lordships belonging to the Church were created in a few years. Clearly the kings had accepted, although reluctantly, the idea that in their struggle against the monopolization of local powers by unruly magnates and especially by the dukes, they had no better weapon than the temporal power of the prelates. It is notable that these ecclesiastical territories were especially numerous and strong where the duchies had been either removed from the map—as in Franconia —or, as in the former Rhenish Lorraine or East Saxony, deprived of all effective control over a part of their old territory. But as things turned out, the policy of the sovereigns proved in the long run to have been illadvised. The long quarrel of the popes and the emperors and the at least partial triumph of ecclesiastical reform caused the German bishops from the twelfth century onwards to look on themselves less and less as officials of the monarchy and, at most, as its vassals. In Germany the ecclesiastical princedom ended by simply taking its place among the elements of disunion in the national state.

In Lombard Italy and—though to a less degree—in Tuscany, imperial policy followed at first the same lines as in Germany. Nevertheless, the concentration of several counties in the hands of the same church was much less common in these regions, and the course of evolution produced very different results. Behind the bishop-count, a new power very quickly arose—that of the urban commune. It was, in many respects, a rival power, but one which was able in the end to use for the furtherance of its own ambitions the weapons prepared by the former lords of the city. It was often as heirs of the bishop or under cover of his name that from the twelfth century the great oligarchic republics of the Lombard cities asserted their independence and extended their lordship over the plain.

In no country was there any very strict legal distinction between a church possessed of counties and one which, while it had received no grants of this kind, none the less had sufficient immunities, sufficient vassals, villeins, persons subject to its jurisdiction to figure as a real territorial power. On every hand the soil of the West was traversed by the frontiers of these great ecclesiastical 'liberties'. Often lines of crosses marked their limits, like so many 'pillars of Hercules' (as Suger put it), impassable for the profane.[1] Impassable, at any rate, in theory. Practice, however, was somewhat different. The patrimony of the saints and the poor provided the lay aristocracy with a favourite form of sustenance for its appetite for wealth and power—by means of enfeoffments, extorted by threats or obtained through the complaisance of over-accommodating friends; sometimes by the most plainly brutal sort of spoliation; lastly— at least within the limits of the former Carolingian state—by the expedient of the *avouerie* or system of lay 'advocacy'.[2]

At the time when the working of immunities was first regularized by Carolingian legislation, it was deemed necessary to provide each immunist church with a lay representative, responsible both for holding the authorized pleas in the lordship itself and for bringing before the count's court those who were required to appear there but who could no longer be directly sought out by the king's own officers on an estate from which the latter were henceforth excluded. The creation of this office answered a double purpose, conformable in its very duality to the fundamental trends of a policy which was very conscious of its ends. It was intended, on the one hand, to prevent the clergy, and in particular the monks, from being diverted by worldly obligations from the duties of their order, and on the other, by giving official recognition to seignorial jurisdictions, to secure their incorporation in a regular, properly supervised, and clearly defined judicial system. Not only, therefore, must every church enjoying immunity possess its 'advocate' (*avoué*) or 'advocates'; but the very choice of these officials was closely supervised by the government. The Carolingian advocate, in short, though he was in the service of the bishop or the monastery, none the less fulfilled in relation to them the rôle of a sort of representative of the crown.

The collapse of the administrative edifice erected by Charlemagne did not entail the disappearance of this institution; but profound changes took place in it. From the beginning, no doubt, the advocate had been re-

[1] Suger, *Vie de Louis VI*, ed. Waquet, p. 228.
[2] There is no detailed study of the post-Carolingian *avouerie* in France. This is one of the most serious *lacunae* in research on the Middle Ages and one of the easiest to fill. In Germany the institution has been examined especially in its relation to the judicial system, though perhaps from a too theoretical point of view.

munerated by the grant of a 'benefit', carved out from the patrimony of the Church. When the notion of public office came to be overshadowed by ties of personal dependence, he ceased as a rule to be regarded as being attached to the king, to whom he did not do homage, and came to be looked on merely as the vassal of the bishop or the monks. His appointment was henceforth entirely in their hands until—and this came about very quickly, in spite of some legal reservations—his fief, like the rest, became in practice hereditary together with his office.

Meanwhile, the rôle of the advocate had grown to a remarkable degree. In the first place, his judicial function had expanded. Since the immunities had monopolized cases involving the death penalty, the advocate henceforth, instead of bringing criminals before the county court, himself exercised the formidable powers of high justice. Above all, he was no longer only a judge. In the troubles of the time the churches were in need of captains to lead their men to battle under the banner of the saint. Since the State had ceased to afford effective protection they needed defenders nearer at hand to protect property which was constantly in danger. They believed that they had found both of these in the lay representatives assigned to them by the legislation of the great Emperor; and these professional warriors themselves were apparently not slow to offer and even to impose their services for tasks which held out a rich prospect of honour and profit. The result was a shifting of the centre of gravity of the office. More and more, when the texts attempt to define the nature of the advocate's office (*avouerie*) or to justify the remuneration claimed by the advocate, they emphasize the factor of protection. There was a corresponding change in the recruitment of these officials. The Carolingian advocate had been an official of fairly modest rank; but in the eleventh century the most powerful individuals, even the members of dynasties of counts, did not disdain to seek a title which only a little while before they would have thought very much beneath them.

Nevertheless, the disintegration which affected so many rights at that time did not spare this one either. In the case of establishments whose possessions were spread over a wide area, Carolingian legislation seems to have provided for one advocate in each county. But soon their number multiplied. In Germany and Lotharingia, where the institution departed least from its original character, these local advocates, frequently called 'sub-advocates' (*sous-avoués*), remained in theory the representatives and as a rule the vassals either of the general advocate of the church, or of one or other of the two or three general advocates between whom it had divided its property. In France, as one might expect, the fragmentation was carried farther: so much so that in the end there was scarcely an estate or group of estates of any size which did not have its particular 'defender' recruited among the neighbouring potentates of middle rank. There again, however, the person—he was usually of higher rank—appointed to protect the bishopric or monastery far surpassed in the extent of his revenues and power the host of petty local protectors. Moreover, this magnate might be not only the advocate of the religious community, but also its 'proprietor' (meaning, principally, that it was he who appointed the abbot), and even occasionally he might himself, although a layman, have assumed the abbot's title—a confusion of ideas very characteristic of an age more impressed by tangible realities than by legal subtleties.

The advocate not only possessed fiefs—frequently very large ones—attached to his office; the office itself allowed him to extend his authority even over the estates of the church and to collect lucrative rents from them. Particularly in Germany, while becoming a protector he remained a judge. Arguing from the old principle which forbade the clergy to shed blood, many a German *Vogt* succeeded in monopolizing almost completely the exercise of high justice within the monastic lordships, and the relative strength of the monarchy and its loyalty to the Carolingian tradition helped to facilitate this appropriation of judicial rights. For, although in Germany also the kings had had to abandon the appointment of the advocates, at least they continued to accord them in theory the investiture of the *ban*, that is to say the right of coercion. Without this delegation of power, which thus passed directly from the sovereign to their vassal, the monks would scarcely have been able to exercise high justice. In practice they barely succeeded in keeping the right to punish the dependants who were attached to them by the closest bonds, their domestics or their serfs. In France, where all ties had been severed between the royal authority and the advocates, the subdivision of jurisdictions worked along more varied lines; and this disorder no doubt served the interests of the Church better than German order.

On the other hand, how many 'exactions'—the term used in the charters—were everywhere levied on the villeins of the churches by their 'defenders', real or pretended! It is true that even in France, where the office of advocate had fallen into the hands of innumerable rural tyrants eager for gain, this protection was not perhaps always as ineffectual as clerical historians would have us believe. A charter of Louis VI, though to all appearance drawn up in an abbey, admits that 'it is extremely necessary and of the greatest utility'.[1] But it was undoubtedly bought at a high price. Service in all its forms, from compulsory labour in the fields to purveyance, from military service to castle-building; dues in oats, in wine, in chickens, in coin, levied on the fields and still more frequently (for it was above all the village that had to be defended) on the cottages—the list of everything that the ingenuity of the advocates was able to extract from peasants of whom they were not the direct lords would be almost interminable. Indeed, as Suger wrote, they devoured them whole.[2]

[1] *Mém. Soc. archéol. Eure-et-Loir*, X, p. 36, and *Gallia christ.*, VIII, *instr.*, col. 323.
[2] *De rebus*, ed. Lecoy de la Marche, p. 168.

The tenth century and the first half of the eleventh was the golden age of the advocate system for the continent (England, where the Carolingian example had not been followed, never knew the institution). Then the Church, revitalized by the Gregorian reform, passed to the offensive. By agreements, by judicial decisions, by redemptions, thanks also to the free grants prompted by repentance or piety, it succeeded in gradually restricting the advocates to the exercise of rights which were strictly defined and progressively reduced. It is true that it had to abandon to them large slices of its ancient patrimony. It is true that the advocates continued to exercise their judicial authority over a number of Church estates and to levy on these certain dues whose origin had come to be less and less understood. Nor did the peasants always derive much benefit from the patient work of their clerical masters; for a rent redeemed by a church did not thereby cease to be collected; it was merely that thenceforth it was paid to the episcopal lord or the monastic lords, instead of going to enrich some neighbouring lay landlord. But once the inevitable sacrifices had been accepted the seignorial power of the Church escaped from one of the most insidious dangers with which it had been threatened.

Those who suffered most from the reform were the petty dynasts and those of middle rank, for they were compelled to abandon the exploitation of resources which were formerly almost indefinitely available to them and without which more than one knightly family of the past would never have succeeded in emerging from its original obscurity. Towards the end of the second feudal age, the local advocates had been rendered practically harmless, but the general advocateships survived. These had always been mainly in the hands of the kings and the greater barons; and the kings had already begun to claim a universal 'guardianship' over the churches within their own realms. Moreover, bishops, cathedral chapters, and monasteries had dared to reject the onerous services of all these petty defenders only because they were henceforth able to depend for their security on the support (which had once more become effective) of the great monarchic or princely governments. Now this protection also, under whatever name it went, had always had to be paid for by very onerous services and money contributions which constantly grew heavier. 'It is fitting that the churches should be rich,' is the naive remark attributed to Henry II of Germany in a forged document; 'for the more that is entrusted to one, the more is demanded.'[1] In theory inalienable, and preserved by their very nature from the perpetual danger of divided succession, the ecclesiastical lordships had constituted from the beginning a remarkable element of stability in an unstable world. From this point of view they were to prove an even more valuable instrument in the hands of the great powers, at the time of the general reconcentration of authority.

[1] *M.G.H., Diplom. regum et imperatorum*, III, no. 509.

XXX

DISORDER AND THE EFFORTS TO COMBAT IT

1 THE LIMITS OF STATE ACTION

WE are accustomed to speak of feudal states, and to the learned in medieval times the idea of the State was certainly not unfamiliar; the texts sometimes employ the old word *respublica*. In addition to obligations to the immediate master, political morality recognized those owed to thus higher authority. A knight, says Bonizo of Sutri, must 'be prepared to die in defence of his lord and to fight to the death for the commonwealth'.[1] But the idea thus evoked was very different from what it would be today; in particular, it was much less comprehensive.

A long list could be made of the activities which we consider inseparable from the idea of the State, but which the feudal states completely ignored. Education belonged to the Church, and the same was true of poor relief, which was identified with charity. Public works were left to the initiative of the users or of petty local authorities—a most palpable breach with Roman tradition and even with that of Charlemagne. Only in the twelfth century did the rulers begin once more to take an interest in such matters, and then less in the kingdoms than in certain precociously developed principalities such as the Anjou of Henry Plantagenet, who built the Loire levees, and Flanders, which owed some of its canals to its count, Philip of Alsace. It was not till the following century that kings and princes intervened, as the Carolingians had done, to fix prices and hesitantly outline an economic policy. Indeed from the second feudal age onwards the real champions of welfare legislation had been almost exclusively authorities of much more limited range, by nature completely alien to feudalism properly so called—namely the towns, which almost from the time when they became autonomous communities concerned themselves with schools, hospitals, and economic regulations.

For the king or the great baron there were virtually only three fundamental duties. He had to ensure the spiritual salvation of his people by pious foundations and by the protection of the true faith; to defend them from foreign foes (a tutelary function to which, when possible, was added

[1] Bonizo, *Liber de vita christiana*, ed. Perels, 1930 (*Texte zur Geschichte des römischen und kanonischen Rechts*, I), VII, 28, p. 248.

conquest, prompted as much by considerations of honour as the desire for power); and lastly to maintain justice and internal peace. Therefore, since his mission required him above all to smite the invader or the evil-doer, he was engaged in making war, meting out punishment, and repressing disorder rather than in the administration of his realm. And this was a sufficiently heavy task.

For one of the common features of all the governments was, not exactly their weakness, but the fact that they were never more than intermittently effective; and this blemish was never more strikingly manifest than where ambitions were greatest and the professed sphere of action widest. When in 1127 a duke of Brittany confessed that he was incapable of protecting one of his monasteries against his own knights, he was merely proclaiming the weakness of a second-rate territorial principality. But even among the sovereigns whose power is most vaunted by the chroniclers, it would be impossible to find one who did not have to spend long years in suppressing rebellions. The least grain of sand was enough to jam the machinery. A petty rebel count entrenches himself in his lair and lo! the Emperor Henry II is held up for three months.[1] We have already noted the principal reasons for this lack of stamina: the slowness and the general difficulties of communication; the absence of monetary reserves; the need for direct contact with men, indispensable to the exercise of genuine authority. In 1157, says Otto of Freising, in the naive belief that he is thereby exalting his hero, Frederick Barbarossa 'returned north of the Alps; by his presence peace was restored to the Franks (i.e. the Germans); by his absence it was denied to the Italians'. To these reasons, naturally, we must add the stubborn competition of personal ties with wider obligations. In the middle of the thirteenth century a French customary still recognizes that there are cases in which the liege vassal of a baron can lawfully make war on the king, by embracing the cause of his lord.[2]

The best minds clearly appreciated the permanence of the State. Conrad II of Germany is credited by his chaplain with having said: 'When the king dies, the kingdom remains, like a ship whose captain has perished.' But the people of Pavia, to whom this admonition was addressed, were undoubtedly much nearer the common opinion when they said that the destruction of the royal palace could not be imputed to them as a crime, because it had taken place during the interregnum. 'We served our emperor while he lived; when he died, we no longer had a sovereign.' Prudent persons always persuaded the new monarch to confirm the privileges granted to them by his predecessor, and in the middle of the twelfth century certain English monks maintained in the king's court that an edict not in conformity with an old custom should be valid only during the

---

[1] *Cartulaire de Redon*, ed. de Courson, p. 298, no. CCCXLVII; cf. p. 449; S. Hirsch, *Jahrbücher des d. Reiches unter Heinrich II*, III, p. 174.
[2] *Ét. de Saint-Louis*, I, 53.

lifetime of its author.[1] In other words, no clear distinction was made between the concrete image of the chief and the abstract idea of power. The kings themselves had difficulty in rising above a strictly limited family sentiment. Consider the terms in which Philip Augustus, on setting out for the Crusade arranges for the disposal of his treasure—the indispensable basis of all monarchic power—in the event of his death on the way to the Holy Land. If his son survives him one half only shall be distributed as alms; but if the child dies before the father the whole shall be so distributed.

But let us not picture a régime of personal absolutism either in law or in fact. According to the code of good government universally accepted at that time, no chief, whatever his rank, could make any serious decision without first taking counsel. This did not mean, of course, taking counsel with the people, which no one considered it necessary to consult either directly or through its elected representatives: were not the rich and the powerful its natural representatives, according to the divine plan? The king or the prince had therefore merely to seek the advice of his principal subjects and personal vassals—in a word, his court, in the feudal sense of the term. The proudest monarchs never failed to recall this necessary consultation in their charters. The Emperor Otto I admitted that a law whose promulgation had been arranged for a particular assembly could not be published there 'on account of the absence of some great men'.[2] How strictly the rule was applied depended on the balance of forces. But it would never have been prudent to violate it too openly; for the sole orders which subjects of a certain social standing believed themselves really bound to respect were those which had been given, if not with their consent, at least in their presence. In this inability to conceive of the political tie otherwise than in terms of personal contact we recognize once again one of the deep-seated causes of feudal disintegration.

2 VIOLENCE AND THE LONGING FOR PEACE

A picture of feudal society, especially in its first age, would inevitably give but an inaccurate idea of the reality if it were concerned exclusively with legal institutions and allowed one to forget that men in those times lived in constant and painful insecurity. It was not, as it is today, the agony of the terrible, but intermittent and collective, dangers inherent in a world of nations in arms. Nor was it—or at least not mainly—the fear of the economic forces which crush the poor or unfortunate. The ever-present threat was one which lay heavy on each individual. It affected one's possessions and, indeed, one's very life. War, murder, the abuse of power—these have cast their shadow over almost every page of our analysis. The reasons why

[1] Bigelow, *Placita Anglo-Normannica*, p. 145.
[2] *M.G.H., Constitutiones regum et imp.*, I, no. XIII, pp. 28-9.

violence became the distinguishing mark of an epoch and a social system may now be summarized in a few words.

'When, after the demise of the Roman Empire of the Franks, various kings shall seat themselves on the august throne, each man will put his trust only in the sword.' These words were uttered in the guise of a prophecy, about the middle of the ninth century, by a cleric from Ravenna who had seen and deplored the disappearance of the great Carolingian dream of empire.[1] Contemporaries were therefore clearly conscious of the evil; and the impotence of governments (which was itself in large measure the result of irrepressible habits of disorder) had helped to unleash it. So had the invasions, which brought murder and pillage to every part of the land, as well as effectively breaking down the old framework of government. But violence was also deep-rooted in the social structure and in the mentality of the age.

It played a part in the economy: at a time when trade was scarce and difficult, what surer means of becoming rich than plunder or oppression? A whole class of masters and warriors lived mainly by such means, and one monk could calmly make a petty lord say in a charter: I give this land 'free of all dues, of all exaction or tallage, of all compulsory services . . . and of all those things which by violence knights are wont to extort from the poor'.[2]

Violence entered into the sphere of law as well; partly on account of the principle of customary law which in the long run resulted in the legalization of almost every usurpation; and also in consequence of the firmly rooted tradition which recognized the right, or even made it the duty, of the individual or the small group to execute justice on its own account. The family feud was responsible for countless bloody tragedies; but there were other threats to public order as a result of people taking the law into their own hands. When the peace assemblies forbade the victim of a material wrong to indemnify himself by personally seizing one of the possessions of the offender, they knew that they were striking at one of the most frequent sources of trouble.

Finally, violence was an element in manners. Medieval men had little control over their immediate impulses; they were emotionally insensitive to the spectacle of pain, and they had small regard for human life, which they saw only as a transitory state before Eternity; moreover, they were very prone to make it a point of honour to display their physical strength in an almost animal way. 'Every day', wrote Bishop Burchard of Worms about 1024, 'murders in the manner of wild beasts are committed among the dependants of St. Peter's. They attack each other through drunkenness, through pride, or for no reason at all. In the course of one year

[1] *M.G.H., SS. rer. Langob. Saec. VI–IX*, p. 385, c. 166.
[2] *Cartulaire de Saint-Aubin d'Angers*, ed. B. de Broussillon, II, no. DCCX (17th September 1138).

thirty-five serfs of St. Peter's, completely innocent people, have been killed by other serfs of the church; and the murderers, far from repenting, glory in their crime.' Nearly a century later an English chronicle, praising the great peace which William the Conqueror had established in his kingdom, could think of no better way to express its plenitude than by naming those two characteristics: henceforth no man may put another to death for a wrong done to him, whatever its nature; and everyone may travel through England with his belt full of gold without danger.[1] This reveals the double root of the most common evils: the practice of private vengeance which, according to the ideas of the time, could plead a moral justification; and brigandage in all its nakedness.

Nevertheless, everyone suffered in the last resort from these brutalities and the chiefs, more than anyone, were aware of the disasters which they brought in their train. And so from the depths of this troubled epoch there arose with all the strength of man's yearning for the most precious and most unattainable of 'God's gifts' a long cry for peace—for internal peace, that is, above all. For a king, for a prince, there was no higher praise than the title of 'peacemaker'. The word must be understood in its most positive sense—not one who accepts peace, but one who imposes it. 'May there be peace in the realm'—this was the prayer on coronation day. 'Blessed are the peacemakers,' exclaimed St. Louis. This concern, common to all rulers, is sometimes expressed with a touching frankness. Listen to the wisdom of King Cnut—that same king of whom a court poet had sung: 'Thou wert still very young, O Prince, when the blazing dwellings of men lit the path of thy advance'. In his laws, he says: 'We require that every man above the age of twelve shall swear never to rob or become the accomplice of a robber.'[2] But precisely because the great temporal powers were ineffectual, there developed, outside the sphere of the regular authorities and at the instance of the Church, a spontaneous effort for the organization of the peace and order which were so much desired.

3 THE PEACE AND TRUCE OF GOD [3]

The peace associations had their origin in meetings of bishops. Among the clergy the sense of human solidarity derived sustenance from the conception

[1] *M.G.H., Constitutiones*, I, p. 643, c. 30; *Two of the Saxon Chronicles*, ed. C. Plummer, I, p. 220; It is impossible to go on retailing anecdotes; but in order to convey the true colour of the period it would be necessary to do so. For example, we are not accustomed to think of Henry I of England as a wild beast. But read in Orderic Vitalis how, when the husband of one of his illegitimate daughters had the eyes of the young son of a royal castellan plucked out, the king in his turn ordered his own granddaughters to be blinded and mutilated.

[2] M. Ashdown, *English and Norse Documents relating to the Reign of Ethelred the Unready*, 1930, p. 137; Cnut, *Laws*, II, 21.

[3] Since works relating to the 'Peaces of God'—notably L. Huberti, *Studien zur Rechtsgeschichte der Gottesfrieden und Landesfrieden*, I, Ansbach, 1892, and G. C. W. Görris, *De denkbeelden over oorlog en de bemoeeiingen voor vrede in de elfde eeuw* (Ideas on

of Christianity as the mystical body of the Saviour. 'Let no Christian kill another Christian,' declared the bishops of the province of Narbonne in 1054; 'for no one doubts that to kill a Christian is to shed the blood of Christ.' In practice, the Church knew itself to be particularly vulnerable. It believed that it had a special duty to protect not only its own members but also all the weak, those *miserabiles personae* whose guardianship had been entrusted to it by canon law.

Nevertheless, despite the ecumenical character of the mother-institution and leaving out of account the tardy support given by the reformed papacy, the movement was in origin very specifically French, and more particularly Aquitanian. It seems to have started about 989 in the neighbourhood of Poitiers, at the council of Charroux, which was soon followed by numerous synods, from the Spanish March to Berry and the Rhône; but it was only in the second decade of the eleventh century that the peace movement spread to Burgundy and the northern parts of the kingdom. Some prelates from the kingdom of Arles and the abbot of Cluny tried, in 1040 and 1041, to win over the bishops of Italy, though apparently without much success.[1] Lorraine and Germany were not seriously affected till towards the end of the century, and England not at all. The peculiarities of this development are easily explained by differences of political structure. In 1023 the bishops of Soissons and Beauvais formed a peace association and invited their colleague the bishop of Cambrai to join them. But that prelate, who was, like them, a suffragan of the archbishopric of Rheims, but personally a subject of the Empire, refused: it was 'unfitting', he said, that a bishop should meddle in matters which pertained to kings. In the Empire, particularly among the imperial episcopate, the idea of the State was still very much alive and the State itself did not appear completely incapable of fulfilling its task. Similarly in Castile and Leon it was only after a disputed succession in 1124 had considerably weakened the monarchy that the great archbishop of Compostela, Diego Gelmirez, was able to introduce conciliar decisions modelled on those 'of the Romans and the Franks'. In France, on the contrary, the powerlessness of the monarchy was everywhere plain to see; but nowhere more than in the anarchic regions of the South and Centre, which had long been accustomed to an almost independent existence. There no principality as solidly constituted as for example Flanders or Normandy had succeeded in establishing itself, so that self-help was necessary if one was not to perish in the disorder.

To suppress violence completely was a vain dream, but at least one might

War and Efforts for Peace in the Eleventh Century), Nijmegen, 1912 (Diss. Leyden)—contain numerous references which are easy to follow up, it is hoped that the reader will understand why in the following pages there are a great number of citations without references.

[1] In the south of the peninsula, the truce of God was introduced by a French pope (Urban II) and the Norman barons (see Jamison in *Papers of the British School at Rome*, 1913, p. 240).

hope to keep it within bounds. At first these efforts took the form—and this was what was properly known as the 'Peace of God'—of extending a special protection to certain classes of persons or objects. The list drawn up by the council of Charroux was still very rudimentary: it was forbidden to enter churches by force or to plunder them; to carry off the peasants' livestock; to strike an unarmed cleric. Later the prohibitions were extended and more clearly defined. Merchants were included among those entitled to protection—for the first time, it seems, at the synod of Le Puy in 990. The list of forbidden acts became more and more detailed—one might not destroy a mill, uproot vines, or attack a man on his way to or from church. Yet certain exceptions were still provided for. Some seemed to be imposed by the necessities of war: the oath of Beauvais of 1023 sanctions the killing of peasants' livestock, if it is done to feed oneself or one's retinue. Other exceptions were explained by the respect for compulsion or even violence, when conceived as legally inseparable from any exercise of authority; 'I will not despoil the villeins,' promised the lords assembled at Anse on the Saône in 1025, 'I will not kill their beasts, except on my own land.' Others, finally, were rendered inevitable by universally respected legal or moral traditions. The right to prosecute the blood-feud after a murder is almost always reserved, either expressly or by pretermission. In fact to prevent the simple and the poor from becoming involved in the quarrels of the powerful; to avert the feud when its only justification, in the words of the council of Narbonne, was a dispute about a piece of land or a debt; above all, to check brigandage—these aims already seemed sufficiently ambitious.

But just as there were persons and things under special protection, so there were also days when violence was prohibited. A Carolingian capitulary had already forbidden the prosecution of the blood-feud on Sunday. This measure was revived—for the first time, apparently—in 1027 by a small diocesan synod held in Roussillon, 'in the Toulonges meadow'. (It is not necessary to assume a direct knowledge of an obscure capitulary, but at least the idea had survived.) Combined as a rule with prohibitions of the other type, it spread with great rapidity. Moreover, people soon began to be dissatisfied with a single day's respite; a similar ban for the Easter period had already made its appearance, in the north this time (at Beauvais in 1023). The 'truce of God', as this periodic armistice was called, was gradually extended, not only to the great feasts, but also to the three days of the week (from Wednesday evening) which preceded Sunday and were considered the preparation for it. Thus eventually there was less time for war than for peace. Virtually no exception was allowed in principle, and no law would have been more salutary—if it had not for the most part remained a dead letter because it asked too much.

The very first councils, like that of Charroux, had confined themselves to the most conventional form of legislation, enforced by religious sanctions. But in 990 Guy, bishop of Le Puy, assembled his diocesans, both knights and villeins, in a meadow and 'besought them to pledge themselves by oath to keep the peace, not to oppress the churches or the poor in their goods, to give back what they had carried off. . . . They refused.' Upon this, the prelate summoned troops whom he had secretly concentrated under cover of darkness. 'In the morning he set out to force the recalcitrants to take the oath of peace and give hostages: which, with the help of God, was done.' [1] This, according to local tradition, was the origin—and it could not be called purely voluntary—of the first 'peace pact'. Others followed, and soon there was scarcely an assembly concerned with limiting violence which was not concluded in this way by a great collective oath of reconciliation and good conduct. At the same time, the pledge inspired by the decisions of the councils became more and more precise in its terms. Sometimes it was accompanied by the handing over of hostages. It was in these sworn associations, which endeavoured to associate in the work of peace the entire population (represented naturally above all by its chiefs, great and small), that the real originality of the peace movement resided.

It remained either to coerce or to punish those who had not taken the oath or who, having done so, had broken their pledges. For to all appearance spiritual penalties were only intermittently effective. As for the temporal punishments which the assemblies also tried to introduce (particularly in the form of compensation for victims and fines), these could have some effect only where there was an authority capable of imposing them.

Reliance seems to have been placed on the existing powers at first. The violation of the peace continued to be subject to the jurisdiction of the local lord, duly bound by his oath and capable of being held to his responsibilities—as was seen at the council of Poitiers in the year 1000—by means of hostages. But this meant returning to the very system which had confessed its impotence. By an almost inevitable evolution the sworn associations, whose sole object had originally been to bind men together by a comprehensive pledge of good behaviour, tended to be transformed into executive organs. They may sometimes, at least in Languedoc, have appointed special judges with a responsibility, beyond the competence of the ordinary courts, for the punishment of offences against good order. It is in any case certain that many of them set up a genuine militia, thus simply regularizing the old principle which recognized the right of a threatened community to pursue brigands. At first this, too, was carried out with evident concern to respect the established authorities: the forces to which the council of Poitiers had entrusted the task of bringing the guilty man to book, if his own lord had not succeeded in doing so, were those of other lords participating in the common oath. But leagues of a new type were soon created which boldly went beyond the traditional limits. By chance we possess a text which has preserved the memory of the

[1] De Vic and Vaissète, *Histoire du Languedoc*, V, col. 15.

confederation instituted by Aimon, archbishop of Bourges, in 1038. All members of the diocese over fifteen years of age were required to take the oath, through the intermediary of their parish priests. The latter, displaying the banners of their churches, marched at the head of the parochial levies. More than one castle was destroyed and burned by this army of the people till at length, ill-armed and reduced, it is said, to using donkeys as mounts for its cavalry, it was massacred by the lord of Déols, on the banks of the Cher.

Unions of this sort were bound to arouse lively hostility, which was not confined to the circles most directly interested in prolonging disorder. For they unquestionably contained an element that conflicted with the social hierarchy; not only because they set up villeins against robber lords; but also and perhaps most of all because they committed men to defending themselves, instead of looking for protection to the regular powers. Not so very long before, in the heyday of the Carolingians, Charlemagne had prohibited the 'gilds' or 'brotherhoods', even when their object was to repress brigandage. The undoubted survival in these associations of practices inherited from German paganism was not the sole reason for their proscription at that time. A state which sought to base itself both on the idea of public office and on relationships of personal subordination pressed into the service of the monarchy could not allow police functions to be taken over by unauthorized groups, which even then, according to the capitularies, consisted in the main of peasants. The barons and lords of feudal times were no less jealous of their rights. Their attitude was displayed with remarkable clearness in an episode which took place in Aquitaine: the last spontaneous effort of a movement already nearly two centuries old.

In 1182, a carpenter of Le Puy, guided by visions, founded a peace brotherhood which spread rapidly in all the regions of Languedoc, in Berry, and even in the district of Auxerre. Its emblem was a white hood with a sort of scarf, the front band of which hung over the breast and bore an image of the Virgin surrounded by the inscription: 'Lamb of God, that takest away the sins of the world, give us peace.' Our Lady herself was supposed to have appeared to the artisan and handed him the emblem with the device. All blood-feuds were expressly prohibited by the group. If one of its members committed a murder the brother of the dead man, if he himself belonged to the *Capuchonnés*, would give the murderer the kiss of peace and take him to his own house where he would feed him, in token of forgiveness. These Peacemakers, as they liked to be called, had nothing Tolstoyan about them, and they fought one bitter and victorious war against the robber-nobles. But it was not long before their spontaneous efforts at law enforcement began to cause anxiety in seignorial circles. With a significant change of attitude we find the same monk who at Auxerre, in 1183, had heaped praises on these good servants of order, denouncing them the following year, as an unruly sect. In the words of another chronicler, they were accused of trying to bring about 'the ruin of the institutions that govern us by the will of God and the ministry of the powerful of this world'. Add to this that unverified revelations to a lay and therefore presumably an ignorant visionary—whether a carpenter Durand or a Joan of Arc—have always, and not without reason, appeared to the guardians of the faith to be fraught with dangers to orthodoxy. Crushed by the combined forces of the barons, the bishops, and the robber-nobles, the *Jurés* of Le Puy and their allies ended as miserably as the Berry militia in the previous century.

These catastrophes were only symptoms (though eloquent enough) of a general setback to the popular peace movement. Incapable of creating out of nothing the good policing and sound justice without which no peace was possible, neither the councils nor the leagues ever succeeded in permanently repressing disorder. 'The human race', wrote Ralph Glaber, 'was like a dog that returns to its vomit. The promise was made; but it was not fulfilled.' In other environments, however, and in diverse forms, the great vanished dream left deep traces.

Punitive expeditions, flying the banners of churches and directed against the castles of the robber lords, heralded the French communal movement at Le Mans in 1070. It all has a familiar ring to the historian of the peace movements—even the name 'holy institutions' by which the young commune of Le Mans described its decrees. Of course the needs which induced the burgesses to unite were many and various; but we should not forget that one of the principal motives of the urban 'friendship'—to use the fine name by which some groups liked to be known—was the repression or reconciliation of vendettas within its own body and the struggle against brigandage without. Above all, we can hardly fail to recall the link existing between the peace pact and the communal pact in the shape of a feature common to both—the oath of equals—whose revolutionary character we have already noted. But unlike the great confederations created under the auspices of councils and prelates, the commune confined itself to bringing together in a single city men bound by a strong class solidarity and already accustomed to living close together. This concentration was one of the main reasons for its strength.

Nevertheless, the king and the princes, from a sense of duty or from self-interest, also sought to establish internal order, and although the peace movement had arisen without their participation, it was inevitable that before long they should seek to turn it to advantage by setting themselves up, each in his own sphere, as 'great peacemakers'—the title expressly adopted by a count of Provence in 1226.[1] It appears that Archbishop Aimon had already planned to make the renowned Berry militia the means

[1] R. Busquet in *Les Bouches du Rhône, Encyclopédie départementale. Première partie,* II. *Antiquité et moyen âge,* 1924, p. 563.

of establishing an actual provincial sovereignty for his own benefit. In Catalonia the counts, who had at first confined themselves to taking part in the synods, soon began to incorporate the decisions of these councils in their own ordinances, giving them at the same time a twist which little by little transformed the peace of the Church into the peace of the prince. In Languedoc and particularly in the dioceses of the Massif Central, the progress of monetary circulation in the twelfth century had enabled the peace associations to put their finances on a regular basis: a subsidy, known as the 'common of peace' or *pezade*, was levied with the twofold object of indemnifying the victims of disturbances and financing expeditions. It was collected through the normal parish machinery and the bishop administered the fund. But this contribution very quickly lost its original character. The magnates—especially the counts of Toulouse, masters and feudal lords of many counties—compelled the bishops to give them a share of the revenues; and even the bishops came to forget the primary purpose of the fund. Thus in the long run—for the *pezade* was to last as long as the Ancien Régime—the most enduring result in France of the great effort of self-defence was to favour the creation of a territorial tax at a remarkably early date.

With the exception of Robert the Pious, who summoned great assemblies for the purpose of taking the oath of peace, the Capetians do not seem to have had much concern for a movement which they may have regarded as a challenge to their own judicial functions. The parochial levies which stormed the lords' strongholds in the reign of Louis VI were in the personal service of the king. As for the solemn ten years' peace which was promulgated by his successor, although it showed the influence of the usual conciliar decisions, it had in itself all the characteristics of an act of monarchic authority. On the other hand, in the strongest principalities of northern France—in Normandy and Flanders—the princes at first considered it advisable to co-operate in the work of the peace associations. In 1030, Baldwin IV of Flanders combined with the bishop of Noyon-Tournai to promote a great collective oath; and in 1047 a council at Caen, influenced perhaps by Flemish texts, proclaimed the Truce of God. But there were no armed leagues; they would not have been tolerated and would have seemed unnecessary. Very soon afterwards the count and the duke—the latter assisted, in Normandy, by certain traditions peculiar to Scandinavian law—assumed the place of the Church as legislators, judges, and guardians of good order.

It was in the Empire that the peace movement had the most far-reaching results and, at the same time, underwent the most curious deviations from its original purpose. We have already seen what opposition it encountered there at first. It is true that there also, from the beginning of the eleventh century, great assemblies were held, in which the various peoples were invited to general reconciliation and abstention from all violence; but these measures were effected in royal diets and through royal decrees, and this state of things continued until the great quarrel between Henry IV and Gregory VII. Then, for the first time in 1082, a Truce of God was proclaimed at Liége by the bishop with the collaboration of the barons of the diocese. The place and the date are equally deserving of attention: Lotharingia was more accessible than Germany proper to influences from the West; and it was barely five years since the first anti-king had been set up against Henry IV. Since it was due to the initiative of an imperialist bishop, the Truce was in no sense directed against the monarchy; Henry indeed confirmed it, though from far away, in the south of Italy. But about the same time, in the parts of Germany where the imperial authority was no longer recognized, the barons felt the necessity of combining to combat disorder. The Church and the local powers were plainly tending to take over the functions of the kings.

Nevertheless the imperial monarchy was still too strong to be forced to abandon this weapon. On his return from Italy Henry IV in his turn began to legislate against violence and henceforth, for several centuries, the emperors or kings from time to time promulgated great peace ordinances, some of them applicable to a particular province, others—and this was most often the case—to the Empire as a whole. This was not purely and simply a return to earlier practices. The influence of the French peace movements, transmitted through Lorraine, had encouraged the replacement of the older kind of very general peace ordinance by a great profusion of more and more detailed rules; and it became increasingly the practice to insert in these texts all sorts of orders which had only a remote relation to their original object. 'The *Friedensbriefe*', a Swabian chronicle of the beginning of the thirteenth century rightly says, 'are the only laws the Germans use.' [1] Among the results of the great effort made by the councils and the sworn associations not the least paradoxical was the fact that, while in Languedoc it helped to give rise to a tax for the benefit of the princes, in Germany it favoured the revival of royal legislation.

England in the tenth and eleventh centuries had its own type of peace association in its peace 'gilds'. The statutes of the London gild, set down in writing between 930 and 940, contain remarkable evidence of the prevailing state of insecurity and violence: rough justice, pursuers hot on the trail of cattle-thieves—we might easily believe we were among the pioneers of the Far West in the great days of the 'Frontier'. But what we have here are the completely secular police arrangements of a rude community, and a popular penal code whose sanguinary severity (as evidenced by an addition to the text) shocked the king and the bishops. The name gilds had been applied in Germanic law to associations of free men formed

---

[1] *M.G.H., SS.*, XXIII, p. 361. Cf. Frensdorff in *Nachr. von der Kgl. Gesellsch. zu Göttingen, Phil. hist. Kl.*, 1894. The same transformation took place in Catalonia and Aragon.

outside the bonds of kinship and intended in some measure to take their place. Their common characteristics were an oath, periodic drinking bouts, accompanied in pagan times by religious libations, occasionally a common fund, and above all an obligation of mutual aid: 'for friendship as well as for vengeance, we shall remain united, come what may,' say the London ordinances. In England, where relationships of personal dependence were much slower than on the continent to pervade the whole of life, these associations, far from being proscribed as in the Carolingian state, were freely recognized by the kings, who hoped to rely on them for the maintenance of order. Where the responsibility of the family or of the lord could not be enforced, it was replaced by the responsibility of the gild for its members. When after the Norman Conquest a very strong monarchy was set up, it borrowed from Anglo-Saxon tradition these practices of mutual surety-ship. But this was to make them in the end—under the name of 'frank-pledge', whose history we have already outlined[1]—one of the cogwheels of the new seignorial system. The original nature of English social develop-ment, which passed directly to a rigorous monarchy from a régime in which the collective action of the free man had never been completely effaced by the power of the lord, had precluded peace institutions of the French type.

On the continent itself the intensity and fervour of the longing for peace were manifested in the councils and the pacts, but it was the kingdoms and territorial principalities which, by bringing about the indispensable recon-centration of authority, finally gave them shape.

[1] p. 271.

XXXI

TOWARDS THE RECONSTRUCTION OF STATES: NATIONAL DEVELOPMENTS

1 REASONS FOR THE RECONCENTRATION OF AUTHORITY

IN the course of the second feudal age political authority, which up to that time was much subdivided, began everywhere to be concentrated in larger organisms. (These were not new, of course, but their effective powers were genuinely revived.) The apparent exceptions, like Germany, disappear as soon as one ceases to envisage the State exclusively in terms of kingship. So general a phenomenon could only have been the result of causes common to the entire West; and a list of these causes could almost be compiled by taking the opposites of those which earlier had led to disintegration.

The cessation of the invasions had relieved the royal and princely powers of a task which exhausted their strength. At the same time it made possible the enormous growth of population to which, from the eleventh century onwards, the progress of land clearance bore witness. The increased density of population not only facilitated the maintenance of order, but also favoured the revival of towns, of the artisan class, and of trade. As a result of a more active and abundant circulation of money taxation reappeared, and with it salaried officials; and the payment of troops began to be substituted for the inefficient system of hereditary contractual services. True, the small or medial lord also profited by the transformations of the economy; he had, as we have seen, his 'tallages'. But the king or the prince almost always possessed more lands and more vassals than anyone else. Moreover, the very nature of his authority provided him with many opportunities to levy taxes, particularly on the churches and the towns. The daily revenue of Philip Augustus at the time of his death was equal in amount to about half the annual revenue returned, a little later, by a monastic lordship which, while not accounted one of the richest, nevertheless owned very extensive properties in a particularly prosperous province.[1]

---

[1] The daily revenue of the French crown at the death of Philip Augustus, according to the testimony of Conon of Lausanne, was 1,200 *livres parisis* (*M.G.H., SS.*, XXIV, p. 782). The annual revenue of the abbey of Sainte-Geneviève in Paris, according to an assessment for the 'tenths' in 1246, was 1,810 *livres parisis* (Bibliothèque Sainte-Geneviève, MS. 356, p. 271). The first figure is probably too high, the second too low. But to restore the correct relation between the figures it should be added that there was apparently a rise in prices between the two dates. In any case, the contrast is striking.

Thus the State from this time onward began to acquire that essential element of its supremacy—financial resources incomparably greater than those of any private person or community.

Corresponding changes took place in the mentality of men. The cultural 'renaissance', from the end of the eleventh century, had made it easier for them to understand the social bond—always a somewhat abstract conception—which is implicit in the subordination of the individual to the government. It had also revived the memory of the great well-ordered monarchic states of the past: the Roman Empire, whose greatness and majesty under absolute rulers were proclaimed by its Codes and its books of history; the Carolingian Empire, embellished by legend. It is true that men sufficiently educated to be influenced by such memories continued to be relatively very few; but in an absolute sense this *élite* had become much more numerous. Above all, education had spread among the laity—not merely the greater aristocracy, but also the knightly class. At a time when every administrator had to be also a military leader, these noblemen of modest fortune were more useful than the clergy; they were also less liable to be diverted by interests alien to the temporal authorities, and they had long been experienced in the practice of law. Hence it was this class which, well in advance of the bourgeoisie, came to form the general staff of the revived monarchies—the England of Henry Plantagenet, the France of Philip Augustus and St. Louis. The practice of writing and the growing interest in its potentialities enabled states to form those archives without which there could be no real continuity of government. Lists of feudal services due from fiefs, periodic accounts, registers of documents dispatched or received—innumerable memoranda of various kinds made their appearance, from the middle of the twelfth century, in the Anglo-Norman state and the Norman kingdom of Sicily and, towards the end of the same century or in the course of the thirteenth, in the kingdom of France and most of its great principalities. Their emergence was the premonitory sign that there was arising a new power, or at least one that had hitherto been confined to the great churches and the papal court, namely the bureaucracy.

Although virtually universal in its fundamental features, this general development nevertheless followed very different lines from country to country. We shall confine ourselves here to considering briefly, and as it were by way of examples, three types of state.

2 A NEW MONARCHY: THE CAPETIANS

The relative strength of the Carolingian monarchy in its heyday had been based on a few general principles: the military service required of all its subjects; the supremacy of the royal court; the subordination of the counts, who at that time were genuine officials; the network of royal vassals, who were to be found everywhere; and finally, its power over the Church. Of all this almost nothing remained to the French monarchy towards the end of the tenth century. It is true that a fairly large number of medial and petty knights continued to do homage directly to the king, especially after the accession to the throne of the Robertian dukes, who brought with them their own retainers. But henceforth they were to be found almost exclusively in that rather restricted area of northern France where the dynasty itself exercised the rights of counts. Elsewhere, apart from the great barons, the crown had only sub-vassals—a serious handicap at a time when the local lord was the only one to whom men felt morally bound. The counts or the officials in control of several counties, who thus became the intermediate link of many vassal chains, did not deny that they held their dignities from the king. But the office had become a patrimony charged with obligations of a new type. Odo of Blois, who had tried to take the count's castle at Melun from another of Hugh Capet's vassals, is reported by a contemporary to have said: 'I did not act against the king; it does not matter to him whether one man or another holds the fief'[1]—meaning, when the relationship is one of lord and vassal. In the same way, a tenant-farmer might say: 'It does not matter who I am, provided the rent is paid.' Yet this rent of fealty and service was often, in cases of this kind, very unsatisfactorily discharged.

For his army the king was normally obliged to depend on his petty vassals, on the 'knights' of the churches over which he had retained some control, and on the rustic levies from the estates of those churches and his own villages. Occasionally one or two of the dukes or greater counts contributed their contingents, though as allies rather than as subjects. Among the litigants who continued to bring their cases to his court we find that it is almost exclusively the same circles which are represented— petty lords bound to the king by direct homage, and royal churches. When in 1023 one of the magnates, the count of Blois, pretended to submit to the judgment of the king's court, he made it a condition that the very fiefs which were the subject of litigation should first be made over to him. More than two-thirds of the bishoprics—along with four entire ecclesiastical provinces (Rouen, Dol, Bordeaux, and Narbonne)—had passed under the domination of the provincial dynasties and were completely outside the control of the crown. True, those that remained immediately subject to the king were still very numerous; and thanks to one or two of these the influence of the monarchy continued to be felt even in the heart of Aquitaine (through Le Puy) and, through Noyon-Tournai, in the very midst of the regions of Flemish domination. But the majority of these royal bishoprics were also concentrated between the Loire and the frontier of the Empire; and the same was true of the 'royal' abbeys, many of which had formed part of the heritage of the Robertians, who in their ducal period were cynical appropriators of monasteries. These churches were to be one of the

[1] Richer, IV, 80.

crown's greatest sources of strength. But the first Capetians seemed so weak that their own clergy attached little value to such privileges as they were able to distribute. Only a dozen charters of Hugh Capet are known to us, from the ten years of his reign; of his contemporary Otto III of Germany, in a reign of less than twenty years—during the earlier of which he was a minor—we know of more than four hundred.

This contrast between the weakness of the monarchy in the West Frankish kingdom and its relative strength in the great neighbouring state did not fail to impress contemporaries. In Lotharingia people were wont to speak of the 'undisciplined manners' of the *Kerlinger*, that is to say the inhabitants of the former kingdom of Charles the Bald.[1] It is easier to note the contrast than to explain it. Carolingian institutions had been originally no less strong in the one kingdom than in the other. Probably the explanation must be sought in fundamental facts of social structure. The great active principle of feudal disintegration was always the power of the local or personal chief over little groups who were thus removed from any wider authority. Now leaving out of account Aquitaine, traditionally insubordinate, the regions which formed in a true sense the heart of the French monarchy were precisely those regions between Loire and Meuse where the manor went back to remote ages and 'commendation' had found its favourite soil. In a country where the immense majority of landed properties were either tenements or fiefs and where, at an early date, the name 'free' came to be applied, not to the lordless man, but to him whose only privilege was the right to choose his master, there was no place for a genuine State.

Nevertheless the very decay of the old public law proved in the end an advantage to the Capetian monarchy. Not that the new dynasty ever contemplated a break with the Carolingian tradition, whence it derived the best part of its moral force. But it was of necessity compelled to replace the old, atrophied organs of the Frankish state with other instruments of power. The kings of the previous dynasty had looked on the counts as their representatives and had not believed it possible to govern any sizeable territory except through their agency. No county directly controlled by the crown seems to have been included in the heritage of the last Carolingians, as received by Hugh Capet. The Capetians, on the contrary, were descended from a family whose greatness was founded on an accumulation of county 'honours' and very naturally they continued the same policy when they were on the throne.

This policy, it is true, was not always very firmly pursued. The early Capetians have sometimes been compared to peasants patiently adding field to field. The picture is misleading in two ways. It expresses very poorly the mentality of these anointed kings who were also great warriors and at all times—like the knightly class whose temperament they shared—dan-

---

[1] *Gesta ep. Cameracensium*, III, 2, in *M.G.H.*, *SS.*, XVII, p. 466; cf. III, 40, p. 481.

gerously susceptible to the glamour of adventure. It also assumes a continuity in their plans which the historian, if he takes a close look at them, seldom finds. If that Bouchard of Vendôme, whom Hugh Capet made count of Paris, Corbeil and Melun, had not lacked any direct heir save a son who had long ago entered a monastery, the most strongly situated of territorial principalities would have been established in the very heart of the Île-de-France. One of the charters of Henry I even envisages, as a not unlikely eventuality, the enfeoffment of Paris.[1] Plainly, it was not easy to break away from Carolingian practices.

Nevertheless from the beginning of the eleventh century the kings acquired one after another a series of counties without appointing any new counts to govern them. In other words the sovereigns, having with good reason ceased to regard these magnates as officials, were less and less reluctant to become their own counts; and so on the estates—inherited from ancestors or recently annexed—where there was now no intermediate power, the only representatives of the royal authority were persons of rather modest status, placed each at the head of a fairly small district. The very insignificance of these 'provosts' (*prévots*) prevented them from being a real danger, and though at first a few of them seem to have succeeded in making their posts hereditary, their masters had no great difficulty in the course of the twelfth century in limiting most of them to farming their offices for a specified term. Then from the time of Philip Augustus, at a higher level of the administrative hierarchy, genuine salaried officials made their appearance—the bailiffs (*baillis*) or seneschals. Because it had adapted itself to new social conditions and modestly based its power on the direct control of fairly restricted groups of men, the French monarchy benefited most by the eventual reconcentration of authority and was able to turn it to the advantage of the very ancient ideas and sentiments which it continued to embody.

But it was not the only power to benefit in this way, for the same phenomenon also occurred within the great territorial principalities which still subsisted. The mosaic of counties, ranging from Troyes to Meaux and Provins, which Odo of Blois about 1022 had succeeded in appropriating by an astute exploitation of family connections, was no less different from the county of Champagne at the beginning of the thirteenth century, with its law of succession based on primogeniture to the exclusion of partition, with its well-defined administrative districts, its officials and its archives, than was the kingdom of Robert the Pious from that of Louis VIII. The organisms thus formed were so strong that even their final absorption by the monarchy failed to disrupt them. Thus it might be said that the kings reassembled France rather than unified it. Observe the contrasts between France and England. In England there was the Great Charter; in France, in 1314–15, the Charters granted to the Normans, to the people of Languedoc, to the

---

[1] Tardif, *Cartons des rois*, no. 264.

Bretons, to the Burgundians, to the Picards, to the people of Champagne, of Auvergne, of the *Basses Marches* of the West, of Berry, and of Nevers. In England there was Parliament; in France, the provincial Estates, always much more frequently convoked and on the whole more active than the States-General. In England there was the common law, almost untouched by regional exceptions; in France the vast medley of regional 'customs'. All these contrasts were to hamper the national development of France. Indeed it seems as if the French monarchy, even when the State had been revived, continued permanently to bear the mark of that agglomeration of counties, castellanies and rights over churches which, in very 'feudal' fashion, it had made the foundation of its power.

3 AN ARCHAISTIC MONARCHY: GERMANY

Noting that 'the perpetuity of fiefs was established in France earlier than in Germany', Montesquieu attributed it to the 'phlegmatic humour and, if I may venture to say so, the mental immutability of the German nation'.[1] As psychological diagnosis this is certainly too sweeping, even when Montesquieu tones it down with a 'perhaps'. But it is a remarkably penetrating piece of intuition, especially if, instead of 'phlegmatic humour', we say simply 'archaism'; for this is the word which must occur to any student of medieval German society, compared period by period with French society. The remark certainly applies, as we have seen, to vassalage and the fief, to the manorial system, to the epic (so truly archaic in its legendary themes and the pagan atmosphere of its marvellous events); and it applies no less to the economic sphere (the 'urban renaissance' in Germany was a century or two later than in Italy, France and Flanders), and is equally valid when we pass to the evolution of the State. No example is more telling than the harmony between social structure and political structure. In Germany, far less profoundly and less uniformly 'feudalized' than France, the monarchy remained faithful much longer to the Carolingian model.

The king governs with the help of counts whose hereditary position is only slowly confirmed, and who, even when this has been established, continue to be regarded as the holders of an office rather than a fief. Even when they are not direct vassals of the king it is from him that in theory, like the advocates of immunist churches, they hold by special grant their power to give orders and to punish—their 'ban', as it was called. It is true that here also the monarchy came up against the rivalry of the territorial principalities—especially in the form of those duchies to whose original structure we have called attention. In spite of the suppressions or divisions carried out by the Saxon dynasty, the dukes continued to be dangerously powerful and insubordinate. But the kings were able to use

[1] *Esprit des Lois*, XXXI, 30.

the Church against them. For, unlike the Capetians, the German heirs of Charlemagne succeeded in retaining control of virtually all the bishoprics of the kingdom. The surrender of the Bavarian bishoprics by Henry I to the duke of Bavaria was only a measure of expediency and was soon revoked; the belated grant of sees beyond the Elbe made by Frederick Barbarossa to the duke of Saxony related only to a missionary field and did not last much longer, and the case of the small Alpine bishoprics, appointment to which was vested in their metropolitan at Salzburg, was an insignificant exception. The chapel royal was the seminary of the prelates of the Empire and it was this personnel of clerics, educated, ambitious, experienced in affairs of state, which more than anything maintained the continuity of the monarchic idea. Bishoprics and royal monasteries, from the Elbe to the Meuse, from the Alps to the North Sea, placed their 'services' at the disposition of the sovereign: contributions in money or in kind; lodging for the king or his followers; above all military service. The contingents of the churches formed the largest and most stable part of the royal army; but they were not the whole of it. For the king continued to demand aid from all his subjects, and although the general levy properly so called—'the call to the country' (clamor patriae)—applied in practice only to the frontier regions in the event of barbarian raids, the obligation to serve with their knights rested on the dukes and counts of the entire kingdom and was in fact fairly satisfactorily fulfilled.

This traditional system, however, never worked perfectly. True, it made possible the great projects of the 'Roman expeditions'; but in so doing— in favouring over-ambitious and anachronistic designs—it had already become dangerous. The internal structure of the country was not really strong enough to support such a load. It is really not surprising that this government which had no taxation other than the few financial 'services' of the churches, no salaried officials, no permanent army—this nomadic government, which possessed no convenient means of communication and which men felt to be physically and morally remote from them, should not always succeed in ensuring the obedience of its subjects. No reign in fact was free from rebellions.

With some delay and many differences, the process by which the powers of the State were broken up into small centres of personal authority triumphed in Germany as in France, The dissolution of the counties, for one thing, little by little deprived the edifice of its necessary basis. Now the German kings, since they were much more than territorial princes, had not provided themselves with anything resembling the restricted, but well-placed, domain of the Robertian dukes who had become kings of France. Even the duchy of Saxony, which Henry I had held before his accession, passed eventually—though reduced in size—out of the hands of the crown. This was one example of a usage which progressively acquired the force of law. Any fief de dignité provisionally falling in to the crown by confiscation or abeyance must be re-granted in fee without delay, and this characteristic principle of the imperial monarchy was especially fatal to its progress. Had it prevailed in France it would have prevented Philip Augustus from keeping Normandy, just as in Germany, some thirty years earlier, it did in fact prevent the annexation by Frederick Barbarossa of the duchies taken away from Henry the Lion. True, it was left to the twelfth century to formulate the principle in its full rigour, under pressure from the baronage. But without any doubt it took its origin from the character of a public office which in Germany was firmly attached to the 'honours' of counts and dukes. How could a sovereign appoint himself his own representative? Certainly, the German king was the direct lord of many villages; he had his own vassals, his *ministeriales*, his castles. But all these were very widely scattered. Belatedly, Henry IV realized the danger, and from 1070 he tried to create in Saxony a veritable Île-de-France, bristling with fortresses. The plan failed; for already the great crisis of the struggle with the popes was at hand, which was to reveal so many sources of weaknesses.

Here again we are faced with an anachronism. Henry IV and Gregory VII had been engaged for several years in an apparently commonplace conflict when in 1076 it suddenly developed into a relentless war. The cause was that dramatic event at Worms—the deposition of the pope pronounced, after consultation with a German council, by a king who had not even as yet been excommunicated. Now this act was only an echo of earlier events. Otto I had deposed one pope; Henry IV's own father and predecessor had deposed three at a single stroke. Since then, however, the world had changed. Reformed by the emperors themselves, the papacy had regained its moral prestige and a great movement of religious awakening was making it the highest symbol of spiritual values.

We have already seen how this long quarrel finally destroyed the hereditary principle in Germany. It ended by throwing the monarchs into the perpetual hornet's nest of Italy; it became a focal point for rebellion and its outcome profoundly affected the royal powers over the Church. Not, of course, that the kings ceased, even in the thirteenth century, to exercise an influence over the appointment of bishops and abbots—an influence which, though it varied greatly with the reign or the moment, continued to be on the whole very extensive. But the prelates, who were henceforth invested by a touch of the sceptre (symbolizing the grant of the fief), ceased to be regarded as holders of a public office, and appeared from now on as ordinary feudatories. Moreover, the development of religious consciousness weakened the idea of the sacred value hitherto attached to the royal dignity and rendered the clergy less willing to submit to attempts at domination which conflicted with their heightened sense of the pre-eminence of spiritual forces. At the same time social changes were in progress which finally transformed the former representatives of the monarchy in the provinces into hereditary lords of subdivided domains, reduced the number of free men (in the original sense of the word), and took away much of the public character of courts which were becoming progressively more subject to the local lords. In the twelfth century Frederick Barbarossa still gave the impression of being a very powerful monarch. The imperial idea, nourished by a richer and more self-conscious culture, had never been expressed more powerfully than during the reign and at the court of this prince. But badly buttressed and ill-adapted to contemporary forces, the monarchic structure was even then at the mercy of the slightest shock.

Meanwhile other powers were preparing to spring up on the ruins of both the monarchy and the old tribal duchies. From the end of the twelfth century territorial principalities, hitherto somewhat loosely held together, gradually emerged as bureaucratic states, relatively well-ordered, subject to State taxation, and possessing representative assemblies. In these states what survived of vassalage was turned to the advantage of their rulers and even the Church was obedient. Politically speaking, there was no longer a Germany; but, as they said in France, 'the Germanies'. On the one hand there was retarded social development, a specifically German characteristic; on the other, there was the advent, common to almost the whole of Europe, of conditions favourable to a concentration of public authority. The meeting of these two chains of causation meant that in Germany the reconcentration of forces was effected only at the cost of a long fragmentation of the ancient state.

4 THE ANGLO-NORMAN MONARCHY: CONQUEST AND GERMANIC SURVIVALS

The Anglo-Norman state was the fruit of a double conquest—the conquest of western Neustria by Rollo and of England by William the Bastard. It owed to this origin a structure much more regular than that of principalities built up piecemeal or of monarchies burdened with a long and sometimes confused tradition. What is more, the second conquest, that of England, had taken place at the very moment when the transformation of economic and intellectual conditions throughout the West began to favour the struggle against disintegration. It is significant that almost from the first this monarchy, born of a successful war, seems to have had at its disposal at an early date an educated personnel and bureaucratic machinery.

Anglo-Saxon England in its latest period had witnessed the creation under its earls of genuine territorial principalities formed, according to the classic pattern, from agglomerations of counties. The war of conquest and the harsh suppression of the subsequent rebellions removed from the scene the great native chiefs; and all danger to the unity of the State from that side might have seemed to be at an end. Nevertheless the idea that it was possible for a king to govern his whole realm directly was then so alien to

men's minds that William believed it necessary to create regional commands
of a similar type. Fortunately for the monarchy, the very faithlessness of
the great barons to whom they were assigned quickly led—with only two
exceptions, the earldom of Chester on the Welsh marches, and the
ecclesiastical principality of Durham on the Scottish border—to the suppression of these formidable political units. The kings continued to create
earls from time to time; but in the counties whose names they bore, they
were thenceforth confined to receiving a part of the proceeds of justice.
The actual exercise of judicial powers, the levying of troops, the collection
of fiscal revenues, belonged to direct representatives of the king, called
sheriffs. These men were not exactly officials in the usual sense. They
farmed their office by paying a fixed sum to the royal treasury (at a time
when economic conditions still precluded a salaried officialdom, this
system was the only alternative to enfeoffment), and a fair number succeeded in making themselves hereditary. But this dangerous development
was suddenly checked by the strong hand of the Angevin sovereigns.
When in 1170 Henry II, at a single stroke, removed from office all the
sheriffs in the kingdom, subjected their administration to an inquest, and
reappointed only a few of them, it was plain to everyone that throughout
England the king was master of those who governed in his name. Because
the public office was not completely identified with the fief, England was a
truly unified state much earlier than any continental kingdom.

Although in certain respects, no state was more completely feudal,
the feudalism was of such a kind as ultimately to enhance the prestige of
the crown. In this country where every piece of land was a tenement, the
king was literally the lord of all the lords. Nowhere was the system of
military fiefs more methodically applied. With armies so recruited the
essential problem was, as we know, to get the direct vassals of the king or
prince to bring with them to the host a sufficient number of those sub-
vassals of whom the bulk of the army was necessarily composed. Now in
the Norman duchy and subsequently on a much larger scale in England
this figure, instead of being left to be decided (as was so often the case elsewhere) by a varying custom, or individual agreements that were more or
less ill observed, was fixed once for all for each barony—at least as to the
required minimum—by the central power. And since it was a recognized
principle that almost every obligation to do something might be replaced
by its equivalent in cash, the kings, from the early years of the twelfth
century, adopted the practice of occasionally demanding from their
tenants-in-chief, instead of soldiers, a tax assessed on the basis of the
number of knights or (to use the contemporary expression) 'shields' which
they would have had to provide.

But this admirably planned feudal organization was linked with traditions derived from a more distant past. In the firm peace established, from
the time of the occupation of the Neustrian counties, by the 'dukes of the

pirates' we can surely recognize the code of an army in cantonment, like those laws which the Danish historian Saxo Grammaticus attributes to the legendary conqueror, King Frode. Above all, we must not underrate the part played by the Anglo-Saxon heritage. The oath of fealty which in 1086 William required of all those in authority in England, 'whose soever men they were', and which his first two successors caused to be renewed—that pledge which transcended and took precedence of all ties of vassalage— was it after all anything else than the ancient oath of the subject, familiar to all the barbarian monarchies and practised by the kings of the West Saxon dynasty, as well as by the Carolingians? Weak as the Anglo-Saxon monarchy in its final period may have seemed, it had none the less been able to maintain—alone among all its contemporaries—a general tax which, from having served at first to pay ransom to the Danish invaders and then to supply the means to fight them, had acquired the name of 'Danegeld'. In this extraordinary survival, which seems to presuppose in England a better monetary circulation than elsewhere, the Norman kings were to find a remarkably effective instrument. Finally, the persistence in England of the ancient courts of free men, associated in so many ways with the maintenance of public order—a Germanic institution if ever there was one—greatly favoured the maintenance and then the extension of royal justice and administrative authority.

Yet the strength of this complex monarchy was entirely relative, and here too the elements of disintegration were present. Service from the fiefs was more and more difficult to obtain because, while the royal government was capable of exercising some measure of coercion over its tenants-in-chief, it could not so easily reach down through them to the mass of often recalcitrant petty feudatories. The baronage was almost continually in-subordinate, and from 1135 to 1154, during the long dynastic troubles of Stephen's reign, the building of innumerable 'adulterine' castles and the recognition of the hereditary position of the sheriffs, who sometimes united several counties under their domination and themselves bore the title of earls, seemed to proclaim the irresistible progress of disintegration. Nevertheless, after the recovery which marked the reign of Henry II, the aim of the magnates in their rebellions was henceforth much less to tear the kingdom asunder than to dominate it. The knightly class, for its part, found in the county courts the opportunity to consolidate itself as a group and appoint its own representatives. The powerful kingship of the con-querors had not destroyed all other powers; but it had forced them to act, even when in opposition to it, only within the framework of the State.

5 NATIONALITIES

To what extent were these states also nations or destined to become nations? Like every problem of group psychology, this question necessitates a careful distinction not only between periods but also between environments.

The growth of national sentiment was hardly possible among the most educated men. All that survived of culture worthy of the name took refuge till the twelfth century among a fraction of the clergy, and there was much in this legacy to alienate these intellectuals from what they would probably have treated as antiquated notions: for example the use of Latin, an international language, with the facilities for intellectual communication which flowed from it, and above all the cult of the great ideals of peace, piety, and unity, which in this world seemed to be embodied in the dual images of Christendom and Empire. Gerbert, although a native of Aquitaine and a former dignitary of the church of Rheims (and therefore in a double capacity a subject of the king of France), certainly did not believe that he was betraying any essential duty by becoming—at the time when the successor of Charlemagne was a Saxon—'a soldier in the camp of Caesar'.[1] In order to discover the obscure foreshadowings of nationalism we must turn to groups of men more simple-minded and more prone to live in the present; not so much, indeed, to the popular masses, of whose state of mind we have no documentary evidence, as to the knightly classes and that half-educated section of the clergy which confined itself, in its writings, to reflecting with sharper emphasis the public opinion of the time.

As a reaction against romantic historiography, it has been the fashion among some recent historians to deny that the early centuries of the Middle Ages had any group consciousness at all, either national or racial. This is to forget that in the crude and naive form of antagonism to the stranger, the 'outsider' (*horsin*), such sentiments did not require a very great refinement of mind. We know today that they manifested themselves in the period of the Germanic invasions with much more strength than Fustel de Coulanges, for example, believed. In the greatest example of conquest offered by the feudal era—that of Norman England—we see them clearly at work. When the youngest son of William, Henry I, had by a characteristic gesture, judged it a shrewd move to marry a princess of the ancient dynasty of Wessex—of the 'direct' line of England, as it was called by a monk of Canterbury—the Norman knights took a derisive pleasure in loading the royal couple with Saxon nicknames. But singing the praises of this marriage, about half a century later, in the reign of the grandson of Henry and Edith, a hagiographer wrote: 'Now England has a king of English race; it finds among the same race bishops, abbots, barons, brave knights, born of both seeds.'[2] The history of this assimilation, which is the history of English nationality, cannot be recounted here even in outline, owing to limitations of space. Leaving aside acts of con-

---

[1] *Lettres*, ed. Havet, nos. 12 and 13.

[2] Marc Bloch, *La vie de S. Edouard le Confesseur par Osbert* in *Analecta Bollandiana*, XLI, 1923, pp. 22 and 38.

quest, it is within the boundaries of the former Frankish Empire, to the north of the Alps, that we must be content to examine the formation of national entities—the birth, so to speak, of France and Germany.[1]

Here, of course, the tradition was unity—a relatively recent tradition, it is true, and to some extent an artificial one, as regards the Carolingian Empire as a whole; but within the narrower limits of the old *regnum Francorum*, many centuries old and based on a real community of civilization. However palpable the differences of manners and language at the lower levels of the population, it was the same aristocracy and the same clergy which had helped the Carolingians to govern the vast state from the Elbe to the Atlantic Ocean. Moreover it was these great families, linked by ties of kinship, which after 888 had provided the kingdoms and principalities resulting from the dismemberment with their rulers, who were only superficially national. Franks disputed the crown of Italy; a Bavarian had assumed that of Burgundy; the successor to the West Frankish throne (Odo) was perhaps of Saxon origin. In the wanderings to which they were committed either by the policy of the kings (to whom they looked for rewards) or by their own ambitions, the magnates took with them a whole body of dependants; with the result that the vassal class itself shared this—so to speak—supra-provincial character. To contemporaries the laceration of the Empire in 840–843 naturally had the appearance of civil war.

Nevertheless, beneath this unity there survived the memory of older groups; and in a divided Europe it was these that first reasserted themselves, in mutual expressions of contempt or hatred. The Neustrians, exalted by their pride in coming from 'the noblest region in the world', are quick to describe the Aquitanians as 'perfidious' and the Burgundians as 'poltroons'; the 'perversity' of the 'Franks' is denounced in its turn by the Aquitanians, and Swabian 'deceit' by the people of the Meuse; a dark picture of Thuringian cowardice, Alemannian rapine, and Bavarian avarice is painted by the Saxons, all of course fine fellows who never run away. It would not be difficult to augment this anthology of abuse with examples drawn from writers ranging from the end of the ninth century to the beginning of the eleventh.[2] For reasons already known to us, antagonisms of this type were particularly deep-rooted in Germany. Far from helping the monarchic states, they were a threat to their unity. The patriotism of the chronicler-monk Widukind, in the reign of Otto I, was

[1] Besides the Bibliography, Section XVII, see F. Lot, *Les derniers carolingiens*, p. 308 *et seq.*; Lapôtre, *L'Europe et le Saint-Siège*, 1895, p. 330 *et seq.*; F. Kern, *Die Anfänge der französischen Ausdehnungspolitik*, 1910, p. 124 *et. seq.*; M. L. Bulst-Thiele, *Kaiserin Agnes*, 1933, p. 3, n. 3.

[2] Abbo, *De bello Parisiaco*, ed. Pertz, I, v. 618; II, vv. 344 and 452; Adhemar of Chabannes, *Chronique*, ed. Chabanon, p. 151; *Gesta ep. Leodensium*, II, 26, in *M.G.H.*, *SS.*, VII, p. 204; Widukind, ed. P. Hirsch, I, 9 and 11; II, 3; Thietmar of Merseburg, ed. R. Holtzmann, V, 12 and 19.

certainly not wanting in fervour or intransigence; but it was a Saxon, not a German, patriotism. What effected the transition from this attitude to a consciousness of nationality adjusted to the new political framework?

It is not easy to form a clear picture of a fatherland without a name. Nothing is more instructive than the difficulty which men so long experienced in giving names to the two principal states carved out of the *regnum Francorum* by the partitions. Both were 'Frances'; but the adjectives East and West by which they were long distinguished were not well fitted to evoke national consciousness. As for the labels Gaul and Germania, which a few writers at an early date sought to revive, they meant little except to the learned. Moreover, they did not correspond to the new frontiers. Recalling that Caesar had made the Rhine the frontier of Gaul, the German chroniclers frequently applied this name to their own provinces on the left bank.[1] Sometimes, unconsciously emphasizing the original artificiality of the boundaries, men fastened on the memory of the first sovereign for whose benefit the kingdom had been carved out: to their neighbours in Lorraine and adjoining territories the Franks of the West remained the men of Charles the Bald (*Kerlinger, Carlenses*), just as the Lorrainers themselves were the men of the obscure Lothar II. German literature long remained faithful to this terminology, probably because it was reluctant to acknowledge the western people's monopoly of the name of Franks or French—the *Chanson de Roland* still employs the two terms indifferently—to which all the successor states seemed to have a legal right.

As everyone knows, however, this restriction of meaning did take place; even at the time of the *Chanson de Roland* the Lorraine chronicler Sigebert of Gembloux regarded it as generally accepted.[2] How did it come about? This great riddle of the French national name has not yet been adequately studied. The usage seems to have been implanted at the time when—in face of an East Frankish kingdom ruled by Saxons—the western kingdom returned to the authentic Frankish dynasty, the Carolingian line. It found support in the royal title itself. By contrast with his rivals who in their charters called themselves simply kings, Charles the Simple, after his conquest of Lorraine, had resumed the old title of *rex Francorum* in order to proclaim his dignity as the heir of Charlemagne. His successors, although they now reigned only over France as we know it today, continued to parade the title more and more generally, even when they had ceased to belong to the ancient line of kings. What is more, in Germany the name 'Franks', as against other tribal groups, preserved almost of necessity a particularist character; it served in current usage to describe the people of the riparian dioceses and the valley of the Main—the region we call today Franconia—and a Saxon, for example, would scarcely have agreed to let himself be so described. On the other side of the frontier, however, there was nothing to prevent the term from being applied, if not to the entire

[1] Cf. Plate XII.   [2] *M.G.H.*, *SS*, VI, p. 339, 1, 41–2.

population of the kingdom, at least to the inhabitants of the region between Loire and Meuse whose customs and institutions continued to be profoundly marked with the imprint of the Franks. Finally, the name was the more easily restricted to the France of the west, because the other France was by a natural process coming to be known by a very different name.

There was a striking contrast between 'Charles's men' and the people of the eastern kingdom—a linguistic contrast, overriding the differences of dialect within each group—in that the language of the former was Romance and that of the latter *diutisc*. This adjective is the word from which the modern German *deutsch* is derived, but at that time in the Latin of the clergy, which abounded with classical memories, it was frequently rendered, in defiance of etymology, by 'Teutonic'. There is no doubt as to its origin. The *theotisca lingua* mentioned by the missionaries of the Carolingian age was none other, in the literal sense, than the speech of the people (*thiuda*), as opposed to the Latin of the Church; perhaps it was also the language of the pagans, the 'Gentiles'. Now since the term 'German', a learned rather than a popular one, had never been deeply rooted in the general consciousness, the label thus devised to describe a mode of speech very soon rose to the dignity of an ethnic name—'the people speaking *diutisc*' is a phrase used already in the reign of Louis the Pious in the prologue to one of the oldest poems written in that language. From this it was an easy step to its employment as the name of a political entity. Usage probably settled the matter long before writers ventured to give recognition to a development so little in accordance with traditional historiography. As early as 920, however, the Salzburg annals mention the kingdom of the Theotisci (or Teutons).[1]

These facts will perhaps surprise those who are inclined to regard emphasis on language factors as a recent symptom of national consciousness. But the linguistic argument in the hands of politicians is not confined to the present day. In the tenth century a Lombard bishop, indignant at the claims—historically well founded—of the Byzantines to Apulia, wrote: 'that this region belongs to the kingdom of Italy is proved by the speech of its inhabitants'.[2]

The use of the same language draws men closer together; it brings out the common factors in their mental traditions and creates new ones. But a difference of language makes an even greater impact on untutored minds; it produces a sense of separation which is a source of antagonism in itself. In the ninth century a Swabian monk noted that the 'Latins' made fun of Germanic words, and it was from gibes about their respective languages

---

[1] Prologue of the *Heliand*, ed. Sievers, p. 3. The distinction between the royal vassals *Teutisci quam et Langobardi* is made in an Italian deed of 845 (Muratori, *Ann.*, II, col. 971); *Annales Juvavenses maximi*, in *M.G.H., SS.*, XXX, 2, p. 738.

[2] Liutprand, *Legatio*, c. 7.

that there arose, in 920, an affray between the escorts of Charles the Simple and Henry I so bloody that it put an end to the meeting of the two sovereigns.[1] Moreover, within the West Frankish kingdom, the curious course of development (not yet adequately explained) which had led to the formation within the Gallo-Romanic tongue of two distinct language groups meant that for long centuries the 'Provençaux' or people of Languedoc, though without any sort of political unity, had a clear sense of belonging to a separate community. Similarly, at the time of the Second Crusade, the knights of Lorraine, who were subjects of the Empire, drew near to the French, whose language they understood and spoke.[2] Nothing is more absurd than to confuse language with nationality; but it would be no less foolish to deny its rôle in the crystallization of national consciousness.

The texts make it plain that so far as France and Germany were concerned this consciousness was already highly developed about the year 1100. During the First Crusade Godfrey of Bouillon who, as a great Lotharingian noble, was fortunate enough to speak both languages, was hard put to it to control the hostility which, we are told, was already traditional between the French and German knights.[3] The 'sweet France' of the *Chanson de Roland* was present in all memories—a France whose frontiers were still a little uncertain, so that it was easily confused with the vast Empire of the Charlemagne of legend, but whose centre was unmistakably situated in the Capetian kingdom. Moreover, among men easily elated by conquests, national pride drew greater strength from being as it were gilded by the memory of the Carolingians; the use of the name 'France' favoured the assimilation, and the legend in its turn helped to fix the name. (The Germans for their part took great pride in the fact that they were still the imperial people.) Loyalty to the crown helped to keep these sentiments alive: it is significant that they are almost completely absent from the epic poems of purely baronial inspiration, like the cycle of Lorraine. We must not suppose, however, that the identification was complete. The monk Guibert de Nogent who, in the reign of Louis VI, wrote a history of the Crusade under the famous title of *Gesta Dei per Francos* was an ardent patriot, but only a very lukewarm admirer of the Capetians. Nationality was nourished by more complex factors—community of language, of tradition, of historical memories more or less well understood; and the sense of a common destiny imposed by political boundaries each of which, though fixed largely by accident, corresponded as a whole to far-reaching and long-established affinities.

All this had not been created by patriotism; but in the course of the

[1] Walafrid Strabo, *De exordiis*, c. 7, in *Capitularia reg. Francorum*, II, p. 481; Richer, I, 20.
[2] Odo of Deuil, in *M.G.H., SS.*, XXVI, p. 65.
[3] Ekkehard of Aura, in *M.G.H., SS.*, VI, p. 218.

second feudal age, which was characterized both by men's need to group themselves in larger communities and by the clearer general consciousness of itself which society had acquired, patriotism became as it were the outward manifestation of these latent realities, and so in its turn the creator of new realities. Already, in a poem a little later than the *Chanson de Roland*, 'no Frenchman is worth more than he' is the praise accorded to a knight particularly worthy of esteem.[1] The age whose deeper history we are endeavouring to trace not only witnessed the formation of states; it also saw true fatherlands confirmed or established—though these were destined still to undergo many vicissitudes.

[1] *Girart de Roussillon*, trans. P. Meyer, §631; ed. Foerster (*Romanische Studien*, V) v. 9324.

PART VIII

Feudalism as a Type of Society and its Influence

XXXII

FEUDALISM AS A TYPE OF
SOCIETY

1 HAS THERE BEEN MORE THAN ONE FEUDALISM?

IN the eyes of Montesquieu, the establishment of 'feudal laws' was a phenomenon *sui generis*, 'an event which happened once in the world and which will perhaps never happen again'. Voltaire, less experienced, no doubt, in the precise formulation of legal definitions, but a man of wider outlook, demurred. 'Feudalism', he wrote, 'is not an event; it is a very old form which, with differences in its working, subsists in three-quarters of our hemisphere.'[1] Modern scholarship has in general rallied to the side of Voltaire. Egyptian feudalism, Achaean feudalism, Chinese feudalism, Japanese feudalism—all these forms and more are now familiar concepts. The historian of the West must sometimes regard them with a certain amount of misgiving. For he cannot be unaware of the different definitions which have been given of this famous term, even on its native soil. The basis of feudal society, Benjamin Guérard has said, is land. No, it is the personal group, rejoins Jacques Flach. Do the various exotic versions of feudalism, which seem to abound in universal history today, conform to Guérard's definition or to Flach's? The only remedy for these uncertainties is to go back to the origins of the problem. Since it is obvious that all these societies, separated by time and space, have received the name 'feudal' only on account of their similarities, real or supposed, to Western feudalism, it is the characteristics of this basic type, to which all the others must be referred, that it is of primary importance to define. But first it is necessary to dispose of some obvious instances of the misuse of a term which has made too much noise in the world not to have undergone many perversions.

In the system which they christened 'feudalism' its first godfathers, as we know, were primarily conscious of those aspects of it which conflicted with the idea of a centralized state. Thence it was a short step to describing as feudal every fragmentation of political authority; so that a value judgment was normally combined with the simple statement of a fact. Because sovereignty was generally associated in the minds of these writers

---

[1] *Esprit des Lois*, XXX, I; Voltaire, *Fragments sur quelques révolutions dans l'Inde*, II (ed. Garnier, XXIX, p. 91).

with fairly large states, every exception to the rule seemed to fall into the category of the abnormal. This alone would suffice to condemn a usage which, moreover, could scarcely fail to give rise to intolerable confusion. Occasionally, indeed, there are indications of a more precise notion. In 1783 a minor municipal official, the market-watchman of Valenciennes, denounced as responsible for the increase in the price of foodstuffs 'a feudality of great country landlords'.[1] How many polemists since then have held up to public obloquy the 'feudalism' of bankers or industrialists! Charged with more or less vague historical associations, the word with certain writers seems to suggest no more than the brutal exercise of authority, though frequently it also conveys the slightly less elementary notion of an encroachment of economic powers on public life. It is in fact very true that the identification of wealth—then consisting mainly of land—with authority was one of the outstanding features of medieval feudalism. But this was less on account of the strictly feudal character of that society than because it was, at the same time, based on the manor.

Feudalism, manorial system—the identification here goes back much farther. It had first occurred in the use of the word 'vassal'. The aristocratic stamp which this term had received from what was, after all, a secondary development, was not strong enough to prevent it from being occasionally applied, even in the Middle Ages, to serfs (originally closely akin to vassals properly so called because of the personal nature of their dependence) and even to ordinary tenants. What was then only a kind of linguistic aberration, especially frequent in somewhat incompletely feudalized regions like Gascony or Leon, became a more and more widespread usage, as familiarity with genuine vassalage faded. 'Everyone knows', wrote Perreciot in 1786, 'that in France the subjects of lords are commonly called their vassals.'[2] Similarly it became customary, in spite of etymology, to describe as 'feudal rights' the burdens to which peasant holdings were subject. Thus when the men of the Revolution announced their intention to destroy feudalism, it was above all the manorial system that they meant to attack. But here again the historian must interpose. Though an essential element in feudal society, the manor was in itself an older institution, and was destined to last much longer. In the interests of sound terminology it is important that the two ideas should be kept clearly separate.

Let us therefore try to bring together in broad outline what we have learned about European feudalism, in the strict sense of the word, from its history.

---

[1] G. Lefebvre, *Les paysans du Nord*, 1924, p. 309.

[2] For example, E. Lodge, 'Serfdom in the Pyrenees', in *Vierteljahrschr. für Soz. und W. G.*, 1905, p. 31; Sanchez-Albornoz, *Estampas de la vida en Leon*, 2nd ed., p. 86, n. 37; Perreciot, *De l'état-civil des personnes*, II, 1786, p. 193, n. 9.

FEUDALISM AS A TYPE OF SOCIETY

2 THE FUNDAMENTAL CHARACTERISTICS OF EUROPEAN FEUDALISM

The simplest way will be to begin by saying what feudal society was not. Although the obligations arising from blood-relationship played a very active part in it, it did not rely on kinship alone. More precisely, feudal ties proper were developed when those of kinship proved inadequate. Again, despite the persistence of the idea of a public authority super-imposed on the multitude of petty powers, feudalism coincided with a profound weakening of the State, particularly in its protective capacity. But much as feudal society differed from societies based on kinship as well as from those dominated by the power of the State, it was their successor and bore their imprint. For while the characteristic relationships of personal subjection retained something of the quasi-family character of the original companionage, a considerable part of the political authority exercised by innumerable petty chiefs had the appearance of a usurpation of 'regalian' rights.

European feudalism should therefore be seen as the outcome of the violent dissolution of older societies. It would in fact be unintelligible without the great upheaval of the Germanic invasions which, by forcibly uniting two societies originally at very different stages of development, disrupted both of them and brought to the surface a great many modes of thought and social practices of an extremely primitive character. It finally developed in the atmosphere of the last barbarian raids. It involved a far-reaching restriction of social intercourse, a circulation of money too sluggish to admit of a salaried officialdom, and a mentality attached to things tangible and local. When these conditions began to change, feudalism began to wane.

It was an unequal society, rather than a hierarchical one—with chiefs rather than nobles; and with serfs, not slaves. If slavery had not played so small a part, there would have been no need for the characteristically feudal forms of dependence, as applied to the lower orders of society. In an age of disorder, the place of the adventurer was too important, the memory of men too short, the regularity of social classifications too uncertain, to admit of the strict formation of regular castes.

Nevertheless the feudal system meant the rigorous economic subjection of a host of humble folk to a few powerful men. Having received from earlier ages the Roman *villa* (which in some respects anticipated the manor) and the German village chiefdom, it extended and consolidated these methods whereby men exploited men, and combining inextricably the right to the revenues from the land with the right to exercise authority, it fashioned from all this the true manor of medieval times. And this it did partly for the benefit of an oligarchy of priests and monks whose task it was to propitiate Heaven, but chiefly for the benefit of an oligarchy of warriors.

443

As even the most perfunctory comparative study will show, one of the most distinctive characteristics of feudal societies was the virtual identity of the class of chiefs with the class of professional warriors serving in the only way that then seemed effective, that is as heavily armed horsemen. As we have seen, of the societies where an armed peasantry survived, some knew neither vassalage nor the manor, while others knew them only in very imperfect forms—as in Scandinavia for example, or the kingdoms of north-western Spain. The case of the Byzantine Empire is perhaps even more significant because its institutions bore the stamp of a much more conscious directing thought. There, after the anti-aristocratic reaction of the eighth century, a government which had preserved the great administrative traditions of the Roman period, and which was furthermore concerned to provide itself with a strong army, created tenements charged with military obligations to the State—true fiefs in one sense, but differing from those of the West in that they were peasant fiefs, each consisting of a small farm. Thenceforth it was a paramount concern of the imperial government to protect these 'soldiers' properties', as well as small-holdings in general, against the encroachments of the rich and powerful. Nevertheless there came a time towards the end of the eleventh century when the Empire, overwhelmed by economic conditions which made independence more and more difficult for a peasantry constantly in debt, and further weakened by internal discords, ceased to extend any useful protection to the free farmers. In this way it not only lost precious fiscal resources, but found itself at the mercy of the magnates, who alone were capable thereafter of raising the necessary troops from among their own dependants.

In feudal society the characteristic human bond was the subordinate's link with a nearby chief. From one level to another the ties thus formed—like so many chains branching out indefinitely—joined the smallest to the greatest. Land itself was valued above all because it enabled a lord to provide himself with 'men' by supplying the remuneration for them. We want lands, said in effect the Norman lords who refused the gifts of jewels, arms, and horses offered by their duke. And they added among themselves: 'It will thus be possible for us to maintain many knights, and the duke will no longer be able to do so.'[1]

It remained to devise a form of real property right suitable for the remuneration of services and coinciding in duration with the personal tie itself. From the solution which it found for this problem, Western feudalism derived one of its most original features. While the 'men of service' who surrounded the Slav princes continued to receive their estates as outright gifts, the fief of the Frankish vassal, after some fluctuations of policy, was in theory conceded to him only for the term of his life. For among the highest classes, distinguished by the honourable profession of arms,

[1] Dudo of Saint-Quentin, ed. Lair (*Mém. Soc. Antiquaires Normandie*, XXIII), III 43–4 (933).

relationships of dependence had assumed, at the outset, the form of contracts freely entered into between two living men confronting one another. From this necessary personal contact the relationship derived the best part of its moral value. Nevertheless at an early date various factors tarnished the purity of the obligation: hereditary succession, natural in a society where the family remained so strong; the practice of enfeoffment which was imposed by economic conditions and ended by burdening the land with services rather than the man with fealty; finally and above all, the plurality of vassal engagements. The loyalty of the commended man remained, in many cases, a potent factor. But as a paramount social bond designed to unite the various groups at all levels, to prevent fragmentation and to arrest disorder, it showed itself decidedly ineffective.

Indeed in the immense range of these ties there had been from the first something artificial. Their general diffusion in feudal times was the legacy of a moribund State—that of the Carolingians—which had conceived the idea of combating social disintegration by means of one of the institutions born of that very condition. The system of superposed protective relationships was certainly not incapable of contributing to the cohesion of the State: witness, the Anglo-Norman monarchy. But for this it was necessary that there should be a central authority favoured, as in England, not only by the fact of conquest itself but even more by the circumstance that it coincided with new material and moral conditions. In the ninth century the forces making for disintegration were too strong.

In the area of Western civilization the map of feudalism reveals some large blank spaces—the Scandinavian peninsula, Frisia, Ireland. Perhaps it is more important still to note that feudal Europe was not all feudalized in the same degree or according to the same rhythm and, above all, that it was nowhere feudalized completely. In no country did the whole of the rural population fall into the bonds of personal and hereditary dependence. Almost everywhere—though the number varied greatly from region to region—there survived large or small allodial properties. The concept of the State never absolutely disappeared, and where it retained the most vitality men continued to call themselves 'free', in the old sense of the word, because they were dependent only on the head of the people or his representatives. Groups of peasant warriors remained in Normandy, in the Danelaw, and in Spain. The mutual oath, strongly contrasting with the oaths of subordination, survived in the peace associations and triumphed in the communes. No doubt it is the fate of every system of human institutions never to be more than imperfectly realized. Capitalism was unquestionably the dominant influence on the European economy at the beginning of the twentieth century; yet more than one undertaking continued to exist outside it.

Returning to our feudal map, we find between the Loire and the Rhine, and in Burgundy on both banks of the Saône, a heavily shaded area which, in the eleventh century, is suddenly enlarged by the Norman conquests of England and southern Italy. All round this central nucleus there is an almost regular shading-off till, in Saxony and especially in Leon and Castile, the stippling becomes very sparse indeed. Finally the entire shaded area is surrounded by blank spaces. In the most heavily shaded zone it is not difficult to recognize the regions where the regularizing influence of the Carolingians had been most far-reaching and where also the mingling of Romanized elements and Germanic elements—more pronounced here than elsewhere—had most completely disrupted the structure of the two societies and made possible the growth of very old seeds of territorial lordship and personal dependence.

3 A CROSS-SECTION OF COMPARATIVE HISTORY

A subject peasantry; widespread use of the service tenement (i.e. the fief) instead of a salary, which was out of the question; the supremacy of a class of specialized warriors; ties of obedience and protection which bind man to man and, within the warrior class, assume the distinctive form called vassalage; fragmentation of authority—leading inevitably to disorder; and, in the midst of all this, the survival of other forms of association, family and State, of which the latter, during the second feudal age, was to acquire renewed strength—such then seem to be the fundamental features of European feudalism. Like all the phenomena revealed by that science of eternal change which is history, the social structure thus characterized certainly bore the peculiar stamp of an age and an environment. Yet just as the matrilineal or agnatic clan or even certain types of economic enterprise are found in much the same forms in very different societies, it is by no means impossible that societies different from our own should have passed through a phase closely resembling that which has just been defined. If so, it is legitimate to call them feudal during that phase. But the work of comparison thus involved is clearly beyond the powers of one man, and I shall therefore confine myself to an example which will at least give an idea of what such research, conducted by surer hands, might yield. The task is facilitated by the existence of excellent studies which already bear the hall-mark of the soundest comparative method.

In the dark ages of Japanese history we dimly perceive a society based on kinship groups, real or fictitious. Then towards the end of the seventh century of our era, under Chinese influence a system of government is founded which strives (exactly as the Carolingians did) to maintain a kind of moral control over its subjects. Finally, about the eleventh century, the period begins which it has become customary to call feudal and whose advent seems (in accordance with a pattern with which we are now familiar) to have coincided with a certain slackening of commercial activity. Here, therefore, as in Europe, 'feudalism' seems to have been preceded by two very different forms of social organization; and, as with us, it was profoundly influenced by both. The monarchy, though it had less connection than in Europe with the feudal structure proper—since the chains of vassalage terminated before reaching the Emperor—subsisted, in law, as the theoretical source of all power; and there also the fragmentation of political authority, which was fostered by very old habits, was held to be a consequence of encroachments on the State.

Above the peasantry a class of professional warriors had arisen. It was in these circles that ties of personal dependence developed, on the model furnished by the relations of the armed retainer with his chief; they were thus, it appears, marked by a much more pronounced class character than European 'commendation'. They were hierarchically organized, just as in Europe; but Japanese vassalage was much more an act of submission than was European vassalage and much less a contract. It was also more strict, since it did not allow plurality of lords. As these warriors had to be supported they were granted tenements closely resembling the fiefs of the West. Sometimes even, on the pattern of our *fiefs de reprises*, the grant was purely fictitious and involved in fact lands which had originally belonged to the patrimony of the pretended recipient. These fighting-men were naturally less and less willing to cultivate the soil, though as in Europe there were to the end exceptional cases of peasant 'vavasours'. The vassals therefore lived mainly on the rents from their own tenants. There were too many of them, however—far more, apparently, than in Europe—to admit of the establishment for their benefit of real manors, with extensive powers over the people. Few manors were created, except by the baronage and the temples, and being widely scattered and having no demesne, they recalled the embryonic manors of Anglo-Saxon England rather than those of the really manorialized regions of the West. Furthermore, on this soil where irrigated rice-fields represented the prevailing form of agriculture, the technical conditions were so different from European practice that the subjection of the peasantry assumed correspondingly different forms.

Although far too brief, of course, and too absolute in its appraisal of the contrasts between the two societies, it seems to me that this outline nevertheless enables us to reach a fairly firm conclusion. Feudalism was not 'an event which happened once in the world'. Like Europe—though with inevitable and deep-seated differences—Japan went through this phase. Have other societies also passed through it? And if so, what were the causes, and were they perhaps common to all such societies? It is for future works to provide the answers. I should be happy if.this book, by suggesting questions to students, were to prepare the way for an inquiry going far beyond it.

XXXIII

THE PERSISTENCE OF EUROPEAN FEUDALISM

1 SURVIVALS AND REVIVALS

FROM the middle of the thirteenth century onwards European societies diverged decisively from the feudal pattern. But a social system, which is simply a phase of a continuous evolution within human groups possessed of memory, cannot perish outright or at a single stroke. Feudalism had its continuations.

The manorial system, on which feudalism had left its mark, long survived it, undergoing many changes, which do not concern us here. It is plain, however, that when manorialism had ceased to form part of a closely related system of political institutions, it was bound to appear more and more pointless in the eyes of the subject populations, and consequently more odious. Of all forms of dependence within the manor, the most genuinely feudal was serfdom, and although it had undergone profound changes and become territorial rather than personal, it nevertheless survived in France till the eve of the Revolution. Who at that time remembered that among those subject to *mainmorte* there were undoubtedly some whose ancestors had voluntarily 'commended' themselves to a protector? And even supposing this remote circumstance had been known, would that knowledge have made an anachronistic state of affairs any easier to bear?

With the exception of England, where the first of the seventeenth-century Revolutions abolished all distinctions between tenure by knight-service and other forms of tenure, the obligations arising from vassalage and the fief were rooted in the soil, and they lasted, as in France, as long as the manorial system or, as in Prussia (which in the eighteenth century proceeded to a general 'allodification' of fiefs), very nearly as long. The State, which alone was capable henceforth of utilizing the hierarchy of dependence, only very slowly abandoned recourse to it for the supply of military forces. Louis XIV summoned the whole body of vassals on more than one occasion. But this was now only an exceptional measure on the part of governments in need of troops; or it might even be a mere fiscal expedient to raise funds through the medium of fines and exemptions. After the end of the Middle Ages the only characteristics of the fief which

448

really retained practical importance were the pecuniary burdens to which it was subject and the special rules which regulated its inheritance. Since there were no more household warriors, homage was henceforth invariably attached to the possession of an estate. Its ceremonial aspect, 'empty' though it might seem in the eyes of jurists nurtured in the rationalism of the new age,[1] was not a matter of indifference to a noble class with a natural concern for etiquette. But the ceremony itself, formerly charged with such profound human significance, now only served—apart from the monetary levies of which it was sometimes the occasion—to establish the ownership of the property, a source of rights which were more or less lucrative, according to the 'custom'. 'Feudal matters' were essentially contentious and a preoccupation of jurisprudence. They supplied a prolific literature of legal theorists and practitioners with splendid themes for dissertations. But that in France the edifice was very decayed, and the profits which its beneficiaries expected from it mostly rather poor, is clearly demonstrated by the ease with which it was overthrown. The disappearance of the manorial system was effected only at the cost of much resistance and not without seriously upsetting the distribution of wealth; that of the fief and of vassalage seemed the inevitable and almost insignificant termination of a long death-agony.

Nevertheless, in a society which continued to be beset with many disorders, the needs which had given rise to the ancient practice of companionage, and then to vassalage, had not ceased to be felt. Among the various reasons which led to the creation of the orders of chivalry which were founded in such great number in the fourteenth and fifteenth centuries, one of the most decisive was undoubtedly the desire of the princes to attach to themselves a group of highly-placed retainers by an especially compelling bond. The knights of Saint-Michel, according to the statutes drawn up by Louis XI, promised the king *bonne et vraye amour* and pledged themselves to serve him loyally in his just wars. The attempt was to prove as vain as that of the Carolingians in an earlier day: in the oldest list of persons honoured by the famous collar, the third place was occupied by the Constable of St. Pol, who was so basely to betray his master.

More effective—and more dangerous—was the reconstitution, during the disorders of the closing years of the Middle Ages, of bands of private warriors, very much akin to the 'satellite' vassals whose brigandage had been denounced by the writers of the Merovingian age. Frequently their dependence was expressed by the wearing of a costume displaying the colours of their chieftain or emblazoned with his arms. This practice was condemned in Flanders by Philip the Bold,[2] but it seems to have been especially widespread in the England of the last Plantagenets, of the

---

[1] P. Hévin, *Consultations et observations sur la coutume de Bretagne*, 1724, p. 343.
[2] P. Thomas, *Textes historiques sur Lille et le Nord*, II, 1936, p. 285 (1385 and 1397); cf. p. 218 (no. 68).

Lancastrians and the Yorkists—so much so that the groups thus formed round the great barons received the name of 'liveries'. Like the household vassals of former days they did not consist exclusively of low-born adventurers, and in fact, the majority were probably recruited from the 'gentry'. When one of these men was involved in a law-suit, the lord extended his protection to him in court. Although illegal, this practice of 'maintenance' was extraordinarily tenacious, as is attested by repeated Parliamentary prohibitions; it reproduced practically feature for feature the ancient *mithium* which the powerful man in Frankish Gaul had extended over his retainer. And since it was also to the advantage of the sovereigns to make use of the personal bond in its new form, we find Richard II seeking to spread through the kingdom—like so many *vassi dominici*—his personal followers, distinguished by the 'white hart' with which their uniform was emblazoned.[1]

Even in the France of the early Bourbons the nobleman who in order to make his way in the world became the servant of a great man assumed a status remarkably akin to primitive vassalage. In a phrase that recalled the vigour of the old feudal language, one said of so-and-so that he 'belonged' to Monsieur le Prince or to the Cardinal. True, the ceremony of homage was no longer performed, though it was often replaced by a written agreement. For, from the end of the Middle Ages, the 'promise of friendship' was substituted for the dying practice of homage. See, for example, this 'letter' addressed to Fouquet on the 2nd June, 1658, by a certain Captain Deslandes. 'I promise and give my fealty to My Lord the Procurator-General . . . never to belong to any but him, to whom I give myself and attach myself with the greatest attachment of which I am capable; and I promise to serve him generally against all persons without exception and to obey none but him, nor even to have any dealings with those whom he forbids me to deal with . . . I promise him to sacrifice my life against all whom he pleases . . . without any exception whatsoever.' It is as though we were hearing, across the ages, the echoes of the most absolute of the formulas of commendation: 'thy friends shall be my friends, thy enemies shall be my enemies'[2]—without even a reservation in favour of the king!

2 THE WARRIOR IDEA AND THE IDEA OF CONTRACT

To the societies which succeeded it the feudal era had bequeathed knighthood, which had become crystallized as nobility. From this origin the dominant class retained pride in its military calling, symbolized by the right to wear the sword, and clung to it with particular tenacity where, as

[1] T. F. Tout, *Chapters in the Administrative History of Mediaeval England*, IV, 1928, p. 62.
[2] Colbert, *Lettres*, ed. P. Clément, II, p. xxx. For an old example of a promise of friendship see J. Quicherat, *Rodrigue de Villandrando*, 1879, Documents, no. XIX.

in France, it derived from this calling the justification for valuable fiscal privileges. Nobles need not pay *taille*, explain two squires of Varennes-en-Argonne about 1380; for 'by their noble status, nobles are obliged to expose their bodies and belongings in wars'.[1] Under the Ancien Régime, the nobility of ancient lineage, in contrast with the aristocracy of office, continued to call itself the nobility 'of the sword'. Even today, when to die for one's country has altogether ceased to be the monopoly of one class or one profession, the persistence of the feeling that a sort of moral supremacy attaches to the function of professional warrior—an attitude quite foreign to other societies, such as the Chinese—is a continual reminder of the separation which took place, towards the beginning of feudal times, between the peasant and the knight.

Vassal homage was a genuine contract and a bilateral one. If the lord failed to fulfil his engagements he lost his rights. Transferred, as was inevitable, to the political sphere—since the principal subjects of the king were at the same time his vassals—this idea was to have a far-reaching influence, all the more so because on this ground it was reinforced by the very ancient notions which held the king responsible in a mystical way for the welfare of his subjects and deserving of punishment in the event of public calamity. These old currents happened to unite on this point with another stream of thought which arose in the Church out of the Gregorian protest against the myth of sacred and supernatural kingship. It was the writers of this clerical group who first expressed, with a force long unequalled, the notion of a contract binding the sovereign to his people—'like the swineherd to the master who employs him', wrote an Alsatian monk about 1080. The remark seems even more full of meaning when taken in the context of the indignant protest of a (moderate) partisan of monarchy: 'the Lord's anointed cannot be dismissed like a village reeve!' But these clerical theorists themselves did not fail to invoke, among the justifications for the deposition to which they condemned the bad prince, the universally recognized right of the vassal to abandon the bad lord.[2]

It was above all the circles of the vassals which translated these ideas into practice, under the influence of the institutions which had formed their mentality. In this sense, there was a fruitful principle underlying many revolts which on a superficial view might appear as mere random uprisings: 'A man may resist his king and judge when he acts contrary to law and may even help to make war on him. . . . Thereby, he does not violate the duty of fealty.' These are the words of the *Sachsenspiegel*.[3] This

---

[1] C. Aimond, *Histoire de la ville de Varennes*, 1925, p. 50.

[2] Manegold of Lautenbach, in *Libelli de lite* (*M.G.H.*), I, p. 365; Wenrich, *ibid.*, p. 289; Paul of Bernried, *Vita Gregorii*, c. 97 in Watterich, *Pontificum Romanorum vitae*, I, p. 532.

[3] *Landr.*, III, 78, 2. The meaning of this passage is disputed by Zeumer in *Zeitschrift der Savigny-Stiftung*, *G.A.*, 1914, pp. 68–75, but is fully confirmed by F. Kern, *Gottesgnadentum und Widerstandsrecht im früheren Mittelalter*, Leipzig, 1914.

famous 'right of resistance', the germ of which was already present in the Oaths of Strasbourg (843) and in the pact between Charles the Bald and his vassals (856), resounded in the thirteenth and fourteenth centuries from one end of the Western world to the other, in a multitude of texts. Though most of these documents were inspired by reactionary tendencies among the nobility, or by the egoism of the bourgeoisie, they were of great significance for the future. They included the English Great Charter of 1215; the Hungarian 'Golden Bull' of 1222; the Assizes of the kingdom of Jerusalem; the Privilege of the Brandenburg nobles; the Aragonese Act of Union of 1287; the Brabantine charter of Cortenberg; the statute of Dauphiné of 1341; the declaration of the communes of Languedoc (1356). It was assuredly no accident that the representative system, in the very aristocratic form of the English Parliament, the French 'Estates', the *Stände* of Germany, and the Spanish *Cortés*, originated in states which were only just emerging from the feudal stage and still bore its imprint. Nor was it an accident that in Japan, where the vassal's submission was much more unilateral and where, moreover, the divine power of the Emperor remained outside the structure of vassal engagements, nothing of the kind emerged from a regime which was nevertheless in many respects closely akin to the feudalism of the West. The originality of the latter system consisted in the emphasis it placed on the idea of an agreement capable of binding the rulers; and in this way, oppressive as it may have been to the poor, it has in truth bequeathed to our Western civilization something with which we still desire to live.

BIBLIOGRAPHY

WHEN the English edition of *Feudal Society* was in preparation, we had to consider what was to be done with the bibliography, which was compiled in 1938–9.

One of two courses seemed open to us: either to attempt to bring it up to date by the inclusion of more recent material, or to print it as it stood, with a supplementary list of titles. There was a strong argument against the first of these alternatives. Bloch's bibliography is a work of personal selection and classification, intended to serve not only as a guide for students, but also as an acknowledgement of his debt to other scholars.[1] To have introduced additional titles into this framework would have been, it seemed to us, an unwarranted interference with Bloch's design, especially as he had made it a principle not to include works of which he had no personal knowledge. We have therefore adopted the second course and reproduced his bibliography as he left it, with the omission of one section only: a list of general histories, the majority of which, we believed, would already be familiar to students of medieval history. A supplement lists more recent publications.[2]

Although this book is based on a profound study of original sources, many of which are referred to in the footnotes, the author in his bibliography has confined himself to listing the standard guides to such material except in the case of the legal sources, which he has enumerated separately. Again, for the intellectual and social 'climate' which he has discussed from a particular point of view in Book II of the volume, his list of secondary authorities is limited to a few special questions. The bibliography is much fuller, however, on the subject of the last invasions and, as might be expected, on the special aspects of social and political development which form the central theme of the book.

Except where otherwise indicated, the place of publication is Paris for a book in French, or London for a book in English.

L. A. Manyon

PLAN OF BIBLIOGRAPHY

I THE EVIDENCE
(1) Standard Guides to Sources.[3] (2) The Linguistic Evidence. (3) Historiography. (4) The Literary Evidence.

II MENTAL ATTITUDES
(1) Modes of Feeling and Thought. (2) 'Terrors' of the Year 1000.

III THE LAST INVASIONS
(1) General. (2) The Saracens in the Alps and the Italian Peninsula. (3) The Hungarians. (4) The Scandinavians. (5) The Conversion of the North. (6) Effects of the Scandinavian Invasions.

IV LEGAL AND POLITICAL STRUCTURE
(1) Original Sources. (2) Modern Works on the History of Law and Institutions. (3) The Legal Mind and the Teaching of Law. (4) Political Ideas.

V TIES OF KINSHIP
(1) The Family and the Vendetta. (2) Economic Solidarity.

VI FEUDAL INSTITUTIONS PROPER
(1) Feudalism in General; Frankish Origins. (2) Feudalism by Countries and Regions. (3) 'Companionage', Vassalage and Homage. (4) *Precaria*, 'Benefit', Fief, and Allod. (5) The Law of the Fief. (6) Plurality of Lords and Liege Homage.

---

[1] See p. xxi, n.   [2] Pp. 478–81.   [3] Excluding literary sources in the vernacular.

BIBLIOGRAPHY

I. THE EVIDENCE

(1) STANDARD GUIDES TO SOURCES

BALLESTER (Rafael), *Fuentes narrativas de la historia de España durante la edad media*, Palma, 1912.
——— *Bibliografia de la historia de España*, Gerona, 1921.
Bibliotheca hagiographica latina antiquae et mediae aetatis, 2 vols. and supplementary vol., Brussels, 1898–1911.
DAHLMANN-WAITZ, *Quellenkunde der deutschen Geschichte*, 9th edn., Leipzig. 2 vols., 1931–2.
EGIDI (Pietro), *La storia medievale*, Rome, 1922.
GROSS (Charles), *The Sources and Literature of English History from the Earliest Times to about 1485*, 2nd edn., London, 1915.
JACOB (Karl), *Quellenkunde der deutschen Geschichte im Mittelalter*, Berlin, 1917 (*Sammlung Göschen*).
JANSEN (M.) and SCHMITZ-KALLENBERG (L.), *Historiographie und Quellen der deutschen Geschichte bis 1500*, 2nd edn., Leipzig, 1914 (A. MEISTER, *Grundriss*, I, 7).
MANITIUS (M.), *Geschichte der lateinischen Literatur des Mittelalters*, 3 vols., Munich, 1911–31 (*Handbuch der klassischen Altertumswissenschaft*, ed. I. MÜLLER).
MOLINIER (Auguste), *Les Sources de l'histoire de France des origines aux guerres d'Italie*, 6 vols., 1901–6.
OESTERLEY (H.), *Wegweiser durch die Literatur der Urkunden-Sammlung*, 2 vols., Berlin, 1886.
PIRENNE (Henri), *Bibliographie de l'histoire de Belgique*, 3rd edn., Brussels, 1931.
POTTHAST (August), *Bibliotheca historica medii aevi*, 2 vols., Berlin, 1875–96.
STEIN (Henri), *Bibliographie générale des cartulaires français ou relatifs à l'histoire de France*, 1907.
UEBERWEG (Friedrich), *Grundriss der Geschichte der Philosophie*, II, 11th edn., Berlin, 1928.
VILDHAUT (H.), *Handbuch der Quellenkunde zur deutschen Geschichte bis zum Ausgange der Staufer*, 2nd edn., 2 vols., Werl, 1906–9.
WATTENBACH (W.), *Deutschlands Geschichtsquellen im Mittelalter bis zur Mitte des dreizehnten Jahrhunderts*, I, 7th edn., Berlin, 1904; II, 6th edn., Berlin, 1894.

BIBLIOGRAPHY

WATTENBACH (W.) and HOLTZMANN (R.), *Deutschlands Geschichtsquellen in Mittelalter. Deutsche Kaiserzeit*, I, Part 1, Berlin, 1938.

(2) THE LINGUISTIC EVIDENCE

ARNALDI (F.), 'Latinitatis italicae medii aevi inde ab anno CDLXXVI usque ad annum MDXXII lexicon imperfectum' in *Archivum latinitatis medii aevi*, X, 1936.

BAXTER (J. H.) *et al.*, *Medieval Latin Word-List from British and Irish Sources*, Oxford, 1934.

BLOCH (Oscar), with the collaboration of W. VON WARTBURG, *Dictionnaire étymologique de la langue française*, 1932.

BRUNEL (C.), 'Le Latin des chartes', *Revue des études latines*, 1925.

—— 'Les Premiers Exemples de l'emploi du provençal', *Romania*, 1922.

DIEFENBACH (L.), *Glossarium latino-germanicum mediae et infimae latinitatis*, Frankfort, 1857. *Novum glossarium*, Frankfort, 1867.

DU CANGE, *Glossarium mediae et infimae latinitatis*, ed. HENSCHEL, 7 vols., 1830–50. New impression, Niort, 1883–7. Further impression, 10 vols. in 5, Graz, 1954.

GAMILLSCHEG (E.), *Etymologisches Wörterbuch der französischen Sprache*, Heidelberg, 1928.

HABEL (E.), *Mittellateinisches Glossar*, Paderborn, 1931.

HECK (Philippe), *Übersetzungsprobleme im früheren Mittelalter*, Tübingen, 1931.

HEGEL (Karl), 'Lateinische Wörter und deutsche Begriffe', in *Neues Archiv der Gesellschaft für ältere deutsche Geschichtskunde*, 1893.

KLUGE (Friedrich), *Etymologisches Wörterbuch der deutschen Sprache*, 11th edn., Berlin, 1934.

MERKEL (Felix), *Das Aufkommen der deutschen Sprache in den städtischen Kanzleien des ausgehenden Mittelalters*, Leipzig, 1930 (*Beiträge zur Kulturgeschichte des Mittelalters*, 45).

MEYER-LÜBKE (W.), *Romanisches Etymologisches Wörterbuch*, 3rd edn., Heidelberg, 1935.

MURRAY (J. A. H.) (ed.), *The Oxford English Dictionary*, 12 vols. and supplement, Oxford, 1888–1928.

NÉLIS (H.), 'Les Plus Anciennes Chartes en flamand', *Mélanges d'histoire offerts à H. Pirenne*, Brussels, 1926, I.

OBREEN (H), 'Introduction de la langue vulgaire dans les documents diplomatiques en Belgique et dans les Pays-Bas', *Revue belge de philologie*, 1935.

OGLE (M. B.), 'Some Aspects of Mediaeval Latin Style', *Speculum*, 1926.

STRECKER (Karl), *Introduction à l'étude du latin médiéval*, translated (into French) by P. VAN DE WOESTIJNE, Ghent, 1933.

TRAUBE (L.), 'Die lateinische Sprache des Mittelalters', in TRAUBE, *Vorlesungen und Abhandlungen*, II, Munich, 1911.

VANCSA (Max), *Das erste Auftreten der deutschen Sprache in den Urkunden*, Leipzig, 1895 (*Preisschriften gekrönt . . . von der fürstlich Jablonowskischen Gesellschaft, histor.-nationalökonom. Section, XXX*).

WARTBURG (W. von), *Französisches etymologisches Wörterbuch*, 1928 ff. (in course of publication).

(3) HISTORIOGRAPHY

BALZANI (Ugo), *Le cronache italiane nel medio evo*, 2nd edn., Milan, 1900.

GILSON (E.), 'Le Moyen-âge et l'histoire', in GILSON, *L'Esprit de la philosophie médiévale*, II, 1932.

HEISIG (Karl), 'Die Geschichtsmetaphysik des Rolandliedes und ihre Vorgeschichte', *Zeitschrift für romanische Philologie*, LV, 1935.

LEHMANN (Paul), 'Das literarische Bild Karls des Grossen, vornehmlich im lateinischen Schrifttum des Mittelalters', *Sitzungsberichte der bayerischen Akademie, Phil.-hist. Kl.*, 1934.

POOLE (R. L.), *Chronicles and Annals: a Brief Outline of their Origin and Growth*, Oxford, 1926.

BIBLIOGRAPHY

SCHMIDLIN (Joseph), *Die geschichtsphilosophische und kirchenpolitische Weltanschauung Ottos von Freising. Ein Beitrag zur mittelalterlichen Geistesgeschichte.* Freiburg im Breisgau, 1906 (*Studien und Darstellungen aus dem Gebiete der Geschichte*, ed. H. GRAUERT, IV, 2–3).

SPÖRL (Johannes), *Grundformen hochmittelalterlicher Geschichtsanschauung*, Munich, 1935.

(4) THE LITERARY EVIDENCE

ACHER (Jean), 'Les Archaïsmes apparents dans la chanson de "Raoul de Cambrai"', *Revue des langues romanes*, 1907.

FALK (J.), *Étude sociale sur les chansons de geste*, Nyköping, 1879.

KALBFLEISCH, Die Realien im altfranzösischen Epos "Raoul de Cambrai", Giessen, 1897 (*Wissenschaftliche Beilage zum Jahresbericht des Grh. Realgymnasiums*).

MEYER (Fritz), *Die Stände, ihr Leben und Treiben dargestellt nach den altfranzösischen Artus- und Abenteuerromanen*, Marburg, 1892 (*Ausgabe und Abhandlungen aus dem Gebiete der roman. Philologie*, 89).

TAMASSIA (G.), 'Il diritto nell' epica francese dei secoli XII e XIII', *Rivista italiana per le scienze giuridiche*, I, 1886.

II. MENTAL ATTITUDES

(1) MODES OF FEELING AND THOUGHT

BESZARD (L.), *Les Larmes dans l'épopée*, Halle, 1903.

BILFINGER, *Die mittelalterlichen Horen und die modernen Stunden*, Stuttgart, 1892.

DORIACHE-RODJESVENSKY, *Les Poésies des Goliards*, 1931.

DRESDNER (Albert), *Kultur- und Sittengeschichte der italienischen Geistlichkeit im 10. und 11. Jahrhundert*, Breslau, 1910.

EICKEN (Heinrich von), *Geschichte und System der mittelalterlichen Weltanschauung*, Stuttgart, 1887.

GALBRAITH (V. H.), 'The Literacy of the Medieval English Kings', *Proceedings of the British Academy*, 1935.

GHELLINCK (J. de), *Le Mouvement théologique du XIIe siècle*, 1914.

GLORY (A.) and UNGERER (T.), 'L'Adolescent au cadran solaire de la cathédrale de Strasbourg', *Archives alsaciennes d'histoire de l'art*, 1932.

HASKINS (Charles H.), *The Renaissance of the Twelfth Century*, Cambridge (Mass.), 1927.

HOFMEISTER (A.), 'Puer, juvenis, senex: zum Verständnis der mittelalterlichen Altersbezeichnungen', *Papsttum und Kaisertum: Forschungen P. Kehr dargebracht*, 1926.

IRSAY (S. d'), *Histoire des universités françaises et étrangères*, I, 1933.

JACOBIUS (Helene), *Die Erziehung des Edelfräuleins im alten Frankreich nach Dichtungen des XII., XIII. und XIV. Jahrhunderts*, Halle, 1908 (*Beihefte zur Zeitschrift für romanische Philologie*, XVI).

LIMMER (R.), *Bildungszustände und Bildungsideen des 13. Jahrhunderts*, Munich, 1928.

PARÉ (G.), BRUNET (A.), TREMBLAY (P.), *La Renaissance du XIIe siècle: les Écoles et l'enseignement*, 1938 (*Publications de l'Institut d'études médiévales d'Ottawa*, 3).

RASHDALL (H.), *The Universities of Europe in the Middle Ages*, 2nd edn. by F. M. POWICKE and A. B. EMDEN, 3 vols., Oxford, 1936.

SASS (Johann), *Zur Kultur- und Sittengeschichte der sächsischen Kaiserzeit*, Berlin, 1892.

SÜSSMILCH (Hans), *Die lateinische Vagantenpoesie des 12. und 13. Jahrhunderts als Kulturerscheinung*, Leipzig, 1917 (*Beiträge zur Kulturgeschichte des Mittelalters und der Renaissance*, 25).

(2) 'TERRORS' OF THE YEAR 1000

BURR (G. L.), 'The Year 1000', *American Historical Review*, 1900–1.

EICKEN (H. von), 'Die Legende von de Erwartung des Weltuntergangs und der Wiederkehr Christi im Jahre 1000', *Forschungen zur deutschen Geschichte*, XXIII, 1883.

BIBLIOGRAPHY

Ermini (Filippo), 'La fine del mondo nell' anno mille e il pensiero di Odone di Cluny', *Studien zur lateinischen Dichtung des Mittelalters, Ehrengabe für K. Strecker*, Dresden, 1931 (*Schriftenreihe der Historischen Vierteljahrschrift*, 1).

Grund (Karl), *Die Anschauungen des Radulfus Glaber in seinen Historien*, Greifswald, 1910.

Orsi (P.), 'L'anno mille', *Rivista storica italiana*, IV, 1887.

Plaine (Dom François), 'Les Prétendues Terreurs de l'an mille', *Revue des questions historiques*, XIII, 1873.

Wadstein (Ernst), *Die eschatologische Ideengruppe: Antichrist-Weltsabbat-Weltende und Weltgericht*, Leipzig, 1896.

III. THE LAST INVASIONS

(1) GENERAL

Lot (Ferdinand), *Les Invasions barbares et le peuplement de l'Europe; introduction à l'intelligence des derniers traités de paix*, 2 vols., 1937.

(2) THE SARACENS IN THE ALPS AND THE ITALIAN PENINSULA

Duprat (E.), 'Les Sarrasins en Provence', *Les Bouches-du-Rhône, Encyclopédie départementale*, 1924.

Latouche (R.), 'Les Idées actuelles sur les Sarrasins dans les Alpes', *Revue de géographie alpine*, 1931.

Patrucco (Carlo E.), 'I Sarraceni nelle Alpi Occidentali', *Biblioteca della Società storica subalpina*, XXXII, 1908.

Poupardin (René), *Le Royaume de Bourgogne (888–1038)*, 1907 (*Bibliothèque de l'École des Hautes Études, Sc. histor.*, 163).

—— *Le Royaume de Provence sous les Carolingiens*, 1901 (*ibid.*, 131).

Vehse (O.), 'Das Bündnis gegen die Sarazenen vom Jahre 915', *Quellen und Forschungen aus italienischen Archiven*, XIX, 1927.

(3) THE HUNGARIANS

Büdinger (Max), *Österreichische Geschichte bis zum Ausgange des dreizehnten Jahrhunderts*, I, Leipzig, 1858.

Caro (G.), 'Der Ungarntribut unter Heinrich I.', *Mitteilungen des Instituts für österreichische Geschichtsforschung*, XX, 1899.

Darko (E.), 'Influences touraniennes sur l'évolution de l'art militaire des Grecs, des Romains et des Byzantins', *Byzantion*, 1935 and 1937.

Jokay (Z.), 'Die ungarische Ortsnamenforschung', *Zeitschrift für Ortsnamenforschung*, 1935.

Kaindl (R. F.), *Beiträge zur älteren ungarischen Geschichte*, Vienna, 1893.

Lüttich (Rudolf), *Ungarnzüge in Europa im 10. Jahrhundert*, Berlin, 1910 (*Ebering's Histor. Studien*, 74).

Macartney (C. A.), *The Magyars in the Ninth Century*, Cambridge, 1930 (reviewed by G. Moravsik, *Byzantinische Zeitschrift*, 1933).

Marczali (Heinrich), *Ungarns Geschichtsquellen im Zeitalter der Arpaden*, Berlin, 1882.

Marquart (J.), *Osteuropäische und ostasiatische Streifzüge*, Leipzig, 1903.

Sauvageot (A.), 'L'Origine du peuple hongrois', *Revue des études hongroises*, II, 1924.

Schönebaum (Herbert), *Die Kenntnis der byzantinischen Geschichtsschreiber von der ältesten Geschichte der Ungarn vor der Landnahme*, Berlin, 1922.

Sebestyen (Charles C. S.), 'L'Arc et la flèche des Hongrois', *Nouvelle Revue de Hongrie*, LI, 1934.

Steinacker (Harold), 'Über Stand und Aufgabe der ungarischen Verfassungsgeschichte', *Mitteilungen des Instituts für Oesterreichische Geschichtsforschung*, XVIII, 1907.

Szinnyei, *Die Herkunft der Ungarn, ihre Sprache und Urkultur*, 2nd edn., Berlin, 1923.

Zichy (Étienne), 'L'Origine du peuple hongrois', *Revue des études hongroises*, I, 1923.

BIBLIOGRAPHY

(4) THE SCANDINAVIANS

ARBMAN (Holger) and STENBERGER (Mårten), *Vikingar i Västerled* (The Vikings on the Western routes), Stockholm, 1935.

BUGGE (Alexander), *Die Wikinger: Bilder aus der nordischen Vergangenheit*, Halle, 1906.

—— 'The Norse Settlements in the British Islands', *Transactions of the Royal Historical Society*, 1921.

CLAPHAM (J. H.), 'The Horsing of the Danes', *English Historical Review*, 1910.

COLLINGWOOD (W. G.), *Scandinavian Britain*, 1908.

CURTIS (E.), 'The English and Ostmen in Ireland', *English Historical Review*, 1908.

DARLINGTON (R. R.), 'The Last Phase of Anglo-Saxon History', *History*, 1937.

FALK (H.), 'Altnordisches Seewesen', *Wörter und Sachen*, IV, 1912.

GARAUD (Marcel), 'Les Invasions des Normands en Poitou et leurs conséquences', *Revue historique*, CLXXX, 1937.

GOSSES (I. H.), 'Deensche Heerschappijen in Friesland gedurende den Noormannentijd', *Mededeelingen der koninklijke Akademie van Wetenschappen, Afd. Letterkunde*, 56, Series B, 1923.

HOFMEISTER (A.), 'Ein angeblicher Normannenzug ins Mittelmeer um 825', *Historische Aufsätze K. Zeumer dargebracht*, Weimar, 1909.

JACOBSEN (Lis), 'Les Vikings suivant les inscriptions runniques du Danemark', *Revue Historique*, CLVIII, 1938.

JORANSON (Einar), *The Danegeld in France*, Rock Island, 1923 (*Augustana Library Publ.*, 10).

KENDRICK (T. D.), *A History of the Vikings*, 1930.

LOT (F.), 'La Grande Invasion normande de 856–862', *Bibliothèque de l'École des Chartes*, 1908.

—— 'La Loire, l'Aquitaine et la Seine de 862 à 866', *ibid.*, 1908.

—— 'Le Monastère inconnu pillé par les Normands en 845', *ibid.*, 1909.

MONTELIUS (Oskar), *Kulturgeschichte Schwedens von der ältesten Zeiten bis zum elften Jahrhundert*, Leipzig, 1906.

—— 'Sverige och Vikingafäderna västernt' (Sweden and the Viking Expeditions to the West), *Antikvarisk Tidskrift*, XXI, 2.

NORDENSTRENG (Rolf), *Die Züge der Wikinger*, trans. L. MEYN, Leipzig, 1925.

OLRIK (Axel), *Viking Civilization*, 1930.

OMAN (Charles W. C.), 'The Danish Kingdom of York', *Archaeological Journal*, XCI, 1934.

PAULSEN (P.), *Studien zur Wikingerkultur*, Neumünster, 1933.

PRENTOUT (Henri), *Étude critique sur Dudon de Saint-Quentin*, 1916.

—— *Essai sur les origines et la formation du duché de Normandie*, Caen, 1911.

SHETELIG (Haakon), *Les Origines des invasions des Normands* (*Bergens Museums Årbog Historisk-antikvarisk rekke*, no. 1).

—— *Préhistoire de la Norvège*, Oslo, 1926. (*Instituttet for sammenlignende Kulturforskning*, Series A, V.

STEENSTRUP (J.), 'Normandiets Historie under de syo fürste Hertuger 911–1066' (with a summary in French), *Mémoires de l'Académie royale des sciences et des lettres de Danemark*, 7th Series, Section des Lettres, V, 1, 1925.

—— *Normannerne*, 4 vols., Copenhagen, 1876–1882. (Part of vol. I has been translated into French as *Études préliminaires pour servir à l'histoire des Normands*, *Bulletin Soc. Antiquaires Normandie*, vol. V, and separately, 1881.)

VAN DER LINDEN, 'Les Normands à Louvain', *Revue historique*, CXXIV, 1917.

VOGEL (W.), *Die Normannen und das fränkische Reich bis zur Gründung der Normandie (799–911)*, Heidelberg, 1906.

—— 'Handelsverkehr, Städtewesen und Staatenbildung in Nordeuropa im früheren Mittelalter', *Zeitschrift der Gesellschaft für Erdkunde zu Berlin*, 1931.

—— 'Wik-Orte und Wikinger: eine Studie zu den Anfängen des germanischen Städtewesens', *Hansische Geschichtsblätter*, 1935.

WADSTEIN, 'Le Mot viking', *Mélanges de philologie offerts à M. Johan Vising*, 1925.

BIBLIOGRAPHY

(5) THE CONVERSION OF THE NORTH

JOHNSON (E. N.), 'Adalbert of Hamburg-Bremen', *Speculum*, 1934.
MAURER (Konrad), *Die Bekehrung des norwegischen Stammes zum Christentume*, 2 vols., Munich, 1855-6.
MOREAU (E. de), *Saint Anschaire*, Louvain, 1930.
SCHMEIDLER (B.), *Hamburg-Bremen und Nordost-Europa vom 9. bis zum 11. Jahrhundert*, Leipzig, 1918.

(6) EFFECTS OF THE SCANDINAVIAN INVASIONS

ANDERSON (Olaf S.), *The English Hundred-Names*, Lund, 1934.
BRÖNDAL (Viggo), 'Le Normand et la langue des Vikings', *Normannia*, 1930.
EKWALL (E.), 'How Long did the Scandinavian Language Survive in England?', *A Grammatical Miscellany Offered to O. Jespersen*, Copenhagen, 1930.
—— *Scandinavians and Celts in the North-West of England*, Lund, 1918 (Lunds Universitets Årsskrift, New Series, Afd. I, vol. 14).
—— 'The Scandinavian Element', in A. MAWER and F. W. STENTON, *Introduction to the Survey of English Place-Names*, I, Cambridge, 1929.
—— 'The Scandinavian Element', in H. C. DARBY, *An Historical Geography of England*, Cambridge, 1936.
EMANUELLI, 'La Colonisation normande dans le département de la Manche', *Revue de Cherbourg*, 1907 ff.
JESPERSEN (O.), *Growth and Structure of the English Language*, 7th edn., Leipzig, 1913.
JORET (C.), 'Les Noms de lieu d'origine non-romane et la colonisation germanique et scandinave en Normandie', *Congrès du millénaire de la Normandie*, Rouen, 1912, II (enlarged edn., separately published, 1913).
LINDKVIST, *Middle-English Place Names of Scandinavian Origin*, Upsala, 1912.
LOT (Ferdinand), 'De l'origine et de la signification historique des noms de lieux en-ville et en-court', *Romania*, 1933 (cf. Marc BLOCH, 'Réflexions d'un historien sur quelques travaux de toponymie', *Annales d'histoire économique*, VI, 1934).
MAWER (A.), *Problems of Place-Name Study*, Cambridge, 1929.
—— 'The Scandinavian Settlements in England as Reflected in English Place-Names', *Acta Philologica*, VII, 1932-3.
PRENTOUT (H.), 'Le Rôle de Normandie dans l'histoire', *Revue historique*, CLX, 1929.
SHETELIG (H.), *Vikingeminner i Vest Europa* (Archaeological Remains of the Vikings in Western Europe), Oslo, 1933 (*Instituttet for sammenlignende kulturforskning*, A, XVI).
SION (Jules), *Les Paysans de la Normandie orientale*, 1908.
SJÖGREN (A.), 'Le Genre des mots d'emprunt norrois en normand', *Romania*, 1928.
STENTON (F. M.), 'The Danes in England', *History*, 1920-1.
—— 'The Danes in England', *Proceedings of the British Academy*, XIII, 1927.

IV. LEGAL AND POLITICAL STRUCTURE

(1) ORIGINAL SOURCES

ACHER (Jean), 'Notes sur le droit savant au moyen âge', *Nouvelle revue historique de droit*, 1906 (Treatise on homage by J. DE BLANOT).
ATTENBOROUGH (F. L.), *The Laws of the Earliest English Kings*, Cambridge, 1922.
BRACTON, *De legibus et consuetudinibus Angliae*. Edited by G. E. WOODBINE, 2 vols., New Haven, 1932 (*Yale Historical Publications, MS. III*); edited by TWISS, 6 vols., London, 1878-83 (*Rolls Series*).
Capitularia Regum Francorum. Edited by A. BORETIUS and V. KRAUSE, Hanover, 1883-97 (*MGH*, quarto).
Formulae Merovingici et Karolini Aevi. Edited by K. ZEUMER, Hanover, 1886 (*MGH*, quarto).
FOURGOUS (J.) and BEZIN (G. de), *Les Fors de Bigorre*, Bagnères-de-Bigorre, 1901. (*Travaux sur l'histoire du droit méridional*, fasc. 1)

BIBLIOGRAPHY

GLANVILL, *De legibus et consuetudinibus regni Angliae*. Edited by G. E. WOODBINE, New Haven, 1932 (*Yale Historical Publications, MS.* XIII).

GULIELMUS DURANDUS, *Speculum judiciale* (written between 1271 and 1276; several times printed).

Le Conseil de Pierre de Fontaines. Edited by A. J. MARNIER, 1886.

LEHMANN (Karl), *Das Langobardische Lehnrecht (Handschriften, Textentwicklung, ältester Text und Vulgattext nebst den capitula extraordinaria)*, Göttingen, 1896.

Les Établissements de Saint-Louis. Edited by P. VIOLLET, 4 vols., 1881-6 (*Soc. de l'Histoire de France*).

LIEBERMANN (F.), *Die Gesetze der Angelsachsen*, 3 vols., Halle, 1903-16 (includes both the Customaries of the Norman period and a valuable historical index).

MUÑOZ ROMERO (T.), *Colección de fueros municipales y cartas pueblas de los reinos de Castilla, León, Corona de Aragón y Navarra*, I, Madrid, 1847.

PHILIPPE DE BEAUMANOIR, *Coutumes de Beauvaisis*. Edited by A. SALMON, 2 vols., 1899-1900 (*Collection des textes pour servir à l'étude . . . de l'histoire*).

ROBERTSON (A. J.), *The Laws of the Kings of England from Edmund to Henry I*, Cambridge, 1925.

Sachsenspiegel. Edited by K. A. ECKHARDT, Hanover, 1933 (*MGH, Fontes juris germanici*, New Series).

SECKEL (E.), 'Über neuere Editionen juristischer Schriften des Mittelalters', *Zeitschrift der Savigny Stiftung, G.A.*, 1909 (on the *Summae feudorum* of the thirteenth century).

TARDIF (Joseph), *Coutumiers de Normandie*, 2 vols., Rouen, 1881-1903.

Usatges de Barcelona, editats amb una introduccio per R. D'ABADAL I VINYALS and F. VALLS TABERNER, Barcelona, 1913 (*Textes de dret catala*, I).

(2) WORKS ON THE HISTORY OF LAW AND INSTITUTIONS

BELOW (Georg von), *Der deutsche Staat des Mittelalters*, I, Leipzig, 1914.

—— *Vom Mittelalter zur Neuzeit*, Leipzig, 1924 (*Wissenschaft und Bildung*, 198).

BESNIER (Robert), *La Coutume de Normandie: Histoire externe*, 1935.

BESTA (E.), Fonti, legislazione e scienza giuridica della caduta dell' impero romano al, secolo XV°, Milan, 1923 (*Storia del diritto italiano . . . di* P. GIUDICE).

BRUNNER (Heinrich), *Deutsche Rechtsgeschichte*, 2nd edn., 2 vols., Leipzig, 1926-8.

CHADWICK (H. M.), *The Origin of the English Nation*, Cambridge, 1924.

—— *Studies in Anglo-Saxon Institutions*, Cambridge, 1905.

CHÉNON (Émile), *Histoire générale du droit français public et privé*, 2 vols., 1926-9.

ESMEIN (A.), *Cours élémentaire d'histoire du droit français*, 14th edn., 1921.

FICKER (J.), *Forschungen zur Reichs- und Rechtsgeschichte Italiens*, 4 vols., Innsbruck, 1868-74.

FLACH (J.), *Les Origines de l'ancienne France*, 4 vols., 1886-1917.

FUSTEL DE COULANGES, *Histoire des institutions politiques de l'ancienne France*, 6 vols. 1888-92.

GAMA-BARROS (H. da), *Historia de la administraçao publica em Portugal nos seculos XII a XV*, 2 vols., Lisbon, 1885-96 (also contains much information on Leon and Castile).

HASKINS (C. H.), *Norman Institutions*, Cambridge (Mass.), 1918 (*Harvard Historical Studies*, XXIV).

HOLDSWORTH (W. S.), *A History of English Law*, vols. I-III, 3rd edn., London, 1923.

JAMISON (E.), 'The Norman Administration of Apulia and Capua', *Papers of the British School at Rome*, VI, 1913.

JOLLIFFE (J. E. A.), *The Constitutional History of Medieval England*, 1937.

KEUTGEN (F.), *Der deutsche Staat des Mittelalters*, Jena, 1918.

KIENER (Fritz), *Verfassungsgeschichte der Provence seit der Ostgothenherrschaft bis zur Errichtung der Konsulate (510-1200)*, Leipzig, 1900.

LEICHT (P. S.), *Ricerche sul diritto privato nei documenti preirneriani*, 2 vols., Rome, 1914-22.

LUCHAIRE (Achille), *Manuel des institutions françaises. Période des Capétiens directs*, 1892.

MAITLAND (F. W.), *Domesday Book and Beyond*, Cambridge, 1921.

BIBLIOGRAPHY

MAYER (Ernst), *Mittelalterliche Verfassungsgeschichte: deutsche und französische Geschichte vom 9. bis zum 14. Jahrhundert*, 2 vols., Leipzig, 1899.
—— *Historia de las instituciones sociales y políticas de España y Portugal durante los siglos V a XIV*, 2 vols., Madrid, 1925–6.
—— *Italienische Verfassungsgeschichte von der Gothenzeit zur Zunftherrschaft*, 2 vols., Leipzig, 1900.
MEYER (Walter), *Das Werk des Kanzlers Gislebert von Mons besonders als verfassungsgeschichtliche Quelle betrachtet*, Königsberg, 1888.
NIESE (Hans), *Die Gesetzgebung der normannischen Dynastie in regnum Siciliae*, Halle, 1910.
OLIVIER-MARTIN, *Histoire de la coutume de la prévôté et vicomté de Paris*, 3 vols., 1922–30.
POLLOCK (F.), *The Land Laws*, 3rd edn., 1896.
POLLOCK (F.) and MAITLAND (F. W.), *The History of English Law before the Time of Edward I*, 2 vols., Cambridge, 1898.
RIAZA (Román) and GALLO (Alfonso García), *Manual de historia del derecho español*, Madrid, 1935.
ROGÉ (Pierre), *Les Anciens Fors de Béarn*, Toulouse, 1907.
SALVIOLI (G.), *Storia del diritto italiano*, 8th edn., Turin, 1921.
SANCHEZ-ALBORNOZ (C.), 'Conferencias en la Argentina', *Anuario de historia del derecho español*, 1933.
—— 'La potestad real y los señorios en Asturias, León y Castilla', *Revista de Archivos*, 3rd series, XXXI, 1914.
SCHRÖDER (R.), *Lehrbuch der deutschen Rechtsgeschichte*, 6th edn., Leipzig, 1919–22.
SOLMI (A.), *Storia del diritto italiano*, 3rd edn., Milan, 1930.
STUBBS (William), *Constitutional History of England*, 3 vols., Oxford, 1895–7 (French translation, with additional notes, by C. PETIT-DUTAILLIS and G. LEFEBVRE, 3 vols., 1907–27).
VIOLLET (Paul), *Histoire des institutions politiques et administratives de la France*, 3 vols., 1890–1903.
VINOGRADOFF (P.), *English Society in the Eleventh Century*, Oxford, 1908.
WAITZ (G.), *Deutsche Verfassungsgeschichte*, vols. I to VI, 2nd edn., Berlin, 1880–96; vols. 7 and 8, Kiel, 1876–8.

(3) THE LEGAL MIND AND THE TEACHING OF LAW

BESTA (E.), *L'opera d'Irnerio*, Turin, 1910.
BRIE (S.), *Die Lehre vom Gewohnheitsrecht, I: Geschichtliche Grundlegung*, Breslau, 1899.
CHÉNON (E.), 'Le Droit romain à la Curia Regis', *Mélanges Fitting*, vol. I, Montpellier, 1907 (reviewed by J. ACHER, *Revue générale de droit*, XXXII, 1908).
CHIAPPELLI (L.), 'Recherches sur l'état des études de droit romain en Toscane au XIe siècle', in *Nouvelle revue historique de droit*, 1896.
CONRAT (Max), *Die Quellen und Literatur des Römischen Rechts im früheren Mittelalter*, Leipzig, 1891.
FLACH (J.), *Études critiques sur l'histoire du droit romain au moyen âge*, 1890.
FOURNIER (P.), 'L'Église et le droit romain au XIIIe siècle', *Nouvelle revue historique de droit*, 1890.
GARAUD (Marcel), 'Le Droit romain dans les chartes poitevines du IXe au XIe siècle', *Bull. de la Société des Antiquaires de l'Ouest*, 1925.
GOETZ (W.), 'Das Wiederaufleben des römischen Rechts im 12. Jahrhundert', *Archiv für Kulturgeschichte*, 1912.
MEYNIAL (E.), 'Note sur la formation de la théorie du domaine divisé . . . du XIIe au XIVe siècle', *Mélanges Fitting*, vol. II, Montpellier, 1908.
—— 'Remarques sur la réaction populaire contre l'invasion du droit romain en France au XIIe et XIIIe siècles', *Mélanges Chabaneau*, Erlangen, 1907.
OLIVIER-MARTIN (F.), 'Le Roi de France et les mauvaises coutumes', *Zeitschrift der Savigny Stiftung*, G.A., 1938.
VINOGRADOFF (P.), *Roman Law in Medieval Europe*, 2nd edn., Oxford, 1929.
WEHRLÉ (R.), *De la coutume dans le droit canonique*, 1928.

BIBLIOGRAPHY

(4) POLITICAL IDEAS

CARLYLE (R. W. and A. J.), *A History of Medieval Political Theory in the West*, vols. I to III, 1903–15.

DEMPF (Alois), *Sacrum imperium: Geschichts- und Staatsphilosophie des Mittelalters und der politischen Renaissance*, Munich, 1929.

KERN (Fritz), 'Recht und Verfassung im Mittelalter', *Historische Zeitschrift*, 1919.

V. TIES OF KINSHIP

(1) THE FAMILY AND THE VENDETTA

BRUNNER (Heinrich), 'Sippe und Wergeld in den niederdeutschen Rechten', in BRUNNER, *Abhandlungen der Rechtsgeschichte*, vol. I, Weimar, 1931 (previously *Zeitschrift der, Savigny Stiftung, G.A.*, III).

CATTIER (F.), 'La Guerre privée dans le comté de Hainaut', *Annales de la Faculté de philosophie de Bruxelles*, I, 1889–90.

DUBOIS (Pierre), *Les asseurements au XIIIᵉ siècle dans nos villes de Nord*, 1900.

ESPINAS (G.), 'Les Guerres familiales dans la commune de Douai aux XIIᵉ et XIIIᵉ siècles', *Nouvelle revue historique de droit*, 1900.

FRAUENSTÄDT (Paul), *Blutrache und Todtschlagsühne im deutschen Mittelalter*, Leipzig, 1881.

HINOJOSA (Eduardo de), 'Das germanische Element im spanischen Rechte', *Zeitschrift der Savigny Stiftung, G.A.*, 1910.

HIS (R.), 'Gelobter und gebotener Friede im deutschen Mittelalter', *Zeitschrift der Savigny-Stiftung, G.A.*, 1912.

PETIT-DUTAILLIS (C.), *Documents nouveaux sur les mœurs populaires et le droit de vengeance dans les Pays-Bas au XVᵉ siècle*, 1908 (with bibliography).

PHILLPOTTS (Bertha Surtees), *Kindred and Clan in the Middle Ages and After: A Study in the Sociology of the Teutonic Races*, Cambridge, 1913 (*Cambridge Archaeological and Ethnological Series*).

ROEDER (Fritz), *Die Familie bei den Angelsachsen*, Part I, Halle, 1899 (*Studien zur englischen Philologie*, IV).

VALAT (G.), *Poursuite privée et composition pécuniaire dans l'ancienne Bourgogne*, Dijon, 1907.

VAN KEMPEN (Georges), *De la composition pour homicide d'après la Loi Salique. Son maintien dans les Coutumes de Saint-Omer jusqu'à la fin du XVIᵉ siècle*, Saint-Omer, 1902.

WILKE (Carl), *Das Friedegebot: ein Beitrag zur Geschichte des deutschen Strafrechts*, Heidelberg, 1911 (*Deutschrechtliche Beiträge*, VI, 4).

YVER (J.), *L'Interdiction de la guerre privée dans le très ancien droit normand* (*Extrait des travaux de la semaine d'histoire du droit normand*), Caen, 1928.

(2) ECONOMIC SOLIDARITY

BRUNNER (H.), 'Der Totenteil in germanischen Rechten', in BRUNNER, *Abhandlungen zur Rechtsgeschichte*, II, Weimar, 1937 (previously *Zeitschrift der Savigny Stiftung, G.A.*, XIX).

CAILLEMER (Robert), 'Les Idées coutumières et la renaissance du droit romain dans le Sud-Est de la France: I, "Laudatio" des héritiers', in *Essays in Legal History*, edited by P. VINOGRADOFF, Oxford, 1913.

—— 'Le Retrait lignager dans le droit provençal', in *Studi giuridici in onore di Carlo Fadda*, IV, Naples, 1906.

FALLETTI (Louis), *Le Retrait lignager en droit coutumier français*, 1923.

FORMENTINI (Ubaldo), 'Sulle origini e sulla costituzione d'un grande gentilizio feodale', *Atti della Società ligure di storia patria*, LIII, 1926.

GÉNESTAL (Robert), 'Le Retrait lignager en droit normand', *Travaux de la semaine d'histoire du droit normand . . . 1923*, Caen, 1925.

LAPLANCHE (Jean de), *La Réserve coutumière dans l'ancien droit français*, 1925.

BIBLIOGRAPHY

PLUCKNETT (Theodore F. T.), 'Bookland and Folkland', *Economic History Review*, VI, 1935–6 (with bibliography).

PORÉE (Charles), 'Les Statuts de la communauté des seigneurs pariers de La Garde-Guérin (1238–1313)', in *Bibliothèque de l'École des Chartes*, 1907, and *Études historiques sur le Gévaudan*, 1919.

SCHULTZE (A.), 'Augustin und der Seelteil des germanischen Erbrechts', *Abhandlungen der sächsischen Akademie der Wissenschaften, Phil.-hist. Kl.*, 28.

TAMASSIO (G.), 'Il diritto di prelazione e l'espropriazione forzata negli statuti dei comuni italiani', *Archivio giuridico*, 1885.

VI. FEUDAL INSTITUTIONS PROPER

(1) FEUDALISM IN GENERAL: FRANKISH ORIGINS

BLOCH (Marc), 'Feudalism (European)', in *Encyclopaedia of the Social Sciences*, VI, 1931.

BOURGEOIS (Emile), *Le Capitulaire de Kiersy-sur-Oise: étude sur l'état et le régime politique de la société carolingienne à la fin du IX⁰ siècle d'après la législation de Charles le Chauve*, 1885.

CALMETTE (J.), *La Société féodale*, 1923 (*Collection A. Colin*).

DOPSCH (A.), 'Benefizialwesen und Feudalität', *Mitteilungen des österreichischen Instituts für Geschichtsforschung*, 1932.

— 'Die Leudes und das Lehnwesen', *ibid.*, 1926.

— *Die Wirtschaftsentwicklung der Karolingerzeit*, 2nd edn., Vienna, 1921–2.

DUMAS (Auguste), 'Le Serment de fidélité et la conception du pouvoir du Iᵉʳ au IXᵉ siècle', *Revue historique de droit*, 1931; cf. LOT (F.), 'Le Serment de fidélité à l'époque franque', *Revue belge de philologie*, 1933; DUMAS (A.), 'Le Serment de fidélité à l'époque franque', *ibid.*, 1935.

GANSHOF (F. L.), 'Note sur les origines de l'union du bénéfice avec la vassalité', *Études d'histoire dédiées à la mémoire de Henri Pirenne*, Brussels, 1937.

GUILHIERMOZ (A.), *Essai sur les origines de la noblesse en France au moyen âge*, 1902.

HALPHEN (L.), 'À propos du capitulaire de Quierzy', *Revue historique*, CVI, 1911.

KIENAST (W.), *Die deutschen Fürsten im Dienste der Westmächte bis zum Tode Philipps des Schönen von Frankreich*, 2 vols., Utrecht, 1924–31.

KRAWINKEL (H.), *Zur Entstehung des Lehnwesens*, Weimar, 1936.

LESNE (E.), *Histoire de la propriété ecclésiastique en France*, 4 vols., Lille, 1910–36.

MAYER (Ernst), 'Die Entstehung der Vasallität und des Lehnwesens', *Festgabe für R. Sohm*, Munich, 1914.

MENZEL (Viktor), *Die Entstehung des Lehnwesens*, Berlin, 1890.

MITTEIS (H.), *Lehnrecht und Staatsgewalt*, Weimar, 1933.

— 'Politische Prozesse des früheren Mittelalters in Deutschland und Frankreich', *Sitzungsberichte der Heidelberger Akademie der Wissenschaften*, 1926.

ROTH (P.), *Feudalität und Unterthanenverband*, Weimar, 1863.

SOCIÉTÉ JEAN BODIN, *Les Liens de vassalité et les immunités*, Brussels, 1936 (and *Revue de l'Institut de Sociologie*, 1936).

VINOGRADOFF (P.), 'Foundations of Society' and 'Feudalism' in *Cambridge Medieval History*, 1911–36, vols. II and III.

WAITZ (G.), 'Die Anfänge des Lehnwesens', in WAITZ, *Gesammelte Abhandlungen*, I, Göttingen, 1896.

(2) STUDIES OF FEUDALISM BY COUNTRIES AND REGIONS

ADAMS (G. B.), 'Anglo-Saxon Feudalism', *American Historical Review*, VII, 1901–2.

BESELER (Georg), *System des gemeinen deutschen Privatrechts*, vol. II, Berlin, 1885.

BROOKE (Z. N.), 'Pope Gregory VII's Demand of Fealty from William the Conqueror', *English Historical Review*, XXVI, 1911.

BRUTAILS (J.-A.), 'Les Fiefs du roi et les alleux en Guienne', *Annales du Midi*, 1917.

CAPASSO (B.), 'Sul catalogo dei feudi e dei feudatari delle provincie napoletane sotto la dominazione normanna', *Atti della reale Accademia di archeologia*, IV, 1868–9.

BIBLIOGRAPHY

CECI (C.), 'Normanni di Inghilterra e Normanni d'Italia', *Archivio scientifico del Reale Istituto superiore di Scienze Economiche . . . di Bari*, VII, 1932–3.

CHEW (H. M.), *The English Ecclesiastical Tenants-in-Chief and Knight Service, especially in the Thirteenth and Fourteenth Century*, Oxford, 1932.

DEL GIUDICE (P.) and CALISSE (C.), 'Feudo' in *Il digesto italiano*, XI, 2, 1892–8.

DILLAY (Madeleine), 'Le "Service" annuel en deniers des fiefs de la région angevine', *Mélanges Paul Fournier*, 1929.

DOUGLAS (D. C.), *Feudal Documents from the Abbey of Bury St Edmunds*, London, 1932 (*Records of the Social and Economic History of England*, VIII); important introduction.

ERDMANN (Karl), 'Das Papsttum und Portugal im ersten Jahrhunderte der portugiesischen Geschichte', *Abhandlungen der Preussischen Akademie, Phil.-hist. Kl.*, 1938.

ESPINAY (G. d'), 'La Féodalité et le droit civil français', Saumur, 1862 (*Rec. de l'Académie de Législation de Toulouse*, Livraison supplémentaire).

HOMEYER (C. G.), 'System des Lehnrechts der sächsischen Rechtsbücher' in *Sachsenspiegel*, ed. HOMEYER, vol. II, 2, Berlin, 1844.

JOLLIFFE (J. E. A.), 'Northumbrian Institutions', *English Historical Review*, XLI, 1926.

JORDAN (Karl), 'Das Eindringen des Lehnwesens in das Rechtsleben der römischen Kurie', *Archiv für Urkundenforschung*, 1931.

KEHR (P.), 'Die Belehnungen der süditalienischen Normannenfürsten durch die Päpste', *Abhandlungen der preussischen Akademie, Phil.-hist. Kl.*, 1934.

—— 'Das Papsttum und der katalanische Prinzipat bis zur Vereinigung mit Aragon', *ibid.*, 1926.

—— 'Das Papsttum und die Königreiche Navarra und Aragon bis zur Mitte des XII. Jahrhunderts', *ibid.*, 1928.

—— 'Wie und wann wurde das Reich Aragon ein Lehen der römischen Kirche', *Sitzungsberichte der preussischen Akademie, Phil.-hist. Kl.*, 1928.

KÖLMEL (W.), *Rom und der Kirchenstaat im 10. und 11. Jahrhundert bis in die Anfänge der Reform*, Berlin, 1935 (*Abhandlungen zur mittleren und neueren Geschichte*, 78).

LAGOUELLE (Henri), *Essai sur la conception féodale de la propriété foncière dans le très ancien droit normand*, 1902.

LA MONTE (J. L.), *Feudal Monarchy in the Latin Kingdom of Jerusalem*, Cambridge (Mass.), 1932 (*Monographs of the Medieval Academy*, 4).

LIPPERT (Waldemar), *Die deutschen Lehnsbücher*, Leipzig, 1903.

MACKECHNIE (W. S.), *Magna Carta: A Commentary*, 2nd edn., Glasgow, 1914.

MENENDEZ PIDAL (R.), *La España del Cid*, 2 vols., Madrid, 1929; English trans. (abridged), *The Cid and His Spain*, 1934.

MONTI (G. M.), 'Ancora sulla feudalità e i grandi domani feudali del regno di Sicilia', *Rivista di storia del diritto italiano*, IV, 1921.

MUNOZ-ROMERO (T.), 'Del estado de las personas en los reinos de Asturias y León', *Revista de Archivos*, 1883.

PAZ (Ramon), 'Un nuevo feudo castellano', *Anuario de historia de derecho español*, 1928.

RABASSE (Maurice), *Du régime des fiefs en Normandie au moyen âge*, 1905.

RICHARDOT (Hubert), 'Le Fief roturier à Toulouse aux XIIe et XIIIe siècles', *Revue historique de droit français*, 1935.

ROUND (J. H.), *Feudal England*, London, 1907.

—— 'Military Tenure before the Conquest', *English Historical Review*, XII, 1897.

SANCHEZ-ALBORNOZ (C.), 'Las behetrias' and 'Muchas páginas más sobre las behetrias', *ibid.*, 1924 and 1927.

—— 'Un feudo castellano del XIII', *ibid.*, 1926.

SECRÉTAN (E.), 'De la féodalité en Espagne', *Revue historique de droit*, 1863.

SCHNEIDER (F.), *Die Entstehung von Burg und Landgemeinde in Italien*, Berlin, 1924 (*Abhandlungen zur mittleren und neueren Geschichte*, 68).

STENTON (F. M.), 'The Changing Feudalism of the Middle Ages', *History*, XIX, 1934–5.

—— *The First Century of English Feudalism (1066–1166)*, Oxford, 1932.

STRAYER (J. R.), 'Knight-Service in Normandy', in *Anniversary Essays by Students of Charles H. Haskins*, 1929.

BIBLIOGRAPHY

TOMASSETTI (G.), 'Feudalismo romano', *Rivista internazionale di scienze sociale*, V, 1894.
WUNDERLICH (Erich), *Aribert von Antemiano, Erzbischof von Mailand*, Halle, 1914.
YVER (Jean), *Les Contrats dans le très ancien droit normand*, 1926.

(3) 'COMPANIONAGE', VASSALAGE, AND HOMAGE

BLOCH (Marc), 'Les Formes de la rupture de l'hommage dans l'ancien droit féodal', *Nouvelle revue historique de droit*, 1912.
BRUNNER (H.), 'Zur Geschichte des fränkischen Gefolgswesens', in *Forschungen zur Geschichte des d. und fr. Rechtes*, Stuttgart, 1894 (previously *Zeitschrift der Savigny Stiftung, G.A.*, IX).
CALMETTE (Joseph), 'Le "Comitatus" germanique et la vassalité', *Nouvelle revue historique de droit*, 1904.
CHÉNON (E.), 'Le Rôle juridique de l'osculum dans l'ancien droit français', *Mémoires de la Société nationale des Antiquaires*, 8th series, VI, 1919–23.
DOUBLIER (Othmar), 'Formalakte beim Eintritt in die altnorwegische Gefolgschaft' in *Mitteilungen des Instituts für österreichische Geschichtsforschung*, Ergänzungsband VI, 1901.
EHRENBERG (V.), *Commendation und Huldigung nach fränkischem Recht*, 1877.
EHRISMANN (G.), 'Die Wörter für "Herr" im Althochdeutschen', *Zeitschrift für deutsche Wortforschung*, VII, 1905–6.
GROSSE (Robert), *Römische Militärgeschichte von Gallienus bis zum Beginn der byzantinischen Themenverfassung*, Berlin, 1920.
HIS (Rudolf), 'Todschlagsühne und Mannschaft', in *Festgabe für K. Güterbock*, Berlin, 1910.
JUD (J.), 'Zur Geschichte und Herkunft von frz. "dru" ', *Archivum romanicum*, 1926.
LARSON (L. M.), *The King's Household in England before the Conquest*, Madison, 1904.
LÉCRIVAIN (C.), 'Les Soldats privés au Bas-Empire', *Mélanges d'archéologie et d'histoire*, 1890.
LEICHT (P. S.), 'Gasindi e vassalli', *Rendiconti della reale Accademia nazionale dei Lincei, Scienze morali*, 6th series, III, 1927.
LITTLE (A. G.), 'Gesiths and thegns', *English Historical Review*, IV, 1887.
MEYER-LÜBKE (W.), 'Senyor, "Herr" ', *Wörter und Sachen*, VIII, 1923.
MIROT (Léon), 'Les Ordonnances de Charles VII relatives à la prestation des hommages', *Mémoires de la Société pour l'Histoire du droit et des institutions des anciens pays bourguignons*, fasc. 2, 1935.
MÜLLER (Martin), *Minne und Dienst in der altfranzösischen Lyrik*, Marburg, 1907.
MYRICK (Arthur B.), 'Feudal Terminology in Medieval Religious Poetry', *Romanic Review*, XI, 1920.
PETOT (Pierre), 'La Capacité testimonial du vassal', *Revue historique de droit*, 1931.
PLATON (G.), 'L'Hommage féodal comme moyen de contracter des obligations privées', *Revue générale de droit*, XXVI, 1902.
RAMOS Y LOSCERTALES, 'La "devotio iberica" ', *Anuario de Historia del derecho español*, 1924.
RICHTER (Elise), 'Senior, Sire', *Wörter und Sachen*, XII, 1929.
SCHUBERT (Carl), *Der Pflegesohn im französischen Heldenepos*, Marburg, 1906.
SEECK (Otto), 'Buccellarii', in PAULY-WISSOWA, *Realencyclopädie der klassischen Altertumswissenschaft*, III, 1899.
—— 'Das deutsche Gefolgswesen auf römischem Boden', *Zeitschrift der Savigny Stiftung, G.A.*, 1896.
WAITZ (G.), 'Über die Anfänge der Vasallität', in WAITZ, *Gesammelte Abhandlungen*, I, Göttingen, 1896.
WECHSSLER (Eduard), 'Frauendienst und Vasallität', *Zeitschrift für französische Sprache*, XXIV, 1902.
—— *Das Kulturproblem des Minnesangs*, I, Halle, 1907.
WINDISCH, 'Vassus und vassallus', *Berichte über die Verhandlungen der königlichen sächsischen Gesellschaft der Wissenschaften*, 1892.

BIBLIOGRAPHY

(4) 'PRECARIA', 'BENEFIT', FIEF, AND ALLOD

BLOCH (Marc), 'Un Problème d'histoire comparée: la ministérialité en France et en Allemagne', *Revue historique de droit*, 1928.

BONDROIT, 'Les "Precariae verbo regis" devant le concile de Leptinnes', *Revue d'histoire ecclésiastique*, 1900.

BRUNNER (H.), 'Die Landschenkungen der Merowinger und Agilolfinger', *Forschungen zur Geschichte des d. und fr. Rechtes*, Stuttgart, 1877 (previously *Sitzungsberichte der preussischen Akademie, Phil.-hist. Kl.*, 1885).

CHÉNON (E.), *Étude sur l'histoire des alleux*, 1888.

CLOTET (L.), 'Le Bénéfice sous les deux premières races', *Comptes rendus du Congrès scientifique international des catholiques*, 1891.

GIERKE (O.), 'Allod', in *Beiträge zum Wörterbuch der deutschen Rechtssprache*, Weimar, 1908.

GLADISS (D. von), 'Die Schenkungen der deutschen Könige zu privatem Eigen', *Archiv für Geschichte des Mittelalters*, 1937.

JOLLIFFE (J. E. A.), 'Alod and fee', *Cambridge Historical Journal*, 1937.

KERN (H.), 'Feodum, fief', *Mémoires de la Société Linguistique de Paris*, II, 1872.

KRAWINKEL (H.), *Feudum*, Weimar, 1938 (*Forschungen zum deutschen Recht*, III, 2).

—— *Untersuchungen zum fränkischen Benefizialrecht*, Weimar, 1936 (*Forschungen zum deutschen Recht*, II, 2).

LESNE (E.), 'Les Bénéficiers de Saint-Germain des Près au temps de l'abbé Irminon', *Revue Mabillon*, 1922.

—— 'Les Diverses Acceptions du mot "beneficium" du VIIIe au IXe siècle', *Revue historique de droit*, 1921.

LOT (Ferdinand), 'Origine et nature du bénéfice', *Anuario de historia del derecho español*, 1933.

PÖSCHL (A.), 'Die Entstehung des geistlichen Beneficiums', *Archiv für katholisches Kirchenrecht*, 1926.

ROTH (P.), *Geschichte des Benefizialwesens von den ältesten Zeiten bis ins zehnte Jahrhundert*, Erlangen, 1850.

SCHÄFER (D.), 'Honor . . . im mittelalterlichen Latein', *Sitzungsberichte der preussischen Akademie, Phil.-hist. Kl.*, 1921.

STUTZ (U.), 'Lehen und Pfründe', *Zeitschrift der Savigny Stiftung, G.A.*, 1899.

WIART (René), *Le Régime des terres du fisc sous le Bas-Empire, Essai sur la precaria*, 1894.

(5) THE LAW OF THE FIEF

ACHER (Jean), 'Les Archaïsmes apparents dans la Chanson de "Raoul de Cambrai" ', *Revue des langues romanes*, 1907.

ARBOIS DE JUBAINVILLE, D', 'Recherches sur la minorité et ses effets dans le droit féodal français', *Bibliothèque de l'École des Chartes*, 1851 and 1852.

BELLETTE (E.), *La Succession aux fiefs dans les coutumes flamandes*, 1927.

BLUM (Edgar), 'La Commise féodale', *Tijdschrift voor Rechtsgeschiedenis*, IV, 1922–3.

ERMOLAEF, *Die Sonderstellung der Frau im französischen Lehnrecht*, Ostermundingen, 1930.

GÉNESTAL (R.), 'La Formation du droit d'aînesse dans la coutume de Normandie', *Normannia*, 1928.

—— *Le Parage normand*, Caen, 1911 (*Bibliothèque d'histoire du droit normand*, 2nd series, I, 2).

—— *Études de droit privé normand. I. La tutelle*, 1930 (*Bibliothèque d'histoire du droit normand*, 2nd series, III).

KLATT (Kurt), *Das Heergewäte*, Heidelberg, 1908 (*Deutschrechtliche Beiträge*, II, fasc. 2).

MEYNIAL (E.), 'Les Particularités des successions féodales dans les Assises de Jérusalem', *Nouvelle Revue historique de droit*, 1892.

MITTEIS (Heinrich), 'Zur Geschichte der Lehnsvormundschaft', *Alfred Schulze Festschrift*, Weimar, 1934.

BIBLIOGRAPHY

Sᴄʜᴜʟᴢᴇ (H. J. F.), *Das Recht der Erstgeburt in den deutschen Fürstenhäusern und seine Bedeutung für die deutsche Staatsentwicklung*, Leipzig, 1851.
Sᴛᴜᴛᴢ (U.), ' "Römerwergeld" und "Herrenfall" ', *Abhandlungen der preussischen Akademie, Phil.-hist. Kl.*, 1934.

(6) PLURALITY OF LORDS AND LIEGE HOMAGE

Bᴀɪsᴛ (G.), 'Lige, liege', *Zeitschrift für romanische Philologie*, XXVIII, 1904, p. 112.
Bᴇᴀᴜᴅᴏɪɴ (A.) 'Homme lige', *Nouvelle Revue historique de droit*, VII, 1883.
Bʟᴏᴏᴍғɪᴇʟᴅ, 'Salic "Litus" ', *Studies in Honor of H. Collitz*, Baltimore, 1930.
Bʀᴜ̈ᴄʜ (Joseph), 'Zu Meyer-Lübke's Etymologischem Wörterbuch', *Zeitschrift für romanische Philologie*, XXXVIII, 1917, pp. 701–2.
Gᴀɴsʜᴏғ (F. L.), 'Depuis quand a-t-on pu en France être vassal de plusieurs seigneurs?', *Mélanges Paul Fournier*, 1929 (review by W. Kɪᴇɴᴀsᴛ, *Historische Zeitschrift*, CXLI, 1929–30).
Pɪʀᴇɴɴᴇ (Henri), 'Qu-est-ce qu'un homme lige?', *Académie royale de Belgique, Bulletin de la classe des lettres*, 1909.
Pᴏ̈ʜʟᴍᴀɴɴ (Carl), *Das ligische Lehensverhältnis*, Heidelberg, 1931.
Zᴇɢʟɪɴ (Dorothea), *Der 'homo ligius' und die französische Ministerialität*, Leipzig, 1917 (*Leipziger Historische Abhandlungen*, XXXIX).

VII. FEUDAL WARFARE

(1) THE ART OF WAR

Bᴀʟᴛᴢᴇʀ (Martin), *Zur Geschichte des deutschen Kriegswesens in der Zeit von den letzten Karolingern bis auf Kaiser Friedrich II*, Leipzig, 1877.
Bᴏᴜᴛᴀʀɪᴄ (Edgar), *Institutions militaires de la France*, 1863.
Dᴇʟʙʀᴜ̈ᴄᴋ (Hans), *Geschichte der Kriegskunst im Rahmen der politischen Geschichte*, III, Berlin, 1907.
Dᴇʟᴘᴇᴄʜ (H.), *La Tactique au XIIIᵉ siècle*, 2 vols., 1886.
Fʀᴀᴜᴇɴʜᴏʟᴢ (Eugen von), *Entwicklungsgeschichte des deutschen Heerwesens*, I, *Das Heerwesen der germanischen Frühzeit, des Frankenreiches und des ritterlichen Zeitalters*, Munich, 1935.
Kᴏ̈ʜʟᴇʀ (G.), *Entwicklung des Kriegswesens und der Kriegsführung in der Ritterzeit*, 3 vols., Breslau, 1886–93.
Oᴍᴀɴ (Charles), *A History of the Art of War: The Middle Ages from the Fourth to the Fourteenth Century*, 2nd edn., 1924.

(2) CAVALRY TACTICS AND EQUIPMENT

Bᴀᴄʜ (Volkmar), *Die Verteidigungswaffen in den altfranzösischen Artus- und Abenteuerroman*, Marburg, 1887 (*Ausgabe und Abhandlungen aus dem Gebiete der roman. Philologie*, 70).
Bʀᴜɴɴᴇʀ (Heinrich), 'Der Reiterdienst und die Anfänge des Lehnwesens', *Forschungen zum d. und fr. Recht*, Stuttgart, 1874 (previously *Zeitschrift der Savigny Stiftung*, G.A., VIII).
Dᴇᴍᴀʏ (G.), *Le Costume au moyen âge d'après les sceaux*, 1880.
Gᴇssʟᴇʀ (E. A.), *Die Trutzwaffen der Karolingerzeit vom VIII. bis zum XI. Jahrhundert*, Basel, 1908.
Gɪᴇssᴇ (W.), 'Waffen nach den provenzialischen Epen und Chroniken des XII. und XIII. Jahrhunderts', *Zeitschrift für romanische Philologie*, LII, 1932.
Lᴇғᴇʙᴠʀᴇ ᴅᴇs Nᴏᴇ̈ᴛᴛᴇs, *L'Attelage et le cheval de selle à travers les âges*, 2 vols., 1931 (cf. Marc Bloch, 'Les Inventions médiévales', *Annales d'histoire économique*, 1935).
Mᴀɴɢᴏʟᴅᴛ-Gᴀᴜᴅʟɪᴛᴢ (Hans von), *Die Reiterei in den germanischen und fränkischen Heeren bis zum Ausgang der deutschen Karolinger*, Berlin, 1922 (*Arbeiten zur deutschen Rechts- und Verfassungsgeschichte*, IV).
Rᴏʟᴏғғ (Gustav), 'Die Umwandlung des fränkischen Heeres von Chlodwig bis Karl den Grossen', *Neue Jahrbücher für das klassische Altertum*, IX, 1902.

BIBLIOGRAPHY

SANCHEZ-ALBORNOZ (C.), 'Los Arabes y los origines del feudalismo', *Anuario de historia del derecho español*, 1929; 'Les Arabes et les origines de la féodalité', *Revue historique de droit*, 1933.

—— 'La caballeria visigoda' in *Wirtschaft und Kultur: Festschrift zum 70. Geburtstag von A. Dopsch*, Vienna, 1938.

SCHIRLING (V.), *Die Verteidigungswaffen im altfranzösischen Epos*, Marburg, 1887 (*Ausgabe und Abhandlungen aus dem Gebiete der roman. Philologie*, 69).

SCHWIETERING (Julius), 'Zur Geschichte vom Speer und Schwert im 12. Jahrhundert', *Mitteilungen aus dem Museum für Hamburgische Geschichte*, 3 (Suppl. 8, Part 2, of *Jahrbuch der Hamburgischen wissenschaftlichen Anstalten*, XXIX, 1911).

STERNBERG (A.), *Die Angriffswaffen im altfranzösischen Epos*, Marburg, 1886 (*Ausgabe und Abhandlungen aus dem Gebiete der roman. Philologie*, 48).

(3) THE MILITARY OBLIGATION

FEHR (Hans), 'Landfolge und Gerichtsfolge im fränkischen Recht', *Festgabe für R. Sohm*, Munich, 1914.

NOYES (A. G.), *The Military Obligation in Mediaeval England*, Columbus (Ohio), 1931.

ROSENHAGEN (Gustav), *Zur Geschichte der Reichsheerfahrt von Heinrich VI. bis Rudolf von Habsburg*, Meissen, 1885.

SCHMITTHENNER (Paul), 'Lehnkriegswesen und Söldnertum im abendländischen Imperium des Mittelalters', *Historische Zeitschrift*, 1934.

WEILAND (L.), 'Die Reichsheerfahrt von Heinrich V. bis Heinrich VI., nach ihrer staatsrechtlichen Seite', *Forschungen zur deutschen Geschichte*, VII, 1867.

(4) CASTLES

ARMITAGE (E. S.), *Early Norman Castles of the British Isles*, 1913 (cf. Round, *English Historical Review*, 1912, p. 544).

COULIN (Alexander), *Befestigungshoheit und Befestigungsrecht*, Leipzig, 1911.

DESMAREZ (G.), 'Fortifications de la frontière du Hainaut et du Brabant au XIIᵉ siècle', *Annales de la Société royale d'archéologie de Bruxelles*, 1914.

ENLART (C.), *Manuel d'archéologie française, Deuxième partie. II. Architecture militaire et navale*, 1932.

PAINTER (Sidney), 'English Castles in the Middle Ages', *Speculum*, 1935.

ROUND (J. H.), 'Castle-guard', *Archaeological Journal*, LIX, 1902.

SCHRADER (Erich), *Das Befestigungsrecht in Deutschland*, Göttingen, 1909.

SCHUCHARDT (C.), *Die Burg im Wandel der Geschichte*, Potsdam, 1931.

THOMPSON (A. Hamilton), *Military Architecture in England During the Middle Ages*, Oxford, 1912.

VIII. TIES OF DEPENDENCE AMONG THE LOWER ORDERS OF SOCIETY

(Cf. Part VI, sec. 2, p. 464: SANCHEZ-ALBORNOZ, 'Las behetrias . . .')

BELOW (G. von), *Geschichte der deutschen Landwirtschaft des Mittelalters*, Jena, 1937.

BLOCH (Marc), *Les Caractères originaux de l'histoire rurale française*, 1931.

—— 'Les "Colliberti", étude sur la formation de la classe servile', *Revue historique*, CLVII, 1928.

—— 'De la cour royale à la cour de Rome: le procès des serfs de Rosny-sous-Bois', *Studi di storia e diritto in onore di E. Besta*, Milan, 1938.

—— 'Liberté et servitude personnelles au moyen âge', *Anuario de historia del derecho español*, 1933.

—— 'Les Transformations du servage', *Mélanges d'histoire du moyen âge offerts à M. F. Lot*, 1925.

BOEREN (P.-C.), *Étude sur les tributaires d'église dans le comté de Flandre du IXᵉ au XIVᵉ siècle*, Amsterdam, 1936 (*Uitgaven van het Instituut voor middeleuwsche Geschiedenis der . . . Universitet te Nijmegen*, 3).

BIBLIOGRAPHY

CATO (G.), *Beiträge zur älteren deutschen Wirtschafts- und Verfassungsgeschichte*, Leipzig, 1905.

—— *Neue Beiträge zur deutschen Wirtschafts- und Verfassungsgeschichte*, Leipzig, 1911.

COULTON (G. G.), *The Medieval Village*, Cambridge, 1925.

HINOJOSA (E. de), *El regimen señorial y la cuestion agraria en Cataluña*, Madrid, 1905.

KELLER (Robert von), *Freiheitsgarantien für Person und Eigentum im Mittelalter*, Heidelberg, 1933 (*Deutschrechtliche Beiträge*, XIV, 1).

KIELMEYER (O. A.), *Die Dorfbefreiung auf deutschem Sprachgebiet*, Bonn, 1931.

LUZZATO (G.), *I servi nelle grande proprietà ecclesiastiche italiane nei secoli IX e X*, Pisa, 1910.

MINNIGERODE (H. von), 'Wachzinsrecht', *Vierteljahrschrift für Sozial- und Wirtschaftsgeschichte*, 1916.

PERRIN (C.-Edmond), *Essai sur la fortune immobilière de l'abbaye alsacienne de Marmoutier*, Strasbourg, 1935.

—— *Recherches sur la seigneurie rurale en Lorraine d'après les plus anciens censiers*, Strasbourg, 1935.

PETIT (A.), *Coliberti ou culverts: essai d'interprétation des textes qui les concernent, IXᵉ–XIIᵉ siècles*), Limoges, 1926.

—— *Coliberti ou culverts: réponse à diverses objections*, Limoges, 1930.

PETOT (P.), 'L'Hommage servile', *Revue historique de droit*, 1927 (cf. the same writer's contribution to Société Jean Bodin, *Le Servage*, see below).

—— 'La Commendise personnelle', *Mélanges Paul Fournier*, 1929 (cf. Marc Bloch, *Annales d'histoire économique*, 1931, pp. 234 ff.).

PIRENNE (Henri), 'Liberté et propriété en Flandre du VIIᵉ au IXᵉ siècle', *Bulletin Académie royale de Belgique, Cl. Lettres*, 1911.

PUIGARNAU (Jaime M. Mans), *Las clases serviles bajo la monarquia visigoda y en los estados cristianos de la reconquista española*, Barcelona, 1928.

SÉE (Henri), *Les Classes rurales et le régime domanial en France au moyen-âge*, 1901.

SEELIGER (G.), 'Die soziale und politische Bedeutung der Grundherrschaft im früheren Mittelalter', *Abhandlungen der sächsischen Gesellschaft der Wissenschaften*, XX, 1903.

SOCIÉTÉ JEAN BODIN, *Le Servage*, Brussels, 1937 (and *Revue de l'Institut de Sociologie*, 1937).

—— *La Tenure*, Brussels, 1938.

THIBAULT (Fabien), 'La Condition des personnes en France du IXᵉ siècle au mouvement communal', *Revue historique de droit*, 1933.

VACCARI (P.), 'L'affrancazione dei servi della gleba nell' Emilia e nella Toscana', Bologna, 1925 (*Reale Accademia dei Lincei. Commissione per gli atti delle assemblee costituzionali*).

VANDERKINDERE, 'Liberté et propriété en Flandre du IXᵉ au XIIᵉ siècle', *Bulletin Académie royale de Belgique, Cl. Lettres*, 1906.

VERRIEST (L.), 'Le Servage dans le comté de Hainaut', *Académie royale de Belgique, Cl. Lettres*, Mémoires in-8°, 2nd series, VI, 1910.

VINOGRADOFF (P.), *Villeinage in England*, Oxford, 1892.

WELLER (K.), 'Die freien Bauern in Schwaben', *Zeitschrift der Savigny Stiftung, G.A.*, 1934.

—— 'Die Frage der Freibauern', *ibid.*

IX. COUNTRIES WITHOUT FEUDALISM

(1) SARDINIA

BESTA (E.), *La Sardegna medioevale*, 2 vols., Palermo, 1909.

RASPI (R. C.), *Le classi sociali nella Sardegna medioevale*, Cagliari, 1938.

SOLMI (A.), *Studi storici sulle istituzione della Sardegna nel medio evo*, Cagliari, 1917.

(2) FRISIA AND DITHMARSCHEN

GOSSE (J. H.), 'De Friesche Hoofdeling', *Mededeelingen der Kl. Akademie van Wetenschappen, Afd. Letterk.*, 1933.

BIBLIOGRAPHY

Köhler (Johannes), *Die Struktur der Dithmarscher Geschlechter*, Heide, 1915.

Marten (G.) and Mäckelmann (K.), *Dithmarschen*, Heide, 1927.

Siebs (B. E.), *Grundlagen und Aufbau der altfriesischen Verfassung*, Breslau, 1933 (*Untersuchungen zur deutschen Staats- und Rechtsgeschichte*, 144).

X. SOCIAL CLASSES IN GENERAL AND THE NOBILITY

(1) ORIGINS AND HISTORY

Bloch (Marc), 'Sur le passé de la noblesse française; quelques jalons de recherche', *Annales d'histoire économique et sociale*, 1936.

Denholm-Young (N.), 'En remontant le passé de l'aristocratie anglaise: le moyen-âge', *ibid.*, 1937.

Desbrousses (X.), *Condition personnelle de la noblesse au moyen-âge*, Bordeaux, 1901.

Du Cange, 'Des chevaliers bannerets. Des gentilshommes de nom et d'armes' (*Dissertations sur l'histoire de saint Louis*, IX and X), in *Glossarium*, ed. Henschel, vol. VII.

Dungern (O. von), 'Comes, liber, nobilis in Urkunden des 11. bis 13. Jahrhundert', *Archiv für Urkundenforschung*, 1932.

—— *Der Herrenstand im Mittelalter*, I. Papiermühle, 1908.

—— *Die Entstehung der Landeshoheit in Österreich*, Vienna, 1930.

Ernst (Viktor), *Die Entstehung des niederen Adels*, Stuttgart, 1916.

—— *Mittelfreie, ein Beitrag zur schwäbischen Standesgeschichte*, 1920.

Fehr (Hans), 'Das Waffenrecht der Bauern im Mittelalter', *Zeitschrift der Savigny Stiftung*, G.A., 1914 and 1917.

Ficker (Julius), *Vom Heerschilde*, Innsbruck, 1862.

Forst-Battaglia (O.), *Vom Herrenstande*, Leipzig, 1916.

Frensdorff (F.), 'Die Lehnsfähigkeit der Bürger', *Nachrichten der königlichen Gesellschaft der Wissenschaften zu Göttingen*, Phil-hist. K., 1894.

García Rives (A.), 'Clases sociales en León y Castilla (Siglos X–XIII)', *Revista de Archivos*, XLI and XLII, 1921 and 1922.

Guilhiermoz (P.), *Essai sur les origines de la noblesse en France au moyen-âge*, 1902.

Heck (Philipp), *Beiträge zur Geschichte der Stände im Mittelalter*, 2 vols., Halle, 1900–5.

—— *Die Standesgliederung der Sachsen im frühen Mittelalter*, Tubingen, 1927.

—— *Übersetzungsprobleme im früheren Mittelalter*, Tübingen, 1931.

Langlois (Charles V.), 'Les Origines de la noblesse en France', *Revue de Paris*, 1904, V (in relation to Guilhiermoz, *Essai . . . , q.v. supra*).

La Roque (de), *Traité de la noblesse*, 1761.

Lintzel (M.), 'Die ständischen Ehehindernisse in Sachsen', *Zeitschrift der Savigny-Stiftung*, G.A., 1932.

Marsay (de), *De l'âge des privilèges au temps des vanités*, 1934, and *Supplement*, 1933.

Minnigerode (H. von), *Ebenburt und Echtheit. Untersuchungen zur Lehre von der adeligen Heiratsebenburt vor dem 13. Jahrhundert*, Heidelberg, 1932 (*Deutschrechtliche Beiträge*, VIII, 1).

Neckel (Gustav), 'Adel und Gefolgschaft', *Beiträge zur Geschichte der deutschen Sprache*, XLVI, 1916.

Neufbourg (de), 'Les Origines de la noblesse', in de Marsay, *Supplement (q.v. supra)*.

Otto (Eberhard F.), *Adel und Freiheit im deutschen Staat des frühen Mittelalters*, Berlin, 1937.

Plotho (V.), 'Die Stände des deutschen Reiches im 12. Jahrhundert und ihre Fortentwicklung', *Vierteljahrschrift für Wappen- Siegel- und Familienkunde*, XLV, 1917.

Reid (R. R.), 'Barony and Thanage', *English Historical Review*, XXXV, 1920.

Round (J. H.), ' "Barons" and "Knights" in the Great Charter', in *Magna Carta: Commemoration Essays*, 1917.

—— 'Barons and Peers', *English Historical Review*, 1918.

Santifaller (Leo), 'Über die Nobiles', in Santifaller, *Das Brixner Domkapitel in seiner persönlichen Zusammensetzung*, I, pp. 59–64, Innsbruck, 1924 (*Schleiern-Schriften*, 7).

Schnettler (Otto), *Westfalens Adel und seine Führerrolle in der Geschichte*, Dortmund, 1926.

BIBLIOGRAPHY

SCHNETTLER (Otto), *Westfalens alter Adel*, Dortmund, 1928.

SCHULTE (Aloys), *Der Adel und die deutsche Kirche im Mittelalter*, 2nd edn., Stuttgart.

VOGT (Friedrich), *Der Bedeutungswandel des Wortes edel*, Marburg, 1909 (*Marburger Akademische Reden*, 20).

WERMINGHOFF (Albert), 'Ständische Probleme in der Geschichte der deutschen Kirche des Mittelalters', *Zeitschrift der Savigny Stiftung, K.A.*, 1911.

WESTERBLAD (C. A.), *Baro et ses dérivés dans les langues romanes*, Upsala, 1910.

(2) DUBBING TO KNIGHTHOOD: THE LITURGIES

ANDRIEU (Michel), *Les Ordines Romani du haut moyen âge: I. Les manuscrits*, Louvain, 1931 (*Spicilegium sacrum lovaniense*, 11).

Benedictio ensis noviter succincti. Pontifical of Mainz: Ms. and ed. cf. ANDRIEU (*Les Ordines . . .*, *supra*), p. 178, and index, *s.v.* 'ensis'; facsimile, MONACI, *Archivio paleografico*, II, n. 73.

Blessing of the sword: Besançon Pontifical, cf. ANDRIEU, p. 445. Ed. MARTÈNE, *De antiquis ecclesiae ritibus*, II, 1788, p. 239; FRANZ, II, p. 294.

FRANZ (A.), *Die kirchlichen Benediktionen des Mittelalters*, 2 vols. Freiburg im Breisgau, 1909.

Liturgy for the dubbing: Reims Pontifical, cf. ANDRIEU, p. 112. Ed. HITTORP, *De divinis catholicae ecclesiae officiis*, 1719, col. 178; FRANZ, II, p. 295.

Liturgy for the dubbing: Pontifical of Gulielmus Durandus, ed. J. CATALANI, *Pontificale romanum*, I, 1738, p. 424.

Liturgy for the dubbing: *Pontificale romanum*, ed. by (among others) CATALANI, I, p. 419.

(3) MEDIEVAL TREATISES ON CHIVALRY

BONIZO, *Liber de vita christiana*, ed. PERELS, 1930 (*Texte zur Geschichte des römischen und kanonischen Rechts*, I), VII, 28.

CHRÉTIEN DE TROYES, *Perceval le Gallois*, ed. POTVIN, vol. II, vv. 2831 ff.

DER MEISSNER, 'Swer ritters name wil empfan . . .', in F. H. VON DER HAGEN, *Minnesinger*, III, p. 107, no. 10.

Lancelot, in H. O. SOMMER, *The Vulgate Version of the Arthurian Romances*, III, 1, pp. 113–15.

L'Ordene de Chevalerie in BARBAZAN, *Fabliaux*, 2nd edn. by MÉON, I, 1808, pp. 59–79.

NAVONE (G.), *Le rime di Folgore da San Gemignano*, Bologna, 1880, pp. 45–9 (*Scelta di curiosità letterarie*, CLXXII).

RAIMON LULL, *Libro de la orden de Caballería*, ed. by J. R. DE LUANCO, Barcelona, R. Academia de Buenos Letras, 1901. English trans., *The Book of the Ordre of Chivalry, translated and printed by W. Caxton*, ed. BYLE;, 1926 (*Early English Text Society*, CLXVIII).

(4) MODERN WORKS ON CHIVALRY AND KNIGHTHOOD

BARTHÉLEMY (Anatole de), 'De la qualification de chevalier', *Revue nobiliaire*, 1868.

ERBEN (Wilhelm), 'Schwertleite und Ritterschlag: Beiträge zu einer Rechtsgeschichte der Waffen', *Zeitschrift für historische Waffenkunde*, VIII, 1918–20.

GAUTIER (Léon), *La Chevalerie*, 3rd edn., s.d.

MASSMANN (Ernst Heinrich), *Schwertleite und Ritterschlag, dargestellt auf Grund der mittelhochdeutschen literarischen Quellen*, Hamburg, 1932.

PIVANO (Silvio), 'Lineamenti storici e giuridici della cavalleria medioevale', *Memorie della reale Accademia delle scienze di Torino*, Series II, LV, 1905, *Scienze Morali*.

PRESTAGE (Edgar) (ed.), *Chivalry: A Series of Studies to Illustrate its Historical Significance and Civilizing Influence*, London, 1928.

ROTH VON SCHRECKENSTEIN (K. H.), *Die Ritterwürde und der Ritterstand. Historisch-politische Studien über deutsch-mittelalterliche Standesverhältnisse auf dem Lande und in der Stadt*, Freiburg im Breisgau, 1886.

SALVEMINI (Gaetano), *La dignità cavalleresca nel Comune di Firenze*, Florence, 1896.

TREIS (K.), *Die Formalitäten des Ritterschlags in der altfranzösischen Epik*, Berlin, 1887.

BIBLIOGRAPHY

(5) ENNOBLEMENT

ARBAUMONT (J.), 'Des anoblissements en Bourgogne', *Revue nobiliaire*, 1866.
BARTHÉLEMY (Anatole de) 'Étude sur les lettres d'anoblissement', *Revue nobiliaire*, 1869.
KLÜBER (J. L.), 'De nobilitate codicillari', in KLUBER, *Kleine juristische Bibliothek*, VII, Erlangen, 1793.
THOMAS (Paul), 'Comment Guy de Dampierre, comte de Flandre, anoblissait les roturiers', *Commission historique du Nord*, 1933; cf. P. THOMAS, *Textes historiques sur Lille et le Nord*, II, 1936, p. 229.

(6) LIFE OF THE NOBLES

APPEL (Carl), *Bertran von Born*, Halle, 1931.
BORMANN (Ernst), *Die Jagd in den altfranzösischen Artus- und Abenteuerroman*, Marburg, 1887 (*Ausgabe und Abhandlungen aus dem Gebiete der roman. Philologie*, 68).
DU CANGE, 'De l'origine et de l'usage des tournois. Des armes à outrance, des joustes, de la Table Ronde, des behourds et de la quintaine' (*Dissertations sur l'histoire de Saint Louis*, VI and VII), in *Glossarium*, ed. HENSCHEL, VII.
DUPIN (Henri), *La Courtoisie au moyen âge (d'après les textes du XII⁰ et XIII⁰ siècle)*, [1931].
EHRISMANN (G.), 'Die Grundlagen des ritterlichen Tugendsystems', *Zeitschrift für deutsches Altertum*, LVI, 1919.
ERDMANN (Carl), *Die Entstehung des Kreuzzugsgedankens*, Stuttgart, 1935 (*Forschungen zur Kirchen- und Geistesgeschichte*, VI).
GEORGE (Robert H.), 'The Contribution of Flanders to the Conquest of England', *Revue belge de philologie*, 1926.
GILSON (Étienne), 'L'Amour courtois', in GILSON, *La Théologie mystique de saint Bernard*, 1934, pp. 192–215.
JANIN (R.), 'Les "Francs" au service des Byzantins', *Échos d'Orient*, XXXIX, 1930.
JEANROY (Alfred), *La Poésie lyrique des troubadours*, 2 vols., 1934.
LANGLOIS (Charles-V.), 'Un Mémoire inédit de Pierre du Bois, 1313; De torneamentis et justis', *Revue historique*, XLI, 1889.
NAUMANN (Hans), 'Ritterliche Standeskultur um 1200' in NAUMANN (H.) and MÜLLER (Gunther), *Höfische Kultur*, Halle, 1929 (*Deutsche Vierteljahrschrift für Literaturwissenschaft und Geistesgeschichte*, Buchreihe, XVII).
—— *Der staufische Ritter*, Leipzig, 1936.
NIEDNER (Felix), *Das deutsche Turnier im XII. und XIII. Jahrhundert*, Berlin, 1881.
PAINTER (Sidney), *William Marshal, Knight-Errant, Baron and Regent of England*, Baltimore, 1933 (*Johns Hopkins Historical Publications*).
RUST (Ernst), *Die Erziehung des Ritters in der altfranzösischen Epik*, Berlin, 1888.
SCHRADER (Werner), *Studien über das Wort "höfisch" in der mittelhochdeutschen Dichtung*, Bonn, 1935.
SCHULTE (Aloys), 'Die Standesverhältnisse der Minnesänger', *Zeitschrift für deutsches Altertum*, XXXIX, 1895.
SCHULTZ (Alwin), *Das höfische Leben zur Zeit der Minnesinger*, 2nd edn., 2 vols., 1889.
SEILER (Friedrich), *Die Entwicklung der deutschen Kultur im Spiegel des deutschen Lehnworts*, II. *Von der Einführung des Christentums bis zum Beginn der neueren Zeit*, 2nd edn., Halle, 1907.
WHITNEY (Maria P.), 'Queen of Mediaeval Virtues: Largesse' in FISKE, C. F. (ed.), *Vassar Mediaeval Studies*, New Haven, 1923.

(7) HERALDRY

BARTHÉLEMY (A. de), 'Essai sur l'origine des armoiries féodales', *Mémoires de la Société des antiquaires de l'Ouest*, XXXV, 1870–1.
ILGEN (T.), 'Zur Entstehung und Entwicklungsgeschichte der Wappen', *Korrespondenzblatt des Gesamtvereins der deutschen Geschichts- und Altertumsvereine*, LXIX, 1921.
ULMENSTEIN (C. U. VON), *Über Ursprung und Entstehung des Wappenwesens*, Weimar, 1935 (*Forschungen zum deutschen Recht*, I, 2).

BIBLIOGRAPHY

(8) SERJEANTS AND SERJEANTIES

(For the German and French literature on this subject earlier than 1925, see the work of Ganshof listed below)

BLOCH (Marc), 'Un Problème d'histoire comparée: la ministérialité en France et en Allemagne', *Revue historique de droit*, 1928.

BLUM (E.), 'De la patrimonialité des sergenteries fieffées dans l'ancienne Normandie', *Revue générale de droit*, 1926.

GANSHOF (F. L.), 'Étude sur les ministeriales en Flandre et en Lotharingie', *Mémoires Acad. royale Belgique, Cl. Lettres*, in-8°, 2nd series, XX, 1926.

GLADISS (D. VON), *Beiträge zur Geschichte der staufischen Ministerialität*, Berlin, 1934 (*Ebering's Histor. Studien*, 249).

HAENDLE (Otto), *Die Dienstmannen Heinrichs des Löwen*, Stuttgart, 1930 (*Arbeiten zur deutschen Rechts- und Verfassungsgeschichte*, 8).

KIMBALL (E. G.), *Serjeanty Tenure in Mediaeval England*, New York, 1936 (*Yale Historical Publications, Miscellany*, XXX).

LE FOYER (Jean), *L'Office héréditaire de Focarius regis Angliae*, 1931 (*Bibliothèque d'histoire du droit normand*, 2nd series, 4).

STENGEL (Edmund E.), 'Über den Ursprung der Ministerialität', in *Papsttum und Kaisertum: Forschungen P. Kehr dargebracht*, Munich, 1925.

XI. THE CHURCH IN THE FEUDAL WORLD: THE 'ADVOCATESHIP'

It has not been considered necessary to include in the following list either general histories of the Church or works dealing with the various problems of ecclesiastical history proper. But the reader may be reminded of the value to the student of feudal society of A. HAUCK's great work (*Kirchengeschichte Deutschlands*, 5 vols., Leipzig, 1914–20) and the fine book of P. FOURNIER and G. LE BRAS (*Histoire des collections canoniques en Occident depuis les Fausses Decrétales jusqu'au Décret de Gratien*, 2 vols., 1931–2).

As many works—particularly German works—do not distinguish clearly between the closely related problems of the 'advocateship' and of judicial institutions in general, the bibliography in Section XII below should also be consulted.

GÉNESTAL (R.), 'La Patrimonialité de l'archidiaconat dans la province ecclésiastique de Rouen', *Mélanges Paul Fournier*, 1929.

LAPRAT (R.), 'Avoué', in *Dictionnaire d'histoire et de géographie ecclésiastique*, V, 1931.

LESNE (E.), *Histoire de la propriété ecclésiastique en France*, 4 vols., Lille, 1910–38.

MERK (C. J.), *Anschauungen über die Lehre und das Leben der Kirche im altfranzösischen Heldenepos*, Halle, 1914 (*Zeitschrift für romanische Philologie*, Beiheft 41).

OTTO (Eberhard F.), *Die Entwicklung der deutschen Kirchenvogtei im 10. Jahrhundert*, Berlin, 1933 (*Abhandlungen zur mittleren und neueren Geschichte*, 72).

PERGAMENI (C.), *L'Avouerie ecclésiastique belge*, Gand, 1907. Cf. BONENFANT (P.), 'Notice sur le faux diplome d'Otton Ier' in *Bulletin–Commission royale histoire*, 1936.

SENN (Félix), *L'Institution des avoueries ecclésiastiques en France*, 1903. Cf. review by W. SICKEL, *Göttingsche Gelehrte Anzeigen*, CLVI, 1904.

—— *L'Institution des vidamies en France*, 1907.

WAAS (A.), *Vogtei und Bede in der deutschen Kaiserzeit*, 2 vols., Berlin, 1919–23.

XII. JUDICIAL INSTITUTIONS

AULT (W. O.), *Private Jurisdiction in England*, New Haven, 1923 (*Yale Historical Publications, Miscellany*, X).

BEAUDOIN (A.), 'Étude sur les origines du régime féodal: la recommandation et la justice seigneuriale', *Annales de l'enseignement supérieur de Grenoble*, I, 1889.

BEAUTEMPS-BEAUPRÉ, *Recherches sur les juridictions de l'Anjou et du Maine*, 1890.

CAM (Helen M.), 'Suitors and Scabini', *Speculum*, 1935.

BIBLIOGRAPHY

CHAMPEAUX (Ernest), 'Nouvelles théories sur les justices du moyen âge', *Revue historique de droit*, 1935, pp. 101–11.

ESMEIN (A.), 'Quelques renseignements sur l'origine des juridictions privées', *Mélanges d'archéologie et d'histoire*, 1886.

FERRAND (N.), 'Origines des justices féodales', *Le Moyen Âge*, 1921.

FRÉVILLE (R. DE), 'L'Organisation judiciaire en Normandie aux XIIᵉ et XIIIᵉ siècles', *Nouvelle revue historique de droit*, 1912.

GANSHOF (François L.), 'Notes sur la compétence des cours féodales en France', *Mélanges d'histoire offerts à Henri Pirenne*, 1926.

—— 'Contribution à l'étude des origines des cours féodales en France', *Revue historique de droit*, 1928.

—— 'La Juridiction du seigneur sur son vassal à l'époque carolingienne', *Revue de l'Université de Bruxelles*, XXVIII, 1921–2.

—— 'Recherches sur les tribunaux de châtellenie en Flandre, avant le milieu du XIIIᵉ siècle', 1932 (*Universiteit de Gent, Werken uitgg. door de Faculteit der Wijsbegeerte en Letteren*, 68).

—— 'Die Rechtssprechung des gräflichen Hofgerichtes in Flandern', *Zeitschrift der Savigny Stiftung, G.A.*, 1938.

GARAUD (Marcel), *Essai sur les institutions judiciaires du Poitou sous le gouvernement des comtes indépendants: 902–1137*, Poitiers, 1910.

GARCIA DE DIEGO (Vicenze), 'Historia judicial de Aragon en los siglos VIII al XII', *Anuario de historia del derecho español*, XI, 1934.

GLITSCH (Heinrich), 'Der alemannische Zentenar und sein Gericht', *Berichte über die Verhandlungen der k. sächsischen Gesellschaft der Wissenschaften, Phil.-histor. Kl.*, LXIX, 1917.

—— *Untersuchungen zur Mittelalterlichen Vogtgerichtsbarkeit*, Bonn, 1912.

HALPHEN (L.), 'Les Institutions judiciaires en France au XIᵉ siècle: région angevine', *Revue historique*, LXXVII, 1901.

—— 'Prévots et voyers au XIᵉ siècle: région angevine', *Le Moyen Âge*, 1902.

HIRSCH (Hans), *Die hohe Gerichtsbarkeit im deutschen Mittelalter*, Prag, 1922.

—— *Die Klosterimmunität seit dem Investiturstreit*, Weimar, 1913.

KROELL (Maurice), *L'Immunité franque*, 1910.

LOT (Ferdinand), 'La "Vicaria" et le "vicarius" ', *Nouvelle revue historique de droit*, 1893

MASSIET DU BIEST (J.), 'A propos des plaids généraux', *Revue du Nord*, 1923.

MORRIS (W. A.), *The Frankpledge System*, New Haven, 1910 (*Harvard Historical Studies*, XIV).

PERRIN (Charles-Edmond), 'Sur le sens du mot "centena" dans les chartes lorraines du moyen âge', *Bulletin du Cange*, V, 1929–30.

SALVIOLI (Giuseppe), 'L'immunità e le giustizie delle chiese in Italia', *Atti e memorie delle R. R. Deputazioni di Storia Patria per le provincie Modenesi e Parmensi*, Series III, V and VI, 1888–90.

—— *Storia della procedura civile e criminale*, Milan, 1925 (*Storia del diritto italiano pubblicata sotto la direzione di Pasquale del Giudice*, III, Part I).

STENGEL (Edmund E.), *Die Immunität in Deutschland bis zum Ende des 11. Jahrhunderts*, I, *Diplomatik der deutschen Immunitäts-Privilegien*, Innsbruck, 1910.

THIRION (Paul), 'Les Échevinages ruraux aux XIIᵉ et XIIIᵉ siècles dans les possessions des églises de Reims', *Études d'histoire du moyen âge dédiées à G. Monod*, 1896.

XIII. THE PEACE MOVEMENTS

ERDMANN (C.), *Zur Überlieferung der Gottesfrieden-Konzilien*, in ERDMANN, *Die Entstehung* . . . (see part VIII, sect. 6 above).

GÖRRIS (G. C. W.), *De denkbeelden over oorlog en de bemoeeiingen voor vrede in de elfde eeuw* (Ideas on War and Efforts for Peace in the Eleventh Century), Nijmegen, 1912 (Leiden dissertation).

HERTZBERG-FRANKEL (S.), 'Die ältesten Land- und Gottesfrieden in Deutschland', *Forschungen zur deutschen Geschichte*, XXIII, 1883.

BIBLIOGRAPHY

HUBERTI (Ludwig), *Studien zur Rechtsgeschichte der Gottesfrieden und Landesfrieden:* I, *Die Friedensordnungen in Frankreich*, Ansbach, 1892.

KLUCKHOHN (A.), *Geschichte des Gottesfriedens*, Leipzig, 1857.

MANTEYER (G. DE), 'Les Origines de la maison de Savoie . . . La paix en Viennois (Anse, 17? juin 1025)', *Bulletin de la Société de statistique de l'Isère*, 4th series, VII, 1904.

MOLINIÉ (Georges), *L'Organisation judiciaire, militaire et financière des associations de la paix: étude sur la Paix et la Trêve de Dieu dans le Midi et le Centre de la France*, Toulouse, 1912.

PRENTOUT (H.), 'La Trêve de Dieu en Normandie', *Mémoires de l'Académie de Caen*, New series, VI, 1931.

QUIDDE (L.), *Histoire de la paix publique en Allemagne au moyen âge*, 1929.

SCHNELBÖGL (Wolfgang), *Die innere Entwicklung des bayerischen Landfriedens des 13. Jahrhunderts*, Heidelberg, 1932 (*Deutschrechtliche Beiträge*, XIII, 2).

SÉMICHON (E.), *La Paix et la Trêve de Dieu*, 2nd edn., 2 vols., 1869.

WOHLHAUPTER (Eugen), *Studien zur Rechtsgeschichte der Gottes- und Landfrieden in Spanien*, Heidelberg, 1933 (*Deutschrechtliche Beiträge*, XIV, 2).

YVER (J.), *L'Interdiction de la guerre privée dans le très ancien droit normand* (*Extrait des travaux de la semaine d'histoire du droit normand* . . . May, 1927), 1928.

XIV. THE INSTITUTION OF MONARCHY

BECKER (Franz), *Das Königtum des Nachfolgers im deutschen Reich des Mittelalters*, 1913 (*Quellen und Studien zur Verfassung des deutschen Reiches*, V, 3).

BLOCH (Marc), 'L'Empire et l'idée de l'Empire sous les Hohenstaufen', *Revue des Cours et Conférences*, XXX, 2, 1928–9.

—— *Les Rois thaumaturges: étude sur le caractère surnaturel attribué à la puissance royale, particulièrement en France et en Angleterre*, Strasbourg, 1924 (*Bibliothèque de la Faculté des Lettres de l'Université de Strasbourg*, XIX).

EULER (A.), *Das Königtum im altfranzösischen Karls-Epos*, Marburg, 1886 (*Ausgaben und Abhandlungen aus dem Gebiete der roman. Philologie*, 65).

KAMPERS (F.), 'Rex und sacerdos', *Historisches Jahrbuch*, 1925.

—— *Vom Werdegang der abendländischen Kaisermystik*, Leipzig, 1924.

HALPHEN (Louis), 'La Place de la royauté dans le système féodal', *Revue historique*, CLXXII, 1933.

KERN (Fritz), *Gottesgnadentum und Widerstandsrecht im früheren Mittelalter*, Leipzig, 1914.

MITTEIS (Heinrich), *Die deutsche Königswahl: ihre Rechtsgrundlagen bis zur Goldenen Bulle*, Baden bei Wien, [1938].

NAUMANN (Hans), 'Die magische Seite des altgermanischen Königtums und ihr Fort-wirken', *Wirtschaft und Kultur. Festschrift zum 70. Geburtstag von A. Dopsch*, Vienna, 1938.

PERELS (Ernst), *Der Erbreichsplan Heinrichs VI.*, Berlin, 1927.

ROSENSTOCK (Eugen), *Königshaus und Stämme in Deutschland zwischen 911 und 950*, Leipzig, 1914.

SCHRAMM (Percy E.), *Die deutschen Kaiser und Könige in Bildern ihrer Zeit*, I, *751–1152*, 2 vols., Leipzig, 1928 (*Veröffentlichungen der Forschungsinstitute an der Universität Leipzig, Institut für Kultur- und Universalgeschichte*, I).

—— *Geschichte des englischen Königtums im Lichte der Krönung*, Weimar, 1937 (English trans.: *A History of the English Coronation* (with general bibliography relating to the royal consecration, in Europe).

—— *Kaiser, Rom, und Renovatio*, 2 vols., Leipzig, 1929 (*Studien der Bibliothek Warburg*, XVII).

SCHULTE (Aloys), 'Anläufe zu einer festen Residenz der deutschen Könige im Mittel-alter', *Historisches Jahrbuch*, 1935.

SCHULTZE (Albert), *Kaiserpolitik und Einheitsgedanken in den Karolingischen Nach-folgestaaten (876–962)*, Berlin, 1926.

VIOLLET (Paul), 'La Question de la legitimité à l'avènement de Hugues Capet', *Mémoires de l'Académie des Inscriptions*, XXXIV, 1, 1892.

BIBLIOGRAPHY

XV. THE TERRITORIAL POWERS

ARBOIS DE JUBAINVILLE (D'), *Histoire des ducs et comtes de Champagne*, 7 vols., 1859–66.

AUZIAS (Léonce), *L'Aquitaine carolingienne (778–897)*, 1937.

BARTHÉLEMY (Anatole de), 'Les Origines de la maison de France', *Revue des questions historiques*, XIII, 1873.

BOUSSARD (J.), *Le Comté d'Anjou sous Henri Plantagenet et ses fils (1151–1204)*, 1938 (*Bibliothèque de l'École des Hautes Études, Sc. Histor.*, 271).

CHARTROU (Josèphe), *L'Anjou de 1109 à 1151*, 1928.

CHAUME (M.), *Les Origines du duché de Bourgogne*, 2 vols., Dijon, 1925–31.

FAZY (M.), *Les Origines du Bourbonnais*, 2 vols., Moulins, 1924.

FICKER (J.) and PUNTSCHART (P.), *Vom Reichsfürstenstande*, 4 vols., Innsbruck, Graz and Leipzig, 1861–1923.

GRIMALDI (Natale), *La contessa Matilde e la sua stirpe feudale*, Florence, [1928].

GROSDIDIER DE MATONS (M.), *Le Comté de Bar des origines au traité de Bruges (vers 750–1031)*, Bar-le-Duc, 1922.

HALBEDEL (A.), *Die Pfalzgrafen und ihr Amt: ein Überblick*. in HALBEDEL, *Fränkische Studien*, Berlin, 1915 (*Ebering's Historische Studien*, 132).

HALPHEN (Louis), *Le Comté d'Anjou au XIᵉ siècle*, 1906.

HOFMEISTER (Adolf), 'Markgrafen und Markgrafschaften im italienischen Königreich in der Zeit von Karl dem Grossen bis auf Otto den Grossen (774–962)', *Mitteilungen des Instituts für österreichische Geschichtsforschung*, VII. Ergänzungsband, 1906.

JAURGAIN (J. de), *La Vasconie*, 2 vols., Pau, 1898.

JEULIN (Paul), 'L'Hommage de la Bretagne en droit et dans les faits', *Annales de Bretagne*, 1934.

KIENER (Fritz), *Verfassungsgeschichte der Provence seit der Ostgothenherrschaft bis zur Errichtung der Konsulate (510–1200)*, Leipzig, 1900.

LA BORDERIE (A. le Moyne de), *Histoire de Bretagne*, vols. II and III, 1898–9.

LAPSLEY (G. T.), *The County Palatine of Durham*, Cambridge (Mass.), 1924 (*Harvard Historical Studies*, VIII).

LATOUCHE (Robert), *Histoire du comté de Maine*, 1910 (*Bibliothèque de l'École des Hautes Études, Sc. histor.*, 183).

LÄWEN (Gerhard), *Stammesherzog und Stammesherzogtum*, Berlin, 1935.

Les Bouches du Rhône, Encyclopédie départementale, part I, vol. II. *Antiquité et moyen âge*, 1924.

LEX (Léonce), *Eudes, comte de Blois . . . (995–1007) et Thibaud, son frère (995–1004)*, Troyes, 1892.

LINTZEL (Martin), 'Der Ursprung der deutschen Pfalzgrafschaften', *Zeitschrift der Savigny Stiftung, G.A.*, 1929.

LOT (Ferdinand), *Fidèles ou vassaux?*, 1904,

MANTEYER (G.), *La Provence du Iᵉʳ au XIIᵉ siècle*, 1908.

PARISOT (Robert), *Les Origines de la Haute-Lorraine et sa première maison ducale*, 1908.

POWICKE (F. M.), *The Loss of Normandy (1189–1204)*, 1913 (*Publications of the University of Manchester, Historical Series*, XVI).

PREVITÉ-ORTON (C. W.), *The Early History of the House of Savoy (1000–1223)*, Cambridge, 1912.

ROSENSTOCK (Eugen), *Herzogsgewalt und Friedensschutz: deutsche Provinzialversammlungen des 9.–12. Jahrhunderts*, Breslau, 1910 (*Untersuchungen zur deutschen Staats- und Rechtsgeschichte*, H. 104).

SCHMIDT (Günther), *Das würzburgische Herzogtum und die Grafen und Herren von Ostfranken vom 11. bis zum 17. Jahrhundert*, Weimar, 1913 (*Quellen und Studien zur Verfassungsgeschichte des deutschen Reiches*, V, 2).

SPROEMBERG (Heinrich), *Die Entstehung der Grafschaft Flandern*. Part I: *Die ursprüngliche Grafschaft Flandern (864–892)*, Berlin, 1935. Cf. F. L. GANSHOF, 'Les Origines du comté de Flandre', *Revue belge de philologie*, 1937.

TOURNADRE (Guy de), *Histoire du comté de Forcalquier (12th century)*, [1930].

VACCARI (Pietro), *Dall' unità romana al particolarismo giuridico del medio evo*, Pavia, 1936.

BIBLIOGRAPHY

VALIN (L.), *Le Duc de Normandie et sa cour*, 1909.
VALLS-TABERNER (F.), 'La Cour comtale barcelonaise', *Revue historique de droit*, 1935.
WERNEBURG (Rudolf), *Gau, Grafschaft und Herrschaft im Sachsen bis zum Übergang in das Landesfürstentum Hannover*, 1910 (*Forschungen zur Geschichte Niedersachsens*, III, 1).

XVI. NATIONALISM

CHAUME (M.), 'Le Sentiment national bourguignon de Gondebaud à Charles le Téméraire', *Mémoires de l'Académie des Sciences de Dijon*, 1922.
COULTON (G. G.), 'Nationalism in the Middle Ages', *Cambridge Historical Journal*, 1935.
HUGELMANN (K. G.), 'Die deutsche Nation und der deutsche Nationalstaat im Mittelalter', *Historisches Jahrbuch*, 1931.
KURTH (G.), 'Francia et Francus', *Études franques*, 1919, vol. I.
MONOD (G.), 'Du rôle de l'opposition des races et des nationalités dans la dissolution de l'Empire carolingien', *Annuaire de l'École des Hautes-Études*, 1896.
REMPPIS (Max), *Die Vorstellungen von Deutschland im altfranzösischen Heldenepos und Roman und ihre Quellen*, Halle, 1911 (*Beihefte zur Zeitschrift für roman. Philologie*, 234).
SCHULTHEISS (Franz Guntram), *Geschichte des deutschen Nationalgefühls*, I, Munich, 1893.
VIGENER (Fritz), *Bezeichnungen für Volk und Land der Deutschen vom 10. bis zum 13. Jahrhundert*, Heidelberg, 1901.
ZIMMERMAN (K. L.), 'Die Beurteilung der Deutschen in der französischen Literatur des Mittelalters mit besonderer Berücksichtigung der Chansons de geste', *Romanische Forschungen*, XIX, 1911.

XVII. FEUDALISM IN COMPARATIVE HISTORY

ASAKAWA (K.), 'The Origin of Feudal Land Tenure in Japan', *American Historical Review*, XXX, 1915.
—— *The Documents of Iriki Illustrative of the Development of the Feudal Institutions of Japan*, New Haven, 1929 (*Yale Historical Publications, Manuscripts and edited texts*, X). With an important introduction.
—— 'The Early Sho and the Early Manor: a Comparative Study', *Journal of Economic and Business History*, I, 1929.
BECKER (C. H.), 'Steuerpacht und Lehnwesen: eine historische Studie über die Entstehung des islamischen Lehnwesens', *Islam*, V, 1914.
BELIN, 'Du régime des fiefs militaires dans l'Islamisme et principalement en Turquie', *Journal Asiatique*, 6th series, XV, 1870.
DÖLGER (F.), 'Die Frage des Grundeigentums in Byzanz', *Bulletin of the International Commission of Historical Sciences*, V, 1933.
ECK (A.), *Le Moyen Âge russe*, 1933.
ERSLEV (K.), 'Europäisk Feudalisme og dansk Lensvaesen', *Historisk Tidsskrift*, Copenhagen, 7th series, II, 1899.
FRANKE (O.), 'Feudalism: Chinese', *Encyclopaedia of the Social Sciences*, VI, 1931.
—— 'Zur Beurteilung des chinesischen Lehnwesens', *Sitzungsberichte der preussischen Akademie, Phil.-hist. Kl.*, 1927.
FUKUDA (Tokusa), 'Die gesellschaftliche und wirtschaftliche Entwickelung in Japan', Stuttgart, 1900 (*Münchner volkswirtschaftliche Studien*, 42).
HINTZE (O.), 'Wesen und Verbreitung des Feudalismus', *Sitzungsberichte der preussischen Akademie, Phil.-Hist. Kl.*, 1929.
HÖTZCH (C. V.), 'Adel und Lehnwesen in Russland und Polen', *Historische Zeitschrift*, 1912.
LÉVI (Sylvain), *Le Nepal*, 2 vols., 1905 (*Annales du Musée Guimet, Bibliothèque*, XVII, XVIII).
LYBYER (A. H.), 'Feudalism: Saracen and Ottoman', *Encyclopaedia of the Social Sciences*, VI, 1931.

BIBLIOGRAPHY

OSTROGORSKY (Georg), 'Die wirtschaftlichen und sozialen Entwicklungsgrundlagen des byzantinischen Reiches', *Vierteljahrschrift für Sozial- und Wirtschaftsgeschichte*, 1929.

RUFFINI AVONDO (E.), 'Il feudalismo giapponese visto da un giurista europeo', *Rivista di storia del diritto italiano*, III, 1939.

SANSOM (J. B.), *Japan: A Short Cultural History*, 1938.

STEIN (Ernst), 'Untersuchungen zur spätbyzantinischen Verfassungs- und Wirtschafts-geschichte', *Mitteilungen zur osmanischen Geschichte*, II, 1923–5.

THURNEYSSEN (R.), 'Das unfreie Lehen', *Zeitschrift für keltische Philologie*, 1923; 'Das freie Leben', *ibid.*, 1924.

UYEHARA (Senroku), 'Gefolgschaft und Vasallität im frankischen Reiche und in Japan' *Wirtschaft und Kultur: Festschrift zum 70. Geburtstag von A. Dopsch*, Vienna, 1938.

WOJCIECHOWSKI (Z.), 'La Condition des nobles et le problème de la féodalité en Pologne au moyen âge', *Revue historique de droit*, 1936 and 1937 (with bibliography).

SUPPLEMENT
TO THE BIBLIOGRAPHY

The following is a list of books and articles on feudal subjects published since 1939. Most of the works listed are concerned with feudalism and feudal institutions in the stricter sense, and this supplement is therefore narrower in scope than the original bibliography. But even within these limits it makes no claim to be exhaustive, and the omission of a publication implies no judgment as to its value.

L.A.M.

BALON (J.), *L'Organisation judiciaire des marches féodales*, 1951.

BARROW (G. W. S.), 'The Beginnings of Feudalism in Scotland' in *Bulletin of The Institute of Historical Research*, XXIX, 1956.

BERGENGRUEN (A.), *Adel und Grundherrschaft im Merowingerreich*, Wiesbaden, 1958.

BLOCH (Marc), *Les Caractères originaux de l'histoire française*, 2nd edn., 2 vols., Paris, 1952 and 1956. (Vol. I is a reprint of the original edition of this fundamental work; Vol. II, *Supplément établi par Robert Dauvergne d'après les travaux de l'auteur*, is a commentary based on Bloch's later writings and the notes he had made in preparation for a new edition.)

BONGERT (Y.), *Recherches sur les cours laïques du Xᵉ au XIIIᵉ siècle*, Paris, 1949.

BOSL (K.), *Die Reichsministerialität der Salier und Staufer*, 2 vols., Stuttgart, 1950–1. (Vol. X of *Schriften der Monumenta Germaniae Historica*.)

—— 'Vorstufen der deutschen Königsdienstmannschaft', *Vierteljahrschrift für Sozial- und Wirtschaftsgeschichte*, XXXIX, 1952, pp. 193–214; 289–315.

BOUSSARD (J.), 'L'Enquête de 1172 sur les fiefs de chevalier en Normandie', *Mélanges Brunel*, Paris, 1955, I, pp. 193–208.

BOUTROUCHE (R.), *Seigneurie et féodalité*, I: *Le premier âge des liens d'homme à homme*, Paris, 1959.

BRUNEL (C.), 'Les Juges de la paix en Gévaudan au milieu du XIᵉ siècle' in *Bibl. de l'École des Chartes*, CIX, 1951, pp. 3–12.

CAHEN (C.), *Le Régime féodal de l'Italie normande*, Paris, 1940.

CAM (H. M.), 'The Evolution of the Mediaeval English Franchise' in *Speculum*, XXXIII, no. 3, July, 1957.

Cambridge Economic History of Europe (ed. J. H. Clapham and Eileen Power), I, *The Agrarian Life of the Middle Ages*, 2nd edn., 1942. (Ch. VI, 'The Rise of Dependent Cultivation', is by Marc Bloch.)

CARABIE (R.), *La Propriété foncière dans le très ancien droit normand*, I, *La propriété domaniale*, Caen, 1943.

COHEN (G.), *Histoire de la chevalerie eu France au moyen âge*, Paris, 1949.

BIBLIOGRAPHY

COULBORN (R.), (ed.), *Feudalism in History* (studies in the comparative history of feudalism by various authors), Princeton, N.J., 1956.

CRONNE (H. A.), 'Historical Revisions, XCI. The Origins of Feudalism' in *History*, XXIV (1940), pp. 251–9.

DAVID (M.), *Le Serment du sacre de IXe au XVe siècle*, Strasbourg, 1951.

DHOUDT (J.), *Études sur la naissance des principautés territoriales en France*, Bruges, 1948.

—— 'Les "solidarités" médiévales. Une société en transition: La Flandre en 1127–1128' (*Annales, E.S.C.*, 1957, pp. 529–60).

DIDIER (N.), *Le Droit des fiefs dans la coutume de Hainaut au moyen âge*, Lille-Paris, 1945.

DILLAY (M.), 'Le "Service" annuel en deniers des fiefs de la région angevine' in *Mélanges Paul Fournier*, Paris, 1949.

DOUGLAS (D. C.), 'The Norman Conquest and English Feudalism' in *Economic History Review*, IX, 1939, pp. 128–43.

DUBY (G.), *La Société aux XIe et XIIe siècles dans la région mâconnaise*, Paris, 1953.

ESLEY (F. N.), 'The *Fideles* in the County of Mâcon' in *Speculum*, XXX, no. 1, 1955, pp. 82–9.

GANSHOF (F. L.), *Qu'est-ce que la féodalité* (3rd edn. revised and enlarged), Brussels, 1957.

—— *Feudalism* (translation of above by Philip Grierson, with foreword by F. M. Stenton), London, 1952.

—— 'Benefice and Vassalage in the Age of Charlemagne' n *Cambridge Historical Journal*, VI, 1939, pp. 149–75.

—— 'Le Roi de France en Flandre en 1127 et 1128' in *Revue historique de droit de français et étranger*, 4th series, XXVII, 1949, pp. 204–28.

—— 'Note sur le rattachement féodal du comté de Hainaut à l'église de Liége' in *Miscellanea Gessleriana*, Antwerp, 1948, pp. 508–21.

—— 'Manorial Organization in the Low Countries in the Seventh, Eighth and Ninth Centuries' in *Transactions of the Royal Historical Society*, 4th series, XXXI, 1949, pp. 29–59.

—— 'A propos de la cavalerie dans les armées de Charlemagne' in *C.R. Acad. Inscript.*, 1952–3, pp. 531–7.

—— 'L'Origine des rapports feodo-vassaliques' in *I Problemi della Civiltà Carolingia*, Spoleto 1954. (Settimane di Studi del Centro Italiano sull'Alto Medioevo, I, 1953).

—— 'Les Relations feodo-vassaliques aux temps post-carolingiens' in *I Problemi communi dell'Europa post-Carolingia*, Spoleto, 1955 (Settimane di Studi del Centro Italiano di Studi sull'Alto Medioevo, II, 1954).

—— 'Note sur l'apparition du nom de "hommage", particulièrement en France', *Aus Mittelalter und Neuzeit. Festschrift für Gerhard Kallen*, Bonn, 1957.

—— 'Charlemagne et le serment' in *Mélanges Louis Halphen*, Paris, 1951.

GAUSEIN (Roger), 'De la seigneurie rurale à la baronnie: l'abbaye de Savigny en Lyonnais', *Le Moyen Age*, vol. LXI, 1955, nos. 1–2, pp. 139–76.

GENICOT (L.), 'Le Destin d'une famille noble du Namurois. Les Noville aux XIIe et XIIIe siecles' in *Annales de la Société Archéologique de Namur*, XLVI (1953), pp. 157–232

—— 'De la noblesse au lignage. Le cas des Boneffe' in *Revue belge de philologie et d'histoire*, XXXI (1953), pp. 39–53

—— *Les Lignes de faite du moyen âge*, Tournai and Paris, 2nd edn., 1952.

—— *L'Economie rurale namuroise au bas moyen âge. I. La seigneurie foncière*, Namur, 1943.

HIGOUNET (C.), 'Les Alaman, seigneurs baslidors et péagers du XIIIe siecle' in *Annales du Midi*, 1956, pp. 227–53.

—— *Le Comté de Comminges de ses origines à son annexion à la couronne*, 2 vols., Toulouse and Paris, 1949.

—— 'Observations sur la seigneurie rurale et l'habitat en Rouergue du IXe au XIVe siecle' in *Annales du Midi*, 1950, pp. 121–34.

HOLLYMAN (M. K. J.), *Le Développement du vocabulaire féodal en France pendant le haut moyen âge, Étude sémantique*, Geneva and Paris, 1957.

479

BIBLIOGRAPHY

KEENEY (B. C.), 'Military Service and the Development of Nationalism in England' in *Speculum*, XXII, 1947, pp. 534–49.

—— *Judgement by Peers*, Cambridge, Mass., 1949.

KIENAST (W.), 'Untertaneneid und Treuvorbehalt', *Zeitschrift der Savigny-Stiftung für Rechtsgeschichte, Germ. Abt.*, LXVI, 1948, pp. 111–47.

—— *Untertaneneid und Treuvorbehalt in Frankreich und England*, Weimar, 1952.

KOCH (A. C. F.), 'L'Origine de la haute et de la moyenne justices dans l'ouest et le nord de la France' in *Revue d'histoire du droit*, 1953, pp. 420–58.

LEICHT (P. S.), 'L'introduzione del feudo nell'Italia franca e normanna' in *Rivista di storia del diritto italiano*, XII, 1939.

—— 'Il feudo in Italia nell'età Carolingia' in *I Problemi della civiltà Carolingia*, Spoleto, 1954 (Settimane di Studi del Centro Italiano di Studi sull'Alto Medioevo, I, 1953).

—— 'LOrganisation des grands domains dans l'Italie du Nord pendant les Xᵉ–XIIᵉ siecles', *Société Jean Bodin, Recueil IV: Le Domaine*, 1949, pp. 165–76.

LEMARIGNIER (J. F.), *Recherches sur l'hommage en marche et les frontières féodales*, Lille, 1945.

—— 'Les Fidèles du roi de France (936–987)' in *Mélanges Brunel*, Paris, 1955, II, pp. 138–92.

LENNARD (R.), *Rural England, 1086–1135*, Oxford, 1959.

LLOYD (L. C.), *The Origins of Some Anglo-Norman Families* (Harleian Society, vol. CIII), London, 1951.

LOT (F.), *L'Art militaire et les armées au moyen âge en Europe et dans le Proche Orient*, 2 vols., Paris, 1946.

LOT (F.) and FAWTIER (R.) (ed.), *Histoire des institutions françaises au moyen âge, I: Institutions seigneuriales*, Paris, 1957.

LOUSSE (E.), *La Société d'Ancien Régime*, I, Louvain, 1943.

LYON (B. D.), 'The Money Fief under the English Kings, 1066–1485' in *English Historical Review*, LXVI, 1951, pp. 161–93.

—— 'Le Fief-rente aux Pays-Bas: sa terminologie et son aspect financier' in *Revue du Nord*, XXXV, 1953.

—— 'The fief-rente in the Low Countries. An Evaluation' in *Revue belge de Philologie et d'Histoire*, XXXII, 1954.

MAYER (T.), *Fürsten und Staat*, Weimar, 1950.

MEYER (B.), 'Das Lehen in Recht und Staat des Mittelalters' in *Zeitschrift für Schweizerische Geschichte*, XXVI, 1946, pp. 161–78.

MITTEIS (H.), *Die Rechtsidee in der Geschichte, gesammelte Abhandlungen und Vorträge*, Weimar, 1957.

MOR (C. G.), *L'età feudale*, 2 vols., Milan, 1952.

NAVEL (H.), *Recherches sur les institutions féodales en Normandie, région de Caen*. (Bull. de la Société des Antiquaires de Normandie, Vol. LI; also published separately Caen, 1951.)

ODEGAARD (C. E.), 'Carolingian Oaths of Fidelity' in *Speculum*, XVI, 1941, pp. 284–96.

—— *Vassi and Fideles in the Carolingian Empire*, Cambridge, Mass., 1945.

OLIVIER-MARTIN (F.), *Histoire du droit français des origines à la Révolution*, Paris, 1948.

PAINTER (S.), *Studies in the History of the English Feudal Barony* (Johns Hopkins University Studies in Historical and Political Science, series LXI, no. 3), Baltimore, 1943.

—— 'Castellans of the Plain of Poitou in the Eleventh and Twelfth Centuries' in *Speculum*, XXXI, no. 2, 1956, pp. 243–57.

—— *French Chivalry: Chivalric Ideas and Practices in Mediaeval France*, Baltimore, 1940.

—— 'The Lords of Lusignan in the Eleventh and Twelfth Centuries' in *Speculum*, XXXVII, no. 1, 1957, pp. 27–47.

—— 'The Houses of Lusignan and Châterrault, 1150–1250' in *Speculum*, XXX, no. 3, 1955, pp. 374–384.

PERRIN (C. E.), 'Chartes de franchise et rapports de droit in Lorraine' in *Le Moyen Age*, 1946, pp. 11–42.

—— 'Le Servage en France et en Allemagne' in *X Congr. Internaz. di Scienze Stor. Relazioni*, III, Florence, 1955, pp. 213–245.

PLUCKNETT (T. F. T.), *A Concise History of the Common Law*, 4th edn., London, 1948.
—— *The Mediaeval Bailiff*, London, 1954.
POOLE (A. L.), *Obligations of Society in the Twelfth and Thirteenth Centuries*, Oxford, 1946.
—— *From Domesday Book to Magna Carta* (The Oxford History of England), Oxford, 1950.
POWICKE (M. R.), 'The General Obligation to Cavalry Service under Edward I' in *Speculum*, XXVIII, no. 4, 1953, pp. 814–33.
PRESTWICH (J. O.), 'War and Finance in the Anglo-Norman State' in *Trans. Royal Hist. Soc.*, 5th series, vol. 4, 1954, pp. 19–43.
RICHARDOT (H.), 'Francs-fiefs: essai sur l'exemption totale ou partielle des services de fief' in *Revue historique de droit français et étranger*, 4th series, XXVII, 1949, pp. 28–63, 229–73.
—— 'Quelques textes sur la reprise de censive en fief' in *Revue historique de droit français et étranger*, 4th series, XXVIII, 1950.
SÁNCHEZ-ALBORNOZ (C.), *En torno a los orígenes del feudalismo*, 3 vols., Mendoza (Argentina), 1942
—— *El 'stipendium' hispano-godo y los orígenes del beneficio prefeudal*, Buenos Aires, 1947.
—— 'España y el feudalismo Carolingio' in *I Problemi della civiltà Carolingia*, Spoleto, 1954 (Settimane di Studi del Centro Italiano di Studi sull'Alto Mediaevo, I, 1953).
SANDERS (I. J.), *Feudal Military Service in England*, 1956.
SCHEIDUNG-WULKOPF (I.), *Lehnsherrliche Beziehungen der fränkisch-deutschen Könige zu anderen Staaten vom 9. bis zum Ende 12. Jahrhunderts*, Marburg, 1948 (*Marburger Studien zur älteren deutschen Geschichte*, Reihe 2, 9).
SCZANIECKI (M.), *Essai sur les fiefs-rentes*, Paris, 1946.
SESTAN (E.), 'L'Italia nell'età feudale' in E. Rota, ed., *Questioni di storia medioevale*, Como-Milan, 1946, pp. 77–122.
STENGEL (E. E.), 'Land- und Lehnrechtliche Grundlagen des Reichsfürstenstandes' in *Zeitschrift der Savigny-Stiftung für Rechtsgeschichte*, Germ. Abt., 1948, pp. 294–342.
STENTON (F. M.), *Anglo-Saxon England* (The Oxford History of England), 2nd edn., Oxford, 1947.
—— 'The Scandinavian Colonies in England and Normandy' in *Transactions of the Royal Historical Society*, 4th series, XXVII, 1945.
STEPHENSON (C.), 'The Origin and Significance of Feudalism' in *American Historical Review*, XLVI, 1941, pp. 788–812.
—— 'Feudalism and Its Antecedents in England' in *American Historical Review*, XLVIII, 1943, pp. 245–65.
Studien und Vorarbeiten zur Geschichte des grossfränkischen und frühdeutschen Adels (published under the direction of G. Tellenbach), Freiburg-im-Breisgau, 1957.
TELLENBACH (G.), *Königtum und Stämme in der Werdezeit des Deutschen Reiches*, Weimar, 1939.
VALDEAVELLANO (L. G. de), 'El prestimonio, contribución al estudio de las manifestaciones de feudalismo en los reinos de León y Castilla durante la Edad Media', *Ann. Hist. Derecho espãn.*, XXV, 1955, pp. 5–122.
VERRIEST (L.), 'Le Servage en Flandre, particulièrement au pays d'Alost', *Revue historique de droit français et étranger*, 1950, pp. 35–66.
YVER (J.), 'Les Caractères originaux du groupe de coutumes de l'ouest de la France', *Revue historique de droit français et étranger*, 1952, pp. 18–79.

INDEX

INDEX

INDEX

Hamburg, 33
hamlets, 242
hands, joined, ceremony of, 151, 162, 183
hanging, 228
Hanno, archbishop, 100
Hanover, 181
Harald Hardrada, 26, 38, 226
Hariulf, chronicle of, 95
harness, as investiture gift, 206
harnessing, 69
Harold II of England, 26
Hartmann von Aue, 294
Hastein, 47
Hastings, Battle of, 26, 99, 184
'hatreds, mortal', 128*f*
Hattentot, 47
hauberk, 291
hawking, 303*f*
health, 72*f*
Hebrides, 21, 38, 51
Heerschilde, 336
heir, principles of choice, 203; *see also* fiefs;
    inheritance; heritability
Heliand, 167*n*
hell, fear of, 87
Helmold, 83
Henri le Liberal, count of Champagne, 104
Henry I, king of Germany, 180, 389, 427,
    435
Henry II, emperor, 384, 407, 409
Henry III, emperor, 79, 92
Henry IV, emperor, 89, 154, 199, 298, 381,
    389, 419, 428
Henry V, emperor, 199
Henry VI, emperor, 200, 201
Henry I, king of England, 227, 381, 412*n*,
    432; Laws of, 232
Henry II, king of England, 112, 119, 134,
    305, 330, 369, 430, 431
Henry III, king of England, 330
Henry I, king of France, 72, 425
Henry the Lion, duke of Bavaria and Saxony,
    180, 229, 428
Henry of England, 'the young King', 304
Herbert de Vermandois, 94, 127, 235
here, 54
heresies, 310
heritability: of fiefs, 190*ff*; of kingship,
    383*ff*; in Germany, 389
Herroi, 172
Hervé 'the Francopol', 296
'hide', 49
Hincmar of Rheims, 113, 191
Histoire des ducs de Normandie, 96
history: place of, in feudal life, 88; writing
    of, 80
Hiung-nu, 8
hlaford, 182
Höflich, 306
Hohenstaufen emperors, 174
Holland, county of, 199
homage: ceremony of, 146*f*; conflicting, 213;
    of ecclesiastics, 348, 349*f*, 352; as ex-
    piatory act, 161*n*; in Germany, 180;
    gradation of acts of, 332; in Italy, 179;

liege, *see* liege homage; 'of mouth and
    hands', 130, 146, 178, 228, 341; obliga-
    tions of, 219*ff*; plural, 211*ff*; post-feudal,
    449; servile, 161; in Spain, 186
homme de corps, 261, 266, 279
homonyms, 140
homunculus, 148
'honours', 176, 192, 335; courts as, 368;
    heritability of, 395
horses: rôle in England, 184; use by North-
    men, 17; war, 152, 290
horse-shoe, 153
'Host, Great', 20
hour-glasses, 73
housecarl, 182
household maintenance, of vassals, 170*f*
households, communal, 131
'housing' vassals, 163, 169*ff*
Hugh Capet, 212, 233, 386, 424, 425
Hugh of Arles, king of Italy, 7, 55, 379
Hugh the Great, duke of France, 386, 396
Hugh, relative of Charles the Fat, 193
humanism, 104
hundred, 363, 364, 370; courts, *see* courts
Hungarians, 3, 8-14, 42, 400; conversion,
    13*f*; methods of warfare, 54; raids by, 9*ff*;
    way of life, 12*f*
Huns, 91
hunting, 72, 303*f*
Huon of Bordeaux, 298
Huy, 90
hygiene, standard of, 73

Ibelin, Sire d', 141, 232
Iberian peninsula: charters of customs, 277;
    colonization of, 69; feudalism in, 186*f*;
    population, 60; *see also* Spain; Portugal
Ibn Khaldun, 54
Iceland, 19, 21, 35, 36, 38; chroniclers, 90;
    genealogies, 285
idiota, 80
Île-de-France, 61, 205, 253, 273, 425
illiteracy, 80
immunity: ecclesiastical, 404; Frankish, 245,
    362*f*; judicial, 362*ff*, 371; from raids, pur-
    chase of, 18; from raids, Western, 56
immutability, 90
Incarnation, era of, 85
indiction, 85
indivisibility of fiefs, 189, 203*f*
Indo-China, 56
infant mortality, 72
infantry, 291
Inge, king of Sweden, 34
ingenuus, 286
Ingleby, 47
inheritance: in France, 194*ff*; in Germany,
    197*ff*; on tenements, 250*f*; *see also* herit-
    ability
initiation ceremonies, 313
insecurity, 410*ff*
insignia, royal, delivery of, 380
institutions, legal, migration of, 187*f*
interpretation, and observation, 83
introspection, 106

489

INDEX

Peter Damian, St., 98, 107
Peter Lombard, 108
'petitory', 115
pezade, 418
Philip I, king of France, 72, 343, 381
Philip II Augustus, king of France, 117, 119, 169, 174, 207*f*, 216, 227, 229, 306, 318, 383, 410, 425, 428; revenue of, 421
Philip III, king of France, 119, 262, 323
Philip IV the Fair, king of France, 80, 119, 130, 235, 323, 324
Philip VI, king of France, 229
Philip I of Alsace, count of Flanders, 225, 438
Philip II the Bold, count of Flanders, 449
philosophy, 108
Picardy, 70, 215, 222, 263, 426
pied poudreux, 63
Pierre des Vaux-de-Cernay, 316
Pilgrim, bishop of Passau, 14
pilgrims, 63; Arab attacks on, 6
pirates: Arab, 5; Greek, 6
Pisa, 7, 19, 118
place-names, 46*f*
Placentinus, 117
placita, 268, 278
Plantagenets, 174, 202, 220; judicial system, 272; *see also* Angevins
Plato, xix
ploughland, 49
plunder, 297
poblaciones, 277
poems, vernacular, 91
poets, Provençal, 233
Poitiers, 195, 413; battle of, 153; Council of, 415
Poitou, 31, 397; count of, 168
Polovtsi, 56
polygamy, 37
polytheism, 32
pomeshchiks, 158
Ponthieu, count(s) of, 314, 400
Poperinghe, 172
Popes: appointment of, and emperors, 392*f*; and homage, 348*n*; and imperial elections, 389; war with Emperors, 428
population: decline in, 60*f*; growth of, 421; *see also* repopulation
populus Francorum, 149
portage of boats, 17
Port-sur-Saône, 376*f*
Portugal, 186, 376
posting service, 64*f*
Pothières, 95
praestitum, 185
Prague, 66
prayer(s), anti-pagan, 41; posture of, 233
preaching, 82
prebends, 68, 337*f*
precaria/precarium, 164
precedent, justice and, 113*f*
prelates: choice of, 348; warrior, 347
prestamo, 187
preux, 306
pride, 292

priests: marriage of, 345; pagan, in Scandinavia, 31; *see also* clergy
primogeniture, 189, 203, 204*f*, 385
princes, 336
principalities, territorial, 394*ff*; development in Germany, 429
prisoners, 297; of Northmen, 18*f*
privilege, equality in, 195
profits, 353
property, real, and tradition, 115
prosody, 76
protection, 148*ff*, 224; of freedmen, 259
Provençal language, 77
Provence, 5–7, 41, 52*f*, 89, 326, 329, 379; counts of, 326, 377; countship of, 131; heresy in, 310; Roman law in, 117
Provins, 425
provosts, 425
prudhomme, 306, 318
Prussia, 448
punishments, 364
purveyance, 250, 278
puszta, 9

Quentovic, 39
Quercy, 77
quest for a lord, 185
Queste du Saint-Graal, 310
Quia Emptores, 208*n*
Quierzy, placitum of, 194, 195
quintaine, 312

Rabanus Maurus, 83
rachat, 206
Radcliffe, Mrs., 302
radmen, 184
ransom/ransoming, 18, 297
Raoul, king, 29, 386
Raoul de Cambrai, 64, 94, 96, 102, 127, 196, 229, 238, 305
Raoul of Gouy, 94
Ravenna, 411; duchy of, 344
Reading, 17
rebellions, 409
reconciliation, of feuds, 129
records, dating of, 74, 84
redemption, right of, by relatives, 133, 139, 142
reeve, 337
referendaries, lay, 80
reform, religious, 91; Gregorian, 106*f*, 116, 252, 308, 345, 347, 350, 352, 381, 407, 451
Regino of Prüm, 9, 89
Reichenau, 211
Reinald of Dassel, 108
relics: Breton, 42; criticism and, 90
relief, 206*f*
relief de l'homme, 129
religion, popular, 83
remarriage, 136
Remi of Auxerre, 55
remuneration: fief as, 166; from honour, 192
renaissance: twelfth-century, 103, 422; urban, in Germany, 426
Renan, Ernest, 381

INDEX